LUTHER'S WORKS

American Edition

VOLUME 49

Published by Concordia Publishing House

and Fortress Press in 55 volumes

General Editors are Jaroslav Pelikan (for vols. 1-30)

and Helmut T. Lehmann (for vols. 31-55)

LUTHER'S WORKS

VOLUME 49

Letters

II

EDITED AND TRANSLATED BY

GOTTFRIED G. KRODEL

GENERAL EDITOR

HELMUT T. LEHMANN

FORTRESS PRESS / PHILADELPHIA

Library of Congress Catalogue Number 55–9893

ISBN 0–8006–0349–4

Printed in the United States of America

GENERAL EDITORS'
PREFACE

The first editions of Luther's collected works appeared in the sixteenth century, and so did the first efforts to make him "speak English." In America serious attempts in these directions were made for the first time in the nineteenth century. The Saint Louis edition of Luther was the first endeavor on American soil to publish a collected edition of his works, and the Henkel Press in Newmarket, Virginia, was the first to publish some of Luther's writings in an English translation. During the first decade of the twentieth century, J. N. Lenker produced translations of Luther's sermons and commentaries in thirteen volumes. A few years later the first of the six volumes in the Philadelphia (or Holman) edition of the *Works of Martin Luther* appeared. But a growing recognition of the need for more of Luther's works in English has resulted in this American edition of Luther's works.

The edition is intended primarily for the reader whose knowledge of late medieval Latin and sixteenth-century German is too small to permit him to work with Luther in the original languages. Those who can will continue to read Luther in his original words as these have been assembled in the monumental Weimar edition (*D. Martin Luthers Werke*. Kritische Gesamtausgabe, Weimar, 1883–   ). Its texts and helps have formed a basis for this edition, though in certain places we have felt constrained to depart from its readings and findings. We have tried throughout to translate Luther as he thought translating should be done. That is, we have striven for faithfulness on the basis of the best lexicographical materials available. But where literal accuracy and clarity have conflicted, it is clarity that we have preferred, so that sometimes paraphrase seemed more faithful than literal fidelity. We have proceeded in a similar way in the matter of Bible versions, translating Luther's translations. Where this could be done by the use of an existing

v

English version—King James, Douay, or Revised Standard—we have done so. Where it could not, we have supplied our own. To indicate this in each specific instance would have been pedantic; to adopt a uniform procedure would have been artificial—especially in view of Luther's own inconsistency in this regard. In each volume the translator will be responsible primarily for matters of text and language, while the responsibility of the editor will extend principally to the historical and theological matters reflected in the introductions and notes.

Although the edition as planned will include fifty-five volumes, Luther's writings are not being translated in their entirety. Nor should they be. As he was the first to insist, much of what he wrote and said was not that important. Thus the edition is a selection of works that have proved their importance for the faith, life, and history of the Christian church. The first thirty volumes contain Luther's expositions of various biblical books, while the remaining volumes include what are usually called his "Reformation writings" and other occasional pieces. The final volume of the set will be an index volume; in addition to an index of quotations, proper names, and topics, and a list of corrections and changes, it will contain a glossary of many of the technical terms that recur in Luther's works and that cannot be defined each time they appear. Obviously Luther cannot be forced into any neat set of rubrics. He can provide his reader with bits of autobiography or with political observations as he expounds a psalm, and he can speak tenderly about the meaning of the faith in the midst of polemics against his opponents. It is the hope of publishers, editors, and translators that through this edition the message of Luther's faith will speak more clearly to the modern church.

J. P.
H. T. L.

CONTENTS

ADB   —*Allgemeine Deutsche Biographie,* edited by Historische Kommission bei der Königlichen Akademie der Wissenschaften, Munich (Leipzig, 1875–1912).

ARC   —*Acta Reformationis Catholicae,* edited by G. Pfeilschifter (Regensburg, 1959–   ).

ARG   —*Archiv für Reformationsgeschichte.*

BA   —*Briefe und Akten zu der Geschichte des Religionsgespräches zu Marburg, 1529, und des Reichs-tages zu Augsburg, 1530,* edited by F. W. Schirrmacher (Gotha, 1876; reprint: Amsterdam, 1968).

C.R.   —*Corpus Reformatorum,* edited by C. G. Bretschneider *et al.* (Halle/Saale, 1834–   ).

DRTA.JR   —*Deutsche Reichstagsakten under Kaiser Karl V.,* edited by Historische Kommission bei der Bayerischen Akademie der Wissenschaften (Gotha, 1893–   ; reprint: Göttingen, 1962–   ).

LCC   —*Library of Christian Classics.* J. T. McNeill and H. P. van Dusen, General Editors (Philadelphia, 1953–1969).

LJB   —*Lutherjahrbuch.*

LThK   —*Lexikon für Theologie und Kirche,* edited by J. Höfer and K. Rahner (2nd ed., Freiburg, 1957–1967).

LW   —American Edition of *Luther's Works* (Philadelphia and St. Louis, 1955–   ).

NB I.Abt.,E.1—*Nuntiaturberichte aus Deutschland.* I. Abteilung: 1533–1559. Ergänzungsband 1: 1530–1531, edited by G. Müller (Tübingen, 1693).

NCE   —*New Catholic Encyclopedia,* edited by The Catholic University of America (New York, 1967).

NDB — *Neue Deutsche Biographie*, edited by Historische Kommission bei der Bayerischen Akademie der Wissenschaften (Berlin, 1953–   ).

PE — *Works of Martin Luther.* Philadelphia Edition (Philadelphia, 1915–1943).

S-J — *Luther's Correspondence*, 2 vols., edited by P. Smith and C. M. Jacobs (Philadelphia, 1913–1918).

SMRH — *Studies in Medieval and Renaissance History.*

St. L. — *D. Martin Luthers sämmtliche Schriften*, 23 vols. in 25, edited by J. G. Walch (2nd ed., St. Louis, 1880–1910).

TP — *Valentin von Tetleben: Protokoll des Augsburger Reichstages, 1530*, edited by H. Grundmann (Göttingen, 1958).

URA — *Urkundenbuch zu der Geschichte des Reichstages zu Augsburg im Jahre 1530*, edited by K. E. Förstemann (Halle, 1833–1835; reprint: Hildesheim, 1966).

WA — *D. Martin Luthers Werke. Kritische Gesamtausgabe* (Weimar, 1883–   ).

WA, Br — *D. Martin Luthers Werke.* Briefwechsel (Wiemar, 1930–1970).

WA, DB — *D. Martin Luthers Werke.* Deutsche Bibel (Weimar, 1906–1961.

WA, TR — *D. Martin Luthers Werke.* Tischreden (Weimar, 1912–1921).

ZKG — *Zeitschrift für Kirchengeschichte.*

INTRODUCTION TO VOLUME 49

Volume 49 of the American Edition of *Luther's Works* is the second volume of letters in this series; it presents 117 letters[1] written by Luther from March, 1522, to October, 1530. This period stretched from the time that Luther, the heretic and outlaw, returned from the Wartburg and re-entered the scene of German history to the Diet of Augsburg in 1530. To get a feeling for the dynamics of this period, one has only to remember that in 1521 Luther stood completely alone before the Emperor and affirmed his evangelical convictions, and that by 1530 a group of Imperial Estates stood before the Emperor and affirmed Luther's evangelical convictions by presenting the *Augsburg Confession* to the Emperor.

Through the excommunication of Luther, the Reformer's energies were channeled into the building of the church of the gospel. And so the years from 1522 to 1530 were for Luther a period of building up, securing, and clarifying his evangelical insight during the emergence of the evangelical church. This process of emergence was a painful one. A new ecclesiastical system had to be organized that would be commensurate with Luther's evangelical insight, and this evangelical insight and interpretation had to be constantly clarified to stand against any interpretation of the gospel which jeopardized Luther's evangelical insight. Further, this emerging evangelical church had to be secured and rooted within a society which was often only too eager to abuse Luther's interpretation of the gospel, and the consequences thereof, for its own purposes. And all this had to be done under the shadow of the Edict of Worms, through which, at least on paper, Luther, his work, and that of his followers were outlawed by Imperial law. The *Augsburg Confession* marks a decisive point in this process of emergence of the evangelical church, inasmuch as the substance of the evangelical church was fixed by this confession.

---

[1] For the organization of the text, see *LW* 48, xiii ff. The letters in *LW* 48 (Letters I) were numbered from 1 to 119; *LW* 49 (Letters II) continues this numbering system, with letters running from 120 to 236.

The highlight in Luther's personal life in this period, a highlight which marked a break in his life as a whole, was his marriage to Catherine von Bora. The monk and professor, who until this time had lived only for his work, now became a husband and family man who was faced with totally new circumstances. Unfortunately not many letters written by Luther to his wife are extant, and of those written by Catherine to her husband, none is extant. This is a great loss for all who are interested in Luther as a person, and no justification need be offered for the fact that all extant letters written by Luther to his wife during the period covered by this present volume have been translated.

Many of the following letters were official ones, briefs, or opinions in which Luther dealt with the major and minor issues of his day. Even the personal letters to his wife or his friends demonstrate how deeply Luther was interested and involved in, or touched by, the general events of his time. A first glance at the selection of letters presented in this volume may give the impression that Luther the person is simply lost in the events of his time. Yet anyone who has even a cursory knowledge of Reformation history in the years from 1522 to 1530 knows that Luther stood at the center of all facets of that history. In selecting the following letters and in allocating the available space, this editor has attempted to familiarize the reader with Luther the builder of the evangelical church, and with Luther the person.

G. G. K.

Bibliographical Note

It would have been impossible to produce this volume without the work done by Ernst Ludwig Enders and his successors,[1] by Otto Clemen,[2] Hanns Rückert,[3] and Theodore G. Tappert,[4] those scholars who have dedicated their energies to editing Luther's letters either totally or in selection. The painstaking work of Hans Volz and Eike Wolgast, who have completed the monumental WA, Br,[5] has also been of fundamental importance in the preparation of this volume.

For the translation and commentary the common technical aids have been used.[6] The general history which is reflected in the letters in this volume is portrayed and analyzed in Ranke's history

---

[1] E. L. Enders et al., Dr. Martin Luther's Briefwechsel (19 vols.; Frankfurt, Leipzig, 1884–1932); hereinafter cited as: Enders, Briefwechsel.

[2] He was the editor of WA, Br 1–11.

[3] H. Rückert, Luthers Briefe. Luthers Werke in Auswahl, Vol. 6; general editor: O. Clemen (2nd ed.; Berlin, 1955); hereinafter cited as: Rückert, LB. Rückert gives his notes to the number of the line of the text. In order to facilitate the citing in the present volume, the line numbers of Rückert have been treated as footnote numbers.

[4] Luther: Letters of Spiritual Counsel. LCC 18 (Philadelphia, 1955); hereinafter cited as: LCC 18.

[5] Volz and Wolgast published in WA, Br 12 additions, and in WA, Br 13 corrections for the whole letter corpus.

[6] To the bibliographical tools cited in LW 48, xviii, n. 5, have to be added the bibliographical reports published annually in LJB; and Bibliographie de la Réforme: 1450–1648 (Leiden, 1960–   ); Bibliographie internationale de l'Humanisme et de la Renaissance (Geneva, 1966–   ). The following technical aids were used for the preparation of the translation and the commentary: C. Lewis, C. Short, A Latin Dictionary (Oxford, 1958); hereinafter cited as: Lewis and Short.—C. du Cange, Glossarium mediae et infimae Latinitatis (7 vols.; Paris, 1840–1850); hereinafter cited as: Du Cange.—A. Götze et al. (eds.), Trübners Deutsches Wörterbuch (8 vols.; Berlin, 1939–1957); hereinafter cited as: Trübner.—A. Götze (ed.), Frühneuhochdeutsches Glossar (5th ed.; Berlin, 1956); hereinafter cited as: Götze.—P. Dietz (ed.), Wörterbuch zu Dr. Martin Luthers Deutschen Schriften (Leipzig, 1870).—F. L. Cross (ed.), The Oxford Dictionary of the Christian Church (New York, 1958); hereinafter cited as: O.D.C.C.—M. Cary et al. (eds.), The Oxford Classical Dictionary (Oxford, 1949); hereinafter cited as: O.C.D.—E. Haberkern, J. F. Wallach (eds.), Hilfswörterbuch für Historiker: Mittelalter und Neuzeit (2nd ed.; Bern, Munich, 1964); hereinafter cited as: Hilfswörterbuch.—E. Brinckmeier, Glossarium Diplomaticum (2 vols.; Gotha, 1856–1863; reprint: Aalen, 1967); hereinafter cited as: Brinckmeier.—B. Altaner, Patrology (New York, 1960); hereinafter cited as: Patrology.—K. Aland, Hilfsbuch zum Lutherstudium (3rd ed.; Witten, 1970).—G. S. Robbert, "A Checklist of Luther's Writings in English," Concordia Theological Monthly 36 (1965), 772 ff. and 40 (1970), 214 ff.—G. Buchwald, Luther-Kalendarium (Leipzig, 1929); hereinafter cited as: Buchwald, LK.

of the Reformation[7] (still the unsurpassed masterpiece for this period), and in the second volume of the *New Cambridge Modern History,* which is edited by Geoffrey R. Elton.[8] This history is documented in the collections prepared by Beresford J. Kidd,[9] Hans Hillerbrand,[10] and Heinz Scheible.[11] Emil Sehling began to collect all the evangelical church ordinances of the 16th century into a monumental corpus, and this task is now being carried on by the Institute for Evangelical Ecclesiastical Law in Göttingen.[12] Hans von Schubert,[13] Walther Friedensburg,[14] and Ekkehart Fabian[15] have analyzed and documented the political activities of those Imperial Estates which supported the Reformation. Karl Schornbaum has supplied careful studies on the margraves of Brandenburg-Ansbach,[16] and on the city of Nürnberg.[17] These two

---

[7] L. von Ranke, *Deutsche Geschichte im Zeitalter der Reformation,* critical edition by P. Joachimsen (6 parts in 3 vols.; Meersburg, Leipzig, 1933); hereinafter cited as: Ranke. Since this Joachimsen edition presents the documentary apparatus it is the only edition which has been used in this present volume. S. Austin has published an abridged English version of Ranke (London, 1905).

[8] *The Reformation: 1520–1559* (Cambridge, 1962); hereinafter cited as: Elton.

[9] *Documents Illustrative of the Continental Reformation* (Oxford, 1911; reprint: Oxford, 1967); hereinafter cited as: Kidd.

[10] *The Reformation: A Narrative History Related by Contemporary Observers and Participants* (New York, Evanston, 1964); hereinafter cited as Hillerbrand.

[11] H. Scheible, *Das Widerstandsrecht als Problem der deutschen Protestanten, 1523–1546* (Gütersloh, 1969); hereinafter cited as: *Widerstandsrecht.*

[12] *Die evangelischen Kirchenordnungen des · XVI. Jahrhunderts* (Leipzig, Tübingen, 1902–   ); hereinafter cited as: Sehling.

[13] *Bekenntnisbildung und Religionspolitik 1529/30* (Gotha, 1910); hereinafter cited as: Schubert, *BRP.*

[14] *Zur Vorgeschichte des Gotha-Torgauischen Bündnisses der Evangelischen, 1525–1526* (Marburg, 1884); hereinafter cited as Friedensburg, *Vorgeschichte GTB.*

[15] *Die Entstehung des Schmalkaldischen Bundes und seiner Verfassung* (Tübingen, 1956 [1st ed.]; 1962 [2nd ed.]) hereinafter cited as: Fabian, *ESBV.* —*Die Abschiede der Bündnis–und Bekenntnistage Protestierender Fürsten und Städte zwischen den Reichstagen zu Speyer und zu Augsburg 1529–1530* (Tübingen, 1960); hereinafter cited as: Fabian, *ABBP.*

[16] *Die Stellung des Markgrafen Kasimir zur reformatorischen Bewegung in den Jahren 1524–1527* (Nürnberg, 1900).—*Zur Politik des Markgrafen Georg von Brandenburg vom Beginne seiner selbständigen Regierung bis zum Nürnberger Anstand, 1528–1532* (Munich, 1906); hereinafter cited as: Schornbaum, *Georg.*

[17] "Zur Politik der Reichsstadt Nürnberg vom Ende des Reichstages zu Speyer 1529 bis zur Übergabe der Augsburgischen Konfession 1530," *Mitteilungen des Vereins für Geschichte der Stadt Nürnberg* 17 (1906), 178 ff.; hereinafter cited as: Schornbaum, Nürnberg.

Estates in south-central Germany, Brandenburg-Ansbach and Nürnberg, though they supported the Reformation, nevertheless played an independent role in Protestant politics. Charles V, the great political counterpoint to the evangelicals, is the subject of Karl Brandi's well written and researched biography which breaks much new ground.[18] The events related to Duke George of Saxony, one of Luther's early and bitter foes, are documented from the Duke's official papers.[19]

The political negotiations between evangelicals and papists in the period immediately following the Diet of Worms are documented in the dispatches of Hans von der Planitz from the Council of Regency.[20] Johannes von Walter has analyzed in a very compact way the history of the Diet of Augsburg,[21] and Wilhelm Gussmann[22] and Michael Reu[23] have investigated and documented the history of the background of the *Augsburg Confession.*

Julius Köstlin,[24] Roland Bainton,[25] Ernest Schwiebert,[26] and

---

[18] *Kaiser Karl V. Werden und Schicksal einer Persönlichkeit und eines Weltreiches.* Vol. 1: Text (5th ed.; Munich, 1959). Vol. 2: Quellen und Erörterungen (2nd ed.; Munich, 1967). Reprint: Darmstadt, 1959–1967. This reprint is hereinafter cited as: Brandi 1 and 2. Because of the documentary apparatus only this edition has been used in this present volume. An English version was published in London, 1939.

[19] F. Gess (ed.), *Akten und Briefe zur Kirchenpolitik Herzog Georgs von Sachsen* (2 vols.; Leipzig, 1905, 1917); hereinafter cited as: *Akten und Briefe.*

[20] E. Wülcker, H. Virck (eds.), *Des Kursächsischen Rathes Hans von der Planitz Berichte aus dem Reichsregiment in Nürnberg, 1521–1523* (Leipzig, 1899); hereinafter cited as: *Planitz Berichte.*

[21] "Der Reichstag zu Augsburg 1530," *LJB* (1930), 1 ff.; hereinafter cited as: Walter, RA.

[22] *Quellen und Forschungen zur Geschichte des Ausgburgischen Glaubensbekenntnisses* (3 parts in 2 vols.; Leipzig, Bern, 1911–1930); hereinafter cited as Gussman, *QFGAG.*

[23] *The Augsburg Confession. A Collection of Sources with an Historical Introduction* (Chicago, 1930). The first part of this vol. (pp. 3–258) presents the introduction, while the second part (pp. 3–513 with asterisk) presents the sources. In order to facilitate the citing, this work is hereinafter cited as: Reu I and Reu II.

[24] G. Kawerau (ed.), *Martin Luther. Sein Leben und seine Schriften* (5th ed., 2 vols.; Berlin, 1903); hereinafter cited as: Köstlin-Kawerau.

[25] *Here I Stand. A Life of Martin Luther* (Nashville, 1950); hereinafter cited as: Bainton.

[26] *Luther and His Times. The Reformation From a New Perspective* (St. Louis, 1950); hereinafter cited as: Schwiebert.

Robert Fife[27] have made the life and work of Luther the topic of profound studies, which supply the details necessary to place many of the presented letters into the the background of Luther's life. The months which Luther spent in 1530 at the Coburg are the subject of a special study by Hans von Schubert.[28]

One of the themes recurring throughout this volume is Luther's controversy with the enthusiasts. Gordon Rupp[29] has analyzed the life and thought of some of the outstanding theologians of the non-Lutheran Reformation, and Hermann Sasse[30] has detailed the Eucharistic controversy.

A selection from the works of Luther's co-worker Melanchthon is now available in a modern edition.[31] Clyde Manschreck[32] has presented a biography of Melanchthon, while Irmgard Höss[33] has made available a biography of Spalatin. The letters of some of the men with whom Luther either worked or corresponded are invaluable sources of information concerning the background of some of Luther's letters presented in this volume.[34]

---

[27] *The Revolt of Martin Luther* (New York, 1957); hereinafter cited as: Fife. —For the history of the Augustinians, see T. Kolde, *Die deutsche Augustiner-Congregation und Johann von Staupitz* (Gotha, 1879); hereinafter cited as: Kolde.—For Luther's theology, see G. Rupp, *The Righteousness of God. Luther Studies* (London, 1953); hereinafter cited as: Rupp, *Luther Studies.*

[28] "Luther auf der Koburg," *LJB* 12 (1930), 109 ff.; hereinafter cited as: Schubert, LaK.

[29] *Patterns of Reformation* (Philadelphia, 1969); hereinafter cited as: Rupp, *Patterns.*

[30] *This is my Body. Luther's Contention for the Real Presence in the Sacrament of the Altar* (Minneapolis, 1959); hereinafter cited as: Sasse.

[31] R. Stupperich *et al.* (eds.), *Melanchthons Werke in Auswahl* (Gütersloh, 1951–); hereinafter cited as: *Melanchthon: Studienausgabe.* For a selection of Melanchthon's works in English, see *LW* 48, xix, n. 18.

[32] *Melanchthon. The Quiet Reformer* (New York, Nashville, 1958); hereinafter cited as: Manschreck.

[33] *Georg Spalatin: 1484–1545. Ein Leben in der Zeit des Humanismus und der Reformation* (Weimar, 1956); hereinafter cited as: Höss, *Spalatin.*

[34] For Melanchthon's correspondence, see *C.R.* 1–10.—For Zwingli's correspondence, see *C. R. Zwingli Werke,* 7–11.—G. Kawerau (ed.), *Der Briefwechsel des Justus Jonas* (2 vols.; Halle, 1884–1885; reprint: Hildesheim, 1964); hereinafter cited as: Kawerau, *Jonas Briefwechsel.*—O. Vogt (ed.), *Dr. Johannes Bugenhagens Briefwechsel* (Stettin, 1888; reprint with additions: Hildesheim, 1966).—J. V. Pollet, *Martin Bucer, Études sur la Correspondance* (2 vols.; Paris, 1958–1962); hereinafter cited as: Pollet.—M. Lenz (ed.), *Briefwechsel Landgraf Philipps des Grossmüthigen von Hessen mit Bucer* (3 vols.; Stuttgart, 1880–1891; reprint: Hildesheim, 1965); hereinafter cited as: Lenz. *BPB.*

The history of the University of Wittenberg is reflected in the official papers,[35] from which much information on persons and events contemporary with Luther can be gained.

Humanism, no less than Luther, shaped the 16th century and influenced the period from 1522 to 1530. The works of Erasmus of Rotterdam, with whom Luther clashed in 1525, are cited according to the early 18th century Clericus edition,[36] while the correspondence of Erasmus has been made available by Percy S. Allen[37] in a masterful modern edition.[38]

---

[35] W. Friedensburg (ed.), *Urkundenbuch der Universität Wittenberg*, Part 1: 1502–1611 (Magdeburg, 1926); hereinafter cited as: *Urkundenbuch.*—W. Friedensburg, *Geschichte der Universität Wittenberg* (Halle, 1917); hereinafter cited as: Friedensburg, *GUW*. See also *LW* 48, xviii, n. 10.

[36] *Desiderii Erasmi opera omnia* (10 vols.; Leyden, 1703–1706); hereinafter cited as: Clericus.

[37] P. S. Allen *et al.*, *Opus epistolarum Desiderii Erasmi Roterodami* (12 vols.; Oxford, 1906–1958); hereinafter cited as: Allen.

[38] For the works of Ulrich von Hutten, see E. Böcking (ed.), *Ulrich von Hutten, Opera omnia* (7 vols.; Leipzig, 1859–1870); hereinafter cited as: Böcking.

Note on Scriptural References

In quoting Scripture, Luther cites only chapter, not verse, since chapters were not yet customarily divided into verses at that time. In the present translation Luther's own citations have been retained —except in the case of the Psalms—and supplemented or corrected as need be in brackets to conform to the versification in the RSV. If there is a major difference between the text offered by the RSV and the text offered by the Luther Bible, or some other version, then the version which comes closest to the passage cited by Luther has been added in parentheses.

Citations from the Psalms present a special problem. In the Vulgate—and in the modern Roman Catholic English versions based upon it—the Psalms are numbered differently than in the AV and RSV, though in both cases the total number of Psalms is 150. The difference parallels that between the Septuagint and the Hebrew text in that for the greater part of the Psalter the numeration of the former is one behind that of the latter; only for Psalms 1–8 and 148–150 is the numeration identical. Further confusion arises from the fact that in modern Latin and German Bibles—following Hebrew precedent—the title or introductory statement attached to many of the Psalms is frequently given a verse number, a practice not followed in the RSV. In the present volume Luther's Psalm citations, if they were correct in terms of the Vulgate of his time, have been altered directly in the process of translation to conform to the chapter numbers of the RSV. The reference to the Vulgate found occasionally in parentheses suggests only that the quoted text is closer to the Vulgate translation than to the RSV.

LUTHER'S WORKS

VOLUME 49

120

To George Spalatin
Wittenberg, March 30, 1522

One of the most important tasks facing Luther when he returned from the Wartburg was the need to clarify his position on the Wittenberg disturbances.[1] Through his famous Invocavit sermons[2] he restored order to the city and peace of mind to his people. The understanding of the liturgy of the Lord's Supper had become a highly controversial issue during Luther's absence from Wittenberg.[3] In response to this situation Luther wrote his booklet Receiving Both Kinds in the Sacrament.[4] Here he developed his understanding of an evangelical communion service. While at the Wartburg, Luther had translated the New Testament from Greek into German; he continued to polish this translation after his return to Wittenberg. Luther now informs Spalatin of this work and engages his help in finding the proper German terms for some difficult passages in Revelation. Luther also comments briefly on some correspondence matters.

On George Spalatin, see LW 48, 8 f.

Text in Latin: WA, Br 2, 489–490.

Mr. George Spalatin, evangelist at Lochau[5]

Greetings. Here is the letter[6] which you wanted, my Spalatin. I do not remember completely what I wrote to Duke John Frederick,[7] except that I am certain that I stated that he should not introduce

---

[1] See *LW* 48, 386, n. 1.

[2] See *Ibid.*, p. 400, n. 2.

[3] See *LW* 48, 324 f.

[4] See *WA* 10^II, 11 ff.; *LW* 36, 237 ff.

[5] The castle at Lochau was the residency of the Saxon elector. Spalatin served there as chaplain and private secretary of Elector Frederick the Wise (see *LW* 48, 49 f.).

[6] This letter cannot be identified with certainty; for possibilities, see *WA*, Br 2, 490, n. 1.

[7] Duke John Frederick of Saxony; see *LW* 48, 181 f. The letter (*WA*, Br 2, No. 461, dated March 18) deals with the question of whether one should receive the Lord's Supper in "both kinds"; see *LW* 48, 143 f., 324 f., 402.

anything new if this could not be done without giving offense to those weak in faith, and that love is to be preferred to everything else.[8] I wrote the same to Duke Charles.[9]

On my Patmos[10] I translated not only the Gospel of John,[11] but the whole New Testament. Philip[12] and I have begun now to polish the whole thing. It will be (God willing) a worthy piece of work. We shall use your services sometime[s] for finding a right word, so be prepared. [But remember] to give us simple terms, not those [used at] the castle or court, for this book should be famous for its simplicity. To begin with, please give us the names and colors of the gems that are mentioned in Revelation 21; or even better, get [the gems] for us from the court or wherever else you can, so that we can see them.[13]

At present, I am working on a little tract on evangelical communion.[14] Even if this should bring me a great deal of trouble, I am not afraid of it. Christ lives, and for his sake we not only have to be a strong fragrance which will cause death for some and life for others,[15] but we may even have to be put to death.[16]

Farewell, and greet all at the court.

From Wittenberg, March 30, 1522   Martin Luther

---

[8] Reference to the disturbances which occurred in Wittenberg in the fall and early winter of 1521, when Karlstadt and Zwilling introduced changes in the communion liturgy there; see *LW* 48, 386, n. 1.

[9] This letter is not extant; it had been included with *WA*, Br 2, No. 464. Duke Charles von Münsterberg was a distant descendent of King Podiebrad of Bohemia (see *LW* 48, 272, n. 3), who had been banned by the church for supporting the request of the Bohemians that the Lord's Supper be celebrated in "both kinds"; see *LW* 48, 143 f. Luther therefore probably discussed problems similar to those mentioned in *WA*, Br 2, No. 461, the letter to which note 7 refers.

[10] I.e., Wartburg; see *LW* 48, 246, n. 8.

[11] What Luther meant here is not clear; for possibilities, see *WA*, Br 2, 490, n. 4. Apparently Spalatin had previously asked Luther to translate, paraphrase, or write a commentary for the Gospel of John. On Luther's translation of the New Testament, see *LW* 48, 352, n. 16.

[12] Philip Melanchthon; see *LW* 48, 77, n. 3. In a letter dated March 30, 1522, Melanchthon informed Spalatin of the revision of the translation of the New Testament; *C.R.* 1, 567.

[13] On May 10, 1522, Luther repeated this request; see *WA*, Br 2, 524.

[14] *Von beider Gestalt des Sakraments zu nehmen* (*Receiving Both Kinds in the Sacrament*) (Wittenberg: J. Grünenberg, April, 1522), *WA* 10^{II}, 11 ff.; *LW* 36, 237 ff. See also *LW* 48, 324 f.

[15] II Cor. 2:16.

[16] Rom. 8:36.

121

To George Spalatin
[Wittenberg,] May 20, 1522

Luther asks for a contribution of some venison for the wedding banquet of Matthew Aurogallus, the professor of Hebrew in Wittenberg. He also comments on possible candidates for a position.
On George Spalatin, see LW 48, 8 f.
Text in Latin: WA, Br 2, 537.

To Master[1] George Spalatin, a servant of Christ,
my brother in the Lord

Grace and peace. My Spalatin: Aurogallus[2] asks that, if possible, he be honored with some venison for his wedding. As you know, he deserves it, and he is far from being the most insignificant member of our University. Do what you can. The wedding will be next Monday, that is, after *Vocem Jucunditatis*.[3]

I am now writing what I promised, as you know. I shall forward it to you tomorrow.[4] [The writing] of letters and the printing arrangements have thus far hindered me from doing this. Farewell.

May 20, 1522   MARTIN LUTHER

Among the Masters of Arts who are here, we cannot find anyone whom we could recommend. Either they are too old [and] do not wish to move there, or they are not qualified for taking over such a position.[5]

---

[1] I.e., Master of Arts. Literally: "To Mr. Master."
[2] Matthew Goldhahn (*ca.* 1490–1543), or Aurogallus, professor of Hebrew, was the successor of Matthew Adrian (see *LW* 48, 132, n. 1). Goldhahn had studied in Leipzig, and in 1521/22 he came to Wittenberg, where he taught Hebrew for the remainder of his life. He was the author of a Hebrew grammar and was of great help to Luther in the translation of the Old Testament. On Matthew Goldhahn, see *NDB* 1, 457.
[3] The name of this Sunday, "The Voice of Joy," is derived from the first words of the introit for the fifth Sunday after Easter. It fell on May 25, 1522; consequently the wedding was to be on May 26.
[4] Luther's reference here is unclear; for possibilities, see *WA*, Br 2, 537 nn. 3, 4.
[5] The circumstances pertaining to this statement could not be clarified. Perhaps Spalatin needed someone with an M.A. to serve in a specific (teaching) position at court.

122

To an Anonymous Addressee
Wittenberg, May 28, 1522

During the Leipzig Disputation and the Wittenberg disturbances, the reserved attitude of Erasmus toward Luther gradually turned into a critical one. Rumors concerning the possibility of a clash between the Reformer and the Humanist spread, and the unclear stand of Erasmus made his position only more suspicious to the Reformers.[1] It was under these circumstances that Luther wrote this letter as a warning for Erasmus. The addressee is unknown, though there has been much speculation about him.[2] Erasmus soon became acquainted with this letter, and on March 11, 1523, he protested to Spalatin.[3] In the summer of 1523, Luther's letter was published in Strassburg, together with other material, as a separate pamphlet entitled: Iudicium D. Martini Lutheri de Erasmo Roterodamo (Dr. Martin Luther's Opinion Concerning Erasmus of Rotterdam).[4] By publishing this letter, friends of the Reformation in Strassburg[5] tried to force Erasmus to make a public statement concerning his stand on the Reformation.

Text in Latin: WA, Br 2, 544–545. The following translation is based on S-J 2, 123–125.

Grace and peace in Christ

I was glad to receive your last letter, distinguished Sir, because it shows how excellently you think, and how you are progressing in your concern for the Christian cause. I hope and pray that the Lord may perfect what he has begun.[6] I am grieved [by the news] of the fury against Christ which prevails among your people.[7] [The

---

[1] See *ARG* 53 (1962), 60 ff.
[2] See *WA*, Br 2, 542 f.; *S-J* 2, 123.
[3] See Allen 5, No. 1348.
[4] See *WA*, Br 2, 429. Erasmus knew of letter No. 122 prior to the publication of this Strassburg edition; consequently, Rückert, *LB*, p. 121, n. 11, has to be corrected accordingly.
[5] Perhaps Nicholas Gerbel; see *LW* 48, 317 f.
[6] Phil. 1:6.
[7] Literally: ". . . among you [plural]."

affair] will develop, however, so that either the Sovereign himself[8] will voluntarily give up his raging, or someone else will make him do so against his will, and that soon.

I knew before that Mosellanus[9] agreed with Erasmus on predestination, for he is altogether an Erasmian. I, on the contrary, think that Erasmus knows less, or seems to know less, about predestination than the schools of the sophists have known. There is no reason why I should fear my own downfall if I do not change my opinion. Erasmus is not to be feared either in this or in almost any other really important subject that pertains to Christian doctrine. Truth is mightier than eloquence, the Spirit stronger than genius, faith greater than learning. As Paul says: "The foolishness of God is wiser than men."[10] The eloquence of Cicero was often beaten in court by less eloquent men;[11] Julian was more eloquent than Augustine.[12] In summary: Truth conquers lying eloquence, even though it only stammers, as it is written: "Out of the mouth of babes and sucklings hast thou perfected strength to destroy the enemy and the avenger."[13]

I shall not challenge Erasmus; if challenged myself once or twice, I shall not hurry to strike back.[14] I think it unwise, however, for him to array the power of his eloquence against me, for I am afraid he will not find in Luther another Lefèvre; he will not be

---

[8] Perhaps Duke George (see *LW* 48, 110, n. 20), since according to tradition and consensus the addressee lived in Leipzig, which was located in Ducal Saxony.

[9] I.e., Peter Schade (1493–1524). He came from a small village in the Moselle valley, and was professor of classical languages at the University of Leipzig. His interests in classics and his opposition to Scholasticism led him into friendship with Erasmus. He presided over one session of the Leipzig Disputation (see *LW* 48, 126), and at that time was more on Luther's side than on Eck's; but he could not overcome his basically Humanistic conceptions, and therefore he never became an open supporter of Luther. On Peter Schade, see *ADB* 22, 358 f.

[10] I Cor. 1:25.

[11] Marcus Tullius Cicero; see *O.C.D.*, pp. 188 ff.

[12] Julian of Eclanum (died *ca.* 454) was the greatest literary champion of Pelagianism; see *Patrology*, pp. 383 f., 442 f.; *O.D.C.C.*, pp. 752 f.

[13] Ps. 8:2.

[14] This feeling was mutual. Though the papists urged Erasmus to write against Luther and thus to clarify his position on controversial issues, and though Erasmus himself clearly realized what separated him from Luther, he did not yet consider challenging Luther at the time Luther made this statement. See Erasmus to Mosellanus: August 8, 1522; Allen 5, No. 1305; see also note 1.

able to glory over me as he glories over [Lefèvre], saying: "The whole world is congratulating me on defeating the Frenchman."[15] But if he casts the die, he will see that Christ fears neither the gates of hell nor the powers of the air.[16] Poor stammerer that I am,[17] I shall parry the eloquent Erasmus with all confidence, caring nothing for his authority, reputation, or good will. I know what is in this man just as I know[18] the plots of Satan;[19] but I expect him to reveal more clearly from day to day what grudge he nurses against me.

I have told you of this at some length, so that you may not be concerned or fearful on my account; don't be alarmed by other people's high sounding bombast. Yes, give my greetings to Mosellanus, for I don't hold it against him that he follows Erasmus rather than me. Indeed, tell him to be boldly Erasmian. The time will come when he will think differently. Meanwhile, we must bear with the poor understanding of matters held by an excellent friend.

Farewell in the Lord to you, too.[20]

Wittenberg, May 28, 1522

123

To George Spalatin
[Wittenberg,] June 7, 1522

Luther is asking (as he so frequently did)[1] for Spalatin's help. In this instance he is interceding on behalf of a fisherman who was caught poaching on the waters of the Elector and sentenced to pay a large fine.

On George Spalatin, see LW 48, 8 f.

Text in German: WA, Br 2, 556. The following translation, with minor changes, is by Theodore G. Tappert and is used by permission from LCC 18, 171–172.

---

15 On Lefèvre d'Etaples, and his controversy with Erasmus, see *LW* 48, 26, n. 15; 55, n. 10.
16 See Matt. 16:18; Eph. 2:2.
17 For a similar statement, see *LW* 48, 118.
18 Literally: "we know."
19 See II Cor. 2:11.
20 I.e., in addition to Mosellanus.
1 See *LCC* 18, 172 ff.

To the reverend gentleman, Master[2] George Spalatin,
Electoral preacher and chaplain,
my especially gracious lord and friend

Jesus

Grace and peace in Christ. Amen. My dear Master Spalatin: A
poor fisherman made a mistake and on only one occasion fished too
close to the waters of my Most Gracious Lord.[3] I interceded in his
behalf with the tax collector,[4] and I am now informed that he
transferred responsibility for the case to my Most Gracious Lord.
I beg you, therefore, to intercede in my name with my Most
Gracious Lord, in order that the penalty be changed. I understand
that a fine of six hundred pieces of silver[5] has been imposed on
him. I do not ask that he go unpunished; his case should serve as
an example to inspire respect and to demonstrate that there is a government. But I ask that his punishment should not deprive him of his
living. I suggest that he be put in prison for several days, or be
made to live on bread and water for eight days so that people may
see that the purpose [of the punishment] is to reform and not
destroy the man. [Moreover,] it seems to me that this would be
a just penalty for a poor man; the rich, on the other hand, may
properly have their purses plucked. I hope that you will take care
of this.

Herewith I commend you to God's keeping.

June 7, 1522   MARTIN LUTHER

---

[2] I.e., Master of Arts.

[3] Here and throughout this letter Luther is referring to Elector Frederick; see
LW 48, 48 f.

[4] Luther wrote *Schosser*; this was the official of the revenue department who
had to collect taxes, fees, and fines.

[5] Luther wrote X *silbern Schock*. A *Schock* generally has sixty pieces. It is
difficult to arrive at a present day equivalent for these six hundred pieces of
silver. Tappert (*LCC* 18, 171) translates the figure as one hundred and twenty
gulden, without, however, giving a source for this sum; for the gulden, see
LW 48, 11, n. 2.

124

To John von Staupitz
Wittenberg, June 27, 1522

Luther and von Staupitz had apparently not exchanged letters since early 1521 (see WA, Br 2, No. 376, dated February 9, 1521; von Staupitz apparently answered this letter about March 5).[1] Von Staupitz, weary of the impact of the Reformation on the Augustinian Order, had resigned in August, 1520, from the office of vicar general,[2] and during the summer of 1521 left the Augustinians altogether to join the Benedictines. On August 2, 1522, he was elected abbot of St. Peter's Benedictine monastery in Salzburg.[3] Luther tells von Staupitz that he has heard of these developments and expresses his disappointment. Nevertheless, although he cannot agree with von Staupitz, he does not want to pass judgment on his former superior. Luther justifies his stand on celibacy, monastic vows, and the mass, and sees God's hand in the development of his own work. He also reports on the fate of the prior of Antwerp and forwards greetings.

On John von Staupitz, see LW 48, 64, n. 1.

Text in Latin: WA Br 2, 567–568. The following translation is based on S-J 2, 129–131.

To Dr. John [von] Staupitz, a preacher at Salzburg

Grace and peace in Christ. Amen. Reverend and excellent Father: I have learned of your abbacy[4] not only through the letter of the prior of Nürnberg,[5] but also through a common rumor which affirms this so persistently that I would have been forced to believe

---

[1] See WA, Br 2, 263.
[2] See LW 48, 171, n. 7.
[3] See Kolde, pp. 332 ff.
[4] See Introduction.
[5] Wolfgang Volprecht, with whom von Staupitz was corresponding, and who in turn kept Luther informed about the developments in the life of the former vicar general. The letter mentioned by Luther is not extant. On Volprecht, see Kolde, pp. 395 f.; WA, Br 4, 457 f.; WA, Br 13, 102, to WA, Br 4, 458, n. 8.

it even if I had not seen your letter.[6] I suppose lies about us are carried to you by the same channels and in the same way. Although I do not want to interfere with God's will,[7] nevertheless in my ignorance I cannot see how it can be God's will that you should become an abbot, nor do I think this advisable. I do not, however, want to oppose, or pass judgment on, your decision. Yet one thing I beg of you: for the sake of Christ's mercies, do not indiscriminately believe the accusations that are made against either Wenceslas[8] or me. You say that my teachings are praised by those who patronize brothels, and that my recent writings have given great offense.[9] I am not surprised or afraid of this. Certainly we have done nothing here other than publicize the pure Word among the people without [creating] a disturbance, and this we are [still] doing. Both the good and the bad are making use of the Word, [and] as you know, it is not in our power to control [how they use it]. We have set ourselves the task of driving out, by means of the Word, that unclean celibacy, the ungodliness of masses,[10] the tyranny of the religious orders,[11] and whatever else has been introduced by men and set up against sound teachings. We will do what Christ predicted when he said that his angels would gather

---

[6] The "common rumor" apparently consisted of two parts. The first part of the gossip was that von Staupitz was a candidate for the abbacy of St. Peter in Salzburg. This was confirmed by von Staupitz in the letter to Volprecht in Nürnberg, who in turn wrote to Luther about it. In addition, something else must have been rumored, perhaps about the reasons which motivated von Staupitz to join the Benedictines, or perhaps some criticism of Luther, because in the next sentence Luther continues to speak of lies about himself, and asks von Staupitz not to believe them. Consequently it must be assumed that Luther considered at least a part of the "common rumor" plain lies.

[7] The text of one manuscript copy has to be translated as follows: "Although I do not wish to draw you away from God's will . . ." In his letter to Volprecht, von Staupitz apparently justified his plan to become a Benedictine abbot by pointing out that this was God's will, which no man can or should resist.

[8] Wenceslas Link; see *LW* 48, 169 f.; 171, n. 7. Luther is here referring to the decisions passed by the Wittenberg convention of the Augustinians in January of 1522 (see *LW* 48, 356, n. 1; 358, n. 4), for which Link was at least partially responsible. These decisions (text: *St. L.* 15, 1948) were a major step toward the disintegration of the German congregation of the Augustinians (see *LW* 48, 6, n. 3). Luther is now asking the former vicar general not to believe any wild stories about this convention and the role played by Link.

[9] This is obviously a reference to the Wittenberg disturbances; see *LW* 48, 386, n. 1.

[10] See *LW* 48, 283 ff., 292 ff., 297 ff.

[11] See *LW* 48, 324 f., 331 ff.

out of his kindom all causes of offense.[12] My Father, I must destroy
that kingdom of abomination and perdition which belongs to the
pope, together with all his hangers-on. He [Christ] is doing this
without us, of course, without the help of a human hand,[13] solely
through the Word. The Lord knows the end of it.[14] The matter is
beyond our power of comprehension and understanding. Therefore
there is no reason why I should delay until someone is able to understand it.[15] Because of the greatness of God, it is most fitting that
there should arise proportionately great disturbance of minds, great
causes of offense, and great monstrosities. Do not let all these things
disturb you, my Father. I am very hopeful. You can see in these
things God's counsel and his mighty hand. Remember how from
the beginning my cause has always seemed to the world to be terrible and intolerable, yet it has grown stronger day by day. It will
also prevail over that which you so greatly fear; just wait a little
while. Satan feels his wound; this is why he is raging this way, and
throwing everything into confusion. But Christ, who has begun this
work, will tread him under foot, and all the gates of hell will strive
against Christ in vain.[16]

James, the prior of Antwerp, has been taken prisoner again.
It is thought that he has been burned at the stake, together with
two others, for it was certain that he would be put to death because
he repudiated his recantation.[17] [Thus] the sophists are swiftly pre-

---

12 Matt. 13:41.
13 See Dan. 8:25.
14 Literally: "The end of it is coming before the Lord."
15 This sentence is translated quite freely.
16 Matt. 16:18 (Vulgate).
17 James Propst; see *LW* 48, 233, n. 34. He was graduated from Wittenberg
University as Licentiate of Theology on August 12, 1521. Then he returned
to Antwerp, where he preached the gospel as he had been taught in Wittenberg, although the Counter-Reformation tried hard to stop the spreading of
the new teachings in the Netherlands. Suspected of heresy, Propst was lured
to Brussels, where he was jailed by the inquisitor general. After a prolonged
and severe imprisonment, Propst recanted in February of 1522. The authorities
of the church sent him to the Augustinian monastery at Ypres, where he soon
began to preach the gospel in the spirit of the Reformation again. This led to
his second imprisonment, on which Luther is now reporting. However, Propst
was able to escape and found refuge in Wittenberg. It cannot be documented
exactly when he arrived there, but apparently it was some time in August of
1522. Luther and his friends were informed about these events in the life of
Propst through a letter of Melchior Mirisch, the prior of the Augustinian
monastery in Ghent. For details, see *LJB* 33 (1966), 55 ff.

paring their own destruction, which will come to them because of the innocent blood they are shedding. Amen. They are planning to burn me at the stake, too. I am daily challenging Satan and his armor all the more, however, so that the Day of Christ may be hastened in which he will destroy the Antichrist.[18]

Farewell, my Father, and pray for me. Dr. Jerome,[19] Rector Amsdorf,[20] and Philip[21] send their greetings. I hope you will excuse Wenceslas;[22] he is a good man and handles the gospel well, and that is a cause of offense to the holy and to the wise men.[23]

Wittenberg, June 27, 1522

Yours,

MARTIN LUTHER

125

To George Spalatin
[Wittenberg, about September 20, 1522][1]

When Luther returned from the Wartburg, he brought along a draft of his translation of the New Testament. Once settled again,

---

[18] See *LW* 48, 104, n. 7; 114, n. 16.
[19] Jerome Schurf; see *LW* 48, 219, n. 2; W. Schaich-Klose, *D. Hieronymus Schürpf. Leben und Werk des Wittenberger Reformationsjuristen* (1481–1554) (St. Gallen, 1967).
[20] Nicholas von Amsdorf who was president of the University at the time; see *LW* 48, 218.
[21] Philip Melanchthon; see *LW* 48, 77, n. 3.
[22] Wenceslas Link; see note 8.
[23] This is perhaps an allusion to I Cor. 1:18 ff.
[1] The extant autograph of this letter is not dated. The date is based on the following observations. On September 4, Luther wrote to Spalatin that the work on the New Testament would be completed by September 21; *WA*, Br 2, 596. On September 25 Luther sent a copy of the New Testament in German— apparently it was the only author's copy that Lotther had made available to him, and he was not too happy about this—to Spalatin (see *WA*, Br 2, 604), and asked him to forward it to Hans von Berlepsch, the castellan of the Wartburg, who had been Luther's kind host from May, 1521, to February, 1522. On September 21 Luther mentioned to John von Schwarzenberg the recently completed translation of the New Testament; see *WA*, Br 2, 601. In the present letter Luther says that "tomorrow" the preface to Paul's Epistle to the Romans, the last part of the work, would be completed. With another, also undated letter (*WA*, Br 2, No. 537), Luther sent to Spalatin the preface to

he reworked his manuscript with the help of Spalatin,[2] Melanch-thon, and others. As soon as a part of the manuscript was reworked, it was given to the publishing house of Melchior Lotther in Witten-berg, who printed the work in fascicles. As early as May 10, the first fascicle came off the press.[3] Only Spalatin, the Elector, and immediate friends in Wittenberg knew of this great enterprise. If we remember that there was no copyright at that time, then it is understandable that Lotther wanted to put a complete copy of his work on the market. The work in Luther's study and at the press progressed rather rapidly. In early summer the Gospels of Matthew, Mark, and Luke, and Paul's Epistles to the Romans and to the Corin-thians were at the publisher, and were being completed.[4] Finally on September 21 the so-called September-Testament was published with the title "Das Newe Testament Deutzsch." The folio-size book of two hundred twenty-two pages provided the German text of the New Testament, an introduction to the whole New Testament, and introductions to the individual books.

In the following letter, written one day before the work on the New Testament was completed, Luther is forwarding the latest fas-cicle to Spalatin, thus giving him the almost completed New Testa-ment in German. He also asks Spalatin to help obtain a raise in John Bugenhagen's salary, pointing out that this could be accomplished by a rearrangement of the University budget.

On George Spalatin, see LW 48, 8 f.

Text in Latin: WA, Br 2, 598. The following translation is based on S-J 2, 140–141.

Mr. George Spalatin,
Christ's servant and faithful steward

Romans, and said that Spalatin now had three complete copies of the New Testament. Since Luther mentioned the completed work for the first time on September 21, we can be sure that the present letter was written on September 20, and that the other undated letter was written on September 21, the target date for the completion of the New Testament in German, as announced by Luther on September 4.

[2] See p. 4.
[3] See WA, Br 2, 525, n. 1.
[4] See WA, Br 2, 573, 580.

Jesus

Grace and peace. Now you have the whole New Testament[5] for yourself and the Elector,[6] except for the preface to Romans, which will be finished tomorrow.[7] I am also sending a copy for the younger Sovereign,[8] which you will please give him in my name; Lucas[9] and Christian[10] have suggested this. I believe Wolfgang Stein[11] has already sent a copy prior to this for the older Sovereign.[12]

It remains for you to accept the task of working on the Elector so that John Pomer[13] may receive one of the salaries that have been previously wasted on the sophists.[14] For next to Philip[15] he is the best professor of theology here in town, and in the world. I hear, I even know, that he might be snatched away to Erfurt.[16] I wish he were rather kept here. Who knows how long I am to remain [here]? More about this, perhaps, at another time.

Farewell, and pray for me.

MARTIN LUTHER

---

[5] See note 1.
[6] Elector Frederick; see LW 48, 49 f.
[7] See note 1.
[8] Duke John Frederick of Saxony; see LW 48, 181 f.
[9] Lucas Cranach; see LW 48, 201.
[10] Christian Düring; see LW 48, 42, n. 8.
[11] Wolfgang Stein was the court chaplain of Duke John in Weimar. Stein had studied at the University of Erfurt at the time that Luther had been a monk and theological student in Erfurt. After a short time as prior of a Cistercian monastery, Stein studied again at Erfurt, this time apparently for a Master of Arts degree. He entered the service of Duke John in the summer of 1520 and in the summer of 1522 spent several months in Wittenberg. As a faithful follower of Luther, he strongly opposed Karlstadt (see LW 48, 79, n. 12), and was involved in the legal proceedings against this hothead. In 1525 Stein helped to introduce the Reformation in Weimar, and in 1529 he became superintendent there. In 1539 he took over this office in Weissenfels. In 1545 he had to abandon this position because of a legal battle between the Elector and the Duke of Saxony (see LW 48, 110, n. 20). He spent the last years of his life as a pastor in Altenburg and in Weimar, and died sometime between 1548 and 1553. See ZKG 45 (1927), 555 ff.
[12] Duke John of Saxony; see LW 48, 269, n. 8.
[13] I.e., John Bugenhagen; see LW 48, 303, n. 44.
[14] I.e., the Scholastic theologians and philosophers and their courses; see also LW 48, Index: Wittenberg, University.
[15] Philip Melanchthon; see LW 48, 77, n. 3.
[16] Sometime in late October, 1522, Melanchthon also informed Spalatin of the attempts of the citizens and the University of Erfurt to obtain Bugenhagen's services; see C.R. 1, 581.

126

To Henning Teppen
Wittenberg, November 21, 1522

Luther is recommending Holy Scripture as the only true comfort in distress; he promises to remember Teppen in his prayers, and asks for Teppen's prayers in his own behalf.
Text in Latin: WA, Br 2, 618.

To Henning Teppen,[1] a priest at Goslar

Jesus

Grace and peace. Through the grace of God you are stronger, my Henning, than to be in need of my comfort. From your letter[2] I can see your great knowledge of Holy Scripture, and I am too loaded down to be able to deal with you at length and in many words. You have the Apostle who shows to you a garden, or paradise, which is full of comfort, when he says: "Whatever was written, was written for our instruction, so that through patience and the consolation of the Scriptures we might have hope."[3] Here he attributes to Holy Scripture the function of comforting. Who may dare to seek or ask for [comfort] anywhere else?

You also ask for my prayer; I will be glad to do whatever is in my power. But I am myself a sinner in need of various things; I, rather than someone else, need help through the prayers of others. May the Lord Jesus Christ strengthen and perfect you; or if it pleases him, may he liberate you from this evil,[4] yet in such a way that you are not led into the old temptation, so that his blessed name may be hallowed forever, Amen.

Farewell in Christ, and you also pray for me.
Wittenberg, November 21, 1522

Yours,
MARTIN LUTHER

---

[1] The identity of this priest is not certain; for a possibility, see WA, Br 2, 618, n. 1.
[2] This letter is not extant.
[3] Rom. 15:4.
[4] The circumstances of this statement could not be identified.

127

To George Spalatin
[Wittenberg, about December 12, 1522][1]

Luther is commenting on the refugee monk Francis Lambert, and on a book by John von Schwarzenberg; he also encloses a letter for the counts of Schwarzburg. The postscript is of major importance. Luther has encountered difficulties in translating certain passages in the Old Testament; he is now requesting Spalatin's help for the identification and translation of the names of certain animals.

On George Spalatin, see LW 48, 8 f.

Text in Latin: WA, Br 2, 630–631.

To my friend in the Lord, George Spalatin, court preacher
at Lochau:[2] *Personal*

Grace and peace. John Serranus[3] seems to be a good man, but there is no need for my advice. Maybe he does not know the disposition

---

[1] The extant autograph is undated. The date is based on the following observations: On December 4 Luther announced the pending end of the work on the Pentateuch translation; see WA, Br 2, 624. Since in the present letter he is engaging Spalatin's help for some difficult passages in the Pentateuch, it may be assumed that this letter was written in the first part of December, after Luther had finished the translating and was polishing his translation; see also WA, Br 2, 625 f. With this letter Luther also enclosed a letter to Count John Henry of Schwarzburg, which was dated December 12; WA, Br 2, No. 554. One can be certain, therefore, that he wrote No. 127 either the same, or the following, day.

[2] The address is rather freely translated. On Lochau, see p. 3, n. 5.

[3] This was the pseudonym of Francis Lambert (1486/7–1530), which he assumed in 1522 when he had to flee the Franciscan monastery in Avignon because of his opposition to monasticism. In the fall of that year he arrived at Eisenach. Here he published theses in which he openly supported the Reformation; he also explained the Scriptures in private to some citizens. Through Spalatin's help, Lambert was able to go to Wittenberg, where he lectured and studied from January, 1523, to February, 1524. Then he moved on, and having vainly tried to introduce the Reformation in Metz, he stayed for some time in Strassburg, apparently in great poverty. In 1526 he was called to Hesse, where in 1527 he was appointed professor of exegesis at the newly organized University of Marburg. Plans to move to France in order to spread the Reformation in this country were shattered by his sudden death. Theologically, Lambert leaned heavily toward the Reformed tradition (which was emerging in the decade from 1520 to 1530), even though he also had strong feelings for Luther's theological position. Lambert is best known for the role he played at the famous synod of Homberg (1526), and for his contribution to the *Refor-*

and ways of the Sovereign;[4] therefore it seems wise to me to leave him at Eisenach, or wherever he can stay, so that he may teach whomever he can attract. For he does not need a so-called "safe-conduct" any more than we. Let God defend him as He does us. Only do not let him be driven away or deported.

It is impossible to answer Lord von Schwarzenberg in detail,[5] As I have previously written to him[6] and Philip [von] Feilitzsch,[7] it is a huge book;[8] in addition, the majority of his questions have already been answered in books that have meanwhile been published. There remains only the one question concerning the authority of the sword. Christ willing, I shall deal with this in a treatise which I will start after the translation of the Pentateuch is finished.[9]

---

matio ecclesiarum Hassiae, a document which was designed to organize Protestantism in Hesse. Lambert envisioned a synodical structure for the cooperation of the individual congregations of the territory, and (perhaps influenced by some Anabaptist concepts) he projected that the congregations represented in this synod should be made up only of true and sanctified believers, who could publicly testify to their faith through word and deed. On Francis Lambert, see *O.D.C.C.,* p. 780; G. Müller, *Franz Lambert von Avignon und die Reformation in Hessen* (Marburg, 1958); *Church History* 35 (1966), 157 ff.

[4] Elector Frederick; see *LW* 48, 49 f. The background of this statement is not clear. Perhaps Lambert expected some particular favor (as a safe-conduct mentioned in the next sentence) from the Elector which was refused to him.

[5] By mistake Luther wrote *Schwarzburg.* John von Schwarzenberg (1463–1528), a member of an old noble family of Franconia (mentioned in 1172 for the first time), was a high official in the service of the bishops of Bamberg. In 1507 he compiled the *Bamberger Halsgerichtsordnung,* the first "modern" criminal code of a German territory, and the forerunner of the famous *Carolina,* the first criminal code of the German Empire. Because of his strong leanings toward the Reformation, he left the service of the bishop of Bamberg in 1522, and joined the government of the margraves of Brandenburg-Ansbach-Kulmbach. Together with others, von Schwarzenberg was instrumental in introducing and organizing the Reformation in the margraviate. In 1526 he was loaned to Margrave Albrecht of Brandenburg (who was then the grandmaster of the Teutonic Order) to set up a new administration for the duchy of (East) Prussia. See *SMRH* 5 (1968), 145 ff., esp. 147, n. 12.

[6] *WA,* Br 2, No. 538, dated September 21, 1522.

[7] The letter to von Feilitzsch (see *LW* 48, 85, n. 8) is not extant.

[8] Von Schwarzenberg's book, or manuscript, mentioned here is not extant; it was forwarded to Luther by von Feilitzsch, who was representing Electoral Saxony at the Council of Regency (see *LW* 48, 70, n. 1) which was then in session in Nürnberg, where von Feilitzsch met von Schwarzenberg.

[9] Luther dealt with this subject in his *Von weltlicher Obrigkeit, wie weit man ihr Gehorsam schuldig sei (Temporal Authority: To what Extent It Should Be Obeyed)* (Wittenberg: N. Schirlenz, March 1523), *WA* 11, 245 ff.; *LW* 45, 75 ff. See also *LW* 48, 258 ff.

Meanwhile, please send my answer for the Counts of Schwarzburg to Anselm of Tettau.[10]

Farewell.

Please make your help available to us, and describe for us the following animals, classifying them by their species:[11]

Birds of prey: kite, vulture, hawk, sparrow hawk, the male sparrow hawk.

Game animals: gazelle, chamois, ibex, wild goat, or forest goat.

Reptiles: Is *stellio* correctly translated as "salamander," and *lacerta limacio* as "orange-speckled toad"?

[Also please name] whatever others of these [three] groups [you know].

Among the Hebrews, Latins, and Greeks, [the names of] these animals are terribly confused, so that we have to guess at what they are on the basis of the genus and species of the animals. If possible, therefore, I want to know the names, species, and nature of all birds of prey, game animals, and venomous reptiles in German.

Let me tell you the poisonous reptiles which I know:

weasel, mouse, toad	Our translator[12] calls [the first
orange-speckled toad	six of these animals] crocodile,
salamander	mygalon and chameleon, and
lizard	classifies them quite carelessly
snail	among the reptiles in Leviticus 11
mole	[:29–30].

There are so many names of night birds: owl, night heron, great horned owl, wood owl, screech owl.

---

10 Count John Henry von Schwarzburg (who was at Luther's deathbed) had sent a letter to Luther, via Anselm of Tettau (a knight who at that time was an aide-de-camp to the Elector, and who later inherited a part of the Schwarzburg domain). The Count asked Luther what to do with the monks who were in charge of the parish church in Leutenberg (a small town in the Schwarzburg domain), where John Henry wanted to introduce the Reformation. Luther's answer (which he apparently wanted to be directed also to John Henry's father, Count Balthasar II, a staunch supporter of the Roman church) is WA, Br 2, No. 554, dated December 12, 1522.

11 This request was caused by the difficulties which Luther encountered in translating, or in revising his translation of, Lev. 11:13–19, 29 f., and Deut. 14:4 f., 12–19. For more linguistic details, see WA, Br 13, 50 ff.

12 Whenever Luther refers to "our translator" in this letter he is referring to the Vulgate.

These birds I know: vulture, kite, hawk, sparrow hawk—although I cannot identify them too well.

These game animals I know: stag, roe deer, chamois (which our translator renders as *bubalus*).

I do not know what our translator is thinking when he mentions among the kosher animals the goat, stag, antelope, and giraffe.[13]

I wish that you would undertake this part of the work. Take a Hebrew Bible and try to find out all about these animals through careful research, so that we can be sure about these things. I do not have so much time.

Farewell, and pray for me.   MARTIN LUTHER

128

To Wenceslas Link[1]
Wittenberg, December 19, 1522

Luther is sending a dog to Link. He comments with sorrow on a letter from von Staupitz, and gives a rather detailed report on the Counter-Reformation in the Netherlands (especially the fate of the Augustinian monastery in Antwerp and its prior, Henry of Zütphen), as well as on the spreading of the gospel in Bremen, Hamburg, and Friesland. Luther then reports briefly on Francis von Sickingen, Duke George, and a certain friar John P., and comments on Melanchthon's exegesis of Genesis 6:7. He also mentions a statement made by the grand-master of the Teutonic Order to the effect that the church is not being helped if people simply burn the books of the Reformers. He expresses his hope that Link will not be burdened much longer with the office of vicar general, and that he

---

13 In Deut. 14:4–5; the first three animals mentioned here seem to be types of antelopes, the last a type of giraffe.
1 The address of the letter (which is extant only in the common editions of Luther's works) is missing in the oldest printed editions of Luther's collected letters. The reference to Link as vicar general, however (see also note 24), makes it obvious to whom the letter was addressed.

will soon visit Wittenberg. He informs Link that he has finished his work on the Pentateuch translation and on a reprint of the New Testament. He concludes by discussing a financial matter.

On Wenceslas Link, see LW 48, 169 f.

Text in Latin: WA, Br 2, 632–633.

Jesus

Grace and peace. I am sending the promised dog, so you no longer need shake your finger at me.[2] You must clean him daily, or every other day, with a comb.

I don't understand [von] Staupitz' letter;[3] I only realize that it is completely void of the Spirit, and that he does not write as he used to. May the Lord set him straight again.

I believe you know what has happened at Antwerp,[4] and that the women have freed Henry[5] by force. The friars were expelled from the monastery; some were held captive at other places; some were dismissed from custody after they had denied Christ; others stand firmly until now. Those who are sons of the city have been forced to live in the House of the Beghards.[6] All utensils of the monastery have been sold. The church and the monastery are closed and sealed, and are even to be demolished. The Host was transferred with great pomp, as if from a heretical place, to the Church of the Blessed Virgin, where it was received with all reverence by Lady Margaret.[7] Some men and women of the city were harassed

---

[2] Literally: ". . . dog, so that my oppressor's [i.e., Link's] rod might be broken." See Isa. 9:4.

[3] This no-longer extant letter of John von Staupitz (see *LW* 48, 64, n. 1) apparently was addressed to Link, who forwarded it to Luther. Luther also mentioned this letter in his letter to Spalatin, dated December 19, 1522; *WA*, Br 2, 635.

[4] See p. 12, n. 17.

[5] Henry of Zütphen; see *LW* 48, 31, n. 21.

[6] The Beghards were members of a religious brotherhood (active especially in the Netherlands) which promoted revivalism. See *O.D.C.C.*, p. 149.

[7] Margaret of Austria (daughter of Emperor Maximilian I and aunt of Emperor Charles V) was in charge of the government of the Habsburg territories in the Netherlands.

and punished. Henry himself, who wanted to come to us, got only as far as Bremen, where he has stayed.[8] Due to the request of the people, he teaches the Word there. The city council ordered it, though the bishop[9] opposed it. The people there are moved by an astonishing desire for and devotion to God's Word; recently some have even sent to us a special bookdealer to bring books from Wittenberg to them. Henry himself has asked for a Certificate of Obedience[10] from you. Since we could not reach you in such a short time, we issued one in your name with the seal of our prior.[11] If you wish, you may confirm our action.

The people of Hamburg also ask for the Word of God after having expelled the ecclesiastical official and his hangers-on, who had tried to prevent this.[12] Friesland, too, requests ministers of the Word.[13] Thus Christ is being sought by the "Gentiles" and condemned among us "Jews."[14]

---

[8] Luther knew of Henry's movements from a November 29 letter written by Henry from Bremen to some Augustinians from the Netherlands, who were then studying in Wittenberg. See WA, Br 2, 633, n. 6; 8, 663; 13, 52, to WA, Br 2, 633, n. 6.

[9] From 1511 to 1558 Christopher of Brunswick-Lüneburg, a staunch foe of the Reformation, was archbishop of Bremen. By 1534, however, his resistance was broken when the city council of Bremen took over the control of ecclesiastical affairs, and officially introduced the Reformation. On Christopher of Brunswick-Lüneburg, see NDB 3, 243 f.

[10] I.e., an official statement that he was released from obedience to Link as vicar general (see note 24).

[11] I.e., Eberhard Brisger; see p. 58, n. 5.

[12] Hamburg was under the ecclesiastical authority of the archbishop of Bremen, who was represented in Hamburg by an official. According to WA, Br 2, 634, n. 11, this expulsion cannot be verified from other sources. According to H. Reincke (Hamburg am Vorabend der Reformation [Hamburg, 1966], pp. 63 ff., 113), Luther is confusing several events here, of which he had perhaps only heard rumors.

[13] This is perhaps a reference to Count Edzard I of Eastern Friesland (1462–1528), who had strong leanings toward the Reformation, and of whom it was known that he was eagerly studying Luther's writings. On Count Edzard, see NDB 4, 317 f.

[14] In 754, while still heathens, the people of Friesland had killed the missionary Boniface (see O.D.C.C., p. 184). Now, however, they are eager to receive Christ and his gospel. Thus, while Christ (i.e., the gospel as understood by the Reformers) is being rejected among "us Jews" (i.e., among those who should long have been believers), he is being accepted by the heathens or Gentiles, the people of Friesland.

Francis [von] Sickingen[15] has declared war against the Count Palatine. This will be a horrible affair. Duke George and his idol at Merseburg[16] act in keeping with their insanity and foolishness.

Philip has also explained the [verse] "I am sorry that I have made. . . ."[17] [He thinks that this] has the meaning of "changing." "I am sorry" means "I shall change what I have previously made." I do not reject the opinion, however, that Scripture speaks of God in such a way that both the ungodly and the godly experience, concerning God, what is called "[God] is angry" when we feel the wrath, or "God is sorry that he has made" when we feel that his works are being changed.

When[18] we wrote about the answer of the sovereigns to the Papal Legate,[19] we were referring to the reply of the [grand-master] of Prussia, the Margrave Frederick.[20] For he had said that he would willingly assist the church, but that condemning open truth and

---

[15] On Francis von Sickingen, see *LW* 48, 244; Schwiebert, pp. 550 ff.

[16] I.e., Duke George of Saxony (see *LW* 48, 110, n. 20) and the bishop of Merseburg. Luther is perhaps thinking of the Duke's order of November 7 which prevented the sale of Luther's translation of the New Testament. The Duke even went so far as to offer reimbursement to those who had already bought a copy if they would bring it to the local authorities. On November 9 Duke George sent this order to the bishops of Merseburg and of Meissen, asking each to issue a similar order and to enforce it. *Akten und Briefe* 1, 386 f.

[17] Gen. 6:6 f. Luther is referring here to Melanchthon's "annotations" on certain difficult passages in Genesis (*C.R.* 13, 760 ff., esp. 791 f.), which had not yet been published when Luther wrote this letter. The circumstances of Luther's statement, especially the "also," are not clear. Luther could have been thinking of a discussion which he might have had with Link, or of a no-longer extant letter by Link, in which Link set forth an interpretation of this passage. Luther could also have been thinking of the way in which he had translated this passage, since in the last paragraph of this present letter he does refer to this translation.

[18] Literally: "What we wrote . . . Legate, has been accomplished by the master of Prussia. . . ." The letter mentioned here is not extant.

[19] Francesco Chieregato, bishop of Teramo, was then the legate of Pope Hadrian VI (see *O.D.C.C.*, p. 601) to the Empire. On Chieregato, see *NCE* 3, 567.

[20] Luther confuses names here. Frederick, duke of Saxony and grand-master of the Teutonic Order, had died in 1510. His successor as grand-master was Albrecht, margrave of Brandenburg-Ansbach-Kulmbach. In autumn of 1522 Albrecht was in Nürnberg to seek military and diplomatic aid from the Council of Regency (see *LW* 48, 70, n. 1) for the fight against Poland.

burning books is not a way to assist the church;[21] they also say that he does not think badly of the gospel.[22]

May God grant that you will be freed from your splendid office of vicar general; you will soon be free if Master[23] Spangenberg, who opposes you in this office, has his way.[24]

John P.[25] fled from here after he had committed a very shameful deed, which is a disgrace to all of us. He was found by the police in a brothel, quite drunk and in lay clothes. As I hear, he

---

[21] On November 19, 1522, Chieregato addressed the Imperial Estates assembled for the second diet in Nürnberg; see DRTA.JR 3, No. 54. Contrary to all expectation, he only touched on the problem of the Reformation. On December 10 the diet granted the floor to the Legate for the second time, and this time Chieregato discussed the whole issue of the Reformation, calling for the immediate enforcement of the Edict of Worms (see LW 48, 216, n. 7; 210). See DRTA.JR 3, No. 73. Notwithstanding this demand, however, a change in attitude toward the Reformation had taken place in Rome since the Humanistically trained Pope Hadrian VI (see note 19) had taken office in January of 1522. Contrary to his predecessor, Leo X (see LW 48, 100), who had little concern for religious problems and consequently no understanding of the challenges presented to the church by Luther, Hadrian was a religiously dedicated person who was fully aware of the needs of the church. Influenced by the *devotio moderna,* a revival movement especially active in the Netherlands (see O.D.C.C., p. 394), and by the Christ-centered mysticism of Bernard of Clairvaux (see O.D.C.C., p. 160), Hadrian wanted to rally all men of good will to a spiritual renewal of Christendom, as well as to rally all political powers to the defence of Christendom against the rapidly advancing Turks. He attempted to solve the problem of the Reformation by urging reform within the church and the strict enforcement of the Edict of Worms. To accomplish the latter Hadrian approached the German Estates through his legate. Luther was kept informed of developments at the Council of Regency and the second Diet of Nürnberg by the chairman of the Electoral Saxon delegation, Hans von der Planitz.

[22] While in Nürnberg, the Grand-Master came under the influence of Lazarus Spengler, a strong supporter of the Reformation (see LW 48, 184).

[23] I.e., Master of Arts.

[24] Link had been vicar general since August, 1520 (see LW 48, 171, n. 7); he resigned from this office in January, 1523, and accepted a pastorate at Altenburg. Luther's statement here should be compared with that in his letter to Link of December 18, 1521 (LW 48, 359), in order to see how rapidly Luther's thoughts and attitudes toward the practical issues connected with the institutions of the papal church (such as the abandoning of monastic life) were developing. John Bethel of Spangenberg (see LW 48, 29, n. 13) can be considered the leader of a minority group of Augustinians who were strongly opposed to Link's pro-Reformation attitudes and policies (see LW 48, 358, n. 4; 359). After much delay (there were not sufficient officers of the Augustinians available to hold an election), Spangenberg was elected vicar general by the remainder of the Augustinians in September, 1523. See Kolde, pp. 391 ff.

[25] This Augustinian friar, apparently one of the few who had remained in the Wittenberg monastery (see LW 48, 337, n. 4), could not be identified.

was even wounded in some part [of his body], but I found this out later, after his escape. Of course I had previously told him, after his evil deed at Zerbst, that he should not come within my sight if he does anything evil again. He has certainly done this. But pray for this poor man—you know how miserable he must be after committing his evil deeds—so that he does not despair and do even worse things. We sit in shame.

All our people [here] greet you, and ask that you visit us at least once.

Farewell in the Lord, and pray for me. I have finished the translation of the Pentateuch.[26] Another edition of the New Testament has also been completed;[27] now [the printers] will start with the Pentateuch.[28] It is amazing how much we need your knowledge of the German language here.[29] I do not know whether your book-dealer has made his payment. Of course, he has given nothing to me, and I ordered him to pay directly to Lotther.[30] Whether he has done so, I cannot find out, since Lotther himself doesn't know. You should know that the letter[31] was given to Mauser.[32]

Wittenberg, December 19, 1522

Yours,

MARTIN LUTHER

129

To the Council of the City of Stettin
Wittenberg, January 11, 1523

Luther gives his opinion on a controversy between the city council and some canons concerning the tax exemption of the clergy. He

---

26 See p. 17, n. 1.

27 See pp. 13 ff.

28 The Old Testament was printed in fascicles.

29 Apparently Luther sought Link's help for the Bible translation.

30 Melchior Lotther was the operator of one of the publishing houses in Wittenberg and the printer of the New Testament in German. The financial transaction mentioned here was perhaps connected with copies of the New Testament.

31 This letter could not be identified. Was it the letter by von Staupitz mentioned in note 3? Or was it this present letter to Link?

32 On Conrad Mauser, see *WA*, Br 10, 79, n. 4.

suggests that, notwithstanding any privileges, the canons ought to pay taxes and thus assume their share of the burdens of the community.

Text in German: WA, Br 3, 13–14.[1]

To the honorable and wise Mayors and
Council of the City of Old Stettin,
who[2] are all so gracious to me

Grace and peace in Christ. Honorable, wise, dear Sirs and Friends. I have received and studied the letter written by Your Honors, together with the information concerning the case between you and the canons.[3] Since you are anxious to know my ideas and opinion, I cannot deny my service to you. First of all, I shall not deal with the contract[4] which was signed between you [and the canons, for] I expect that the law, as established in the contract, will certainly support you in your claim.[5] Even if no contract had ever been signed the matter in itself is such that if the canons want to conduct themselves in a Christian, godly way, then they should voluntarily submit to bearing the common tax burden of the city like other citizens, notwithstanding all their Imperial and papal privileges, contracts, law, and customs.[6] They ought to do this according to the gospel, for in Matthew 17 [:24–27] Christ pays tax to the emperor, and in Matthew 22 [:21] he says: "Render to Caesar the things that are Caesar's." In Romans 13 [:1 ff.] Paul says: "Let every person be subjected to the governing authority," and, "Pay

---

1 The letter is extant in many manuscript copies, and in the common editions of Luther's works. Soon after Luther had written this letter it was printed several times, both in Wittenberg and elsewhere. For bibliographical information, see WA, Br 3, 13; 8, 663; 13, 53, to WA, Br 3, 13, Fundorte.

2 The last portion of the address (from "who are") is translated quite freely.

3 I.e., the canons of the collegiate chapters of St. Otto and St. Mary in Stettin.

4 In 1492/3 the city and the canons had settled a quarrel on the following terms: The city council granted a tax exemption for some of the property of the canons, who in turn canceled certain yearly rents which were to be paid by the city. Now the city was attempting to revoke this contract and make the canons pay the tax anyway. See WA, Br 3, 12 f.; Enders, *Briefwechsel* 4, 61, n. 1.

5 It is questionable whether Luther's judgment would stand up in court. Luther may have felt this, and for that reason may have continued to focus on the matter of the case rather than its legal form.

6 For Luther's position, see also SMRH 5 (1968), 197 ff.

taxes to whom taxes are due and revenue to whom revenue is due."
St. Peter teaches in the same way.[7] No one is exempt from this
commandment, be he priest or layman, unless he wishes not to be
a Christian.

The canons may argue that the emperor and the secular authorities have given their agreement and consent in this matter.[8]
It is obvious, however, that the emperor cannot give away that
which does not belong to him,[9] or grant something which would
be against God's commandment. Furthermore, even if [the abandoning of the right to tax the clergy] could be justified, [it must
be said] that in the meantime the tax exemption [of the clergy] has
turned into a burden too big for the whole world to bear, and has
come to be intolerably abused. It is against God, conscience, and
love, as well as against reason and right, to tolerate such privileges
any longer. Therefore [the clergy] is obligated to renounce their
privileges so that hardship for the community be avoided. But they
are people who do not intend to live in a brotherly or Christian
way. They run full tilt at everything until they are overburdened
with hatred.

Therefore, I do not know of any other counsel here than that
Your Honors remind them in a friendly way of their Christian duty.
If this does not help, then see to it, by means of a public proclamation, that they be subjected to the governing authority, in accordance with the gospel. For it is un-Christian, even unnatural, to derive benefit and protection from the community and not also to
share in the common burden and expense, to let other people work
but to harvest the fruit of their labors.[10] This is especially the case
because it has become clear now that we do not need canons, and
they do not do anything to disprove this fact, but so far they have
only led us astray with their ecclesiastical racket.[11]

With this I commend you to God; may he grant Your Honors

---

[7] I Pet. 2:13 ff.
[8] I.e., they have agreed not to tax the clergy.
[9] I.e., the obligation (see Rom. 13:1 ff.) to obey secular authority.
[10] See note 6. Luther had developed similar thoughts in 1519; see WA 2,
743 ff.; LW 35, 49 ff.
[11] Luther wrote: mit yren geystlichen Jarmerken. I.e., "with their [the canons']
spiritual [i.e., ecclesiastical] fairs." A Jahrmarkt is a trade fair, which is an
opportunity for profit making, but also for fun and entertainment.

his grace to conclude this and all other matters in a Christian and blessed way. Amen.

Written at Wittenberg, January 11, 1523

MARTIN LUTHER

130

To the Council of the City of Leisnig[1]
Wittenberg, January 29, 1523

In the Middle Ages the income of the individual parish came predominantly from three sources.[2] The first was the tithe, a special tax levied upon all members of the parish. The second was the income derived from endowments with the income from real estate or highway tolls, bridge tolls, water rights, minings rights, etc. Individual contributions, either as cash gifts or as endowments, formed the third source of income. The entire income was generally administered solely by the clergy, and not always in the most correct ways. As a result of mismanagement, or corruption, the underprivileged in a parish often suffered. Toward the end of the Middle Ages, therefore, individuals, or independent religious brotherhoods, or even secular authorities gradually stepped into the field of charities.

The Reformers attempted to organize a proper administration of the parish moneys, and to set up a system for the local care of the poor and sick. Luther was convinced that it was the right and the duty[3] of a local parish, as the congregation of believers, to set

---

[1] The address is missing in the extant witnesses. From the content and background of the letter, however, it is obvious to whom it was addressed.

[2] The following introduction is based on *SMRH* 5 (1968), 197 ff.

[3] This right is the application of Luther's conviction (derived from I Cor. 2:15) that the spiritual man (i.e., the believer who is overcome by the presence of Christ through the power of the Holy Spirit) has the divine right to judge all things, including the legal and organizational problems of the church. Another application of this conviction (this time to the individual Christian) would be the idea of the priesthood of all believers, which Luther had developed in his book *To the Christian Nobility of the German Nation* (*WA* 6, 404 ff.; *LW* 44, 115 ff.). The criteria for setting up a system for handling the finances of the parish were, of course, valid for the organizational life of the parish as a whole. If applied to the pastoral office, e.g., they result in the right of the parish to call its pastor; see note 15. For details, see *SMRH* 5 (1968), 152 ff., 173 ff.

up a system for handling the finances of the parish, and he developed three criteria for such a system: the administration of the finances of the parish had to serve the spiritual center of the parish (that is, the preaching of the Word and the administration of the sacraments); had to acknowledge the basic Christian rights of equality, freedom, and brotherly love; and had to be conducted in an orderly fashion. According to Luther this right of the parish to run its own affairs superseded all other previous legal arrangements.[4]

The Ordnung der Stat Wittenberg (Wittenberg City Ordinance) of January 24, 1522[5] (which was drawn up by Karlstadt but was based on some suggestions of Luther) pulled all ecclesiastical finances of Wittenberg into a Common Chest under the control of both laymen and clergymen; its revenues were to be used exclusively for paying the clergy, maintaining buildings, and for charities. According to this ordinance, these finances were to be handled by parties who were responsible to secular authorities, that is, to the department of revenue of the Electoral government and the city council.

Many cities, both Imperial cities and those which were under the authorities of a territorial ruler, were eager to follow this example set by Wittenberg. As closely knit communities (sometimes even political entities all by themselves, as was the case

---

[4] This right applied not only to finances but to all laws in the church. This is the reason for Luther's strong opposition to the Canon Law of the Roman church. Luther, therefore, encouraged the citizens of Leisnig to break with the traditional ways. The abbot of the Cistercian monastery Buch (close to Leisnig) controlled all aspects of the ecclesiastical affairs of the Leisnig parish. A Master John Gruner and apparently also a Henry Kind, a monk of Buch (see however WA, Br 3, 22, n. 2), preached the gospel to an enthusiastic audience in Leisnig, with the result that in the summer of 1522 the traditional religious life gradually died out. The people of Leisnig invited Luther to visit them; he did so in September of that year, and advised the people to make use of their Christian rights of freedom, equality, and brotherly love for a fundamental reorganization of the parish. Through a joint undertaking of the people of all social classes this was done. The priest appointed by the abbot of Buch was prohibited from celebrating mass and was boycotted, while Gruner and Kind were considered by the people to be their pastors, to be maintained through voluntary contributions. The cancellation of all endowments of the parish and the organization of a Common Chest was also considered. For documentation, see WA 12, 3 ff.

[5] Text: A. Richter (ed.), *Die evangelischen Kirchenordnungen des sechzehnten Jahrhunderts,* 2 (Weimar, 1846), 484 f.

with the Imperial cities),[6] the citizens and the city governments were aware of the corruption that had crept into the handling of the finances of the church; they were also unwilling to tolerate the existing situation which had been stripped of its religious foundation by the Reformers' criticism. In addition many city governments had a keen interest in controlling the wealth of the parishes by incorporating it into the city treasury, if possible.[7] In the early 1520s a number of cities, therefore, adopted ordinances for a Common Chest;[8] among them was Leisnig, a small city in Electoral Saxony.

In letter No. 130, Luther is congratulating the city council of Leisnig upon its newly-adopted ordinance;[9] he also promises his cooperation for the organization of the office of the pastor and for the drawing up of a new liturgy.

Text in German: WA, Br 3, 23.

Grace and Peace in Christ

Brave, honorable dear Sirs and Friends: I was pleased and de-

---

[6] An instructive study in relationship to Nürnberg is presented by H. von Schubert, *Lazarus Spengler und die Reformation in Nürnberg* (Leipzig, 1934); see also V. Vajta (ed.), *Luther and Melanchthon in the History and Theology of the Reformation* (Philadelphia, 1961), pp. 32 ff.; C. S. Meyer (ed.), *Luther for an Ecumenical Age. Essays in Commemoration of the 450th Anniversary of the Reformation* (St. Louis, Mo., 1967), pp. 108 ff. The situation in Nürnberg, the most important Imperial city in southern Germany, was typical of many cities, though not too many were as successful as Nürnberg in incorporating church administration into the political structure of the city and thus controlling the former.

[7] Unfortunately, far too many secular authorities rushed to secularize the resources of the church, and thus alienated church property from ecclesiastical tasks. They were often in no hurry at all to turn these monies or lands over to the Common Chest. In Leisnig, e.g., the mayor refused to make available to the Common Chest certain properties that had belonged to the parish, and the ten *Kastenvorsteher* (a position which combined the present-day office of a deacon, or elder, in the Lutheran church with that of an auditor) appealed to the Elector and to Luther for help. Luther sharply criticized the mayor and urged the Elector to make a decision in the form of an executive order favoring the Common Chest. For reasons unknown, however, the Elector delayed such a decision. See also pp. 45 ff. The result of this tangled situation was that the preachers could not be paid their wages. The visitations that were conducted later were designed to clear up, among other matters, such difficulties regarding finances.

[8] E.g., Augsburg, March, 1522; Nürnberg, September 1522; Kitzingen, 1523; Strassburg, September 1523; the texts of these ordinances are now being made available in the monumental Sehling.

[9] Text: *LW* 45, 176 ff.; Kidd, No. 64.

lighted to receive your Christian writing and statement through Sir Sebastian von Kötteritzsch and Francis Salbach.[10] I am highly pleased with your ordinance and the institution of a Common Chest. I also hope it[11] may both glorify God and serve many people as a fine example of Christian faith and love.[12] I wish and pray that God may bless, strengthen, and perfect your hearts and plans[13] out of the wealth of his grace. Amen.

I willingly make my services available on the other two points for which you, dear Friends, have asked my help: namely, to organize[14] the office of pastor on the basis of Scripture,[15] and to prepare an ordinance for singing, praying, and Scripture reading[16]— although by God's grace you have among yourselves the God-given talent to do this, and are not in need of my poor abilities. Yet God

---

[10] Kötteritzsch was a member of the local nobility of Leisnig (see WA, Br 3, 23, n. 3), who often acted as a spokesman for the people. With Francis Salbach, one of the outstanding citizens of Leisnig, he had visited Luther in Wittenberg after January 25. It is controversial whether "writing" refers to the Leisnig Ordinance, or to the letter written to Luther by the councilors and inhabitants of the city of Leisnig and the incorporated villages (WA, Br 2, No. 576, dated January 25), which was the credential for the delegates. It is certain, however, that through this visit Luther became thoroughly familiar with the events at Leisnig and the plans of the people there.

[11] I.e., the issuance of the Ordinance and the organization of the Common Chest.

[12] This hope apparently was the motivation for Luther to publish the Leisnig Ordinance, together with a preface of his own; see WA 12, 8; LW 45, 169 ff.

[13] In early 1523, the people of Leisnig undertook a complete reorganization of their parish life. They established the Common Chest; called Kind and Gruner (see note 4) as their own pastors and charged them with faithful service; boycotted the priest who remained faithful to the abbot of Buch (continuing to pay him some wages, however); and abolished private masses, all liturgical vestments, and many of the festival days; see WA 12, 6.

[14] Literally: "to put on solid foundation [or: to fortify]."

[15] The Leisnig people wanted a theology of the pastoral office and its relationship to the parish. Luther was to document from Scripture that the parish, the congregation of believers, has the inherent right to call and appoint its pastor and to judge its teachings. Luther fulfilled his promise with his Dass ein christliche Versammlung oder Gemeine Recht und Macht habe, all Lehre zu urtheilen und Lehrer zu berufen . . . (The Right and Power of a Christian Assembly or Congregation to Judge All Teaching and to Call Teachers) (Wittenberg: Cranach and Düring, May 1523), WA 11, 408 ff.; PE 4, 75 ff. This pamphlet of eight pages in quarto encouraged many parishes to introduce the Reformation, even against the will of the authorities, either secular or ecclesiastical. For one example, see SMRH 5 (1968), 151 ff.

[16] Luther fulfilled this promise with his Von Ordnung Gottesdiensts in der Gemeine (Concerning the Order of Public Worship) (Wittenberg: Cranach and Düring, Spring 1523), WA 12, 35 ff.; LW 53, 11 ff.

wills that in dealing with each other we should be humbled and served by one another. By his grace we will yield to this procedure.

With this I commend you all to the grace of our Lord Jesus Christ; may he perfect the good work which he has begun in you until his Day.[17] Amen.

Wittenberg, January 29, 1523　　　　　　MARTIN LUTHER

131

To Eobanus Hessus
[Wittenberg,] March 29, 1523

Luther is extending congratulations on a poem Eobanus Hessus has written. Commenting on the relationship of Humanistic learning to theology, Luther points out that a solid training in the Humanistic studies is a prerequisite for a sound theology.

Eoban Koch (1488–1540), who used the name Eobanus Hessus, was a Humanistic poet who had studied at the University of Erfurt, where he had received his Master of Arts degree in 1509. After a short period in the service of the bishop of Pomesanian, a year of studying law in Frankfurt/Oder, and a short stay in Leipzig, Hessus settled down in Erfurt. Here he was the uncrowned king of the poets, and from 1517 held a chair for Latin in the University. In 1521 he openly endorsed the Reformation, and although never a leader of the movement, he nevertheless remained faithful to Luther. From 1523 to 1526 he studied medicine in Erfurt, and from 1526 to 1533 he taught poetry and rhetoric at the Gymnasium in Nürnberg. After a short stay in Erfurt, he went to the University of Marburg in 1536, to be professor of history. Hessus is known for his Captiva, and for a metric edition of the book of Psalms.

Text in Latin: WA, Br 3, 49–50; the following translation is based on S-J 2, 175 ff.

Martin Luther to Eobanus Hessus, a faithful poet in Christ, my dearest brother: Greetings

Grace and peace! Our dear Crotus,[1] who is traveling with James

---

[17] Phil. 1:6.
[1] Crotus Rubeanus; see LW 48, 143, n. 7.

Fuchs and Peter,[2] has given me your most enjoyable letter;[3] Philip,[4] however, showed me the *Captiva*.[5] Perhaps this much would have been enough for the unpolished Luther[6] to write as a reply to you, excellent Eobanus. For what else should I write, since I wish you to read nothing which is not worthy of your muses?[7] Of course, I know the sincerity of your heart, [and] that you do not scorn poorer writings.

What I think of the *Captiva* you can judge for yourself. You are not of such hard fiber that you do not know [it] yourself, and you are not so conceited[8] as to flatter yourself that you have surpassed even yourself. Yet in this one thing you will not surpass yourself. You will not get yourself to believe that the *Captiva* displeases either me or you. It will be published shortly.[9] Even without our help, it will portray what sort of man its author is, and it doesn't need to be afraid, even of envy. By the way, if I did not know that you would reply that you did it for the sake of propriety, I would protest that in this remarkable [poem] too much glory

---

[2] Peter Eberbach was an Erfurt Humanist; the reference to James Fuchs is unclear. For details, see *WA*, Br 3, 50, n. 1; Enders, *Briefwechsel* 2, 323, n. 1.

[3] This letter is not extant.

[4] Philip Melanchthon; see *LW* 48, 77, n. 3.

[5] Hessus was accused of leanings toward the Roman church not only by some pro-Reformation hotheads in Erfurt, but also by the rather sober and careful Lang (see *LW* 48, 14); see *WA*, Br 2, 566, n. 12. Apparently for the champions of the Reformation in Erfurt Hessus was not outspoken enough in his support of the new movement. In order to demonstrate his support of Luther, Hessus composed the poem which Luther here calls *Captiva,* and sent it to Luther, via Melanchthon; see also note 9.

[6] In corresponding with the Humanists, Luther repeatedly pointed out his lack of polish and eloquence. Luther was not the only one to practice such false modesty; it was typical of the people of the sixteenth century to deprecate their own stylistic abilities, sometimes to gain a compliment. See also *LW* 48, xiv.

[7] Luther used *Musae.* Apparently he was thinking of Calliope and Erato. Since the plural of *musa* is often used to designate (philosophical) studies and poetry, one could translate Luther's phrase also: ". . . worthy of your poetry [or: studies]."

[8] In the text this word is written in Greek.

[9] Melanchthon gave the manuscript to John Setzer, a printer in Hagenau, who had visited Wittenberg and was in the process of returning home. Setzer published the manuscript with the title: *Ecclesiae afflictae epistola ad Lutherum* (*A Letter to Martin Luther by the Afflicted Church*); for bibliographical information, see *WA*, Br 3, 50, n. 3.

has been ascribed to me. Give to others (says the poet)[10] the honor of such a glorious name. Yet I shall endure this undeserved glory, since I have become accustomed to bearing so much disgrace, which I have deserved.

Do not worry that we Germans are becoming more barbarous than we ever have been, or that our theology causes a decline of learning.[11] Certain people are often afraid when there is nothing to fear. I myself am convinced that without the knowledge of the [Humanistic] studies,[12] pure theology can by no means exist, as has been the case until now: when the [Humanistic] studies were miserably ruined and prostrate [theology] declined and lay neglected.[13] I realize there has never been a great revelation of God's Word unless God has first prepared the way by the rise and the flourishing of languages and learning, as though these were forerunners, a sort of [John] the Baptist. Certainly I do not intend that young people should give up poetry and rhetoric. I certainly wish there would be a tremendous number of poets and orators, since I realize that through these studies, as through nothing else, people are wonderfully equipped for grasping the sacred truths, as well as for handling them skillfully and successfully. Of course, wisdom makes the tongues of infants eloquent;[14] but [wisdom] does not wish the gift of language to be despised. Therefore I beg also you to urge your young people at my request (should this have any weight) to study poetry and rhetoric diligently. [As] Christ lives, I am often angry even with myself, that [these] times and ways of living do not give me leisure for an occasional reading of poets and orators. Once I [even] bought an edition of Homer in order to become a Greek.[15]

---

[10] Horace *Satires* i. 4, 44.

[11] This fear was prevalent among the Humanists when they examined Luther's course after the Leipzig Disputation, and the events which were triggered by Luther's tireless production of books and pamphlets. For details, see *ARG* 53 (1962), 60 ff.

[12] Luther wrote *literae*. The context makes obvious that he was thinking of the *bonae literae;* this was the technical term for the Humanistic studies.

[13] See also *LW* 48, 37 f., 42, 56 ff.

[14] Wisdom of Solomon 10:21.

[15] Preserved Smith discovered a copy of Homer's *Iliad* and *Odyssey* owned by Luther; see *ZKG* 32 (1911), 112 f. This copy is now in the library of Columbia University; according to a dedicatory inscription it was given to Luther by Melanchthon; see *ARG* 45 (1954), 228. In the light of Luther's statement

Now I have bothered you enough with these trifles. Think well of Luther, as you can also think well of your *Captiva*.

Farewell and be strong in Christ. Amen.[16]

March 29, 1523

132

To Elector Frederick[1]
Wittenberg, May 29, 1523

Soon after the Diet of Worms, the Imperial government realized the impossibility of enforcing the Edict of Worms.[2] Therefore, the Council of Regency[3] and the Diets of Nürnberg[4] had to find some other solution to the upheaval in church and state that the Reformation was causing. This was especially necessary since the papacy and its hotheaded supporters in the Empire were not willing to sit still and watch the Reformation rapidly spread while the edict was not being enforced. In the spring of 1523 the Council of Regency and the Diet of Nürnberg dropped the problem into the Pope's[5] lap by urging him to call a general council of the church to meet within one year, somewhere convenient to the German nation. The authorities also promised the Pope to do all in their power in the meantime to prevent Luther and his followers from writing and

---

above it is clear that Luther owned at least two copies of Homer's works. Smith's presentation (see also S-J 2, 177, n. 2) has to be balanced with the material presented in *ARG*, *loc. cit.* For Luther's knowledge of the classical authors, see *WA*, Br 13, 55, to *WA*, Br 3, 51, n. 7.

[16] Hessus published Luther's letter almost immediately; for bibliographical information, see *WA*, Br 3, 49. In this original edition the signature is missing because Luther as author had been identified in the title.

[1] The address is missing in the extant autograph, perhaps because Luther did not consider this document to be a letter but rather a brief, or because the document was not "mailed," but was taken along by Schurf personally (see note 8).

[2] See *LW* 48, 210.

[3] See *LW* 48, 70, n. 1.

[4] First Diet of Nürnberg: March 26, 1522–April 30, 1522. Second Diet of Nürnberg: November 17, 1522 (official opening convocation; the work of the diet had begun during the last weeks of October) to February 9, 1523. Third Diet of Nürnberg: January 14, 1524–April 18, 1524.

[5] I.e., here and throughout the letter Hadrian VI; see p. 24, n. 21.

publishing any new books. The authorities decided that in the meantime "only the pure gospel is to be preached;" the term "pure" was, however, qualified by a reference to those writings which were sanctioned by the church. An Imperial mandate to this effect was issued on March 6, 1523,[6] and a special letter[7] was sent to Elector Frederick of Saxony, admonishing him to take the necessary steps to enforce the mandate. The Elector dispatched Jerome Schurf[8] to Wittenberg, along with copies of the letter and the mandate,[9] for a conference with Luther and the University authorities. Schurf was to inform Luther of the Elector's request that Luther and his followers abide by the mandate. The following letter, intended to be used as a public, political document,[10] is Luther's reaction to these developments.

In the first part of the letter Luther reviews the events that led to the writing of his letter, and in the second part he gives his reaction. As proof of his good will he refers first to his prior offers to live in peace. Then he justifies the harshness of his writings by referring to his vocational responsibility, which forces him to promote God's Word and serve the Christian people. And finally, Luther assures the Elector of his willingness to abide by the mandate. In view of the latest publications of some of his foes, however, Luther sees little hope that he will be able to obey the mandate, for, as he underscores, his vocational responsibility makes it impossible for him to be silent if the Word of God is slandered. He sees the possibility that the mandate is designed to silence him and to brand his efforts as evil, while approving the efforts of his opponents. Yet he glosses over this, and focuses on the passage in the mandate concerning the preaching of the gospel, taking it to mean that he would be justified in issuing a rebuttal of his opponents at any time, should they attack the truth of the gospel.

On Elector Frederick, see LW 48, 49 f.

Text in German: WA, Br 3, 75–77.

---

[6] *DRTA.JR*, 3, No. 84. The mandate was not delivered to Elector Frederick until May 6 or 7; see note 25; *Planitz Berichte*, pp. 433 f.

[7] *Planitz Berichte*, No. 160, dated March 6, 1523; see note 25.

[8] Jerome Schurf; see *LW* 48, 219, n. 2.

[9] See *Planitz Berichte*, p. 434.

[10] See the second paragraph from the end of the letter.

First of all, grace and peace in Christ! Most Serene, Noble Sovereign, Most Gracious Lord! In[11] the past days Your Electoral Grace has informed me that His Roman Imperial Majesty's regents, sovereigns and other councilors of the Council of Regency[12] have written[13] to you [as follows]:

When[14] at the most recent Diet of Nürnberg[15] the Pope, through his Legate,[16] solicited and asked for help for the crown of Hungary,[17] this same Legate afterwards dealt[18] verbally (and by using a papal brief and an instruction)[19] with my various writings and teachings, and with those of my followers. [He stated] that necessity required the early consideration of measures to counteract these writings and teachings, which are intended to lead to revolution. [He added] the request that said Imperial Estates set forth and communicate to the Pope their ideas and judgment concerning ways and means of countering my undertakings. Thereupon the honorable regents, electors, sovereigns, and Estates, having long

---

[11] The following translation, especially of the first two paragraphs of the letter, had to be quite free in some instances because Luther's text is very rough. The first four paragraphs of the translated text are all in one sentence in the original. The roughness of the text might be explained by the fact that Luther anticipated that the Electoral chancellery would put this letter into the proper form if it were to be made public.

[12] See note 3.

[13] See note 7.

[14] Here begins an almost verbatim reproduction of portions of the letter written by the Council of Regency on March 6, 1523, to Elector Frederick (see note 7).

[15] I.e., the second Diet of Nürnberg; see note 4.

[16] I.e., here and throughout the letter Francesco Chieregato; see p. 23, n. 19.

[17] On November 19 the Legate addressed a plenary session of the diet on this matter for the first time; see *DRTA.JR* 3, No. 54. The Turks were at that time threatening to overrun Hungary; see *ibid.*, No. 35.

[18] Literally: ". . . Legate did the admonishing and recalling to memory afterwards . . ."

[19] The parentheses have been added by this editor. Luther refers here to the December 10 plenary session of the diet, during which the Legate once more solicited help for Hungary, and then discussed the problem of the Reformation at great length. See *DRTA.JR* 3, 301; *Planitz Berichte*, p. 267 (dated December 11). For the Legate's address, see *DRTA.JR* 3, No. 73. Text of the papal instruction for the Legate, see *DRTA.JR* 3, 388, n. 1. In this December 10 meeting the Legate did not produce a papal brief, nor did he give permission to the Estates to read the instructions to which he referred several times. Finally in a plenary session on January 3 he presented his instructions (different from those of December 10) and a brief. Text of the papal instructions presented on January 3: *DRTA.JR* 3, No. 74; text of the brief: *ibid.*, No. 75.

considered and evaluated the present situation,[20] were unable to come up with a more promising solution than that the Pope, with the consent of [His] Roman Imperial Majesty,[21] should call a free Christian council at a place convenient to the German nation, and should arrange that this council be convened no later than a year from now. Accordingly, the aforementioned regents, electors, sovereigns, and other Estates had their judgment and opinion recorded and sent to the Pope.[22] In addition,[23] they offered in the meantime, until the council convenes, to do everything possible especially insofar as Your Electoral Grace is concerned, since I and some of my followers are living within Your Electoral Grace's territory, to insure that henceforth within this period I and my followers neither write nor have published anything which is new. [The Estates did this] in the confidence that Your Electoral Grace, as an honest elector and as is fitting, would assist in this matter. Likewise every elector, sovereign, and all the other Estates of the Empire are to ordain that in the meantime in the territories subject to them nothing be preached but the holy gospel, according to the explanation set forth in those writings which are approved and accepted by the Christian church, and also that nothing new be printed or sold unless it is first inspected and approved by some learned people who are to be especially appointed for this task. Since said regents, electors, sovereigns, and Estates were prevented from communicating[24] [this program] to Your Electoral Grace because of the hurried departure,[25] and thus from using all diligence

---

[20] Literally: "evaluated the form and occurrence of all matters of the present time." For the lengthy and sometimes quite heated discussions, see *DRTA.JR* 3, 385 ff.

[21] I.e., here and throughout the letter Charles V; see *LW* 48, 175 f.

[22] The Estates apparently turned over their answer to the Legate on February 5; text: *DRTA.JR* 3, No. 82.

[23] Luther is now referring to the mandate and the letter to the Elector; see notes 6, 7.

[24] Literally: "writing." I.e., they could not write to the Elector via von der Planitz, the Elector's ambassador at the diet; see also note 25.

[25] Luther does not specify who departed. This could be a reference to the sudden departure of von der Planitz, the Electoral Saxon ambassador to the Council of Regency and the diet, who from April 20 to May 23 was away from Nürnberg. Using the previous portion of the sentence ("were prevented from communicating"; see also note 24), one could understand this phrase to mean that the Estates were prevented from communicating "this program" to the Elector because the Elector's ambassador had suddenly left

to hinder me and my followers from writing or having anything new published until the expected council [convenes], they approached the Council of Regency and ordered [it] to write Your Electoral Grace.[26] [The Council of Regency was to tell Your Grace of] this promise made to the Pope, and also of the resolution and decision passed by the Estates, and was to urge Your Electoral Grace to comply with [this program] as much as it is within [Your Grace's] power to do so. The request was to be added that Your Electoral Grace make the necessary arrangements,[27] as was commanded above, to prevent me and my followers from writing or having anything printed in the meantime regarding the place of the above mentioned future council. In this way the tentative promise given to the Pope, that Your Electoral Grace would surely cooperate in this, would be kept; and further, under these circumstances the above mentioned resolution might the more certainly be enforced, etc.[28]

In view of this Your Electoral Grace has urgently informed me[29] that it is your wish for me to comply blamelessly [with this

---

Nürnberg. This interpretation is strengthened by the observation that as late as April 16 the letter to the Elector had not yet been issued (see *Planitz Berichte*, p. 426). When the letter was finally completed is not known, but it was dated back to March 6, obviously to bring it into agreement with the date of the mandate. Consequently, according to the letter itself, one reason for the letter of the Council of Regency to Elector Frederick was supposed to have been the fact that von der Planitz was not available in Nürnberg. This "reason" is phoney, however, and reveals the fact that the Council dated the letter back to March 6, because on March 6, or prior to that date (i.e., at the time that the decision concerning the Luther problem was made), von der Planitz was present in Nürnberg. One can arrive at another possible interpretation of this phrase by viewing it against the background of the end of the diet. On February 9 the final resolution was presented to the diet, a resolution against which the city delegates and other delegates protested. Since this protest was not accepted by the majority, the city delegates left the diet. Consequently no resolution could be promulgated, and the diet simply faded away. See *DRTA.JR* 3, 736. "Hurried departure" would then refer to the fact that, because of these circumstances (i.e., the departure of certain delegations, and the fact that no resolution could be proclaimed), the Estates were prevented from communicating with von der Planitz (see note 24), and therefore approached the Council of Regency to write the letter.
[26] The Council of Regency did this with the letter which was dated March 6, but which actually was written later; see note 25.
[27] Literally: "ordain, forestall, and prevent."
[28] Here Luther's review of the events of the past based on the letter of the Council of Regency to the Elector ends.
[29] See Introduction.

decision], so that, since Your Electoral Grace has just now published this Imperial mandate,[30] no one should have reason to complain of anything done contrary to this order. Many thoroughly deliberated reasons [supported Your Grace's wish]; it would take too much time to cite them all, and might be boring to Your Electoral Grace to read them.

In reply to this, Most Gracious Lord, I shall not keep my humble opinion from Your Electoral Grace. I have humbly and gratefully received[31] Your Electoral Grace's request. With good reasons, without boasting, and in line with several earlier [statements] made in public,[32] I am able to write Your Electoral Grace that my mind and intention have never been—nor are they even now—set on slandering anyone of high or low position, nor on writing, teaching, or preaching anything which could cause disturbance, disunity, or rebellion in the Holy Roman Empire, or could lead Christians into error. I have often written and preached harshly against these things.[33] However, my sole purpose from beginning to end has been and still is to write, teach, preach, do, and promote nothing else but that which serves, and is necessary and useful for, the strengthening of God's Word and honor, and also of the holy, true faith, of the love of one's neighbor, and consequently of the well-being of all of Christendom. In this matter, with God's help, I can stand with a good conscience before my God.

That up to now I wrote so harshly and earnestly against some people of various standings is not without reason; yet it was done by me without hatred or an un-Christian heart. To be sure, I certainly know that my harsh writing has been and still is distasteful to and opposed by many of my friends and enemies, including Your Electoral Grace; in addition, at various times Your Electoral Grace has opposed me, and told me to abstain from such activity. But it is also true that I at first entered this arena without Your Electoral Grace's counsel, knowledge, or consent. At my own risk I returned last year to Wittenberg. I did not intend to be a burden

---

[30] For the mandate, see note 6. On May 25 the Elector issued the mandate to his officials for the promulgation of the Imperial mandate; see DRTA.JR 3, 448, n. 1.

[31] Literally: "I have in all things humbly . . ."

[32] See LW 48, Index: Luther, Martin: Offers to present himself.

[33] See, e.g., LW 48, 351, n. 9; 355, n. 18.

to anyone on earth, but only to take care of the small flock which God has entrusted to me, and to serve the whole Christian congregation with my poor ability, as I am obligated to do out of Christian duty.[34]

From the bottom of my heart I would be inclined to refrain from any further writing, especially harsh writing. However, since some of those who are ill disposed toward me [are not silent]— especially Sir John Faber (the vicar of the bishop of Constance),[35] [who] has written a big book in Latin against me, which was recently published at Leipzig, and also Emser,[36] [who] publishes one book after the other in German against me, [books] which do not do much good and also do not harm me, [yet] are full of all kinds of slander not only against my reputation as a Christian but also against the holy gospel—it will be extremely difficult for me, as Your Electoral Grace and all Christian people can understand, to tolerate such slander against God, my Lord, and to tolerate the fact that the wanton writings of my opponents should be considered honorable writings, and that my own rebuttal, which is necessary and which they force me to make, should be [considered] malicious, bad, and even be prohibited. Nevertheless I shall be of firm con-

---

[34] See also *LW* 48, 388 ff.

[35] The parentheses have been added by this editor. John Faber (1478–1541), or Fabri (sometimes called "The Hammer of the Heretics"), had studied theology and Canon Law at Tübingen and Freiburg/Breisgau, and in 1518 was appointed vicar general of the bishop of Constance. As an admirer of Erasmus of Rotterdam, Faber was an ardent promoter of the Humanistic reform program. Initially he was friendly with Zwingli and Melanchthon, and could even criticize Eck for his malicious opposition to Luther. From 1521 Faber strongly opposed the Reformation, however, and as early as August, 1522, he published in Rome his *Adversus dogmata Martini Lutheri* (*Against Martin Luther's Teachings*), the first in a series of broadsides against the Reformation. (This is the "big book in Latin" mentioned by Luther above. Luther refers to it in the reprint which was published in Leipzig in April, 1523. For bibliographical information, see *WA* 12, 81 f.) In 1523 Faber became chaplain to Archduke Ferdinand I of Austria. In this capacity Faber gained the confidence of Ferdinand, who used him for many missions in connection with ecclesiastical and secular affairs. As reward for Faber's services, Ferdinand saw to it that Faber was appointed bishop of Vienna in 1530. In this capacity Faber worked hard to improve the quality of the clergy under his jurisdiction, and dedicated himself to preaching and writing for the spiritual betterment of the people, and for the purpose of combating the Reformation. On John Faber, see *LThK* 3, 1333; *NDB* 4, 728 f.; *NCE* 5, 782.

[36] Jerome Emser; *LW* 48, 137, n. 19; 264 ff. His latest attack against Luther had been published in January, 1523; see Enders, *Briefwechsel* 4, 146, n. 3.

fidence and hope in God, since the Imperial mandate,[37] now issued, clearly states, among other things, that only the holy gospel is to be preached and taught, and further, that teachers and preachers are to be wisely instructed in such a way that [the mandate] may not be misunderstood as hindrance or oppression of the evangelical truth. [Therefore] it should also not be forbidden to me, and no one may reproach me, if I have to protect the divine evangelical truth, rather than my own innocence, in a written defense.

In humble obedience I did not wish to withhold this information from Your Electoral Grace any longer. In all obedience I request that [Your Grace] graciously accept my humble reply and forward it [to whom] Your Electoral Grace pleases.[38] For, God be praised, I am not afraid in what I am doing, and I cannot be ashamed of this cause and of God's Word.

May the eternal God enlighten and strengthen Your Electoral Grace's heart with his divine grace and mercy. Amen.

Wittenberg, May 29, 1523

> Your Electoral Grace's humble servant,
> MARTIN LUTHER

133

To John Oecolampadius
Wittenberg, June 20, 1523

The growing alienation between Luther and Erasmus (the latter was living in Basel at that time) caused considerable uneasiness for some people like Oecolampadius, and Luther tried to keep his position clear and understandable in the minds of his friends. Oecolampadius, having abandoned monastic life in January, 1522, moved to Basel in November, 1522, where he worked for a publishing house while also lecturing to the people on Isaiah. Luther is now briefly commenting on Oecolampadius' abandonment of monasti-

---

[37] See note 6. The passage to which Luther is referring can be found in *DRTA.JR* 3, 449, lines 25 ff.

[38] On June 20 the Elector forwarded a copy of this letter to von der Planitz in Nürnberg; see *Planitz Berichte*, p. 469.

cism, and urging him not to be dismayed by the fact that Erasmus is displeased with him. Luther acknowledges the linguistic ability of Erasmus, but he does not hesitate to state that he has little use for Erasmus' theology, and expresses the hope that Oecolampadius might not become overwhelmed by Erasmus' prestige. In closing Luther mentions Oecolampadius' translation of a work by Chrysostom, and tells of the time and energy he is spending in taking care of monks and nuns who have abandoned their orders and come to him for help.

On Oecolampadius, see LW 48, 230, n. 14.

Text in Latin: WA, Br 3, 96–97.

To the learned and devout man, Mr. John Oecolampadius,
a disciple and faithful servant of Christ,
my brother in the Lord

Grace and peace in Christ. First, I want to ask you, excellent Oecolampadius, not to attribute to ungratefulness or laziness the fact that so far I have not written anything to you. I myself have not received a letter from you since you shook off [St.] Bridget.[1] At the same time I thought that since Christ has strengthened you with the power of such great courage—so that you, conquering the superstition [which bothered your] conscience, were able to free yourself from this yoke of Satan—you have become too great a man for me to expect a letter from you, or that I, in turn, could strengthen you with a letter. Of course, we have highly approved of your courage and the great deed. Philip[2] does not cease extolling you to me each day, rejoicing with special delight in the recollections he has of you.[3]

May the Lord strengthen you in your task of lecturing on

---

[1] In January, 1522, Oecolampadius had left the St. Bridget monastery in Altomünster (in Upper Bavaria). He then went to the Ebernburg, one of Francis von Sickingen's castles (see LW 48, 244), and in November, 1522, went to Basel. See E. Staehelin (ed.), *Briefe und Akten zum Leben Oekolampads* (Leipzig, 1927/34), 1, 175, n. 1; 2, 781 f. None of Oecolampadius' letters of his time in Altomünster seems to be extant.

[2] Philip Melanchthon; see LW 48, 77, n. 3.

[3] In 1513 Oecolampadius and Melanchthon were studying Greek together in Tübingen; see C.R. 1, 26; 4, 720; Staehelin, *op. cit.*, 1, 23.

Isaiah,[4] even though this irritates Erasmus,[5] as someone has written
to me. Do not be disturbed by his displeasure. What Erasmus
thinks, or pretends to think, in his judgment of spiritual matters
is abundantly shown in his booklets from the first to the last. Although I myself feel his stings all over,[6] yet since he pretends not
to be my open foe[7] I, too, pretend not to understand his cunning;
however, I understand him better than he thinks. He has accomplished what he was called to do: he has introduced among us
[the knowledge of] languages,[8] and has called us away from the
sacrilegious studies.[9] Perhaps he himself will die with Moses in the
plains of Moab,[10] for he does not advance to the better studies
(those which pertain to piety). I greatly wish he would restrain
himself from dealing with Holy Scripture and writing his *Paraphrases*,[11] for he is not up to this task; he takes the time of [his]
readers in vain, and he hinders them in studying Scripture. He has
done enough in showing us the evil. He is (in my opinion) unable
to show us the good and to lead us into the promised land. But
why do I talk so much of Erasmus? Only so that you will not be
influenced by his name and authority, but rather be happy when
you feel that something displeases him in this matter of Scripture.
For he is a man who is unable to have, or does not want to have,
a right judgment in these matters, as almost the whole world is beginning to perceive of him.[12]

---

[4] Since April, 1523, Oecolampadius had been lecturing on Isaiah. For this
lecture, see Staehelin, *op. cit.*, 1, 219, n. 7.

[5] The channels through which Luther found out about this could not be
verified. Luther made a similar statement in a letter to Nicholas Gerbel in
Strassburg (see *LW* 48, 317 f.), which was written perhaps at the beginning
of June, 1523; see *WA* 12, 53 ff.

[6] Luther made a similar statement in May, 1522; see *WA*, Br 2, 527. Luther
based his opinion on some of the material published by Erasmus at that time;
see *ibid.*, 528, n. 6; *ARG* 53 (1962), 63 ff.

[7] See pp. 7 f., and the letter quoted in note 6.

[8] See *LW* 48, 52 f.

[9] I.e., the Scholastic studies; for a similar statement, see *LW* 48, 40.

[10] Deut. 34:1, 5.

[11] Since 1517 Erasmus had been publishing his *Paraphrases* (Clericus 7) of
the individual books of the New Testament. They were rather free paraphrases
of the text, and were designed as a theological supplement to the linguistic
commentary which he had furnished in his edition of the New Testament (see
LW 48, 23).

[12] Erasmus soon knew of this letter—we do not know how—and voiced his
indignation in letters to some of his friends; see Allen 5, Nos. 1384, 1397.

I have not yet seen your translations from Chrysostom.[13] I hope you will kindly tolerate my verbosity, since I know that you do not need such comforters. Christ, who dwells in you and works through you, will not forsake you. Please, pray for me too, for I am so occupied with external business that there is a danger that I, who began in the spirit, will be worn out by the flesh.[14] The nuns and monks who have left [their orders] steal many hours from me,[15] so that I serve everyone's needs—to say nothing of the mixed multitude of people who claim my services in many ways.

Farewell, excellent Oecolampadius, and the grace of Christ be with you. Greet all our friends.

Wittenberg, June 20, 1523   MARTIN LUTHER

134

To Elector Frederick
Leisnig, August 11, 1523

In August, 1523, Luther went to Leisnig to investigate some problems that had arisen there in connection with the establishment of the Common Chest.[1] In the following letter he reports on his findings, and urges the Elector to intervene in favor of the congregation and against the city council, which was retaining certain properties which at one time belonged to the church.

On Elector Frederick, see LW 48, 49 f.

Text in German: WA, Br 3, 124–125.

To the Most Serene and Noble Sovereign and Lord,
Sir Frederick, duke in Saxony, elector, etc.,
margrave in Meissen and landgrave in Thuringia,
my Most Gracious Lord

Grace and peace in Christ. Most Serene, Noble Sovereign, Most

---

[13] Oecolampadius' *Psegmata Joannis Chrysostomi* (Basel: A. Cratander, March 1523), is a selection from the works of Chrysostom in Latin translation. (On Chrysostom, see *Patrology*, pp. 373 ff.; *O.D.C.C.*, pp. 282 f.) On this translation, see Staehelin, *op. cit.*, 1, 207 ff.

[14] This is perhaps an allusion to Gal. 3:3.

[15] See also Luther's April 10 letter to Spalatin; WA, Br 3, 54.

[1] See p. 30, n. 7.

Gracious Lord! I am now in Leisnig because of the discord about
their Common Chest, and I have learned what the situation of this
affair is. All the disputed points have been settled except one,
namely, that the property, which so far has belonged to the local
parish, and of which much was used for ungodly endowments[2]
and [other] abuses, has not yet been handed over [to the Common
Chest].[3] Some of the city councilors wish a decree from Your Electoral Grace, and want to wait for it.[4] The situation being what it
is, any extended delay is dangerous, for through wicked tongues
Satan is making the matter more bitter and worse on both sides,
and eventually may cause an explosion among the mob, which is
an unsure animal if not tamed and made certain of its place.[5]

Therefore it is my humble request to Your Electoral Grace
that Your Electoral Grace issue a decree, so that not only the present disgrace[6] (which wicked mouths and hearts already force upon
the gospel) but also any future glee of our enemies may be avoided;
for these people continually wait for the chance to mock and to
say: "Aha, Aha! our eyes have seen it."[7] David and many prophets
prayed heartily to God to oppose this, and we ought likewise to
pray that it be checked by your Electoral Grace (since it is [Your
Grace's] task).[8] For any disgrace to the gospel is disgrace to God,
which justly ought to upset us. Even a child knows very well that
the city council has no right to retain under its own power those

---

[2] I.e., endowments for the celebration of masses for the dead.

[3] *Leisnig Ordinance,* Art. II, 1–3; Kidd, p. 123.

[4] See p. 30, n. 7.

[5] The Wittenberg disturbances (see *LW* 48, 386, n. 1) caused in Luther a
deeply rooted suspicion of all spontaneous expression of the people's will. In
addition Luther knew well that masses of people can be led to all sorts of
actions—even contradictory actions—if aroused by agitation. Although the
Reformation was introduced in Leisnig in a peaceful way through a consensus
of the people, irrespective of their social class, Luther, knowing how easily
people can change their minds, now voices his fear that the good beginnings of
Leisnig may be destroyed by Satan through mob action.

[6] I.e., that the institution of the Common Chest does not work, and that consequently the old order in ecclesiastical affairs is replaced by chaos.

[7] Ps. 35:21 (Vulgate).

[8] It was Luther's conviction that God has charged secular authority with the
maintaining of law and order within society, and that secular authority must
help to restore proper order in the external affairs of the church. Luther was
equally emphatic in pointing out, however, that secular authority has no legal
or administrative rights or privileges within the church; all that it can do is
help to secure the three basic spiritual rights of the Christian (see p. 29,
n. 4). See *SMRH* 5 (1968), 153, n. 33; 191, n. 117; 192 f.

properties which have been freed through the demise of un-Christian endowments, but that [such properties] must be diverted again to Christian use,[9] or to whatever [use] the government determines.[10]

I am disturbed to realize—and I have now experienced it first hand—that the city councilors are so embittered that they would rather tolerate, and would even be willing to reintroduce and re-establish—contrary to the gospel—all the un-Christian practices and endowments which have already been abolished. May the grace of God grant that Your Electoral Grace energetically oppose this. Even if Christ should let them begin this, I hope he will not permit them to complete it.

Another reason for approaching Your Electoral Grace is that if the property of the parish is not handed over [to the Common Chest], then the [institution of the] Chest must soon come to an end, since there is nothing in it and not enough comes in to provide for [the pastor][11] according to the ordinance.[12] For the sake of God's honor, therefore, may Your Electoral Grace decide this matter most beneficially, and not give an opportunity to the enemies of the Word for rejoicing, and a reason to the poor for mourning.[13]

May God's mercy instruct and rule Your Electoral Grace's mind and heart. Amen.

Leisnig, August 11, 1523   Your Electoral Grace's

dedicated

MARTIN LUTHER

---

[9] Throughout his life Luther was strongly opposed to *Kirchenraub*, i.e., any kind of secularization of properties or economic rights of a local parish by secular authorities without due compensation.

[10] See note 8.

[11] Luther wrote: *die person, i.e.,* the person. Were we better informed about the situation in Leisnig we could interpret Luther's statement more adequately. Did the Leisnig parish have deacons, janitors, musicians? Then one would have to translate: ". . . provide for the personnel [of the parish] . . ." Or were there only two pastors (see p. 29, n. 4) who had to be maintained? Then the interpretation "pastor" or "pastors" would suffice. In any case, it is clear what Luther meant here.

[12] I.e., the *Leisnig Ordinance,* Art. V; see Kidd, p. 124.

[13] Having returned to Wittenberg, Luther repeated his plea on August 19; WA, Br 3, No. 647. For some unknown reason, however, no decision was made by the Elector. In November, 1524, Luther complained to Spalatin that the Leisnig people will force their pastor to leave because they have let him starve. Why does the Elector procrastinate about making a decision? See WA, Br 3, 390. It was not until 1529 that the issue was settled when the visitation commission came to Leisnig and confirmed the institution of the Common Chest. See WA 12, 7.

135

To John von Staupitz
Wittenberg, September 17, 1523

Luther is expressing not only his disappointment about von Staup-
itz' apparent continued adherence to monasticism, but also his hope
that his former superior might soon make a clear break with the
papacy by leaving the monastery at Salzburg. Luther is also won-
dering whether von Staupitz' attitude toward him has changed.
Notwithstanding any doubt and disappointment, Luther assures
von Staupitz of his continued affection, gratitude, and prayer. He
also intercedes in behalf of a certain monk who has left the Salz-
burg monastery without permission.
On John von Staupitz, see LW 48, 64, n. 1.
Text in Latin: WA, Br 3, 155–156.

To the Reverend Father in Christ, Doctor John,
abbot of St. Peter's Benedictine monastery in Salzburg,
my superior, father, and teacher in the Lord

Grace and peace in Christ Jesus our Lord! Reverend Father in
Christ: Your silence is quite unjust, and you can judge for yourself what I am forced to think of it. Yet even if I have lost your
favor and good will, it would not be right for me to forget you or
to be ungrateful to you, for it was through you that the light of
the gospel first began to shine out of the darkness into my heart.[1]

I also have to say that it is true that it would have been more
agreeable to me had you not become an abbot.[2] But since you
have, let us be considerate of each other, and each grant the other
his opinion. I, indeed, together with your best friends, have not
so much taken it ill that you are estranged from us as that you
have put yourself into the hands of that infamous monster, your
Cardinal.[3] He does whatever he pleases and whatever he can get

---

[1] See *LW* 48, 65 ff.; *WA*, TR 1, No. 173: "I have all my [wisdom] from
Doctor Staupitz."
[2] See pp. 10 f.
[3] I.e., here and throughout this letter, Matthew Lang; see *LW* 48, 99, n. 14.
Von Staupitz was only a figure in the game of church politics played by Lang,

away with; the world hardly can endure it any longer, but now you have to tolerate it and be silent. It will be a miracle if you do not fall into the danger of denying Christ. Therefore we earnestly wish and pray that you may be released from this tyrant's jail and given back to us, and we hope that this is also your intention. Insofar as I have known you up to this time, I am unable to make any sense out of these two contradictions: that you should still be the same man you were, yet have decided to stay there; or if you are still the same man, that you are not constantly planning to get away from there.[4] For the latter, however, we still have good hope, since we all think the best of you and wish the best for you; of course, this hope has been rather badly shattered by your long silence.

For this reason I have dared to write this letter to you in behalf of Brother Achatius,[5] who was once a prisoner at your monastery, but I hope is now a free man in Christ. If you are still what you have been to us, then I not only dare to ask pardon for him for fleeing without permission (I hope you will richly grant that to him), but I also beseech you earnestly to give him something of the great wealth of your monastery [at Salzburg],[6] so that the poor and needy man can start a better way of leading a new life. He has asked me to do this. Although I was doubtful and uncertain about doing so, I finally took more hope and agreed to do it, since thus far I still assume the best of you. But if you have become another man toward us—Christ forbid (to be frank with you)—I will waste no more words, but invoke God's mercy on you and on us all. You see, therefore, Reverend Father, with what great doubts I am writing, because through your extended silence you have left us uncertain for such a long time about your feelings toward us. On the other hand, you can be most certain about our thoughts

---

who had obtained from Rome the necessary permissions for the former vicar general of the Augustinians to join the Benedictines, and who had succeeded in having him elected abbot of St. Peter. See Kolde, pp. 329 ff.

[4] Whether von Staupitz ever had the intention of leaving Salzburg cannot be verified, but it seems highly doubtful.

[5] This former member of St. Peter's monastery in Salzburg can not be identified with certainty; for a possibility, see Kolde, p. 349, n. 2.

[6] Luther was mistaken here, for St. Peter's monastery was quite poor; see Kolde, p. 334.

and feelings.[7] I am sure you do not really despise us, although we may displease you in everything. I shall certainly not cease wishing and praying that you will be turned away from your Cardinal and the papacy as I am, and as certainly you yourself once were. May the Lord hear me and take you to himself, together with us. Amen.

Wittenberg, September 17, 1523

Your son,

MARTIN LUTHER

136

To Gregory Brück
Wittenberg, October 18, 1523

In 1523 James Strauss,[1] a preacher in Eisenach, published fifty-one theses on the subject of lending money at interest. He based his

---

[7] For Luther's last extant letter to von Staupitz, see pp. 10 ff. On April 1, 1524, von Staupitz answered either the present letter or another (no-longer extant) letter by Luther; see WA, Br 3, No. 726. The present letter and von Staupitz' reply of 1524 are the last extant letters exchanged between Luther and his former superior, who died on December 28, 1524.

[1] James Strauss (*ca.* 1480–1533) was one of the Reformation hotheads who now and then appeared in the early sixteenth century. He was apparently born in Basel and studied in Freiburg/Breisgau, where he was graduated as Doctor of Theology in 1516(?). From 1521 to May, 1522, while preaching in the Inn valley against the abuses of the papal church, he found an enthusiastic audience, especially among the middle and lower classes. He was forced to leave this area because of the increasing pressure put on the political authorities by the ecclesiastical officials. Upon Luther's recommendation Strauss became the chaplain of Count George of Wertheim but was soon pushed out again due to personal difficulties. At the end of 1522 he became a preacher in Eisenach, where he forcefully introduced the Reformation, but at the same time offended people by his lack of tact. He directed his attention not only to abuses in religious life, but also to social problems. In a series of sermons he dealt with the lending of money at interest. He summarized his position in fifty-one theses which he published under the title: "*Haubstuck und Artickel Christenlicher leer wider den vnchristlichen wucher* (*Main Argument and Articles of Christian Teaching against Un-Christian Usury*), the book to which Luther is referring; for bibliographical information, see WA, Br 3, 177, n. 1. Through his opposition to the paying of interest, Strauss became one of the champions of the peasants. Although he tried to calm the peasants, and indeed separated himself from them, his call for self-help (see the text of the letter) identified him as one of the spirtual fathers of the peasants' rebellion (a mark which clung to him for the rest of his life), so that he could no longer remain in Electoral Saxony. After a period of wandering, always haunted by his associa-

arguments on Deuteronomy 15:1–11 and categorically rejected any interest payment as usury, and thus as contrary to God's Word; he also admonished the people not to pay any interest on a loan lest they become involved in sin. He accused the governmental authorities of sinning because they tolerated the lending of money at interest, a practice which, according to Strauss, played right into the greedy hands of the papal clergy. The clergymen in Eisenach reacted to Strauss's broadside by complaining about him to the Electoral government, which in turn asked Luther for an opinion on this matter.

In his evaluation of Strauss's position, Luther points out that the practice of lending money at interest is basically un-Christian, but that it is the responsibility of governments to abolish this practice. Until this has been accomplished the evil has to be endured. Luther charges Strauss with stirring up the people by encouraging them to take the situation into their own hands and by telling them to refuse to pay interest. He also charges Strauss with unsound theological thinking. Since not all people operate by Christian principles, all the evils connected with interest payment will not simply disappear, especially not if people take matters into their own hands.

Gregory Brück (1483?–1557) studied law at the Universities of Wittenberg and Frankfurt/Oder. As a result of his splendid academic career and professional prestige, Brück was eventually called by Elector Frederick to be his legal counselor. Soon thereafter Brück met Luther, and became a wholehearted supporter of the Reformer's cause. After the Diet of Worms, where he headed the Electoral Saxon delegation, Brück became chancellor. In this position he shaped the policy of Electoral Saxony for almost the next quarter-century, first as chancellor, and then later as chancellor emeritus. The last years of his life he spent in developing the University of Jena. Brück became famous for his steadfastness at the Diet of Augsburg in 1530, where he aided in drafting the Augs-

---

tion with the peasants, he finally became ecclesiastical advisor to the margrave of Baden-Baden. Little is known of the remainder of his life, except for his literary outbursts against Oecolampadius and Zwingli in connection with the controversy on the Lord's Supper. Strauss was no doubt a man of good will; theologically he was close to Karlstadt and is to be classified among the religious enthusiasts. On James Strauss, see *LThK* 9, 1109.

burg Confession and, through careful yet shrewd negotiations, suc-
ceeded in having it read before Emperor Charles. He faithfully
upheld the position of the Reformation during all the diplomatic
moves at the diet, thus serving as a counterbalance to Melanchthon,
who was willing to discuss terms of compromise between the
Roman party and the representatives of the Reformation. He ener-
getically developed the Smalcaldic League into a powerful block of
Estates, which the Emperor constantly had to take into considera-
tion. Through his administrative work, Brück had permanent influ-
ence on the shaping of the constitutions and governments of some
of the German Protestant territorial churches. On Brück, see NDB
2, 653 f.; E. Fabian, Dr. Gregor Brück (Tübingen, 1957).

Text in German: WA, Br 3, 176–177.

To Gregory Brück, Doctor and chancellor, etc.

Grace and peace in Christ. Highly learned, honorable, dear Mr.
Chancellor: I have read through the booklet by Doctor Strauss,
and [want to] inform you now what my opinion of it is, so that
you can pass this opinion along to my Gracious Lord.[2]

To begin with, it is true that lending money at interest,[3] as
it has thus far customarily been practiced,[4] is un-Christian.[5] It is
probably not even possible that this practice could ever be curbed
and turned into a decent system, since all the world is greedy, and

---

[2] I.e., Duke John of Saxony; see *LW* 48, 269, n. 8.

[3] Luther wrote *Zinskauf*. This was the technical term for lending money at
interest.

[4] It is impossible to give any details on the history and legalities of the lending
of money at interest. The papal church had outlawed as usury any monetary
profit that was derived from any other source than labor. But in reality there
were many ways to get around this theory, and the papal church was only too
often one of the big money lenders, entering into sharp competition with
rising banking companies, such as the Fuggers. As a result, throughout the
fourteenth and fifteenth centuries many popular preachers charged the church
with approving of usury. The diets of the fifteenth and sixteenth centuries tried
to regulate this matter, but with little success. For details, see *NCE* 14, 498 f.;
LThK 10, 1245, 1374 f.; B. N. Nelson, *The Idea of Usury* (Princeton, 1949);
J. T. Noonan, *The Scholastic Analysis of Usury* (Cambridge, Mass., 1957).

[5] For Luther's position on this subject, see his personal letter to Strauss, which
apparently also was written on October 18 (*WA*, Br 3, No. 674), and his
Long Sermon on Usury (1520), *LW* 45, 273 ff.; see also *LW* 45, 233 ff.

always looks out for its own interest. The best and only way to help here is to abolish the practice altogether. It would be a noble, Christian accomplishment if sovereigns and lords would get together and abolish it.[6]

Doctor Strauss does not do justice to the problem, however. He just skims over the top and does not sufficiently deal with [the element of] risk (which is the only excuse for this business).[7] Therefore this book could not stand if it were challenged by opponents.[8] On the other hand, by using high-sounding words, he makes bold the common man, who could not challenge his book [anyway]. Perhaps he thinks the whole world is [full of] Christians, or perhaps even that Christ is the common possession of all, so that as soon as he says something it will be put into practice.[9]

The most dangerous point in this booklet, however, is Strauss's teaching that the debtor ought not pay the interest to the usurious

---

[6] In principle Luther agreed with Strauss. Both wanted to abolish the paying of interest on borrowed money. The difference between their positions lies in the framework of their arguments. Strauss substantiated his view mainly with Deut. 15:1–11. For Strauss, as for many of his religiously enthusiastic contemporaries, the social laws of the Old Testament had to be the laws of the Christian community. Consequently, since paying interest on borrowed money was contrary to Scripture, and since the authorities did nothing to stop this evil, the debtor *had* to refuse to pay the interest; even more, the Christian, trusting the Lord to care for him, could under no circumstances borrow money.
[7] Luther has a realistic view of man's wickedness ("The whole world is not full of Christians") and realizes that the creditor takes a risk. The theological problem which apparently Luther wants to have aired is the following: Does a creditor who is also a Christian have the duty (out of love for his neighbor) to risk the loss of his money? Is this duty unconditional? Or are there certain circumstances which could justify demanding security and reimbursement for the risk taken, i.e., could justify payment of interest?
[8] Literally: "Therefore this book would not endure the thrust [as from a sword], should it be attacked by enemies."
[9] This sentence is not clear. Luther wrote: *oder Christus soll je so ein gemein Ding sein, dass es so bald leben müsse, wann er's geredet hat.* The problem arises from *er's,* i.e., he [has spoken] it. Does this refer to Christ? Then one would have to paraphrase: Perhaps Strauss thinks . . . that Christ is the common possession of all people, so that when he, Christ, says something it will at once be done because the people abide by what Christ says. Or does *er's* refer to Strauss himself? Then one would have to paraphrase: Perhaps Strauss thinks . . . that Christ . . . so that when he, Strauss (as Christ's minister and based on God's Word), says something it will be done at once because the people mind God's Word. Notwithstanding this ambiguity, the general meaning of Luther's argument is clear: Not all people operate by Christian principles; consequently Strauss is unrealistic if he expects all the evils connected with borrowing or lending money at interest simply to disappear if the Word is proclaimed.

creditor for then he would be agreeing with the usurious creditor and would sin along with him.[10] This is not right. For the debtor has acted correctly, and is free of sin, if he tells the creditor that [the business transaction] is usury, and points out its iniquity. Yet the debtor should take no revenge, but should consent to pay the unjust creditor, just as I ought to be willing to yield my body, property, and honor to the murderer; Matthew 6.[11] Certainly no debtor would pledge himself to pay interest if necessity did not force him to do so. Doctor Strauss thinks, however, that a man should believe that God will provide for him. [Under these circumstances] he who is being robbed also might say that he does not wish to be robbed, or that he does not consent to it, [and] that God will certainly rescue him.[12]

If Doctor Strauss has preached this, as it seems, then it is necessary that my Gracious Lords[13] order him to get this out of the peoples' heads again. For although true Christians have not been led astray by this, yet the common herd, which is insolent anyhow, likes to hear such things and [immediately] to put them to work, for no other reason than its own profit.

There is not enough time now to show what the sovereigns should do to abolish the lending of money at interest, for the [practice of] lending money at interest varies greatly from one territorial state to the other, so that the matter cannot be settled [with one stroke of the pen].[14] In the meantime people should be encouraged to endure this wrong in a Christian way for awhile, and to pay the interest until things are improved. If they want to oppose it on legal grounds, they should be allowed to come for hearings and bring their charges; they should be judged in accordance with fairness[15] and the gospel. I do not know whether a

---

10 For Strauss's argument, see WA, Br 3, 177, n. 10. Luther considered this argument not only a danger for personal salvation but also for society, because it could be used as justification for taking matters into one's own hands.
11 The reference is to Matt. 5:39 f.
12 Another possible translation would be: "He [i.e., Strauss] could just as well say [to someone] who is being robbed that he should not let himself be robbed, or consent to it, and that God will certainly rescue him."
13 I.e., the sovereigns of Electoral Saxony.
14 Literally: "For the lending of money at interest is so confused . . . that one is not to drive into it so [easily]."
15 Or: "justice."

general edict should be issued, for the devil has too amazingly confused this matter. Here the gospel must help us.

Herewith I commend you to God.

Wittenberg, October 18, 1523   Martin Luther

137

To Nicholas Hausmann
[Wittenberg, end of October, 1523][1]

In addition to the problem of reorganizing the finances of those congregations which joined the Reformation movement,[2] Luther and his friends were faced with the problem of creating an order of worship that would be in accordance with their understanding of the gospel. In this letter Luther is giving some of his ideas on a revision of the liturgy of the mass, and announces that it seems wise to him to write a new order for the communion service. He also tells of the stand taken by the Bohemian Brethren in regard to the Lord's Supper.

On Nicholas Hausman, see LW 48, 399 f.

Text in Latin: WA, Br 3, 184.

To the learned and devout man, Mr. Nicholas Hausmann, pastor of the congregation at Zwickau, my friend in the Lord

Grace and peace. Your messenger is now returning to you, excellent Nicholas. I believe, however, that my last letter[3] has reached you. In the meantime, I have considered your wish,[4] and it seems wise to me that I should shortly publish something setting forth

---

[1] The extant autograph of this letter is undated. For the suggested date, see WA, Br 3, 182 f.

[2] See pp. 28 ff.

[3] Apparently this is WA, Br 3, No. 678. Luther had given this letter to a messenger who went to Zwickau some days prior to the day on which the present letter was being written.

[4] In 1523 Hausmann had contacted Luther several times regarding a form of worship (especially one to be used for the celebration of the Lord's Supper) that would be commensurate to the understanding of the gospel which Luther had developed; see WA 12, 197. On August 19, 1523, Luther asked Hausmann to tell him again which topics Hausmann wanted clarified; see WA, Br 3, 136. It is interesting to observe that later Hausmann urged Luther to suggest to the Electoral Saxon government that it conduct the visitations; see p. 135, n. 23.

(as I have written)[5] a form for the celebration of the mass.[6] Meanwhile, abolish all private masses[7] if you can, or as many [as possible]. As a next step I shall revise the Canon, and some of the ungodly prayers. But I do not see why we should alter the rest of the ritual, together with the vestments, altars, and holy vessels, since they can be used in a godly way and since one cannot live in the church of God without ceremonies.[8] In other booklets, I have written at length on the other matters.

This is how the Picards[9] feel about the sacrament [of the altar]: Christ is not present under the bread corporeally, as some say, so that they could see there blood and a child, etc.,[10] but [he is there] in a spiritual or sacramental manner. This means that whoever receives the bread [and the wine] in a visible manner truly receives the natural [body and] blood of him who is seated at the right hand of the Father, but [receives it] in an invisible manner. I cannot condemn them for this, for so we, too, understand [the sacrament]. Further, regarding the fact that they do not venerate [the consecrated elements], they refer to the same idea, namely, that Christ is not present [in the consecrated elements] in a visible manner, as in visions, but in an invisible manner, that is, at the right hand of the Father.

Please accept this short letter written by a busy man.

MARTIN LUTHER

---

[5] In the letter mentioned in note 3.

[6] This is a reference to Luther's *Formula missae et communionis,* which Luther sent to Hausmann on December 4, 1523; see *WA, Br* 3, 199; *WA* 12, 205 ff.

[7] See *LW* 48, 281, n. 26; 317; 324 f.

[8] This was one of Luther's arguments against the religious enthusiasts who, on the basis of a spiritualistic interpretation of religion in general, devalued the liturgy and ceremonies of the church. For Luther's basic position on liturgy and ceremonies, see the references cited in *LW* 48, 325.

[9] The work of the Bohemian Reformer, John Huss (1369?–1415; see *LW* 48, 143), eventually resulted in the existence of two churches in Bohemia in addition to the Roman Catholic church: The Utraquist Church and the Bohemian Brethren; the latter were often referred to as "Picards." Between these two groups were various splinter groups, which occasionally were also called Picards. See P. Brock, *The Political and Social Doctrines of the Unity of Czech Brethren in the 15th and Early 16th Centuries* (The Hague, 1957); for the Eucharistic theology of the Bohemian Brethren, and Luther's relationship to the Brethren and their theology, see *LW* 36, 271 ff.; Sasse, pp. 70 ff.

[10] For details regarding this materialistic type of Eucharistic piety, see A. Franz, *Die Messe im deutschen Mittelalter* (Freiburg, 1902; reprint: Darmstadt, 1963), pp. 88 f., 100 ff.

138

To Elector Frederick
[Wittenberg, mid-November, 1523][1]

Luther's strong criticism of the papal church caused many people to become so unruly that they refused to fulfill their external obligations to the institutions of the church, such as the payment of rents. Consequently many ecclesiastical institutions were faced with financial difficulties. In addition, there was the question of what was to be done with the buildings which formerly had been occupied by members of the papal church but which for one reason or the other had been abandoned. In the same way as a Common Chest[2] had to be established to care for the external needs of the local parish, so a way had to be found to care for monasteries. In this letter Luther is briefly reporting on the economic difficulties of the Augustinian monastery in Wittenberg, and asking for the cancellation of a grain debt. He also suggests that the Elector accept the monastery with all assets and liabilities, and asks for the personal favor that he and the Prior, the only remaining inhabitants of the monastery, be permitted to use some of the monastery's facilities as their personal quarters.

On Elector Frederick, see LW 48, 49 f.

Text in German: WA, Br 3, 196–197.

Grace and peace in Christ!

Most Serene, Noble Sovereign and Lord: Your Electoral Grace this year permitted us to borrow some grain from the tax collector.[3]

---

[1] The letter is extant in the common editions of Luther's works. In the earliest witnesses the address and the date are missing. From the content of the letter it is, however, obvious to whom the letter was written. The date is based on the observation that on November 6 Luther wrote to Spalatin about the economic plight of the monastery; see WA, Br 3, 185 f. It may be assumed that Spalatin suggested (in his no-longer extant reply to Luther) that Luther contact the Elector about this matter. It may further be assumed that, in view of the urgency of the situation, Luther wrote to the Elector immediately after receiving Spalatin's letter, i.e., sometime in the middle of November. See WA, Br 3, No. 687, Introduction.

[2] See pp. 28 ff.

[3] Luther wrote *Schösser;* see p. 9, n. 4.

Now the tax collector daily admonishes us severely [to repay it], yet we cannot do so since our rents do not come in; they have not yet been paid. In order to settle this matter I therefore humbly ask that Your Electoral Grace cancel our debt for this grain with the aforementioned tax collector. I think and hope it will not be necessary to do so again.

Further, Most Gracious Lord, I am now living alone[4] in this monastery with the Prior[5] (not counting some who were exiled by the enemies of the gospel [and] whom we lodge here out of Christian love). I have delayed this Prior more than a year to serve me; I cannot and do not wish to prolong his stay here any further, since his conscience requires him to change his [way of] life.[6] In addition, I cannot endure the daily moaning of the people whom I must admonish to pay the rents.[7] Therefore we are inclined to relinquish and hand over the monastery with all its property to Your Electoral Grace, as the last heir.[8] For if the Prior leaves, then I no longer have any business here; I have to see where God will provide for me.

I humbly request Your Electoral Grace graciously to grant, either to this Prior or directly to me, the property next to the hospital, which had been purchased by our monastery for . . . gulden,[9] so that we, the last, do not depart from the monastery absolutely empty-handed.[10] I do not mean that Your Electoral Grace should

---

[4] For the mass exodus of monks from the Wittenberg monastery, see *LW* 48, 337, n. 4; 358 f.; Kolde, pp. 376 ff.

[5] The last prior of the Wittenberg monastery was Eberhard Brisger from Mühlheim, near Koblenz, who had matriculated at Wittenberg University in July of 1518. He apparently remained with Luther in the monastery until the end of 1525, though this cannot be verified. Later Brisger went as pastor to Altenburg. See *WA*, Br 1, 371, n. 18; 3, 408. On Eberhard Brisger, see *NDB* 2, 618.

[6] Brisger's conscience was forcing him to abandon monastic life.

[7] As early as 1516 Luther had had to collect the fees for real estate and certain rights (such as fishing rights) which the monastery had rented out; see *LW* 48, 28.

[8] The Wittenberg monastery had been founded by the Ernestine family (see *LW* 48, 110, n. 20), either by Elector Frederick himself, or by his immediate predecessor; see Kolde, p. 147, n. 1. Since the monastery could no longer fulfill the purpose envisioned by the founders, the facilities should return to the founders, or to their heirs, namely, to Elector Frederick.

[9] In the no-longer extant autograph the sum was obviously spelled out; see Schwiebert, p. 226 f.

[10] Luther requested permission to live in the so-called *Spitalraum;* see *WA*, Br 3, 197, n. 3; Schwiebert, p. 226.

make a public grant or issue a deed for it, since I well know what problems this could cause Your Electoral Grace. I only ask Your Electoral Grace to look the other way so that we might take it over quietly, yet with good conscience. In this way we would be protected, and could oppose X[11] if this property stood in my name. If X should become somewhat greedy, or make its own manipulations to get it, we could then appeal to Your Electoral Grace as if to acquire the permission at that time. Meanwhile [perhaps] God will also make an open bequest possible.[12]

Responsibility and love force me to ask for this, since, because of the persecution of the gospel, the Prior must forego his inheritance from his father, which is located in the territory of the bishop of Trier. Under other circumstances he would be rich enough.

May God's Grace protect Your Electoral Grace. Amen.

Your Electoral Grace's dedicated
MARTIN LUTHER

139

To Margrave Albrecht of Brandenburg, Grand-Master of the Teutonic Order [Wittenberg, December, 1523][1]

In late November and early December, 1523, Margrave Albrecht, the grand-master of the Teutonic Order, visited Luther in Wittenberg and questioned him on the relationship of the papal office to the church. This letter is Luther's answer to the Grand-Master's questions.

According to the earliest collection of Luther's letters,[2] the no-longer extant autograph was in Latin. The available Latin version

---

[11] Apparently in the no-longer extant autograph Luther wrote *Rat*, i.e., city council; see Schwiebert, p. 226.
[12] Luther was permitted to live in the monastery, and eventually was given the deed to the whole property as a wedding present; see Schwiebert, pp. 226 f.
[1] For the address, date, and signature see note 4.
[2] I.e., Aurifaber's collection which was published in Eisleben in 1565.

of this letter (WA, Br 3, 209–214) offers a text which in some portions is quite different from a German version of the letter. However, Otto Clemen has suggested[3] that the German version is the original, and the following translation is based on the German version.[4]

Margrave Albrecht (1490–1568), a member of the Brandenburg-Hohenzollern family,[5] became grand-master of the Teutonic Order in 1511. This Order occupied the territory that was once known as East Prussia. Since 1515 Albrecht had been in feudal relationship to the crown of Poland, and, in spite of great diplomatic and military efforts, was able to break neither these ties nor the grip which, since the days of the Peace of Torun (1466), Poland had on East Prussia. During his attendance at the first Diet of Nürnberg (1522), Albrecht came into direct contact with the Reformation.[6] Through Luther (with whom the Margrave stayed in close contact)[7] Albrecht became convinced that monasticism, even in the military form of the Teutonic Order, was against Scripture. As a result, in 1525 Albrecht resigned from his office in the Order, and changed Prussia into a secular duchy[8] to be ruled by him and his heirs, with the Polish king as feudal overlord. In 1544 Albrecht founded the University of Königsberg, which became a stronghold of the Reformation in Prussia, as well as its missionary center for the Eastern countries.

On Albrecht of Brandenburg, see NDB 1, 171 ff.; O.D.C.C., p. 30. Text in German: WA Br 3, 214–219.

---

[3] WA, Br 3, 207.

[4] The Latin version preserves the form of a letter by giving the address, a date (which has to be corrected), and the signature. The German version gives neither address, signature, nor date. Luther is identified in the title of the printed versions of this text as the writer of the letter, and the addressee can be established on the basis of the relationship between the Latin and the German versions of the letter. The approximate date can be established on the basis of the Grand-Master's itinerary; see WA, Br 3, 207.

[5] Casimir and George, margraves of Brandenburg-Ansbach-Kulmbach, were some of his brothers; Albrecht, archbishop of Mainz and Joachim I, elector of Brandenburg were some of his uncles.

[6] See pp. 23 ff.

[7] Many of the letters exchanged between Luther and Albrecht are extant, and in contrast to letters from other correspondents a large number of Albrecht's letters to Luther are extant.

[8] For details, see ARG 43 (1952), 145 ff.

Question [I]

Has Christ built his congregation,

or church,[9] on Peter and the succeeding

popes?

Answer:

No, [the church] is built only on Jesus Christ, the Son of God.

Proofs:

1. I Corinthians 3 [:11]: "No other foundation can anyone lay than that which has been laid, which is Jesus Christ."
2. II Corinthians 4 [:5]: "We preach not ourselves, but Jesus Christ as Lord, with ourselves, however, as your servants for Jesus' sake."
3. Matthew 16 [:18]: "You are Peter, and on this rock I will build my church, and the gates of hell shall not prevail against it."

That Peter and the popes cannot be this basis or rock, and that this passage cannot be understood in this way, is substantiated by the following points:

1. The "gates of hell" have prevailed against Peter and the popes, when they have fallen and have sometimes sinned. To "prevail" does not mean to take away honor, riches, health, or temporal life, for this robbers and murderers also can accomplish; rather it means that faith and man's holiness in the Spirit [cannot be] defeated. Therefore a foundation or rock is needed which does not waver at any time, nor is able to waver, does not sin, nor is able to sin. But Christ alone is [such a foundation].
2. The church, or congregation, is in the Spirit, and is holy in all things. As we say: "I believe in the Holy Christian Church, or congregation." But the thing in which one be-

---

[9] Luther used the terms *Gemeinde* and *Kirche* (i.e., "congregation" and "church") interchangeably. Throughout this letter, e.g., he used the term "congregation" quite often. Since to the modern reader "congregation" connotes more the church in its local setting than the church at large, the term "church" has been adopted. Even when using "congregation" Luther often was not focusing as much on the *local* gathering of believers as present usage of this term suggests, but rather on the gathering of believers as such, i.e., the church. For more information on Luther's understanding of the church, see H. Preuss, *The Communion of Saints. A Study of the Origin and Development of Luther's Doctrine of the Church* (Minneapolis, Minn., 1948).

lieves cannot be seen or felt, because faith concerns things which are not seen; Hebrews 11 [:1]. How then can Peter or the popes rule or preserve this church if they cannot know who is holy, can never see this church, but can only believe as we all do? Christ alone sees this church; he alone gathers and keeps it together, and he alone preserves it.

3. Neither Peter nor the popes can give to this church faith, love, and the other gifts of the Holy Spirit; they also cannot take away these gifts or change them, nor rule the church according to these gifts. If the church is not ruled by faith, love, and the other gifts of the Holy Spirit, however, then it is not a church or congregation of Christ, but rather an assembly of Satan.[10] Thus Christ alone rules his congregation [through the Holy Spirit]. Therefore also he alone is [the] ruler and head, shepherd, foundation, and master of this [church], as he himself says in Matthew 23 [:8]: "You have one master, Christ, but you all are brethren." This is to say: "You all are equal; but I alone am your master and supreme lord."

4. Even Peter and the popes were in need of this foundation; they needed faith, love, and the Holy Spirit, and other similar gifts.

Now one may ask whether Peter and the popes have another foundation, another faith, love, and Spirit than all the rest [of the Christians]. If they have these same gifts, then they share them equally with us. Then they cannot be superior to anyone in this church. If they should not have these gifts, however, they would not be in this church, since there is no other foundation of this church in the whole world than this one Christ.

Question [II]
What then is the power of popes and bishops?
[Answer:]

If one asks what the popes and bishops are and what their power in the church is, Paul answers this in I Corinthians 4 [:1]: "This is how one should regard us: as servants of Christ and stewards of

---

10 See Rev. 2:9.

the mysteries of God." That is, we are not lords of this church and do not distribute own own mysteries,[11] but those of God. We are servants through whose words God's mystery comes to the church.

This is what Paul calls[12] God's mystery: the secret and hidden things in us, that is, the foundation, [which is] Christ, [and further,] faith, the Spirit, love, and the other gifts and possessions of the church. For these things are internal, in the Spirit. They are given and granted to us internally through the Word of the gospel, [which is] preached and taught externally. For while the apostle, preacher, or bishop is teaching the gospel externally, Christ is at the same time internally [present], and gives and distributes in the heart the mysteries of God, according to the word which is spoken and taught externally; so we read in Acts 10 [:44 ff.] that the hearts of the Gentiles were cleansed through Christ by faith on the basis of the words and the sermon of Peter.

From this it truly follows that the Christian church cannot or should not hear, teach, know, or receive any other teaching than that by which the mysteries of God are distributed. Those who teach or distribute other things than the mysteries of God are neither apostles nor bishops, but thieves and murderers who destroy the sheep. On them Paul, in Galatians 1 [:9], utters this curse and malediction: "If anyone would teach you differently than we have preached to you, let him be accursed."

The church (which is a matter of the Spirit)[13] is not born or preserved, it cannot exist, work, conquer, continue, or do any other [suitable] thing unless it is based on its foundation which is Christ alone; that is, the church must have Christ for its ruler, who rules it through faith, the Spirit, and the other gifts of his Spirit. From this it necessarily follows that [only] such preaching and teaching which are concerned exclusively with these matters and these mys-

---

[11] As freer translations one could suggest: ". . . administer our own [things] but the sacraments of God." Or: ". . . preach our own wisdom, but that of God." For the understanding of "mystery," see Luther's following sentences; see also Erasmus' notes to Eph. 5:32 f. (Clericus 6, 855) and his paraphrase of this passage (Clericus 7, 987).

[12] Luther was apparently not thinking of any specific passage. For passages where Paul does speak of the mystery, or mysteries of God, in a way that Luther could have alluded to, see Eph. 1:9; 3:3 ff.; 6:19; Col. 2:2; I Tim. 3:16.

[13] Literally: "a spiritual thing."

teries should be done in the church; for only that should be preached in the church by which alone it is preserved and continues to exist. Therefore one should preach Christ alone and establish him as foundation, and teach the faith and those matters which are related to the faith, as Paul has said above: "We do not preach ourselves, but Jesus Christ our Lord."[14]

Question [III]

What then is the meaning of the laws and precepts
of the popes and councils concerning fasting, holy days, vestments, [sacred]places, and other external matters?

Answer:

None of these things comes from Christ, nor does any one of them provide the foundation, or give the Spirit. None of these matters is a distribution of the mysteries of God. Therefore we can have Christ and all the other things that belong to the congregation or church, without any of these external matters. But without Christ all these things are valueless since they do not give faith, the Spirit, or whatever belongs to the life of the Spirit. [These latter things] are given to you only by Christ and not by your fasting, cowl, monastery, or any of the other things set up by the popes and monasteries.

If, then, the pope taught that his precepts were such that they would lead to salvation if obediently observed, or damnation if despised, then he would be the true Antichrist, making himself the foundation of eternal salvation, with Christ being expelled.

Proof:

As already mentioned, life, the Spirit, salvation, and all the possessions of this church come from and originate in Christ alone, [and come to us] by means of the proclaimed Word of the gospel, which is grasped and accepted in faith; as a result, they do not come from the laws of the popes. If they come through the precepts of the popes, however, then they cannot come from Christ, since there is only one Christ. Therefore the pope has to preach only Christ. If he also preaches his own cause, then he is expelling Christ and setting himself in Christ's place. This is precisely what he is doing. For this is the reason that the pope is called Christ's vicar, because

---

14 II Cor. 4:5.

he has set himself up as the foundation of the church in place of the expelled Christ.

Question [IV]

What should one, then, do with the pope's laws?

Answer:

Like any other external matter, they are to be placed outside of [the] church.

Example: As you do with eating, drinking, dressing, and other external matters, so do also with the precepts of popes and councils. What do you do? You place eating, drinking and clothes outside the church; that is, you believe that you live because of Christ alone, and that you are saved by him. These are the mysteries of God which are given to you through the word of the apostles and preachers. Therefore you do not have any more or less of Christ whether you eat or fast, or wear these or those clothes. You may use these things in freedom, as you see fit, provided they belong to you and you have not stolen them from your neighbor.

You ought to deal likewise with all regulations and ceremonies [that were established by] the popes, councils, and monastic orders, since those regulations or precepts are not [a part of] Christ or the mystery of God. For I am not in the church, nor do I have eternal life, just because I observe these regulations, nor am I dead, or cut off from the church, if I do not observe but neglect them. Therefore, they are optional, free, and make no difference, as are all other external things which serve the body. This is what St. Paul states in Romans 14 [:17]: "The kingdom of God is not eating and drinking, but faith, peace, and joy in the Holy Spirit."

If the pope, councils, and monastic orders declared their laws and regulations to be a matter of choice, and did not require the church and congregations to fulfill them as something necessary and useful for salvation or life, then they could be tolerated. But if they preached in this manner, their kingdom would not last. They want their regulations to be considered necessary so that they have something with which they can coerce the people. Thus they are like adversaries of Christ; the pope is the real Antichrist, a vile abomination which stands in the holy place, as Christ says in Matthew 24 [:15]. It is utterly absurd and shocking that anyone should want to rule this church through works and laws that deal with external matters such as eating, drinking, clothes, times, [sacred] places, and similar things. The church, after all, does not derive its life from these matters, nor can it be upheld by them, since they will perish. Rather the church lives out of the one eternal Christ who makes the church alive by his Spirit through the proclaimed word of faith.

These external matters should be regulated by parents and secular sovereigns, because it is their task to rule bodies and material possessions. No salvation or damnation is involved here, but only peace among the citizens of this world. A bishop should care for those things, however, through which the souls are ruled in the Spirit. That is, he should preach Christ, that [Christ] alone is the Saviour, and set up him alone as the foundation, and from this develop the fruits of love.

From this one may easily see whether the pope, with or without the councils, has been given the authority to pass laws which go beyond God's commandments, and by which man should be saved if he observes them, or condemned if he despises them. Neither the pope nor his councils have the authority to do this. This would also not be fitting for any angel or any other creature, since the salvation or damnation of man is based on faith alone, as is clearly expressed by Christ in the last chapter of Mark [16:16]: "He who believes will be saved, he who does not believe will be condemned." When Christ sent out his disciples, he said: "Go and proclaim the kingdom of God! He who hears you hears me; he who despises you despises me."[15] And in another passage: "Go and preach the gospel to all creatures."[16]

So if the pope or the councils preach Christ, or faith, or the gospel (which are the mysteries of God), then one necessarily will have to listen to them. If they preach something else, however, then man may choose whether or not to listen. But if they want to force us, then we should not listen to them. For the Father's decree concerning Christ, Matthew 17 [:5], is still valid: "Obey Him."[17]

---

[15] See Luke 9:2; 10:16.

[16] Mark 16:15.

[17] This is a literal translation. Luther, in the September-Testament and in later revisions of the New Testament translation, and the RSV always translate this passage as: "Listen to him." This translation is suggested also by the following sentence.

In the church nothing should be heard but the Word of God, which teaches the mysteries of God, I Peter 4 [:11]: "When someone speaks, he should speak as the Word of God."

Question [V]

May the pope and the councils, then, change
God's commandments, or explain, or interpret them arbitrarily
or as they see fit?

Answer:

No. Paul says: "Let him be accursed who teaches differently."[18] Christ says, Matthew 5 [:19]: "Whoever annuls one of the least of these commandments and teaches men so, shall be called least in the kingdom of heaven."

How then can the crowd of papists say that this or that commandment of Christ is not a commandment but a counsel?[19] In matters of the Spirit the pope and the councils have no other authority than to proclaim these same [commandments] to others through the Word. Besides this, every child in the cradle has just as much power as Peter and all the other apostles in matters concerning Christ, faith, Spirit, and in all other matters of the church. For in Christ we are all brethren and equal, since we have one faith, Spirit, life, salvation, and one God. It is only externally that one teaches these things and the other listens, for we all could teach, learn, and listen.

It is then definitely clear that the pope and all the other servants of the church should be concerned with nothing in the church other than the mysteries of God, the Word of life, and the teachings of faith. In summary, they should do only those things that are based on God's Word. To it the pope and all the other servants of the church are subject. Since it is God's Word, everyone ought to know it, and must know it for the sake of salvation.

This has the incontrovertible consequence that everything which the pope has thus far done, decreed, and set up in the church

---

18 Gal. 1:9.
19 In the Middle Ages the ethical precepts of the New Testament were broken down into two categories: (a) Precepts which were valid for all Christians; e.g., the commandment to love God and the neighbor. (b) Counsels of perfection which were valid only for those Christians who wanted to attain the status of perfection; e.g., the renunciation of all property in order to follow Christ's example more fully. See LThK 3, 1245 ff.; NCE 4, 383 f.

is contrary to or without [basis in] the Word of God. It has been undertaken by him or his councils in an unjust and un-Christian way, however hard he may defend himself with usages, customs, old traditions, and resolutions of councils. Through all these things he has exalted himself above everything that belongs to God or is the true worship of God (II Thessalonians 2 [:4]),[20] since he does all these things against, in spite of, and without God's Word.

140

To George Spalatin[1]
[Wittenberg, end of 1523]

In connection with his attempt to improve the form of worship, Luther is discussing his intention of writing psalm hymns in German, and is requesting Spalatin's and von Dolzig's help for this task.
   On George Spalatin, see LW 48, 8 f.
   Text in Latin: WA, Br 3, 220.

Grace and peace

[Our] plan is to follow the example of the prophets and the ancient fathers of the church, and to compose psalms for the people [in the] vernacular, that is, spiritual songs, so that the Word of God may be among the people also in the form of music. Therefore we are searching everywhere for poets. Since you are endowed with a wealth [of knowledge] and elegance [in handling] the German language, and since you have polished [your German] through much use, I ask you to work with us[2] on this project; try

---

[20] The parentheses have been added by this editor.
[1] Address, date, and signature are missing in the extant autograph. Spalatin noted on the autograph, however, that it was written by Luther in 1524. This date suggests perhaps the time when Spalatin received the letter. The possibilities for the date are further narrowed down through Luther's statement in his letter dated January 14, 1524, that he has recently written to Spalatin about the German hymns; see p. 70.
[2] This is a reference to some of Luther's Wittenberg friends who were at that time busy writing hymns. For details, see LW 53, 191 ff.

to adapt any one of the psalms for use as a hymn, as you may see [I have done] in this example.[3] But I would like you to avoid any new words or the language used at court.[4] In order to be understood by the people, only the simplest and the most common words should be used for singing; at the same time, however, they should be pure and apt; and further, the sense should be clear and as close as possible to the psalm. You need a free hand here: maintain the sense, but don't cling to the words; [rather] translate them with other appropriate words.[5] I myself do not have so great a gift that I can do what I would like to see done here. So, I shall find out whether you are a Heman, or an Asaph, or a Jeduthun.[6] I would like to ask the same of Hans [von] Dolzig,[7] [whose German] is also rich and elegant. Nevertheless [you people should work] on this only if you have the leisure, which I suspect is not the case just now.[8] You have my *Seven Penitential Psalms* and the commentaries on them,[9] from which you can catch the sense of the psalm. If this is satisfactory to you, either the first one[10] can be assigned to you, "O Lord, [do not rebuke me] in [Thy] anger," or the seventh,[11] "Hear my prayer, O Lord." To Hans [von] Dolzig I would assign the second:[12] "Blessed are they whose [transgressions

---

3 This "example" cannot be identified with certainty; for possibilities, see *WA*, Br 3, 221, n. 4; Enders, *Briefwechsel* 4, 274, n. 4.

4 See also p. 4.

5 The statements here should be compared with the ideas Luther developed in 1530 in his *On Translating: An Open Letter* (*LW* 35, 181 ff.).

6 Heman was supposed to have been the author of Psalm 88. Asaph of Psalm 77, and Jeduthun the cantor of Psalms 39 and 77.

7 Hans von Dolzig (*ca.* 1485–1551; see *LW* 48, 169, n. 8; 314, n. 12) began his service for the Electoral Saxon government in the department of revenue. Together with Deginhard Pfeffinger (see *LW* 48, 32, n. 28), von Dolzig paid the money for Luther's graduation as Doctor of Theology; see S-J 1, 26. In 1519 von Dolzig became marshall of the court; while he held this position he was sent on many diplomatic and military missions. He became a close friend of Luther, to whose marriage he was invited; see p. 116. In 1545 he was appointed governor for the district of Saalfeld. On John von Dolzig, see *NDB* 4, 64.

8 In November, 1523, Spalatin, and apparently also von Dolzig, had accompanied Elector Frederick to the third Diet of Nürnberg (see p. 35, n. 4). The Electoral Saxon delegation returned to Weimar at the beginning of March, 1524; see *WA*, Br 3, 221, n. 6.

9 See *LW* 48, 19, n. 6.

10 Of the Penitential Psalms; i.e., Psalm 6.

11 Of the Penitential Psalms; i.e., Psalm 143.

12 Of the Penitential Psalms; i.e., Psalm 32.

are forgiven]." I have done "Out of the depths,"[13] and "Have mercy on me"[14] has already been given to someone else.[15] If these [psalms] are too difficult then take these two: "I will bless the Lord at all times," and "Rejoice in the Lord, O you righteous," that is, Psalms 33 and 32.[16] Or [you may take] Psalm 103, "Bless the Lord, O my soul." But let us know what we can expect from you.

Farewell in the Lord.

141

To George Spalatin
Wittenberg, January 14, 1524

Luther is waiting for the hymns which Spalatin was to write as adaptations of particular psalms. He also comments on the activities of Karlstadt, Eck, and Emser. He tells of the visit of an official of Ferdinand of Austria, from whom he has learned of the lies about himself that were circulating at Ferdinand's court.

On George Spalatin, see LW 48, 8 f.

Text in Latin: WA, Br 3, 234–235. The following translation is based on S-J 2, 212–213.

Master[1] George Spalatin, court evangelist, my
dearest friend in the Lord

Grace and peace! I have no news to write, my Spalatin, except that I am waiting for your German poems, about which I recently wrote to you.[2]

Karlstadt[3] behaves as usual. He has had his material published by a newly founded publishing house in Jena, and, so it is rumored,

---

[13] Ps. 130. From this Psalm came Luther's well-known *Out of the Depths I Cry to Thee;* see *WA* 35, 97 ff., 419 f.; *LW* 53, 221 ff.
[14] Ps. 51.
[15] To a certain Erhard Hegenwald; see *WA, Br* 3, 221 n. 12.
[16] According to the Vulgate; Psalms 34 and 33 according to the *RSV.*
[1] I.e., Master of Arts. Literally: "Mr. Master George."
[2] See letter No. 140. "German poems," i.e., literally: "German muses."
[3] Andrew Karlstadt; See *LW* 48, 79, n. 12.

he will still bring out eighteen more books.[4] Eck[5] is not worth answering; this is not only my opinion but that of everyone else as well. They think that [that] sophist was among the Lapiths,[6] and was drunk when he spewed out this slime.[7] The King of England, the "Defender of the Church," is worthy of such a defender; and Emser in turn is the right defender for Eck. Let them therefore protect each other.[8]

I am sending you a poem written by Provost Justus Jonas.[9]

An ambassador, or something else, of Ferdinand[10] has visited

---

[4] After Luther returned from the Wartburg he curbed the Wittenberg disturbances (see LW 48, 386, n. 1) and restored peace to the city. He voided some of the new practices which had been introduced by Karlstadt and Zwilling (see LW 48, 39, n. 3). This created great tension between Luther and Karlstadt. The latter felt betrayed by Luther, and gradually drifted away from his former colleague and friend. Disappointed with the turn taken by the Reformation, Karlstadt withdrew to Orlamünde; the parish of this small town was a part of the endowment of his chair at the University of Wittenberg. Here he developed his thoughts, and put them to work (see Bainton, pp. 256 ff.), while at the same time agitating against Luther. How critical the situation between the two men actually was may be seen from the rumor which Luther is here reporting. In 1524 the preliminary skirmishes erupted into open hostility.

[5] John Eck; see LW 48, 80, n. 13.

[6] This is perhaps a reference to Ovid's (Roman poet, 43 B.C.–A.D. 17; see O.C.D., pp. 630 f.) Metamorphoses xii. 210, 536; xiv. 670. The Lapiths were a brave, fierce people of Greek mythology whose victorious fight with the Centaurs is reported by Ovid. For details, see O.C.D., p. 179; Paulys Realencyclopädie der classischen Altertumswissenschaft, 12[I] (Stuttgart, 1924), 784 ff.

[7] King Henry VIII of England (1509–1547) had written a defense of the sacraments of the Roman church against Luther's On the Babylonian Captivity of the Church (see WA 6, 497 ff.; LW 36, 11 ff.). As a result Pope Leo X bestowed on the King the title "Defender of the Faith." Luther's reply to the King's attack (see WA 10[II], 180 ff.) was challenged by Eck, who in May, 1523, published a defense ("this slime") of the King's position; for bibliographical information see WA, Br 3, 235, n. 4.

[8] Jerome Emser published a German translation of the King's attack on Luther in March, 1523. Luther thus considers Emser a "worthy" defender of both the King and Eck, not only because of this translation, but perhaps also because of his generally critical attitude toward the Reformation. Emser had published several attacks on Luther. His latest effort to discredit the Reformation had appeared in May, 1523; for bibliographical information, see WA 10[II], 178. Here Emser prefaced and edited certain letters exchanged by Henry VIII, Elector Frederick, and Duke George, in which letters the King complained about Luther.

[9] Justus Jonas, the provost of the All Saints' Chapter at Wittenberg's Castle Church (see LW 48, 275, n. 3), had just completed the hymn Were God Not With Us At This Time; see WA 35, 124 f., 440. See also LW 53, 245 f.

[10] Ferdinand I; see LW 48, 217, n. 17. No details could be verified about the incident reported by Luther.

me to see what kind of a man I am and what I am doing. He said that I have quite a reputation with his lord for supposedly walking around armed and with a bodyguard, and for spending my time with harlots, and dice, and in taverns. I do not know what other honors are attributed to me in that court, but I have become sufficiently used to lies.

Live in the Lord; farewell in him, and pray for me.[11]

Wittenberg, January 14, 1524   Martin Luther

142

To George Spalatin
Wittenberg, March 14, 1524

Luther is expressing his grief over the course Karlstadt has taken with the radical reforms at Orlamünde, and tells of the administrative and legal steps which are planned to counter Karlstadt. Against the background of Karlstadt's ideas, Luther discusses briefly whether the Mosaic laws are valid for people who are not Jews, and who are not living in the Holy Land.

On George Spalatin, see LW 48, 8 f.

Text in Latin: WA, Br 3, 254.

To the venerable Master[1] George Spalatin, minister of the
gospel at the court of Saxony, my friend in the Lord

Grace and peace! Lucas[2] has brought the bundles of your letters,[3] my Spalatin, from which I have learned all that I wanted to know.

Besides this I have read [about] Karlstadt's[4] monstrosities[5]

---

[11] Literally: "Live, and farewell in the Lord, and pray for me."

[1] I.e., Master of Arts. Literally: "Mr. Master George."

[2] This Lucas could not be identified; perhaps it was Lucas Cranach (see *LW* 48, 201).

[3] These letters could not be identified. Spalatin had left Nürnberg (see p. 69, n. 8) on February 26. The letters mentioned by Luther were apparently a last shipment of letters from Nürnberg.

[4] Andrew Karlstadt; see *LW* 48, 79, n. 12.

[5] The letters mentioned at the beginning of this letter brought, or confirmed, news (see *WA*, Br 3, 256) of the radical reforms undertaken by Karlstadt in his parish in Orlamünde: destruction of images, abolishment of Eucharistic

with grief. God withstood the Jews for a while so that they would not kill his Son. Finally when they were unwilling to desist, God gave him into their hands, letting them not only kill him, but also condemn him to the most shameful of deaths. Thus the iniquities of the Amorites[6] were completed and God's wrath against the Jews was fulfilled. In the same way, through us, Christ has long resisted Karlstadt; yet that man will not stop, but continues to speed his own destruction. I am afraid that, by compelling us even to pray against him, he will finally earn the permission to do the damage [necessary] for his perdition. May Christ prevent [this] by his grace, Amen. An untamed desire for glory and fame is consuming this man. Please pray for him, too!

First of all, in the name of the University we shall call him from that place to which he was not called[7] back to this office of the Word which he ought [to exercise] here at Wittenberg.[8] Should he not come, then we shall finally arraign him [before the Sovereign].[9] Perhaps I myself shall also admonish him in a letter. Yet this also is a relic of the Cross,[10] and the legitimate fate of the Word, that he who has eaten Christ's bread should lift his foot against him.[11] But Christ lives and is lord, even over Satan.

---

and other clerical vestments, etc. Karlstadt based his actions on a confusion of the dialectic relationship of the law to the gospel, on a spiritualistic interpretation of religion (according to which the Spirit cannot operate through earthen vessels, or have anything to do with matter), and on a literal understanding of the Old Testament laws, especially those which forbid the making of images. For further details, see WA 18, 72 f., 76 f.; LW 40, 89 f., 92 f.

[6] Gen. 15:16.

[7] I.e., the University did not officially release Karlstadt from his lecture obligation. On the other hand, this statement must be questioned. The parish at Orlamünde was a part of the endowment of Karlstadt's chair in the University, and was incorporated into the office of archdeacon at the All Saints' Chapter, which office was held by Karlstadt. The University had only the right to nominate the vicar who, residing at Orlamünde, would take care of the parish, while the pastor would reside in Wittenberg and fulfill his obligation to the University. Karlstadt, cited by the University, did appear in Wittenberg in April, 1524, and defended his action. At that time Karlstadt agreed to return to Wittenberg after certain matters in Orlamünde were settled. Karlstadt changed his mind, however, and did not return to Wittenberg. For documentation, see WA, Br 3, 255, n. 5; ARG 11 (1914), 69 ff.; C.R. 1, 652.

[8] With his move to Orlamünde Karlstadt abandoned the fulfillment of his duties as professor and archdeacon of the All Saints' Collegiate Chapter at Wittenberg's Castle Church.

[9] Elector Frederick; see LW 48, 49 f.

[10] See LW 48, 387.

[11] John 13:18.

Those who want to praise the judicial system of Moses are to be rejected. We have our own civil law[12] under which we live. Neither Naaman the Syrian,[13] nor Job,[14] Joseph,[15] David,[16] nor any other Jew observed his own laws when outside his country, but the laws of the people among whom he was staying. The laws of Moses were binding for the Jewish people only in the country which God had chosen for them. Now they are a matter of choice. Were all the laws [of Moses] to be kept, then there is no reason why we should not also be circumcised and observe all the laws concerning ceremonies.

Farewell, and pray for me.

Wittenberg, March 14, 1524   MARTIN LUTHER

143

To Elector Frederick
Wittenberg, March 23, 1524

Luther is requesting the Elector to change Melanchthon's teaching assignment from the teaching of Greek to that of lecturing on the Bible. Luther justifies this request by pointing out that he himself is overworked because he is devoting so much time to the Bible translation, that Melanchthon is especially gifted for lecturing on the Bible, and that the University owes this service to the students, many of whom, despite great hardship, have registered for the sole purpose of studying God's Word. Luther adds the warning that now is the time to take full advantage of every opportunity to train young men in God's Word, for no one can know how long this opportunity may last.

On Elector Frederick, see LW 48, 49 f.

Text in German: WA, Br 3, 258–259.

---

12 Luther evidently uses the term "civil law" in the broadest possible sense.
13 II Kings 5.
14 Because Job is not considered to be an Israelite, or to have lived within the boundaries of the Promised Land.
15 I.e., during his stay in Egypt.
16 I.e., during those times when David had to stay outside the borders of the Promised Land.

To the Most Serene, Noble Sovereign and Lord,
Sir Frederick, duke in Saxony, elector, landgrave
in Thuringia, and margrave in Meissen,
my Most Gracious Lord

Grace and peace in Christ! Most Serene, Noble Sovereign, Most
Gracious Lord! Your Electoral Grace undoubtedly knows that by
God's grace there are fine young men[1] here who have come from
distant countries because they are hungry for the saving Word and
who endure great poverty because of this, so that some of them
have only water and bread to eat. I have proposed to Master[2]
Philip[3] that he lecture on Scripture, since he is richly endowed by
God's special grace to a greater extent than I myself am. Although
I would willingly give these lectures, it would mean neglecting the
Bible translation.[4] [I suggest therefore] that he undertake the
teaching of Scripture instead of the teaching of Greek. This is the
earnest desire of the whole University and faculty.[5] Melanchthon
objects to this with only one excuse, namely, that he is called and
paid by Your Electoral Grace to teach Greek; therefore he has to
fulfill this obligation, and may not neglect it.

I humbly beg, therefore, on behalf of the whole University,
that Your Electoral Grace consider—for the good of the precious
youth, and the further promotion of God's gospel—whether it might
be possible for Your Electoral Grace to designate that Melanchthon's salary be paid for lecturing on Holy Scriptures. We have
many young people here who could excellently handle the teaching
of Greek. It is not fitting that Melanchthon always deals [only]
with this childish course in Greek[6] while he neglects a more important one in which he could create much fruit, and which could

---

[1] Literally: "a fine youth."
[2] I.e., Master of Arts.
[3] Philip Melanchthon; see LW 48, 77, n. 3.
[4] See pp. 18 ff.
[5] Since the Urkundenbuch does not provide any material on this subject, it
could not be verified whether Luther is exaggerating here and in the first
sentence of the next paragraph, or whether his statement is based on a University resolution of which no evidence is extant.
[6] Luther is generalizing here, for since Melanchthon had come to Wittenberg
he had periodically given lectures in theology. See Friedensburg, GUW, p. 166.

not be rewarded with any money or salary. Would to God that we had more such men [as Melanchthon], who are such good lecturers. Unfortunately there are enough [instructors] who drivel and really waste the time of the students who are here by God's grace.[7] The time will come again, as has been the case before, that one has to neglect [Biblical lectures] even if one does not like to do so, because there is a shortage of such [qualified] people. Therefore we must see to it that we train [young] men as long as we can, and do the best for our future generations.

If Your Electoral Grace is willing to do so, then I ask that Your Grace strictly command Philip to lecture diligently on Scripture. Even if one has to raise his salary, he must do this job.[8]

Your Electoral Grace be commended to God's mercy. Amen.
Wittenberg, March 23, 1524

Your Electoral Grace's dedicated servant,
MARTIN LUTHER

144

To Erasmus of Rotterdam
Wittenberg, [about April 18,] 1524[1]

This letter, and Erasmus' answer,[2] are the last extant pieces of correspondence exchanged between the Reformer and the Humanist in a more-or-less friendly atmosphere. Shortly thereafter the two clashed in the controversy on free will. In an earlier letter to an unknown addressee (No. 122) Luther had warned Erasmus indirectly to keep out of the religious controversy; in this letter Luther re-

---

[7] Another possible translation would be: ". . . [instructors], here by God's grace [of course], who drivel . . . the students." Luther's statement that these instructors are here by God's grace would then be sarcastic.
[8] As early as March 31, 1524, Elector Frederick replied affirmatively to the University; see *Urkundenbuch*, No. 133. In September of 1525 Melanchthon's salary was raised by one hundred gulden (see *LW* 48, 11, n. 2) on the condition that Melanchthon would also take over the task of lecturing in the department of theology; see *Urkundenbuch*, No. 139.
[1] For the address and the date, see note 3.
[2] *WA*, Br 3, No. 740, dated May 8, 1524; S-J 2, No. 624.

peats his warning, this time to Erasmus directly. Luther expresses his disappointment that Erasmus will not support him, but he is able to accept this. Luther says he will restrain himself from attacking Erasmus in public, even though he feels the sting of the Humanist's pen. He admonishes Erasmus to show similar restraint and to cease his tongue-lashings, for some people will not put up with his attacks but will fight back. In closing, Luther commends Joachim Camerarius to Erasmus.

On Erasmus, see LW 48, 116 f.

Text in Latin: WA, Br 3, 270–271.[3]

Grace and peace from our Lord Jesus Christ!

I have been silent long enough, excellent Erasmus. For although I was expecting you, as the greater and older man, to break the silence, since I have waited so long in vain,[4] I think charity itself compels me to take the initiative.

To begin, I am saying nothing about the fact that you have behaved quite peculiarly toward us, so that your relationship with my enemies, the papists, would be unimpaired and safe. To continue, I was not especially offended by the fact that you have bitingly attacked and sharply needled [me][5] in several places in the

---

[3] The autograph of this letter is no longer extant. In May, 1524, Erasmus, having copied the autograph, gave it to John Laski (a Polish nobleman), apparently together with copies of letters Nos. 122 and 133. Laski was to show these documents to Sigismund I, king of Poland, so that the King could realize that Erasmus and Luther had nothing in common. For documentation, see WA, Br 3, 268. Letter No. 144 is extant in manuscript copies, and in the common editions of Luther's works. The address is missing in all manuscript copies; see Enders, *Briefwechsel* 4, 319. The content of the letter, however, makes obvious to whom it was addressed. The suggested date is based on the following circumstances: Camerarius (see note 22) and others, leaving Wittenberg sometime between April 16 and 19 (see Enders, *Briefwechsel* 4, 322, n. 1), accompanied Melanchthon to his hometown of Bretten; he took the letter along and, making a side trip to Basel to visit Oecolampadius and Erasmus, delivered the letter personally. April 18 seems, then, to be a good assumption for the date of this letter. As can be deduced from other letters of this period, it was general knowledge in Wittenberg that Luther would use this opportunity to send a letter to Erasmus; see WA, Br 3, 268 f. Erasmus' answer (see note 2) arrived in Wittenberg in June, again via Camerarius.

[4] The last extant letter of Erasmus to Luther was dated August 1, 1520; WA, Br 2, No. 321. Luther's reply is not extant, but is mentioned in Luther's letter to Spengler, dated November 17, 1520; see LW 48, 185.

[5] Literally: "us."

booklets you have published[6] in order to gain the favor of [my enemies], or to mitigate their fury against you.[7] For we realize that you have not yet been given by the Lord such courage, or rather such a disposition, that you, together with us, could openly and confidently fight these monsters around us; nor are we the kind of people who would dare to demand from you what would be beyond your strength and way of doing things. Indeed we have endured your weakness and respected the "measure of God's gift within you."[8] For certainly the whole world cannot deny that it is God's wonderful and glorious gift through you that those studies[9] through which one arrives at an unadulterated reading of the Biblical books[10] now flourish and have authority. For this we ought to give thanks. Therefore, I for one have certainly never wished that you would desert or neglect your gift and join our camp, although you could have profited [our] cause greatly through your genius and eloquence; nevertheless, since your heart is not in it, it was safer [for you] to serve where your gift lies. [Among us] this one fear exists: that, induced by our enemies, you might publicly[11] attack our teachings, and that necessity would then compel us to "oppose you to your face."[12] We have already restrained some who wanted to draw you into the arena with books that have already been prepared. This was also the reason why I would have preferred that Hutten's *Expostulatio*, and even more your *Spongia*, had not

---

[6] Erasmus did this more in his letters than in his books. Since many of his letters were published, either by himself or by friends or enemies, his private statements became public. See *ARG* 53 (1962), 60 ff.; 63, n. 16; 64, n. 17; C. R. Thompson, *Inquisitio de fide. A Colloquy by Desiderius Erasmus Roterodamus, 1524* (New Haven, 1950), pp. 12 ff. For the passages on which Luther could have focused, see Rückert, *LB*, p. 122, n. 18.

[7] Erasmus was caught between the Roman and the Reformation parties. His declared intention to remain a neutral critic and judge, uninvolved in the struggle, irritated both sides. See *ARG* 53 (1962), 60 ff.

[8] Eph. 4:7.

[9] Luther wrote *literae*; see p. 34, n. 12. One manuscript copy and one of the earliest printed editions of this letter offer a text which has to be translated: ". . . cannot deny the fact that through you [i.e., your efforts] those [studies] flourish. . . ."

[10] See also p. 34.

[11] Literally: "by means of published booklets."

[12] Gal. 2:11. On August 8, 1522, Erasmus wrote to Mosellanus that the Emperor (Charles V), the King of England (Henry VIII), and the cardinals in Rome want him, Erasmus, to attack Luther; see Allen 5, No. 1305. See also *ARG* 53 (1962), 63 ff.

been published.[13] Unless I am wrong, [I think in writing the *Spongia*] you realized how easy it is to write on moderation and criticize Luther's immoderation, but how hard or even impossible it is to practice this unless one has received a special gift of the Spirit. Believe it or not, [but] Christ is my witness: I feel heartily sorry for you that the hatred, or the zeal, of so many and important people is stirred up against you.[14] I cannot believe that you are not troubled by this (since your human strength is no match for such great difficulties). However, perhaps a just zeal moves [your opponents], and they may think that you have provoked them in shameful ways. Indeed (to speak frankly), since they are people who are unable to bear your satire and pretense (which you would like to have considered as prudence and moderation) because they are weak, they certainly have just cause for indignation. If they were of a more steadfast disposition they would have no such reason.

Although I myself am easily provoked, and have often been prodded into writing sharply, yet I have done this only against those who are obstinate and without restraint. In other respects I think that my mildness and gentleness with sinners and ungodly people, however insane and wicked they may be, is sufficiently attested to not only by the witness of my own conscience, but also by the experience of many people. So I have thus far held back my pen whenever you have needled me. I have even written in letters to friends[15]—which you too have read—that I would restrain myself until you attack me in public. For although you do not side with

---

[13] In the *Expostulatio* (*A Challenge*), published in the first half of July, 1523, Ulrich von Hutten (see *LW* 48, 163, n. 1) had sharply attacked Erasmus for what seemed to him and many others to be a wavering between allegiance to the papal church and criticism of it. Hutten had also challenged Erasmus to take a stand on the controversial issues that were separating the Reformers and the papists, or to disappear, lest he be forced to take a stand which might endanger his life. (For the text, see Böcking 2, 180 ff.) Erasmus replied just as caustically with his *Spongia* (*A Sponge*), published in September, 1523; see Allen 5, No. 1378, Introduction. (For the text, see Clericus 10, 1631 ff.)

[14] See note 7.

[15] See p. 7. For documentation of the fact that Erasmus had read this letter, see Erasmus' letter to Melanchthon, dated September 6, 1524; Allen 5, No. 1496 (p. 549); S-J 2, 249. According to this letter to Melanchthon, Luther's statement (that he would not attack Erasmus if Erasmus in turn did not attack him) was one of the reasons that Erasmus finally did publish something against Luther, for he wanted to avoid the impression that he had made a deal with Luther.

us, and condemn most of the main teachings of piety either in an ungodly or deceitful way, or take no definite stand [on them], I still cannot charge you with obstinacy, nor do I want to.

But what shall I do now? The affair is highly exasperating for both sides. If I could be a mediator,[16] I would wish that your enemies, too,[17] would cease attacking you with such great vehemence and grant that you, in your old age, could peacefully fall asleep in the Lord. In my opinion, they certainly could do this if they considered your weakness and weighed the magnitude of the cause, which has long since outgrown your stature—especially since the affair has progressed to such a stage that there is little danger to be feared for our cause, even if Erasmus should fight us with all his might, much less if he only stings occasionally [or] merely bares his teeth. On the other hand, my Erasmus, you should remember your opponents' weakness and should abstain from your biting and bitter sounding figures of speech. If you absolutely cannot and dare not join our cause, then leave it alone and stay with your own things. For (even according to your own judgment) your opponents have good reason not to bear your carping patiently, since human weakness knows and greatly fears the name and authority of Erasmus. There is quite a difference between being stung once by Erasmus and being attacked simultaneously by all the papists.

I wanted to say this, excellent Erasmus, as a testimony of my sincerity toward you. I wish that a disposition which is worthy of your fame would be given to you by the Lord. If the Lord defers giving this to you, then I ask you, if you can do nothing else, in the meantime to be only a spectator of our tragedy. Only do not give comfort to my enemies and join their ranks against us. Above all, do not publish booklets against me, as I shall publish nothing against you. Finally, remember that those who seek to attack you in Luther's name are human beings like you and me, who are to be tolerated and forgiven, as Paul says: "Bear one another's burdens."[18] There has been enough snarling; now we must see to it

---

[16] Luther placed this portion of the sentence in parentheses after "I would wish."
[17] I.e., as Luther does not attack Erasmus.
[18] Gal. 6:2.

that we "do not devour each other."[19] This would be too miserable a drama, since it is absolutely certain that neither side really wishes to do any damage to piety, and [that both wish] to please everyone without pertinacity on the part of either.

Pardon my lack of eloquence,[20] and farewell in the Lord. I[21] commend to you this young man Joachim,[22] who is like our own Philip.[23] If you accept him, he will put himself in an even better light.

Wittenberg, 1524   MARTIN LUTHER

145

To Nicholas Gerbel[1]
Wittenberg, May 6, 1524

This is a personal greeting which includes a brief report on the spread of the Reformation in Germany and a reference to the rise of the Spiritualists.

---

[19] Gal. 5:15.

[20] Literally: "Take my childishness in good part, and . . ."

[21] The sentences from "I" to "light" are missing in some witnesses.

[22] See also note 3. Joachim Kammermeister (1500–1574), or Camerarius, was born in Bamberg, and studied in Leipzig, Erfurt (where he was a member of the local circle of Humanists), and Wittenberg, concentrating on classical languages. While in Wittenberg, he became an admirer of Melanchthon, and also of Luther, and began to affirm the Reformation principles, which he understood, however, in the light of his Humanistic background. Recommended by Melanchthon, Camerarius became an instructor in Greek and Latin at the *Gymnasium* in Nürnberg in 1526. From there he went as professor to the University of Tübingen in 1535, and to the University of Leipzig in 1541; he taught there for the remainder of his life. Shaped by Melanchthon's irenical approach to the problems created by the Reformation, Camerarius played a major role in the various unity discussions between the Reformers and the champions of the papal church. How much Camerarius was considered as standing apart from the dissenting parties can be seen from the fact that at one time Emperor Maximilian II even called him to Vienna to introduce certain reforms in the church in Austria. Camerarius is best known for his contributions to the Humanistic reorganization of the University of Leipzig, and for his biography of Melanchthon. This latter work is not only a history of Melanchthon's life but a broad history of the times. On Joachim Camerarius, see *NDB* 3, 104.

[23] Philip Melanchthon; see *LW* 48, 77, n. 3.

[1] The oldest available source of this letter is Aurifaber's collection of Luther's letters (published in 1565), and in this source the address is missing. The content of the letter makes obvious, however, to whom Luther was writing.

On Nicholas Gerbel, see *LW* 48, 317 f.
Text in Latin: *WA, Br* 3, 284.

Grace and peace in the Lord!

I have nothing to write about, excellent Gerbel. Yet since this letter carrier was available it seemed good that I should send you greetings and ask you to greet all the brothers and sisters in the Lord, to encourage them, and to ask them to remember me in their prayers. For I hear that the Word almost rules among you.[2] Here, around us, the more it is forbidden, the more it spreads far and wide. It has already taken over Magdeburg and Bremen;[3] soon it will pass over into Brunswick, I hope, especially since that Sovereign Henry,[4] who once was extremely hostile, seems to became a different man.

I think our Lonicer[5] has received my letter, and I hear that he has a new master. May the Lord not forsake him.

Satan is setting up a sect among us, at yet another place,[6] and this sect[7] supports neither the papists nor us. [The members of this sect] boast that they are being moved by pure spirits, without the testimony of Holy Scripture. This shows that our word is truly the Word of God, since it is being harassed not only by force, but also by new heresies.

---

2 On March 7 Gerbel wrote to Justus Jonas (see *LW* 48, 275, n. 3) about the willingness and eagerness of the Strassburg people to listen to God's Word and to study it; see Kawerau, *Jonas Briefwechsel* 1, 89 f. For details, see M. U. Chrisman, *Strasbourg and the Reform* (New Haven, 1967), pp. 131 ff.

3 See also p. 22.

4 On May 11, 1524, Luther wrote to Spalatin that Duke Henry of Brunswick was beginning to accept the gospel, and that a member of "our order" had been called by the Duke to preach the gospel; see *WA, Br* 3, 292. The duke mentioned by Luther was Duke Henry the Younger of Brunswick-Wolfenbüttel (see *NDB* 8, 351 f.), who ruled from 1514 to 1568. Luther's statement here was too optimistic. Henry never supported the Reformation; to the contrary, he became one of the champions of the Dessau Federation (see p. 119, n. 24).

5 John Lonicer; see *LW* 48, 164, n. 4; *WA, Br* 13, 28, to *WA, Br* 2, 99, n. 10. He was working as an editor in Strassburg, and at that time was leaving one publishing house to work for another. Luther's letter is not extant.

6 I.e., not in Wittenberg.

7 It is not clear whether Luther is referring here to Thomas Münzer in Allstedt (see *LW* 40, 45 ff.), the Nürnberg enthusiasts (see pp. 96 ff.), or Karlstadt in Orlamünde (see p. 72, n. 5).

Stay always well, you and your Rib,[8] and greet everyone in the Lord.

Wittenberg, May 6, 1524   MARTIN LUTHER

146

To Wolfgang Stein
Wittenberg, [beginning of September,][1] 1524

On March 14, 1524, Luther wrote to Spalatin[2] that Karlstadt[3] would be summoned from Orlamünde to appear before the University Senate to defend his action in leaving Wittenberg. This meeting took place on April 4, 1524.[4] Although Karlstadt promised to take up residence in Wittenberg, he did not keep this promise once he had returned to his parish in Orlamünde. On August 14 Karlstadt wrote to Duke John of Saxony[5] saying that if the Duke suspected him of false teachings he would be willing to debate and be corrected if proven wrong.[6] Through his court chaplain, Wolfgang Stein, the Duke asked Luther what Karlstadt should be told. The present letter is Luther's reply to Stein to the effect that the Duke should not deal with Karlstadt at all, but simply insist that Karlstadt cease his activities.

On Wolfgang Stein, see p. 15, n. 11.

Text in Latin and German: WA, Br 3, 343.[7]

To Wolfgang Stein, ducal preacher at Weimar,[8]
my brother in the Lord

---

[8] I.e., Gerbel's wife; this is obviously an allusion to Gen. 2:22.
[1] For the suggested date, see *WA*, Br 3, 342 f.
[2] See p. 73.
[3] Andrew Karlstadt; see *LW* 48, 79, n. 12.
[4] See p. 73, n. 7.
[5] Duke John of Saxony; see *LW* 48, 269, n. 8.
[6] For Karlstadt's letter, see *WA*, Br 3, 342 f.
[7] The letter is extant in one manuscript copy, and in the common editions of Luther's works.
[8] Elector Frederick (see *LW* 48, 49 f.) and his brother, Duke John of Saxony (see note 5), were co-rulers of Electoral Saxony. Frederick held the electoral office, and usually resided in the castle at Lochau, or at Wittenberg, or at Torgau, while Duke John usually resided at Weimar.

Grace and peace! I have both written and told the younger Sovereign[9] what should be said to Andrew Karlstadt when he is summoned. Now one may reply to [Karlstadt's] letter as follows, either when he is summoned or by a letter: Dear Doctor! You started this affair before you consulted us and received the gulden from Doctor Martin.[10] Why do you now, at long last, ask us for grace or favor, since previously you have always done as you were pleased? If you handle the matter well the outcome will be satisfactory.

With reference to the other point, that is, [Karlstadt's] offer to be questioned and to submit to a disputation, one should reply as follows: My most gracious Lord[11] is greatly surprised [by this offer], since Karlstadt has so often been summoned to Wittenberg to debate, lecture, and preach [there] in accordance with [the terms of] his office, [as] he is obligated to do according to the appointment issued by the Sovereign.[12] Now, however, he first magnifies his [willingness to] debate as if someone had hindered him [from debating], or even prohibited it. Yet he knows very well that so far no one could even drag him there. In the future he should not

---

[9] I.e., Duke John Frederick; see *LW* 48, 181 f. Karlstadt's August 14 letter to Duke John (see Introduction) was delivered to the Duke's councilors on August 15, while Duke John was absent from Weimar. On August 21 Luther was in Weimar and in the absence of Duke John discussed Karlstadt's letter with Duke John Frederick; for documentation, see *WA*, Br 3, 342 f. Luther then apparently wrote a short memorandum (seemingly no longer extant), to which he is now referring. After he returned to Wittenberg, Luther received Duke John's request (made through Stein) for an official statement on the matter.

[10] On August 22, 1524, Luther met Karlstadt in Jena and challenged him to state and defend his views publicly. As a token of this invitation, Luther gave him a gulden (see *LW* 48, 11, n. 2), which Karlstadt accepted. See *WA* 15, 339 f.; 18, 134; *LW* 40, 144.

[11] It is not clear whether Luther is thinking here of Duke John or Elector Frederick. Luther usually used the superlative ("my most gracious Lord") only for the Elector; see *WA* 11, 245, n. 1. Clemen (see note 1) suggests that in the autograph this phrase was most probably abbreviated, and that the copyist of the only extant manuscript copy (the one on which the *WA*, Br text is based) made a mistake in transcribing the abbreviation. On the other hand, Luther may very well have thought of the Elector, since at the end of this sentence he refers to the Elector as the person who had appointed Karlstadt.

[12] Elector Frederick (see note 8) was the patron of the University and the All Saints' Collegiate Chapter at Wittenberg's Castle Church, and Karlstadt had obligations to both institutions: to the former as a professor, to the latter as archdeacon.

pester my most gracious Lord[13] with such nonsense but conduct himself in such a way that he can bear [the full] responsibility for it.

Because the things [Karlstadt] believes about God are so stupid, he first wants to consult the Sovereigns.[14] If his actions are based on God's inspiration, why does he hesitate? Why does he procrastinate? Why does he consult men? Here you realize how certain that wicked spirit is about his being driven by God in what he is doing. Oh madness! But let him come!

Farewell to you and to all.

[*Written*] *hurriedly, Wittenberg, 1524*

MARTIN LUTHER

147

To the Council of the City of Zerbst
[Wittenberg,] October 8, 1524

The Roman Catholic church of the Middle Ages regulated both marriages and the married life. Secular law supported the church by lending its executive power to the church and by shaping the matrimonial laws accordingly.[1] With the development of the Reformation the legal authority of the papal church was increasingly disregarded, and secular authorities had little idea how to handle cases concerning marriages or the married life. The laws of the state had been issued in conformity with the regulations set forth by Canon Law. Yet Canon Law was no longer to be valid.[2] In this situation Luther and the University of Wittenberg were asked for advice. In the present letter Luther is answering one of these requests by reporting on the way in which adulterers were punished in Wittenberg.

Text in German: WA, Br 3, 355.[3]

---

[13] See note 11.

[14] I.e., of Saxony; see note 8.

[1] See *O.D.C.C.*, p. 873; H. E. Feine, *Kirchliche Rechtsgeschichte: Die Katholische Kirche* (4th ed.; Köln-Graz, 1964), pp. 543 ff.

[2] For a detailed discussion of the validity of Canon Law for the Reformation, see *Zeitschrift der Savigny-Stiftung für Rechtsgeschichte. Kanonistische Abteilung* 51 (1965), 190 ff.

[3] For Luther's position on questions related to marriage and sex, see also *LCC* 18, 258 ff.

To the Honorable and Wise Mayor and Councilors of the City of Zerbst, my Dear Sirs and Friends

Grace and peace in Christ! Honorable, Wise, Dear Sirs! I have talked to the gentlemen and doctors here[4] about your letter regarding adultery. This is our reply: According to the law of Moses,[5] [adulterers] were stoned; yet this law was only given to the Jews. We, who are living among the Gentiles and have a Gentile government, are obligated to behave and to punish according to the same Gentile law,[6] although, unfortunately, that same law and government are not strong and are of little use.[7] Therefore here at Wittenberg, we have let the honorable city council punish adulterers by flogging them and expelling them from the city.[8] [We use] this milder punishment, since the one which the Imperial law prescribes is not used here.[9]

Your Honors may follow this example of the people of Wittenberg, if you like it, or use the strict punishment of the Imperial law.

---

[4] I.e., the members of the Law Faculty and perhaps also of the Theological Faculty.

[5] Lev. 20:10; Deut. 22:22.

[6] For a similar statement, see pp. 74, 385 ff.

[7] Luther wrote: *recht und regiment ligt und wenig ynn brauch ist.* Literally: ". . . law and government lie down [or: are trodden down; or: give up] and are in little use." Luther wanted to say, apparently, that there is no strong government which enforces the law concerning the married life, be it Imperial (see the last sentence of this paragraph) or territorial.

[8] In later years Luther's opinion changed. In a Table Talk recorded for February, 1546, Luther argued that adulterers, just as thieves and robbers, should be beheaded; see *WA*, TR 6, No. 6934.

[9] When Luther speaks of Imperial law, he means either the Roman Law, or certain regulations set up by the different emperors or worked out by a specific commission of the diet (see *LW* 48, 70, n. 1) and recommended to the Estates for enforcement. Since the Imperial Estates jealously guarded their independence, any Imperial criminal or civil laws had little prospect of being generally enforced throughout the Empire. At Luther's time there was no criminal code which was valid for all of Germany. The first one (issued in 1532) was the *Carolina,* the criminal code compiled under the direction of Charles V. This code was by no means designed, however, to jeopardize the laws of the territories; see *Carolina,* Preface. It was to be regulatory only, and was to be an example for territorial laws. This confusion, which was even worse prior to the *Carolina,* is perhaps the reason why Luther complained about the weakness of secular law. In the *Carolina,* adultery was stipulated to be a crime punishable by death. For the pre-*Carolina* period, see *Corpus iuris civilis. Novellae constitutiones,* CXVII: cap. VIII; CXXXIV: cap. X. For the *Carolina,* see Art. CXX.

Herewith I commend [Your Honors] to God.

October 8, 1524   MARTIN LUTHER

148

To Nicholas Hausmann
Wittenberg, November 17, 1524

Luther informs Hausmann that he will reply to Erasmus' book on free will, but that he will postpone writing on the Lord's Supper until Karlstadt has further elaborated his position on this issue. He also mentions that Zwingli and Jud have the same understanding of the Lord's Supper as Karlstadt.

Then Luther spells out some ideas on how to reshape the liturgy.[1] He would like the mass to be celebrated in German, yet he also admits that thus far he has been unable to write an order of service. He rejects any notion that a general council[2] should regulate the order of worship to be followed by the individual congregations, and maintains that each congregation has the privilege[3] of establishing its own order for public worship, provided that the unity of the Spirit in the faith and the Word is maintained among all the congregations.[4] In closing, Luther mentions the martyrdom of a certain Caspar Tauber, and of a bookdealer named George.

On Nicholas Hausman, see LW 48, 399 f.

Text in Latin: WA, Br 3, 373–374. The following translation is based on S-J 2, 258–260.

To the faithful and prudent servant of Christ, Mr. Nicholas Hausmann, bishop at Zwickau,[5] my superior in the Lord

---

[1] See *LW* 48, 143 f., 324 f.

[2] For Luther's stand on the councils of the church, and the conciliar form of ecclesiastical government, see K. Skydsgaard (ed.), *The Papal Council and the Gospel* (Minneapolis, 1961), pp. 37 ff.

[3] See also pp. 28 ff.

[4] This idea is also expressed in Article VII of the *Augsburg Confession* of 1530, and thus incorporated into the official doctrine of the Lutheran church.

[5] Throughout his life, Luther was convinced that the pastor of a congregation was its shepherd and bishop, that all pastors or bishops were equal, and that within the church none of them had any special spiritual, or even any special legal, privileges. See also *SMRH* 5 (1968), 205 ff.

Grace and peace in the Lord. I have not forgotten you,[6] my Hausmann, though it is true that my memory is somewhat weakened by the various matters with which I have to deal, and by advancing years.

I shall answer Erasmus,[7] not for his sake, but for the sake of those who abuse his authority in their glorying against Christ. I am putting off writing the book on the Eucharist which you previously requested of me[8] until Karlstadt[9] has poured out his poison, as he promised me to do when he accepted the gulden from me.[10] However, I am already familiar with the more important parts of his ridiculous arguments.[11] Among the Swiss, Zwingli at Zürich[12]

[6] Luther's last extant letter to Hausmann is dated June 15, 1524; WA, Br 3, No. 751.

[7] At the end of August the tension which had been latent between Erasmus and Luther since the summer of 1519 finally erupted when Erasmus published his De libero arbitrio (On Free Will). Text: Clericus 9, 1215 ff.; a critical edition was published by J. von Walter (Leipzig, 1935); English translation in LCC 17. Luther did not issue an immediate rebuttal. Apparently he considered the Eucharistic controversy with Karlstadt more urgent, for he postponed answering Erasmus until the second half of 1525 and, instead, began working on a book dealing with Karlstadt and the Lord's Supper almost immediately.

[8] Hausmann's letters to Luther have not survived and, therefore, we do not know exactly what kind of a book on the Eucharist Hausmann had asked Luther to write.

[9] Andrew Karlstadt; see LW 48, 79, n. 12.

[10] See p. 84, n. 10.

[11] In at least one of the pamphlets published by Karlstadt after the fall of 1523 (see WA 18, 38, 42), Karlstadt's main point was that when Christ said, "This is my body, given for you," he was not referring to the bread, but to himself (who was to die the following day), and was pointing to his body; consequently, Karlstadt maintained, Christ is not present in the Lord's Supper. For details, see Lutheran Quarterly 12 (1960), 152 ff.

[12] Ulrich Zwingli (1484–1531), the Reformer of Zürich and of the German-speaking parts of Switzerland, had studied at the Universities of Vienna and Basel, and was graduated as Master of Arts from the University of Basel in 1506. In the summer of 1506 he studied theology in Basel, and was ordained into the priesthood in September of that year. From 1506 to 1516 he was pastor in Glarus, and from 1516 to 1518 Leutpriester (people's priest, i.e., chief pastor and preacher) in Einsiedeln. At the end of 1518 he was called as Leutpriester to the Grossmünster (cathedral) in Zürich, a position he held for the remainder of his life. Through the influence of Erasmus, Zwingli developed from a religiously unconcerned papistic preacher into a reform-minded Christian Humanist. And so while at Einsiedeln, Zwingli preached against some of the abuses within the papal church, while seriously studying the New Testament and St. Augustine. In the fall of 1519 Zwingli was very ill with the plague, and at the time became familiar with some of Luther's writings. Christian Humanism, St. Augustine, Luther, and the experience of being near death—all these caused Zwingli to become a Reformer himself. In Lent of 1522 he broke officially with the papal church by disregarding the regulations on

and Leo Jud[13] share the same opinion as Karlstadt,[14] so widespread

fasting. The Zürich city council asked the ecclesiastical superior of the city, the bishop of Constance, to call a provincial synod to deal with Zwingli's arguments against fasting and other customs of the church, as well as with his arguments against some of the more important teachings of the papal church. Since the bishop refused to call a synod, the city council stepped into the matter, and sponsored the famous First Zürich Disputation (January 29, 1523). The result of this disputation was a clear victory for Zwingli, who, with the consent of the city council, introduced the Reformation to Zürich. By 1526 the Reformation had completely taken over the city, and as a result of Zwingli's efforts the cause of the gospel was being spread to other Swiss city republics, especially Bern. The papacy was of course not standing idle. In May of 1526 the assembly of the Swiss republics, dominated by a pro-papal majority, excommunicated and banned Zwingli, and the pro-papal republics (supported by the Hapsburgs) began a political drive against Zürich. Zwingli, through tireless diplomatic and even military efforts, tried successfully to head off any possible danger and to strengthen Zürich's position. With great political wisdom he attempted to bring about an anti-Hapsburg, anti-Roman alliance not only of all Protestant territories of the Empire (including Switzerland) but even of Europe. In spite of strong support for such a plan on the part of Strassburg and Philip of Hesse and many attempts on the part of Martin Bucer to bridge discrepancies, the plan did not materialize. Zürich, isolated from the Protestants in the Empire, had to face the pro-papal Swiss republics alone, and was defeated; Zwingli died in the battle at Cappel on October 11, 1531. Though Zwingli was deeply impressed with Luther and had many theological concepts in common with the Wittenberg Reformer, he nevertheless steered an independent course, and thus became one of the fathers of the Reformed tradition. The main point at issue between Zwingli and Luther was their understanding of the Lord's Supper. In November, 1524, Zwingli wrote a letter to a certain Matthew Alber in Reutlingen. This letter soon was circulated in Germany (in five hundred manuscript copies, it was said), and in this letter Zwingli contended that Christ is not present in the elements of the Lord's Supper; in the spring of 1525 Zwingli published his theological masterwork, the *Commentarius*. Here he developed his symbolic understanding of the Eucharist in great detail. After some preliminary yet important skirmishes between the friends of Luther and the friends of Zwingli, the controversy between Zwingli and Luther himself erupted in 1527. When both men finally met in October, 1529, in Marburg, Luther clearly stated the basic difference between himself and the Zwinglians in his famous statement: You have a different spirit.

13 Leo Jud (1482–1542) worked hard and faithfully with Zwingli in organizing the Reformation in Zürich. He dedicated much of his effort to translating the works of St. Augustine, Zwingli, and Erasmus (especially the *Paraphrases*). He was also responsible for the translation of the prophets and Apocrypha in the *Zürich Bible* (published in 1529), the first complete translation of the Bible into German, i.e., the Swiss-German. In April of 1526, when the controversy on the Lord's Supper was increasingly separating Wittenberg and Zürich, Jud published a dialog, which he hoped would serve to bridge the discrepancies. After Zwingli's death, Jud and Henry Bullinger guided the course of the Reformation in the German-speaking parts of Switzerland. On Jud, see *NCE* 8, 1.

14 This opinion was not based on a solid knowledge of any of Zwingli's writings (it is almost impossible that Luther had already seen Zwingli's letter to Alber; see note 12), but on vague secondhand information. On August 27,

is this evil. But Christ reigns—to say nothing of the fact that he fights back.

I desire a German mass more than I can promise [to work on an order for it].[15] I am not qualified for this task, which requires both a talent in music and the gift of the Spirit. Meanwhile I charge each one to use his judgment until Christ gives us something different. I do not consider it sufficiently safe to call a council of our party for establishing unity in the ceremonies.[16] It would set a bad example, however praiseworthy the zeal with which it might be attempted, as all the councils of the church prove from the beginning. Even the Council of the Apostles[17] dealt almost more with works and traditions than with faith. In the later councils, in fact, there was never any discussion of faith, but only of opinions and questions. As a result, the word "council" is almost as suspect and distasteful[18] to me as the term "free will."[19] If in these external matters one congregation[20] does not voluntarily want to follow another, why should it be compelled to do so by decrees of councils, which are soon converted into laws and snares for souls? Of its own accord a congregation should, therefore, follow another one, or else be allowed to enjoy its own customs; only the unity of the Spirit should be preserved in faith and in the Word, however great may

---

1524, a preacher in Wertheim named Franz Kolb wrote to Luther about Zwingli's understanding of the Lord's Supper; WA, Br 3, No. 769. Apparently on the basis of this information Luther suspected that Zwingli would be supporting Karlstadt, although Zwingli's views on the Lord's Supper were different from those of Karlstadt, especially in regard to the exegesis of the Words of Institution. Karlstadt and Zwingli had two points in common, however: (a) they held that the Words of Institution were not directly applicable to the elements; (b) they maintained a spiritualistic concept of God, according to which God, or the Holy Spirit, used no earthly symbols (such as sacraments) to accomplish his purpose. On the basis of these two points Luther put Karlstadt and Zwingli into the same category. For references to details, see p. 94, n. 6; for Zwingli's position, see C. Gestrich, *Zwingli als Theologe. Glaube und Geist beim Züricher Reformator* (Zürich, 1968).

[15] See pp. 55 f.

[16] Apparently Hausmann had suggested this in a no-longer extant letter. The same desire for uniformity in liturgical matters was also expressed to Luther by the leaders of the Reformation in Strassburg; see WA, Br 3, 384.

[17] Acts 15:1 ff.

[18] See note 2.

[19] This was an issue between Luther and the Scholastic theologians, and had just been emphasized again in the book by Erasmus, mentioned in note 7.

[20] Luther wrote *ecclesia*, i.e., church; see p. 61, n. 9.

be the diversity and variety in respect to the flesh and the elements of the world.

I believe you have seen the story concerning Caspar Tauber,[21] who has recently become a martyr in Vienna. [It is written] there that he was beheaded and burned on account of the Word of God. The same thing has happened in Budapest, Hungary, to a book-seller by the name of George;[22] he was burned at the stake, to-gether with his books which were placed around him, and he suffered most courageously for the Lord. Blood touches blood,[23] and it will choke the pope along with his kings and their kingdoms.

Farewell, and pray for me, a sinner.

Wittenberg, November 17, 1524   MARTIN LUTHER

149

To George Spalatin[1]
Wittenberg, November 30, 1524

Luther is encouraging Spalatin not to resign from the position of court chaplain unless he is forced to do so by very urgent matters, such as wedding plans. Commenting on a particular letter written by Argula von Grumbach, Luther points out that at this time he has no wedding plans, since he daily expects death. In a postscript Luther inquires about the members of the present Electoral Saxon delegation to the Council of Regency; he hopes they might be in a position to do something for a certain Augustinian, John Mantel. He also asks for Spalatin's help regarding the latest supplication of "poor Sophie."

---

[21] Tauber, a merchant in Vienna, was executed on September 17, 1524; see WA, 18, 224. His fate was the subject of a little book (for bibliographical information, see WA, Br 3, 368, n. 8; 13, 69, *ad loc.*), to which Luther is referring.

[22] On this bookdealer "George," see WA, Br 3, 374, n. 11; Enders, *Brief-wechsel* 5, 54, n. 9. Luther also mentioned this incident in WA, 18, 224.

[23] Hos. 4:2.

[1] The letter is extant in manuscript copies, and in the common editions of Luther's works. Even though the address is missing in the manuscript copies, the content of the letter makes clear to whom Luther was writing.

On George Spalatin, see LW 48, 8 f.
Text in Latin: WA, Br 3, 393–394.

Grace and peace!

To your request for my advice regarding your possible resignation from your position at court,[2] my Spalatin, I have this to say: There is of course some reason for resigning if people do not listen to the Word, as the sage says: "Waste not your word where no man listens."[3] But one should not cease [preaching] if anyone at all is listening. Otherwise I would have long ago been silent on account of the great contempt for the Word. Unless you have some other reason which burdens your conscience, the wickedness and malice [of men] is not a sufficient reason for deserting your place and vocation, or for doing anything at all.[4] For unless marriage moves you from this place, I cannot imagine any reason that should. You now know the court completely by experience, and can be of great value to the people around the Sovereign.[5] Whereas if a novice takes over, what can he accomplish until he becomes acquainted with the court? Suppose that he did distinguish himself in all things similarly, how long might it be before he would enjoy the high confidence and esteem of the Sovereign which you have? These are things which have come about through long association. Therefore remain, or if you leave, do so only because you are forced to by marriage plans! Perhaps you are afraid of mentioning this reason, and wish to pretend something else instead. I do not see what good this would do, since the real reason would come out anyway when you married.

---

[2] On November 25 Spalatin had asked Elector Frederick for a discharge. He based his request on his lack of necessary qualifications for a court chaplain, his poor health, and his intention to marry. Spalatin's letter to Luther is not extant. But, as can be deduced from Luther's answer, Spalatin explained his desire to leave the court to Luther by pointing to the poor response which his gospel ministry created at the court. Spalatin at that time was physically exhausted and consequently was depressed; thus he was unable to cope with the roughness of some of the courtiers who made him, his small stature, and his way of preaching the target of their jokes. For documentation, see Höss, *Spalatin*, pp. 270 ff.; WA, Br 3, 394, n. 1.

[3] Ecclesiasticus 32:6.

[4] In some witnesses the last portion of this sentence ("or for doing . . .") is missing.

[5] I.e., here and throughout the letter Elector Frederick; see LW 48, 49 f.

I am grateful for what Argula[6] writes about my wedding plans;[7] I am not surprised about such gossip, since so many other bits of gossip are around concerning me. Nevertheless give her my thanks and tell her I am in God's hand as a creature whose heart God may change and rechange, kill and revive again at any moment. Nevertheless, the way I feel now, and have felt thus far, I will not marry. It is not that I do not feel my flesh or sex, since I am neither wood nor stone, but my mind is far removed from marriage, since I daily expect death and the punishment due to a heretic. Therefore I shall not limit God's work in me, nor shall I rely on my own heart. Yet I hope God does not let me live long.

Farewell, and pray for me.

Wittenberg, November 30, 1524　　　Martin Luther

I[8] wish to know who the representatives of the Sovereign at the Council of Regency[9] in Esslingen are, for I was asked to intercede for Mr. Mantel,[10] who is imprisoned, [and to find out] if, with their help, he could be released. According to news from Esslingen, a promise was given by Ferdinand's[11] people. I also commend to

---

[6] Argula von Grumbach; see p. 313, n. 11.

[7] This letter, as well as others exchanged between Argula von Grumbach and Luther, is not extant.

[8] In some manuscript copies and in Aurifaber's edition of Luther's letters (published in 1565) the postscript is missing. In one manuscript copy the postscript is separated from the body of the letter. Rückert, *LB*, No. 66, does not reproduce the postscript. Clemen (*WA*, Br 3, 394) and Enders, *Briefwechsel* (5, 77) add the postscript without giving any reason for doing this. Thus they follow de Wette's edition of Luther's letters (2, 569 ff., published in Berlin in 1826), in which apparently for the first time the postscript has been added to the body of the letter. On the basis of the extant witnesses it has to remain an open question whether the postscript belongs to this letter, or to another letter. The fact that the postscript is dated by itself is inconclusive, because the copyist could easily have made a mistake.

[9] Literally: "Senate of the Empire." On the Council of Regency, see *LW* 48, 70, n. 1. After the last Diet of Nürnberg (see p. 35, n. 4) the Council had moved from Nürnberg to Esslingen.

[10] John Mantel was a former Augustinian. From August, 1523, he had been imprisoned by the Austrian government because he had openly proclaimed a year of jubilee in which all debts were to be canceled (see Ex. 21:2; Deut. 15:1 ff.); this was considered by the authorities to be an incitement to rebellion. See *WA*, Br 1, 202, n. 1; 3, 393, n. 7; 13, 15, to *WA*, Br 1, 202, n. 1.

[11] I.e., Ferdinand of Austria (see *LW* 48, 217, n. 17), in whose custody Mantel was.

you this latest supplication of poor Sophie;[12] maybe you can do something. Farewell, and pray for me!

Wittenberg, November 30, 1524   M. L.

150

To the Christians in Strassburg
[Wittenberg, about December 15, 1524]

During Luther's exile at the Wartburg, the first major internal crisis of the Reformation erupted when the Wittenberg disturbances occurred.[1] By 1526 the one Reformation movement had become split into three different groups: the Lutheran; the Zwinglian; and that composed of the evangelical Anabaptists, the religious enthusiasts and spiritualists, and the social radicals.[2] Luther called this last group Schwärmer,[3] but quite often also included Zwingli and his followers in this group. Inevitably the different camps had to clash. Luther's controversies with Karlstadt[4] and Münzer[5] were one phase of this battle; the controversy on the Lord's Supper[6] was the other phase. This controversy began as a tug-of-war between Wittenberg and Zürich over the position of Strassburg, for by 1526 Wittenberg, Nürnberg, Strassburg, and Zürich had come to be major centers from which the ideas of the Reformation were being spread. Wittenberg was dominated by Luther, Zürich by Zwingli, and

---

[12] Nothing could be established about the background of this statement.

[1] See *LW* 48, 386, n. 1.

[2] On this third group, which Roland Bainton has called "The Left Wing of the Reformation" (*Journal of Religion* 21 [1941], 124 ff.), and which George H. Williams has called "The Radical Reformation" (*The Radical Reformation* [Philadelphia, 1962]), see *The Encyclopedia of the Lutheran Church* (Minneapolis, 1965), 1, 783 ff,

[3] On Luther's relationships with the *Schwärmer*, see the ref. to the *Encyclopedia of the Lutheran Church*, cited in note 2; see further, J. S. Oyer, *Lutheran Reformers Against the Anabaptists. Luther, Melanchthon and Menius and the Anabaptists of Central Germany* (The Hague, 1964).

[4] See Rupp, *Patterns*, pp. 49 ff.

[5] On Luther's controversy with Münzer, see *LW* 40, 47 ff. On Thomas Münzer, see E. W. Gritsch, *Reformer Without a Church. The Life and Thought of Thomas Muenzer. 1488–1525* (Philadelphia, 1967); Rupp, *Patterns*, pp. 157 ff.

[6] On this controversy, see W. Köhler, *Zwingli und Luther* (2 vols.; Leipzig-Gütersloh, 1924, 1953); Sasse, *passim*.

Nürnberg, after a brief period of indecisiveness, whole-heartedly supported Luther. The situation in Strassburg, however, was not as clear-cut. Here were not only those who supported either Luther or Zwingli, but there were also those who supported the Schwärmer. Therefore Karlstadt was well received in Strassburg after he had been expelled from Electoral Saxony. Since the local preachers had difficulty understanding Karlstadt's teachings, they approached Zwingli[7] and Luther[8] for advice on and interpretation of Karlstadt's views. Although Zwingli criticized certain of Karlstadt's tenets, he nevertheless endorsed Karlstadt's position as a whole, since it was so much closer to his own than that of Luther; thus Zwingli attempted to consolidate the anti-Luther forces in Strassburg. Letter No. 150 is Luther's official reply in the form of an open letter addressed to the Christians in Strassburg.[9] Luther at once followed this public statement with several private letters.[10]

Luther begins his letter by encouraging the Christians of Strassburg to stand fast in the true faith even though the powers of darkness might assail them. The main thrust of the letter is Luther's description of the points on which he and Karlstadt disagree. Luther vigorously argues that breaking images, denying the real presence of Christ in the Lord's Supper, and rejecting the baptism of infants are acts which any "rascal" can do, but which never make a person a Christian. He characterizes Karlstadt's teachings concerning the Lord's Supper as a demonic temptation, and admits that in the past he himself had to struggle against this temptation.

---

[7] WA 15, 384. Zwingli's answer won greater favor in Strassburg than did Luther's answer.

[8] WA, Br 3, No. 797, dated November 23, 1524. On the position of Strassburg, see Pollet 2, 54 ff. Luther received the shipment from Strassburg on December 14, and on that day forwarded the letter (together with other material) to Spalatin; he also told Spalatin that within two days he would publish an answer. See WA 15, 383.

[9] Luther's letter was printed, and apparently one of these printed copies was sent to Strassburg. One can arrive at an approximate date for Luther's letter by taking as point of departure Luther's December 14 letter to Spalatin (see note 8), and Luther's December 17 letters to Nicholas Gerbel and to Catherine Zell (see note 10).

[10] Luther's personal answer to the Strassburg preachers (see Enders, *Briefwechsel* 5, 83, n. 1) is no longer extant. On December 17 Luther wrote also to Nicholas Gerbel (see *LW* 48, 317 f.; *WA*, Br 3, No. 807; *S-J* 2, No. 651) and to Catherine Zell (*WA*, Br 3, No. 808), the wife of Matthew Zell, a preacher in Strassburg.

Luther also discusses briefly some of the events which preceded Karlstadt's expulsion from Electoral Saxony. In a lengthy conclusion Luther admonishes his readers to walk in the narrow path of truth, to abandon both Karlstadt and himself and to look to Christ alone, and to understand Christ not as an example for life—as Karlstadt does—but as God's gift of strength, wisdom, righteousness, sanctification, and redemption.

Text in German: WA 15, 391–397; translation by C. Bergendoff, LW 40, 65–71.

151

To Lazarus Spengler
Wittenberg, February 4, 1525

In the fall of 1524 the Nürnberg city council investigated Hans Denck (the master of the school at St. Sebald's Church in Nürnberg)[1] and three members of the famous painters' guild[2] for "godless" teachings.[3] In January of 1525 all four suspects were punished

---

[1] John Denck (*ca.* 1500–1527) was the most profound thinker of the early *Schwärmer* movement (see p. 94) in southern Germany. He had studied at the University of Ingolstadt, and after a brief period of teaching on what today would be considered the secondary level, he went to Basel to work for one of the publishing houses there. Recommended by Oecolampadius (see *LW* 48, 230, n. 4), Denck became master of the school at St. Sebald's Church in Nürnberg in September, 1523. On January 21, 1525, Denck was expelled from Nürnberg because of his "seditious and un-Christian teachings." For the remainder of his life he found in Augsburg, Strassburg, and Basel only brief respite from wandering around and from being hunted from one place to the other because of his association with the Anabaptists. In August, 1527, Denck attended a meeting of leading Anabaptists in Augsburg, and they apparently sent him as a missionary into the areas of Basel and Zürich. While visiting Basel in November of 1527, Denck died of the plague. On John Denck, see *NDB* 3, 599 f.; *The Mennonite Encyclopedia* 2 (Scottdale, Pa., 1956), 32 ff.; W. Fellmann (ed.), *Hans Denck, Schriften*, Part II: *Die religiösen Schriften* (Gütersloh, 1956), 8 ff.

[2] A certain George Pentz, and the brothers Sebald and Barthel Beheim; see also note 3. All three were "students" of Albrecht Dürer. On Dürer's relationship to the Reformation, see *Zeitschrift für bayerische Kirchengeschichte* 25 (1956), 40 ff.; *Historische Zeitschrift* 206 (1968), 22 ff.

[3] See note 10. For the documents of this investigation, and for details, see *Kirchengeschichtliche Studien Hermann Reuter zum 70. Geburtstag* (Leipzig, 1888), pp. 228 ff.; *Beiträge zur bayerischen Kirchengeschichte* 8 (1902), 1 ff., 49 ff.; *Zeitschrift für bayerische Kirchengeschichte* 25 (1956), 40 ff.; *Mit-*

by expulsion from the city. Apparently before this verdict was is-
sued Spengler forwarded to Luther some records of the investiga-
tion, and asked for Luther's advice regarding the treatment of these
people.[4] *In his answer Luther mentions that he had always sus-*
pected that Münzer's position might eventually be affirmed by other
people,[5] *but that until now he was not aware that this had already*
happened. Luther states that secular government may punish these
people only if they promote revolution; otherwise they are to be
considered as Turks, or Christians who have denied their name, a
fact for which they are not to be punished by secular authorities.

On Lazarus Spengler, see LW 48, 184.

Text in German: WA, Br 3, 432–433.

To the prudent and wise Lazarus Spengler, chancellor[6] of the
City of Nürnberg, my kind lord and good friend

---

teilungen des Vereins für Geschichte der Stadt Nürnberg 50 (1960), 120 ff.;
The Mennonite Quarterly Review 39 (1965), 25 ff.; Fellmann, *op. cit.*, 20 ff.;
A. Evans, *An Episode in the Struggle for Religious Freedom. The Sectaries of*
Nuremberg, 1524–1528 (New York, 1924).

[4] Spengler's letter is not extant. Clemen (*WA*, Br 3, No. 824, Introduction)
argues that Spengler apparently forwarded to Luther all the records of this
investigation. It is not clear whether Spengler did this before or after the
verdicts had been issued on January 21 against Denck, and on January 26 or
27 against the "godless" painters. That Luther saw some material is obvious
from this letter to Spengler, and also from Luther's February 4 letter to
Briessmann; *WA*, Br 3, 433. If Spengler had sent the material to Luther *after*
the verdicts had been issued, then it is not clear why Spengler asked Luther
for counsel on how to treat these "godless" people. On the basis of Luther's
answer, it must be assumed that Spengler asked Luther whether the secular
government has the right or duty to punish physically these "godless" people.
Would this have made sense if a verdict had already been issued? One has to
assume, therefore, that Spengler sent the records prior to the date that the
verdict was issued.

[5] See also note 13.

[6] In addressing Spengler, Luther used various titles; e.g., *Ratsschreiber, Stadt-*
schreiber (so on November 17, 1520; see *LW* 48, 184), or *Syndicus*, as in the
letter here. A literal translation of these titles cannot reproduce the meaning of
the position held by Spengler in the Nürnberg city government. In *LW* 48,
184, Spengler's title *Stadtschreiber* (city clerk) has been explained as that of
the legally trained counselor and liaison man between the city council and
the major. This explanation is not specific enough. The title "chancellor"
seems best able to communicate to the present-day reader the position held by
Spengler in Nürnberg, and to avoid the ambiguities connected with a literal
translation of the titles used by Luther.

Grace and peace in Christ! Prudent, kind, dear Sir and Friend! I was both pleased and dismayed by your most recent letter[7] to me: pleased that Christ is so active among you[8] and is watching the wolves; dismayed that through the emissaries of the devil this catastrophe[9] has progressed so far that such articles[10] are being doubted and denied, while at the same time a Christian concern is pretended.[11] Even though I was always suspicious of the "spirit of Allstedt,"[12] [thinking] he might eventually reach this point,[13] yet

---

[7] This letter is not extant; see notes 4, 8.

[8] Spengler apparently informed Luther of the progress the Reformation was making in Nürnberg. As early as July, 1522, the city fathers began to reorganize the care for the poor in the city, and in August/September, 1523, following the examples set by Wittenberg and Leisnig, they published an ordinance concerning the Common Chest; text: Sehling 11, 23 ff. In the spring of 1524, the two great parishes, St. Sebald and St. Lawrence, conducted major religious and liturgical reforms (see Sehling 11, 46 ff.), and the two chief pastors defended these reforms in a highly detailed brief; text: W. F. Schmidt, K. Schornbaum (eds.), *Die Fränkischen Bekenntnisse* (Munich, 1930), pp. 157 ff. In March, 1525, a disputation on the major issues raised by Luther was sponsored by the city council, and was conducted in the beautiful great city hall (which was destroyed during the Second World War). On March 16, 1525, the city council officially introduced the Reformation by ordering that from then on all churches were to cease celebrating mass according to the papal liturgy, and by strongly urging all ecclesiastical institutions within the city's jurisdiction to adopt the liturgy which had been used by the two great city parishes since the spring of 1524. For documentation and for details, see G. Pfeiffer, *Quellen zur Nürnberger Reformationgeschichte* (Nürnberg, 1968); G. Strauss, *Nuremberg in the Sixteenth Century* (New York, 1966), pp. 154 ff. No doubt, Spengler was informing Luther of some details in this development.

[9] I.e., the spreading of the *Schwärmer* (see p. 94) and their beliefs.

[10] See note 4. Since Spengler's letter to Luther is not extant, and since it cannot be established with certainty which documents Luther had available, it can also not be established to which "articles" Luther is here referring. In his letter to Briessmann (see note 4), Luther mentions that some citizens in Nürnberg deny the validity of Christ, of God's Word, of baptism and the Lord's Supper, and of secular power. On the basis of all available evidence (see note 3), it can be assumed that Luther referred in the Briessman letter to the statements made by the painters. For the statements made by Denck, see Fellmann, *op. cit.*, 11, 20 ff.

[11] I.e., Denck and the painters argued that their consciences compelled them to affirm their teachings in order to be Christians.

[12] I.e., Thomas Münzer, who had been the pastor at Allstedt/Thuringia. Luther suspected that Münzer had influenced Denck and the "godless" painters. On the one hand this was a close guess, since Münzer was indeed at that time in Nürnberg, where he had some of his writings printed. However, no specific connections between Münzer and Denck can be documented; see Fellmann, *op. cit.*, 10. The painters were more under Karlstadt's influence than that of Münzer; *WA*, Br 3, 434, n. 7; *Beiträge* (see note 3), 64. In his letter to

I did not think that it had already happened. It is good, however, that such abomination comes out into the open, so that the folly and the plans of such spirits can become known and crushed.

But you ask me how they[14] should be punished.[15] I do not yet consider them to be blasphemers, but to be like the Turks, or apostate Christians, who are not to be punished by secular authorities, especially not by means of corporal punishment.[16] If they do not want to acknowledge and obey the secular government, however, then they have forfeited their rights to property and person. For then there is certainly rebellion and murder in their hearts. In that case, secular government must act against them. No doubt, your gentlemen[17] will know how to proceed in that situation.

Pray to God for me! May his grace be with you all. Amen.

Wittenberg, February 4, 1525   MARTIN LUTHER

152

To Theobald Billicanus
Wittenberg, March 5, 1525

Replying to a letter from Billicanus, Luther develops his understanding of the relationship of the Word to the sacrament in the

Briessmann (see note 4), Luther made Münzer *and* Karlstadt responsible for the Nürnberg heresies. This suggests that one should perhaps not give too much attention to Luther's statement here, in the letter to Spengler, that *Münzer* influenced the Nürnberg heretics.
[13] I.e., the heresy as it was affirmed by the Nürnberg heretics. The text could also justify the following translation: "Even though I was always suspicious of the "spirit of Allstedt," that he would go there [i.e., to this area, southern Germany], just as Karlstadt did, yet . . ."
[14] In the following sentences "they," "them," "their," etc., refer to Denck and the "godless" painters.
[15] For the following see K. Holl, *Gesammelte Aufsätze zur Kirchengeschichte,* I: *Luther* (6th ed.; Tübingen, 1932), 370, n. 2; J. Heckel, *Lex charatatis. Eine juristische Untersuchung über das Recht in der Theologie Martin Luthers* (Munich, 1953), pp. 151, 193, n. 1504; R. Götze, *Wie Luther Kirchenzucht übte* (Berlin, 1959); F. E. Cranz, *An Essay on the Development of Luther's Thought on Justice, Law and Society* (Cambridge, Mass., 1959); R. H. Bainton, *Studies on the Reformation* (Boston, 1966), pp. 20 ff.
[16] Literally: ". . . especially not in the body." In the text "blasphemers" is written in Latin.
[17] I.e., the members of the Nürnberg city government.

consecration of the Lord's Supper. He points out that the validity
of the sacrament as such does not depend on the qualities of the
minister or the recipient of the sacrament, but exclusively on the
power of God's Word; further, he shows that faith is necessary in
order to receive the benefit of the sacrament.

Theobald Gerlach (1490?–1554) of Billigheim (hence Billicanus)
near Landau/Palatinate studied theology in Heidelberg, where he
also became a canon. From 1518, when Luther was visiting Heidelberg, Billicanus was attracted by the Reformer and supported him;
as a result, so Billicanus said, he was not admitted to the doctoral
examination in Heidelberg, and had to leave town. In 1522 he became a preacher in Nördlingen. The area around Nördlingen was
influenced both by the Lutherans (from Nürnberg) and by the
Zwinglians (from Strassburg and Zürich). It was also a stronghold
of the Schwärmer. Billicanus was wavering between Zwingli and
Luther; although he opposed Karlstadt's iconoclasm, he was nevertheless for some time open to Karlstadt's interpretation of the Lord's
Supper. He was so vacillating that in 1529 he affirmed his allegiance
to the papal church, and in 1530 rejected all Reformation "heresies."
In 1535 he resigned from his pastoral office in Nördlingen and went
to Heidelberg, where he studied and taught law. From 1544 to the
end of his life he taught rhetoric at the University of Marburg.

On Theobald Billicanus, see NDB 2, 238.

Text in Latin: WA, Br 3, 451–452.

Mr. Theobald Billicanus, an evangelist in Nördlingen,
my dearest brother in Christ

Grace and peace in the Lord! I think, my Theobald, that your
long letter[1] to me has been sufficiently answered in my booklet

---

[1] In January, 1525, the restlessly wandering Karlstadt (see LW 48, 79, n. 12),
who at that time had found a home in Rothenburg, visited Billicanus in Nördlingen; he intended to push the Reformation in that city into a radical direction, and to gain Nördlingen's support for himself and his ideas. Although
Billicanus (and his colleagues) rejected Karlstadt's iconoclasm, he was nevertheless apparently sufficiently impressed by Karlstadt's interpretation of the
Lord's Supper that he wrote a no-longer extant "long letter" to Luther. For
documentation, see WA, Br 3, 452, n. 1; Enders, Briefwechsel 5, 110, n. 4.

on the sacrament against Karlstadt.[2] I take your recent statement to Philip[3] concerning the office of consecrating the Lord's Supper to mean, however, that an ungodly man could not consecrate or bless the bread. I am of a different opinion on this matter. The Word of God is God's Word, not on the basis of our holiness, but on the basis of its own power, and it does what it does, not because of our merit, but because of its own nature. You certainly know that in Romans 1 [:16] the gospel is called by the Apostle the "power of God which saves those who believe;" and yet not all people obey the gospel, according to Romans 10 [:16]. Finally, according to Philippians 1 [:15], the gospel is preached by envious and strife-torn people; yet it does not cease being the Word and power of God because of their unworthiness or their unbelief. Let [God's Word] be weak and foolish to the ungodly, yet it is wise and powerful to the godly.[4] Consequently the Word of God is neither changed nor made better through the faith of the godly, nor made worse through the unbelief of the ungodly. Otherwise God would not be a bear or a lion[5] to the ungodly, and salvation and life to the godly.

Therefore, since the sacrament has been instituted through the power of the Word, and also is consecrated through that same power, one need not take into consideration the minister who consecrates [the sacrament], if one is concerned with the sacrament as such; if one is concerned with the minister's own salvation, however, then one has to consider [his faith]. For Christ himself instituted and blessed the sacrament, not through the power of his holiness, but through the power of the Word. Therefore, as the Word of God is a mighty power of God wherever it may be, even if the ungodly derive no blessing from this power, so also the sacra-

---

[2] Luther does not answer Billicanus' letter, mentioned in note 1, but refers to his *Against the Heavenly Prophets*; WA 18, 62 ff., 134 ff.; LW 40, 79 ff., 144 ff. This book was written and published in two parts. Part I was published on January 2, 1525, or shortly before this date, while part II was published at the end of January, 1525; see WA 18, 43 f.

[3] Philip Melanchthon; see *LW* 48, 77, n. 3. Having written to Luther, Billicanus apparently also wanted to sound out Melanchthon on Karlstadt's interpretation of the Lord's Supper; in the no-longer extant letter to Melanchthon, Billicanus made the statement to which Luther is now replying in detail.

[4] See I Cor. 1:18.

[5] Hos. 13:8.

ment is a complete sacrament wherever it is consecrated, even if the ungodly derive no blessing from this consecration. For in administering the Word of life and the sacraments of salvation, we are planters and sprinklers, but we are not the givers of growth.[6] We do administer, however, the same Word and sacrament that Christ administered. Just as he himself accomplished nothing among the Jews with the Word, so he vainly gave the sacrament to Judas Iscariot. Nevertheless he taught [the Jews] the true Word, and gave [Judas Iscariot] the real sacrament. Otherwise, if one has to consider the faith of those who administer the sacrament and those who receive it, everything would become uncertain; since no one's faith is a certain thing, one would have to wonder whether the Word and the sacrament would be anywhere. Now, however, the validity of Word and sacrament is not based on the law, nor on our merits, but on the promise, so that the holy ministry may be known to be strong and reliable among God's people. This is what I wanted to tell you; may you receive it in the best way.

Pray to Christ for me; may his grace be with you. Amen.

Wittenberg, March 5, 1525   MARTIN LUTHER

153

To George Spalatin
[Wittenberg,] April 16, 1525

Commenting briefly on a business transaction, Luther mentions a trip to Eisleben which he is about to make for the purpose of organizing a Christian school. He uses this opportunity to impress upon Spalatin how much the Electoral Saxon government neglects the University of Wittenberg, while other governments are eager to organize schools and for this purpose are drawing competent people away from Wittenberg. In the second paragraph Luther deals in a humorous way with the fact that thus far he has not married.

---

[6] See I Cor. 3:6.

On George Spalatin, see LW 48, 8 f.
Text in Latin: WA, Br 3, 474–475.

Mr. George Spalatin, a servant of Christ
at the Saxon court, my dearest brother in the Lord

Grace and peace! I have entrusted our Lucas[1] with everything, and
he is to see to it that one hundred copies are shipped to the head-
master,[2] for at this hour I am leaving for Eisleben with Philip[3] and
Master[4] Eisleben.[5] We have been summoned there by Count Adel-
berd[6] for the purpose of setting up a Christian school,[7] while you
people[8] are not interested in and neglect ours.[9] I am beginning to
make plans for Philip[10] to start a similar school at Nürnberg.[11] The

---

[1] I.e., apparently Lucas Cranach (see also note 2); see *LW* 48, 201.
[2] I.e., a hundred copies of Luther's booklet *Christliche Schrift an W. Reissenbusch, sich in den ehelichen Stand zu begeben* (*A Christian Writing for W.
Reissenbusch, Encouraging Him to Marry*) (Wittenberg: Cranach and Düring,
1525), *WA* 18, 275 ff.; *LCC* 18, 272 ff. This booklet was originally a letter
written by Luther on March 27, 1525, to Wolfgang Reissenbusch, the head-
master in the St. Anthony House in Lichtenberg (see *LW* 48, 180). For details
on Reissenbusch, see *WA* 18, 273.
[3] Philip Melanchthon; see *LW* 48, 77, n. 3.
[4] I.e., Master of Arts.
[5] I.e., John Agricola; see *LW* 48, 220.
[6] I.e., Count Albrecht III (1486–1560) of Mansfeld, Luther's territorial lord.
The counts of Mansfeld were one of the very old noble families in the Empire,
and at one time played a major role in German political affairs. In Luther's
time the family had lost much of its prestige (mostly because of several divisions and subdivisions of the land and privileges the family had held), and
was in feudal relationship to the elector of Saxony and the bishops of Magdeburg and Halberstadt. Since 1519 Albrecht and his brother Gebhard had been
strong supporters of Luther. On Albrecht, see *ADB* 20, 215 ff.; *Beiträge zur
sächsischen Kirchengeschichte* 25 (1911), 1 ff. On the counts of Mansfeld,
see also *WA*, Br 12, 364 ff.
[7] The invitation was no doubt a result of Luther's book (published in 1524)
*To the Councilmen of all Cities in Germany That They Establish and Maintain
Christian Schools; LW* 45, 347 ff. The purpose of Luther's trip was to discuss
the steps necessary for organizing a Latin school (a secondary, "college pre-
paratory" school) in Eisleben. The school did not function until August, 1525,
when Agricola moved to Eisleben to organize the school and be its first principal. See *WA*, Br 3, 475, n. 2; Enders, *Briefwechsel* 5, 158, n. 3.
[8] "You [plural]," i.e., the people at the Electoral Saxon court.
[9] I.e., the University of Wittenberg, which at that time was experiencing a
serious crisis. See also *WA*, Br 3, 500, 501 f., 519 ff.; *S-J* 2, 317; Friedensburg,
GUW, pp. 173 ff.
[10] See note 3.
[11] In October, 1524, the Nürnberg city council offered Melanchthon the position of principal and professor of rhetoric at the *Gymnasium*, which was then

people at Magdeburg have called Caspar Cruciger,[12] and the people at Danzig have called Master[13] Arnold.[14] Thus we are scattered, and our school[15] falls to pieces. What will become of me I do not know. Of course I know that in this matter you are free from any guilt.[16] Satan alone is at the bottom of it.

Incidentally, regarding what you are writing[17] about my marrying[18] [let me say the following]: I do not want you to wonder that a famous lover like me does not marry. It is rather strange that I, who so often write about matrimony[19] and get mixed up with

---

in the process of being organized (in response to Luther's exhortation made in the book cited in note 7). This *Gymnasium* was to function in addition to the four Latin schools which at that time were in operation in Nürnberg. Nürnberg tried hard to obtain Melanchthon's services, yet without success. Melanchthon did help, however, with the organization of the *Gymnasium*, especially its curriculum. While Melanchthon's contribution to the Nürnberg *Gymnasium* is well known, no details could be established concerning any direct contribution (see above) to this project from Luther. In May of 1526 Melanchthon delivered the inaugural address at the opening convocation of the *Gymnasium*. During its history of over four hundred years the *Gymnasium*, which today bears Melanchthon's name, developed into a university and then regressed again to a *Gymnasium*. For details, see *Melanchthon*, Studienausgabe 3, 64 ff. (Melanchthon's famous inaugural address); W. Maurer, *Der junge Melanchthon zwischen Humanismus und Reformation* 2 (Göttingen, 1969), 462 ff.; Manschreck, pp. 131 ff.; *Die Nürnberger Hochschule im Fränkischen Raum* (Nürnberg, 1955), pp. 11 ff.; H. Steiger, *Das Melanchthongymnasium in Nürnberg, 1526–1926* (Munich-Berlin, 1926); Strauss, *op. cit.* (see p. 98, n. 8), pp. 236 ff.

[12] Caspar Cruciger (1504–1548) was born in Leipzig and studied in Wittenberg. In 1524 Melanchthon tried without success to have Cruciger appointed to the University of Wittenberg. From 1525 to 1528 Cruciger was principal of a newly organized Latin school in Magdeburg, and from 1528 to his death he was the preacher at Wittenberg's Castle Church and a professor on the Theological Faculty. He assisted Luther with the translation of the Bible, and later was one of the editors of the Wittenberg edition of Luther's works. On Caspar Cruciger, see *NDB* 3, 427 f.

[13] See note 4.

[14] I.e., a certain Arnold Warwick of Buren/Westphalia (hence Burenius); see *WA*, Br 3, 475, n. 5.

[15] See note 9.

[16] Perhaps Luther is being sarcastic.

[17] This letter is not extant. Apparently it was Spalatin's answer to Luther's letter of April 10 (*WA*, Br 3, No. 854) in which Luther wrote: "Why don't you go on and get married? I urge matrimony on others [see note 2] with so many arguments that I am myself almost moved to marry [Is this a hint?], though our enemies do not cease to condemn that way of life, and our wiseacres laugh at it all the time." S-*J* 2, 304.

[18] See also pp. 115 f.

[19] See e.g., note 2, and *LW* 44, 7 ff., 251 ff.; 45, 7 ff., 17 ff., 141 ff., 385 ff.

women,[20] have not yet turned into a woman, to say nothing of not having married one. Yet if you want me to set an example, look, here you have the most powerful one, for I have had three wives simultaneously,[21] and loved them so much that I have lost two who are taking other husbands; the third[22] I can hardly keep with my left arm,[23] and she, too, will probably soon be snatched away from me. But you are a sluggish lover who does not dare to become the husband of even one woman. Watch out that I, who have no thought of marriage at all, do not some day overtake you too eager suitors—just as God usually does those things which are least expected. I am saying this seriously to urge you[24] to do what you are intending.

Farewell, my Spalatin.

April 16, 1525   MARTIN LUTHER

---

[20] This is apparently a reference to the circumstances mentioned by Luther on p. 45.

[21] Rückert, *LB*, p. 127, n. 16, states that no definite explanation can be given of this and of the following statements. It seems to be certain, however, that Luther is referring here to some of the nuns who had left the nunnery and had come to him for help, and for whom he felt responsible. See *WA*, Br 3, 54 f.; *S-J* 2, 179 f.; Köstlin-Kawerau 1, 558 ff., 728 ff. Among those nuns were two sisters, Ave and Margaret von Schönfeld, whom Luther had lodged with the Cranach family (see *LW* 48, 200). According to a Table Talk (*WA*, TR 4, No. 4786), Luther at one time had had an eye for Ave von Schönfeld, but did not wish to pursue the matter, and Ave later married a young physician, a certain Basilius Axt. Ave von Schönfeld could then indeed be one of the "lost wives." The other one could perhaps be a certain Ave Alemann, whom, on January 2, 1526, Luther referred to as his bride; see *WA*, Br 4, 3. If Luther was thinking here of Ave Alemann, then it would not be clear why he considered her to be lost, since she was still single in January of 1526.

[22] This is perhaps a reference to Catherine von Bora (who was also among the escaped nuns; see note 21), whom Luther had lodged with the family of the Wittenberg city clerk Reichenbach, and whom he was trying hard to marry either to Jerome Baumgärtner of Nürnberg (see *WA*, Br 3, No. 782; *S-J* 2, No. 642), or to Caspar Glatz, who was then the pastor at Orlamünde (see *ibid.*, Köstlin-Kawerau 1, 729). On Catherine von Bora, see p. 115, n. 1.

[23] "Marriage at the left hand [or: arm]" was the technical term for concubinage; see Trübner 3, 312.

[24] Literally: "I am saying this so that I may urge you without joking . . ."

154

To John Rühel[1]
Seeburg, May 4, 1525[2]

On April 16 Luther traveled to Eisleben for discussions concerning the establishment of a Latin school.[3] While in Eisleben Luther wrote his Admonition for Peace[4] as a reply to the Twelve Articles of the Swabian Peasants.[5] When Luther wrote this pamphlet he knew little of the peasants' uprising. Therefore he urgently reminded all sovereigns of their duty to listen to the complaints of the peasants and to heed the peasants' demands as a call to repentance. At the same time Luther admonished the peasants to abstain from violence. As soon as Luther had completed this pamphlet he sent it to Wittenberg to have it printed. While he was still in Eisleben, however, Luther became increasingly aware of the dimensions which the uprising was taking, even in the immediate neighborhood. Luther apparently left Eisleben on April 21; he traveled through Thuringia for the purpose of visiting his parents, friends, and relatives,[6] and of trying to restore peace to the countryside. Luther preached almost daily against violence and admonished the population to maintain peace, law, and order, yet without success.[7] In addition he became familiar with some of the atrocities committed by

---

[1] The letter is extant only in the common printed editions of Luther's works. It is clear that Rühel is the addressee by the identification in the heading of the text, and by the way in which Luther addressed Rühel here (see note 14) and in other letters (see *WA*, Br 3, 507, 515, 522).

[2] For the date, see note 41. Seeburg is located southeast of Eisleben.

[3] See p. 103.

[4] Luther had planned this pamphlet as soon as he became familiar with the *Twelve Articles;* see *WA* 18, 281; *C.R.* 1, 739. For the text of the *Admonition* (of which the autograph is extant), see *WA* 18, 291 ff.; *LW* 46, 17 ff.

[5] Text: Kidd, No. 83; *LW* 46, 8 ff. On the Peasants' War, see G. Franz, *Der deutsche Bauernkrieg* (4th ed.; Darmstadt, 1956) and his *Quellen zur Geschichte des Bauernkrieges* (Darmstadt, 1963); E. G. Bax, *The Peasants' War in Germany* (London, 1903); Elton, pp. 88 ff.; Ranke 1^{II}, 106 ff. On the *Twelve Articles,* see Bainton, pp. 273 f. On Luther's relationship to the Peasants' War, see P. Althaus, *Luther's Haltung im Bauernkrieg* (Reprint from *LJB* 7 [1925], 1 ff.: Darmstadt, 1952); Bainton, pp. 270 ff.; K. A. Strand (ed.), *The Dawn of Modern Civilization* (Ann Arbor, Mich., 1962), pp. 129 ff.; *Lutheran Church Quarterly* 19 (1946), 115 ff.

[6] On this trip and the sermons preached by Luther, see *WA* 17^I, xxxi f.; Köstlin-Kawerau 1, 702 ff.; Buchwald, *LK,* pp. 39 f.; Schwiebert, pp. 564 ff.

[7] See Köstlin-Kawerau 1, 709.

the peasants, and in some cases had to experience the contempt of the masses.[8] He made one last attempt to bring the peasants to their senses.[9] When this appeal fell on deaf ears, he firmly opposed the peasants as rebels, and developed plans for his Against the Robbing and Murdering Hordes of Peasants.[10] On his way home, Luther met John Rühel, a councilor of Count Albrecht of Mansfeld (in whose territory the uprising was fermenting), and received further news. While continuing his journey home,[11] Luther wrote the present letter. Addressing Count Albrecht through Rühel, Luther encourages the Count to use all force available to curb the activities of the peasants. Luther sees in the peasants perjurers, rebels, robbers, and hypocrites who try to cover up their actions with the gospel. The Count's task is, Luther underscores, to wield the sword as a punishment for the wicked. Luther sees in the uprising of the peasants an attempt of the devil on his own life and work, and expresses his determination to spite the devil by marrying his Katie.

John Rühel (or Rühl) had studied at the Universities of Wittenberg and Bologna, and was graduated as Doctor of Both Laws from the University of Bologna in 1515. Prior to entering the service of the counts of Mansfeld (at a date which could not be established), he served the Elector of Saxony. As early as January, 1517, Rühel clashed with John Tetzel,[12] and it seems that he was one of the earliest supporters of Luther. While Luther was in Augsburg in 1518, Rühel had close contacts with the Reformer, contacts which were deepened through family ties, and which are documented in many extant letters. Rühel attended Luther's wedding, and be-

---

[8] See Köstlin-Kawerau 1, 709 f.

[9] Even though the date of this action cannot be established, Luther's publication (with a preface and a concluding admonition) of the peace treaty, signed in the middle of April by the Swabian League and some groups of the upper German peasants (WA 18, 336 ff.), has to be considered Luther's last appeal to the peasants.

[10] See ARG 33 (1936), 126 ff. For the text, see WA 18, 357 ff.; LW 46, 49 ff. Luther published his Against the Robbing . . . Peasants together with his Admonition (see note 4); WA 18, 345, edition A. This fact, no doubt, was in part responsible for the bad publicity which Luther received from his actions in connection with the peasants' uprising.

[11] Luther returned to Wittenberg on May 6 in the early evening; see WA, Br 3, 487; Buchwald, LK, p. 40.

[12] See H. Volz, Martin Luthers Thesenanschlag und dessen Vorgeschichte (Weimar, 1959), p. 63, n. 13.

came godfather of Luther's second son, Martin.[13] *On John Rühel,
see Enders, Briefwechsel 17, 177, n. 1.*

Text in German: WA, Br 3, 480–482.

Grace and peace in Christ

Honored, dear Doctor and Relative:[14] During this whole trip I
have constantly been mulling over the news[15] which you told me
in parting; therefore I must write to you now from here concerning this matter.[16]

To begin with, I urge you not to influence my gracious Lord,
Count Albrecht,[17] to be soft in this affair.[18] Let His Grace continue[19] as he has begun, even though the devil becomes angrier
as a result and rages more through the demonic members of his
body. For we have God's Word, which does not lie; it says in
Romans 13 [:4]: "He does not bear the sword in vain," etc. So there
can never be any doubt that the count's office was decreed and ordained by God. Therefore, as long as life is in him, His Grace
ought to use his sword for punishing the wicked. Should the sword
be forcibly struck from His Grace's hand, then we must endure this
and leave it in God's hands; he first gave the sword and he may

---

[13] See p. 115, n. 2; WA, Br 6, 220.

[14] Luther wrote *Schwager*, i.e., literally "brother-in-law." In a wider sense it
can mean any relative through marriage, or it can also mean friend. See
Trübner 6, 250. Luther used the term to mean relative; Rühel was not his
direct brother-in-law, but was apparently married to one of Luther's distant
relatives, who had been a relative by marriage only; see Enders, *Briefwechsel*
12, 95, n. 1.

[15] It cannot be established with certainty to what Luther is referring here.
"News" could be any news concerning the peasants' uprising. On the basis of
the second sentence in the next paragraph ("Let His Grace continue . . ."), and
the second sentence of the last paragraph ("Encourage His Grace to continue
. . ."), however, it may be assumed (as Clemen, WA, Br 3, No. 860, Introduction, has done), that "news" pertained to information concerning the
"victory" which Count Albrecht of Mansfeld had won over a group of peasants
near Osterhausen on May 5. See also note 41.

[16] I.e., the peasants' uprising.

[17] I.e., here and throughout this letter, Count Albrecht III of Mansfeld; see p.
103, n. 6.

[18] I.e., in dealing with the peasants.

[19] There is some ambiguity in the text here; the subject of "continue" is left
indefinite and could refer to Count Albrecht (as we have translated), or it
could possibly refer to "affair," i.e., to the peasants' uprising and the way in
which the Count should deal with it.

take it back when and by what means he wishes. As a result His Grace may have a good conscience, and until death pursue and be dedicated to the duties of his office for the sake of God's Word; God's Word has ordained this office for as long as the Word[20] is valid. This is the same as the fact that no one is to abandon any good work unless it is knocked from his hands by force, and no one is to forego an advantage in battle, or stop fighting unless he is overcome.

If there were thousands more of the peasants, they would still be altogether robbers and murderers, who take the sword simply because of their own insolence and wickedness, and who want to expel sovereigns [and] lords, and [to destroy] everything, and to establish a new order in this world. But for this they have neither God's commandment, authority, right, or injunction, as the lords have it now.[21] In addition, the peasants are faithless and are committing perjury toward their lords.[22] Above all this, they borrow the authority of the divine Word and gospel [for covering up] their great sins, and thus disgrace and slander [God's name].[23] If God in his wrath really lets them reach their goal (for which they by no means have God's authority or command)[24] then we shall have to endure it, just as when in other circumstances someone endures, or has to endure, injustice, but does not agree that they [who are making him suffer] are doing the right thing. I still firmly hope that the peasants will not be victorious, or at least not remain so, although God occasionally plagues the world with the most desperate characters, as he has done and is still doing with the Turks.[25]

It is a mockery on the devil's part when the peasants pretend that they do not hurt or harm anyone. Is it not doing harm when

---

[20] Another possible translation would be: ". . . as long as the institution of the office is valid [or: a valid one]."

[21] I.e., the lords have this authority on the basis of Romans 13.

[22] I.e., the peasants did not take their oath of fealty in good faith.

[23] I.e., the peasants pretended to act as good Christians who obey God's Word. In his *Against the Robbing and Murdering Hordes of Peasants,* Luther accused the peasants of breaking the oath of loyalty and obedience sworn to the lords, of rebellion, murder and plundering, and of covering up their deeds with the gospel. See WA 18, 357; LW 46, 49 f.

[24] The parentheses have been added by this editor.

[25] LW 46, 18, n. 1; ARG 47 (1956), 145 ff.; see also J. W. Bohnstedt, *The Infidel Scourge of God: The Turkish Menace as seen by German Pamphleteers of the Reformation Era* (Philadelphia, 1968).

they drive out and kill their lords? If they do not wish to hurt anyone, why do they gather in hordes and demand that one yield to
their demands? To hurt no one and yet to take everything—that's
the way the devil too would do good and hurt no one, if one would
let him do as he pleases. Pure insolence is the [peasants'] only
reason for driving out their lords. Why does one not rather improve
what is wrong [with the system]? Look at the government of the
S.[26] It also began this way,[27] and is now worse than it has ever
been. There is no discipline or obedience [among the S.], and they
are nothing but mercenaries.[28]

In short: if God wants to pour out his wrath upon us and
devastate Germany, then these enemies of God, these blasphemers,
robbers, and murderers, these unfaithful and perjuring peasants are
suitable for this. In that case we [will] endure this and call them
lords, as Scripture calls the devil a sovereign and lord.[29] But may
God protect all devout Christians from consenting to something
like this, or worshipping it—as he tempted Christ to do, Matthew
4:1 ff.—but [rather make us] resist [the peasants] in word and
deed as long as we are able to do so, and die for this in God's name.
If the peasants should offer not to harm anyone as long as we yield
to them, then we, in turn, should offer to surrender to them, and
if necessary to state publicly[30] that they rule over us as unfaithful,
lying blasphemers and robbers, and that they do not have God's
right on their side, but only inspiration from the sovereign of this
world.[31] [For] the devil boasts in Matthew 4 [:8 f.], that he holds
the entire world's power and glory, and is able to give it to whom
he wishes. Both are true, if God ordains it and does not prevent it.

I (for whom this[32] is also meant, since the devil definitely
wants to have me dead) am well aware that the devil is angry,
since up to now he has been unable to accomplish anything, either

---

[26] Luther was apparently thinking of the Swiss. In his *Whether Soldiers, Too,
Can Be Saved,* he made a similar negative remark; see WA 19, 635; LW 46,
109 f.
[27] I.e., with the 1291 "uprising" against the Hapsburgs.
[28] This is apparently a reference to the fact that many Swiss were selling their
services as soldiers to whichever foreign sovereign paid the most.
[29] See John 14:30; Eph. 6:12.
[30] Literally: "confess."
[31] I.e., from the devil; see John 12:31; 16:31.
[32] I.e., Luther takes the peasants' uprising to mean the devil's attack against
his person and his work; see also LW 46, 18, n. 1.

by fraud or force. He is set to get rid of me, even if he has to attempt the worst and confound the whole world altogether. I almost believe and think that it is because of me that the devil is making such a mess in the world, in order that God might vex the world. Well, if I get home I shall prepare for death with God's help, and await my new lords, the murderers and robbers, who tell me they will not harm anyone. They are like the highway robber who said to the good coachman: "I shall do you no harm, but give me all you have and drive where I tell you; and if you don't you will die!" Beautiful innocence! How magnificently the devil decorates himself and his murderers! But I would rather lose my neck a hundred times[33] than approve of and justify the peasants' actions; may God help me with his grace to do this. If I can manage it, before I die I will still marry my Katie[34] to spite the devil, should I hear that the peasants continue. I trust they will not steal my courage and joy. Their own god,[35] and no one else, may believe their statement that they are not like Münzer.[36]

I am writing this so that you[37] may be comforted and can comfort others, especially my gracious lord, Count Albrecht. Encourage His Grace to continue courageously, to entrust this matter to God, and to act according to God's divine command in using the sword for as long as he can. For the conscience is on firm ground in this case,[38] even if one has to perish for it. On the other hand,

---

[33] Literally: "lose a hundred necks before."

[34] Catherine von Bora. This statement seems to be the first definite suggestion that Luther had decided to marry Catherine von Bora. Von Amsdorf (see LW 48, 218) reports the following incident which apparently occurred during his visit to Wittenberg sometime after the middle of March (see LJB 7 [1925], 59 f.) Catherine von Bora complained to von Armsdorf about Luther's intention to marry her to Dr. Glatz (see p. 105, n. 22), whom she apparently considered a miser; she would be willing, however, to marry either von Amsdorf, or Luther himself. Obviously von Amsdorf told Luther about this; how Luther reacted is not known. See Köstlin-Kawerau 1, 729 f.; Bainton, pp. 287 ff. Apparently while visiting with his parents (see Introduction) Luther made the decision to ask for Catherine's hand; see WA, Br 3, 541, 531; Bainton, p. 288.

[35] I.e., the devil.

[36] On the role played by Thomas Münzer in the Peasants' War, see G. Franz (ed.), Thomas Müntzer, Schriften und Briefe (Gütersloh, 1968), pp. 453 ff., 543 ff.; Bainton, pp. 277 ff.; Franz, Quellen, pp. 475 ff.; Franz, Bauernkrieg, pp. 248 ff.

[37] Literally: "so that you, too, may be."

[38] Apparently this statement has to be seen against the background of the general confusion which existed regarding the question of a moral right to fight the peasants. This confusion is best documented by the letter, written on April

even if the peasants served God's wrath in punishing and destroying the sovereigns, God would nevertheless reward them with the fire of hell. In a short while the true judge will come, who will meet[39] both the peasants and us: us with grace if we endure their violence and wickedness; them with wrath, since on their own they take up the sword, by which they will also perish, as Christ has already pronounced the judgment [in] Matthew 26 [:52]. Indeed, their actions and success cannot remain nor stand for long.

Give my greetings to your dear Rib.[40]

Written at Seeburg, May 4, 1525[41]

D. MARTIN LUTHER

155

To Nicholas von Amsdorf
Wittenberg, May 30, 1525

Luther is commenting on the fact that certain people are saying that he is a toady to sovereigns, an opinion which is the result of his book against the peasants. He sees in this opinion Satan's attack against the gospel, and he expresses his intention to trample Satan under foot. He points out that in view of the continuous rebellion on the part of the peasants it is better that the peasants be crushed than that the lords be defeated; for under the government of the lords the two kingdoms can exist, while under the peasants everything would be devastated. Therefore Luther affirms he will have nothing to do with those who favor the peasants.

14 by Elector Frederick of Saxony (see *LW* 48, 49 f.) to his brother (see *LW* 48, 269, n. 8), Duke John (Franz, *Quellen,* No. 167), and by the inability of many authorities to deal constructively with the peasants' demands. See also Köstlin-Kawerau 1, 695 ff.

39 Literally: "who will find both."

40 This is obviously an allusion to Gen. 2:21 f.; see also *WA,* Br 3, 482, n. 16.

41 This date seems to be wrong; either Luther erred, or the error occurred in the process of handing the letter down. On June 23 Luther wrote to Rühel (see *WA,* Br 3, 508; *S-J* 2, 318) that he had departed from Rühel on the day on which Elector Frederick (see *LW* 48, 49 f.) died. The Elector died on May 5; see *WA,* Br 3, 508, n. 6. In view of this fact, and on the basis of the observation made in note 15, it may be suggested that the date of this letter is May 5. See also *WA,* Br 3, No. 860, Introduction.

On Nicholas von Amsdorf, see LW 48, 218.
Text in Latin: WA, Br 3, 517–518.

Sir Nicholas [von] Amsdorf, my friend in the Lord

Grace and peace! You inform me of a new honor, my Amsdorf,
namely, that I am called a toady to the sovereigns.[1] Satan has
conferred many such honorary titles upon me in these years. But
I do not pity our know-it-alls; while they judge me they betray
their own blood-thirsty and seditious spirits. Therefore rejoice that
Satan is so indignant and breaks out into such blasphemies whenever I touch him. For what are these [know-it-alls] but the voices
of Satan, by which he tries to disgrace me and the gospel? He,
who has thus far so often beaten Satan under my feet,[2] and has
broken to pieces the lion and the dragon, will not allow the basilisk
to tread on me.[3] So, let them roar. My[4]conscience is certain that
whatever came from my lips in this matter is right before God.
Let [my words] be crucified, let them displease those who feel
superior to our efforts and the name of the gospel, so that they dishonor us and pay us their gratitude as [this] adulterous generation[5]
is accustomed to doing. But they are raised up in order to be cast
down, and their end will be utter destruction.[6] Perhaps the time
will come when even I may say: "You all shall be offended this
night [because of me]."[7] How swiftly we have forgotten the blessings we have received! How proud we are, and how quick to judge
even those from whom we have learned! But Christ, who began his
work without our advice, will complete his work even against all
our advice. Admonish the brethren, then, not to act rashly according to their own wisdom and by stirring up the sinful mind, since
they have heard so often from the gospel that man is nothing, and

---

[1] This opinion was caused by Luther's *Against the Robbing . . . Peasants* (see
p. 107, n. 10). It could not be established on what date this pamphlet was released by the press. As early as May 26, John Rühel mentioned this pamphet
and the charge on which Luther now comments. See WA, Br 3, 511.
[2] See Rom. 16:20.
[3] See Ps. 91:13.
[4] Literally: "Our."
[5] Matt. 12:39.
[6] Phil. 3:19.
[7] See Matt. 26:31.

that the flesh-oriented mind must be killed. It is God who acts above and counter to, underneath and outside, our ability to understand.[8]

I definitely cannot come to you now, since I am so busy and occupied with various tasks; otherwise there is nothing I would prefer doing.

In my opinion it is better that all of the peasants should be killed rather than that the sovereigns and magistrates should be destroyed, because the peasants take up the sword without God's authorization. The consequence of this wickedness of Satan can only be the satanic devastation of the kingdom of God and of the world. Even if the sovereigns exceed [their authority], yet they at least carry the sword by God's authority;[9] under their government it is still possible for both kingdoms[10] to exist. Those peasants, who do not quiet down when they have been warned, who do not surrender even when the fairest terms have been offered to them, but only continue to confound everything with the furor of Satan, as those peasants in Thuringia and Franconia do, deserve no mercy or patience, but rather the wrath and indignation of God and of men. To justify their actions and to have mercy on them, or to favor them, would be the same as to deny and blaspheme God, and to throw God out of heaven. Tell this to those preachers of yours;[11] they may dare [to favor these peasants], they may attempt to do this, but it will be without my consent. Indeed I will curse their efforts in the name of the Lord. Afterwards the Lord will judge which spirit is from the devil, theirs or mine. But I am grieved that we handed over the office and knowledge of the Word to those blasphemous people. May God convert and enlighten them, or depose them from their throne again. Amen.

Farewell in the Lord.

Wittenberg, May 30, 1525   MARTIN LUTHER

---

[8] See Eph. 3:20.

[9] See *LW* 48, 258 ff.

[10] I.e., the earthly, political community, and God's kingdom as present on earth. For further information on this basic concept in Luther's thought, see *Lutheran Quarterly* 15 (1963), 239 ff.; Rupp, *Luther Studies*, pp. 286 ff.; *LJB* 24 (1957), 40 ff.

[11] Some of the preachers in Magdeburg, where von Amsdorf lived, were sympathizing with the peasants; see Enders, *Briefwechsel* 5, 183, n. 3.

156

To George Spalatin
Wittenberg, June 21, 1525

The year 1525 brought a major change into Luther's life—his marriage to Catherine von Bora. In this letter Luther is inviting Spalatin to the wedding banquet. He is also returning a letter of the King of Denmark.

On George Spalatin, see LW 48, 8 f.

Text in Latin: WA, Br 3, 540.

Mr. George Spalatin, a servant of Christ, my dearest brother
in the Lord

Grace and peace in the Lord! The wedding banquet for me and my Catherine[1] will be held this coming Tuesday, that is, after the festival of St. John the Baptist.[2] I am inviting you, my Spalatin,

---

[1] Catherine von Bora (Jan. 29, 1499–Dec. 20, 1552) came from a noble family from outside Leipzig. Because of the death of her mother in 1504, Catherine was placed into a Benedictine nunnery in Brehna, and later into the Cistercian nunnery Nimbschen, near Grimma. About 1515 she herself became a nun. Around 1520 she and some of her fellow sisters became increasingly acquainted with Luther's writings. In April of 1523 she escaped from the nunnery with eleven nuns, supposedly under quite dramatic circumstances. The nuns came to Wittenberg where, upon Luther's recommendation and urging, they were taken in by some families. One after the other of the nuns was married or left Wittenberg, and thus was taken care of, while all attempts to marry Catherine von Bora to some suitable gentleman failed. Consequently Luther occasionally teased her by saying that he was stuck with her, or she with him. On Catherine von Bora and her marriage, see *NDB* 2, 454; E. Kroker, *Katharina von Bora. Martin Luthers Frau* (5th ed.; Berlin, 1959); Bainton, pp. 287 ff. Catherine and her marriage are the subject of many books, the majority of which are of little value for the historian; E. J. Mall's, *Kitty, my Rib* (St. Louis, 1959) and J. Klepper's, *Das ewige Haus* (Stuttgart, 1951), are the exceptions.

[2] I.e., June 27, 1525. Luther had decided to marry Catherine von Bora sometime at the end of April, or beginning of May; see p. 111, n. 34). On June 13, in the evening, the legally binding wedding ceremony was conducted in Luther's home (the former Augustinian monastery) in the presence of John Bugenhagen (see *LW* 48, 303, n. 44), Justus Jonas (*op. cit.*, 275, n. 3), Mr. and Mrs. Lucas Cranach (*op. cit.*, 201), and Dr. Apel (a professor of law; see p. 310). The banquet was to be the public celebration and declaration of the wedding. Luther invited his parents and many friends for this occasion; among them were John Rühel (*WA*, Br 3, No. 890), Spalatin (*WA*, Br 3, No. 892; S-J 2, No. 693; and the present letter), Wenceslas Link (*WA*, Br 3, No.

to this [banquet] so that I may see for myself that you really rejoice in my marriage. Please do not miss it. I have also written to the Marshall[3] for venison, and invited him at the same time. Please try hard to see if you can accomplish something.

I am returning the letter of the King of Denmark.[4] I know nothing, however, about the books of the King of England.[5] As much as I can, I shall pray [for him], and in due time I shall write [him]; at the moment I cannot. Please inform me when there is time and opportunity to send a messenger.[6]

Farewell, and pray for me.

Wittenberg, June 21, 1525   MARTIN LUTHER

157

To Nicholas von Amsdorf[1]
[Wittenberg,] June 21, 1525

Luther confirms the truth of the rumor that he has married Catherine von Bora; he gives some reasons for his marriage, and invites

896; S-J 2, No. 693), John von Dolzig (see note 3), Nicholas von Amsdorf, (see letter No. 157), and a certain Leonard Koppe of Torgau (WA, Br 3, No. 898; S-J 2, No. 694), who supposedly helped Catherine and the other nuns escape from the nunnery. The banquet was to be on June 27, in the late morning, after a short service at the door steps of the City Church, during which the couple would be publicly recognized as husband and wife. For details and documentation, see Schwiebert, pp. 581 ff.; Bainton, pp. 288 ff.; Köstlin–Kawerau 1, 734 ff.; LJB 7 (1925), 40 ff.

[3] Hans von Dolzig; see p. 69, n. 7. Text of Luther's letter (also dated June 21): WA, Br 3. No. 897.

[4] King Christian II of Denmark apparently wrote not only to Luther (see WA, Br 3, No. 872, dated May 20, 1525) but also to the Elector, or to Spalatin; the latter forwarded the letter to Luther, who was now returning it.

[5] I.e., Henry VIII; see p. 71, n. 7. It is not clear to which books Luther is referring here. Perhaps King Christian had written about some books against Luther, published in England under Henry's name. Christian apparently also mentioned the fact that Henry was beginning to be favorably inclined toward the gospel (hence Luther's statement that he will pray for Henry), and apparently also said that Henry had nothing at all to do with these books.

[6] I.e., for a letter either to Henry or to Christian. The former possibility seems to be nearer to the circumstances, since as early as May 15, Luther had sent to Spalatin, for his opinion, a draft of a letter to Henry; see WA, Br 3, 500.

[1] The letter is extant only in one manuscript copy and in the common editions of Luther's works. The address and signature are missing in the earliest witnesses. The content of this letter makes clear, beyond any doubt, however, who wrote the letter, and to whom it was addressed.

von Amsdorf to the wedding banquet. Luther also reports facts and rumors concerning the recent development of the Peasants' War, mentions a pending meeting between Duke George of Saxony and the Elector of Brandenburg and the Archbishop of Mainz, and tells of the rumor that Duke George might sue for Luther's extradition.

On Nicholas von Amsdorf, see LW 48, 218.

Text in Latin: WA, Br 3, 541.

Grace and peace in the Lord!

I was looking for a messenger to carry this letter to you, my Amsdorf, and look, a messenger brings your letter[2] to me.

Indeed, the rumor is true that I was suddenly married to Catherine;[3] [I did this] to silence the evil mouths which are so used to complaining about me. For I still hope to live for a little while.[4] In addition, I also did not want to reject this unique [opportunity to obey] my father's wish for progeny, which he so often expressed.[5] At the same time, I also wanted to confirm what I have taught by practicing it; for I find so many timid people in spite of such great light from the gospel. God has willed and brought about this step. For I feel neither passionate love nor burning for my spouse, but I cherish her. To give a [public] testimony of my wedding I shall give a banquet this coming Tuesday,[6] where my parents will be present. I definitely wish that you, too, will be there. Therefore, since I wanted to invite you, I am inviting you now and ask you to be there if you can possibly do so.

The rumor concerning the Elector[7] is wrong.[8] The people of

---

[2] This letter is no longer extant. On the basis of Luther's answer it is safe to assume that von Amsdorf had heard of Luther's marriage, and that he consequently asked Luther about it. Apparently von Amsdorf had also heard a rumor about Elector John and the Peasants' War and mentioned this rumor, too, when writing to Luther.

[3] See p. 115, n. 2.

[4] See p. 111.

[5] Luther made a similar statement in his letter to John Rühel and others, dated June 15, 1525; WA, Br 3, 531; S-J 2, 323.

[6] June 27, 1525. See also p. 115, n. 2.

[7] Elector John of Saxony, see LW 48, 269, n. 8.

[8] The "rumor" to which Luther is referring here could not be verified. Certainly it had to do with the Peasants' War and the military actions taken by

Meiningen,[9] Mellrichstadt,[10] Neustadt,[11] [and] Münnerstadt,[12] along with ten other cities,[13] have unconditionally surrendered to the Elector. He is trying to settle everything there peacefully with them. Yes, it is true that in Franconia eleven thousand peasants were killed at three different places, that sixty-one intact cannons were captured,[14] [and that] the castle of Würzburg has been liberated.[15] Margrave Casimir rages against his peasants since they have twice broken their word to him.[16] In the Duchy of Württemberg six thousand peasants were killed; elsewhere in Swabia ten thousand, in different places. Rumor has it that the Duke of Lorraine has killed twenty thousand in the Alsace.[17] Thus the poor peasants

the Elector against the peasants. For the Elector's campaign against the peasants, see WA, Br 3, 542, n. 7; Franz, Bauernkrieg (see p. 106, n. 5), pp. 268 ff.

[9] Located in western Thuringia, at the Werra river, north of Würzburg.

[10] Located between Meiningen and Schweinfurth.

[11] Located at the Saale river.

[12] So according to Enders, Briefwechsel, 5, 205, n. 4; located south of Neustadt/Saale.

[13] Several of them are named by Spalatin in his biographies of some of the Saxon electors; see WA, Br 3, 542, n. 7. All cities were located near the Saxon-Franconian border. On June 1 Elector John ended a major campaign against the peasants in western Thuringia by having some of their leaders executed in Eisenach (WA, Br 3, 520, n. 1); then he pushed south without meeting much resistance.

[14] To what degree these figures are reliable could not be verified.

[15] In Franconia the peasants' uprising originated in the Tauber valley, and from there moved into the area of Würzburg. After the peasants of the Tauber valley had united with the peasants from the Odenwald and from the area north of the Main river, they laid siege to the city of Würzburg, which thereupon joined the peasants rather than risk "annihilation." The castle of Würzburg, however, which was the residency of the bishop of Würzburg and a last stronghold of the Franconian nobility, did not surrender. The peasants unsuccessfully tried to storm it, and then settled down to bombard it and to starve it into surrender. While doing this, the morale among the peasants fell drastically, and on June 4 they were catastrophically beaten by the army of the Swabian League which came to the rescue (i.e., Luther's "liberation") of the Würzburg castle. See Franz, Bauernkrieg, pp. 203 ff.

[16] Margrave Casimir of Brandenburg-Ansbach-Kulmbach, who in April and May of 1525 had done nothing to oppose the peasants, finally entered the war against the peasants after they had been defeated by the Swabian League at the beginning of June. Between June 5 and July 2, Casimir had eighty people decapitated and sixty-nine blinded, or crippled in some other way. See Franz, Quellen (see p. 106, n. 5), No. 130. The reference to the peasants breaking their word cannot be exactly verified; apparently Luther had heard of some of the fruitless negotiations between Casimir and the peasants which were designed to bring about some form of peace. See also SMRH 5 (1968), 160 f.

[17] The estimate of the number of victims in Württemberg is supported by other witnesses, as are the other numbers; see WA, Br 3, 542, nn. 8, 9;

are being killed everywhere. One can predict what the people at Bamberg will have to suffer.[18] Nevertheless the peasants continue rebelling in the Breisgau and in the County of Tyrol, so that from Innsbruck to Trent everything is in commotion, and the bishops of Trent and Brixen have fled.[19]

This coming Monday[20] Duke George[21] will meet with the Margrave and the [Arch]bishop of Mainz[22] in Dessau.[23] There is a rumor that Duke George, inflated by his success,[24] wants to sue

Enders, *Briefwechsel* 5, 205, nn. 8, 9. The incidents reported by Luther pertain to the battles that took place in May. See Franz, *Bauernkrieg*, pp. 221, 146 ff.

[18] After the Swabian League had defeated the western Franconian peasants and liberated Würzburg (see note 15), the troops of the Swabian League turned east and liberated the bishop of Bamberg, who was besieged by a group of eastern Franconian peasants; the troops of the league defeated them on June 17, and executed a number of people. Luther thus far knew only that the troops of the League were turning toward Bamberg. See Franz, *Bauernkrieg*, pp. 208 ff; Franz, *Quellen*, Nos. 131, 132.

[19] Contrary to the peasants' uprising in central and southern Germany, the movement in Tyrol was able to be handled by compromises, and without much bloodshed. See Franz, *Bauernkrieg*, pp. 156 ff.

[20] June 26, 1525.

[21] Duke George of Saxony; see *LW* 48, 110, n. 20.

[22] I.e., Elector Joachim I, margrave of Brandenburg (see *LW* 48, 56, n. 3) and his brother, Cardinal Albrecht, archbishop of Mainz (see *LW* 48, 44 f.).

[23] On June 10, 1525, Duke George (in agreement with Cardinal Albrecht) invited the Elector of Brandenburg for June 26 (i.e., "this coming Monday") to Dessau. Since Joachim could not be present at that date, the meeting was postponed to July 5; see *Akten und Briefe* 2, 289, 300. See note 24.

[24] I.e., inflated by his military success over the peasants. Duke George and Landgrave Philip of Hesse had defeated the peasants near Frankenhausen on May 15, 1525. See Franz, *Quellen*, No. 184; Franz, *Bauernkrieg*, pp. 268 ff. Elector John joined the two sovereigns, and all three, on May 25, stormed Mühlhausen, the "capital" of the rebellious peasants in Thuringia. Münzer, the spiritual leader of the central German peasants, was captured, and this was the end of the peasants' uprising in Thuringia. Following this victory, Elector John swung south for the mop-up action mentioned above. While still encamped at Mühlhausen Duke George laid plans to wipe out Luther, whom he considered to be the root of the evil and the spiritual father of Münzer and the peasants. See Ranke 1[II], 137. The Duke's first goal was to secure the cooperation of Philip of Hesse and of Elector John. He gained the good will of both sovereigns by emphasizing the necessity that all three sovereigns should work together in order to forestall any further uprisings on the part of the peasants, or any other enemies of the public peace. Consequently at the end of May the three sovereigns signed an agreement which created an alliance to maintain jointly the common peace; see *Akten und Briefe* 2, 254 f. Contrary to the purpose of this alliance and agreement, Duke George used the alliance as basis for promoting his anti-Lutheran policies by inviting (see note 23) Albrecht of Mainz, Joachim of Brandenburg (some of Luther's most vociferous enemies), and the dukes of Brunswick, Eric and Henry, to a meeting which

for my extradition from Wittenberg;[25] he thinks that I am like Münzer in what I teach.[26] But Christ will give grace. Watch out that Duke George does not sue for Magdeburg's extradition.[27]

Farewell, and pray for me.

June 21, 1525

158

To John Briessmann
Wittenberg, [after August 15,][1] 1525

In addition to congratulating Briessmann on his marriage, Luther mentions some of his letters written to Königsberg, warns of Zwingli and Karlstadt (the latter of whom had stayed with him for some time), evaluates the outcome of the Peasants' War, and in this connection tells of his own wedding. Luther also briefly reports on

---

was designed to work out plans for maintaining law and order by wiping out the Lutheran heresy. See also *Akten und Briefe* 2, 288 f. At a meeting in Dessau (July 19–24), which was not attended by the Elector and the Landgrave, a league was established between Ducal Saxony, Mainz, Brunswick, and Brandenburg to wipe out the "cursed Lutheran sect." See *Akten und Briefe* 2, 352 f. This Dessau League was parallel to the Regensburg League of July, 1524; see p. 126. Both leagues clearly demonstrated that the papal church and its supporters in the Empire were seeking a political, military solution to the issues raised by Luther; they also demonstrated how the German nation was split by papal actions into two political camps. On the reaction of Electoral Saxony and Hesse to the Dessau League, see pp. 123 f., 127; on the general political situation, see Ranke 1^II, 136 ff.; on the Dessau League, see Friedensburg, *Vorgeschichte GTB*, pp. 11 ff.

[25] It is not clear whether Luther is referring to rumors about the planned meeting at Dessau, or to some legalities between Ducal and Electoral Saxony (see *LW* 48, 110, n. 20). Although both territories existed independently from one another as sovereign entities within the Empire, nevertheless the dynastic law which had set up both states included the clause that the enemies of the one were to be considered also the enemies of the other. Since Duke George considered Luther his enemy (and this from the days of the Leipzig Disputation, June/July, 1519), the Duke had the technical right to demand Luther's extradition. See Enders, *Briefwechsel* 5, 206, n. 14.

[26] Thomas Münzer; see p. 111, n. 36; see also note 24.

[27] It is not clear what Luther had in mind here. Perhaps he was warning von Amsdorf (who was living in Magdeburg) that Duke George might demand that von Amsdorf be extradited; or perhaps he was envisioning the possibility that the Duke might undertake a military campaign against Magdeburg, since it had developed into a stronghold of the Reformation.

[1] The letter is extant only in printed form. For the date, see note 25.

the Dessau League, and mentions the intention of some of the
Imperial cities to stay on the side of the gospel. In closing, he sends
greetings to Briessmann's wife and to the Bishop of Samland.

John Briessmann (1488–1549/50), the Reformer of East Prussia
and Livonia, was a Franciscan friar who had studied theology at
the University of Frankfurt/Oder. In 1518 he transferred to the
University of Wittenberg, from which he was graduated as Doctor
of Theology in 1522. While in Wittenberg, Briessmann came under
Luther's influence, and in 1523 Luther recommended him to Mar-
grave Albrecht of Brandenburg (the grand-master of the Teutonic
Order),[2] who was then looking for an evangelical preacher. Briess-
mann went to Königsberg where he spread the Reformation[3] by
means of learned publications and simple yet powerful preaching.
After a brief stay in Riga (1527–1531), where he helped to organize
the Reformation, Briessmann returned to Königsberg as chief
preacher at the cathedral in 1531. In 1544 he worked hard to help
form and develop the University of Königsberg, and from 1546–
1549 he administered the Samland diocese as "president." In addi-
tion to organizing the Reformation, Briessmann was especially in-
volved in various theological battles with Schwenckfeld, Osiander,
and the Roman Catholics who tried not only to curb the Reforma-
tion movement in East Prussia, but to bring East Prussia back
under the authority of the papal church. On John Briessmann, see
NDB 2, 612 f.; Jahrbuch für Brandenburgische Kirchengeschichte
34 (1939), 3 ff.

Text in Latin: WA, Br 3, 555–556.

To [my] very dear brother in Christ, John Briessmann,
an evangelist in Königsberg, Prussia

Grace and peace in Christ! May Christ bless your marriage,[4] my
Briessmann. Sometime ago I wrote a letter about Martin Cellarius,[5]

---

[2] See p. 60.

[3] For the history of the Reformation and the Lutheran Church in East Prussia,
see R. Stupperich, *Die Reformation im Ordensland Preussen* (Ulm, 1967);
W. Hubatsch, *Geschichte der Evangelischen Kirche Ostpreussens* (3 vols.,
Göttingen-Zürich, 1968).

[4] For Briessmann's marriage, see *WA, Br 3, 532, n. 1.*

[5] Martin Keller (or Cellarius, or Borrhaus), a friend of the Zwickau prophets
(see *LW, 48, 365 ff.*), had arrived in Königsberg sometime in May of 1525

and now also a longer letter to the Sovereign Adelbert[6] concerning the ceremonies which should be instituted.[7] Therefore I am now writing you only briefly, since I am loaded down with so much that has to be written.

Should Karlstadt's[8] or Zwingli's[9] poison on the sacrament come to you people, then watch out and be on guard. That miserable man[10] found a secret refuge in my house. Now the whole world is not big enough for him; he is under such attack everywhere that he was finally forced to seek protection from his enemy.[11] I treated

---

(see WA, Br 3, 527, 532) in search of a pastorate. Since his involvement with the Zwickau prophets was known in Königsberg, and since he was suspected in that city of being of the same mind as Karlstadt and Münzer (see the last two references), it was only natural that the people of Königsberg were hesitant to give Keller a job, and that they wanted to know Luther's opinion about Keller. Apparently Keller was not given the red carpet treatment in Königsberg during the second half of 1525, for in February, 1526, he promised to go "within three days" to Wittenberg in order to receive instruction by Luther. On Martin Keller, see *The Mennonite Encyclopedia* 1 (Scottdale, Pa., 1955), 538 f.; WA, Br 3, 527, n. 1.

[6] I.e., Duke Albrecht of Prussia; see note 2.

[7] None of the letters mentioned here is extant. On June 16, 1525, Briessmann mentioned to Luther a letter from Duke Albrecht (also no longer extant) concerning Keller; see WA, Br 3, 532. And Spalatin mentioned a letter (also no longer extant) written by Albrecht (see WA, Br 3, 533, n. 7), in which Luther was invited to come to an assembly of the territorial Estates of East Prussia. This assembly was to meet on August 24, and was to organize the Reformation in East Prussia, i.e., deal with matters of liturgy (Luther's "ceremonies") and faith. Certainly the letters mentioned here by Luther were answers to these letters from East Prussia. It cannot be established whether the first letter, too, was addressed to Briessmann, to the Duke, or to someone else. It is safe, however, to assume that Luther's letters dealt with Keller, and with Albrecht's invitation to come to Königsberg.

[8] Andrew Karlstadt; see LW 48, 79, n. 12.

[9] Ulrich Zwingli; see p. 88, n. 12. Apparently Luther was thinking of Zwingli's *Commentary on True and False Religion*, published in March, 1525; see *C. R. Zwingli Werke* 3, 628 ff.; S. M. Jackson et al. (eds.), *The Latin Works and Correspondence of Huldreich Zwingli* (Philadelphia, 1929) 3, 44 ff. In chapter 18 of the *Commentary* Zwingli developed his understanding of the Lord's Supper. In February, 1526, Zwingli published a popularized version of his understanding of the Lord's Supper, which is translated in LCC 26, 185 ff.

[10] I.e., Karlstadt.

[11] ". . . his enemy," i.e., Luther. After Karlstadt had been expelled from Electoral Saxony, and had been restlessly wandering through southwestern Germany and Franconia, he finally settled down for a while in the Imperial city of Rothenburg. At once he became involved with the rebellious peasants. After their defeat he was again on the run. From Frankfurt/Main he wrote to Luther on June 12, 1525, asking for forgiveness and for help in returning to Electoral Saxony; see WA, Br 3, No. 889. At the end of June Luther gave Karlstadt asylum in his house for about eight weeks; see WA, TR 2, No. 2064;

that man in as friendly a way as I could, and helped him. But, as is usual with this type of spirit, he does not abandon his opinion, even when he is convicted [of error]. So be careful of him and his teaching. I have found out that all [his writings] are valueless, especially in this matter.[12]

Münzer and the peasants[13] have done much damage to the gospel here, [and] have revived the spirits of the papists so much, that it seems we have to begin building all over again. This is the reason that I have now testified to the gospel not only by word but also by a deed: I have married a nun[14] to spite the triumphant enemies who yell "Hurrah, hurrah!" [I have done this] so that it does not seem that I am yielding. Even though I am old and foolish, I shall, if I can, still do other things which will pain them, and [thus] confess the Word.

Duke George, Margrave [Joachim] of Brandenburg, and the two sovereigns of Brunswick have held a small council and have formed a conspiracy to restore the *status quo ante.*[15] Our Sovereign John,[16] who was strongly urged by Duke George to join the conspiracy, thus far stands firm; and so that man[17] becomes almost in-

---

LJB 7 (1925), 67. In a July 19 letter to John Hess in Breslau (see *LW* 48, 143, n. 5), Luther mentioned that he had not yet given up hope of convincing Karlstadt of a more sound understanding of the Lord's Supper; see *WA*, Br 3, 544. On July 25 Karlstadt drafted a statement which, though it was quite ambiguous, could have strengthened Luther's optimism, an optimism which was not blind, however, as Luther's statement to Briessmann (see above) demonstrates. Nevertheless on September 12 Luther supported Karlstadt's request to the Electoral government for a temporary residence permit. See *WA*, Br 3, 565 f., 572, 599. And on September 17 the Elector issued instructions to Spalatin for discussions with Luther, which were designed to lead to a general pardon for Karlstadt; see *WA*, Br 3, 573 f., 576.
[12] I.e., Karlstadt's understanding of the Lord's Supper.
[13] On Thomas Münzer and the Peasants' War, see p. 111, n. 36.
[14] For the general reaction to Luther's wedding, see *S-J* 2, Nos. 689, 692; Köstlin-Kawerau 1, 731.
[15] See p. 119, n. 24.
[16] Elector John; *LW* 48, 269, n. 8. On August 11, at a meeting in Naumburg, Duke George presented to the Elector the constitution of the Dessau League (see p. 119, n. 24), interpreting it as the development of the Mühlhausen agreement. The Duke also encouraged the Elector to join the Dessau League. The Elector protested this misinterpretation of the Mühlhausen agreement, and requested time for consulting with the Landgrave. See Fabian, *ESBV* (2nd ed.), p. 25; Friedensburg, *Vorgeschichte GTB*, pp. 14 ff.
[17] I.e., Duke George of Saxony, the champion of the Dessau League; see *LW* 48, 110, n. 20.

sane, and threatens to burst with wrath. I believe that the Landgrave of Hesse[18] also remains firm, although he is under pressure from the Duke of Brunswick, who functions as a legate of this small council. The Imperial cities are now already consulting together to be able to remain on the side of the gospel in spite of the great threats made against them by the furious sovereigns.[19] In short, it looks as if an even bigger war[20] will develop and will destroy the ungodly sovereigns, unless God prevents it.

Duke George thinks that he can do anything now that Frederick is dead.[21] But so far Christ nicely ridicules him, and will ridicule him even more if you people will join with us in prayer.

The affair of the peasants has quieted down everywhere after almost a hundred thousand have been killed, so many orphans

---

[18] Philip (1504–1567) was (since 1518) the energetic landgrave of Hesse who declared his allegiance to the Reformation in 1524, and who officially organized the Reformation in Hesse in 1526. Being an ambitious politician whose moves in eccesiastical matters were heavily influenced by political considerations, he was quite ready to settle the Reformation issues by means of military power. As a result, he gave the necessary political backbone to the Reformation in Germany, even though his moves were at times ill considered. Theologically seen, Philip stood between Luther and Zwingli, though it was Martin Bucer (see *LW* 48, 247, n. 13) who ultimately was Philip's theological teacher and advisor in ecclesiastical matters. In addition to being a far-sighted politician, Philip was also somewhat of a ladies' man; yet because of his religious feelings his conscience bothered him and took some of the enjoyment out of his escapades. Luther always suspected Philip of being a political hothead who would endanger the very essence of the Reformation by his political maneuvers. Nevertheless the two men kept in close contact with each other, and more than once Luther functioned as spiritual counselor to the Landgrave. The best known incident in this connection is Luther's spiritual counsel with which Philip justified his bigamy. (For details, see *American Journal of Theology* 17 [1913], 206 ff.; H. Eells, *The Attitude of Martin Bucer toward the Bigamy of Philip of Hesse* [New Haven, 1924].) Duke Henry of Brunswick was charged by the Dessau League (see p. 119, n. 24) to influence the Landgrave so that he would join the league. As late as September 30, Henry reported to Duke George that thus far he had not been successful in contacting the Landgrave, but that he would continue trying hard to make the Landgrave join the league. See *Akten und Briefe* 2, 356, 403. On Philip of Hesse, see *NCE* 11, 275 f.; R. Hauswirth, *Landgraf Philipp von Hessen und Zwingli* (Basel, 1968); *Church History* 35 (1966), 157 ff.

[19] It is not clear to which specific event Luther is referring. See also Ranke 1[II], 143.

[20] I.e., than the war against the peasants.

[21] Elector Frederick (see *LW* 48, 49 f.) had passed away on May 5, 1525. He was succeeded by his brother, Duke John (see *LW* 48, 269, n. 8). Apparently Duke George of Saxony considered himself in an advantageous position due to this change in the administration.

made, and the rest so robbed of their livelihood that the appearance
of Germany was never more miserable than now. The victors rage[22]
in such a way that they complete the wickedness [of the peasants].

Greet your new spouse and the Most Reverend Father, the
Bishop of Samland.[23] Since I was unable to write more extensively
at this time, I wanted at least to write briefly.

Farewell in the Lord to you, too,[24] and pray for me!
Wittenberg, after the Ascension,[25] *1525*

MARTIN LUTHER

159

To Elector John[1]
Wittenberg, September 6, 1525

*The victory of the Imperial army over France at Pavia in 1525
and the peace treaty signed with France in Madrid in 1526 allowed
Charles V*[2] *again to direct his attention for a short time to the conditions in Germany, and to consider the possibility of enforcing
the Edict of Worms.*[3] *As compared with 1521, the situation in Germany had completely changed. The religious concerns set forth
by Martin Luther, the Augustinian professor who some seven years*

[22] See e.g., p. 118, n. 16.
[23] On June 16, 1525, Briessmann reported to Luther that George von Polentz
(or Polenz), the bishop of Samland, had married a noble lady; WA, Br. 3,
532. Von Polentz (1487–1550), a member of an old Saxon noble family, rose
to prestige in the diplomatic service of Pope Julius II, of Emperor Maximilian
I, and of the Teutonic Order. In 1519 he became bishop of the diocese of
Samland. In 1522 he became interested in Luther and the Reformation, and
under Briessmann's influence he developed into a stern supporter of the Reformation. His marriage was a public testimony to his affirmation of the Reformation. Through a visitation program and the introduction of an evangelical
church ordinance, he created an evangelical diocese of Samland. On George
von Polentz, see *LThK* 8, 588.
[24] I.e., in addition to Briessmann's wife and George von Polentz.
[25] On the basis of the events mentioned in the letter, "Ascension" must refer
to the day of the Assumption of the Virgin Mary, i.e., August 15, and not to
the day of the Ascension of Christ; see *WA, Br* 3, No. 911, Introduction.
[1] The letter is extant only in manuscript copies and in many editions. The
address is already missing in the earliest manuscript copies of this letter; the
content of the letter and its background make clear to whom it was addressed.
[2] See *LW* 48, 175 f., 210, 315, n. 18.
[3] See *LW* 48, 210, 216, n. 7.

prior to 1525 had been totally unknown, had developed into a religious and political movement of such strength that the Council of Regency and the diets[4] were unable even to consider any uniform enforcement of the Edict of Worms. In April, 1524, the diet, which was meeting in Nürnberg, passed a resolution[5] which charged the Imperial Estates with the task of finding a solution for the problems created by the "Lutheran" movement. According to this resolution the Edict of Worms was to be enforced by the Estates as strictly as possible; the diet was to convene again in November in order to settle all ecclesiastical affairs, and such settlement was to be in effect until a general council of the church would decide the issues raised by Luther. In order to prepare for the diet, the Estates were ordered to draw up abstracts of the issues which were controversial between the followers of Luther and the adherents of the papal church. While these preparations for the diet were being made, the Reformation spread rapidly throughout Germany. Obviously the papal church was unwilling to watch this development idly. In Regensburg, in July of 1524, Lorenzo Campeggio,[6] the papal legate to Germany, concerned about the lack of decisive action against Luther and the Reformation movement on the part of the diet and the Council of Regency, negotiated an alliance of south-German sovereigns and bishops who were willing to curb the Lutheran heresy, if necessary even with arms.[7] The Dessau League of July, 1525,[8] was a parallel to this Regensburg League for the northern portions of Germany. Through these political maneuvers on the part of the papacy, the religious issues raised by Luther became highly politicized, and Germany was split into two

---

[4] See *LW* 48, 70, n. 1, and in this vol., pp. 35 ff.

[5] Text: *DRTA.JR* 4, No. 149 (pp. 603 f.). See also Ranke 1[II], 78 ff.

[6] Lorenzo Campeggio (1472–1539) was a member of an old noble Italian family. He taught law at the University of Bologna, and after his wife's death in 1509 became a clergyman, and entered the service of the papal court. Because of his professional ability he was rapidly advanced and became a cardinal in 1517. In 1513 he represented the pope at the court of Emperor Maximilian I, and later he was papal legate to England. In January of 1524 he replaced Chieregato as legate to Germany. In 1527/28 he was the presiding judge in the "trial" for annulment of the marriage of Henry VIII. Then he was again papal legate to Germany at the time of the Diet of Augsburg, 1530. On Lorenzo Campeggio, see *NCE* 2, 1113; *NB* I. Abt., E. 1, xlvii ff.

[7] See *ARC* 1, Nos. 123, 124; Kidd, No. 73; Ranke I[II], 92 ff.

[8] See p. 119, n. 24.

religious-political camps: one which was the tool of the ambitions of Rome, the other which tried to protect Luther and his work.[9] During the summer of 1524 and thereafter, the possibility of civil war for religious reasons hung over Germany like a dark cloud, and finally exploded into the Smalcaldic War of 1546/47.

In the summer of 1525 Elector John of Saxony and Landgrave Philip of Hesse declined to join the Dessau League.[10] In so doing they gave a public testimony to their affirmation of the Reformation, an action which could have involved the greatest political danger. Seeking political support in order to meet any possible danger from the Dessau League, Elector John looked to Margrave Casimir of Brandenburg-Ansbach-Kulmbach, his neighbor to the south (who could protect the southern frontier of Electoral Saxony).[11] Both sovereigns had cooperated against the peasants, and Casimir had refused to join the Regensburg League, although strongly urged to do so.[12] In addition, a strong Reformation movement was developing in the Margraviate. Casimir did not hesitate to use this movement for his political purposes, notwithstanding the fact that he had no clear position, or convictions, regarding the issues raised by the Reformation.[13] Using the resolution of the Nürn-

---

[9] For the motivations of some of the Estates which supported Luther, see p. 30.

[10] The letter in which the Elector and the Landgrave informed Duke George of their decision not to join the Dessau League was dated September 15; see Fabian, *ESBV* (2nd ed.), p. 26, n. 48.

[11] On Margrave Casimir, see *SMRH* 5 (1968), 157 f.—According to the discussions conducted at Mühlhausen (see p. 119, n. 24), Elector John and Landgrave Philip were to contact, among others, Margrave Casimir in an attempt to gain him for the Mühlhausen alliance for the prevention of further disturbances; see *Akten und Briefe* 2, 255, 288 f. It cannot be established at what date Elector John developed the plan to use this task as an opportunity for finding out whether Casimir would be willing to work with him also in ecclesiastical matters. As early as June 20, however, the Elector started negotiations with the dukes of Lüneburg (with whom the Elector later entered into a league for the sake of defending the territory if the members of the league were attacked because of their support of the Reformation); see Fabian, *ESBV* (2nd ed.), p. 333. These negotiations suggest that toward the end of June the Elector was engaged in trying to use the Mühlhausen decision for creating an alliance both to maintain law and order, and to protect the cause of the gospel particularly against the threats which might arise from Duke George's maneuvers, i.e., from the Duke's interpretation of the Mühlhausen alliance as a tool to crush the Reformation.

[12] See *SMRH* 5 (1968), 168, n. 64.

[13] *Ibid.*, 156 ff.

berg diet of April, 1524, Casimir called a meeting of his territorial Estates in Ansbach in September, 1524.[14] During this meeting a commission drew up the Evangelische Ratschlag.[15] This brief expressed the theology of those clergymen and laymen in the territory who had come to embrace the gospel as Luther understood it.

In early August, 1525, after the peasants had been defeated, Elector John and Margrave Casimir met in Saalfeld to discuss how to prevent further disturbances.[16] Elector John used this opportunity to promote an alliance with Casimir for possible cooperation in religious and other issues at a future diet. (It cannot be established whether the Elector envisioned at that meeting the possibility that such a cooperation might easily balance the probable political and military impact of the Dessau League.) Margrave Casimir enthusiastically took up the Elector's plan, and suggested an exchange of documents so that each partner of the future alliance could learn the other's position on religious issues. While the Elector was in no position to present such a document, Casimir forwarded the Evangelische Ratschlag to the Elector on August 21, 1525. The Elector in turn sent it to the Theological Faculty of the University of Wittenberg for an opinion, which was delivered in the present letter. Apart from a minor difference concerning the evaluation of religious pictures and statues, Luther and his colleagues wholeheartedly approved the Ratschlag.[17]

On Elector John, see LW 48, 269, n. 8.

Text in German: WA, Br 3, 569–570.

Grace and peace in Christ!

---

[14] *Ibid.*, 158 ff.

[15] I.e., a brief dealing with a particular issue under discussion. For the text of this *Ratschlag*, see *Die Fränkischen Bekenntnisse, op. cit.* (see p. 98, n. 8), pp. 183 ff. See also *SMRH* 5 (1968), 172 ff.

[16] On this meeting, see *ARG* 25 (1928), 41; *ZKG* 29 (1908), 323 ff., 342 ff; 30 (1909), 28 ff.

[17] The Elector forwarded the judgment of the Wittenberg theologians to the Margrave. Unfortunately the contacts established in Saalfeld were not pursued, since Margrave Casimir's enthusiasm for an alliance with the two sovereigns who championed the Reformation politically was suddenly replaced by an eagerness to gain the good will of the Hapsburgs, who were championing the papal cause. See *SMRH* 5 (1968), 168 ff.

Most Serene and Noble Sovereign, Most Gracious Lord! We have received Your Electoral Grace's letter,[18] together with the enclosed booklet,[19] and studied [both] diligently; in humble obedience we are now sending to Your Electoral Grace our answer and judgment.

Everything that is discussed and stated in this booklet pleases us tremendously. It is of our currency and carries the right imprint;[20] it is what we have taught and promoted in the last five years. We thank God with joy that there are such people elsewhere[21] who maintain the total truth so steadfastly, and keep it so faithfully in their hearts. We are certain that wherever this *Ratschlag*[22] is read it will stand up with all honor, not only against the papists but also against the gates of hell.[23] We wish to join and stand with those who are affirming such articles as we have thus far stood by our teaching, and as we ought to do. For this [document expresses] the genuine truth. On this Your Electoral Grace and the Sovereign[24] who forwarded this document to Your Electoral Grace may wholeheartedly rely, if God gives grace and strength.

In the one article in which [the authors] oppose images,[25] we do not completely agree with them. Although we also do not attach any importance to images,[26] yet we think that people who have pictures painted for themselves, or who own them, should not be condemned as if they acted contrary to God['s will]. Christ himself did not oppose the emperor's coin but used it,[27] even

---

[18] This letter is not extant.

[19] I.e., the Ansbach *Evangelische Ratschlag*, which was available in several printed editions; for bibliographical details, see WA Br 3, 569, n. 1.

[20] I.e., the Wittenberg theologians consider that, in its way, the *Ratschlag* is as valid as the currency which is used in Electoral Saxony and which shows as imprint a picture of the sovereign.

[21] For the spread of the Reformation see, e.g., pp. 22, 82.

[22] See note 19.

[23] Matt. 16:18.

[24] I.e., Margrave Casimir; see Introduction.

[25] In Article 20, Section 155, of the *Ratschlag* it is stated: "Since the creation of images and their possession is undertaken without any specific commandment of God, [and] to the contrary, is done against God's expressed prohibition and the threat of [his] punishment, it is only right that such open, prohibited, sacrilegious abuse of the idols be abolished. . . ." See *Fränkische Bekenntnisse, op. cit.*, pp. 314 f.

[26] Literally: "idols." For Luther's opinion on this issue, see also LW 48, 401, and his *Against the Heavenly Prophets* (see p. 101, n. 2).

[27] Matt. 22:19.

though it bore images and still does today. However, since this booklet is only a *Ratschlag*[28] from which a final solution should be drawn, we cannot censure the opinion and proposal of these devout people, especially since they state in such a Christian manner that they are willing to be shown and to be instructed; this[29] fine and good booklet should not be rejected just because of one small mistake.

This is what we have wanted to answer, in humble diligence, in response to Your Electoral Grace's letter and request. We leave it to Your Electoral Grace's pleasure and good will to defer or decide [on this subject],[30] as God will grant [Your Grace wisdom].

With this we commend Your Electoral Grace to God's blessing and favor, Amen.

Wittenberg, September 6, 1525

Your Electoral Grace's dedicated
MARTIN LUTHER
JUSTUS JONAS[31]
JOHN BUGENHAGEN POMER[32]
PHILIP MELANCHTHON[33]

160

To Elector John
Wittenberg, October 31, 1525

One of Luther's constant concerns was the welfare and development of his University.[1] The Wittenberg disturbances[2] and the ris-

---

[28] See note 19.
[29] Literally: "such a fine."
[30] This apparently was a reference to the negotiations between the Elector and the Margrave for an alliance. The issue for the Elector would have been whether to go ahead and press for an alliance with a sovereign in whose territory the doctrine expressed in the *Ratschlag* was affirmed. From a theological point of view there was unity between the Wittenberg Reformers and those of Ansbach, and consequently there were no theological objections to the alliance.
[31] See *LW* 48, 275, n. 3.
[32] See *LW* 48, 303, n. 44.
[33] See *LW*, 48, 77, n. 3.
[1] See e.g., *LW* 48, 154; 160; 165 f.; 269, n. 3; 275; 308.
[2] See *LW* 48, 386, n. 1.

ing pressure of the Roman Catholics[3] caused a decline in student registration; the leading men of the University, especially Melanchthon, were often called to other universities, or towns, or territories, to organize and to teach at new schools—and this usually at higher salaries.[4] The financial foundation of Wittenberg University was shaky; courses could not be conducted because of a lack of instructors, and students were poor.[5] On April 16, 1525, on the eve of the war against the peasants, Luther complained to Spalatin that the government was grossly neglecting the University and that it would gradually disintegrate.[6] Apparently as a result of this complaint, Luther was given the task of drafting a memorandum for Elector Frederick on the improvement of the University.[7] Before Luther discharged this responsibility, however, Elector Frederick died on May 5, 1525,[8] and this created a completely new situation.[9] Would Frederick's successor, his brother, Duke John, be willing to help the University overcome its dilemma? What effect would the Peasants' War have on the economic condition of the land in general, and on the University in particular? Because of these uncertainties Luther deferred drafting his memorandum.[10] He finally sent it off via Spalatin on May 20, together with a no-longer extant letter to Elector John;[11] he also enlisted the help of the Elector's son, Duke

---

[3] E.g., the Regensburg League (see p. 126) decided to forbid its subjects to study at Wittenberg; see *ARC* 1, 332.

[4] See *WA, Br* 3, 474, 583.

[5] On the financial conditions of the University, see Schwiebert, pp. 256 ff.; on the situation in 1524/25, see Friedensburg, *GUW*, pp. 169 ff.; on the lack of instructors, see *WA, Br* 3, 501, 575; on the students, see *WA, Br* 3, 567, n. 7; 575.

[6] See pp. 103 f.

[7] Since the memorandum is no longer extant, little can be said about its origin and content. Luther apparently mentioned the memorandum for the first time on May 15; see *WA, Br* 3, 500. A note in the Weimar archive, where the memorandum was deposited, informs us that Elector Frederick had requested the memorandum of Luther and Melanchthon, that it was written by Luther, and that it dealt with financial matters and with academic chairs; see *WA, Br* 3, 502, n. 1; Enders, *Briefwechsel* 5, 174, n. 1.

[8] See p. 124, n. 21.

[9] On May 7 the University was officially informed of Frederick's death; see *Urkundenbuch*, No. 136.

[10] So according to Luther's letter to Spalatin, dated May 15, 1525; *WA, Br* 3, 500.

[11] *WA, Br* 3, 502; the personal letter to Duke John is also mentioned in the letter to Duke John Frederick (see note 12).

John Frederick, to gain the Elector's good will for the University.[12]
The Elector took no decisive action on Luther's memorandum, but
he was sufficiently concerned to dispatch Spalatin to Wittenberg
to assure the faculty of the good will of the government.[13] *Luther*
continued to remind the court of this matter,[14] *and this apparently*
displeased the Elector. In the present letter, written after the Elector
had finally acted,[15] *Luther defends the fact that he had constantly*

---

[12] WA, Br 3, No. 870; S-J 2, No. 684.

[13] Elector John's answer to Luther is dated June 1, 1525, WA, Br. 3, No. 880. The Elector assures Luther and the faculty of his continued good will toward the University, asks Luther to be patient until he returns from the campaign against the peasants, and asks that Luther encourage the faculty to be dedicated teachers. After the war against the peasants and all its problems are settled, the Elector says, he will gladly dedicate himself to the organization of the University affairs. The Elector sent his reply to Spalatin in Torgau, requesting that Spalatin go to Wittenberg, deliver the letter to Luther personally, assure the faculty that the Elector would not let the "praiseworthy undertaking" (i.e., the University) perish, but ask that for the time being the faculty be patient. *Urkundenbuch*, No. 137. Spalatin was in Wittenberg on June 6, and reported to the Elector on this visit on June 12. He briefly assures the Elector that the University and the city are calm and are operating peacefully, and that the leading men of the faculty are most gratified with the Elector's promise to aid the University. *Urkundenbuch*, No. 137, n. 2; WA, Br 3, 520, n. 2.

[14] The patience which the Elector asked the faculty to exercise must have been needed longer than the two sides had anticipated. Apparently the diplomatic activity following the war against the peasants involved the Elector so completely that any work on the University affairs had to be postponed. On the other hand, Luther's marriage and the necessary rearrangements in his life occupied him fully. Therefore, the summer passed and the University affairs were not improved. Luther apparently did approach the court at one time, although no record is extant, for when he mentioned the University affairs again, on September 6, he asked Spalatin whether the Elector had been alienated because of "our" reminders; see WA, Br 3, 567. On September 15 Luther wrote directly to the Elector, reminding him of his promise given on June 1, and pointing out the faculty's patient trust in this promise; WA, Br 3, No. 921.

[15] Even before Elector John had received Luther's letter of September 15, he had already again taken up the matters of the University. On September 17 he issued detailed instructions to Spalatin (*Urkundenbuch*, No. 139), and gave him the necessary credentials (WA, Br 3, No. 922). Spalatin was to go on a fact-finding mission to Wittenberg, and then to report to the Elector on it. Spalatin had authority to confirm whatever arrangements the faculty had made, and he was to come to terms with the faculty regarding future plans. He was to admonish especially the Law Faculty to be diligent in its work. The dates of Spalatin's visit to Wittenberg could not be verified. Spalatin was in Wittenberg, however, sometime after September 17 (the day he received his credentials), and before September 28, for on that day Luther wrote to Spalatin that the University had now been set in order (WA, Br 3, 583); on October 1 Spalatin reported to the Elector on his visit and made further sug-

urged the Elector to do something for the University. He also calls the Elector's attention to two tasks that now have to be undertaken: the one is the organization of the external structure of the parishes; and the other is a careful supervision of local government, and of administrative officials. Luther makes some detailed suggestions on how these matters could be accomplished.

On Elector John, see LW 48, 269, n. 8.

Text in German: WA, Br 3, 594–596.

To the Most Serene, Noble Sovereign and Lord, Sir John,
duke of Saxony, elector, etc., landgrave in Thuringia,
margrave in Meissen, my Most Gracious Lord

Grace and peace in Christ! Most Serene, Noble Sovereign, Most Gracious Lord! I most humbly beg Your Electoral Grace kindly not to hold it against me that I must so often bring trouble and disquiet to the court with my letters, since I certainly get nothing out of it for myself except much trouble and disquiet. I would also be glad to spare Your Electoral Grace all of this; but because of the position of authority which I hold, I cannot allow myself to be tired of it.

To begin with, Most Gracious Lord, I apologize for having been so insistent on the organization of the University, for I have heard that Your Electoral Grace was quite offended by my solicitous urging [of this project], perhaps thinking that I did not put sufficient confidence in Your Electoral Grace's promise.[16] Of course it is not true that I distrusted Your Electoral Grace; had that been the case, my doubts would certainly have caused me to give up my urging. It is because I did not doubt Your Electoral Grace's promise that I kept on urging, so that the matter would not be deferred merely because of the profusion of business, as had frequently been the case under our previous most gracious lord, etc.[17]

---

gestions (*Urkundenbuch*, No. 141). We know that prior to October 11 the Elector acted upon these suggestions by dispatching Hans von Dolzig and Hans von Gräfendorf to Wittenberg (see *Urkundenbuch*, No. 143). Both were in Wittenberg at least from October 11 (see WA, Br 3, 588) to October 15 (see *Urkundenbuch*, No. 146).

16 See Introduction.

17 I.e., Elector Frederick the Wise; see LW 48, 49 f., and above, notes 8, 9.

People at court have many things to do, and it is necessary to keep after them, as the saying goes.[18] In addition to this, I was also being urged by others and there was need for haste, since people were leaving the University, and it seemed as if the school were breaking up.

However it may have been, even if I had insulted Your Electoral Grace through mistrust on my part, I would not repent too much of such a sin in view of the good result which was brought about by this. The result is worthy of much more sins. I would be willing to sin even more in this way against Your Electoral Grace, if in so doing I could accomplish such good. I am fully confident that Your Electoral Grace not only will graciously forgive, but also will be pleased with these [sins], since it is certain and inevitable that Your Electoral Grace must feel in your heart that such work is good and God-pleasing. And even though Your Grace seeks neither merit nor reward in this, much less honor and glory in the world, yet the conscience must rejoice and faith must be strengthened through the fact that God has accomplished such good results through Your Electoral Grace, and that he has used Your Grace as an instrument, and has indicated that he intends to continue using this instrument for the purpose of his divine, gracious will. For this we heartily pray and wish. Amen.

Most Gracious Lord: the University has now been organized,[19] and the order of worship is now also being composed and is about

---

[18] In his letter to Duke John Frederick, dated May 20 (see note 12), Luther asked for the Duke's help in countering the possible intrigues of the *Hofschranzen*, i.e., the courtiers.

[19] Luther made the same statement in his September 28 letter to Spalatin; see note 15. During his visit to Wittenberg (see note 15) Spalatin had adjusted the salaries of the faculty—Melanchthon received a major increase, the salaries of the other professors and lecturers were raised—and revised the teaching assignments of the individual instructors. In addition he established two new courses for the law school. In order to finance this development, Spalatin suggested to the Elector on October 1 that all the endowments of the All Saints' Chapter at Wittenberg's Castle Church be sequestrated and marked for the University budget. Spalatin also suggested to the Elector that he send some officials to Wittenberg to incorporate the finances of the Chapter in an orderly way into the University budget. The Elector followed this suggestion, and dispatched von Dolzig and von Gräfendorf to Wittenberg; they transferred the Chapter's finances to the University's exchequer. They assigned one-third of the Chapter's revenues to the upkeep of the Chapter and two-thirds to the University. See *Urkundenbuch*, Nos. 141, 143; Friedensburg, *GUW*, pp. 175 ff.

to go into use.[20] There remain, however, two matters which require the attention and action of Your Electoral Grace as the secular authority.

The first matter is that everywhere the parishes are in such poor condition. No one contributes anything, no one pays for anything, mass fees[21] have been abolished, and there are either no rents or they are too small. The common man pays so little attention and respect to preachers and pastors that in a short time there will not be a parsonage, a school, or a pulpit functioning, and thus God's Word and worship will perish, unless Your Electoral Grace passes strict laws, and carefully regulates the maintenance of parishes and pulpits. For this reason, may Your Electoral Grace continue to allow God to use Your Grace, and to be God's faithful instrument. This will bring great comfort to Your Electoral Grace's own conscience, because it is God who asks and requires this action of you through us and through the emergency situation[22] itself. Your Electoral Grace will certainly find means to deal with this situation. There are enough monasteries, collegiate chapters, benefices, endowments, and [other] similar things that can be used for this purpose, if only Your Electoral Grace will issue an order that they be inspected, accounted for, and set in order. God will give his blessing to [such an undertaking] and prosper it, so that, if it be God's will, the ordinances concerning the souls of men—as for instance the higher schools and the worship—will not be obstructed by need and neglect of the poor stomach. For this we beseech His divine grace. Amen.[23]

---

[20] See p. 90. On October 29 the Wittenberg City Church had used Luther's German order for the mass for the first time, and after Christmas, 1525, this German order was the standard form of worship in Wittenberg. At the turn of the year this order was also published: *Deutsche Messe und Ordnung des Gottesdienstes (The German Mass and Order of Service)* (Wittenberg: M. Lotther, 1525/26), WA, 19, 72 ff.; LW 53, 53 ff.

[21] I.e., fees previously used for the now abolished private masses.

[22] On this term, see note 23.

[23] With this paragraph Luther fulfilled a promise given to Nicholas Hausmann (see LW 48, 399 f.) on September 27, when he wrote: "I know that a reformation of the parishes and the institution of a uniform order of worship are necessary; I am now trying to crack this nut, and I shall solicit the Sovereign's help for this." WA, Br 3, 582; S-J 2, 338. In the midst of the peasants' uprising, Hausmann drew up a memorandum for Duke John (the future elector), proposing ways of spreading the gospel. He suggested that the privilege of appointing pastors should be taken away from the papistic patrons, and that

The second matter is that Your Electoral Grace should also have the [local] secular governments inspected, as I once discussed with Your Electoral Grace at Wittenberg.[24] [One ought to find out] how the city councils and all other [district] officials rule over, and deal with, the commonweal. For there is everywhere great complaint about bad government, both in the towns and in the countryside. As head and ruler of the territory, it is Your Electoral Grace's duty to look into this. Perhaps there might be fewer correspondence cases and complaints reaching the court if such a visitation and good discipline were carefully practiced.

May Your Electoral Grace graciously accept all [these thoughts]

---

the right of electing their own pastors be given to the congregations. Since the bishops were refusing to do anything about abolishing the blasphemous ceremonies, or about instituting the preaching of the pure gospel, Hausmann argued, the territorial sovereign would have to interfere in this situation, conduct a thorough visitation of the parishes in his domain, introduce the Reformation in them, and thus prevent the eternal damnation of his subjects. For documentation see WA, Br 3, 582, n. 2; WA 26, 177. Hausmann here exactly followed Luther's line. As early as 1520, in his *Address to the German Nobility*, Luther had said that in view of the refusal of the papal bishops to establish in the parishes the preaching of the pure gospel, the secular authority had the right and the duty to function in ecclesiastical matters, and to abolish the papal ways of worship and preaching. The sovereign was to function as a *Notbischof*, i.e., an emergency bishop, as Luther later said. In 1523 Luther advocated the right of the individual parish, as the communion of the true believers, to elect its own pastors and teachers, and to exercise control over them; see pp. 28 ff.; *SMRH* 5 (1968), 191 ff.; *Church History* 22 (1953), 113 ff. Luther apparently discussed Hausmann's suggestions with Spalatin (who had independently approached Elector Frederick as early as May 1, 1525 with a similar idea; see Höss, *Spalatin*, p. 276) when the latter was in Wittenberg at the end of September (see note 15). For in his report to the Elector, dated October 1, Spalatin mentioned the visitation program as the first item. See *Urkundenbuch*, No. 141; Höss, *Spalatin*, p. 322. In his letter to Spalatin dated October 28 Luther mentioned that the visitation program was the next necessary undertaking, now that the University was set in order; WA, Br 3, 583. Whether the Elector took up Spalatin's suggestions in connection with the Dolzig-Gräfendorf mission to Wittenberg (see note 15) cannot be established; it is very dubious that he did so, however, since the visitation program is mentioned neither in Dolzig's instruction nor in his report to the Elector (*Urkundenbuch*, Nos. 143, 146, 147). Nevertheless Luther mentioned the matter again on October 11. On that day he reported to Hausmann that the Elector's councilors were then in Wittenberg to deal with the form of worship at the All Saints' Chapter, and that when this matter was settled the problem of setting the parishes in order would finally be attacked; WA, Br 3, 588. Did Luther and the Electoral officials discuss the visitation program? If so, then apparently there were no positive results, for Luther now, on October 31, approached the Elector directly.
24 On this visit to Wittenberg, July 13–16, see WA, Br 3, 546, n. 1.

as humble suggestions on my part, since Your Electoral Grace sees and is well aware that I mean well. May God graciously put his Spirit into Your Electoral Grace's heart regarding these undertakings, with all the light and power necessary to do what is well pleasing to Him. Amen.

Wittenberg, October 31, 1525

Your Electoral Grace's dedicated
MARTIN LUTHER

161

To Elector John[1]
Wittenberg, November 30, 1525

Elector John replied to Luther's letter of October 31 (No. 160) on November 7, 1525, and asked Luther's opinion on financial matters concerning pastors and parishes.[2] In the present letter Luther answers the Elector with suggestions for the visitation program and for the care of pastors and parishes. In closing, Luther points out the necessity of caring for elderly pastors and for those who are unable to fulfill their pastoral duties.

On Elector John, see LW 48, 269, n. 8.

Text in German: WA, Br 3, 628–629.

God's grace and peace in Christ!

Most Serene, Noble Sovereign, Most Gracious Lord: Your Electoral Grace has replied[3] to my suggestion of caring for the parishes in all matters. Now, it is not my idea that all parishes should be maintained by Your Electoral Grace's treasury.[4] However, since

---

[1] The letter is extant only in printed form. The address is missing even in the earliest witnesses. The content of the letter (esp. the way in which Luther addressed the person to whom he was writing), however, makes it clear to whom the letter was written.

[2] WA, Br 3, No. 944; S-J 2, No. 714.

[3] See note 2.

[4] See note 2.

Your Electoral Grace has graciously requested my judgment on how this matter should be handled, I submit my humble opinion:

Your Electoral Grace should have all the parishes in the whole territory inspected. If one finds that the people wish to have evangelical preachers but the parish assets are insufficient for their support, then Your Electoral Grace should command that this community provide a certain sum yearly, be it from city hall,[5] or in any other way. For if the people want to have a pastor, it is Your Electoral Grace's duty to see to it that they also reward the laborer, as the gospel sets forth.[6]

Such inspections could be undertaken in the following way: Your Electoral Grace could divide the whole territory into four or five districts and send into each district two men, perhaps [a representative] of the nobility and [one] of the district officials. They should inform themselves about the parishes and [the parishes'] assets, and find out the needs of the local pastor. They should also present Your Electoral Grace's command concerning the annual tax.[7] If the expense and trouble connected with such a procedure are too much for Your Electoral Grace, then one could use citizens from the towns, or one could summon [a meeting of representatives of] the important towns of the territory and discuss the matter with them. But whatever is most agreeable to Your Electoral Grace should be done.

In addition to this, one should also make provisions for the old pastors and those who are otherwise incapacitated. If they are devout people in other respects, or not opposed to the gospel, they

---

[5] I.e., from the treasury of the community. Luther apparently envisioned an annual tax to be collected by the city and to be used as subsidy for the budget of the parish.

[6] Matt. 10:10; Luke 10:7.

[7] The suggestions made here by Luther were temporarily shelved. Only sporadically were fact-finding missions undertaken by some of the Elector's councilors or advisors, especially Spalatin; see Höss, *Spalatin*, p. 323. Since the visitation of a parish was the privilege and duty of the bishop in whose diocese the parish was located, Luther here suggested a basic interference with the Canon Law of the papal church and with the traditional structure of the state-church relationship. To do this on a territorial level was something apparently too hot to handle even for Elector John, whom Protestant historiography has come to call "The Constant." It was not until the Diet of Speyer had issued its famous resolution (see p. 156) that the Elector felt that he had a basis in public law for conducting the visitations. Therefore in the late autumn of 1526 Luther's suggestions were again taken up.

ought to be obligated (if they are unable to preach) either to read the gospels with the *Postil*[8] to the people, or arrange to have them read. Thus a true ministry of the gospel would be given to the people, whom the pastors ought to nourish. For it would not be good to put these men out [of their offices] without any recompense, if they are not against the gospel.

I wanted humbly to present to Your Electoral Grace these suggestions at Your Electoral Grace's request.

[Your Grace] be herewith commended to God.

Wittenberg, November 30, 1525

> Your Electoral Grace's dedicated
> MARTIN LUTHER

162

To Michael Stifel[1]
Wittenberg, December 31, 1525

At the end of August, 1524, through his book On Free Will, Erasmus publicly disassociated himself from the Reformation. The increasing controversy on the Lord's Supper and the turmoil created by the peasants did not allow Luther immediately to reply to Erasmus.[2] In the summer of 1525 Luther finally composed his rebuttal, On the Bound Will, which came off the press in December. Luther is sending a copy of this work to Stifel along with the present letter. He also comments briefly on the Eucharistic controversy, pointing out that the lack of doctrinal unity among the enthusiasts appears to him to be a sure sign that their teachings are inspired by the devil. In closing, he sends greetings to Stifel's patroness, Dorothy Jörger.

---

[8] I.e., the *Wartburg Postil* (with its two parts containing sermons for the Advent and Christmas seasons; see *LW* 48, 237 ff.), to which Luther had added the *Lent Postil* (*WA* 17[II]) in 1525.

[1] The letter is extant in manuscript copies, and in the common edition of Luther's works. The address is missing in all witnesses. Besides the fact that Luther addresses a Michael, there seems to be no other basis for substantiating Stifel as the addressee, as the text tradition has established.

[2] See p. 88, n. 7.

Michael Stifel (1486?–1567), or Stiefel, was an Augustinian friar from Esslingen who in 1522 openly supported Luther. For this he had to flee to Wittenberg; while there, a close personal friendship between him and Luther developed. Upon Luther's recommendation Stifel became a preacher in Mansfeld, and then later on in Tollet (in Upper Austria). From 1528 he held several pastorates in Electoral Saxony. Forced to leave Saxony during the Smalcaldic War, Stifel found a new home in East Prussia. In 1554 he returned to Wittenberg, and at once became involved in a controversy with Melanchthon. From 1559 to the end of his life Stifel taught mathematics at the University of Jena.Stifel had strong leanings toward apocalyptic speculation, which he combined with keen interest in and solid knowledge of mathematics. Consequently he could not resist attempting to determine when the world would come to an end. In 1532 he published a booklet in which he established that the world would come to an end and that Christ would return in glory on October 19, 1532. The enthusiasm with which he defended his theories and conclusions repeatedly caused him trouble, and Luther had to help him out of more than one tight situation. On Michael Stifel, see ADB 36, 208 ff.; Jahrbuch für Geschichte der oberdeutschen Reichsstädte, 14 (1968), 30 ff.; L. R. Froom, The Prophetic Faith of our Fathers 2 (Washington, D.C., 1948), 320 ff.

Text in Latin: WA, Br 3, 653.

Grace and peace in the Lord

I am sending you, my Michael, my rebuttal of Erasmus,[3] which I completed as best I could in a short time and in a hurry.

I like your idea[4] that the ruler of this world[5] is so powerful

---

[3] On September 27, 1525, Luther wrote to Hausmann that he was working on a rebuttal of Erasmus; WA, Br 3, 582; S-J 2, 338. It seems that Luther finished the manuscript between November 11 and 18; see WA 18, 581. The printing began while Luther was still working on the manuscript. In December, 1525, Hans Lufft in Wittenberg released Luther's *De servo arbitrio (On the Bound Will)* WA 18, 600 ff.; LCC 17, 101 ff. For Luther's statement that he had written this book in great hurry, see WA 18, 581 f.

[4] The letter in which Stifel expressed this idea is not extant. Apparently Luther had just received it (see Luther's statement), and answered it at once in order to give his answer to the messenger who had brought Stifel's letter.

[5] See John 12:31; 16:11.

in obstructing any fruit of the Word (although he is forced to allow men to hear the Word)[6] and in sowing sects of the ungodly, that is, his own weeds.[7] The error concerning the sacrament has three sects,[8] but they agree with each other. Zwingli fights Karlstadt with one set of arguments; Valentine from Silesia fights both of them, and everyone else, with another set. You will hear more about this in due time.[9] This quarrel among the sects is a sign that their teachings are of Satan, since the Spirit of God is not a spirit of discord, but of peace.[10]

Please give my greetings to your Lady[11] and her sons, and my thanks for the present she sent,[12] although it has not yet arrived, and perhaps may never arrive. But that does not matter; , is the good will that counts.

Farewell, and pray for me.

Wittenberg, December 31, 1525, [the day] on which I received your letter[13]

MARTIN LUTHER

---

[6] The parentheses have been added by this editor.

[7] See Matt. 13:25.

[8] I.e., the followers of Ulrich Zwingli, of Andrew Karlstadt, and of Valentine Krautwald (who was a friend of the Silesian nobleman Caspar von Schwenckfeld).

[9] It is not clear how this sentence is to be connected with the preceding one. The text leaves unanswered the question whether Stifel will hear more about the whole controversy or about Krautwald's arguments.

[10] See I Cor. 14:33.

[11] Stifel's patroness was the recently widowed Dorothy Jörger of Tollet in Upper Austria, whose late husband, Sir Wolfgang Jörger, was governor of an Austrian district. The Jörgers had asked Luther for an evangelical preacher, and Luther had sent Stifel to them. One of the Jörger sons, Christopher, to whom Luther recommended Stifel (see WA, Br 3, No. 884, dated June 3, 1525), later rose to a high administrative position in Austria. Dorothy and her sons were firm followers of Luther and demonstrated a deep insight into the nature of the gospel as Luther was teaching it. See WA, Br 3, 524, n. 1.

[12] Nothing could be established about the background of this statement.

[13] See note 4.

163

To Gabriel Zwilling
Wittenberg, January 2, 1526

Through his marriage to Catherine von Bora, Luther had changed from a monk and a professor who lived only for his work into a family man who had to face all the problems that accompany married life.[1] In the present letter Luther is sending the measurements for a mattress which Zwilling (who was at that time pastor in Torgau) was supposed to arrange to have made. Luther also reports the loss of a small amount of money.

On Gabriel Zwilling, see LW 48, 39, n. 3.

Text in Latin: WA, Br 4, 4.

To Master[2] Gabriel Zwilling

Grace and peace! My Gabriel, I am sending the measurements for the length and width of the mattress as I would like to have it made. If there are any people [in your town] who know how to make one, please give the measurements to them. I shall pay whatever will have to be paid.[3]

Recently you returned some money[4] by placing it into my Psalter.[5] But since the little book was thrown into the wagon, [the coins] were lost; we could hardly find one or two. It would have been better if you had left them for the household servants than that I should have lost them in such a way.

Farewell, and pray for me!

Wittenberg, January 2, 1526   MARTIN LUTHER

---

[1] Bainton, pp. 290 ff., gives a fine picture of Luther the family man.

[2] I.e., Master of Arts.

[3] In later years Luther discussed similar household needs with Zwilling. On February 10 and March 19, 1539, e.g., he requested Zwilling's aid in obtaining a linen cabinet; see WA, Br 8, 369, 395.

[4] Luther wrote *grossulos*. It is extremely difficult, if not impossible, to give any equivalent figure in modern currency. Suffice it to say that in Germany the *Groschen* was the particular unit of currency next to the smallest unit, the penny; in Luther's days the *Groschen* was generally a silver coin. On the *Groschen*, see Trübner 3, 244 f.

[5] The background and the book to which Luther refers here are unclear; for possibilities, see WA, Br 4, 4, n. 3.

164

To George Spalatin
[Wittenberg,] March 27, 1526

In the first part of the letter Luther comments on the fact that he has not written for quite some time, and forwards to Spalatin certain letters of King Christian II of Denmark, which contained sad news. The major part of Luther's letter, however, is dedicated to a discussion of certain political manipulations by Duke George of Saxony and "the bishops," the latest publication of Erasmus of Rotterdam against Luther, and the controversy with the enthusiasts over the Lord's Supper. Luther mentions briefly the Syngramma Suevicum, and Pirckheimer's attack on Oecolampadius. Pointing out that regarding the Lord's Supper six heresies have developed during the last year, Luther briefly sketches the interpretations of the Lord's Supper held by some of his major opponents among the enthusiasts.

On George Spalatin, see LW 48, 8 f.

Text in Latin: WA, Br 4, 41–42.

To my dearest friend in Christ, George Spalatin, a most
faithful servant of Christ in Altenburg[1]

Grace and peace in Christ! It is true, dearest Spalatin, that we exchange letters very rarely.[2] Make sure that you do have a reason for this, since I have a very good one. Why should I want to disturb rudely the joys of a newly married husband, and not rather let the honeymoon be spent undisturbed[3]—especially since the news I have to write is not very pleasant. But joking aside, letter carriers are scarce; otherwise I would have long ago sent to you this most sad letter from King Christian[4] (who is now an extremely

---

[1] See note 3.
[2] Luther's last extant letter to Spalatin was dated December 9, 1525; see WA, Br 3, No. 953.
[3] In August, 1525, Spalatin had left his position at court and accepted a pastorate in Altenburg; in November he married; see WA, Br 3, 637, n. 1; Höss, *Spalatin*, pp. 292 ff.
[4] This letter of Christian II, king of Denmark, to Spalatin is no longer extant. The King added this letter to his letter to Luther (see note 7), and asked the

miserable man,[5] yet wonderfully living only for Christ),[6] together with the letter which he has sent to me,[7] and the most lamentable news in it.[8] God will now at last call [birds] (as they say), that is, call a king and a queen to heaven;[9] of course it will be that king of whom the human mind would least have expected it, so that God's glory might be shown in making sport of our judgment.

You can hardly imagine what great things Satan is setting in motion through Duke George[10] and the bishops. I shall soon give you a little sample of Satan's wickedness through a booklet which is already on the press.[11] Unless the Lord prevents it, you will have

---

Reformer to forward this enclosure to Spalatin. Luther is finally doing this. The letter to Spalatin apparently was not sealed; consequently Luther was in a position to read it and state now that it is a "most sad" letter.

[5] Because of the death of Queen Isabella on January 19, 1526; see WA, Br 4, 25, n. 1.

[6] The parentheses have been added by this editor.

[7] King Christian II of Denmark to Luther: January 28, 1526; WA, Br 4, No. 976. In this letter the King reports of the sickness and death of his wife, Queen Isabella. The Queen was a sister of Charles V (see LW 48, 175 f.). Having been exiled from Denmark, the royal couple lived with the Queen's aunt, Margaret (see p. 21, n. 7), in the Netherlands. On the basis of the available material (see WA, Br 4, 25, n. 1) it seems that the Queen had strong sympathy for the Reformation. More important than this, however, is the fact that in his letter to Luther (and probably also in the letter to Spalatin) the King claimed that he and his Queen were strong supporters of the gospel, apparently in an attempt to gain the good will of the Wittenbergers, and through them the good will of Elector John. The King's evangelical convictions were not as deep as Luther thought.

[8] It is not clear to what "most lamentable news" refers. Is it only the news concerning the Queen's death which was in Luther's letter and which apparently was also the core of the King's letter to Spalatin?

[9] Literally: "God will now at last call game (as they say), that is . . ." Luther occasionally used the German proverb: In heaven sovereigns are rare game. Perhaps he is referring to this proverb here. See LW 48, 295; WA, TR 3, 219; 5, 507, 576; WA, Br 13, 40, to WA, Br 2, 382, n. 18.

[10] Duke George of Saxony; see LW 48, 110, n. 20.

[11] At the end of 1525 the sovereigns of the Dessau League (see p. 119, n. 24) requested the Emperor to bring an end to the "damned Lutheran teachings;" see WA 19, 252; Friedensburg, Vorgeschichte GTB, pp. 98 f. On November 14, 1525, the leading clergy of the Archdiocese of Mainz issued a Ratschlag (brief), and sent it with a special delegation to the Emperor. In this brief the Emperor was also called upon to put down the Lutheran heresy. In February, 1526, Elector John asked Luther for a commentary on this brief. Luther at once wrote his Against the Mainz Brief (WA 19, 260 ff.), and as early as March 27 the manuscript was on the press. In this booklet Luther settled accounts not only with the Archbishop of Mainz, but also with Duke George. In order to avoid difficulties with Duke George Elector John stopped the printing, after he had tried in vain to influence Luther to adopt a conciliatory tone of writing; see WA, Br 4, 45 f.

to admit that the rebellion and slaughter of the peasants[12] were only a prelude to the destruction of Germany. I earnestly beg you, therefore, to pray along with me, using all our strength, to the Father of mercies[13] that he prevent such plots, and subdue the fury [of Duke George and the bishops], especially by indicting Duke George, a man who (I fear) is lost and to be deplored; [let us pray] that God may convert him, or if he be unworthy of such grace, [that God may] take him from our midst. Otherwise that beast will not rest; he is almost Satan himself, not just because of his own fury but also because he incites the bishops. Indeed, it torments this man that Luther is not killed, so much that there is reason to fear he may perhaps be worn away with this single sickness of his soul. He can neither sleep nor be awake.

Dear God, how much our Sovereign[14] has to endure, not only from [Duke George], but also from the intrigues and evil counsels of his own most wicked nobility. I have much to tell you which I cannot entrust to letters. In addition, that enraged viper, Erasmus of Rotterdam, is again writing against me.[15] How much eloquence this vainglorious beast uses up this time in trying to knock Luther down!

I believe you have read what those very learned men of Swabia[16] have written against Oecolampadius;[17] it is wonderful how popular [their] booklet is.[18] Willibald Pirckheimer has also written against Oecolampadius with more spirit and zeal than I would have expected from such an important man. I thought

---

[12] See pp. 117 ff.

[13] II Cor. 1:3.

[14] Elector John; see *LW* 48, 269, n. 8.

[15] In March, 1526, Erasmus published the first part of his *Hyperaspistes* (Clericus 10, 1249 ff.), in which he refuted Luther's *On the Bound Will*.

[16] So on the basis of one witness; see *WA, Br* 13, 82, to *WA, Br* 4, 41 f.

[17] John Oecolampadius; see *LW* 48, 230, n. 14. Luther is referring here to Oecolampadius' book *On the Original Meaning of the Words of Institution according to the Testimonies of the Fathers of the Church* (published in late summer of 1525; see *WA* 19, 447), in which Oecolampadius affirmed a figurative interpretation of the Lord's Supper; see Sasse, pp. 140 f. The book was dedicated to the clergy of Swabia in an attempt to gain their support.

[18] Luther is referring here to the *Syngramma Suevicum (Swabian Symposium)* of October, 1525, in which some pastors of Swabia, led by John Brenz, rejected Oecolampadius' position. See *WA* 19, 449; Sasse, pp. 141 f.

[Pirckheimer] was too much wrapped up in other things.[19] Yet others keep rising. If I am not wrong, then this sacramentarian sect has already produced six heads in one year.[20] A wonderful spirit, thus to disagree with itself! Karlstadt's [exegesis of] "this" [in the Words of Institution] was one [head] which has already fallen;[21] Zwingli's was the second one, which is falling now.[22] The figurative exegesis of Oecolampadius was the third one which will fall.[23] The fourth one, by C . . . , has fallen, too;[24] when he was attacked, he rearranged the words in the following way: "That which is given for you is my body." The fifth one is rising now

---

[19] Willibald Pirckheimer was one of the outstanding patricians of Nürnberg, and a highly learned Humanist; in various lengthy writings he clashed with Oecolampadius on the latter's understanding of the Lord's Supper. On Willibald Pirckheimer, see L. W. Spitz, *The Religious Renaissance of the German Humanists* (Cambridge, Mass., 1963), pp. 155 ff.

[20] See also p. 141, and *WA*, Br 4, 33; *WA*, 19, 458. "Heads" is perhaps an allusion to Rev. 12:3; 13:1. In *S-J* 2, 367, the following sentences are translated in such a way that the picture of heads which have been produced, and which have fallen (see Rev. 17:10), or which will fall, is maintained. While it is most probable that Luther had this picture in mind—and this is the reason why the meaning of the *S-J* translation has been retained for the present translation—the translation offered in *S-J* is quite free. In a literal translation of the following sentences, "head" would have to be replaced with "sect," or "opinion."

[21] Andrew Karlstadt; see *LW* 48, 79, n. 12. Luther considered Karlstadt refuted ever since the publication of *Against the Heavenly Prophets* (see p. 101, n. 2).

[22] On March 28 and 29 Luther preached three sermons in which he developed his understanding of the Lord's Supper. He indirectly contrasted his teaching to that of Zwingli, and demonstrated how and where Zwingli's opinion was contrary to Scripture; he did not, however, attack Zwingli personally. Nevertheless he could consider these sermons to be a means by which Zwingli would be refuted. In the fall of 1526 these sermons were published: *Sermon von dem Sakrament des Leibes und Blutes Christi, wider die Schwarmgeister (The Sacrament of the Body and Blood of Christ—Against the Fanatics)* (Wittenberg: H. Lufft, October, 1526), *WA* 19, 482 ff. *LW* 36, 335 ff.

[23] In his book mentioned in note 17, Oecolampadius had established the figurative explanation of the Lord's Supper. Luther apparently believed that Oecolampadius' interpretation would be refuted through Pirckheimer's book, and also through the *Swabian Symposium* (see note 18), which he himself prefaced and published in the first half of 1526; see *WA* 19, 457 ff.

[24] The text is obscure here, and this name cannot with certainty be identified. *S-J* 2, 367, n. 3, suggests that "C . . ." is identical with a certain Michael Cellarius, or Keller, or Köllner, a preacher in Augsburg who supported Karlstadt. For other possibilities, see *WA*, Br 4, 43, n. 14. The "rearrangement" of the Words of Institution (which Luther ascribes to "C . . .") is typical of Karlstadt, so that Smith's thesis (*S-J* 2, *loc. cit.*) seems well founded. On Keller, see F. Roth, *Augsburgs Reformationsgeschichte* (2nd ed.; Munich, 1901, 1911), 1, 200 ff.; *NDB* 3, 181.

and exists in Silesia; its producers are Valentine Krautwald and Caspar [von] Schwenckfeld,[25] who changed the words in this way: "My body which is given for you is this, namely, a spiritual food." These people vex us tremendously with [their] writings, and are troublesome babblers. I wish my gallstones to these fellows, who think they are so strong![26] The sixth one is that of Peter Aloet in Cologne. I have not yet seen anything [written] by him, except for a letter which is in Philip's hands.[27] Wow, how [Peter] reproaches Luther! I know, he says, that Luther is forsaken by the Lord.

All these diverse spirits condemn each other with crafty arguments, all boast of revelations which they obtained by prayers and tears, and, in essence, all agree anyhow. Good for us, that Christ has made them fight each other from the very beginning.[28]

See what sad news I have had to write to you! He who adds to someone's knowledge also adds to his pain. But in this way I want to compensate for my silence with prolixity.

Farewell to you and to your Rib![29]

March 27, 1526   Yours,

MARTIN LUTHER

---

[25] Valentine Krautwald and Caspar von Schwenckfeld; see pp. 148 ff.

[26] Throughout the spring of 1526 Luther repeatedly suffered from kidney stone or gallstone attacks. It was not until June that he got some relief; see *C. R.* 1, 801.

[27] It is not certain that this Peter Aloet is identical with Peter Fuchs (a printer in Cologne), as S-J 2, 368, n. 1 suggests. Clemen cannot identify this person or trace the letter; see *WA, Br* 4, 44, n. 19. On Melanchthon, see *LW* 48, 77, n. 3.

[28] Literally: "Good for us through Christ, who for us has made them fight each other immediately, from the beginning."

[29] This is obviously an allusion to Gen. 2:22. On Spalatin's wife, Catherine Heidenrich of Altenburg, see Höss, *Spalatin,* pp. 297 f., 394 ff.

165

To Caspar von Schwenckfeld[1]
Wittenberg, April 14, 1526

In this letter Luther is rejecting von Schwenckfeld's interpretation of the Lord's Supper and is asking him to abandon his false teachings.

Caspar von Schwenckfeld (1489–1561), offspring of an old Silesian noble family, studied theology (and probably also Canon Law) at the Universities of Cologne and Frankfurt/Oder, but apparently was never graduated. Sometime after 1518, while serving at the court of the Duke of Liegnitz, he experienced a religious conversion, apparently while studying Luther's writings. He always gratefully acknowledged Luther's influence in spite of the sharp differences which eventually separated the two men. (Luther, for his part, considered von Schwenckfeld one of the most dangerous of the enthusiasts.) From 1521 von Schwenckfeld worked in Silesia to further the Reformation. His special concern was to emphasize the ethical fruits of faith and the spiritualization of the whole religious life. Insisting that he had received a new understanding of the Lord's Supper through a special revelation, he interpreted the sacrament as a reference to the glorified Christ, whose flesh is the spiritual food of the soul.[2] He rejected any possibility of a mediation between God and man by means of anything creaturely, and, under the influence of Mysticism and Humanism, developed a strictly individualistic, spiritualistic understanding of faith, and a sectarian understanding of the church. Rejecting both Luther and the Reformed Reformers, as well as the papal church, von Schwenckfeld considered his own theology the true "heavenly philosophy of salvation," on which all people could and should agree. Upholding this notion he became one of the first major advocates of religious tolerance, and this in an age which was not ready for tolerance.

---

[1] The letter is extant in one manuscript copy, and in the common editions of Luther's works. The address and the signature are missing in the earliest witnesses. But the contents of the letter, especially the references to von Schwenckfeld's teachings on the Lord's Supper, make clear to whom Luther was writing this letter.

[2] On von Schwenckfeld's teachings on the Lord's Supper, see *LCC* 25, 161 ff.; Sasse, p. 301, n. 8.

Consequently he had to spend the remainder of his life in continuous controversies with his theological opponents, and in continuous search for refuge and for peace. In 1529 he left Silesia and, living on a small pension derived from his paternal inheritance, he restlessly roamed through southwest Germany; his continuous controversies with the Reformers made him unwelcome almost everywhere. Finally, he found refuge in Ulm, where he was protected by a small number of noble families who were converted to his teachings, and where he eventually died. On Caspar von Schwenckfeld, see O.D.C.C., p. 1229; NCE 12, 1189; The Mennonite Encyclopedia 4 (Scottdale, 1959), 1120 ff.

Text in German: WA, Br 4, 52–53.

Grace and peace in Christ!

My dear Sir and Friend: I have long deferred answering [you], so that you certainly can see that we did not read your material[3] carelessly. Now we return it again by your messenger.[4]

But what should I say? Perhaps it is God's will that you should fall like this. You promised me that you[5] would try to prove that the Words of Institution agree and are identical with the sixth

---

[3] At the beginning of December, 1525, von Schwenckfeld was in Wittenberg to discuss his understanding of the Lord's Supper with Luther. (For Schwenckfeld's report on these discussions, see *Corpus Schwenckfeldianorum* 2 [Leipzig, 1911], 237 ff.) It is not clear to what "material" refers. It is certain that, while in Wittenberg, von Schwenckfeld gave to Luther a lengthy letter written by Valentine Krautwald to von Schwenckfeld; see WA, Br 3, No. 951. Apparently von Schwenckfeld also left with Luther a manuscript of a treatise by Krautwald. See *Corpus Schwenckfeldianorum* 2, 224 ff., 292. Luther was to study this material and then to give von Schwenckfeld and Krautwald an evaluation of their position. Valentine Krautwald (*ca.* 1470–1545) was a canon in Neisse prior to his appointment as a canon in Liegnitz and as the principal of a school there. In Humanistic circles he was well known for his knowledge of Hebrew. On Valentine Krautwald, see *Corpus Schwenckfeldianorum* 2, 177 ff.; *The Mennonite Encyclopedia* 1 (Scottdale, 1955), 732 f.

[4] The background of this statement could not be verified. Did von Schwenckfeld send a special messenger to Luther in order finally to get an answer?

[5] This is a reference to the discussions between Luther and von Schwenckfeld. Luther is not correct here, since it was not von Schwenckfeld who was to prove the correctness of his teachings, but Krautwald, who (in his writings mentioned in note 3) was to prove the correctness of the teachings which he, Krautwald, *and* von Schwenckfeld affirmed. See WA, Br 4, No. 995, Introduction, and Luther's April 14 letter to Krautwald; WA, Br 4, No. 996.

chapter of John.[6] This you did not do, and never will be able to do. What good is it that you inform us in great detail on "the two kinds of food, the figurative and the true,"[7] but omit all documentation which could demonstrate that these two types of food can be found in the Lord's Supper? Of course you say that this is so, but you do not prove it. As a result, we cannot believe you and rest our souls on your word. It is therefore my courteous request that you renounce this obvious error, and do not join those who now lead the world so miserably astray. If this should not happen, then God's will be done. Although I am heartily sorry, yet I am not responsible for your blood,[8] nor for the blood of all those whom you lead astray with [your teachings]. May God convert you. Amen.

Wittenberg, April 14, 1526

166

To John Agricola
[Wittenberg,] May 11, 1526

Luther is having some amusing difficulties in trying to send a little pewter dish to Agricola. He mentions his controversy with Erasmus, the progress of Agricola's school, and gives some news of mutual friends.

On John Agricola, see LW 48, 220.

Text in Latin: WA, Br 4, 73–74.

To my brother in the Lord, John Agricola, a servant of Christ at Eisleben

Grace and peace! I am sending that little pewter dish with the glass inset before it finds another owner, for my Katie is trying hard to get it.[1]

---

[6] "John" is written in Latin.
[7] The quotation is written in Latin.
[8] Matt. 27:24.
[1] It appears that Nicholas Hausmann (see LW 48, 399 f.) had sent this dish to Luther, asking that he forward it to Agricola, who had once seen something like it and expressed to Hausmann a desire to have such a piece; see WA, Br 4, 40, 55.

I am pleased with your judgment of Erasmus,[2] but even more [pleased] with the progress of your school.[3] This is at least one good word to hear in the great confusion of this age. Wendelin[4] is not here, but he will hurry to you from Halle. We wrote him accordingly and sent your letter to him. Do help this man as he deserves, and as you know [how to help him]. Tell your Else, if she does not yet know it, that Doctor Draco[5] has married, and that it is said that this Syrus has the same hope.[6]

Farewell to you and yours, and pray for me!

May 11, 1526   MARTIN LUTHER

Now look, just as I wanted to give the letter to the carrier and as I searched for the little dish, [I see that] my Katie, this stealthy woman, has hidden it. I would have searched for it, but I am prevented from doing this by a conspiracy on the part of our Provost[7] and of our Pastor,[8] who perhaps are hiding it. Just wait until the dish is freed by Katie's confinement to childbed;[9] then I will steal it and carry it off.

167

To John Rühel
[Wittenberg,] June 8, 1526

Forwarding a "little Psalter" with this letter, Luther comments briefly on some of his work. He also announces the birth of his son John, his first child.

---

[2] I.e., concerning Luther's controversy with Erasmus regarding free will.

[3] See p. 103, n. 7.

[4] I.e., Wendelin Faber, a teacher whom Luther had recommended for Agricola's school in Eisleben; see *WA*, Br 4, No. 998. Agricola had offered Wendelin a position and had asked him to come to Eisleben.

[5] John Draco, a pastor from a nearby town; see *LW* 48, 223, n. 7. The connection of Draco to Else Eisleben is not clear. See *NDB* 4, 95.

[6] "Syrus" must have been the letter carrier. Who it was cannot be identified; it was perhaps a pseudonym. For further information on this rather obscure passage, see *WA*, Br 4, 74, n. 4.

[7] Justus Jonas (see *LW* 48, 275, n. 3) was provost of the All Saints' Chapter in Wittenberg.

[8] John Bugenhagen (see *LW* 48, 303, n. 44) was the pastor of the City Church.

[9] See p. 152.

On John Rühel, see pp. 107 f.
Text in German: WA, Br 4, 87.

To my lord and relative,[1] Doctor John Rühel at Eisleben,
written with affection

Grace and peace in Christ! I am sending the little Psalter[2] to you
along with this letter, dear Doctor and Relative; as far as I am
able, I shall from now on work on the Psalms.[3] To serve you I
have attacked the Anathema and discovered where it is wrong.
Therefore be satisfied [for now].[4]

Please tell Master Eisleben[5] on my behalf, that yesterday, on
the day which is called *Dat*[6] in the calendar, at two o'clock, my
dear Katie, by God's great grace, gave to me a Hansen Luther.[7]
Tell him not to be surprised that I approach him with such news,
for he should bear in mind what it is to have sun[8] at this time of
year.

---

[1] Luther wrote *Schwager;* see p. 108, n. 14.
[2] I.e., *Vier tröstliche Psalmen an die Königin von Ungarn* (*Four Comforting
Psalms for the Queen of Hungary*) (Wittenberg: H. Barth, 1526), WA 19,
552 ff.; *LW* 14, 207 ff.
[3] It is not clear to what Luther is referring here.
[4] It is not clear to what Luther is referring here.
[5] I.e., John Agricola; see *LW* 48, 220.
[6] I.e., "he [she, it] gives," written in Latin. This is the name given to June 7
by an old calendar in which the names of dates were taken from rhymes
composed from the initial syllables of the names of the important saints of
each month. On this calendar, called the Cisiojanus, see H. Grotefend, *Taschen-
buch der Zeitrechnung des deutschen Mittelalters und der Neuzeit* (10th
ed.; Hannover, 1960), p. 20.
[7] See also p. 323, n. 7. John Luther was born on June 7, 1526, in the early
afternoon (between 1:00 and 2:00 P.M., see *WA*, Br 4, 87, n. 4). In 1542 he
attended Latin school at Torgau, and in 1543 he matriculated at the University of Wittenberg, where he later studied law. Supported by Duke Albrecht
of Prussia, John studied from *ca.* 1549 to 1551 at the University of Königsberg. He returned to Wittenberg because his mother demanded it, and "more
from respect for his father's memory than recognition of any ability on his
part" John was employed in the chancellery at Weimar (Schwiebert, p. 602).
Soon thereafter he became a member of the chancellery of the Elector of
Brandenburg, in whose service he undertook several diplomatic missions. On
one of these missions he died on October 27, 1575, in Königsberg. On John
Luther, see J. Luther, *Johannes Luther, des Reformators ältester Sohn* (Berlin,
1930).
[8] This is a play on words: June is the time when there is much *Sonne,* i.e.,
sun; it is appropriate therefore to have a *Sohn* (son).

Please greet your dear sun-bearer[9] and Eisleben's Else. I commend you herewith to God. Amen. Just as I am writing this, my weak Katie is asking for me.

June 8, 1526   MARTIN LUTHER

168

To Michael Stifel[1]
Wittenberg, August 11, 1526

In this apparently hastily written letter, Luther sends his greetings and those of his wife. Luther's obvious reason for writing the letter is to tell of the birth of his son John; at the same time he briefly yet proudly praises his wife. In addition, Luther communicates some incidental news.

On Michael Stifel, see p. 140.

Text in Latin: WA, Br 4, 108–109.

Grace and peace in the Lord!

Since I have come upon this messenger who is going all the way to your place, my Michael, I wanted to send these greetings to you, since besides this there is almost nothing else to write about. I plan to write against the sacramentarian sects,[2] if God grants me so much leisure. I am expecting a heap of arguments from Erasmus.[3] As of now, I know nothing about the diet,[4] except that the

---

[9] I.e., son-bearer; see note 8.

[1] The letter is extant in manuscript copies, and in the common edition of Luther's works. The address is already missing in the earliest witnesses. The name mentioned in the first sentence of the text seems to be the only substantiation for the traditional assumption that Stifel was the recipient of this letter. See also p. 141, n. 11.

[2] See pp. 141, 145 f. Here Luther mentions for the first time his intention to write *Dass diese Worte Christi "Das ist mein Leib" noch fest stehen wider die Schwärmgeister* (*That These Words of Christ, "This Is My Body," Still Stand Firm Against the Fanatics*) (Wittenberg: M. Lotther, April, 1527), WA 23, 64 ff.; LW 37, 3 ff.

[3] In August, 1527, Erasmus published the second part of his *Hyperaspistes;* Clericus 10, 1337 ff. Here he once again tried to refute Luther's teachings on the bondage of the will. Luther is now anticipating this book.

[4] See Excursus.

bishops are trying hard to restore their former governmental authority. The Sovereign[5] is vigorously fortifying our town.[6]

God in his great goodness has blessed me with a healthy and vigorous son, John, a little Luther.[7] Katie, my rib,[8] sends her greetings and her appreciation that you have honored her with such a kind letter.[9] She is well, by God's grace, compliant, and in every way is obedient and obliging to me, more than I had ever dared to hope (thank God), so that I would not want to exchange my poverty for the riches of Croesus.[10]

Greet your hostess and your hosts[11] in my name, and farewell to you in Christ![12]

Wittenberg, August 11, 1526   MARTIN LUTHER

---

[5] Elector John; see *LW* 48, 269, n. 8.

[6] Perhaps to meet an attack of the sovereigns of the Dessau League; see p. 119, n. 24.

[7] John Luther; see p. 152, n. 7.

[8] See Gen. 2:22.

[9] This letter is not extant.

[10] I.e., a king of Lydia who died in 546 B.C. and who was, according to legend, extremely rich; see *O.C.D.*, page 243.

[11] Literally: "your lady and your lords." The reference is to Dorothy Jörger and her sons; see p. 141, n. 11.

[12] Literally: "Greet your lady and your lords in my name in Christ, and farewell!"

Excursus

In the extant letters Luther takes comparatively little notice of the first Diet of Speyer, which was in session from June 25 to August 27, 1526. (On this diet, see W. Friedensburg, *Der Reichstag zu Speyer, 1526, im Zusammenhang der politischen und kirchlichen Entwicklung Deutschlands im Reformationszeitalter* [Berlin, 1887]; *LJB* 8 [1926], 120 ff.; Ranke 1[II], 208 ff.) The statement in the letter to Stifel, and a remark about the carousing of the sovereigns who attended the diet (*WA*, Br 4, 109), seem to be the only statements which Luther made about this important diet.

According to the Emperor's plans, and those of the papal party in the Empire (see Kidd, No. 88), this diet, finally, was to enforce the Edict of Worms (see *LW* 48, 210) uniformly throughout the Empire, and to begin to take care of the grievances against the Roman church (see Ranke 1[II], 212 f.). The evangelicals in the Empire were ready to meet this situation. To balance the political or military threats which might come from the Dessau League, Elector John of Saxony and Landgrave Philip of Hesse on May 2, 1526, signed a defense alliance, and thus created the Gotha-Torgau League. This league had been discussed by the Elector and the Landgrave at a meeting which took place at the end of February, 1526, in Gotha, and had been ratified on May 2 in Torgau. (For details, see Friedensburg, *GTB;* Fabian, *ESBV* [2nd ed.], pp. 26 f.; Ranke 1[II], 210 f., 3[II], 81 ff.) At a meeting in Magdeburg on June 12 this league was joined by other sovereigns of northern and central Germany, and shortly thereafter by the city of Magdeburg. (See Fabian, *ESBV* [2nd ed.], pp. 27 ff.; Ranke 1[II], 211 f.) The immediate purpose of this Magdeburg League was joint action at the Diet of Speyer. (See Ranke 1[II], 212.) Indeed, the evangelicals at the diet in no way acted like a group of people which stood under the threat of the Imperial ban. In spite of harassment, the evangelical preachers who were attached to the individual delegations preached publicly, sometimes even attracting large crowds. And over the doors of their quarters and on the coatsleeves of their jackets the evangelicals displayed the large letters: *V.D.M.I.E.* (*Verbum Domini manet in eternum*; see Isa. 40:8; Ps. 119:89), thus demonstrating their willingness to affirm the Word of God as Luther was teaching it.

From the very beginning the intentions of the Emperor and of the papal party ran into difficulty, mostly because of a strong anti-ecclesiastical mood, which was especially dominant in the College of the Cities. (See Ranke 1[II], 212 ff.; Kidd, No. 89; *LW* 48, 70, n. 1.) The secular members of all three colleges were determined to do something about a general reform of the church; their attention was centered more on the grievances against the church than on the enforcement of the Edict of Worms. And the ecclesiastical members of the diet, especially the bishops, were equally determined not to give an inch; hence Luther's statement above. (See also Ranke 1^{II}, 213 f.)

The political developments outside the Empire struck the death-blow to the plans of the Emperor and the papal party. On May 22, 1526, Pope Clement VII, Francis I (king of France), Venice, and Milan signed the League of Cognac (see Kidd, No. 87; Ranke 1^{II}, 205 ff.) against Charles V, and immediately hostilities broke out in northern Italy. And yet another enemy confronted the Emperor: the Turk. Francis I was able to influence Sultan Suleiman II, the Magnificent, to join in the campaign against Charles V. The Sultan planned a two-pronged attack, by sea against Spain, by land against northern Italy via Hungary and Austria. (See Ranke 1^{II}, 245 ff.; Elton, pp. 346 ff.) On April 23, 1526, the Sultan and his splendid, powerful army left Constantinople. On September 10, 1526, the Sultan conquered Budapest after he had defeated the outnumbered and technically inferior army of the Hungarian king, Louis II, in the battle at Mohacs on August 29. At that moment all of Hungary seemed lost to the Turks. But because of internal difficulties, the Sultan was forced again to withdraw his troops to the Danube line.

As early as July 27 the Emperor's policies regarding the Reformation were radically changed (see the Emperor's July 27 letter to his brother Ferdinand; Ranke I^{II}, 219 f.). He needed the help of Germany against the Pope and his ally, the French King, and against the Turk. Political considerations forced the Emperor to bypass the question of the uniform enforcement of the Edict of Worms and to postpone the whole Reformation issue until a general council of the church would deal with it. Consequently on August 27 the diet adopted a resolution according to which, in matters relating to the Edict of Worms, the Estates of the Empire would so live and govern that each Estate would hope to be able to answer for its actions to God and to His Imperial Majesty. (The resolution in excerpt: Kidd, No. 90.) This resolution, which was to be in effect until a council had decided the issues raised by the Reformation, shifted the enforcement of the Edict of Worms from the Empire to the Estates; thus it contributed to Germany's political division on a religious basis. While this resolution did not furnish a legal basis for the Reformation, it was understood by many territorial sovereigns to be precisely that.

169

To Wenceslas Link[1]
[Wittenberg,] January 1, 1527[2]

Luther is commenting on his correspondence with King Henry VII. of England. He asks Link for seeds so that he can do some garden ing in the spring, and also for some tools.

On Wenceslas Link, see LW 48, 169 f.

Text in Latin: WA, Br 4, 147–148.

To my superior in the Lord, Wenceslas Link, a faithful evangelist in Nürnberg

Grace and peace in the Lord! You preach to me, my Wenceslas, that Christ is set for the fall and rising [of many].[3] Thus one sermon follows the other. Persuaded by the King of Denmark, I wrote a suppliant and humble letter to the King of England; I certainly had high hope and [wrote] with a guileless and candid heart. He has answered me with such hostility that he sounds just like Duke George, and as if he rejoiced in the opportunity to have his revenge.[4] These tyrants have such weak, unmanly, and totally sordid characters that they are worthy of serving the rabble. But thanks

---

[1] The letter is extant in only one manuscript copy, and in the common editions of Luther's works. The signature is missing in all witnesses. That Luther wrote this letter, as the tradition has established, can be substantiated on the basis of the following facts: the references to Christian II and Henry VIII (see note 4); the reference to Wolfgang Seberger (see note 7); Luther's subsequent letters to Link, dated January 23 (WA, Br 4, 162), and July 5 (see p. 167), in which Luther mentions the seeds (see letter, second paragraph) and his gardening efforts.

[2] On the date of this letter, see note 12.

[3] Luke 2:34.

[4] Luther had heard from King Christian of Denmark that King Henry VIII of England might now be favorably inclined toward the gospel; see p. 116, n. 5. In his letter to Henry, dated September 1, 1525 (WA, Br 3, No. 914; S-J 2, No. 700), Luther apologized for the sharp tone which he had used against the King in their clash regarding *On the Babylonian Captivity*. The King's printed answer (WA, Br 4, No. 1046; WA 23, 18) was sent to Luther on December 21, 1526, via Duke George of Saxony, Luther's bitter foe (see LW 48, 110, n. 20); see WA, Br 4, 142 f. The Duke also sent a copy of this work to Erasmus of Rotterdam (see Allen 6, No. 1776; see also Allen 6, No. 1773), and at once had the work reprinted. For bibliographical information on the King's answer, see WA, Br 4, 125 f., 143, n. 1.

be to Christ, I am sufficiently avenged, for I disdain them and their god, who is Satan, and this is my joy.

I appreciate that you also promise to send seeds in the spring.[5] Send as many as you can, for I really want them and look forward to having them. If I can do anything in return, command it, and be sure it will be done. For even if Satan and his members rage, I shall laugh at them and in the meantime I will turn my attention to the gardens, that is, to the blessings of the Creator, and enjoy them to his praise.[6]

Since among us barbarians there is neither art nor style of life, I and my servant Wolfgang[7] have taken up the art of operating a lathe. We are enclosing a gold gulden[8] and asking that you be so kind as to send us at your convenience some tools for boring and turning, and also two or three [of those tools] which they call "screws;"[9] any lathe operator can easily tell you what this is. We do have tools, but we want some of a more elegant form, that is, the kind that is used in your artistic Nürnberg. Please do this—unless it is too much of a bother—and if you spend more, it will be repaid,[10] for I believe prices are lower where you are. If the world

---

[5] On January 23 Luther repeated this hope; WA, Br 4, 162. Apparently Luther had "also" asked some of his other friends in Nürnberg for seeds.

[6] For similar statements, see WA 49, 434.

[7] Wolfgang Seberger (or Sieberger) was a very poor, perhaps even lame (and apparently not too bright or industrious) student from Munich. In 1515 he matriculated at Wittenberg. From that time he had in Luther a faithful friend, who in 1517 found him shelter in the monastery. Seberger became a *famulus* of Luther (see LW 48, 164, n. 4). After Luther married, he became attached to the Luther household as a servant. He and his wife stayed with the Luther family until his death in 1547. Seberger's attempts at operating a lathe were apparently not too successful. On May 19, 1527, Luther wrote to Link that he now had sufficient tools to operate the lathe, unless the Nürnbergers had invented tools to do the work by themselves while Wolfgang was lazy or sleeping; WA, Br 4, 203. Luther put up with Seberger's inefficiency with good humor. When in an attempt to trap some birds Seberger built a big bird cage in the yard of the Wittenberg monastery (the residence of the Luther household), Luther wrote a delightful little work in which the birds complain to him, Luther, about Seberger's lack of attention to and respect for them; see WA 38, 292 ff. Luther obtained for Seberger a yearly gift of wheat from the Elector; he also bought a little garden and a house for his servant, the rent money of which went to Seberger; see WA 38, 290, n. 2; WA, Br 12, 421, n. 10. See also Köstlin-Kawerau 2, 492 f.

[8] On the gulden, see LW 48, 11, n. 2.

[9] Luther used the German *Schraube*. For a lathe operator a *Schraube* is some kind of a clamp. On these tools, see also WA, Br 8, 670, to WA, Br 4, 203, n. 1.

[10] Luke 10:35.

should indeed not want to feed us on account of the Word that we preach, then we shall learn how to obtain our bread through the work of our hands, and to serve unworthy and ungrateful people according to the example of our Father in heaven.[11]

The grace of God be with you!

January 1, 1523[12]

170

To Nicholas Hausmann
[Wittenberg,] January 10, 1527

Luther is briefly reporting on the Elector's desire to speed up the beginning of the visitation program. He tells of his own work (commentary on Zechariah, book against the sacramentarians), comments on Oecolampadius and Rhegius, and mentions the campaign of the Imperial army in northern Italy.

On Nicolas Hausmann, see LW 48, 399 f.

Text in Latin: WA, Br 4, 159.

Mr. Nicholas Hausmann, faithful bishop of the
congregation[1] in Zwickau, my superior in the Lord

Grace and peace in Christ,[2] my dearest Nicholas. I have no other news except that the Sovereign has replied to the University that

---

[11] See Matt. 5:45. Did Luther learn how to operate a lathe for the sake of having a hobby, as is suggested, or was he seriously thinking that he, a man with family responsibilities, might have to earn a living by using his hands rather than his head, as is also suggested? See WA, Br 4, 148, n. 6; Rückert, LB, p. 147, n. 17; Bainton, p. 291. Rückert (*loc. cit.*) cites a passage of a February 29, 1520 letter to Spalatin (WA, Br 2, 58), and Clemen (WA, Br 2, 58, n. 7) refers to a passage in the *Second Lectures on the Psalms* (WA 5, 449), and both passages suggest that Luther was indeed serious about the possibility that he might have to earn a living with his hands. And further, one may not take lightly those statements in which Luther affirmed that, if necessary, he would leave Wittenberg and seek somewhere else a place to live; see e.g., LW 48, 88, 90, 94, and in this vol. pp. 15, 58.

[12] This date is given in the oldest extant manuscript copy. The material presented in note 4 makes clear that 1527 must be the correct date, and that the copyist made an error.

[1] See pp. 87, n. 5; 61, n. 9.

[2] This sentence is written in German.

he wishes to speed up the visitation of the parishes.[3] When that has been accomplished, and the congregations[4] have been set in order, then the usage of excommunication can be discussed.[5] But what can be undertaken now while everything is upside down?

Zechariah is now on the press, ready for publication; the book is growing daily under my hands.[6] At the same time I am attacking the sacramentarians.[7] Please pray that Christ may guide my pen successfully and advantageously against Satan. I also greatly rejoice over your testimony that you are still untouched by this leaven [of evil],[8] for I always believed this about you. I am deeply grieved that Oecolampadius,[9] that excellent man, has fallen into this abyss, pushed by Satan through such empty and ridiculous arguments. May the Lord pull him out again! Urbanus Rhegius[10] is either

---

[3] Elector John; see LW 48, 269, n. 8. See also in this vol., p. 138, n. 7. In November, 1526, Luther urged the Elector to take up the visitations; see WA, Br 4, 133 f.; S-J 2, 383 f. The Elector replied promptly (WA, Br 4, 136 f.), assuring Luther of his cooperation. Luther is now informing Hausmann of this latest development. The visitations of the parishes in the neighborhood of Wittenberg, the *Kur-Kreis*, finally began in February, 1527.

[4] Luther wrote *ecclesia* (see p. 61, n. 9). This can refer to the local parish, and this is apparently what Luther meant here; see ZKG 48 (1929), 230, n. 2.

[5] In a no-longer extant letter Hausmann apparently had suggested that the evangelical congregations practice this old disciplinary measure.

[6] *Der Prophet Sacharja ausgelegt* (*Explanation of the book of the Prophet Zechariah*) (Wittenberg: M. Lotther; the printing of the individual installments of the manuscript was begun in December of 1526, or January of 1527, and was not completed, due to Luther's illness and other work, before the end of November), WA, 23, 485 ff.

[7] See p. 153, n. 2.

[8] See I Cor. 5:7 f.

[9] John Oecolampadius; see LW 48, 230, n. 14. In a letter to Nicholas Gerbel (see LW 48, 317 f.) Luther made a similar statement about Oecolampadius; see WA, Br 4, 63.

[10] Urbanus Rieger (1489–1541), or Rhegius, a Humanist and poet laureate, had studied theology in Freiburg and Ingolstadt, and had become a preacher in Augsburg in 1520/21. In his capacity as preacher he helped to introduce the Reformation in Augsburg. Even though he wholeheartedly affirmed Luther's teachings and rejected Karlstadt's position on the Lord's Supper, Rhegius was attracted to Zwingli's symbolic interpretation of the sacrament, and publicly endorsed it in 1526. This flirtation with the symbolists lasted, however, only a short time. In 1530 Rhegius went to Brunswick-Lüneburg, where, in close cooperation with Wittenberg, he organized and guided the church of the Reformation. He was especially concerned with the development of a clergy which would be highly educated and which would be dedicated to good preaching and responsible day-by-day care of souls. On Urbanus Rhegius, see ADB 28, 374 ff.; *Die Religion in Geschichte und Gegenwart* 5 (3rd ed.; Tübingen, 1961), 1081 f.

sinking into the same calamity or has already fallen into it. May the Lord preserve his own!

I believe you have heard that the cause of the Emperor in Italy has developed successfully.[11] The Pope[12] is afflicted from all sides, so that he will be ruined, for his end and his hour have come, although persecution rages everywhere and many are being burned at the stake.

My Katie sends respectful greetings.

January 10, 1527   Yours,

MARTIN LUTHER

171

To Nicholas Hausmann[1]
[Wittenberg,] March 29, 1527

Luther is sharply criticizing the conduct of a pastor in Zwickau who had indulged in personal polemics from the pulpit. While Luther does not suggest how to deal with this particular pastor, he details his thoughts on church discipline in general. Basing his

---

[11] See Rückert, *LB*, p. 156, n. 6. The anti-Imperial League of Cognac brought about the second war between Charles V (see *LW* 48, 175 f.) and France and its Italian allies. In the fall of 1526 the Imperial army, led by George von Frundsberg, occupied northern Italy without meeting much resistance. See Ranke 1[II], 223 ff.; Elton, pp. 343 f.

[12] Clement VII (1523–1534) was born in 1478, an offspring of the famous Medici family. As a protégé of Pope Leo X (*LW* 48, 100), he became a cardinal in 1513. In 1523 he became pope as a result of the influence of the Emperor among the cardinals. As pope Clement tried unsuccessfully to play France against the Emperor in an attempt to promote the interests of the Papal States and of the Medici family. After the Emperor was victorious over France in the battle at Pavia (1525), Clement initiated the Holy League of Cognac against the Emperor, which in turn led to the Pope's defeat. In his attitude toward the Reformation he was exclusively guided by political considerations. He steadfastly rejected a general council of the church, yet he repeatedly *promised* a general council; but finally in 1532 he postponed it indefinitely. Always concerned with the power of the Emperor and its possible influence on papal prestige and politics, Clement VII often openly opposed the Emperor's policies, and thus aided the cause of the Reformation. On Clement VII, see *O.D.C.C.*, p. 298; *NCE* 3, 931 f.; G. Müller *Die römische Kurie und die Reformation. Kirche und Politik während des Pontifikates Clemens VII.* (Gütersloh, 1969).

[1] The letter is extant in one manuscript copy, and in the common editions of Luther's works. The address and the signature are missing in all witnesses.

position on I Timothy 5:1 and Matthew 18:15 ff., Luther points out that the congregational meeting, and not the service, is the place where Christians should exhort each other, and if necessary should punish the sinner.

On Nicholas Hausmann, see LW 48, 399 f.

Text in German:[2] WA, Br 4, 180–181.

Grace and peace in Christ!

Reverend, dear Pastor. I have definitely been told—and X[3] has indicated the same—that one of your preachers began[4] to speak offensively in the pulpit, and in a provoking way attacked some members of the city council, which of course pleases[5] the rabble.[6] Thus the

---

[2] Luther generally wrote to Hausmann in Latin; since Hausmann was to inform the city council of this letter, Luther made an exception and wrote in German in anticipation of the fact that Hausmann might show the letter to the council.

[3] I.e., the Mayor of Zwickau, who had written to Roth and thus (indirectly) informed Luther about the events in Zwickau, while Roth "told" Luther about the events; see note 6.

[4] Another possible translation would be: ". . . preachers claimed the right [or: dared] to speak . . ."

[5] Literally: "pleases and fools the rabble."

[6] On March 15, 1527, the Mayor of Zwickau informed Stephen Roth, one of Zwickau's students at Wittenberg, of the offensive actions of the preacher Paul Lindenau (for biographical information, see WA, Br 4, No. 1091, Introduction; Enders, *Briefwechsel* 6, 33, n. 2), and asked Roth to bring this matter to Luther's attention; see WA, Br 4, 181 ff. Lindenau was publicly criticizing some of the decisions of the city council; even more, he apparently openly acted contrary to these decisions. In addition, he attacked the Mayor from the pulpit and censured him for his immoral conduct. It seems that there were two points of irritation for Lindenau. One was his opposition to being pushed around in ecclesiastical affairs by the orders of the city council. And the other one was a personal irritation, and involved Lindenau's wife, for on October 31, 1526, he and his wife were relieved of the "directorship" of the city "girls' school." In the letter to Roth (which was, of course, indirectly addressed to Luther) the Mayor and the council said that their action in respect to the girls' school was the result of the urgent requests made by Lindenau and his wife; see WA, Br 4, 183. Yet the pastor's wife seemed to have been extremely unhappy with this development, and was not at all reluctant to say so. On December 8 the city council, therefore, decided to tell Lindenau to stop his wife's inflammatory ranting, and this did not make the pastor happy. By March, 1527, the situation in Zwickau had become decidedly uncomfortable for everyone. Unfortunately no material is extant in which the pastor's side of this story is presented. In the Mayor's report to Roth (and through him to Luther), the pastor is the culprit; therefore, Luther's reply is based exclusively on one-sided information, a fact which must be kept in mind when reading Luther's letter. Further, it should be pointed out that Luther does not address himself directly to the situation in Zwickau—did Luther have second thoughts

spirit which seeks its own honor and followers still [haunts us].[7] Therefore it is my friendly request that you, together with the city council, give attention to this matter so that sleep and negligence do not again cause us trouble. By God's grace you certainly know that such censuring of a person should be done only in a meeting of Christians.[8] At present [that kind of] a meeting, which we hope will be instituted by the visitation, has not yet been set up among you. Yet even if such a meeting were already arranged, such a scolding would not be right, since St. Paul says: "Do not rebuke an older man, but exhort him as you would a father."[9] And Christ commands, in Matthew 18 [:15 ff.], that admonition in private should first take place. He who[10] does not comply with this order is up to no good.

In the sermon preached in public, where Christians and non-Christians stand together and listen, as is the case in the church,[11] one should censure all kinds of unbelief and vice in general, [but one should] not point to someone in particular. For the sermon is for everyone, and should remain so; no one should[12] be embarrassed and shamed in front of the others until he has been separated and brought into the meeting. Here he can be admonished, besought, and censured in the proper way. If this preacher is eager to censure in public, then he should do it to those who have at-

---

about the Mayor's letter?—but developed his ideas on the handling of church discipline in general terms.

[7] This sentence, and the next one, are references to the Zwickau prophets and the disturbances they had created in Zwickau and in Wittenberg; see LW 48, 364, n. 28. In his report, the Mayor had quite cleverly suggested that Lindenau might be another Thomas Münzer; see WA, Br 4, 182. On Münzer and the Zwickau prophets, see P. Wappler, Thomas Müntzer und die "Zwickauer Propheten" (2nd ed.; Gütersloh, 1966).

[8] A member of the church was not to be upbraided in public, but only within the privacy of a meeting of those who were truly Christians. Luther hoped that the visitations would eventually prepare the ground for the practice of ecclesiastical discipline; see also the introduction to Luther's German Mass (1526), WA 19, 74 f.; LW 53, 63 f.

[9] I Tim. 5:1; this quotation is written in Latin.

[10] Literally: "The spirit that does not."

[11] Luther wrote Kirchen. This could refer to the church in general, as Clemen (WA, Br 4, 159, n. 3) and Rückert (LB, p. 155, n. 24) suggest, yet it does not necessarily do so. Luther could very well have been thinking here of the church in its local setting, i.e., the parish. In fact, the reference to the congregational meeting suggests that Luther was thinking of the parish.

[12] Literally: "For it is a common sermon; it also should remain common, and no one should . . ."

tacked him in public first, as I do to the papists and enthusiasts.[13] Otherwise he should restrain himself, and should not seek a following or cause contempt of anyone. Such censuring improves no one, but only panders to the rabble and satisfies the critic's appetite.

Please communicate this to the honorable city council on my behalf, and on behalf of the [other] preachers, and yourself. Take diligent care of this matter, for Satan never sleeps, but constantly strives to cause misery.

With this I commend you to God. Amen.

March 29, 1527

172

To Wenceslas Link[1]
[Wittenberg, about May 4,] 1527[2]

Luther is tartly commenting on Zwingli's latest letter and booklet the Amica exegesis. He evaluates a translation of the prophets which had been published in Worms, mentions his own work on the prophets, and reports on some family matters.

On Wenceslas Link, see LW 48, 169 f.

Text in Latin: WA, Br 4, 198.

Grace and peace!

The only news I have to write, my Wenceslas, is that Zwingli has sent me a letter[3] along with his most foolish booklet;[4] [the letter is] in his own handwriting, and is worthy of his haughty spirit. He raged, foamed, threatened, and roared with such "moderation"

---

[13] Luther wrote *Schwärmer;* see p. 94.

[1] The letter is extant only in printed form. Even though the address is already missing in the earliest witnesses, the content of the letter ("Wenceslas," Spengler, seeds) makes clear to whom Luther was writing.

[2] The approximate date of this letter can be established by comparing its content with Luther's letter to Spalatin dated May 4, 1527; see *WA*, Br 4, No. 1099.

[3] Ulrich Zwingli to Luther: April 1, 1527; *WA*, Br 4, No. 1092.

[4] Zwingli's answer to Luther's sermons (mentioned on p. 146, n. 22) was entitled: *Amica exegesis, id est expositio eucharistiae negotii* (*Friendly Exegesis, that is, an Exposition of the Eucharistic Problem*). It was published in February, 1527; *C. R. Zwingli Werke* 5, 562 ff.

that he seems to be incurable, and condemned by self-evident truth. My verbose booklet[5] has indeed profited many people.

I do not condemn the German translation of the prophets published in Worms,[6] except that the German is quite confusing, perhaps due to the local dialect. The translators were diligent,[7] but who can manage to do everything? I myself am now getting ready to translate the prophets into German,[8] and at the same time I shall lecture on Isaiah,[9] so that I may not be idle. Pray to the Lord for me, and for his church!

May Christ grant that I hear that a healthy child has been born to you.[10] Amen. My Katie has nausea again from a second pregnancy.[11] Greet Spengler[12] and thank him, for all the seeds you[13] sent us[14] have sprung up; only the melons and gourds have not, although they, too, are sprouting—but only in other people's gardens.

Farewell.

1527   MARTIN LUTHER

---

[5] See p. 146, n. 22.

[6] This is the so-called Worms translation of the prophets published in Worms in April of 1527. It was the work of Ludwig Hätzer (see *The Mennonite Encyclopedia* 2 [Scottdale, Pa., 1956], 621 ff.) and Hans Denck (see p. 96, n. 1). For bibliographical information, see G. Baring (ed.), *Hans Denck, Schriften* 1, *Bibliographie* (Gütersloh, 1955), 32 ff. Through his own work in translating the prophets Luther acquired a less favorable opinion of this Worms translation; see *WA* 30[II], 640; *LW* 35, 194. On Luther and this Worms translation of the prophets, see also *WA*, DB 11[II], cxiii ff.; G. Krause, *Studien zu Luther's Auslegung der Kleinen Propheten* (Tübingen, 1962), pp. 15 ff. Since Denck had run into difficulties in Nürnberg because of his strong spiritualistic tendencies (see pp. 96 ff.), there was a movement in Nürnberg, which finally succeeded, to prohibit the sale of the Worms translation; see George Regel to Ulrich Zwingli: May 15, 1527; *C. R. Zwingli Werke* 9, 133 ff. Had Link asked Luther for an opinion on this matter? Or was Luther just reporting on his first impression of the work?

[7] This is perhaps a reference to the statement made in the preface by the translators to the effect that they used all diligence possible; see also Enders, *Briefwechsel* 6, 47, n. 5.

[8] See *WA*, DB 2, xi f., 512; 11[II], xiv ff.

[9] From May 1528 to 1529/30, Luther periodically lectured on Isaiah; see pp. 175, n. 26; 181; *WA* 25, 79 ff.; 31[II], vii ff.; *WA*, Br 13, 89, to *WA*, Br 4, 198, n. 5; *WA*, DB 11[II], xix ff.; *ARG* 45 (1954), 209 ff.

[10] See p. 166.

[11] See p. 181.

[12] Lazarus Spengler; see *LW* 48, 184.

[13] "You" singular.

[14] See p. 158. Apparently Spengler had also sent seeds; hence Link was to express Luther's appreciation to Spengler. The singular "you" suggests that Spengler shipped the seeds to Luther either together with those of Link, or by means of a messenger dispatched by Link.

173

To Wenceslas Link[1]
[Wittenberg,] July 5, 1527

This is a letter of one family man to another. Luther is congratulating Link on the birth of a daughter. He expresses his appreciation for tools and gifts sent by his friends in Nürnberg, and tells Link of his gardening efforts. Luther offers to send copies of some of his books to Nürnberg as a token of his friendship, and gives some information on his business relationship with his printers.

On Wenceslas Link, see LW 48, 169 f.

Text in Latin: WA, Br 4, 220. The following translation is based on S-J 2, 402–403.

Grace and peace

I congratulate you on the birth of your daughter Margaret, who has been given to you as a gift of God. I have looked forward to this with great eagerness so that you, too, might experience "the natural affection of parents for their children;" see how suddenly I have become a barbarous Greek.[2]

By the way, we have received[3] the tools for the lathe, together with the quadrant and the clock.[4] I shall try to give you an idea

---

[1] The letter is extant only in printed form. The address is already missing in the earliest witness. The content (Link's daughter, the gifts from Nürnberg, the seeds) makes clear, however, to whom Luther was writing.

[2] The material in quotation marks is written in Greek by Luther and may have been a quotation.

[3] As early as May 19, 1527, Luther had confirmed the receipt of this whole shipment; see WA, Br 4, 203. On the tools for the lathe and garden seeds, see pp. 158, 165.

[4] On April 22, 1527, Luther thanked a certain Frederick Pistorius in Nürnberg for a clock sent to him by Link on behalf of Pistorius; see WA, Br 4, No. 1096; S-J 2, No. 756. The "quadrant" was an instrument for measuring altitudes in astronomy and navigation. It is not clear who sent this instrument. Was it attached to Pistorius' clock? This is suggested by Luther's letter of May 19 (see note 3) in which Luther also mentioned a quadrant. Further, it could not be established whether the tools for the lathe, quadrant, clock, and seeds came in one shipment, or in separate shipments.—Frederick Hass (1485–1553), or Pistorius, was the last abbot of the St. Aegidius Benedictine monastery in Nürnberg. In July of 1525 he turned the administration of the monastery over to the city council. He continued to live in the monastery and to use the title "abbot." Luther dedicated his *Confitemini* to Pistorius.

of my cup, but it could not be done quickly.[5] Give Nicholas Endrisch[6] many greetings [from me]; tell him he should feel free to ask me for copies of any of my books [which he may want]. For we, too,[7] are very poor as far as money goes, but I make use of a certain modest claim on the printers. Since I take nothing from them for my various works,[8] I occasionally take a copy of a book if I want to. I think [the printers] owe this to me, since other authors, and even translators, receive a gulden for a fascicle. Therefore I have ordered my Wolfgang[9] to get at once whichever of my books poor Endrisch may ask for; he can count on this.

Farewell to you and all of yours. The melons, or pumpkins, are growing and want to take up an immense amount of space;[10] so do the gourds and watermelons. Don't think you sent the seeds in vain! Again farewell.

July 5, 1527   MARTIN LUTHER

174

To Nicholas Hausmann
[Wittenberg,] July 13, 1527

Luther is briefly giving his opinion on a particular marital situation. He also tells Hausmann that the visitations have begun, phi-

---

[5] This sentence is not clear. Luther apparently had a cup. Had he made it with the tools sent by Link? Had Link asked him for a sketch so that a similar cup could be made in Nürnberg for Link? Or had Link, upon an inquiry made by Luther, written that a cup could be made in Nürnberg, but that a sketch was necessary? See also WA, Br 11, 327, to WA Br 4, 221, n. 2.

[6] This is apparently the former Nürnberg Carmelite Nicholas Endrisch, or Eudrisch, who in 1515 had matriculated at the University of Wittenberg. Since May of 1525 the Nürnberg Carmelite monastery had been dissolved. This could have caused some hardship for "poor" Endrisch. Apparently Endrisch had asked Luther for a copy of one of his books, and had explained this request by pointing to his own poverty. On Endrisch, see M. Simon (ed.), *Nürnbergisches Pfarrerbuch* (Nürnberg, 1965), No. 298.

[7] I.e., just as Endrisch.

[8] In contrast to Erasmus, e.g., who "lived" from his writing, Luther was proud that he neither demanded nor received any author's fees.

[9] Wolfgang Seberger; see p. 158, n. 7.

[10] See p. 165.

*losophizes over the sacking of Rome, extends the greetings of his
family, and mentions a severe fainting spell he has had.*
   On Nicholas Hausmann, see LW 48, 399 f.
   Text in Latin: WA, Br 4, 222.

To the venerable and devout[1] man, Mr. Nicholas Hausmann, pastor
   of the congregation[2] at Zwickau, my superior in the Lord

Grace and peace. If that man's case is as he described it, my Nicholas, then I think he may lawfully keep this wife, since the former
husband deserted her such a long time ago and exposed himself
and her, too, to all kinds of danger. This is my opinion in this case.[3]

   The visitation has begun. Eight days[4] ago Dr. Hero[5] and
Master[6] Philip[7] set out upon this work. May Christ guide them.
Amen.

---

[1] Literally: "holy."
[2] Luther wrote *ecclesia;* see p. 61, n. 9.
[3] Nothing could be established about the background of this paragraph.
[4] At the beginning of July, 1527, the visitations of the parishes of Electoral
Saxony (outside the *Kur-Kreis;* see p. 106, n. 3) finally began; see pp. 159 f.
According to *C. R.* 1, 880, the Wittenberg members of the visitation commission left Wittenberg on July 5; see *WA, Br* 4, 222, n. 2.
[5] It is not clear whom Luther identified as *"D. Hero."* It could be Jerome
Schurf of Wittenberg (see *LW* 48, 219, n. 2), so that *"D. Hero"* would be
an abbreviation for *"Doctor Hieronymus."* Since Schurf was a member of the
visitation commission (see *WA, Br* 4, 222, n. 1) and lived in Wittenberg, he
very likely was the *"D. Hero"* who set out from Wittenberg with Melanchthon.
On the other hand, *"Hero"* could be a corruption of *heros* (demi-god, hero,
knight), so that Luther would be thinking here of one of the Electoral administrative officials (knights or noblemen) who participated in the visitations. On
April 11, 1528, Luther mentioned to Hausmann *"Heroem a Plawnitz,"* i.e.,
Hans von der Planitz; see *WA, Br* 4, 440. Since von der Planitz (see p. 24,
n. 21) was also a member of the visitation commission, Luther could be referring here to him, in which case *"D. Hero"* would mean *"Dominus Hero,"*
i.e., Sir Knight.
[6] I.e., Master of Arts.
[7] Philip Melanchthon; see *LW* 48, 77, n. 3. Melanchthon summarized his ex-
periences during this first part of the visitations, and made suggestions for
conducting the program and improving the conditions existing in the parishes
in his *Articuli de quibus egerunt per visitatores in regione Saxoniae (Articles
Which Were Dealt with by the Visitors in the Territory of Saxony),* which
was at once printed, even though Melanchthon did not authorize it. In the
summer, Wittenberg University was evacuated to Jena to escape the plague
(see p. 175, n. 26); from here Melanchthon and others visited the parishes of
western Thuringia. Parallel to his fieldwork, Melanchthon wrote his *Unterricht
der Visitatoren (Instructions for the Visitors).* He had finished this work by
the end of August and turned it over to the Elector, who forwarded it to

Rome and the pope have been terribly laid waste.[8] Christ reigns in such a way that the emperor who persecutes Luther for the pope is forced to destroy the pope for Luther. It is evident that all things serve Christ and those who belong to him, and [are directed] against their enemies. Otherwise there is nothing new.

My Katie and little John[9] send greetings. Farewell in Christ. I have had a severe fainting spell,[10] so that even now my head compells me[11] to abstain from reading and writing.

July 13, 1527   MARTIN LUTHER

175

To Elector John
[Wittenberg,] September 16, 1527

One of the problems with which the Reformers were constantly confronted was the question of what to do with ecclesiastical properties, or endowments, which could no longer be used for the purpose for which they had once been intended or used. The Ordinance for a Common Chest was one way of handling this problem.[1] In this letter Luther is asking the Elector's help in changing the deserted Franciscan monastery in Wittenberg into an asylum for the poor and sick.

On Elector John, see LW 48, 269, n. 8.

Text in German: WA, Br 4, 248. The following translation, with minor changes, is by Theodore G. Tappert, and is used by

---

Luther, who, in turn, made some corrections; it was finally published in February/March of 1528, together with a preface by Luther; see *Melanchthon, Studienausgabe* 1, 215 ff.; *WA* 26, 195 ff.; *LW* 40, 263 ff. See also Manschreck, pp. 137 ff.

[8] This is a reference to the sack of Rome, the conquest and plundering of Rome by the Imperial army on May 6, 1527; see Ranke 1[II], 236 ff.; Elton, p. 344.

[9] John Luther; see p. 152, n. 7.

[10] On July 6 Luther suffered from a spiritual *Anfechtung* (see *LW* 48, 28, n. 10), which was followed by severe illness; see *WA*, Br 4, 221, and *ibid.*, n. 4.

[11] Literally: "my head is compelled to abstain."

[1] See pp. 28 ff.

permission from LCC 18, 324–325. Published 1955, The Westminster Press.

To my Most Gracious Lord, Duke John, elector in Saxony, etc.,
to his Electoral Grace: *Personal*

Grace and peace in Christ Jesus! Most Serene, Noble Sovereign, Most Gracious Lord: Your Electoral Grace recently gave the city council of Wittenberg permission to use the local Franciscan monastery as a refuge for the sick.[2] Accordingly, we—the Pastor[3] and I—together with the city council, inspected it and discovered that Gregory Burger[4] has secured from Your Electoral Grace the best and most useful parts, such as the well, cistern, bathrooms, brewhouse, and other important rooms and areas, without which the rest of the monastery can be of little use. When we spoke to him about this, he indicated his willingness to abandon the property for the sake of the poor people and in the hope that Your Electoral Grace might grant him another property in return.

Inasmuch as even the burial places of both Jews and Gentiles are held in great honor, and since this monastery is an old burial site for sovereigns,[5] [this monastery] cannot be put to better use than to set it aside for the service of God and of poor people, in whom Christ himself is served. Therefore, together with the city

---

[2] For the background, see *LJB* 9 (1927), 105; *WA*, Br 13, 93, to *WA* Br 4, 248 (not 249 as in the text), n. 1. On February 21, 1526, Luther reported to the Elector on the miserable condition of the Wittenberg Franciscan monastery and the poverty of the few friars who existed there. See *WA*, Br 4, No. 983. Soon the monastery was completely deserted, and the city council asked the Elector for permission to use the monastery as an asylum for the poor and sick. Gregory Burger (see note 4) had been faster, however, and already in early 1526 had secured for himself some of the choice buildings and assets of the monastery. On August 21, 1527, the Elector finally granted the city council's request; the monastery was to become an asylum for those poor people who were not afflicted by contagious diseases (leprosy, syphilis); see *WA*, Br 4, 248, n. 1.

[3] I.e., John Bugenhagen; see *LW* 48, 303, n. 44.

[4] From 1520 to 1522, Gregory Burger was the *Schösser* (see p. 9, n. 4, and thereafter was the *Gleitsmann* (see *LW* 48, 397, n. 7) in Wittenberg; on Gregory Burger, see *WA*, Br 3, 302, n. 4; 4, 249, n. 2.

[5] The chapel of the Wittenberg Franciscan monastery had served as a burial site for the old ruling Saxon family, the Ascanians. In 1435 Barbara, the wife of Elector Rudolph III, was buried there; she was the last to be buried there. See Enders, *Briefwechsel* 6, 90, n. 5; *WA*, Br 13, 93, to *WA*, Br 4, 249, n. 3.

council, I humbly request Your Electoral Grace to appoint and give the monastery, including Gregory Burger's areas and buildings, to our Lord Jesus Christ as an asylum and home for his poor members (for he says: "What you do to the least of my brethren you do to me").[6] Further, [I humbly request Your Grace] also earnestly to command the council to put the monastery into usable condition without damaging it, lest in time grasping hands should fall upon it and tear it down.[7]

Herewith I commend Your Electoral Grace to God. Amen.

September 16, 1527   Your Electoral Grace's dedicated

MARTIN LUTHER

176

To Justus Jonas[1]
[Wittenberg, about November 10, 1527][2]

In the first half of this letter Luther expresses his grief over the bitter attacks made against him by Erasmus and the sacramentarians, and meditates on the meaning of this for him. Then he reports on the situation caused by the plague in Wittenberg: he is worried about his wife, due soon to deliver their second child; he tells of the illness of his son John; and he mentions some friends he has taken in. He reports some of the affairs of Christian Goldschmidt, and mentions his desire to complete the work on Ecclesiastes.

On Justus Jones, see LW 48, 275, n. 3.

Text in Latin: WA, Br 4, 279–280.

---

[6] Matt. 25:40.

[7] On October 11 the Elector ordered the city council to put the monastery into good condition and make it available to the poor. For unknown reasons, however, the monastery was not made a part of the Common Chest (see note 1) until 1535. See WA, Br 4, 249, n. 6, and WA, Br 13, 93, *ad loc.*

[1] The letter is extant only in printed form. The address is already missing in the earliest witness; but since Luther mentioned the addressee in the letter it is clear to whom he was writing.

[2] For the date of this letter, see note 20.

Grace and peace in the Lord Jesus, the Savior!

I thank you, my Jonas, that you pray for us and occasionally write us a letter. I believe that the letter which I sent yesterday[3] has reached you in the meantime.

I have not yet read Erasmus[4] or the sacramentarians,[5] except about three fascicles of Zwingli's book.[6] These people are right in despising me, miserable one that I am, to follow the example set by Judas. They also force me to lament with Christ: "He persecuted the poor and needy, and the brokenhearted to his death."[7] For I am enduring God's wrath because I have sinned against him.[8] Pope and emperor, sovereigns and bishops, and the whole world hate and attack me; and this is not enough, even my brothers torment me, so that my sins, death, and Satan with all his angels rage[9] without ceasing. What could save and console me if Christ, too, should abandon me, [he] for whose sake they all hate me? But up to the end Christ will not abandon me, the most miserable sinner; for I consider myself to be the least of all men.[10] Oh, that

---

[3] For this letter see note 20.

[4] See p. 153, n. 3. Luther made a similar statement on October 27; see *WA, Br* 4, 272.

[5] This is a reference to Zwingli's and Oecolampadius' replies to Luther's book which is cited on p. 153, n. 2. The title of Oecolampadius' book was *Luther's Incorrect Interpretation of the Eternally True Words "This is my Body" Will Not Stand Up to Criticism*, which was published in June of 1527. Luther made a similar statement on the books of the sacramentarians in his letter to Justus Menius, dated August 12, 1527; *WA, Br* 4, 229. Apparently at that date Luther had not yet seen the works by Oecolampadius and Zwingli; see *WA, Br* 4, 235.

[6] I.e., Ulrich Zwingli's book *These Words of Christ "This is my Body which is given for you" Will Retain Their Only and Original Meaning*, published in June of 1527; *C. R. Zwingli Werke* 5, 805 ff. Luther had known of Zwingli's book at least since August 12, 1527; see note 5. By November 1 he definitely had a copy, loaned to him by von Amsdorf. On that day he also mentioned a reply which he had to delay because of illness; *WA, Br* 4, 275. In the first days of November he studied Zwingli's book, and had finished three signatures, or fascicles, by the time he wrote to Jonas. Already on November 22 he reported to Link that he was answering the enthusiasts with the "confession of my faith"; *WA, Br* 4, 284; *S-J* 2, 424. At the end of March, 1528, he published his *Vom Abendmahl Christi, Bekenntnis* (*Confession Concerning Christ's Supper*), *WA* 26, 261 ff; *LW* 37, 151 ff.

[7] Ps 109:16.

[8] Micah 7:9.

[9] II Cor. 12:7.

[10] See I Cor. 4:9.

God would grant—and again [I say], oh, that God would grant—
that Erasmus and the sacramentarians could experience the anguish
of my heart for only a quarter of an hour! How surely would I
then declare them to be most genuinely converted and healed.
Now my enemies are strong and alive; they even add grief upon
grief,[11] and persecute him whom God has smitten.[12] But this is
enough—lest I be one who complains about and is impatient with
God's rod, for he smites and heals, kills and makes alive,[13] and is
blessed in his holy and perfect will. It is impossible that one whom
the world and its ruler[14] hate so much would not be pleasing to
Christ. If we were of the world, the world would love its own.[15]

I am concerned about the delivery of my wife,[16] so greatly
has the example of the Deacon's wife terrified me.[17] But He who
is mighty has done great things for me;[18] and so the endurance
of great things also is required of me. May my Christ, whom I
have purely taught and confessed, be my rock and fortress. Amen.

My little John cannot now send his greetings to you because
of his illness,[19] but he desires your prayers for him. Today is the
twelfth day that he has eaten nothing;[20] he has been somehow

---

[11] See Phil. 2:27.
[12] Ps. 69:26 f.
[13] Deut. 32:39; see also Isa. 9:4.
[14] I.e., Satan; see John 12:31.
[15] John 15:19.
[16] See pp. 165, 181.
[17] Hanna, the wife of the Wittenberg deacon George Rörer (on Rörer, who
was one of the collectors of Luther's works, see Enders, *Briefwechsel* 6, 112,
n. 8; *ADB* 53, 480 ff.; *Die Religion in Geschichte und Gegenwart* 5 [3rd ed.;
Tübingen, 1961], 1149), and a sister of John Bugenhagen (see LW 48, 303,
n. 44), had come down with the plague and passed away on November 2,
shortly after she gave birth to a stillborn child. This event was a great shock
to Luther and his friends; see also WA, Br 4, 276 (dated November 4). Apparently there would have been a slight possibility of saving the child's life by
a caesarian; WA, Br 4, 275, 276. According to WA, Br 4, 275, n. 13, it was
a custom to perform a caesarian on a dead woman; caesarian operations on a
living woman, however, were not performed prior to the sixteenth century.
[18] Luke 1:49.
[19] Luther was not certain whether his son John (see p. 152, n. 7) was
suffering from the plague or was teething; see WA, Br 4, 275, 276. In view of
the length of the boy's illness the former seems to be more probable; at least
on November 7 Luther counted John among the people in his house who
were afflicted with the plague; WA, Br 4, 277.
[20] This statement supplies information for establishing the date of this letter.
In a letter to von Amsdorf written on November 1, Luther mentioned that
John had been ill for three days; WA, Br 4, 275. On November 4 Luther re-

sustained only by liquids. Now he is beginning to eat a little bit. It is wonderful to see how this infant wants to be happy and strong as usual, but he cannot because he is too weak.

Yesterday the abscess of Margaret von Mochau was operated on.[21] Since the pus has drained away[22] she is beginning to feel better. I have confined her in our usual winter room, while we are living in the big front hall. Hänschen[23] is staying in my bedroom, while the wife of Augustine [Schurf][24] is staying in his.[25] We hope

---

ported to Jonas that John had been ill for eight days (WA, Br 4, 276), and on November 7, he said that John had now been ill for over eight days; WA, Br 4, 277. According to these dates, John became sick on about October 28 or 29. In the present letter to Jonas Luther mentions that John has been ill for twelve days, which would date this letter November 9 or 10. This raises the question of the no-longer extant letter to Jonas, mentioned at the beginning of this letter. Luther says that he had sent a letter "yesterday." The WA, Br editor argues that this letter is no longer extant; so does Rückert, LB, p. 216, n. 18. Enders does not deal with the matter at all. L. de Wette (Dr. Martin Luthers Briefe, Sendschreiben und Bedenken [Berlin, 1827] 3, 220) suggests that the letter which Luther says he sent "yesterday" might be the one of November 4 (WA, Br 4, No. 1165). This suggestion jeopardizes the approximate date established for this present letter (ca. November 10), as de Wette pointed out. This need not be the case, however, if one considers that Luther could very well have written to Jonas on November 4, but—in view of the plague situation—could not send off the letter until "yesterday," i.e., ca. November 9. Another possibility would be to assume that Luther's memory tricked him—a good possibility—and that "yesterday" is not to be taken literally. In the opinion of this editor, the letter to Jonas mentioned by Luther at the beginning of this letter of ca. November 10 is the one of November 4 (WA, Br 4, No. 1165). A comparison of the content of the letters of November 4 and that of ca. November 10 could substantiate this assumption in more detail. See also note 29.

[21] Margaret von Mochau was a sister-in-law of Andrew Karlstadt (see LW 48, 79, n. 12); see H. Barge, Andreas Bodenstein von Karlstadt (2nd ed.; Nieuwkoop, 1968), 2, 18, n. 38; 1, 364. She was taken in by the Luther family when the plague became increasingly severe.

[22] Literally: "pure pestilence having been drained away."

[23] I.e., John Luther. This word is written in German. See also p. 323, n. 7.

[24] Anne, the daughter of the mayor of Torgau, Matthew Moschwitz, was married to Augustine Schurf in approximately 1522. Augustine Schurf (the brother of Jerome Schurf; see LW 48, 219, n. 2) had been teaching medicine in Wittenberg since 1521, and performed the first dissection of a human head at Wittenberg University. On Augustine Schurf, see ARG 7 (1909/10), 360 ff.

[25] On the rooms of the Luther house (which was the former Augustinian monastery), see ARG 17 (1920), 301 ff. Notwithstanding the danger involved, the Luthers took in people during this plague epidemic, even if they were sick, so that Luther said his home was beginning to be a hospital; WA, Br 4, 275. In addition to the people mentioned here, the Bugenhagens had moved in after November 2, having been greatly shocked by the dramatic passing of George Rörer's wife, who had died in the Bugenhagen home; WA, Br 4, 276.

for the end of the plague.[26] Farewell, and give a kiss to your son[27] and a hug to his mother[28] [from me], and remember us in your prayers.

To write some news,[29] I have seen the letter which the young

---

[26] It finally came. On November 22 Luther reported that the plague had disappeared; see WA, Br 4, 284. This seems to have been a somewhat overly optimistic statement; see WA, Br 4, 287 (November 29), 288 (December 13). But by December 10, the situation seems definitely to have improved; see WA, Br 4, 294.—It is difficult to say much about the plague epidemic without going into great medical details. The bubonic, pneumonic, and septicemic forms of the plague, the forms in which the plague occurred during the later Middle Ages and the sixteenth and seventeenth centuries, were highly contagious, and were accompanied by a high rate of mortality caused by a combination of intense fever, swellings, abscesses, and even paralysis. The plague broke out in Wittenberg in the summer of 1527. On August 15 the University was evacuated to Jena, and from there to Schlieben, near Wittenberg. It did not return to Wittenberg until April of 1528. See *Urkundenbuch,* Nos. 151–155; Köstlin-Kawerau 2, 171. Luther and his family and Bugenhagen (the city pastor) and his family remained in the plague-infested city (on the plague in Wittenberg, see also G. Buchwald, *Zur Wittenberger Stadt- und Universitäts-Geschichte in der Reformationszeit* [Leipzig, 1893], pp. 3 ff.), even though Luther himself was physically weak and had been urged by the Elector on August 10 to leave the city; WA, Br 4, No. 1127; S-J 2, No. 769. With both word and deed Luther ministered to the sick; he assisted the city council; he lectured (see p. 181) to a small group of students who for unknown reasons had not left town; and he wrote his beautiful long pastoral letter addressed to John Hess in Breslau (see LW 48, 143, n. 5), which is entitled: *Whether One May Flee From a Deadly Plague*; WA 23, 338 ff.; LW 43, 113 ff. Luther's actions during these months of danger and distress, together with this treatise, give some of the strongest testimony of Luther's understanding of the responsibilities a pastor has toward his flock, and a Christian toward his brother. Some scholars have argued that during these weeks of the plague, in which also the tenth "anniversary" of the posting of The Ninety-five Theses fell, Luther composed his A Mighty Fortress is Our God; see Enders, *Briefwechsel* 6, 112, n. 9. There are indeed striking similarities between the hymn and Luther's life and work in the plague-infested city. See, however, *Luther* 19 (1937), 4 ff.; PE 6, 306; LW 53, 283 ff.

[27] The text incorrectly reads *filiam,* i.e. daughter. Jonas had only a son, Justus, who was born on December 3, 1525; see WA, Br 3, 630, n. 1. Justus, who later brought much grief to his father (see Enders, *Briefwechsel* 7, 302, n. 4), was the second-born. A first-born son, John, died in the summer of 1527; see WA, Br 4, 232 (dated August 19); Kawerau, *Jonas Briefwechsel* 1, No. 102.

[28] On February 9, 1522, Jonas had married a certain Catherine Falcke (or Falck, or Falk), who died in 1542; see Enders, *Briefwechsel* 4, 98, n. 6; WA, Br 8, 446, n. 1.

[29] Luther apparently felt the information which he had communicated thus far was *not* "news," because in his November 4 letter to Jonas (WA, Br 4, No. 1165) he had told Jonas much of what he tells in this present letter. A closer examination of both letters could substantiate the argument that in the letter of *ca.* November 10, Luther brings Jonas up to date by continuing to report on those events which he had mentioned for the first time on November 4.

man, the brother of Mrs. Christian Goldschmidt,[30] has written. In this letter he states that he is engaged to Dorothy Falken[31] for a stable and true marriage, if [the relatives] on both sides give their permission, and asks his sister and Christian for advice and help. I do not know what should be done in this case. You can tell this to his sister,[32] as a certain piece of news.

I do not want Rome to be burned, for that would be a great monstrosity.[33] I wish that we could live together again,[34] and could publish our work on Ecclesiastes before we die.[35] Remember me in your prayers. Christian and his family had moved to Berlin[36] but Margrave Joachim[37] ordered him out of his whole territory on

---

[30] The wife of Christian Düring (see LW 48, 42, n. 8), or Goldschmidt, was a certain Barbara Blankenfeld. She was a grand-daughter of Thomas Blankenfeld, who had been mayor of Berlin several times. See WA, Br 3, 514, n. 4, and WA, Br 13, 74 ad loc.; 4, 280, n. 22. Apparently she had a brother, who had written to the Goldschmidts, and Luther had seen this no-longer extant letter. This brother could be identical with John Blankenfeld of Berlin, who had matriculated in Wittenberg in 1516; see WA, Br 4, 280, n. 22.

[31] A certain Caspar Falk, or Falcke, was a brother-in-law of Jonas; WA, Br 8, 446, n. 1. Did Dorothy Falken have any relation to this Caspar Falk and thus to Jonas?

[32] The text does not make clear whose sister this was supposed to be; one can assume, however, that it was another sister of John Blankenfeld, who indeed had at least two more sisters; see WA, Br 3, 514, n. 4 and WA, Br 13, 74, ad loc. But did any one of them live in Nordhausen, where Jonas lived at that time? Or does one have to think of a sister of Christian Goldschmidt?

[33] See p. 169. This passage could also be translated: ". . . for that would be a momentous omen." But "omen" of what? The answer closest at hand would be that "omen" was intended to be connected with God's judgment over the world, and thus with the end of this world. According to WA, Br 4, 223, n. 4, the author of a contemporary pamphlet (not available to this editor) saw in the sack of Rome God's judgment over the papacy.

[34] In the middle of August Jonas and his family had gone to Nordhausen to escape the plague and also to take care of some private matters. See WA, Br 4, 232, 268. Jonas stayed there till the end of January, 1528. See Kawerau, Jonas Briefwechsel 1, Nos. 107, 121, 122.

[35] In the summer and fall of 1526 Luther had lectured on Ecclesiastes; WA, Br 4, 110, 122. These lectures were not published until 1532, and then were published by some of Luther's friends (and only on the basis of students' notes); WA, 20, 1 ff. It is not clear what role Jonas (who was living in Nordhausen) was to play in this project. Was he to be the editor? Was he to supply a German translation? Had Luther discussed this translation with him? The latter possibility seems logical, since Jonas did indeed publish, in 1533, a German translation of these lectures; see WA 20, 4.

[36] The aunt of Christian Düring's wife (see note 30), Catherine Hornung, lived in Berlin as a mistress of Margrave Joachim I; see WA, Br 4, No. 1179, Introduction. See also p. 326, n. 11.

[37] Margrave Joachim I, elector of Brandenburg and one of Luther's earliest foes, afraid that the plague would be brought to his territory, expelled the

the same day, under the pretext of the danger of the plague. Behold the wickedness of Satan and men! Thus we Wittenbergers are the object of hate, disgust, and fear of all, as the Psalmist says: "A reproach of men and despised by the people,"[38] but (we hope) "the crown and joy"[39] of angels and saints. Amen.

MARTIN LUTHER, dirt for Christ's sake[40]

177

To John Brenz
Torgau,[1] November 28, 1527

With this letter Luther begins his correspondence with John Brenz. He extends greetings and expresses his pleasure that Brenz is walking so steadfastly in the way of truth and maintaining the true teaching concerning the Lord's Supper.

John Brenz (1499–1570) met Luther for the first time at the Heidelberg Disputation in 1518,[2] and saw him again at the Marburg Colloquy in 1529.[3] In 1522 Brenz gradually introduced the Reformation in Schwäbisch Hall, where on Christmas Day, 1525, the first evangelical Lord's Supper was celebrated, and where Brenz organized the Reformation by creating an evangelical church ordinance in 1526.[4] From 1534 Brenz was responsible for guiding the development of the Reformation in the Duchy of Württemberg. After the Smalcaldic War, Brenz had to flee from Schwäbisch Hall in 1548 in order to avoid imprisonment. Christopher, the duke of Württemberg, called Brenz back and appointed him to the position

---

Dürings. Luther interpreted this as an act of hostility toward his city of Wittenberg.

[38] Ps. 22:7.

[39] Phil. 4:1.

[40] Literally: "Christ's mud." For "dirt" Luther wrote *lutum,* and this was obviously a pun on his name.

[1] See note 22.

[2] See *LW* 48, 60 ff.

[3] See pp. 234 ff.

[4] Text: Richter, *op. cit.* (see p. 29, n. 5), 1, 40 ff.; on this ordinance, see also M. Brecht, *Kirchenordnung und Kirchenzucht in Württemberg vom 16. bis zum 18. Jahrhundert* (Stuttgart, 1967), pp. 11 ff.

of supreme superintendent in 1553; and in 1559 Brenz undertook a complete reorganization of the church in Württemberg on the basis of a church ordinance which he had drafted. From the days of the Heidelberg Disputation until the end of his life, Brenz was a staunch adherent of Luther's teachings. In the controversy on the Lord's Supper he sided with Luther, and through the Syngramma Suevicum[5] swung the northern areas of Württemberg to Luther's position. He was no blind follower of Luther, however, and consequently he searched for new ways of expressing the concerns of Luther, ways which could unite the diverse Lutheran territorial churches of Germany. On John Brenz, see O.D.C.C., p. 195; NDB 2, 598 f.

Text in Latin: WA, Br 4, 285–286.

To my very dear brother and lord in Christ, John Brenz, a devout[6] disciple of Christ and a faithful preacher of the congregation in Schwäbisch Hall

Grace and peace in Christ Jesus, our Lord! My dearest Spalatin[7] has shown me your letter to him.[8] I have certainly read it with joy, my Brenz, seeing that the grace of God lives in you through Christ, his Son, because you serve and teach the Word of God in such a steadfast and faithful way in the midst of this wicked and perverse nation.[9] Blessed be God and the Father of our Lord Jesus Christ,[10] who permits me, in the midst of so many evil things,

---

[5] See p. 145, n. 18.
[6] Literally: "holy."
[7] George Spalatin; see LW 48, 8 f.
[8] For Brenz's letter to Spalatin, dated September 29, 1527, see O. Clemen, *Beiträge zur Reformationsgeschichte* 2 (Berlin, 1902), 108 f. In this letter, Brenz wrote that even though he would like to write to Luther directly, he was hesitant to do so in view of Luther's busy schedule; Spalatin would therefore do him a great favor if he gave Luther his greetings. When Luther was in Torgau at the end of November (see note 22), Spalatin showed the letter to Luther, who in turn wrote the present letter. Thus began a cordial friendship, which even though it was sometimes strained (especially during the Diet of Augsburg, 1530), lasted to the end of the Reformer's life. Brenz was grateful that Spalatin had opened up the friendship with Luther; see Brenz's April 15, 1532, letter to Spalatin, T. Pressel (ed.), *Anecdota Brentiana* (Tübingen, 1868), p. 121.
[9] Phil. 2:15.
[10] See e.g., II Cor. 11:31.

to see that at least some brethren are the true and right seed of Israel. Otherwise there are nothing but furious and raging monsters everywhere. We have thus far been holding Karlstadt in our bosom with sufficient kindness[11] with the reasonable hope that he might return to the [true] way; but day by day this poor man gets more hardened, although he is forced by his cowardice to be silent. He still holds on to his [exegesis of] "tuto,"[12] though it has been repudiated even by his own friends.[13] So great is [God's] wrath, when someone has[14] opposed the Word of God. I pray Christ to preserve you and your brethren with us in his purity and simplicity until the day of his glory. Amen.

Spalatin has wrung this letter out of me (although I wrote it willingly and spontaneously, he still did wring it out),[15] so that by writing letters I may gain your friendship. By the grace of God, we are already most closely united in spirit and in our way of thinking.[16] But you and your brethren pray that Christ may complete and perpetuate this joy among us.[17] Pomer[18] sends greetings; he is my only companion, since all others have gone because of fear of the plague.[19] Commend us, especially me, poor sinner, to your congregation, for Satan has been let loose upon me, and tries to tear me away from Christ through his devious manipulations in my private life, since he sees that he cannot tear me away from confessing the Word in public. I wonder what kind of a man Zwingli[20] is, since he is so ignorant of grammar and dialectic, to say nothing of the other [liberal] arts, yet ventures to boast of victories. That kind of glory quickly leads to embarrassment.

---

11 See p. 122, n. 11.

12 I.e., "This is my body. . . ." See also p. 88, n. 11.

13 Oecolampadius, in his book cited on p. 172, n. 5, criticized Karlstadt's exegesis of the Words of Institution. And Zwingli had criticized Karlstadt's position as early as 1524; see WA, Br 4, 286, n. 5; Rückert, LB, p. 221, n. 14.

14 According to some witnesses, one has to add "once."

15 See note 8. In the text, the parentheses are closed after "spontaneously."

16 Luther obviously arrived at this judgment on the basis of the Syngramma Suevicum (see note 5) and of Brenz's letter to Spalatin (see note 8).

17 See John 16:24.

18 I.e., John Bugenhagen; see LW 48, 303, n. 44.

19 See p. 175, n. 26.

20 Ulrich Zwingli; see p. 88, n. 12. Luther arrived at this judgment on the basis of his study of Zwingli's work cited on p. 172, n. 6.

Farewell to you, my very precious joy and crown[21] in Christ Jesus, our master and Lord, and also farewell to all the brethren.
Torgau, at Spalatin's,[22] *November 28, 1527*

Most cordially yours,[23]

MARTIN LUTHER

178

To Justus Jonas[1]
[Wittenberg,] December 10, 1527

Luther is happily announcing the birth of his daughter Elizabeth, and the recovery of the Wittenbergers from the plague. He details the suicide of a councilor of the Archbishop of Mainz, reports on his meeting with Melanchthon and Agricola in Torgau, and vents his anger over the preface to Emser's German translation of the New Testament. In a postscript he mentions rumors concerning the political and military developments in Europe.

On Justus Jonas, see LW 48, 275, n. 3.

Text in Latin: WA, Br 4, 294–295.

Grace and peace

---

[21] See Phil. 4:1.

[22] Luther and Bugenhagen were called by Elector John to Torgau for a conference with Melanchthon (see LW 48, 77, n. 3) and Agricola (see LW 48, 220). Agricola rejected the interpretation of the law which Melanchthon had developed in his writings on the visitations (see p. 168, n. 7). Luther was in Torgau from November 25–29 (see Buchwald, LK, p. 54) to settle this so-called first Antinomian controversy. Spalatin, who had a house in Torgau (see WA, Br 4, 286, n. 9, and WA, Br 13, 95, *ad loc.*), was also present. On this controversy, see WA, Br 4, 272; S-J 2, 418 f.; J. Rogge, *Johann Agricolas Lutherverständnis* (Berlin, 1960), pp. 114 ff.; *Die Religion in Geschichte und Gegenwart* 1 (3rd ed.; Tübingen, 1957), 452; LW 47, 102 f.

[23] Literally: "Your brother from the heart."

[1] The letter is extant only in printed form. Even though the address is already missing in the earliest witness, it is clear to whom Luther was writing since he sends greetings to little Justus, the son of Jonas; see below. And further, this letter is a continuation of letter No. 176. Finally, Jonas' answer to this present letter is extant; WA, Br 4, No. 1199; S-J 2, No. 787.

At this hour, ten o'clock, when I returned home from a lecture, I received your letter.[2] I had read only ten lines of it when at that very moment I was told that my Katie was delivered of a little daughter.[3] Glory and praise be to the Father in heaven. Amen. The mother in childbed is well but weak. And our little son John is also well and happy again; the wife of Augustine [Schurf] is well, too; and finally, Margaret von Mochau has, against all expectations, escaped death.[4] Instead of these people we have lost and given up five pigs.[5] May Christ, our own comfort, allow the plague to be content with this tribute, and cease. My own condition is just what it has been, namely, as the Apostle says: "As dead, and behold I live."[6]

Similar statements were said and written to us concerning Emser and Teutleben.[7] The affair of K.[8] is a long story. In sum-

---

[2] This letter by Jonas is not extant; obviously it must have been a reply to Luther's letters of the beginning of November (see p. 173, n. 20). Even though the University had been evacuated because of the plague (see p. 175, n. 26), Luther had continued his classroom work with a small group of students who, for reasons unknown, had remained in Wittenberg. From August 19 to November 7 he lectured on I John; from November 11 to December 13 on Titus; from December 16 to 18 on Philemon; see WA 20, 592; 48, 313; 25, 1; 48, 301; 25, 2.

[3] See pp. 165, 173. Elizabeth Luther was born around 9:00 A.M.

[4] See pp. 173 ff.

[5] The plague affected even the animals.

[6] II Cor. 6:9.

[7] Jerome Emser; see LW 48, 137, n. 19. See also note 21. Were Jonas' letter (mentioned in note 2) available, the background of this statement would be clearer. It seems to be certain, however, that among other things Jonas wrote about the death of Emser, about the Preface (see note 22), about news concerning a certain Teutleben, and in turn asked for information about "the affair of K." It is not clear who this Teutleben, or Tetleben, was. In connection with Luther, two brothers by this name are important. Caspar von Tetleben was teaching law at Wittenberg University, and was one of Luther's close friends. See Enders, Briefwechsel 7, 130, n. 1; WA, Br 5, 112, n. 1; TP, pp. 10 f. Valentin von Tetleben (one of Luther's bitter enemies), a councilor of Cardinal Albrecht of Mainz and the author of TP, became bishop of Hildesheim in 1536. See TP, 11 ff., esp. 30. What statements were made about "Teutleben" is unknown.

[8] This is apparently a reference to John Krause, a theological councilor of Cardinal Albrecht of Mainz (see LW 48, 44 f.). Together with other councilors, he received the Lord's Supper with bread and wine from a pastor George Winkler in Halle. After the Archbishop had prohibited this, Krause alone complied, while some of the other councilors protested. Luther and Melanchthon refer often to this suicide and the ways in which it was explained. For documentation and details, see Enders, Briefwechsel 6, 147, n. 9; WA, Br 4, 296, n. 8, and WA, Br 13, 96, ad loc.; P. Redlich, Kardinal Albrecht von Brandenburg und das neue Stift zu Halle (Mainz, 1900), p. 61.

mary [this is what happened]: He was cut up with eight wounds, of which only one was fatal. Some say that his conscience was disturbed because he had denied Christ, that is, [he wouldn't permit] the "two kinds"[9] to be distributed [in the Lord's Supper]. Others add that it was also because he had advised that George of Halle[10] be either killed or expelled. He had locked himself alone in his room, counted all his money, and made plans, and had written down how he wanted it used. In the morning when he was, as usual, called by his daughter, he refused to come out or to let her in. Asked whether something was wrong, he answered: "Much too much."[11] He was again called at lunchtime, but did not answer; when the door was broken down, see, he was lying dead on the steps leading to his bed, with his boots and topcoat on, next to a dagger. No wounds were to be seen, except one at the throat. After he was undressed, however, the other wounds in the chest and side could be seen. Who knows, maybe he repented at the final moment, since he passed away with such a sound mind and in such composed fashion?

Our famous discussion[12] at Torgau scarcely amounted to anything. The one topic, of which you have heard from Eisleben,[13] was discussed and soon settled, and we nicely agreed on everything. In a short time the whole visitation [material] will even be printed.[14] The most important thing that we accomplished was to burden the Sovereign[15] with expenses. The finest result, however, is the fact that the rumor or suspicion concerning a discord [among us] was buried [in Torgau]. God be praised and thanked for this! The reason why I didn't write you anything about this "tragedy"

---

[9] See LW 48, 143 f.

[10] This is apparently George Winkler, a preacher in Halle (see note 8), who at one time had been a protégé of Cardinal Albrecht. After Winkler had celebrated the evangelical Lord's Supper, and also had married, he was accused of heresy. Summoned to appear before the Archbishop's court, he was only reprimanded, but not removed from office. Returning from his trial, Winkler was ambushed and killed. For documentation, see WA, Br 4, 209, n. 4.

[11] This word is written in German.

[12] Literally: "discord." See p. 180, n. 22.

[13] I.e., John Agricola; see LW 48, 220.

[14] This is a reference to Melanchthon's Instructions for the Visitors, and perhaps also to his Articuli; see p. 168, n. 7.

[15] Elector John; see LW 48, 269, n. 8.

was that it actually didn't amount to anything, and that I didn't consider it of any consequence.[16]

I am glad that the tyranny of your stone[17] has been mitigated. I wish you could come here just to walk with me through town, so that you could see that the plague did no harm, thanks be to God. Only two are left in the hospital, and they are convalescing well. Neither the doctor nor the deacons[18] are busy with sick people in town, which of course is a definite sign that the plague has ceased.

Please give my respectful regards to Michael,[19] your host and mine. You cannot imagine how I rejoice that he has been allowed to be on the side of the Word. May Christ increase and perfect this, his gift in Michael, to his glory. Amen. Also tell [him] that I had considered writing a letter of sympathy to Duke George.[20] I was very angry that the name of their own Sovereign should be so shamelessly abused by those who live under his shadow. If those people were not willing to spare their own Sovereign, they at least ought to have had some respect for the honor of the common Saxon name and of the ruling family. For I am not pleased but disgusted when the name of a sovereign—even if he be my enemy—is so dishonorably and shamefully polluted by the eternal disgrace of that *Preface*.[21] But now since Emser is dead and

---

[16] Luther was wrong, as the second Antinomian controversy was to demonstrate.

[17] I.e., kidney stones.

[18] On October 19 Luther quite proudly reported to Jonas that of the forty people under the medical care of Master Bohemus only six had died; *WA, Br* 4, 269; *S-J* 2, 417. On this doctor, see Buchwald, *op. cit.* (p. 175, n. 26), pp. 10, 48. The deacons were George Rörer (see p. 173, n. 17) and John Mantel (see Enders, *Briefwechsel* 4, 294, n. 5; *WA, Br* 3, 248, n. 7).

[19] This is a reference to Michael Meienburg, who had been city clerk of Nordhausen since 1520, and who became mayor of that town in 1540; see *ADB* 52, 286 ff.; *WA, Br* 10, 102, n. 3. It cannot be determined when Luther was his guest. Clemen suggests (*WA, Br* 4, 296, n. 18) that during his visit in Nordhausen in the spring of 1525 (see p. 106; *WA, Br* 3, 479, n. 5) Luther might have stayed with Meienburg. Apparently Jonas, in his no-longer extant letter (see note 2), mentioned Meienburg as a source of some of the information concerning Emser, or the *Preface*, or Duke George (see notes 21, 22).

[20] Duke George of Saxony; see *LW* 48, 110, n. 20.

[21] Luther is referring here to the *Preface* of Emser's (see note 7) translation of the New Testament of 1527. This *Preface* was (supposedly) written by Duke George himself, yet Luther was "convinced" that the Duke's name was only added to give more weight to the *Preface* and to the translation which was endorsed in the *Preface*. Text: *Akten und Briefe* 2, 775 ff.; *St. L.* 19,

Duke George sick,[22] I have changed my mind.

Deacon John intends to move out of your house and return to the parsonage.[23] Pomer[24] will await his wife's confinement at my place. The students gradually return.[25] Dr. Jerome[26] expects to arrive around Christmas, if the situation with the plague remains the way it is now. May Christ gather us together again at one place. Amen. Even weddings are becoming more frequent here [again]. In the outlying fishermen's quarters nothing has been heard of the plague or of death for almost two months now.[27]

The Lord keep you, and shortly bring you and yours back to us. Amen. On my behalf greet little Justus and his mother, to whom I am also writing.[28] The grace of God be with you. Amen.

December 10, 1527   Yours,

MARTIN LUTHER

---

494 ff. Luther angrily rejects the idea that the Duke's name should have been used to "authorize" Emser's polemics against Luther's own translation of the New Testament. Consequently Luther wanted to write a letter expressing his "sympathy" for the Duke, whose name had been abused by Emser. Whether Luther here is sarcastic would depend on the depth of his conviction regarding the fact that Emser abused the Duke's name.

[22] Emser had died on November 8. The evangelicals saw in this death God's judgment, since the death had supposedly occurred while Emser was sitting at his desk writing a "poisonous" booklet against Luther; see Enders, *Briefwechsel* 6, 148, n. 17; WA, Br 4, 269, n. 21. Duke George was apparently seriously ill, since it was even rumored that he had passed away; see WA, Br 4, 297, n. 22.

[23] After the parsonage had been infested with the plague, and Rörer's wife had died (see p. 173), Bugenhagen moved in with the Luthers, and Luther moved Deacon John Mantel's family into Jonas' house, which had not yet been contaminated; WA, Br 4, 287. Mantel himself (and also Rörer) remained in the parsonage, apparently in order to avoid long contact with his family, and thus to lessen the chance of passing on the plague.

[24] I.e., John Bugenhagen; see LW 48, 303, n. 44. On December 31, Luther reported that a son, John, was born to Bugenhagen; WA, Br 4, 313. Just as Elizabeth Luther soon died (see p. 203, n. 4), so did John Bugenhagen, Jr. and a son of Deacon John Mantel; see WA, Br 4, 463, n. 6; Enders, *Briefwechsel* 6, 170, n. 5; 271, n. 5.

[25] The greater number of students had left town because of the plague (see p. 175, n. 26). Some had remained, and Luther had continued to lecture to them (see note 2), and others were now returning since the worst seemed to be over.

[26] Jerome Schurf; see LW 48, 219, n. 2.

[27] The plague apparently had broken out in July in the outlying sections of town, especially in the fishermen's quarters (WA, Br 4, 232; August 19); then it came into the town proper. Luther had already made a similar statement on November 4; WA, Br 4, 276.

[28] The letter mentioned here is not extant.

There is a rumor here that the Emperor has come to an understanding with the Pope and the Frenchmen, in which both the Englishmen and the Venetians are supposedly included.[29] Also, that the Turk is preparing an extremely extensive campaign. It is uncertain whether it will be directed against Apulia[30] or Hungary;[31] if against Hungary, it will certainly strike Germany with fear, and put Ferdinand[32] to flight.

179

To Justus Jonas
[Wittenberg,] December 30, 1527[1]

While asking for Jonas' prayer in his behalf, Luther mentions his spiritual trials and his longing for the companionship of his friends who have left the city because of the plague. He tells of the cessation of the plague and extends greetings. In a postscript Luther asks Jonas to return certain books written by the enthusiasts.

On Justus Jonas, see LW 48, 275, n. 3.

Text in Latin: WA, Br 4, 312.

---

[29] This is a reference to the peace negotiations between Charles V and Pope Clement VII, which were successfully concluded on November 26. See Ranke 2^{III}, 14. At that time there were no negotiations between the Emperor and the other members of the League of Cognac mentioned by Luther, namely, Venice and France, or between the Emperor and England which in April of 1527 had become an ally of the French (see Ranke 2^{III}, 10).

[30] I.e., southeast Italy, the "spur" and "heel" of the Italian "boot."

[31] Since the battle at Mohacs (August 29, 1526) the southeastern border of the Empire was vulnerable to an invasion by the Turks. Luther is here referring to rumors concerning the military preparations which eventually climaxed in the (unsuccessful) attack on Vienna in 1529.

[32] Ferdinand I; see LW 48, 217. Through the dynastic arrangement made by Maximilian I (Ferdinand's grandfather), Ferdinand obtained the right to succeed the Hungarian king after the latter's death in the battle at Mohacs. Thus Ferdinand became responsible also for the defense of Hungary against the Turks. This task was extremely difficult, since a large portion of the Hungarian people and nobility rejected Ferdinand as a foreigner and saw in John Zapolyai (the ruler of Transylvania) the champion of their nationalistic hopes. Zapolyai, in turn, was seeking coexistence with the Turks in an attempt to gain help against Ferdinand.

[1] For the date, see note 9.

To my dearest brother in Christ, Justus Jonas, a sincere servant of Christ in Nordhausen

Grace and peace in Christ! Please do not cease praying for and struggling along with me, my Jonas (for sometimes my spiritual trials are weaker, but in time they return with even greater violence),[2] so that Christ may not abandon me nor permit this[3] to be a torment of the ungodly people but [rather a testing] of his children, and that my faith may not cease to the end. If only you all were here again.[4] We have prayed to the Lord to avert the plague, and it does seem that we have been heard. Definitely no further cases of the plague are reported, not even in the outlying fishermen's quarters, and the air is pure and wholesome again.[5]

Pray also that [God] will glorify his Word among us, since it is exposed to danger and disgrace by our dispersion.[6] Satan and his followers rejoice that we are thus separated from each other. Greet all our friends, especially your Katie.[7] Pomer[8] sends many greetings; so does my Katie. Christ be with all of you, and with us. Amen.

December 30, 1528[9]

The books of the enthusiasts aren't available here yet.[10] Therefore you will do well if you return them to me.

MARTIN LUTHER

---

[2] The weeks of extreme tension, hardship, and misery, during which he himself became physically run-down and ill, coincided for Luther with a period of extreme spiritual trial (*Anfechtung;* see *LW* 48, 28, n. 10); see *WA, Br* 4, 299 (December 14), 288 (November 29), 275 (November 1).

[3] I.e., the trials and tribulations should be a means of testing, purifying, and maturing the faith of God's children.

[4] The impact of the plague scattered Luther's friends; see p. 175, n. 26.

[5] See p. 184.

[6] See note 4.

[7] "Your Katie," i.e., Jonas' wife Catherine, in contrast to "my Katie" in the following sentence.

[8] I.e., John Bugenhagen; see *LW* 48, 303, n. 44.

[9] Luther wrote "1528." Luther used a way of dating his letters in which the beginning of a year was figured differently than it is on a modern calendar.

[10] Since the beginning of November Luther had had two copies of Zwingli's work cited on p. 172, n. 6. One had been sent to him by von Amsdorf; Luther mentioned it on November 1 (*WA, Br* 4, 275), and *ca.* November 10 (see p. 172). The other, received on November 11 (*WA* 26, 261), either was purchased by Luther or was sent to him by the publisher, or even by the author.

180

To Nicholas von Amsdorf[1]
[Wittenberg,] April 16, [1528]

In this fragment of a letter Luther is requesting some information about von Amsdorf's visit to Goslar. He also reports on an action taken by the Duke of Bavaria against the sacramentarians, and tells of the recent marriage of Oecolampadius.

On Nicholas von Amsdorf, see LW 48, 218.

Text in Latin: WA, Br 4, 443.

If you are back from Goslar,[2] my A., I would enjoy knowing and wish to know what Christ has accomplished through you, or what Satan has prevented.

In upper Germany [Satan] rages unbelievably through the Anabaptists.[3] The Duke of Bavaria has ordered that my books

Somehow he received a copy, or copies, of Oecolampadius' book. At the end of December the books by the enthusiasts, i.e., Zwingli and Oecolampadius, were not yet available at the Wittenberg "bookstores." Whatever copies Luther had, he must have received through private channels. Apparently Luther had lent Jonas a copy of Zwingli's work and one of Oecolampadius' work. Luther now asks that Jonas return these copies; apparently Luther wanted them available when his friends finally returned to Wittenberg.

[1] The fragment is extant in one manuscript copy which has been edited by Gustav Kawerau in *Lutherstudien zur 4. Jahrhundertfeier der Reformation veröffentlicht von den Mitarbeitern der Weimarer Lutherausgabe* (Weimar, 1917), p. 9. Enders, *Briefwechsel* 17, 220 f., reproduces this text. The name of the person addressed by Luther is abbreviated with "A." This fact alone of course does not justify the assumption that von Amsdorf was the recipient of the letter. It is known, however, that von Amsdorf was in Goslar during the first quarter of 1528 attempting to organize an evangelical church there. When he met with some initial resistance he decided to leave (hence Luther's statement about Satan). However the congregation urged him to remain, so he stayed for three more weeks. On April 3, 1528, he again asked for permission to leave Goslar, and apparently returned to Magdeburg shortly before Easter (April 12). For documentation, see WA, Br 4, 443, n. 1. This material is sufficient justification for believing von Amsdorf to be the addressee of this letter, and for dating the letter in the year 1528. That Luther was the writer of this letter has been assumed since the earliest extant witness. This assumption is somewhat corroborated by the reference to the events in Bavaria.
[2] See note 1. Apparently von Amsdorf's visit to Goslar was more successful than either he or Luther had assumed. For on July 14, 1528, Luther reported to Link that Goslar had accepted the gospel; see WA, Br 4, 497.
[3] It is not clear whether Luther is thinking of the *Schwärmer* in general, or of the evangelical Anabaptists in particular. The reference to "my books against the sacramentarians" only complicates the problem. He could speak of "my

187

against the sacramentarians be sold and read throughout his terri-tory.[4] Thus I have become the protector even[5] of the papists, and they—who persecute me—defend themselves with my help. See the wonderful works of God!

On Laetare[6] Oecolampadius married a widow,[7] a wealthy one, they say. Good for him!

Do pray to Christ for me!

April 16[8]

---

books against the sacramentarians" only with reference to his writing against Zwingli (see pp. 146, n. 22; 153, n. 2), since he had published only one work which dealt specifically with the question of baptism as raised by the Anabaptists: *Von der Wiedertaufe, an zwei Pfarrherrn* (*A Letter to Two Pastors Concerning Rebaptism*) (Wittenberg: H. Lufft, February, 1528), WA 26, 144 ff.; LW 40, 229 ff. Or was Luther thinking that his *Against the Heavenly Prophets* was also directed against the Anabaptists? One could as-sume that here Luther was referring to the evangelical Anabaptists in partic-ular. Louis Hätzer was very active in upper Germany at this time, and in neighboring Austria Balthasar Hubmaier had been executed in Vienna on March 10, 1528. And from autumn of 1527 a strong Anabaptist movement had been active in Bavaria; see *Church History* 28 (1959), 367 ff.; *The Mennonite Encyclopedia* 1 (Scottdale, Pa., 1955), 251. But how then is the plural *books* to be explained?

[4] The background of this statement cannot be clarified. It seems highly dubious that Luther was correctly informed when he made this statement. William IV, one of the then ruling dukes of Bavaria, was a convinced papist and an op-ponent of Luther. Starting November, 1527, a wave of persecution of all non-conformists went over Bavaria. While the Anabaptists were especially hunted down, "there was no slackening in the campaign against real or alleged Lutherans" (*Church History* 28 [1959], 369), nor is any law or pronouncement known in which Luther's books were ordered to be sold in the duchy or read by the people of Bavaria. For details, see *Church History* 28 (1959), 367 ff.; *Zeitschrift für bayerische Kirchengeschichte* 30 (1961), 121 ff.; H. Rössler, *Geschichte und Strukturen der evangelischen Bewegung im Bistum Freising* (Nürnberg, 1966), pp. 7 ff.

[5] Luther considered himself to be "protector" only of the gospel.

[6] I.e., March 22, 1528. Luther does not seem to be correctly informed about the date of this wedding. According to Staehelin, *op. cit.* (see p. 43, n. 1), 2, 143, n. 1, the wedding took place sometime between March 12 and 15.

[7] John Oecolampadius (see LW 48, 230, n. 14) married Wilibrandis Rosen-blatt, widow of the Basel master craftsman Louis Keller, and daughter of a former colonel of the Imperial army.

[8] On the date, see note 1.

181

To Elector John
[Weimar, May 1 or 2, 1528]¹

After the successful ending of the first war of Charles V against France,² the Emperor was determined to put an end to the Reformation.³ The second war against France occupied him so much, however, that he was unable to concentrate on the events in Germany. As a result, the first Diet of Speyer in 1526 ended in a compromise so far as the cause of the Reformation was concerned.⁴ This was a chance for further development of the Reformation in Electoral Saxony, Hesse, Brandenburg-Ansbach, various northern German territories, and some Imperial cities. This progress of the Reformation was suddenly endangered through the political maneuvers of Landgrave Philip of Hesse,⁵ through which Germany was brought to the brink of war. The events which led to this point are shrouded in darkness, and sound like a cloak-and-dagger story.⁶ In 1528 Otto von Pack, an official of Duke George of Saxony,⁷ turned over a copy of a document to Philip of Hesse. This document (signed by the leading pro-papal Estates of the Empire on May 15, 1527, in Breslau) was intended to provoke the Estates which supported the Reformation to war against the papists, for it described an alliance of the most powerful pro-papal sovereigns of the Empire⁸ for the purpose of stamping out the Lutheran heresy by means of military force. What motivated von Pack is unclear.⁹

---

¹ For the place from which Luther wrote this letter and for its date, see note 15.
² See p. 125.
³ See pp. 155 f.
⁴ See note 3.
⁵ See p. 124, n. 18.
⁶ The events are called the Pack affair, or the Landgrave's campaign against the bishops. For details, see Ranke 2ᴵᴵᴵ, 23 ff.; Elton, p. 93; K. Dülfer, *Die Packschen Händel* (Marburg, 1958); for a substantial critique of Dülfer's book, see Fabian, *ESBV* (2nd ed.), pp. 33 ff., and esp. 338 ff.
⁷ See *LW* 48, 110, n. 20.
⁸ Ferdinand, archduke of Austria, king of Bohemia, viceroy of the Empire and brother of Emperor Charles V; the dukes of Bavaria and Saxony; the archbishops of Mainz and Salzburg; the bishops of Bamberg and Würzburg; the Elector of Brandenburg.
⁹ It seems that money played a major role in the transactions between von Pack and the Landgrave; see Fabian, *ESBV* (2nd ed.), p. 341.

It is further unclear whether Duke George or any other pro-papal sovereign had a hand in this transaction. All Estates which supposedly had joined in this Breslau League loudly denied having had anything to do with it, or ever having thought of such a plan.[10] Was the hotheaded Landgrave Philip responsible for this document? Was he attempting to create legal and moral justification for a surprise attack against the papists? Even though Philip protested such insinuations, there is strong evidence putting him behind the Pack affair.[11] After all was said and done, von Pack was blamed with having forged the document.[12]

With the news about this alliance Philip hurried to Electoral Saxony. On March 9 a military alliance was signed between the Landgrave and the Elector, and both territories mobilized and planned to begin a surprise war as early as June 1.[13] The matter developed further, and the Landgrave tried to make this date even earlier.[14] At the end of March the Electoral government consulted with Luther.[15] Although he could not know any of the circum-

---

[10] See Fabian, *ESBV* (2nd ed.), p. 34. Yet the Leagues of Regensburg and Dessau (see pp. 126, 119, n. 24) document that the pro-papal Estates of the Empire were indeed capable of developing such a plan.

[11] In contrast to Dülfer, who saw the culprit in von Pack, Fabian has suggested that the Landgrave might be the culprit; he also has convincingly demonstrated that, as early as December, 1527, the Landgrave was seriously considering a military action against some bishops. See Fabian, *ESBV* (2nd ed.), pp. 32 f., 339 f. And further, Herbert Grundmann (*Landgraf Philipp von Hessen auf dem Augsburger Reichstag 1530* [Gütersloh, 1959]) has sufficiently documented the fact that in political matters the Landgrave had a highly pragmatic approach to the question of truth. It is known that in the Pack affair, for example, Philip could stretch the truth so that it would fit his plans. In order to convince Elector John of Saxony of the danger of the situation, Philip affirmed that he had *seen* the *original* of the document, while as late as March 15 von Pack was still promising to send it to the Landgrave; see *WA*, Br 4, 430, n. 2.

[12] See p. 197.

[13] See *WA*, Br 4, No. 1246, Introduction to Document No. I.

[14] The Landgrave contacted Brandenburg-Ansbach and Nürnberg for help, and received only neutrality, or at best, concession; see Schornbaum, *Georg,* pp. 20 ff.

[15] Luther was confronted with the Pack affair for the first time when he was in Altenburg on March 19 and 20 for a meeting of the Electoral Saxon Estates, to which he had been called by the Elector. While very little is known about the position which Luther took at that meeting, apparently he strongly opposed the idea of a surprise military attack on any one of the members of the Breslau League, pointed out the moral wrong of such an action, and even threatened to leave Electoral Saxony in order to avoid having his work loaded down with the infamy of such an action. See in this present letter, at the

stances, he stringently opposed any thought of a surprise military attack; he encouraged his Sovereign to pursue a wait-and-see policy, and suggested diplomatic and legal steps to settle the crisis. In the meantime the public had become aware of the mobilization in Electoral Saxony and Hesse. At this point the Council of Regency[16] stepped in and issued a mandate (dated April 16)[17] to the effect that, under threat of severest punishments, the public peace was to be maintained under any circumstances, and that all difficulties were to be settled in a legal way. Letter No. 181 is Luther's and Melanchthon's reaction to this mandate. In this jointly issued statement the Elector is urged to abide by the mandate and to use it as a means for maintaining peace. Luther and Melanchthon point out that if the Elector rejected the mandate, he could be charged with rebellion, a fact which would have serious consequences for the preaching of the gospel. On the other hand, if the Elector were to abide by the mandate and the members of the Breslau League did not, then they could be charged with rebellion.

---

end. Luther returned from Altenburg *ca.* March 26 (Buchwald, *LK,* p. 57; *WA,* Br 4, 421) but was called immediately to Torgau for consultation. Here, on March 28, he issued his first brief on the Pack affair; *WA,* Br 4, No. 1246, pp. 421–424; *S-J* 2, No. 793. In this brief Luther rejected the idea of a surprise attack, urged the Elector to abandon the plan of striking first, and suggested that the Elector seek to untangle the situation through negotiations. The Elector adopted Luther's position, much to the Landgrave's anger. In a brief of April 11 (*WA,* Br 4, No. 1246, pp. 425–429; *S-J* 2, No. 794) the Landgrave tried to nullify Luther's arguments, and in an April 12 letter the Landgrave informed the Elector that he would insist on the arrangements made on March 9, and that he hoped to go to war in about five weeks; see *WA,* Br 4, 425. On April 28, the Elector, the Landgrave, Luther, and Melanchthon met in Weimar for a summit meeting (Buchwald, *LK,* p. 58), during which Luther, together with Melanchthon, issued a second brief; *WA,* Br 4, No. 1246, pp. 431–433. On April 30 a new alliance between Saxony and Hesse was signed which was a slightly modified version of the March 9 alliance. Under the influence of Luther's second brief, it was decided not to strike first, but to give an ultimatum to the sovereigns of the Breslau League to the effect that they declare their intentions and keep the peace; if they refused to keep peace, then Saxony and Hesse would consider themselves to be at war with them; see *WA,* Br 4, 433. After this second alliance was signed, the Imperial mandate arrived in Weimar; see *WA,* Br 4, No. 1258, Introduction. Since Luther says that the mandate arrived "yesterday," and since Luther was in Weimar until May 2 (see *ARG* 25 [1928], 6), place and date of the following brief was Weimar, May 1 or 2. It is extant in Melanchthon's handwriting, and was written on paper which at that time was used in the Electoral chancellery.

[16] See *LW* 48, 70, n. 1.

[17] See note 15. On this mandate, see *WA,* Br 4, No. 1258, Introduction.

On Elector John, see LW 48, 269, n. 8.
Text in German: WA, Br 4, 448–450.

To the Most Serene, Noble Sovereign and Lord, Sir John, duke in
Saxony, elector, etc., landgrave in Thuringia, margrave in Meissen;
to our Most Gracious lord: *Personal*

Most Serene, Noble Elector, Most Gracious Lord! We have learned
that yesterday a mandate issued in the name of His Imperial
Majesty arrived from the Council of Regency.[18] [This mandate]
orders all Estates of the Empire to maintain peace. We are extremely pleased by this, since we, though we understand little
[of such matters], hope that this [mandate] will be a fine and excellent reason for finding that peace which, after all, we want and
for which we are yearning. It seems to us that God is listening to
our prayers and intends to be gracious to us.[19] For he certainly
is friendly to us,[20] if only we receive [his message] and respond
to him accordingly. Obviously we should have searched high and
low for such an opportunity [for making peace], which now comes
into our midst[21] without any effort [on our part]. And whether
it is true or not that the sovereigns of the league[22] themselves are
responsible for that mandate,[23] it is nevertheless a good basis from
which one may directly negotiate for peace with them, or [take
the necessary steps] at the Council of Regency against them, etc.[24]
Our humble opinion is, therefore, not to disregard this Imperial
mandate (although we know that in Your Grace's sovereign wisdom
Your Electoral Grace does not need our advice).

First, so that God, who shows himself by this mandate to be
graciously inclined toward peace, should not be held in contempt.

---

[18] See notes 15 and 16.
[19] Literally: "intends to be graciously at [our side]."
[20] Literally: "For he [i.e., God] certainly greets us kindly, if . . ."
[21] Literally: "comes to us into the house."
[22] See Introduction.
[23] I.e., in an attempt to forestall military actions for which they were not
prepared.
[24] Literally: ". . . basis [or: opportunity] with which one may negotiate with
them [i.e., the sovereigns of the Breslau League], or at the Council of
Regency against them [i.e., the sovereigns of the Breslau League] for peace,
etc."

Second, because this mandate was issued by our regular governmental authority, which has been established by God, and which we are duty bound to obey;[25] and this is especially so since in [this mandate] no evil is commanded, only good and peace, and neither our [interests]nor those of the other party are considered, but only the common good of the Empire is being sought and is being offered to us, etc.

We fear that if this mandate were to be disregarded or thrown to the winds, the sovereigns of the league [could] by this action create[26] for themselves a tremendously favorable impression and reputation throughout the Empire, while [at the same time] they could load on us the greatest disgrace in the eyes of the whole world. [They could show themselves] as those who offered peace and wanted to be obedient to His Imperial Majesty, but who because of their obedience are attacked[27] by those who are disobedient, those who are rebels against His Imperial Majesty. They would charge us immediately with the crime of lese majesty. In addition, they would continue to work against us at the Council of Regency and secure the [Imperial] ban [against us]. The case of our party would get so far that [we][28] would have no good conscience before God, no legal ground before the Empire, and no honor before the world. This would be dreadful and terrifying.

To summarize: we are afraid that Satan has a more terrible thing in mind than is obvious to us. For he does not want to attack the gospel in parts; but just as Haman wanted to extinguish the whole Jewish people,[29] so Satan, too, now wants to turn all of Germany·upside down and thus to extinguish the gospel. Not for nothing is Satan so busy around us, fighting and resisting, so that we have become heavy and lazy, yes, even unwilling to search for peace and to accept it when God orders us to do so and offers [us a chance].

Your Electoral Grace is no doubt aware[30] what an unfortunate event it would be, even if all things worked out and were success-

---

25 Rom. 13:1 f.
26 Literally: "lift up and produce."
27 Literally: "offended."
28 Literally: "it [i.e., our party]."
29 Esther 3:13.
30 Literally: ". . . Grace no doubt put into consideration . . ."

fully arranged, if one were to shed so much blood needlessly, [and do so] contrary to conscience and His Imperial Majesty ['s order]. Should it—God forbid—be undertaken and carried out with such a bad conscience and in [such] disobedience anyway, then, even though we should regret the need to do so, we would be compelled[31] to speak out and to testify against Your Electoral Grace, our most beloved Lord, by whom to this day we have been graciously fed, protected, and overwhelmed with such great deeds of kindness and favors as if by a father. In addition, as I, Martin, declared to Your Electoral Grace at Altenburg,[32] we would have to leave Your Electoral Grace's territory and emigrate. [We would have to do this] for the sake of the gospel, in order to avoid having all this disgrace appear to fall justifiably on the innocent Word of God.[33] What could grieve our hearts more than that we and perhaps many fine people along with us should have to be separated from such a father and patron? Certainly the devil has this, and even bigger distress, in his mind. God, however, now graciously offers an opportunity to stop him; later one might perhaps be willing to give [an entire] territory for such an opportunity, but then one will not find it anywhere. [If this mandate is rejected] we cannot imagine how, in the eyes of the whole world, our party would not justly be considered as preferring war to peace, and bloodshed to good government. We who have and boast of God's Word should avoid such suspicion more than all the other sovereigns who do not have God's Word, etc.

It is our humble opinion, therefore, that an impressive delegation be sent to the Council of Regency. [This delegation] should declare [to the Council] the obedience of Your Electoral Grace and of my gracious lord, the Landgrave;[34] it should accuse the

---

[31] Literally: ". . . we would have to, and would be compelled to speak out and to testify against . . ."
[32] See note 15, and WA, Br 4, No. 1241, Introduction. From the very beginning Luther apparently made it clear that he could not sanction a surprise attack, and that the Elector's first duty was to explore all avenues for peace, even if the Landgrave opposed this; see also WA, Br 4, 423 (Luther's first brief). Luther did not, however, oppose a war of defense in this matter; see WA, Br 4, 422.
[33] Since the bloodshed and the disobedience to the Imperial government would be blamed on Luther's understanding and teaching of God's Word.
[34] Philip of Hesse; see note 5.

sovereigns of that league [of seeking war], and take other steps, etc.; Your Electoral Grace certainly knows how to do this much better than we can advise.

Your Electoral Grace's dedicated
MARTIN LUTHER[35]
PHILIP MELANCHTHON[36]

182

To Duke John Frederick
Wittenberg, May 18, 1528

Soon after the meeting at Weimar[1] the Elector informed Luther and Melanchthon (in a no-longer extant letter) about developments in the Pack affair, and said that he would continue to seek peace. He also wrote that he had sent his son, the Electoral prince, Duke John Frederick, to Landgrave Philip in an attempt to convince the Landgrave of the wisdom of pursuing a wait-and-see policy rather than of rushing into military action.[2] In the present letter Luther and Melanchthon encourage the Electoral prince regarding this mission.

On Duke John Frederick, see LW 48, 181 f.

Text in German: WA, Br 4, 465. The letter is extant in Luther's handwriting, Melanchthon having only signed the letter.

To the Serene, Noble Sovereign and Lord, Sir John Frederick, duke in Saxony, landgrave in Thuringia, margrave in Meissen, my Gracious Lord

Grace and peace in Christ! Serene, Noble Sovereign, Gracious Lord: We have heard that Your Grace has departed on a mission to our gracious lord, the Landgrave,[3] to promote peace and to

---

[35] See note 15. Luther's signature is in his own handwriting.
[36] See note 15; *LW* 48, 77, n. 3.
[1] See p. 190, n. 15.
[2] See *WA*, Br 4, 464, n. 1.
[3] Philip of Hesse; see p. 124, n. 18.

prevent war. This pleases us extremely, and we pray that God may grant Your Grace mercy and success in this undertaking, so that such peaceful means and arguments may be of greater effect than any zeal and provocation for war. We know, of course, that young sovereigns are passionately interested in rooting out such guile and provocation. Yet God has promised great mercy to those who seek peace and endure guile when he says: "Blessed are the meek, for they shall inherit the earth."[4] War does not gain much, but loses much and risks everything. Gentleness, however, loses nothing, risks little, and gains everything. Therefore [God] says in Psalm 34 [:12, 14]: "Shun evil, do good, seek peace and pursue it; then you will have good days." May Christ grant that Your Grace earnestly seek peace, because time will bring enough wars (which will prove unavoidable); therefore, we do well to make peace wherever we can.

Wittenberg, May 18, 1528

Your Grace's dedicated
MARTIN LUTHER
PHILIP MELANCHTHON[5]

183

To John Hess[1]
Wittenberg, [about June 13,][2] 1528

Luther is commending the carrier of this letter. He also comments on the development of the Pack affair.

On John Hess, see LW 48, 143, n. 5.

Text in Latin: WA, Br 4, 480

---

[4] Matt. 5:5.
[5] See *LW* 48, 77, n. 3.
[1] The letter is extant only in printed form. The earliest witness (to be found in a sixteenth century edition of Luther's letters) does not give an addressee for this letter. Without giving any reasons, all editors have assumed that Luther was writing to John Hess in Breslau. While there is next to no material available that would *compel* us to see in John Hess the addressee of this letter, there seems to be no material available that would compel us to abandon the established tradition that John Hess was the addressee.
[2] On the date of the letter, see note 12.

Grace and peace

The carrier of this letter, whom you had once recommended to me, is now returning to you,[3] my Hess. He is a man worthy of your recommendation, and indeed of ours [too]. May Christ grant that he may not have been here in vain.

I think you have heard of the league of the ungodly sovereigns and of their excuses, which are colder than ice, and which no one believes except their own followers.[4] Finally the nobles of Duke George[5] openly admit that this league has not at all been imaginary, but that indeed the letters and the copy [of the document] are available. About this material they now want to pretend that it has been drawn up with the unauthorized use of the names of the sovereigns and with counterfeit seals.[6] They consider that Sir Otto von Pack is being held prisoner because of this. But since this councilor of Duke George has been captured by the Landgrave,[7] this imprisonment seems to me rather an escape

---

[3] This carrier could not be identified.

[4] See Introduction to letter No. 181; see also below, note 6.

[5] Duke George of Saxony; see *LW* 48, 110, n. 20.

[6] As a result of the special delegation sent by Electoral Saxony and Hesse to the Council of Regency (see p. 194), the Council requested the Estates which supposedly had formed the Breslau League to dissolve this alliance immediately and to refrain from any hostile action against Electoral Saxony or Hesse. Consequently (see however also note 9) these Estates individually issued statements (Luther's "excuses") to the effect that they never had planned or participated in such an alliance; see *St. L.* 16, 389 ff. Duke George issued his statement (in the form of a letter to Landgrave Philip) as early as May 21, immediately after the Landgrave had sent a copy of the league document to him; see *St. L.* 16, 382. In his letter to Link of June 14 (*WA*, Br 4, 483, *S-J* 2, 444 f.) Luther wrote that he believed these "excuses," especially Duke George's, to be phony; he saw in them admissions of guilt. Since Duke George in some mysterious way received a copy of this letter to Link, Luther and the Duke became engaged in a fierce literary battle; see *WA*, Br 4, No. 1285, Introduction.

[7] In view of the tense situation, Landgrave Philip had imprisoned von Pack, who supposedly was the only person to have seen the original of the document constituting the Breslau League, and who had supplied the copy of it to Philip. If the Landgrave was the culprit in this affair, then by imprisoning von Pack he wanted to make sure that he had a scapegoat available. If he was not the responsible party, then by imprisoning von Pack he wanted to make sure that he had available the person who was to be blamed for the highly embarrassing situation in which he found himself. It is interesting to point out that even though Duke George, in his "excuse" (see note 6), demanded a confrontation with the informer, the Landgrave refused to do this; so according to Enders, *Briefwechsel* 6, 294, n. 3.

and a voluntary imprisonment so that he might be safe from the tyranny of his Phalaris.[8] But these secrets will soon be revealed more and more. It seems impossible to me that such things as these could only be dreamed up by people. Further, it is certain that even today these sovereigns would be only too willing to do something like this. They have demonstrated this thus far through edicts, force of arms, and every conceivable ruse and violence, so that they cannot be considered free of guilt. But perhaps you know all these things better than we.

The bishops of Bamberg and Würzburg have made peace.[9] The Landgrave is still bearing arms against [the Archbishop of] Mainz, [but] there is hope for peace there, too, unless the Archbishop[10] shouldn't want it. Nothing further has been heard from Italy.[11]

---

[8] I.e., Duke George of Saxony. Phalaris was a cruel tyrant who ruled over western Sicily about 550 B.C.; See *O.C.D.*, p. 674.

[9] Either because of the Imperial mandate (see p. 191, n. 17) or because they were not ready to defend themselves against the combined troops of Electoral Saxony and Hesse, those members of the Breslau League who were exposed to the military threat of Saxony and Hesse came to the conference table, and a peace treaty was worked out in Smalcald in the first days of June. The bishops of Bamberg and Würzburg, against whom the Landgrave was leading his army in late May, were the first to make peace. The Archbishop of Mainz followed. Little is known about the negotiations with Brandenburg and Ducal Saxony, the two other members of the League, whose territory directly bordered on Hesse and Electoral Saxony. Elector Louis (the count palatine) and Archbishop Richard of Greifenklau (the elector of Trier; he seems to have been busy in peace negotiations as early as the beginning of May; see Enders, *Briefwechsel* 6, 286, n. 2) functioned as mediators. On June 5 Hesse-Saxony signed the peace treaty with the bishops of Bamberg and Würzburg at Smalcald. The major condition of the peace was the restitution of the expenses incurred by Saxony-Hesse for the mobilization. Electoral Saxony abandoned its claim, however; Bamberg-Würzburg eventually paid sixty thousand gulden (see *LW* 48, 11, n. 2) to Hesse. See *WA, Br* 4, 476, n. 1; Fabian, *ESBV* (2nd ed.), p. 36, n. 118. This willingness to pay for the mobilization expenses raises some serious questions: Did the bishops have a bad conscience in this matter? Or were they not prepared for war and, therefore, glad to get away so easily? Or did they feel blackmailed, and feel that they had to "buy" peace? If they did feel blackmailed, why did the bishops not seek legal redress from the Imperial government?

[10] Luther actually wrote "bishop" rather than "archbishop." The Archbishop of Mainz, Cardinal Albrecht of Brandenburg (see *LW* 48, 43 f.), also participated in the peace negotiations at Smalcald (see note 9); he refused to pay any reparations, however, and at once asked the Swabian League for military help. The Archbishop of Trier and the Count Palatine stepped into the situation and mediated peace between Saxony-Hesse and Mainz on June 11; the Cardinal, too, paid a reparation of forty thousand gulden.

[11] See p. 185, n. 29.

Commend us [to God] in your prayers, and in those of your people. Farewell in Christ.

Wittenberg, 1528[12]   MARTIN LUTHER

184

To Nicholas Gerbel[1]
[Wittenberg,] July 28, 1528

Luther is expressing his anger about Bucer's latest actions in connection with the controversy on the Lord's Supper. He is also briefly commenting on the congregation and University in Wittenberg, on Karlstadt, and on a campaign of Elector Joachim of Brandenburg against a robber baron.

On Nicholas Gerbel, see LW 48, 317 f.

Text in Latin: WA, Br 4, 508. The following translation is based on S-J 2, 450–451.

Grace and peace in Christ!

In the past I have known enough, and more than enough of Bucer's wickedness,[2] my Gerbel. So I am not surprised that he

---

[12] The approximate date of this letter can be established on the basis of the following observations: on June 9 Elector John reported to Luther about the negotiations of Smalcald; peace had been made between Bamberg-Würzburg and Saxony-Hesse; Mainz had been informed of this development, and it was hoped that Mainz, too, would make peace. See WA, Br 4, No. 1280. Since Luther is now informing Hess of this development, it seems safe to date this letter some days after Luther could have received the Elector's letter. In letters dated June 13 and 14 (WA, Br 4, Nos. 1282, 1284, 1285; S-J 2, No. 798) Luther made statements which are similar to, or sometimes even exactly the same as, those made in this letter to Hess, in which he discussed the most recent developments of the whole Pack affair. Therefore it seems safe to include the present letter to Hess in this group, and to date it *ca.* June 13.

[1] The letter is extant in manuscript copies and in the common editions of Luther's works. Even though the address is already missing in the earliest witnesses, it is clear to whom Luther was writing, since he greets Gerbel in the opening sentence of the letter; and further, the letter is Luther's answer to Gerbel's letter of June, 1528 (WA, Br 4, No. 1290).

[2] Martin Bucer; see LW 48, 247, n. 13. On Luther's relationship to Bucer prior to this statement, see Sasse, p. 142; *Bucer Werke. Deutsche Schriften* 2 (Gütersloh, Paris, 1962), 177 ff.

turns my own sermon (to which he refers)[3] against me. Following St. Augustine's opinion, I spoke in this sermon of the flesh of Christ [in such a way that I argued] not against, but for the sacrament. As is known to the whole world, we do not condemn the statements of the fathers, even if they conflict with one another [though they do] not [conflict] at this point),[4] as long as they are not quoted to oppose true piety. In a word, had Zwingli[5] said such a thing, there would have been *epieikeia*[6] ready to interpret it in a friendly way, and in fairness; but because Luther said it, it was soon subject to the most violent calumnies. May Christ visit these vipers, and either convert them or render them their just due.

[Bucer] has really produced quite a stench in this latest *Dialogue*,[7] in which he blithely ignores all my arguments and shows

---

[3] The parentheses have been added by this editor. In June of 1528 (for the date, see *WA*, Br 4, No. 1290, Introduction) Gerbel had informed Luther (*WA*, Br 4, 491) that the *Confession Concerning the Lord's Supper* (see p. 172, n. 6) had created wide divergence of opinion in Strassburg. While Caspar Hedio wanted to convince the citizens that the *Confession* clearly demonstrated that unity could be accomplished between Zwingli and Oecolampadius on the one side and Luther on the other, "someone else" charged that the book contained nothing of St. Paul's spirit. Bucer voiced his strong criticism of Luther's statement that in the Lord's Supper even an impious person would participate in Christ's body and blood (*manducatio impiorum*; see *WA* 26, 287 f.; *LW* 37, 188; Sasse, p. 141, n. 10). Gerbel continued to report that "our" (i.e., the Strassburg) theologians were going to great lengths to make the people suspicious of Luther's teachings on the Eucharist. From the pulpit Bucer charged Luther with contradictory teachings. In a sermon preached in 1523 Luther proclaimed, according to Bucer, something quite different regarding John 6:63 (". . . the flesh is of no avail . . .") than he wrote in his *Confession*. The passages discussed by Bucer can be found in *WA* 26, 372 ff.; *LW* 37, 248 ff.; *WA* 12, 580 ff., esp. 582 f. In his *Dialogue* (see note 7) Bucer once more dealt with this "contradiction," and also discussed Luther's opinion on the *manducatio impiorum;* see *Bucer Werke, op. cit.*, 336 ff., 355 ff.

[4] I.e., the point cited by Bucer. According to *St. L.* 21a, 1180, one would have to translate: ". . . even if they [i.e., the statements of the fathers] conflict with one another (in more than one point) . . ."

[5] Ulrich Zwingli; see p. 88, n. 12.

[6] The Greek word for clemency, gentleness, graciousness.

[7] *Vergleichung D. Luthers und seins gegentheyls vom Abentmal Christi. Dialogus, Das ist eyn freundtlich Gesprech* (Compromise [or: Comparison] of the Opinions held by Dr. Luther and his Opposition on Christ's Supper. A Dialogue, that is, a Friendly Discussion) (Strassburg: Wolf Köpphel, 1528; June 21 is the date of the preface); *Bucer Werke, op. cit.*, 305 ff. The purpose of the *Dialogue* was to promote the possibility of unity between Luther and the upper German Reformers. Perhaps following the example set by Erasmus

himself as a mere slanderer, [has he not]? Among other things, he throws at me the figurative mode of speech, [that is,] synecdoche, which I have not only not denied in my book, but have discussed in the greatest detail.[8] But let these vipers thrive! May Christ keep you safe (I pray with greatest fervor for this), since you dwell in the midst of such wild beasts, vipers, female lions, and leopards, [and are] in almost greater peril than Daniel in the den of lions.[9]

Christ is keeping the congregation[10] here at peace and of one mind, and is keeping the University flourishing in letters and studies.[11] As a result, Satan is ready to burst. Karlstadt,[12] that

in his colloquy *Inquisitio de fide* (see p. 78, n. 6), Bucer created two figures which represented Bucer's interpretation (Arbogast) and Luther's (Sebolt) interpretation of the Lord's Supper. The whole discussion centers on the thesis that Luther's *Confession* (see note 3) proves that Luther and Zwingli could agree concerning the presence of Christ if they were of good will. As the *Dialogue* unfolds, Arbogast, who in addition to representing Luther's opponent also represents Bucer's concern for unity, and who is portrayed as the greater intellectual light, convinces Sebolt of the correctness of the thesis that unity is possible between Luther and Zwingli if both agreed on Bucer's teachings. The *Dialogue* ends with the wish that one day both partners in the controversy would be able to dicuss their differences in person. Bucer's work was not the first dialogue published between 1520 and 1530 for bringing about unity among the Reformers, (Leo Jud had published a similar work in 1526), or even in western Christendom, but certainly next to Erasmus' work, Bucer's *Dialogue* was the most impressive one. It helped prepare the way which eventually led to Marburg, and thus to the only direct conversation between Luther and Zwingli. When Luther studied Bucer's *Dialogue* for the first time, however, the atmosphere had already been so poisoned that Luther could see only the negative sides of Bucer's well-meant undertaking. On the other hand it has to be pointed out that Bucer, in his overeagerness for unity, did not do justice to all of Luther's concerns, or to those of Zwingli either. Bucer did not see—whether he was unable or unwilling to do this would be another question—that the whole controversy on the Eucharist was not merely a matter of good will, but primarily one of religious (should one use the highly abused and ambiguous term "existential"?) concerns.

[8] See Bucer's *Dialog, Bucer Werke, op. cit.,* 310 f., and Luther's *Confession,* WA 26, 444 f.; *LW* 37, 301 ff.

[9] Dan. 6:16.

[10] Luther used *ecclesia;* see p. 61, n. 9. Luther apparently wanted to point out the difference between what was going on in Wittenberg and in Strassburg (see note 3).

[11] How much weight one may place on this statement has to remain an open question. For the registration figures which in 1528 reached a new height of approximately one hundred and forty, see C. E. Förstemann (ed.), *Album academiae Vitebergensis* 3 (Halle, 1905), 804. Luther's statement has to be seen against the background of the plague and the impact which it had on the day-by-day operations of the University; see also p. 175, n. 26.

[12] Andrew Karlstadt; see *LW* 48, 79, n. 12.

viper in our bosom, is the only one who mutters a little; but he does not dare to come out. I wish he would stay with your fanatics,[13] so that we could be rid of him!

All our friends send you greetings. There is no news here except that the Margrave[14] is attempting to subdue a certain knight who invaded his territory and committed a robbery.

Dearest friend, farewell in Christ to you and your Rib.[15] Amen.

July 28, 1528   MARTIN LUTHER

185

To Nicholas Hausmann[1]
Wittenberg, August 5, 1528

On behalf of his son John, Luther is sending thanks for a rattle. He mentions his decision to write something about the war against the Turks, and informs Hausmann briefly of the status of the plans to "kidnap" a certain nun. In the balance of the letter, Luther expresses his sorrow over the death of his daughter Elizabeth two days earlier.

On Nicholas Hausmann, see LW 48, 399 f.

Text in Latin: WA, Br 4, 511.

Grace and peace

---

13 I.e., the upper German Reformers.

14 Elector Joachim I, margrave of Brandenburg, was attempting to subdue Nickel von Minkwitz, who, breaking the peace of the land, had plundered the city of Fürstenwalde in Brandenburg; see WA, Br 4, 501; Enders, *Briefwechsel* 6, 305, n. 15.

15 This is obviously an allusion to Gen. 2:22. Gerbel had been married for the second time on December 11, 1525, but nothing is known about his bride except that her name was Dorothy; see *NDB* 6, 249.

1 The letter is extant only in printed form. Even the earliest witness gives no address for this letter. The name "Nicholas," mentioned by Luther in the opening sentence of the letter, is of little help in identifying the addressee, since Luther was corresponding with several men who had this name. The circumstances mentioned in note 5, however, justify identifying Hausmann as the addressee of this letter.

My little John thanks you, excellent Nicholas, for the rattle.[2] He is very proud of it, and delighted with it.

I have decided to write something on the Turkish war, and I hope it will be useful.[3]

My baby daughter, little Elizabeth, has passed away.[4] It is amazing what a sick, almost woman-like heart she has left to me, so much has grief for her overcome me. Never before would I have believed that a father's heart could have such tender feelings for his child. Do pray to the Lord for me. In him, farewell.

Wittenberg, August 5, 1528

Nothing is being done about the woman who was to be kidnapped from Freiberg;[5] it was merely an idea, so your mind can be at ease.

MARTIN LUTHER

---

[2] The text would also justify the translation "toys."

[3] Here Luther mentions for the first time his plans to write his *Vom Kriege wider die Türken* (*On War Against the Turk*) (Wittenberg: H. Weiss, April, 1529), WA 30II, 107 ff.; LW 46, 161 ff.

[4] Elizabeth Luther was born December 10, 1527 (see p. 181), and passed away on August 3, 1528 (see also WA, Br 4, 511, n. 2). Although, as far as we know, Catherine Luther had not had the plague herself, there is a strong probability that Elizabeth was weakened by her mother's exposure to the plague, which had been raging in Wittenberg shortly before Elizabeth's birth. See also p. 184, n. 24.

[5] This person cannot be clearly identified. On June 29, 1528, however, Luther had written to Hausmann that one day he would need Hausmann's help for a nun who wanted to escape from a nunnery in Freiberg/Saxony; WA, Br 4, 488. Replying to Luther, Hausmann apparently pointed out some difficulties, so that for the time being the whole idea was shelved. Yet on October 20, 1528, Luther informed Spalatin that three nuns who had escaped from a Freiberg nunnery were staying with him; see WA, Br 4, 586. One of them was the Duchess of Münsterberg (see WA, Br 4, 587, n. 2; Enders, *Briefwechsel* 7, 2, n. 1). It has to remain open whether she was the one of whom Luther was thinking in this present letter to Hausmann.

186

To Lazarus Spengler[1]
[Wittenberg,] August 15, 1528

In March of 1525 a disputation was sponsored by the Nürnberg city council, during which the Reformation principles were defended against the attacks of the traditionalists. On March 16 the city council issued a mandate, according to which the celebration of the papal mass was prohibited and that of the evangelical mass was ordered.[2] The liturgy which was to be used was the one drawn up by the chief pastors in the parish churches of St. Lawrence and St. Sebald and had been used in these churches for some time.[3] Thus the Reformation was officially introduced and legally secured within Nürnberg. A traditional custom, however, was retained: the evangelical mass was celebrated every day. If no communicants were available, the celebrant alone communed. Some of the pastors seized the initiative and took steps to eliminate this leftover of the papal church; the city council, however, did not approve of this, much to the dismay of the pastors. Other pastors made declarations to the effect that the duty to commune posed a serious constraint on their consciences.[4] Finally in January, 1527, the chief preacher of St. Sebald, a certain Dominicus Schleupner,[5] drafted a brief[6] for the city council in which he discussed the issue, defending those among his colleagues who wanted to remedy the situation. By issuing this brief he called on the city fathers to sanction further reforms. But as in the past, so now too the council was slow to move, and shelved the whole matter for a year or more. Then, in May of 1528, Lazarus Spengler

---

[1] Even though the signature is missing in all the witnesses, except in the Wolfenbüttel manuscript copy (see note 10), the whole tradition has assigned this letter to Luther. This is sufficiently justified by the signature in the Wolfenbüttel copy, and by the circumstances surrounding Luther's reply (see note 8).

[2] On the Reformation in Nürnberg, see p. 98, n. 8.

[3] See *Jahrbuch für Liturgik und Hymnologie* 1 (1955), 1 ff.

[4] See *WA*, Br 4, No. 1307, Introduction; Enders, *Briefwechsel* 6, 359, n. 1.

[5] On Dominicus Schleupner, see *Nürnbergisches Pfarrerbuch, op. cit.* (see p. 167, n. 6), No. 1211.

[6] Text: U. G. Haussdorf, *Leben-Beschreibung eines Christlichen Politici, nehmlich Lazari Spengler* (Nürnberg, 1741), pp. 154 ff.

forwarded a copy of this brief to Luther, asking for the Reformer's opinion on the matter. The present letter is Luther's reply to Spengler.[7] Luther affirms Schleupner's arguments,[8] and suggests how this matter should be handled and how often communion should be celebrated. In addition Luther gives some details concerning his understanding of the pastoral office.

On Lazarus Spengler, see LW 48, 184, and in this vol. p. 97, n. 6.

Text in German: WA, Br 4, 534–536. The letter is extant in manuscript copies, in the common editions of Luther's works, and in some separate editions.[9] While all witnesses principally agree with each other, there is extant in Wolfenbüttel one manuscript copy which is quite different from the other witnesses.[10] Since the background of this Wolfenbüttel copy is unclear, the following translation is based on the text furnished in WA, Br, which in turn is based on all those witnesses which principally agree with on another.

To the prudent and wise Lazarus Spengler at Nürnberg, etc. my friend and lord, who is so favorably inclined toward me

Grace and peace in Christ! Prudent, dear Lord and Friend! I received your letter, together with the document[11] concerning the mass, and studied it diligently. Although I arrived at the conclusion that you do not need my counsel since God himself has provided you with such people in Nürnberg [who can advise you on this matter], yet at your request I shall willingly also add my voice.

First of all, it is proper and prudent not to compel anyone to come to or abstain from the sacrament, or to appoint particular times or places for it, thus trapping the consciences. Since St. Paul teaches, however, [in] I Corinthians 14 [:40, that] among Chris-

---

[7] Spengler approached Luther and Melanchthon in May, 1528; see *C. R.* 1, 894, 977.
[8] See the material presented in WA, Br 4, 533, n. 1.
[9] See also WA, Br 13, 104, to WA, Br 4, 533, No. 1307.
[10] The text of this Wolfenbüttel copy is edited in Enders, *Briefwechsel* 6, 356–359.
[11] See note 6; Spengler's letter is not extant.

tians all things should be done in an orderly fashion, it seems good to me that the Provosts[12] and ministers[13] should get together and decide on a common and free procedure for this matter. The honorable city council should then see to it that this procedure is used, and thus preserve unity and uniformity. If I were asked for advice regarding such a procedure, I would suggest the following:

First, that all masses without communicants should be completely abolished;[14] it is only right that they should be abolished, as their brief[15] itself announces.

Second, that one or two masses should be celebrated on Sundays or on the days of the saints in the two parish churches, depending on whether there is a great or small number of communicants. If there were a need for it, or if it were considered desirable, the same could be done at the *Spital*.[16]

Third, during the week mass could be celebrated on whatever day there is a need for it, that is, if there are some communicants present who ask for it and desire it. In this way no one would be forced to come to the sacrament, and yet everyone would be served [with the sacrament] in an orderly and sufficient way.

---

[12] I.e., the chief pastors of the two city parishes: George Pessler of St. Sebald and Hector Pömer of St. Lawrence; see *Nürnbergisches Pfarrerbuch, op. cit.,* Nos. 996, 1029.

[13] I.e., all the clergy functioning at the various ecclesiastical institutions of the city, and also the clergy of the countryside.

[14] For Luther's opinion on this issue, see, e.g., *LW* 48, 317.

[15] I.e., Schleupner's brief (see Introduction), which Luther assumed had been issued in the name of all the Nürnberg clergy.

[16] The Holy Spirit *Spital* (a combination of old folks' home, home for the poor, and hospital) was one of Nürnberg's best endowed ecclesiastical foundations, and dated back to the year 1339. Originally it was a church to which a hospital room, the so-called *Sutte*, was attached. Later the *Sutte* was separated from the church and was located in an impressive building spanning the Pegnitz river, which flows through the center of downtown Nürnberg. In use since 1518, the building had a house-chapel, and housed approximately two hundred and fifty inmates who were served by two *Sutten*-chaplains who served under the *custos*, or chief pastor of the Church of the Holy Spirit. In the fall of 1524, one of the chaplains, a certain Andreas Döbner, or Döber (see *Nürnbergisches Pfarrerbuch, op. cit.,* No. 240), composed an evangelical mass which was structured for the particular needs of the hospital setting; text: Sehling 11, 51 f. Elements of this liturgy were adopted by the clergy of the Church of the Holy Spirit, when in January of 1525 an evangelical mass liturgy in the vernacular was introduced at that church; text: Sehling 11, 56 f. See also *Zeitschrift für bayerische Kirchengeschichte* 28 (1959), 143 ff.

If the ministers complain about this,[17] however, alleging that they are thus forced [to celebrate the Lord's Supper], or lamenting that they are unworthy [to celebrate the Lord's Supper], I would tell them that no one compels them except God himself through his call. For since they have the office, they are already obliged and compelled (on the basis of their calling and office)[18] to administer the sacrament when it is requested of them; thus their excuses are void. This is the same as their obligation to preach, comfort, absolve, help the poor, and visit the sick, as often as these services are needed and demanded.

It also does not matter that someone may pretend to be unworthy because of his weak faith, shortcomings in his life, or coldness in devotion. He ought to look at his vocation and office, or even [better], at the Word of God which has called him. He may be impure and unworthy, yet the office and the call, or the Word, is sufficiently pure and worthy. And if he really believes he has been called, then he himself is, through this faith, worthy enough. For whoever believes he is called to the office of the church definitely also believes that his office and his work, and he himself in such an office, are acceptable and just before God; if he does not believe this, then it is also certain that he does not believe that his vocation and office are entrusted to him by God.

Those who doubt that they are called to such an office should be kept far away from [the office of the church], for they are no good. Those who are certain that they have such an office entrusted to them by God through the urging of the governing authorities or the prayer of the brethren[19] should enter into such a vocation with joy and confidence, and not look at any worthiness or unworthiness of their own. For faith in the calling is necessarily connected with faith in justification because it is a faith which is trusting and courageous on the basis of the Word of God who does the calling.[20]

Whoever believes in his vocation will definitely have all nec-

---

[17] I.e., the number of communions to be administered.
[18] The parentheses have been added by this editor.
[19] This last portion of the sentence could perhaps also be translated as: ". . . entrusted to them by God, as well as demanded [of them] by the governing authorities, or by request of the brethren . . ."
[20] This sentence is written in Latin, except for the initial "for."

essary devotion, desire, and daring, because it is impossible for him who is certain of his calling not to take into consideration the power of grace.[21] After all, such a man cannot say: I shall go and commit adultery, or some other evil. But he must say: I shall go and take care of my office. But what else is this than saying: I want to be obedient to my God and serve my neighbor? This intention, however, is devotion; it is the desire to become devout and to do good or to improve oneself—unless it could not be called devotion or the desire [to be devout], if I am willing to obey God.

It is of course true that whoever wants to examine himself and decide whether he is worthy or unworthy, [or] make himself worthy, without regard for this Word of his calling and faith in his office, does nothing but judge himself in terms of human work and feeling. These persons certainly must lament that they are not always worthy; as a matter of fact, they are at all times unworthy. After all, until now we have preached to the laymen not to pray, or to receive the sacrament, to rule, or serve, or do anything worthwhile on the basis of their own worthiness or unworthiness;[22] rather in all things they should hold on to God's promise, command, calling, or coaxing, and based on this undertake and do whatever has to be done. How then could the ministers of the church be unworthy—they who are called and made worthy by God through the Word, provided [only that] they believe this? Certainly my dear gentlemen and friends themselves[23] will know better [than I can suggest] how to deliberate further on all such matters.

Such an innovation[24] may cause quite some commotion among

---

[21] The last part of this sentence, the portion following "daring," is written in Latin.

[22] See e.g., Luther's sermon of 1518 *De digna praeparatione cordis pro suscipiendo sacramento eucharistiae* (*On the Right Preparation of the Heart for Receiving the Sacrament of the Eucharist*), WA 1, 329 ff.; *Eine kurze Unterweisung wie man beichten soll*, 1519 (*A Short Instruction on Confession*), WA 2, 59 ff.; J. N. Lenker (ed.), *The Standard Edition of Luther's Works* 24 (Minneapolis, 1907), 328 ff.; *Ein Sermon vom würdigen Empfang des heiligen wahren Leichnams Christi*, 1521 (*Sermon on Receiving Properly the True and Sacred Body of Christ*), WA 7, 692 ff.; B. L. Woolf (ed.), *Reformation Writings of Martin Luther* 2 (New York, 1956), 102 ff.

[23] I.e., the Nürnberg clergy.

[24] I.e., the final abolishing of masses celebrated without communicants; see also note 14.

the common people, but this is a risk which must be taken and put into the hands of God. But one must do everything to quiet any such commotion. This could be done in the following way: The undertaking of the visitation[25] provides a good opportunity to admonish [the people] from the pulpit and to impress upon them that, as they themselves and the whole world well know, there have been many abuses in the worship, which we intend to correct. Therefore they should be calm and not so outraged[26] when some things are changed. Also in things which are of concern to all, no one should consider his own opinion to be the best. Rather all should devoutly help [and] pray to God, who does not wish anything in his church done according to man's opinion, work, or word, but according to God's Word and work (as St. Peter teaches),[27] so that through His Spirit all things may be arranged in a blessed and good way.

For nothing is improved by much judging and back-biting, but only by humble prayer and a humble unanimity. Certainly my dear gentlemen[28] will know well how to press these points and explain them effectively [to the people]. In this way, it is God's work; he will be [with this work] if we desire it, and if we do not act in it in an insolent fashion. [Let us not act] as if our reason or ability could accomplish anything without God's power and aid, as do those who do not pray, and only insolently pass judgments, and extol their own opinions.

I have nothing better to say now. May Your Honor be content with this. I pray to God, the Father of all wisdom and power,[29] to grant Your Honor a rich portion of His Spirit, so that [Your

---

[25] In the summer and fall of 1528 the Imperial city of Nürnberg, in cooperation with the Margraviate of Brandenburg-Ansbach-Kulmbach, conducted a visitation of all the parishes within its boundaries. Luther apparently knew of this visitation through Link, for on July 14, 1528, he expressed to Link his joy over this visitation; WA, Br 4, 496; S-J 2, 446 f. On this visitation, see *Zeitschrift für bayerische Kirchengeschichte* 35 (1966), 7 ff.; Sehling 11, 113 ff.

[26] Or: "offended."

[27] The parentheses have been added by this editor. It is not clear to which particular passage Luther was referring. Perhaps this is an allusion to I Pet. 1:5, or to II Pet. 1:3–7.

[28] I.e., the Nürnberg clergy, especially the members of the visitation commission.

[29] See Dan. 2:20; I Cor. 1:24.

Honor] may do and accomplish what is well pleasing to Him, in Christ Jesus, his Son. Amen.

August 15, 1528

187

To Elector John
[Wittenberg,] September 3, 1528

Luther is suggesting Michael Stifel as the new pastor of Lochau, and expresses his hope that Stifel might care for the widow of the previous incumbent.

On Elector John, see LW 48, 269, n. 8.

Text in German: WA, Br 4, 546.

To the Most Serene, Noble Sovereign and Lord, Sir John,
duke in Saxony and elector, etc., landgrave in Thuringia,
margrave in Meissen, my Most Gracious Lord

Grace and peace in Christ! Most Serene, Noble Sovereign, Most Gracious Lord. Master Francis, the pastor at Lochau,[1] has departed from this life in God. The village people have asked me to install the old revenue collector [as their pastor].[2] Since I have nothing to say in this matter, I referred the people to Your Electoral Grace.[3]

I would like to keep Mr. Michael Stifel in the territory,[4] since he is devout and very capable in [handling] Scripture and

---

[1] Francis Günther; see LW 48, 173, n. 8.

[2] Thomas Windisch; see WA, Br 4, 551; 13, 105, to WA, Br 4, 546, n. 2. It is not clear why the people wanted this man to be their pastor.

[3] The people of Lochau also approached the Elector, apparently at the same time that they wrote to Luther. Near the village of Lochau was one of the Electoral castles, and the Elector, as patron of the village church, had the right to appoint the pastor.

[4] Michael Stifel (see p. 140) saw his life in Upper Austria threatened in the aftermath of the Pack affair (see WA, Br 4, 343, n. 1), and with the permission of his employer, Dorothy Jörger, left Tollet and sought refuge with Luther in Wittenberg. His presence in Wittenberg from January 6, 1528, has been established; see WA, Br 4, No. 1203.

preaching. Provided that this met with the approval of Your Electoral Grace, some of us thought that it would be wise to make him the pastor at Lochau until something else came up for him. For this good man is bothered in his conscience by the thought that he might be a burden to me because he is staying with me; [therefore] he constantly wishes to leave, so that I have a hard time keeping him [here]. I would prefer to see devout and learned people remain here, since too many of them leave. If [Stifel] were to become the pastor one could try to see whether he wouldn't also for God's sake take care of the poor forsaken pastor's widow and the two children. She is really in great misery, and more hardship will await her in the future. If [Stifel is] not [willing to do this], then God's will be done.

I leave all this up to Your Electoral Grace and ask for a gracious reply. I am presupposing that the name Michael Stifel is known to Your Electoral Grace; he accompanied me on the trip to Weimar, and Your Electoral Grace presented him with five gold gulden,[5] etc.

Christ be always with Your Electoral Grace. Amen.[6]

September 3, 1528   Your Electoral Grace's dedicated
MARTIN LUTHER

---

[5] On the gulden, see *LW* 48, 11, n. 2. On this meeting at Weimar, which took place on May 6 in connection with the Pack affair, see *WA*, Br 4, No. 1259, Introduction; *ARG* 28 (1931), 267.

[6] According to the Elector's reply (see *WA*, Br 4, No. 1319), Luther and Melanchthon were to examine Windisch (see note 2). If Windisch met their approval, the Elector would appoint Windisch to the Lochau parish, while Stifel was to get another parish. The Elector apparently changed his mind, for at the beginning of October Luther expressed his joy to Stifel that the latter would settle down in Lochau; *WA*, Br 4, 584. And on October 25/26 Luther was in Lochau to marry Stifel and Günther's widow, and to install Stifel in the parish; *WA*, Br 4, 593.

188

To John Agricola
[Wittenberg,] September 11, 1528

Luther is asking for information about a rumor to the effect that Agricola was teaching that faith can exist without producing good works.

On John Agricola, see LW 48, 220.
Text in Latin: WA, Br 4, 558.

To [my] brother, venerable in Christ, Master[1] John Agricola,
faithful instructor of the young people at Eisleben

Grace and peace! Someone has recently told me a story concerning you, my Agricola. He was so sure about it that he would not stop affirming [the story] until I said I would write to you and investigate [the matter]. The story goes that you are starting to affirm and fight for a new doctrine, namely, that faith can exist without good works. He said you presented this idea and tried to sell it with great effort of rhetoric and ingenuity, and even by using Greek words.[2] I, who have been taught by the harassing of Satan to be fearful even in safe matters, am writing now not only because of [my] promise [to that man],[3] but also to admonish you in all seriousness to watch Satan and your own flesh. For you know that no protection, no defense, is sufficient against the snares of Satan unless we are under the constant and eternal protection of heaven. There is such poison and danger in these snares that a great fire can arise from a spark, or, as Paul used to say,[4] a little yeast leavens the whole lump. Therefore, we should not play

---

[1] I.e., Master of Arts.
[2] According to Agricola's answer (see WA, Br 4, 563), this accusation was based on several of his sermons which he had preached in Altenburg. He had been called to that town to join the party of the Electoral prince, Duke John Frederick (see LW 48, 181 f.), who was then traveling to Prague, where Ferdinand of Austria (see LW 48, 217, n. 17) was residing. The "someone" who informed Luther about Agricola's sermons was either a member of that party, or perhaps Spalatin or Brisger, who were both in Altenburg at that time.
[3] I.e., the informer.
[4] I Cor. 5:6.

around or experiment with such an important thing, no matter how slightly, since this enemy usually penetrates the smallest cracks, and then will do no less damage than if he had broken in where all doors stood open.

[Please] accept this warning with good will, since you know from what kind of heart it comes. And [further] please report to me (if you have time) on the status of this matter. For what was further from my mind than that Oecolampadius,[5] Rhegius,[6] and the others would fall? And what don't I now fear, even from my most intimate friends here?[7] So it is not strange at all that I fear for you, with whom I should least want to disagree.

Farewell in the Lord, and greet your Else with her cluster of grapes.[8] The Lord has taken my little Elizabeth,[9] that she may not see any evil.

September 11, 1528

Yours,
MARTIN LUTHER

189

To Nicholas von Amsdorf[1]
Wittenberg, November 1, 1528

In this note Luther expresses his wonder about von Amsdorf's silence. Then he reports briefly on the plague in Wittenberg, and mentions the poverty which he encountered while conducting the visitation of the parishes.

On Nicholas von Amsdorf, see LW 48, 218.

Text in Latin: WA, Br 4, 597. The following translation is based on S-J 2, 460–461.

---

[5] John Oecolampadius; see *LW* 48, 230, n. 14.
[6] Urbanus Rhegius; see p. 160, n. 10.
[7] It is not clear to what Luther is referring here.
[8] See Ps. 128:3.
[9] See p. 203.
[1] The letter is extant only in printed form. Even though the address is already missing in the earliest witness, it is clear to whom Luther was writing since he greets von Amsdorf by name in the opening sentence of the letter.

Grace and peace in the Lord Jesus Christ

Your silence is astonishing, my Amsdorf; it is not your custom, nor do I deserve to be treated by you in this way, especially in this age which is so full of trials and dangers.

The plague is no longer ruling among us, yet it still comes out every now and then, and shows itself in one corner or another.[2] May Christ keep you in good health in the midst of this fire.[3] Amen.

We are visitors,[4] that is, bishops,[5] and have found poverty[6] and need everywhere. May the Lord send workers into his harvest.[7] Amen.

I beseech you, pray to the Lord for me, and farewell. Our friends send you their greetings.

Wittenberg, November 1, 1528　　　　　　MARTIN LUTHER

190

To Wenceslas Link
[Wittenberg,] March 7, 1529

Luther mentions his decision to refrain from a new literary attack on Duke George of Saxony, and he voices his criticism of the behavior of Erasmus of Rotterdam. Then Luther reports on certain celestial apparitions, which he interprets as signs of the impending

---

[2] See p. 183.

[3] What Luther had in mind when he wrote this sentence is not clear. Was von Amsdorf ill? Or was it just a general wish?

[4] In the fall of 1528 the visitation program was again speeded up. On October 15 Melanchthon left for the visitations in Thuringia (WA, Br 4, 584), and on October 22 Luther and others began to visit the parishes in the immediate neighborhood of Wittenberg; WA, Br 4, 586. Luther was not absent too long, however, but shortly thereafter returned again to Wittenberg.

[5] In the papal church it was the privilege and duty of a bishop to visit and inspect the parishes under his jurisdiction.

[6] This passage perhaps suggests that in mentioning "poverty" Luther was thinking of poverty in the area of theology and piety. If this was indeed the case then Luther wrote the catechisms in an attempt to eliminate this poverty.

[7] Matt. 9:38.

end of the world. In a postscript he asks for the return of certain
letters.

    On Wenceslas Link, see LW 48, 169 f.

    Text in Latin: WA, Br 5, 28.

To [my] brother, venerable in Christ, Doctor Wenceslas Link,
a faithful servant of the Lord in Nürnberg

Grace and peace in Christ. I have received two letters filled with
news,[1] my Wenceslas. I have begun to despise my Moab,[2] however, and shall no more reply to his slander. What Erasmus[3] is
doing is worthy of him, in that he rails at the Lutheran name;[4]
[yet] it is only under this name that he is now living securely.[5]
Why doesn't he go to his Dutchmen, Frenchmen, Italians, [or]
his Englishmen? He smells danger [there].[6] With this flattery he
is, of course, preparing a place for himself, but he will not find it;
he will fall between the two chairs.[7] If the Lutherans hated him

---

[1] These letters could not be identified. They obviously contained some comments on Luther's latest controversy with Duke George (see note 2), and on
Erasmus' latest actions (see note 5).

[2] I.e., Duke George of Saxony; see *LW* 48, 110, n. 20. Apparently thinking of
Isa. 16:6, Luther several times applied the name "Moab" to the Duke; for
documentation, see *WA, Br* 5, 28, n. 1. Luther wrote a letter to Link in which
he was highly critical of Duke George's connection with the Pack affair; see
p. 197, n. 6. A copy of this letter reached the Duke, who in turn demanded
an explanation from Luther; *WA, Br* 4, No. 1343. Luther answered rather
tartly (*WA, Br* 4, No. 1346; *S-J* 2, No. 811), and at once published a sharp
pamphlet against the Duke (*WA* 30^II^, 25 ff.), to which the Duke replied; see
WA, Br 4, 626; *S-J* 2, 462; *WA, Br* 5, 7. Apparently influenced by some of his
friends (see *WA, Br* 5, 17; dated February 12, 1529), Luther decided not to
pursue the matter further, and now informs Link accordingly.

[3] Erasmus of Rotterdam, see *LW* 48, 23, 116 f.

[4] The background of this statement could not be verified. For a critique of
the explanation given by Enders, *Briefwechsel* 7, 63, n. 2, see *WA, Br* 5, 28,
n. 3, and *S-J* 2, 469, n. 4. *S-J, loc. cit.,* suggests that Luther was thinking of a
letter of Erasmus to Pirckheimer in Nürnberg, and that Luther became
acquainted with this letter through Link. See Allen 7, No. 1977.

[5] Erasmus was at that time living in Basel, one of the centers of the Reformation in the German-speaking areas of Switzerland. Luther generalizes here
when he applies the term "Lutheran name" to the Reformation as a whole
without differentiating between "his" Reformation and that of Oecolampadius
in Basel, or that of Zwingli in Zürich.

[6] Literally: "He smells mice." This sentence is written in German. See also
WA 51, 676, No. 90.

[7] See also *WA* 51, 679, No. 114; *LW* 48, 160. Erasmus had recorded this
saying in his *Adagia;* see Clericus 2, 262 f. What Luther warns may happen

215

as those [friends] of his do, then certainly he could stay in Basel [only] with his life in danger.[8] But Christ will judge this atheist[9] and Epicurean Lucian.

There is nothing new here. Concerning the apparitions of which one hears in Bohemia, nothing is certain; many [people] deny [that they have occurred].[10] It is certain, however, that the northern light,[11] which has been [seen] here and which I, too, have seen on the Saturday after Epiphany[12] at eight in the evening, has been seen in many places, even as far away as the ocean. In addition Doctor Hess[13] writes that in December the sky above the cathedral of Breslau was fiery during the night, and that on another day two flame-like roof frames[14] were seen with a burning broom in the midst of them. I think that through these fires it is signified that the Last Day may be at hand.[15] Rome falls, kings fall, popes fall, and obviously the world will tumble, just as a big house which is about to collapse usually begins its decay with little

---

had in fact already happened. Many among the papists distrusted Erasmus, were highly critical of him, and openly harassed him; and the number of Reformers who openly supported or admired the great Humanist was rapidly dwindling.

[8] Even though Oecolampadius and the Basel city council assured Erasmus of their friendship and esteem, the Humanist neither felt safe in that city any longer, nor did he want to sanction with his presence the Reformation in Basel. Consequently he moved to Freiburg/Breisgau in the middle of April, 1529.

[9] In the extant autograph this word is written in Greek; see Enders, *Briefwechsel* 7, 62. On Lucian, see *O.C.D.*, p. 515.

[10] This could not be identified.

[11] This could not be identified. Luther wrote *chasma*, i.e., a chasm, abyss, or an opening either in the earth or the sky. It was apparently some kind of meteor, or a comet, or northern lights; the last is suggested by Clemen (*WA*, Br 5, 14, n. 9) on the basis of *St. L.* 21a, 1270. In a letter (dated January 31, 1529) to John Hess in Breslau, Luther said that through the *chasma* the whole night was illuminated; see *WA*, Br 5, 14.

[12] I.e., January 9.

[13] John Hess; see *LW* 48, 143, n. 5. The *WA*, Br editor suggests that, on January 31 (see note 11), Luther perhaps answered this no-longer extant letter of Hess.

[14] This could not be identified since Hess' letter is not extant. Luther wrote *contignationes*, i.e., something made of beams which were joined together, or a floor composed of joists and boards, or one story of a house, or a floor with a frame already up for a roof. *St. L.* 21a, 1270, suggests floor, or story, and this is adopted in *WA*, Br 5, 28, n. 9. Perhaps Luther was thinking of something like a burning frame of a roof, which in turn "appeared" in the sky above the roof of the cathedral.

[15] See *LW* 48, 104, n. 7; 114, n. 16.

cracks. Only the Turk, the final[16] Gog and Magog, is to glory in his supreme victory and is [then] to perish, together with his companion, the pope.[17]

Pray for me, a sinner; give my greetings to the Lord Abbot,[18] and ask him to remember me in his prayers. May Christ make the delivery of your wife a happy one. Grace be with you.

March 7, 1529   MARTIN LUTHER

I do not wish my letters on despair to be printed, unless perhaps they are checked over and [improved] by me so that they may appear in a form more worthy of light and audience. You may therefore return them, for I did not keep a copy of them.[19]

---

[16] According to Ezek. 38, in the latter days Gog (the King of Magog) will invade Judah and will come against the people of Israel like a cloud covering the land. In his initial triumph Gog does not realize that he is only the instrument of God who uses him "that the nations may know me [i.e., God] when through you, O Gog, I vindicate my holiness before their eyes" (Ezek. 38:16). Consequently God himself will interfere with Gog's evil plans and will prevent their completion. On his day God will shatter Gog's army to pieces and devastate Magog (Ezek. 38:17 ff.; 39:8, 11) so that "the house of Israel shall know that I am the Lord their God . . . And the nations shall know that the house of Israel went into captivity for their iniquity. . . ." (Ezek. 39:22 f.). The purpose of these two chapters is to illustrate God's triumph over all evil and all ungodly powers, and to reveal to all people God's universal lordship. Luther—who in 1531 published a brief explanation of these two chapters (WA 30[II], 223 ff.)—apparently wants to say that before the world comes to its end it will be necessary for an enemy from outside Christendom to triumph over Christendom, just as, according to Ezek. 38–39, Gog of Magog was to invade and to triumph over Israel. Luther sees this enemy of Christendom in the Turks, for in 1527 it had been rumored among Luther's friends that the Turks were mobilizing for a military expedition against the Empire; see e.g., p. 185; Kawerau, *Jonas Briefwechsel* 1, No. 126.
[17] Luther sees the collapse of the world as coinciding with the perishing of Christendom's enemies, both the external enemy and the internal enemy, i.e., the Turk and the pope. Luther apparently identifies the pope and his hangers-on with those elements in Israel who were jeopardizing God's lordship, and who caused God's judgment to come over the people of Israel.
[18] I.e., Frederick Pistorius; see p. 166, n. 4.
[19] These letters cannot be identified with certainty. For possibilities, see WA, Br 5, 28, n. 14.

191

To Nicholas von Amsdorf[1]
[Wittenberg,] May 5, 1529

Luther announces the birth of his daughter, Magdalen, and asks von Amsdorf to be the godfather of the infant.
On Nicholas von Amsdorf, see LW 48, 218.
Text in Latin: WA, Br 5, 61.

Grace and peace

The last letter to you, [the one] concerning that deceptive[2] groom,[3] I wrote in the presence of Katie, who soon thereafter began to moan and to go into labor. Three hours after I had written the letter she gave birth to a healthy baby daughter without difficulties.[4] The Lord has blessed us so richly that she had an uncomplicated delivery; to him be glory forever. Amen.

What I did not dare [to state] in your presence, I am putting forward in your absence:[5] Honorable,[6] reverend Sir: God, the

---

[1] The letter is extant in manuscript copies, in the common edition of Luther's works, and in some special editions. Even though the address and signature are missing in all witnesses, there is sufficient evidence (reference to Katie; notes 3, 5) to adopt the assumption of the tradition that this letter was written by Luther and was addressed to von Amsdorf.

[2] The translation is based on a conjecture suggested by de Wette (*Dr. Martin Luthers Briefe, Sendschreiben und Bedenken* 3 [Berlin, 1827], 447).

[3] Von Amsdorf apparently had contacted Luther regarding a certain groom who had contended that his engagement (which in Luther's time was a legally binding act, just as marriage is today) was void. Luther gave his opinion on the mater in a May 4, 1529, letter to von Amsdorf; see WA, Br 5, 60.

[4] Literally: ". . . she, a healthy one, gave birth to a healthy baby daughter." Magdalen Luther was born on May 4, 1529, and died on September 20, 1542.

[5] On March 29 Luther had invited (see WA, Br 5, 45) von Amsdorf to come to Wittenberg for the April 7 wedding of Bruno Brauer (who was a pastor in Dobien, and who also lived near Luther; see Enders, *Briefwechsel* 6, 123, n. 2; WA, Br 12, 237 ff., 411 ff.). Von Amsdorf apparently did come to Wittenberg, since Luther now refers to this occasion; see also ARG 30 (1933), 84. In this same March 29 letter Luther wrote that von Amsdorf would become a poor man if Katie's delivery and this wedding should coincide, i.e., if von Amsdorf had to spend money for a wedding present as well as for a gift for the newborn child. Perhaps Luther was then already thinking of von Amsdorf as godfather. Since it was customary in Germany to give a *Patentaler* (a gold coin of substantial value), and for the godfather to assume full

Father of all grace,[7] has graciously presented a baby daughter to me and my dear Katie. I am therefore asking Your Honor for God's sake to assume a Christian office, to be the spiritual father of the said little heathen, and to help her to the holy [Christian faith][8] through the heavenly, precious sacrament of baptism. Thus you would be the catechist of my daughter. Henry Dichlensis, the provost's vicar, will in the meantime stand in your place.[9]

The Lord be with you, and pray for us!

May 5, 1529, in the morning

192

To Wenceslas Link[1]
[Wittenberg,] May 6, 1529

In this letter Luther acknowledges the receipt of a clock, and expresses his appreciation for this gift. He also announces the birth of his daughter, Magdalen, comments briefly on the outcome of

---

responsibility (guardianship) should something happen to the parents, it is understandable that Luther did not want to discuss this matter with von Amsdorf at a time when the latter's budget might have been strained by a wedding present.

[6] This sentence and the following are written in German.

[7] See II Cor. 1:3.

[8] Literally: "help her to holy Christendom."

[9] This sentence is unclear. Who is the provost? Luther wrote: *Henr. Deldensis* [some witnesses read *Dichlensis*] *praepositus vicarius erit tuo interim loco.* Enders (*Briefwechsel* 7, 91, n. 3) suggests that an otherwise unknown vicar of Justus Jonas, the provost of the All Saints' Chapter in Wittenberg (see LW 48, 275, n. 3), who was at that time away from Wittenberg for the visitations, would function as proxy for von Amsdorf. Clemen (*WA*, Br 5, 61, n. 6) suggests that a certain Henry Benegringk, a provost in Magdeburg, would function as temporary replacement for von Amsdorf while the latter was in Wittenberg for the baptism. Clemen asks, however, whether it would be probable to assume that Luther would have suggested to von Amsdorf a replacement for the few days that he was to be in Wittenberg. The translation is based on the text made available by de Wette (*op. cit.*, 448), in which *praepositus vicarius* is placed between commas.

[1] This letter is extant in manuscript copies and in the common editions of Luther's works. Even though the address is already missing in the earliest witnesses, since Luther greets a Wenceslas, and since Link is the only Wenceslas with whom Luther frequently corresponded, it seems safe to assume that this letter was addressed to Link.

the Diet of Speyer, and reports some news he has received from Italy concerning the relationship of the Venetians and the French to the Turks.

On Wenceslas Link, see LW 48, 169 f.

Text in Latin: WA, Br 5, 62–63.

Grace and peace in Christ[2]

The clock[3] which you presented [to me], my Wenceslas, has arrived. Perhaps worn out from the trip, or unaccustomed to its new home, it is sometimes quiet; but it seems, as time goes on, that it resumes its movement. My thanks to you. I, a poor man, have nothing to give in return, for I assume that the books which I recently published[4] have already reached you people some time ago; in addition they are not worthy of being called a present, for they are [only] old material issued in a new form.

The Lord has enlarged my family with a little daughter, Magdalen; the mother is healthy, and had an uncomplicated delivery.[5]

The diet has come to an end again,[6] but with almost no results[7] except that those who chastise Christ and tyrannize the soul were unable to vent their fury. It is sufficient for us to have received such [a gift] from the Lord, for we have no hopes concerning a council that is being talked about [now].

A certain man from Venice[8] is staying with me. He affirms

---

[2] This sentence is written in German.

[3] In the spring of 1527 Luther had already received a clock from his friends in Nürnberg; it was given to him by Frederick Pistorius and forwarded to him by Link; see p. 166. In Luther's time Nürnberg was famous for the manufacture of clocks. In fact one Nürnberger, a certain Peter Henlein (*ca.* 1485–1542), is credited with having put together the first pocket watch, the famous *Nürnberger Ei.* See NDB 8, 534.

[4] It is unclear to which books Luther was referring here.

[5] See p. 218.

[6] The second Diet of Speyer was opened on March 15, 1529, and was adjourned on April 24.

[7] Due to lack of information, Luther underestimated the importance of this diet; it was this diet which brought forth the famous Protest which gave the name Protestants to the evangelicals.

[8] I.e., Martin Richter, who came to Wittenberg as emissary of Jakob Ziegler. The latter was a Humanist who was especially interested in mathematics and geography. Living in Rome and Ferrara since 1521, Ziegler had become increasingly disenchanted with the profane ways of the papal clergy; he decided to move to Germany and seek the company of the Humanists and Reformers

that a son of the Doge of the Venetians is at the court of the Turks.[9] Thus we are fighting against the Turks to the point that the Pope, the Venetians, and the French have become openly and shamelessly Turks. [This man] even says that eight hundred Turks were recently in the French army at Pavia, of whom three hundred —those not wounded but war-weary—have returned home.[10] I assume that these monstrosities are unknown to you, since you write nothing about them. Yet I was informed about these things under such circumstances that I believe them to be true. Thus midnight is at hand when the cry will be heard: "The bridegroom comes; come out to meet him!"[11]

Pray for me, and farewell to you and your Flesh.[12] Greet all our friends.

May 6, 1529

Yours,

MARTIN LUTHER

193

To Elector John
Wittenberg, May 22, 1529

The sack of Rome in May, 1527,[1] nullified the political ambitions of Pope Clement VII, and was one of the decisive blows against

there. Consequently he sent Richter, a friend and co-worker, on a mission to Germany to establish contacts. For details, see WA, Br 5, 65, n. 5; Enders, *Briefwechsel* 7, 95, n. 4.

[9] This is a reference to Louis, or Aloisio, Gritti (a son of Doge Andrew Gritti), who was Venetian ambassador to the court of the sultan; see Enders, *Briefwechsel* 7, 96, n. 6. In this position he gained the confidence of Sultan Suleiman, and thus was able to participate responsibly and decisively in the shaping and execution of the Turkish policy. In 1529, e.g., he accompanied the Sultan's army during the invasion of Hungary, and in the name of the Sultan installed Zapolyai as king of Hungary on September 14, 1529 in Ofen. See p. 241, n. 5.

[10] This is apparently a reference to the French conquest of Pavia in northern Italy in September of 1528. In a letter to Justus Jonas, also dated May 6, Luther tells the same story, adding, however, that five hundred of the Turkish auxiliary contingent were killed; WA, Br 5, 63. Nothing is known about these Turkish troops in Northern Italy. See Ranke 2[III], 20.

[11] Matt. 25:6.

[12] This is an allusion to Matt. 19:5.

[1] See p. 169.

the League of Cognac.[2] *Even though the military situation in Italy remained unclear during 1528,*[3] *both Pope and Emperor began cautiously to negotiate for peace.*[4] *These negotiations culminated in the peace treaty signed on June 29, 1529, in Barcelona.*[5] *Since in 1528/29 the military and diplomatic fortunes of the Emperor had gradually improved, and since in June of 1529 the French were finally decisively defeated in northern Italy, the road to peace with France was also open. In August of 1529 the peace between the Emperor and the French was finally established at Cambrai.*[6] *This positive outcome of the second war of Charles against France and France's Italian allies enabled the Emperor to turn his attention to Germany, which was then just getting over the Pack affair.*[7]

Meanwhile in 1528 the Imperial vice-chancellor, Balthasar Merklin von Waldkirch,[8] *made a special trip through southern Germany to proclaim the Emperor's intense displeasure with the Reformation; he also made loud threats against those sovereigns who, on the basis of the resolution of the 1526 Diet of Speyer,*[9] *had officially sanctioned and organized the Reformation within their territories.*[10] *In a letter written in October, 1528, the Pope admonished the Emperor to deal with the Reformation more zealously than in the past.*[11] *At the end of November the Emperor called for the diet to convene on February 21, 1529, in Speyer.*[12] *He placed on the agenda, among other issues, preparations for a war against the Turks (who were threatening to overrun Hungary), and the Reformation issue.*

The von Waldkirch mission and the Pack affair had strengthened the pro-papal Estates of the Empire. Consequently they eagerly

---

[2] See p. 156.
[3] See Ranke 2^{III}, 14 ff., 71 ff.; Elton, pp. 344 f.
[4] See p. 185, n. 29.
[5] See Kidd, No. 108; see also Ranke 2^{III}, 74 f.; Elton, pp. 345 f.
[6] See Ranke 2^{III}, 78 ff.; Elton, p. 345.
[7] See pp. 189 ff.
[8] On Balthasar Merklin von Waldkirch, see Allen 5, No. 1382, n. 25.
[9] See p. 156.
[10] On Merklin's mission and its effect, see *DRTA.JR* 7^{I}, 342 ff.; Ranke 2^{III}, 70, 90; Schornbaum, *Georg*, pp. 37 ff.
[11] See Ranke 2^{III}, 90 f.
[12] Text: *DRTA.JR* 7^{II}, No. 70; in excerpt, Kidd, No. 103. On this Diet of Speyer, see J. Kühn, *Die Geschichte des Speyrer Reichstages, 1529* (Leipzig, 1929); *ARG* 31 (1934), 1 ff.

looked forward to this pending diet, and when the diet was finally convened on March 15, 1529, they held a majority. In view of the lack of any final settlement with France and the Pope,[13] the Emperor's proposal for this diet (dispatched from the Imperial court on December 25, 1528) was worded in a conciliatory fashion.[14] The Emperor envisioned a national council of the church in Germany, which was to work out a Humanistically oriented compromise between the Reformation party and the papal party.

This proposal arrived in Speyer too late, however, and was never brought to the floor for action, because Ferdinand, as viceroy, had in the meantime issued a proposal of his own, pretending that it was the Emperor's proposal. Encouraged by the positive accomplishments of the Imperial policies, and eager to strike out against the Reformation, Ferdinand adopted a hard-line policy in his proposal.[15] He promised a general council which would deal with the Reformation issue, and demanded the nullification of the resolution of the 1526 Diet of Speyer and an end to any further spread of the Reformation.

Since this proposition found favorable hearings in the various colleges and committees of the diet, in which the Reformation party was in the minority,[16] the sovereigns and city delegates of the Reformation party filed a minority report on April 19, in which they solemnly protested the proposal and its adoption.[17] Notwithstanding this protest, the diet adopted Ferdinand's proposal in a resolution passed on April 22.[18] In the evening of this same day

---

[13] See Ranke 2[III], 19 ff. It was not until the latter part of spring, 1529, that the Emperor's cause finally triumphed; the peace treaties were not signed until long after the diet had been adjourned. The relationship between Pope Clement VII and Emperor Charles V had again become tense in view of the desire of Henry VIII to obtain from the Pope permission to divorce Catharine of Aragon, the Emperor's aunt. This development, among others, placed the Pope in an excellent position to negotiate with the Emperor, who considered Henry's desire a personal affront and an act of political impudence. On the relationship of this divorce affair to the Pope, and to Charles's policy toward the Pope, see Ranke 2[III], 11 ff., 80 ff.

[14] Text: DRTA.JR 7[II], No. 72.

[15] Text: DRTA.JR 7[II], No. 104; in excerpt, Kidd, No. 104; Reu II, No. 3.

[16] Text of the majority resolution in excerpt: Kidd, No. 105; Reu II , No. 4.

[17] Text of the Protest: DRTA.JR 7[II], No. 137; in excerpt, Kidd, No. 107a. Text of the final version, dated April 20: DRTA.JR 7[II], No. 143; Reu II, No. 5 (with the wrong date).

[18] Text of the resolution: DRTA.JR 7[II], No. 148.

*Landgrave Philip of Hesse, Elector John of Saxony, and the dele-
gates of the cities of Nürnberg, Ulm, and Strassburg signed a preliminary draft of a secret alliance for the purpose of mutual assistance if any one of them were attacked for the sake of his faith; a
conference was soon to follow in which the plans for the alliance
should be completed.*[19] *On April 25 the signers of the April 19
protest made their protest legal by having it notarized and by filing
an appeal to the Emperor and to a general council of the church,
seeking justice for their cause.*[20] *As long as this appeal was pending,
the resolution of the diet was de jure ineffective and unenforceable.
The "Protestants" also decided to send an emissary to the Emperor
to hand over their Protest and Appeal.*

*The present letter is Luther's reaction to the Protestants' secret
defense alliance of April 22. As Melanchthon had done after his
return from Speyer,*[21] *so Luther, too, rejects the alliance. Luther
gives three reasons for his position: (a) At present the alliance is
both unnecessary and dangerous; it might provoke the opposition
to actions which could perhaps be avoided if the alliance were not
made. (b) The alliance blasphemes God and jeopardizes the preaching of the gospel since it includes people (that is, some of the enthusiasts) who oppose God's Word. (c) The alliance is a sign of
lack of trust in God and his gracious help and guidance.*

On Elector John, see LW 48, 269, n. 8.

Text in German: WA, Br 5, 76–77.

To the Most Serene, Noble Sovereign and Lord, Sir John,
duke in Saxony and elector, landgrave in Thuringia, margrave
in Meissen, etc., my Most Gracious Lord

Grace and peace in Christ! Most Serene, Noble Sovereign, Most
Gracious Lord! Master[22] Philip[23] has brought to me from the diet,

---

[19] Text of the alliance document: *DRTA.JR* 7[II], No. 152; Reu II, No. 6. For
details, see Fabian, *ESBV* (2nd ed.), pp. 42 ff.
[20] Text of the Appeal: *DRTA.JR* 7[II], No. 167; in excerpt, Kidd, No. 107b.
See also J. Ney, *Die Appellation und Protestation der evangelischen Stände
auf dem Reichstage zu Speier 1529* (Leipzig, 1906, reprint: Darmstadt, 1967).
[21] On May 17 Melanchthon wrote to Lazarus Spengler, the chancellor of
Nürnberg, urging him to block any further action on the alliance envisioned
by Philip of Hesse; *C.R.* 1, 1069.
[22] I.e., Master of Arts.
[23] Philip Melanchthon; see *LW* 48, 77, n. 3.

among other [news],[24] the word that supposedly a new alliance has come into being, in particular between my gracious lord, the Landgrave[25] in Hesse, and some cities.[26] I am quite disturbed about this because a year ago,[27] when God by miraculous grace rescued us from that dangerous alliance, I was [once] burnt [so that I am now doubly careful].[28] Even though I am confident that God will continue to protect us, and [continue] to give his spirit and counsel to Your Electoral Grace, [that Your Grace may] be safe from this and similar alliances, nevertheless, because of excessive anxiety and the pressure of my conscience, I could not hold back from writing Your Electoral Grace about this matter; for I know through experience that one cannot sufficiently and studiously enough anticipate the devil and his aims. Through our prayers Christ our Lord will grant that, even though the Landgrave might yet continue to develop this alliance[29] (may God graciously prevent this), Your Electoral Grace may nevertheless not let yourself get involved in this and caught up in it; for what kind of evil will result from [such undertakings] we cannot even imagine.

First of all, it is certain that such an alliance is neither made by God nor by trust in God, but rather by human ambition and for the sole purpose of seeking human aid, and depending upon it. [Such an alliance] does not have a good foundation, and in addition cannot bring forth any good fruit, in view of the fact that such

---

[24] On May 4 and 6 Luther wrote about the anticipated return of Melanchthon from the Diet of Speyer; see WA, Br 5, 60, 63. Melanchthon apparently did not return from Speyer until about May 14; see WA, Br 5, 61, n. 3. Then Luther finally received an accurate report (see p. 220) about the events which had occurred in Speyer.

[25] I.e., here and throughout the letter, Landgrave Philip of Hesse; see p. 124, n. 18. For "cities" see Introduction.

[26] I.e., Ulm and Strassburg; see Introduction.

[27] I.e., in connection with the Pack affair. See pp. 189 ff.

[28] Literally: "because a year ago I was burnt." This part of the sentence could also be taken to mean that Luther was "burning" with worry. Since Luther used the same phrase on some other occasion, however (see WA, 51, 685, No. 152), where he obviously intended it to have the meaning given it here in the translation, and since the whole context here—with Luther warning the Elector of the Landgrave's hotheadedness—seems to make it impossible to assume that Luther is referring to past worries, it seems justifiable to render Luther's phrase with the familiar English colloquialism, even though the second part of the phrase ("so that . . .") had to be added by this editor.

[29] Literally: ". . . even though the Landgrave might continue with his making of an alliance . . ."

an alliance is unnecessary. For the papistic crowd neither is in a position nor has the courage to do so much as even begin something [against us]—and God has already protected us against them with the wall of his might. The result of such an alliance is simply that the opponents are led also to make an alliance; perhaps, in addition, for the sake of defense and protection, they might do what they would otherwise have left undone. There is the further worry—and this may be more than a possibility—that the Landgrave, once he has created such an alliance, and since he is a hotheaded young sovereign, might not be content [with this alliance] but, as happened last year,[30] might find some reason not only to defend [himself] but also to attack [the opponents]. It would certainly not be in accordance with God's will for us to act in this way, for as yet no one is attacking or pursuing us.[31]

Second, the worst thing is that in such an alliance we are forced to include those who work against God and the sacrament [of the altar] as wanton enemies of God and his Word.[32] In so doing we are forced to load upon us, participate in, and fight for all their vice and blasphemy, so that certainly no more dangerous alliance could be made to blaspheme and impede the gospel, and to condemn us, both soul and body.[33] Unfortunately this is what the devil is after.

---

[30] I.e., as happened in connection with the Pack affair. See note 27.

[31] On April 24 the sovereigns of both the majority and the minority parties issued promises to maintain peace; see *DRTA.JR* 7[II], Nos. 164, 165. It is possible that this action is the background for Luther's statement here.

[32] Luther considered Strassburg and Ulm, both members of the secret alliance, to be strongholds of an incorrect understanding of God's Word, since the theologians of both cities, especially Bucer in Strassburg, stood closer to Zwingli than to Luther in their understanding of the Lord's Supper. And further, the Landgrave's ambition was to draw into this alliance all the protesting cities in southwestern Germany; he even hoped to include the (Zwinglian) cities of the German-speaking portions of Switzerland. See Fabian, *ESBV* (2nd ed.), pp. 40 f.

[33] Luther's main concern regarding the alliance with the upper-German cities, which were strongholds of Zwinglianism, was his opposition to the symbolic interpretation of the Lord's Supper which he believed was affirmed in these cities. Even though it is true that the theologians of the upper German cities maintained a Eucharistic theology which was more Zwinglian than Lutheran, there were nevertheless definite degrees of difference in both directions. By 1529 the Eucharistic controversy between the Lutherans and the Zwinglians had developed to such a state, however, that both parties saw only the divisive elements, and were unwilling, and perhaps even unable, to do justice to each other's position. For Luther the whole issue was one of personal salvation; a

If it cannot be otherwise, then may God grant that Your Electoral Grace abandon the Landgrave and stand aside, as I hear my gracious lord, Margrave George, has said he will do and is doing.[34] Our Lord Jesus Christ, who until now has wonderfully protected Your Electoral Grace without the Landgrave, even against the Landgrave,[35] will certainly continue to help and counsel [Your Grace].

Third, God has at all times in the Old Testament condemned such alliances of human aid, as [in] Isaiah 7, 8, 30[36] when he says: "If you are calm and trusting, you shall be helped."[37] For we are to be children of faith in God, in honest trust. If we are to have alliances, however, [God] will provide them for us without our seeking or our worry, as he promises [in] Matthew 6 [:25, 33]: "Do not be anxious, all such things shall come to you, provided that you seek first the kingdom of God." And St. Peter says: "Cast all your anxieties on him, for he cares about you.[38] And Isaiah [says]: "Who are you, that you are afraid of mortal men?"[39] One cannot put this kind of trust in the Landgrave, who was once so terribly wrong,[40] especially since up to now he has experienced neither a change [of mind] nor any contrition or sorrow about it.[41]

I wanted to present this humbly to Your Electoral Grace, hoping that Christ has already inspired Your Electoral Grace's heart

---

"wrong" faith can lead only to damnation. Consequently no unity—whether ecclesiastical or political is unimportant—can be established with those who affirm any such "wrong" faith. It was of secondary importance to him, and here he differed from Melanchthon, that the upper German cities were havens for all kinds of zealots, political dreamers, and "trouble makers."

[34] Margrave George of Brandenburg-Ansbach-Kulmbach did not join the secret alliance, although he had joined in the Protest and Appeal, and although in Speyer he had been invited to become a member of this alliance. He did maintain contacts with the members of the Speyer alliance, however, and did attend the subsequent conference. He had political reasons of his own for his aloofness, to be sure, but he was also in basic agreement with Luther that it was impossible to enter any political union unless there was also agreement among the members concerning matters of faith. See Schornbaum, *Georg*, pp. 70 ff.

[35] I.e., against Philip's hotheadedness and its possible catastrophic outcome in connection with the Pack affair; see note 27.

[36] This is a reference to Isa. 7:4–7; 8:12 f.; 30:15.

[37] See Isa. 7:9, 30:15.

[38] I Pet. 5:7.

[39] Isa. 51:12.

[40] I.e., in connection with the Pack affair; see note 27.

[41] I.e., the Landgrave has learned nothing from the Pack affair.

[with such thoughts, only] better and more abundantly. We are praying and shall continue to pray, and shall be heard, that God, the Father of all mercies,[42] will counsel us, [and] will protect Your Electoral Grace against all deceitful attacks and plans of the devil. Amen. May Your Electoral Grace graciously receive this, my letter.

Wittenberg, May 22, 1529

Your Electoral Grace's dedicated
MARTIN LUTHER

194

To Landgrave Philip of Hesse
[Wittenberg,] June 23, 1529

Luther and Melanchthon strongly opposed the alliance of the Protestants which had been planned on April 22 in Speyer.[1] In the weeks following the diet, Melanchthon worked hard in an attempt to block any further negotiations aimed at the completion of this alliance.[2] At the end of May, 1529, the ambassadors of the protesting Estates met in Nürnberg for the purpose of sending the Protest and Appeal to the Emperor via a special delegation.[3] During this meeting, and then again later during a meeting in Rodach,[4] near Coburg (when, according to the secret document signed by some of the Protestant Estates in Speyer on April 22,[5] the details of the Speyer alliance were to be worked out), it became clear that the discrepancies between Luther and Zwingli concerning the Lord's Supper doomed any further negotiations. Consequently sometime in late May or early June[6] Landgrave Philip of Hesse[7] approached

---

[42] See II Cor. 1:3.
[1] See letter No. 193.
[2] On Melanchthon's activities in this connection, see note 19; Fabian, *ESBV* (2nd ed.), pp. 46 ff.
[3] See Fabian, *ABBP,* pp. 22 ff.; Fabian, *ESBV* (2nd ed.), pp. 52 ff.
[4] See Fabian, *ABBP,* pp. 29 ff.; Fabian, *ESBV* (2nd ed.), pp. 54 ff.; Reu II, No. 7.
[5] See p. 224.
[6] For the approximate date, see note 15.
[7] See p. 124, n. 18.

Luther (in a no-longer extant letter), suggesting that Luther come to Marburg for a discussion of the whole matter with some of the upper German Reformers. The Landgrave apparently pointed out the political and military dangers which would be created for the Reformation if these discrepancies were not overcome, and the alliance could not materialize.[8] The Landgrave forwarded this letter to Luther via the Electoral Saxon court, and Elector John added a (also no-longer extant) letter of his own, in which he urged Luther to give a positive answer to the Landgrave's feeler.[9] In the present letter Luther replies to Landgrave Philip, and reluctantly agrees to come to Marburg for the suggested meeting.

On Landgrave Philip of Hesse, see p. 124, n. 18.

Text in German: WA, Br 5, 101–102.[10]

To the Illustrious Sovereign and Lord, Sir Philip,
landgrave in Hesse, count in Katzenellenbogen, Nida, and
Ziegenhain, my Gracious Lord

Grace and peace in Christ! Illustrious Sovereign, Gracious Lord! I was pleased to receive Your Sovereign Grace's letter and request, which was surely sent to me out of a Christian [and] gracious attitude. I have also received the letter of my most gracious lord, Duke John,[11] elector, etc., in which His Electoral Grace also strongly urges me to give Your Sovereign Grace a positive answer in the hope that the matter[12] might thus be improved, in case God should give his grace so that such discord among us concerning the sacrament [of the altar] might be dissolved. For this purpose Your Sovereign Grace has suggested that I arrive in Marburg[13]

---

[8] So on the basis of the last paragraph in Luther's letter. The Landgrave's letter can be reconstructed on the basis of Luther's answer, and of other letters written by the Landgrave at that time. See also Lenz, *BPB* 1, 12 f.

[9] See the first paragraph of Luther's letter.

[10] Luther's letter is available in two versions. The autograph, which even bears Luther's seal, is deposited in the Marburg archive. This text is reproduced in *WA* 5, No. 1438, pp. 101–102, and is the basis for the following translation. The text of the first draft of this letter is also extant, and is reproduced in *WA, Br* 5, No. 1438, pp. 104–105.

[11] Elector John, see *LW* 48, 269, n. 8.

[12] "The matter," i.e., here and throughout the letter, the Eucharistic controversy.

[13] I.e., the city in which the residency of the Landgrave was located.

on St. Michael's Day,[14] to confer in a charitable way and in secret with the opposition.[15]

I am indeed absolutely convinced that Your Sovereign Grace is completely sincere and has the best of intentions. For this reason I, too, am ready and willing to render my services in this, Your Sovereign Grace's Christian undertaking, though I fear [my services] may be futile and perhaps dangerous for us. I too, of course, desire and love that peace about which the others talk so much with their mouths and pens but put into jeopardy with their actions.

I shall now frankly tell your Sovereign Grace, however, what I think [of this plan]. It looks to me as if the opposition seeks to make this, Your Sovereign Grace's effort, something from which no good can come; that is, [I believe] that they hope to extoll themselves later [by saying that] it was not their fault, that they had [even] engaged such an important sovereign, etc., so that they may disgrace us in Your Sovereign Grace's name, [and blame us] for not wishing peace and truth, in order to put themselves into the best light. I know the devil well; may God grant that I am not a prophet. It is now twelve years since I have learned to be cautious about such matters and plots, and often I have been badly burned. If this were not a plot, and if they really and earnestly wished [to have peace with us], then they would not have to use such a grandiose way of operating, that is, [deal with us] through great and important sovereigns (who certainly have other things to do). They would only need a little pen, especially since we are not of such high birth, are also not so barbarous and uncouth, that they could not long ago have announced to us their great zeal for peace and unanimity (as they brag).

Consequently, if Your Sovereign Grace can do something, and

---

[14] September 29.
[15] "Opposition," "they," i.e., here and throughout the letter the representatives of the symbolic interpretation of the Lord's Supper; see also note 12. As early as the beginning of 1528, Landgrave Philip envisioned a colloquy between Luther and the Zwinglians in order to settle the Eucharistic controversy and to prepare the way for unity among the Reformers; see *C.R. Zwingli Werke*, 9, No. 687 (dated February 11, 1528). On April 22, 1529, he contacted Zwingli from Speyer regarding this matter; Zwingli's positive answer was dated May 7, and reached Philip around May 25. Encouraged by Zwingli's readiness to attend a conference with Luther, the Landgrave then approached the Wittenbergers. See Enders, *Briefwechsel*, 7, 123, n. 2; Lenz, *BPB* 1, 10 ff.

since Your Sovereign Grace is willing to deal with this matter [at all], I would like to suggest that [Your Grace] inquire of them whether they would be willing to abandon their opinion, so that in the long run the matter does not become worse. For Your Sovereign Grace can easily see that all discussions are futile and the meeting vain, if both parties come with the intention of conceding nothing. Thus far I have found nothing other than that they want to insist on their position, though they have become very familiar with the basis of our position. On the other hand, having also become familiar with the basis of their position, I certainly know that I am unable to yield, just as I know that they are wrong. If we should part from one another in discord, then not only Your Sovereign Grace's expense and troubles would be lost, in addition to our time and efforts, but [our opponents] would also continue their bragging, as they have been doing until now; thus they would force us again to give an account [of our position]. Then it would be better had we let the matter rest as it is now, and let it take its own course, wherever it goes. For in short, I cannot expect anything good from the devil, no matter how nicely he may appear to act.[16]

Since Your Sovereign Grace is concerned that bloodshed may follow from such discord, Your Sovereign Grace should also know that whatever of [such discord] may follow (may God prevent it), we shall not be guilty of any of it. It is nothing new that the enthusiasts cause bloodshed. They have proven this before in connection with Francis von Sickingen, and through Karlstadt, and Münzer;[17] and yet by God's grace we have been found totally innocent in these cases. But may Christ, our Lord, crush Satan under his and all our feet.[18] Amen.

June 23, 1529   Your Sovereign Grace's willing
                                                MARTIN LUTHER[19]

---

[16] Luther considered any attempt to establish unity at the expense of what he believed was the truth to be a demonic temptation.

[17] See *LW* 48, 244 f.; 79, n. 12; and in this vol., p. 111, n. 36.

[18] See Rom. 16:20.

[19] Since the meeting in Speyer, Melanchthon had been aware of the Landgrave's desire to bring about unity between Luther and the symbolists by way of a conference. Since for reasons of his own he was opposed to the idea, he suggested to Elector John as early as May 14 that the Elector should refuse to grant a leave of absence to the Wittenbergers; in this way they would be

195

To Thomas Löscher
[Wittenberg,] August 26, 1529

One of the questions which arose in the church of the Reformation[1]
was how properly to handle heretics and unbelievers. Since the
Canon Law, which had regulated these matters, was rejected by
the church of the Reformation,[2] new guidelines necessarily had
to be developed. Luther was convinced that no one could or should
be forced to believe in Christ, an idea which he maintained
throughout his life.[3] This conviction contributed little to a legal
solution of the matter, however, for, as Luther had experienced
both in his own case and in the case of the peasants, all "heresy"
has social, legal, and political implications.

Thomas Löscher, the pastor of Mylau (a small village near
Wittenberg),[4] wrote Luther a letter, which is unfortunately no
longer extant, about certain "blasphemers" who despised the gospel
or the Christian faith. He asked for Luther's advice on how to
handle the matter.[5] The following letter is Luther's answer. The Re-
former maintains that no one can be or should be forced to faith.

---

prevented from attending the planned conference; see Fabian, *ESBV* (2nd
ed.), p. 48. When the Landgrave approached Luther about the conference, he
also wrote a no-longer extant letter to Melanchthon. Melanchthon, in his
reply dated June 22 (*C.R.* 1, 1077 f.), also reluctantly accepted the invitation; he added, however, that the Landgrave, as he had promised in Speyer,
was also to invite some Roman Catholic theologians to this meeting. Satisfied
with the Wittenbergers' acceptance of the idea of the colloquy, the Landgrave
issued the official invitations for the Marburg Colloquy to Luther and Melanchthon on July 1, 1529 (*WA,* Br 5, No. 1441; Lenz, *BPB* 1, 15 f.), and Luther
and Melanchthon officially accepted this invitation on July 8 (*WA,* Br 5, No.
1443).

[1] See *LW* 48, 211 f.
[2] See *LW* 48, 186 f., and in this vol., pp. 85 ff.
[3] See e.g., *WA* 30[I], 349.
[4] For some information on this otherwise unknown pastor, see *WA,* Br 5,
138, n. 1.
[5] Nothing could be ascertained either about the identity of these "blasphemers"
or about their actions. Were they stubborn papists? Or enthusiasts? On July
18, 1528, Löscher mentioned a pastor who had been jailed because of
blasphemy; see *WA,* Br 5, 138, n. 1. However, we do not know whether
Löscher's inquiry to Luther was related to this affair. Whatever the event
that prompted Löscher to write to Luther it must have been shocking, for
both the pastor and the lord of the village approached Luther for advice;
see *WA,* Br 5, No. 1466.

If after careful interrogation and counseling the "blasphemers" con-
tinue in their error, Luther says, then they should be compelled to
be silent so that their teachings and conduct would stir up no
trouble in the community. The "blasphemers" should further be
compelled to attend sermons on the commandments and the Cate-
chism in which matters concerning public and private life are ex-
pounded.
Text in Latin: WA, Br 5, 137.

To [my] brother, venerable in Christ, Thomas Löscher,
pastor in Mylau, a faithful and upright minister of the Word

Grace and peace in Christ. This is my opinion, my brother[6] in
the Lord, about what you write concerning those despising blasphemers: As no one is to be compelled to [accept] the faith and
the gospel, so they should not be allowed under the same government[7] to blaspheme. But they should be called and heard, and they
[themselves] should listen; if they can give no explanation [for
their conduct] and have no wish to believe, they should by all
means be forced to silence, so that no seed of civil discord be nourished. For he who wants to speak against [the Christian faith]
should do this in public, and he should be checked through the
authority of the government either publicly or privately. This is
the way we do it, and the way we advise [handling this matter].

From this you will already understand that under the same
government[8] such people are by no means to be permitted to do in
the church[9] what you write. For this[10] is the hissing of the serpents
which flee the light. So call them before the public, that they may
be either victorious or defeated. In addition, since the Decalogue
and the Catechism also teach matters pertaining to the political
commonwealth and the management of household affairs, and since
such matters must often be dealt with in sermons, these people

---

[6] Luther wrote *vir*, i.e., man.
[7] I.e., a government which supports the "correct" faith cannot tolerate blasphemy against the faith, or religious disunity among the people, since such
toleration could not help but lead to unrest.
[8] See note 7.
[9] Luther wrote *ecclesia;* see p. 61, n. 9.
[10] I.e., whatever the "blasphemers" had done.

should be compelled to attend those sermons in which they can learn secular obedience and the [proper way] of managing a household—regardless of whether they believe the gospel or not—so that they are not a cause of offense to others, and so that they do not despise the teachings concerning the state and the household in the same way [that they despise the gospel]. For if they want to live as a part of the community,[11] they should learn and listen to the law of this community[12]—even if they do so unwillingly—not only for their own good but also for the good of their children and households.

Christ will give you further instruction; in him, farewell.

August 26, 1529   MARTIN LUTHER

196

To Mrs. Martin Luther
[Marburg,] October 4. 1529

Encouraged by Luther's willingness to attend a conference with representatives of the symbolic interpretation of the Lord's Supper,[1]

---

[11] Literally: "live among the people."

[12] Literally: "law of this people."

[1] See pp. 228 ff. The Landgrave's (see note 2) political astuteness is worthy of note. To Luther he always mentioned only "Oecolampadius and some of his followers" as being the men with whom Luther was to confer, even though he had already negotiated with Zwingli for the conference; see p. 230, n. 15. The Landgrave was apparently well aware that Luther might not attend a meeting with Zwingli, due to the hard feelings that existed between Luther and Zwingli. On the other hand, Oecolampadius had been more gentlemanly in his polemics against Luther, so that the Landgrave could hope that Luther would attend a colloquy with the Reformer of Basel; therefore as early as his first feeler toward Luther, the Landgrave mentioned only Oecolampadius. And Luther in the first draft of his reply (see p. 229, n. 10) expressed his willingness to meet with Oecolampadius, see WA, Br 5, 104. The Electoral Saxon court, apparently knowing of Philip's efforts to get Zwingli and Luther to the conference table, and apparently informing Luther accordingly, corrected Luther's draft, so that in the final version Luther mentions no one by name and speaks only of the "opposition," with which he would be willing to meet; see p. 230. The Landgrave kept up the facade, however, and in his official invitation (see p. 231, n. 19) he again mentioned only Oecolampadius and his followers. Luther, in his official acceptance of the invitation (see note 3), again mentioned no one by name. If Luther knew of the Landgrave's

Landgrave Philip of Hesse[2] issued the official invitation to Luther on July 1, 1529, and Luther, in turn, officially accepted it on July 8.[3] Between September 30 and October 1 an illustrious company of theologians arrived at the castle of the Landgrave in Marburg. After preliminary discussions the conference[4] began at 6:00 A.M. on October 2 in the private chambers of the Landgrave, under the chairmanship of the Hessian chancellor, Christian Feige,[5] and in the presence of the Landgrave. The conference continued until the late afternoon of October 3, when it was more or less officially closed; it had become clear to all participants that, notwithstanding the cordial atmosphere of the conference, the discrepancies between Luther and Zwingli could not be bridged. The Landgrave was not so easily discouraged, however, and upon his initiative the discussions were renewed in the evening of October 3, now in the more informal atmosphere of a dinner meeting. The conference participants continued their discussions through October 4, and finally adopted the Marburg Articles.[6] On October 5, in the afternoon, Luther and Melanchthon departed from Marburg.

In the following letter, written apparently before the Marburg Articles were adopted,[7] Luther briefly characterizes the events which had taken place since the conference had been officially closed on October 3 in the afternoon. Luther quotes some of the main arguments of the opposition, names some of the participants in the conference, and reports on an outbreak of English fever in Marburg. He also sends greetings to Bugenhagen and kisses to his own children.

Text in German: WA, Br 5, 154.[8]

---

real intentions, and there is not the slightest reason to assume that he did not, then, in view of the Landgrave's deceptive actions, it is no wonder that Luther distrusted the Landgrave, and went to Marburg more apprehensively than he would have, had he been weighed down only by theological considerations.
[2] See p. 124, n. 18.
[3] See p. 231, n. 19.
[4] On the Marburg Colloquy, see Köhler, *op. cit.* (see p. 94, n. 6), 2, 84 ff.; Sasse, pp. 215 ff.; LW 38, 15 ff. For the participants, see note 28.
[5] On Christian Feige, see *NDB* 5, 55 f.
[6] Text: WA 30[III], 160 ff.; Sasse, pp. 269 ff.
[7] See note 11.
[8] For a commentary on this letter, and for references to other letters dealing with the Marburg Colloquy, see Köhler, *op. cit.*, 2, 139 ff. See also Rückert, *LB*, pp. 241 ff.

To my kind, dear lord, Catherine Luther, a doctor and preacher[9] in Wittenberg

Grace and peace in Christ. Dear Sir[10] Katie! You should know that our amiable colloquy at Marburg has come to an end, and we are in agreement on almost all points, except that the opposition insists on affirming that there is only simple bread in the Lord's Supper, and on confessing that Jesus Christ is spiritually present there. Today the Landgrave is negotiating [to see] if we could be united, or whether, even though we continue to disagree, we could not nevertheless mutually consider ourselves brethren, and members of Christ. The Landgrave works hard on this matter.[11] But we do not want this brother-and-member business, though we do want peace and good [will]. I assume that tomorrow or the next day we shall depart from here and travel to our Gracious Lord[12] in Schleiz/ Vogtland, where His Electoral Grace[13] has ordered us [to go].[14]

---

[9] See note 10.

[10] Or "Lord," or "Mr." To the modern reader this form of address may sound quite awkard, especially since Catherine Luther was neither a doctor nor a preacher. These phrases lose their point, however, if they are interpreted as jokes, or as an allusion to Catherine Luther's noble birth. Catherine Luther had become for Luther a person of extreme importance, not only as mistress of his house (who looked after him, something which the professor needed so badly; see Bainton, p. 290), or as mother of his beloved children, but, and this above all, as spiritual companion. In her quiet, direct, confident, and sometimes blunt way she was both preacher and teacher to Luther, their children, and their friends; more than once she helped Luther to deal with his religious tensions and fears. Luther signed this letter with "Your obedient servant." This is a major comment on the relationship between husband and wife as Luther understood it—the same Luther who took literally St. Paul's statement that wives should be subordinate to their husbands, and who would never have dreamed of joining the chorus of the Humanists who clamored for the social and intellectual emancipation of the female. For more material on Luther's views on marriage in general and on his own in particular, see the fine statements in Bainton, pp. 290 ff.

[11] This sentence suggests that the work on the *Marburg Articles* (see note 6) was still going on, and that the Landgrave's diplomatic machinery was going full speed. Perhaps Luther wrote this letter during the lunch recess. In another letter, also dated October 4 (see *WA, Br* 5, No. 1477; *S-J* 2, No. 850), Luther mentions the *Marburg Articles* as being completed.

[12] I.e., Elector John; see LW 48, 269, n. 8.

[13] See note 12.

[14] While in Marburg, Luther received by special messenger the order of Elector John (dated September 28; *WA, Br* 5, No. 1475) that immediately

Tell Mr. Pomer[15] that the best arguments[16] have been, in Zwingli's case, that a[17] body cannot exist without a location, therefore Christ's body is not in the bread, [and] in Oecolampadius' case,[18] [that] this[19] sacrament[20] is a sign of Christ's body. I assume that God has blinded them so that they had nothing else to offer.

I am very busy, and the messenger is in a hurry. Say "good night" to all, and pray for us! We are all still[21] alert and healthy,

---

after the close of the Marburg Colloquy Luther (with Melanchthon and Jonas) was to travel to Schleiz; if the Elector had by then already left Schleiz, then Luther and his party were to follow further instructions. Elector John met in Schleiz from October 3 to October 7 with Margrave George of Brandenburg-Ansbach-Kulmbach and a representative of Landgrave Philip of Hesse, in order to re-examine the possibility of an alliance of the Prostestants in the light of the newest developments. The meeting of the Prostestants at Rodach (see p. 228) torpedoed the plans for the secret alliance which had been made at Speyer. The sore point was the Eucharistic teaching. The Landgrave concentrated his efforts on the idea of a compromise through the Marburg Colloquy; Melanchthon, Luther, the Electoral Saxon government, Nürnberg, and Margrave George, however, worked on the idea of a political-military alliance based on doctrinal agreement. For this purpose Melanchthon drew up the so-called *Schwabach Articles* (text: WA 30[III], 178 ff.; Reu II, No. 8). All parties concerned were to meet in Schleiz to discuss an alliance based on these articles. The Landgrave (who was also invited to Schleiz) could not attend this meeting since it jeopardized the purpose of the Marburg Colloquy; consequently he sent only some minor officials to Schleiz. In view of the general situation it is understandable that Elector John wanted a first-hand report about the Marburg Colloquy while he was still in Schleiz. Even though no dramatic decisions emerged from this meeting in Schleiz because of the Landgrave's absence, Electoral Saxony and Brandenburg-Ansbach came to a full agreement on the *Schwabach Articles*, on the planned alliance, and on other matters. See Fabian, *ABBP*, pp. 63 ff. A meeting with the representatives of Nürnberg, Ulm, Strassburg, and other Protestant cities was scheduled for mid-October in Schwabach, at which time the city delegates were to be informed of the idea of an alliance based on the *Schwabach Articles*. This meant that either the upper German cities would have to affirm a strict Lutheran interpretation of the Lord's Supper or be excluded from the alliance. For details, see Fabian, *ESBV* (2nd ed.), pp. 59 ff; Reu I, 26 ff.

[15] I.e., John Bugenhagen; see *LW* 48, 303, n. 44.

[16] This is to be understood as sarcasm.

[17] From here on the text is written in Latin.

[18] Luther wrote: *des Oecolampadii.*

[19] This word is written in German.

[20] From here on to the end of the sentence the text is written in Latin. Then Luther continues in German. Catherine Luther had mastered some Latin and, according to the *Table Talks*, was capable of participating in a discussion conducted in Latin; see *WA*, TR 3, No. 3298b; 4, No. 4860; 5, No. 5567. On the theological issues involved, see Köhler, *op. cit.*, 2, 87, 107 ff.

[21] See note 29.

and live like kings.[22] Kiss Lenchen [23] and Hänschen[24] on my behalf.

October 4, 1529   Your obedient servant,

MARTIN LUTHER

John Brenz,[25] Andrew Osiander,[26] [and] Doctor Stephen[27] from Augsburg have also come here.[28]

The people here have become almost mad with fear of the

---

[22] The Landgrave treated his guests royally, and Luther's statement may be a reference to the banquet held in the evening of October 3.

[23] Magdalen Luther; see p. 312, n. 6.

[24] John Luther; see p. 323, n. 7.

[25] John Brenz from Schwäbisch Hall; see pp. 177 f.

[26] Andrew Osiander (1498–1552) was the chief preacher at Nürnberg's famous St. Lawrence Church. In this position he worked hard and successfully for the introduction and organization of the Reformation in Nürnberg, and was one of the authors of the *Brandenburg-Nürnberg Church Ordinance* of 1533. In 1549 he became a professor at the University of Königsberg, where he taught for the remainder of his life. Osiander, who is said to have been a specialist in the Hebrew language and the *Cabala,* and to have been influenced by the Humanist Reuchlin, was one of the most independent thinkers of the Reformation in Germany (in addition to being a somewhat arrogant churchman). His basic contribution to Protestant thought was a fundamental re-interpretation of Luther's doctrine of justification. While attending the Diet of Augsburg, 1530, and then again later while teaching in Königsberg, Osiander rejected the forensic understanding of justification and replaced it with an understanding according to which in justifying faith a *substantial transference* of Christ's righteousness to the sinner' takes place. After Luther's death, Osiander became involved in bitterly fought doctrinal controversies which harassed the Reformation in Germany for decades to come. On Osiander, see *O.D.C.C.,* p. 996; G. Seebass, *Das reformatorische Werk des Andreas Osiander* (Nürnberg, 1967).

[27] Stephen Kastenbauer, or Agricola, a former Augustinian, is one of the many lesser known men of the Reformation in Germany. He was born *ca.* 1491 in Abensberg/Bavaria, and died in 1547 in Eisleben. In 1522 he was imprisoned because of his (open?) support of Luther, yet he was able to escape from prison, and found a home and pastorate in Augsburg in 1524. He was invited by the Landgrave to attend the Marburg Colloquy as theological representative of the evangelical clergy in Augsburg. Because of his outspoken opposition to Zwingli, Agricola had to leave Augsburg in 1531. He took over a parish in Hof, and later one in Sulzbach (Upper Palatinate) from which he had to flee during the Smalcaldic War. From 1546 to the end of his life he was a pastor in Eisleben. On Stephen Agricola, see *NDB* 1, 105 f.

[28] In addition to Brenz, Osiander, and Agricola, the Marburg Colloquy was attended by Melanchthon (see *LW* 48, 77, n. 3), Jonas (see *LW* 48, 275, n. 3), Zwingli (see p. 88, n. 12), Oecolampadius (see *LW* 48, 230, n. 14), Bucer (see *LW* 48, 247, n. 3), Hedio (a pastor in Strassburg), and Luther. The theologians listed here were the actual participants in the colloquy who signed the *Marburg Articles.* In addition a host of hopefuls had come to Marburg seeking admittance, if only as audience, or at the very least to snatch up news.

English fever;[29] about fifty people fell ill yesterday, of whom one or two have [already] passed away.

197

To Nicholas von Amsdorf[1]
[Wittenberg,] October 27, 1529

Luther says that he shares von Amsdorf's satisfaction with the results of the Marburg Colloquy. He also reports news concerning the final attack of the Turkish army against the city of Vienna, and the end of the Turkish siege of that city. In closing he discusses von Amsdorf's question whether it is objectionable that the Saxon Elector enter into an alliance with other Estates, even if they are godless, or are adversaries of the Word. Luther affirms that for the sake of defending the country such an alliance is permissible.

On Nicholas von Amsdorf, see LW 48, 218.

Text in Latin: WA, Br 5, 167–168.

Grace and peace in the Lord

I rejoice that you, my Amsdorf, are so happy with our Marburg synod,[2] which, to be sure, looked insignificant, but was effective

---

[29] The English fever (*Englischer Schweiss*, an epidemic fever which had been brought into Germany at the beginning of the sixteenth century by English sailors) was feared by the people even more than the plague, probably because it was still less known. See Enders, *Briefwechsel* 7, 142, n. 9. According to Melanchthon and others (see WA, Br 5, 154, n. 3; 13, 115, *ad loc.;* Enders, *Briefwechsel* 7, 168, n. 4) the outbreak of this disease in Marburg caused the Landgrave to hurry the discussions and to be satisfied with the *Marburg Articles,* instead of continuing to press for marathon negotiations which might have resulted in the eventual compromise between Luther and Zwingli that the Landgrave was hoping for.

[1] Even though the address is missing in all witnesses, it is clear to whom Luther was writing, since he greets von Amsdorf by name in the opening sentence of the letter.

[2] On the Marburg Colloquy, see letter No. 196. On October 19 Luther had written briefly to von Amsdorf about the Marburg Colloquy; in that letter he also mentioned verbal reports which von Amsdorf had received; WA, Br 5, 163; S-J 2, 502. Von Amsdorf apparently immediately wrote back to Luther a no-longer extant letter, so that Luther could now, on October 27, refer to von Amsdorf's opinion about the Marburg Colloquy as expressed in that letter.

in the matter itself. This has been accomplished by the prayers of the faithful: [the opposition,] confused as it was, was feeble and was humiliated. Praise and glory be to God.

Yesterday we heard that by a great miracle of God the Turk[3]

---

[3] Since the fall of Constantinople (1453) the Ottoman Turks had controlled the Balkans south of a line approximately marked from the west to the east by the Save and Danube rivers. In the eastern parts of the Balkans they had already gone beyond the Danube, subjugating the principalities of Wallachia and Moldavia. Under Sultan Suleiman II (see R. B. Merriman, *Suleiman the Magnificent, 1520–1566* [Cambridge, Mass., 1944]) the Turks started their military drive into central Europe with the conquest of Belgrade in 1521. In the famous battle at Mohacs the small Hungarian army was defeated, and on September 10 Ofen (Budapest) was conquered. All of Hungary would have been lost to the Turks, had not a civil war in Asia Minor forced the Sultan to cut short his campaign. In the battle of Mohacs, King Louis II of Hungary was killed. He was married to Mary, a sister of Charles V and Ferdinand of Austria; this marriage had remained without children. On the basis of dynastic arrangements negotiated by Emperor Maximilian I, Ferdinand of Austria was to succeed to the Hungarian throne, were Louis to pass away without heirs. But the Hungarian nobility split over this issue. The majority elected John Zapolyai, the woiwode (duke) of Transylvania, while the minority accepted Ferdinand. These dynastic affairs of the Hapsburgs on the one hand, and the inner German affairs on the other hand, clouded the dangerous situation, so that little or nothing was done for an effective defense of Hungary against the Turks; see Ranke 2^{III}, 117. In May of 1529 Suleiman began his second campaign against central Europe with an army of overwhelming size. The Hungarian nobility, justly feeling abandoned by Ferdinand because of his squabbles with the Protestants (see Ranke 2^{III}, 117) and following the example set by Zapolyai, surrendered and commended themselves to the Sultan. When Ferdinand and his followers were unable to protect even the sacred St. Stephen's crown (the national symbol of highest emotional value), the last resistance collapsed; see Ranke 2^{III}, 118 f. The small Austrian garrison in Budapest was cut down, some of the other fortresses were stormed, and the way to Vienna, and thus to the center of Europe, was open. On September 26 the Turkish siege of Vienna began. Even though the German sovereigns, regardless of their religious convictions, started to mobilize and come to the aid of Ferdinand, for the time being Vienna was on its own. In view of the fact that only a small mercenary army could be organized on such short notice, and in view of the general disrepair of the fortifications of Vienna, it seemed highly unlikely that Vienna could resist the Sultan's army for any length of time. The only assets of the Viennese were their brave determination to hold the city and their highly sophisticated artillery. Once developed as a hobby of the Hapsburg Emperor Maximilian I (at an expense which almost bankrupted the country), this artillery was now to contribute to the rescue of the city, and thus stop the Turkish invasion of Central Europe. See Ranke 2^{III}, 116 ff.; Elton, pp. 346 ff.; St. Fischer-Galati, *Ottoman Imperialism and German Protestantism 1521–1555* (Cambridge, Mass., 1959); *The Slavonic and East European Review* 38 (1960), 493 ff.; *Studies in the Renaissance* 10 (1963), 60 ff. Luther heard of the Turkish siege of Vienna while returning from the Marburg Colloquy. He had been ordered by Elector John to go from Marburg to Schleiz (see p. 236, n. 14), but his party was redirected to

has, on the eve of the feast,[4] departed from Vienna for Hungary.[5] For after he had attacked the city itself in vain for almost the twentieth time,[6] he undermined the ground in three places, put

---

Torgau (the seat of the Electoral Saxon government), since the Electoral party had left Schleiz for Torgau by October 8. While in Eisenach on October 7, Luther's party received word from the Elector about the siege, and after their arrival in Torgau on October 17 they learned the details. While in Torgau they also experienced all the excitement of a hurried mobilization. See *C.R.* 1, 1108; 4, 971; *ARG* 25 (1928), 45. Luther was deeply distressed about the events, but even more about the lack of military effort to stop the Turks and defend the countryside. As early as October 20 he mentioned that he was working on an exhortation to the German people regarding the defense against the Turkish attack; *WA*, Br 5, 164. And on October 26 he informed Hausmann in Zwickau that he would publish his sermon against the Turks, and that Melanchthon and Jonas were working on a similar project; *WA*, Br 5, 166; *S-J* 2, 502 f.; see also *WA*, Br 5, 170; *S-J* 2, 504.

[4] The Turkish army began its retreat during the night of October 14–15; see Ranke 2[III], 128; *WA*, Br 5, 168, n. 4. It was not until October 18 that the last of the Turkish contingents were breaking camp. "Feast" could designate the day of St. Gallus (October 16), or the day of St. Luke the Evangelist (October 18), and the "eve" (see *LW* 48, 76, n. 18) could thus designate October 15 or October 17. Since in the following sentences Luther reports the events which had taken place on October 14, the "eve" of the feast was apparently the eve of St. Gallus (or October 15), i.e., the day during which the first part of the Turkish retreat, which had begun during the night of October 14–15, took place.

[5] The Turks retreated to central Hungary, where they installed Zapolyai (see note 3) as a puppet king. Here parts of the army were disbanded, and Suleiman returned to Constantinople. Even though the Sultan had not accomplished his goal, he nevertheless could be satisfied with the results of his campaign. The Save-Danube line of the Ottoman Empire was no longer the border of the Turkish Empire; almost all of Hungary was secured for the Turkish Empire and was governed by a vassal whose throne, at least for the time being, depended on Turkish weapons for protection against either interior or foreign enemies. The Hapsburg-Hungarian kingdom was restricted to a small corridor stretching in a northeastern-southwestern direction along the (Zapolyai-) Hungarian border.

[6] On October 9, 11, and 12 the Turks succeeded in opening major gaps in the Viennese defenses. On October 9 and 11 the second attack wave of the Turks collapsed, however, before the point-blank fire of the Viennese artillery and the bravery of the German and Austrian *Landsknechte* (mercenaries); see Ranke 2[III], 126 f. On October 12 the Turkish attack did not even get off the ground after a part of the city wall had been dynamited; see Ranke 2[III], 127. The "twenty" attempts to storm the city, mentioned by Luther, must either refer to initial skirmishes or else Luther had been misinformed. The "mining" (see note 7), mentioned by Luther as a last resort of the Turks, was in fact routinely used by them in laying siege to a fortress. They used it against Vienna at least as early as October 2 (see Ranke 2[III], 126), i.e., shortly after the actual siege had begun; it is dubious that in such a short period the Turks made twenty attempts to storm the city.

powder [into the tunnels], blasted the ground,[7] and made an opening.[8] But through no power could he force his army, terrified by God, into a head-on attack, so that [the army] was willing to let itself be cut down by its leaders rather than attempt this very last head-on attack. Some believe that [the Turk] departed confused by fear of the big guns,[9] and by our approaching army.[10]

---

[7] The Turks, too, had artillery (see note 3); it seems that compared with the Viennese they had more light and highly movable fire power, but less heavy stationary artillery. What was new to the western armies was the practice of digging tunnels under the walls, filling them with powder, and igniting the charge, thus bringing the walls down, or at least weakening them. The Turks were experts in this technique, and the "mining engineer battalion" had a place of special honor in the Turkish army; see Ranke 2^{III}, 125 f. The Viennese, at first taken completely by surprise, rapidly learned from their enemies, and started to dig tunnels toward the camps of the Turks; often it was a race to see who could blast whom first. As early as October 2 the Viennese beat the Turks at their own game, destroying an almost completed Turkish tunnel; see Ranke 2^{III}, 126.

[8] I.e., apparently into the city wall. The following sentence makes clear that Luther was reporting on the events of October 14. As early as October 12 it had become clear that the Turkish army, being accustomed to easy and quick victory, was completely demoralized by the resistance of the Viennese garrison. After the charges in the tunnels had been detonated on October 14 and parts of the city wall had tumbled to the ground, the Turks were confronted with the point-blank firing of the Viennese artillery and the squares of Landsknechte, and they panicked. "In short, they did not want to bite the fox," states a German battle record; see Ranke 2^{III}, 128, n. 1. Contemporary records confirm that the Turks had to be forced by their leaders to attack. The Turkish attack completely collapsed in the late afternoon, and by night the Sultan ordered the retreat.

[9] See note 3.

[10] Relief troops were indeed organized. A small Hapsburg army slowly approached from the north (i.e., from Moravia), and the first contingent of the Imperial army approached from the west; see Ranke 2^{III}, 123 f., 127 f. To what degree these armies could have threatened the Turks with a two-front war, or could have been a threat to the Turks once they had conquered Vienna, are open questions. (How poorly organized the efforts of the Empire against the Turks were, how small the insight into the military and tactical situation on the part of the men in charge, and how unimportant these relief troops really were, can be seen from the following facts: The relief troops were unable to disrupt the Sultan's more-or-less orderly retreat, or to follow the retreating armies and push the Sultan out of Hungary, or to depose Zapolyai, the Sultan's puppet in Hungary. And the mobilization in the Empire was stopped immediately after the Sultan's retreat; see, e.g., ARG 25 [1928], 45.) The Sultan and his staff were too skilled as military leaders to take any unnecessary risks. It was late autumn; the army was encamped in campaign areas rather than in fortified places; the countryside was literally barren of anything which could be used for food; the supply lines from the well-administered areas behind the Danube were too long; the morale of the troops was terrible. It was a combination of circumstances and excellent statesmanship which caused the Turkish retreat, rather than the military or

Others are of a different opinion. [In any case] God has obviously fought for us this year. [The Turk] has lost twenty-six thousand men, while it is said that six thousand of our men have been killed, having perished in the counterattacks.[11] I wanted to tell you this, if you haven't already heard other [news], so that we can be grateful and pray together. For the Turk who has become our neighbor[12] will not allow us to live in peace for ever.[13]

Regarding your question whether it is safe and permissible for our Sovereign[14] to ally himself with the godless and with the adversaries of [God's] Word,[15] we believe that this is possible because this is [a matter of] common defense; it would be impossible if one were to start a war or alliances when [not attacked]. For likewise[16] if the house of a godless man is on fire, or if your enemy is starving, feed him,[17] help him. In an emergency we have to do good even to our enemies.

Farewell in the Lord, and pray for me.

Written on October 27, 1529

Yours,

MARTIN LUTHER

---

political efforts on the part of the Empire. The strength of the Sultan's position and the weakness of Ferdinand's can be seen from the fact that the Sultan was able to hold on to Hungary by creating a puppet government, and that as early as May, 1530, Ferdinand sent an embassy to Constantinople in the hope of regaining Hungary by diplomatic negotiations; see Ranke 2[III] 248.

[11] These figures can be questioned.

[12] See notes 3, 5.

[13] See p. 265.

[14] I.e., Elector John; see *LW* 48, 269, n. 8.

[15] In the no-longer extant letter (see note 2), von Amsdorf apparently brought up for discussion the whole situation which led to the Marburg Colloquy, and perhaps also discussed the meeting at Schleiz (see p. 236, n. 14). He apparently also asked the question whether, in view of the Turkish danger, Elector John had the right to cooperate with the pro-papal sovereigns for the purpose of defending the Empire against the Turks.

[16] The translation is based on a conjecture suggested in *St. L.* 21a, 1372.

[17] Rom. 12:20.

198

To Elector John
[Wittenberg,] November 18, 1529

The alliance negotiations among the Protestant Estates following the 1529 Diet of Speyer failed because of two problems: the theological discrepancy between Luther and Zwingli regarding the Lord's Supper,[1] and the question whether the protesting Estates, if attacked for the sake of their faith, had the right to defend themselves by taking up arms, not only against their fellow Estates, but also against the emperor himself.[2]

While preparing themselves for the conference in Schwabach,[3] both Elector John of Saxony[4] and Margrave George of Brandenburg[5] were in agreement that they indeed had the right, even the duty, to protect themselves and their subjects against any military action on the part of the emperor taken on account of their own religious convictions, or those of their subjects; and Philip of Hesse[6] was always ready to fight the emperor.[7] In view of Emperor

---

[1] See pp. 228 ff., 234 ff.

[2] For "emperor," see p. 274, n. 22. The Nürnberg city government, led by its chancellor, Lazarus Spengler (see *LW* 48, 184), was opposed to any ideas of armed resistance to the emperor from the very beginning of the negotiations. As early as May, 1529, Lazarus Spengler, in his draft of an alliance constitution which was to be discussed in Rodach (see p. 228), made it clear that the Estates have the right to take up arms against other Estates, but not against the emperor as overlord; see Schornbaum, Nürnberg, 196, n. 2; Fabian, *ESBV* (2nd ed.), pp. 53 f.

[3] See p. 236, n. 14.

[4] See *LW* 48, 269, n. 8.

[5] See p. 60, n. 5.

[6] See p. 124, n. 18. In September, 1529, the Landgrave asked the Elector if he could rely on the Elector's military support if he were attacked by Emperor Charles V for reasons of the faith. See Schornbaum, Nürnberg, 195. As soon as the Landgrave knew that the Protestants' delegation to the Emperor had been jailed (see note 9), he was ready to fight back; see Fabian, *ESBV* (2nd ed.), p. 66.

[7] As a result of the Landgrave's inquiry, mentioned in note 6, and prior to the meeting in Schleiz (see p. 236, n. 14), Elector John approached his theologians in Wittenberg for counsel on this matter. Since Luther and Melanchthon had already left for Marburg, Bugenhagen (see *LW* 48, 303, n. 44) had to reply to the Elector. In a brief, dated September 29, Bugenhagen argued that if an emperor acted like a Turk and murderer, then he was no longer a lord, and that then the Word of God is the lord who is to be obeyed. Bugenhagen pointed out, however, that his opinion should be subject to revision by

Charles's[8] attempts to bring the Protestants to heel,[9] the three Protestant sovereigns felt that they could justify taking up arms even against the Emperor in the defense of their own faith and that of the people of their territories; and some of the upper German cities joined the sovereigns in this conviction. At the end of October or the beginning of November, however, the Nürnberg city government openly rejected any idea of armed resistance to the Emperor.[10] Even though the Nürnberg city fathers were ready to fight their fellow Estates in order to defend themselves if attacked because of matters of faith, they were absolutely against the idea of armed resistance to the emperor, if the latter were to make war on the Protestants for the sake of their faith. They buttressed their position with a host of biblical passages. They drew especially on Romans 13, identifying the emperor with that governing authority to which Paul says every person is to be subject. They saw the emperor as the major (original) governing authority, and the Estates as the minor (derivative) governing authorities. Relying on Paul, who said that "every person" is to be subject to the governing authorities, and equating the Estates with Paul's "every person," the Nürnberg officials came to the conclusion that the Estates were to be obediently subject to the emperor, and consequently could under no circumstances take up arms against the emperor. The

---

more learned people. Based on Bugenhagen's opinion, and on briefs issued by the Electoral Saxon chancellery, the Elector and the Margrave agreed in Schleiz on the right of armed resistance to the emperor if necessary, i.e., if attacked because of their religious convictions; they also instructed their ambassadors to Schwabach accordingly. See Fabian, ESBV (2nd ed.), pp. 59 f. For Bugenhagen's brief, see Widerstandsrecht, pp. 25 ff.; see also Ranke 2[III], 112 f.; for the instruction drafted in Schleiz, see Fabian, ABBP, pp. 70 ff., esp. p. 72.

[8] See LW 48, 175 f., and in this vol., p. 222.

[9] The Emperor was unwilling to put up with the Protest and Appeal of the Protestants (see p. 223). On July 12 in Barcelona he issued a mandate against the Protestants, demanding that they withdraw their Protest and Appeal; see DRTA.JR 7[I], 880, n. 1; WA, Br 5, 180. And on October 24 the Nürnberg city government received the news (dated October 13) that the Emperor had jailed the delegation which was to turn over the Protest and the Appeal of the Protestants to the Emperor. Nürnberg immediately informed the other participants of the Protest; see Schornbaum, Nürnberg, 188; Fabian, ESBV, (2nd ed.), pp. 65 f.

[10] For the discussions in the Nürnberg city council, see Schornbaum, Nürnberg, 189 f. In mid-November Lazarus Spengler (see note 2) drafted a major brief in which he summarized the Nürnberg position; text: Widerstandsrecht, pp. 29 ff.; see also Schornbaum, Nürnberg, 196.

arguments of the Nürnberg officials eventually caused Margrave George and Elector John to have second thoughts regarding the right of armed resistance to the emperor.[11] *So by early November, 1529, the Speyer plans for an alliance among the Protestants— even in the modified form which developed during the summer and fall of 1529*[12]*—were completely doomed to failure.*

Yet the political situation was demanding some effective action on the part of the Protestants. On October 19 the Protestant delegates, assembled in Schwabach,[13] *decided to meet again in the middle of December in the Electoral Saxon town of Smalcald.*[14] *This meeting was to bring about a decision on an alliance based on the Schwabach Articles. Obviously at this meeting the problem of resistance to the emperor would have to be discussed. In view of the news which arrived from the Imperial court,*[15] *Nürnberg, in cooperation with Elector John, took the initiative, and on November 1 and 2 scheduled the Smalcald meeting for November 28.*[16] *This meeting was to deal first of all with the Protestants' reaction to the Emperor's treatment of the delegation which the Protestants had sent to the Emperor for the purpose of delivering the Protest and Appeal,*[17] *and then secondly with the matter of the alliance. In view of the importance of the situation all the Estates which had joined in the Protest and Appeal were invited to Smalcald, so that,*

---

[11] When the officials of Brandenburg-Ansbach and Electoral Saxony saw Spengler's brief (see note 10) for the first time cannot be established. On November 15 Spengler informed the chancellor of Ansbach, George Vogler, that he would soon send this brief; see Schornbaum, Nürnberg, 196, n. 5. The instructions which Margrave George of Brandenburg-Ansbach issued for his delegates to the Smalcald meeting (see note 16) do not yet show any influence of Spengler's brief; see Schornbaum, Nürnberg, 196, n. 6; Reu II, No. 13. Also the Elector's request, to which Luther replies in the present letter, does not demonstrate any knowledge of the Nürnberg position; at least Luther's reply does not document that the Nürnberg position was at issue between the Electoral court and Luther. Apparently it was in Smalcald that Spengler's brief became generally known. And then throughout December and January Landgrave Philip exchanged letters with Margrave George in which the Margrave represented the Nürnberg position regarding the right of armed resistance to the emperor; see Schornbaum, Nürnberg, 196, n. 6; Schornbaum, *Georg*, pp. 95 ff., 103 ff.

[12] See p. 236, n. 14.

[13] See note 3.

[14] Text: Fabian, *ABBP*, pp. 95 ff.; Reu II, No. 10.

[15] See note 9.

[16] See Fabian, *ESBV* (2nd ed.), pp. 67 f.

[17] See note 9.

for the time being at least, the one big issue which divided the Protestants, the Lord's Supper, was once more removed to the background. In order to prepare himself for this important meeting, Elector John dispatched Gregory Brück[18] to Wittenberg with instructions to obtain from Luther and his colleagues a judgment on the situation, especially regarding the planned alliance.[19]

The present letter is Luther's reply, given also in behalf of his colleagues. Luther opposes the alliance, as he had in the past.[20] Regarding the political dangers that could result from the lack of an alliance, Luther admonishes the Elector to be steadfast in the faith. He further points out that in the present situation it is the task of the Christian to stand up for his belief, even if this might result in suffering, and adds that in matters of faith it is not the task of the Christian to engage in bloodshed, but rather to suffer.[21]

On Elector John, see LW 48, 269, n. 8.

Text in German: WA, Br 5, 181–183.

To the Most Serene, Noble Sovereign and Lord, Sir John, duke in Saxony and elector, etc., landgrave in Thuringia and margrave in Meissen, my Most Gracious Lord

Grace and peace in Christ! Most Serene, Noble Sovereign, Most Gracious Lord! The honorable and highly learned sir, Gregory Brück,[22] doctor, etc., has presented to the four of us[23] credentials issued by Your Electoral Grace, and on this basis we received from him Your Electoral Grace's opinion. We have put our best judg-

---

[18] See pp. 51 ff.

[19] The right of armed resistance to the emperor was not a specific issue for this Smalcald meeting, apparently because the Nürnberg position was not yet generally known. Luther's reply does not deal in a detailed way with this issue. Luther deals only with the alliance and with the problems surrounding taking up arms for the defense of one's faith.

[20] See pp. 223 ff.

[21] Brück worked Luther's letter into a lengthy brief, which guided the Elector at his negotiations in Smalcald; text: Reu II, No. 13. See also Fabian, *ESBV* (2nd ed.), p. 72.

[22] See note 18.

[23] This translation is based on the WA, Br text. According to Enders, *Briefwechsel* 7, 190, n. 2, one would have to translate: "the three of us." According to Fabian, *ESBV* (2nd ed.), p. 72, the present brief was issued by Luther, Melanchthon, and Bugenhagen. Clemen (WA, Br 5, 181) adds Jonas as the fourth author.

ment in writing, to be turned over to Your Electoral Grace, and ask that Your Electoral Grace graciously receive from us said judgment.[24] For according to our consciences we can neither approve of such an alliance nor advise [that it be initiated], in view of the fact that, if [this matter] developed and perhaps some bloodshed or some other catastrophe came from it, we could not get out of it, even if we wished to, and would have to bear all such misfortune as an intolerable burden. We would rather wish to be ten times dead than to have on our consciences the thought that our gospel[25] should have been the cause of such bloodshed and damage, done because of us.[26] We are to be those who suffer, and as the prophet says [in] Psalm 44 [:22], we are to be considered as the sheep for the slaughter, and not avenge or defend ourselves, but give way to God's wrath; Romans 12 [:19].

It does no harm that Your Electoral Grace should be in the midst of danger because of this.[27] Our Lord Christ is powerful enough, [and he] can easily find ways and means [to see] that such danger will do nothing to Your Electoral Grace; he can very well nullify the plans of the ungodly sovereigns;[28] Psalm 33 [:10]. For we also feel that such an undertaking of the Emperor[29] is only a threat of the devil, which will be without power and will finally grow into a catastrophe for the opposition, as Psalm 7 [:16] says:[30] "His mischief returns upon his own head, and his violence will descend upon him." In addition, Christ tries us (as is right and necessary) through this [danger to see] whether or not we, too, [31] take his word seriously and uphold it as firm truth. For if we wish to be Christians and have life eternal in the world to

---

[24] For the following, see also pp. 225 ff.

[25] I.e., the way "we" understand and teach the gospel.

[26] I.e., because "we" have understood and taught the gospel in such a way that a "hostile" opposition emerged, a fact which in turn led "us" to make an alliance, which in turn could result in bloodshed.

[27] I.e., that no alliance was made.

[28] I.e., those sovereigns who during the Diet of Speyer had joined Ferdinand, as viceroy, in demanding the nullification of the resolution of the 1526 Diet of Speyer (see p. 156), and who might go to war against the Protestants in order to enforce this resolution.

[29] See notes 8, 9.

[30] Literally: "sings."

[31] I.e., that "we" take God's Word as seriously as the author of Psalm 7 did.

come,[32] then we cannot [in this world] be better off than our Lord himself and all his saints were and still are. Christ's cross must always be carried; the world does not want to carry it, but wants to place it on others; but we Christians have to carry it so that it does not lie around without an owner, or is good for nothing.[33] Your Electoral Grace has till now sincerely shared in carrying [the burden of Christ's cross] both in the case of the insurrection,[34] and in the case of the great spiritual temptation,[35] envy, hatred, and evil treachery by friends and foes. Yet God has always graciously helped, has given Your Electoral Grace firm courage, and has not abandoned [Your Grace] without comfort, both physical and spiritual. Rather, in a miraculous way God has uncovered, torn up, and brought to nothing all the devil's evil treachery and snares. He will also do [us] no harm in the future, provided we believe and pray.[36] Indeed we know positively, [and] we have also experienced up to now, through God's manifest help, that our cause is not our's, but that of God himself. This [fact] is our defiant boast and our consolation because as a faithful father [God] has cared for and defended these, his affairs, in such a way that we have to confess that it[37] has been beyond our skill and might, and that we could not have directed, defended, or done it[38] in this way with our own wisdom.

Therefore I humbly plead and exhort Your Electoral Grace to be calm and undismayed in this danger. If God wills it, then we shall accomplish more with prayer and pleading to God than [our enemies] will accomplish with all their threats, if only we keep our hands clean from bloodshed and crime. And if it should come to the point (which I doubt) that the Emperor[39] should continue to press and demand my extradition, or any others', then by God's grace we shall stand up for ourselves, [and] shall not expose Your

---

[32] Literally: "there."
[33] See also LW 48, 12 ff., 387.
[34] I.e., the Peasants' War. See also LW 48, 387.
[35] Luther wrote Anfechtung; see LW 48, 28, n. 10.
[36] See Isa. 7:9. This sentence is ambiguous. "He" could refer either to God or the devil.
[37] See note 38.
[38] I.e., "our" work, which is that of God. The reference is to "these, his affairs."
[39] See note 8; see also LW 48, 392.

Electoral Grace to any danger in our behalf, as I have previously often told Your Electoral Grace's brother—God bless him—my most gracious lord, Duke Frederick.[40] For Your Electoral Grace is not to defend my faith, or that of anyone else. [Your Grace] cannot do any such thing. But if it gets to the point that our overlord, that is, the emperor, wants to attack us [then] each one has to defend his own faith for himself, and has to believe or not believe in the face of his own risk, and not because of danger to someone else. In the meantime much water will run [down the river], and God will indeed find a way so that things will not turn out as [our enemies] plan.

May Christ, our Lord and comfort, richly strengthen Your Electoral Grace. Amen.

November 18, 1529   Your Electoral Grace's dedicated
                             MARTIN LUTHER

199

To Landgrave Philip of Hesse
[Wittenberg,] December 16, 1529

The Smalcald meeting of all the Estates which had joined in the Speyer Protest and Appeal marked the collapse of all further negotiations among all the Protestants.[1] At Smalcald it was decided[2] that only those Estates which would subscribe to the Schwabach Articles[3] could join the alliance; however, no concrete decisions were made about what could be done in reaction to the Emperor's treatment of the delegation which was to deliver to him the Protest and Appeal.[4] A new meeting was scheduled for January, 1530, in Nürnberg, at which there were to be further negotiations regard-

---

[40] I.e., Elector Frederick, see *LW* 48, 49 f., 391; for other references, see *WA*, Br 5, 183, n. 6.

[1] On this meeting at Smalcald (November 28–December 4, 1529), see p. 246; Fabian, *ESBV* (2nd ed.), pp. 71 ff.

[2] Text of the resolution: Fabian, *ABBP*, pp. 101 ff.

[3] See p. 236, n. 14.

[4] See p. 245, n. 9.

ing the alliance and the Emperor's treatment of the delegation; to this meeting were to come only those Estates which were ready to subscribe to the Schwabach Articles.

In order to avoid the necessity of having each of the Protestant Estates face the Emperor's displeasure about the Protest and Appeal, or do so all alone, the Estates developed plans of their own. The Nürnberg city council, for instance, at one time apparently even seriously considered withdrawing from the Protest and Appeal.[5] And Landgrave Philip of Hesse (abandoning his ambition to create an alliance of all Protestant Estates) speeded his alliance negotiations with Strassburg and Zürich.[6] He also forced a showdown with Margrave George of Brandenburg-Ansbach on the question of the right of armed resistance to the emperor; in the process it became clear that he could expect no help from the Margrave if Emperor Charles or his deputies attacked Hesse because of the gospel.[7] Furthermore, Philip wanted to go on the political offensive. Immediately after the Smalcald meeting he approached Luther,[8] asking for support for a plan which was politically farsighted. He suggested that the sovereigns who were affirming the gospel should refuse to aid the Emperor against the Turks[9] unless the Emperor would promise, by means of a public proclamation, not to make war on the Protestants for the sake of the gospel, and thus, by Imperial law, guarantee the existence of the Reformation.

---

[5] See Schornbaum, Nürnberg, 189 ff., 198 f., 202 f.; Fabian, *ESBV* (2nd ed.), p. 74.

[6] See Fabian, *ESBV* (2nd ed.), p. 74.

[7] See Schornbaum, *Georg*, pp. 102 ff.

[8] Philip of Hesse to Luther: December 9, 1529; *WA*, Br 5, No. 1503; *S-J* 2, No. 861.

[9] In November, 1529, the Council of Regency (see *LW* 48, 70, n. 1) met in Speyer to discuss the threat posed to the Empire by the Turks, and decided to support Ferdinand's military efforts against the Turks. Even though the immediate danger for the Empire was eliminated by the withdrawal of the Turks, Ferdinand of Austria continued the campaign against the Turks in Hungary, though with little success (see p. 242, n. 10). For this campaign he was seeking the support of the Estates. The Emperor considered it his duty not only to defend the borders of the Empire against the infidels, but also to defeat them. Consequently he placed the matter of the war against the Turks, as the external enemy of Christendom, on the agenda of the Diet of Augsburg; see Reu II, p. 69. Behind such a grandiose design of a crusade-like campaign against the Turks lay hidden, however, rather primitive dynastic interests, namely, making all of Hungary a part of the Hapsburg dynastic lands.

Philip wanted Luther to promise that if Elector John approached him for counsel, Luther would advise him along the lines that Philip had suggested.

The following letter is Luther's reply to the Landgrave, and it is rather vague. Luther points out that he knows nothing of the matter concerning aid in the fight against the Turks, and that the Electoral court has not asked for his advice. Were he to be asked for advice, he would of course give his best counsel. How Luther really felt about the defense of the Empire against the Turkish invasion can clearly be seen from his writings on the Turkish war.[10] Luther was too much of a German to side with a plan that in the long run might weaken the military strength of the Empire. And further, he could not have supported the idea of using political power (that is, pressuring the Emperor, or almost blackmailing him) for the purpose of attaining a religious goal (that is, the legally guaranteed right to proclaim and affirm the gospel as the Reformers had come to understand it). This goal itself was not a purely religious matter, however; it was also a political and legal matter which could rapidly develop into a military matter. So, while on the one hand one has to admire Luther's willingness to suffer for the sake of the gospel rather than to tinge the cause of the gospel with politics,[11] on the other hand one cannot help but see in him a certain political naïveté, a blindness, or perhaps even an unwillingness to come to terms with power politics.

On Philip of Hesse, see p. 124, n. 18.

Text in German: WA, Br 5, 203–204.

To the Serene, Noble Sovereign and Lord, Sir
Philip, landgrave in Hesse, count in Katzenellenbogen,
Ziegenhain, Dietz and Nida, my Gracious Lord

Grace and peace in Christ! Serene, Noble Sovereign, Gracious Lord! By this messenger I have received Your Sovereign Grace's letter and learned what nonsense is being fed to the Emperor by

---

[10] See pp. 203, n. 3; 240, n. 3.
[11] See also pp. 249 f.

the priests.[12] I hope to God, who in the Psalter is praised[13] as the one who nullifies the plots of godless sovereigns and people, that he will now also listen to us and nullify such plots [as these], especially since the clergy is now so puffed up and arrogant because of the Emperor's and other peoples' support for its cause, cares absolutely nothing about God, and does not call on him [for help]. May God only grant that we do not presume on our cleverness or strength, but rather seek his help and wait for it; then it surely will come.[14]

Your Sovereign Grace has also requested that, if I am asked for advice, I will help to influence my Most Gracious Lord[15] in such a way that [he] not approve the Emperor ['s request] for assistance against the Turks unless a common peace has first been promised and established, etc. Until now I have not been asked [for counsel on this matter]. I also know nothing at all of the way this matter was recently handled at Speyer,[16] or at Smalcald,[17] or what the current situation concerning this matter may be; consequently at this point I am unable to say anthing concerning the matter. Should it come to the point that my advice is requested, I shall of course, if God wills it, assist in offering the best possible counsel. For counsel on such a matter will [have to be governed by] my conscience, and I shall be compelled to give the most honest[18] advice. In the meantime I shall pray as much as I may and can, with God's grace, that not the clergy's will but God's will be done. Amen.

---

[12] I.e., here and throughout the letter, Emperor Charles V; see *LW* 48, 175 f. Literally: ". . . what nonsense is being brewed by the priests into the Emperor." Luther apparently is not thinking of any specific action on the part of the papal clergy or the Emperor, for the Landgrave, in his letter (see note 8), too, did not single out any specific action by the opposition, but commented only in general terms on the recent dealings of the Emperor with the Protestants (see p. 245, n. 9).

[13] Literally: "praises himself." This is apparently a rather general statement based on passages such as Ps. 2:2 ff.; 18:3; 33:10; 146:4; see also Job 5:12.

[14] See also p. 227.

[15] I.e., Elector John; see *LW* 48, 269, n. 8.

[16] See note 9.

[17] During the Smalcald meeting (see note 1) the decision of the Council of Regency regarding support of the campaign against the Turks was apparently discussed. The issue was not mentioned, however, in the resolution (see note 2).

[18] Literally: "best."

I commend Your Sovereign Grace to the grace of Christ. Amen.
December 16, 1529   MARTIN LUTHER

200

To Elector John
[Wittenberg,] December 24, 1529

*In the days following the Smalcald meeting of the Protestants,[1]
Landgrave Philip of Hesse[2] forced Margrave George of Brandenburg-Ansbach[3] and Elector John of Saxony[4] to come to terms with
the problems concerning the right of armed resistance to the emperor.[5] In view of the way Emperor Charles[6] had treated the Appeal
delegation,[7] the Protestants had to expect the worst from the Emperor. As the Landgrave saw it,[8] it was the duty of the sovereigns
to protect their subjects against any possible attacks by the Emperor, and to avoid having their subjects forced to return to the
papal church. Landgrave Philip tried to circumvent the possible
application of Romans 13 to the situation at hand by pointing out
that the territorial sovereigns were the governmental authorities of
which Paul spoke in this chapter,; and that the emperor was only
primus inter pares on the basis of a treaty with the sovereigns, a
treaty which Emperor Charles would break were he now to make
war on the Protestants on account of their faith. On December 9
the Landgrave wrote a letter to Elector John, requesting that the
Elector come to a decision about the right of armed resistance to
the emperor.[9] The Elector in turn requested Luther's opinion on
this matter, and the following letter is Luther's reply to the Elector.*

---

[1] See p. 250.
[2] See p. 214, n. 18.
[3] See p. 246, n. 11.
[4] See *LW* 48, 269, n. 8.
[5] See note 9, and p. 247, n. 22.
[6] See *LW* 48, 175 f.
[7] See p. 245, n. 9.
[8] See the Landgrave's letter to Margrave George of Brandenburg-Ansbach, dated December 21, 1529, in Schornbaum, *Georg*, p. 102, and *ZKG* 30 (1909), 287 ff.
[9] See Schubert, *BRP*, p. 222.

Strongly emphasizing that the situation is not as critical as it seems, Luther suggests that prior to jumping into war, every possibility for achieving peace must be exhausted. Luther says that to mobilize the troops is to bait the opposition unnecessarily; to do this is to be recalcitrant toward the Emperor, and furthermore is a sign of a lack of faith. Maintaining that the emperor is the governmental superior of the territorial sovereigns, Luther nevertheless gives qualified approval of the right to resist the emperor with arms, even though he does not come to terms with the problems which this position creates. Luther underscores four points: (a) As long as Emperor Charles has acted no worse than in the past, there is no reason to react in such a way as to provoke a war. (b) The present circumstances by no means justify any thoughts of armed resistance to the Emperor. (c) To mobilize the troops against the Emperor (or any other Estate) for a preventive war would be the greatest perversion of what is right, and would do great damage to "our" cause. (d) Rather than be concerned with matters of armed resistance to the emperor, the Elector should make every effort to come to an understanding with Emperor Charles. Such an undertaking would demand much courage and trust in God.[10]

On Elector John, see LW 48, 269, n. 8.

Text in German: WA, Br 5, 209–211.

To the Most Serene, Noble Sovereign and Lord, Sir John, duke in Saxony and elector, landgrave in Thuringia and margrave in Meissen, my Most Gracious Lord

---

[10] Whether or not Luther evaluated the whole situation correctly cannot be decided. By intuition he was correct in his judgment; for even though the Emperor and the Pope were never on better terms than in the summer and fall of 1529, and the Emperor was committed to defend Christendom against its internal (i.e., heretics) and external (i.e., the Turks) foes, nevertheless the Emperor was at that time far from pursuing a bend-or-break policy, as his summons for the Diet of Augsburg, signed on January 21, 1530 (see Reu II, No. 15), clearly demonstrates. For Luther's position on the right of armed resistance to the emperor, see note 25; J. Heckel, *Lex charitatis. Eine juristische Untersuchung über das Recht in der Theologie Martin Luthers (Abhandlungen der Bayerischen Akademie der Wissenschaften. Philosophisch-historische Klasse*, New Series, 36 [Munich, 1953]), pp. 184 ff.; *Widerstandsrecht, passim; The Lutheran Quarterly* 6 (1954), 338 ff.; *Zeitschrift der Savigny Stiftung für Rechtsgeschichte. Kanonistische Abteilung* 6 (1916), 331 ff.

Grace and peace in Christ! Most Serene Noble Sovereign, Most Gracious Lord! Since Your Electoral Grace has made known to me what my gracious lord, the Landgrave, etc.,[11] has written to Your Electoral Grace,[12] and since His Sovereign Grace[13] is willing to have Your Electoral Grace listen to my opinion in this matter,[14] and further, [since] accordingly Your Electoral Grace requests me to put my thoughts into writing [I have the following to say]:

First, I advise that Your Electoral Grace, together with the other sovereigns and cities who are united in their faith,[15] give a humble reply to the Emperor, and in all humility sue for peace from His Imperial Majesty.[16] I hear that in a short time councilors are to come together in Nürnberg for just this purpose.[17] At the present time the mandates referred to and cited in the Emperor's answer (which he had given to the delegation) have not yet been issued.[18] And since (as Scripture says)[19] the king's heart stands in God's hands, it is quite possible that by God's grace the Emperor's mind has changed since the time that the delegation was with His Imperial Majesty, and that His Imperial Majesty will not act so quickly.[20] Who knows whether God does not influence and change all these things which have thus far occurred and are still occurring so marvelously, in order that he may test our faith? If the Emperor be given a reply which might seem harsh and obstinate, greater ill will, which otherwise could be avoided, would be caused.[21] In addition, according to God's law[22] it behooves us to be humble to-

---

[11] I.e., Philip of Hesse; see p. 124, n. 18.

[12] See note 9. The Landgrave also wrote to Luther on December 9; see p. 251, n. 8.

[13] I.e., Philip of Hesse.

[14] I.e., the right of armed resistance to the emperor; see Introduction.

[15] Literally: "who are one in the undivided faith." This is a reference to the Protestant Estates who were willing to subscribe to the *Schwabach Articles* (see p. 236, n. 14).

[16] I.e., here and throughout the letter, Emperor Charles V; see note 6. "Reply" refers to the steps which the Protestants should take in response to the Emperor's reaction to the Protest and Appeal (see p. 245, n. 9).

[17] On this meeting, see pp. 250 f. Luther, with Melanchthon, issued a brief for this meeting; see *WA*, Br 12, 106 ff.

[18] See p. 245, n. 9; Schubert, *BRP*, p. 187.

[19] Prov. 21:1.

[20] Literally: ". . . will not drive [or: ride] so quickly."

[21] See also p. 226.

[22] Literally: "It also behooves us, before God, to act with humility toward the Emperor as our government. . . ."

ward the emperor as our governmental authority, as much as this is possible,[23] and not be eager to be obstinate, for indeed it is written in God's will and commandment: "You are to honor the king." I Peter 2[24] [:17].

Second, even if it were the Emperor's intention to proceed against the gospel with force, [and] without a [general] council [of the church] and a hearing [of our party],[25] nevertheless one may not with a good conscience bring the troops to the battlefield.[26] May God grant that the Emperor continue to give ungracious replies, or no reply at all.[27]

The reason[28] is:

First, that such [an undertaking] is unjust[29] and also against the natural law. For to bring the troops to the battlefield and to put up resistance are to be avoided, unless there is actual violence, or an unavoidable necessity. But this early moving out [for war], and [this] determination to resist will not be regarded as self-

---

[23] Luther here envisions a situation in which any such humble obedience would have to be canceled.

[24] Luther wrote "I Peter 3" by mistake.

[25] I.e., a hearing concerning the Protest and Appeal, as required by Imperial law; see K. Müller, *Luthers Äusserungen über das Recht des bewaffneten Widerstandes gegen den Kaiser* (*Sitzungsberichte der Königlichen Bayerischen Akademie der Wissenschaften.* Philosophisch-philologische und historische Klasse, 8 [Munich, 1915]), pp. 15 ff.

[26] Luther wrote: *zu Felde ziehen,* which literally means "to move into the field [of battle, or war]." Luther used this phrase several times throughout this letter and the same translation is used for it wherever this phrase occurs. The phrase is the technical term used to designate the second stage in preparing for war (as opposed to general mobilization, or the calling out of the troops, which would be the first). The idea behind this term is that the troops would be encamping in the field, poised for combat, but not yet actually engaged in battle. As such the term designates readiness for battle and can be synonymous with the declaration of war, or at least with being in a state of war.

[27] Luther wrote: *Gott gebe, der keiser gebe weiter vngnedige odder gar kein antwort.* The background of this statement is unclear. *St. L.* 21a, 1385, has amended the text so that it would have to be translated: "God grant that the Emperor give neither an ungracious answer, nor any [answer] at all."

[28] I.e., for the fact that at this point one may not, with good conscience, bring the troops together for battle.

[29] Luther wrote: *unbillich,* i.e., something which is contrary to what is right, or what is just, or what is one's due. On the way in which the terms "billich," and "unbillich" were understood by Luther, by Erasmus, and by other Humanists, see Heckel, *op. cit.,* pp. 83 ff., 163, n. 1297; G. Kisch, *Erasmus und die Jurisprudenz seiner Zeit. Studien zum humanistischen Rechtsdenken* (Basel, 1960), *passim.*

defense, but rather as a challenge to and insolence toward those who are still sitting calmly and have done nothing. It is now indeed obvious that His Imperial Majesty has not yet issued mandates against these sovereigns;[30] and even if [mandates] had been issued, or were issued, this would not yet mean the issuing of the ban.[31] In the meantime much water can run [down the river],[32] and God can easily find many means [toward peace, and] perhaps establish peace even through the other party. Therefore for the sake of the afore-mentioned reason[33] one may not start a war or bring the troops to the battlefield, even if the emperor were a sovereign of equal standing.[34]

Someone might say in this connection that, even though one is of course to trust in God, nevertheless one is not to gloss over those means available at the right time, lest one tempt God;[35] this would all be true. But one is not to seek such means by oneself, but rather to pray and to wait [until] God makes [such means] available; then one should grasp them firmly, and not follow one's own ideas; and [one must also carefully consider] whether these means are such as can be used with God ['s blessing], and not against God. Otherwise if one searches so anxiously for [suitable]

---

[30] I.e., the sovereigns who had joined in the Protest and Appeal.
[31] I.e., by the ban the Protestants would be outlawed, and this ban could be enforced through a campaign against the Protestants. To issue the ban without a hearing on the Protest and Appeal would be unconstitutional, and would obviously create a new situation. If this happened the Emperor would be acting contrary to Imperial law, and then the Protestant sovereigns would have the duty to protect their subjects from the unconstitutional acts of the Emperor.
[32] See also p. 250 and Ernst Thiele, *Luthers Sprichwörtersammlung* (Weimar, 1900), No. 196.
[33] I.e., in view of the lack of decisive action by the Emperor, (a) the Protestants are not in an emergency situation, and consequently (b) the bringing together of the troops for battle would not be a matter of self-defense, but of provocation, even rebellion.
[34] I.e., even if one were to affirm the Landgrave's position that the emperor is by treaty only *primus inter pares* (see Introduction), one could not bring the troops together for battle under the present circumstances.
[35] In his December 9 letter to Luther (see p. 251, n. 8), Landgrave Philip had stated, in connection with the idea of blackmailing the Emperor regarding help in fighting the Turks, that one should not despise the means now available for securing the right to preach the gospel; see WA, Br 5, 198; S-J 2, 508.

means, this certainly jeopardizes[36] trust in God. For the Jews of old also might have said the same when they made alliances with foreign kings and pretended to trust in God, but [in reality] they were searching for [safety] through such alliances. And so[37] they were severely punished for this. To bring the troops to the battle-field would be [a sign of] glory-seeking, and something which at this point is unnecessary and premature, etc.

Further, the emperor, of course, is the lord and governmental superior of these sovereigns.[38] Indeed none of [these sovereigns] would wish to have his own subjects put up such premature resistance to him, as in this case would be done against the Emperor, so that the whole matter would indeed be one of rebellion and disobedience. Therefore one has to advise that the efforts that are being used to find means of resistance be used instead to find means [of making peace], especially through humility and submissiveness to [His] Imperial Majesty. Then God will give grace (especially if the sovereigns and we ask for grace in all sincerity), and our worries will be taken care of, for he has promised us, and he does not lie to us, [in] Psalm 55[39] [:22]: "Cast your burden on the Lord, he will sustain you." And also in I Peter 5 [:5]: "He opposes the proud and gives his grace to the humble."

Second, it[40] would be futile, even dangerous and damaging. Let us suppose that we had already taken to the field[41] in resistance to [the Emperor]. What would happen, however, if the Emperor sat still or stayed away, and left us to exhaust ourselves on the field and to get tired of resistance? What would we have gained by this but irreparable damage, together with the whole world's

---

[36] Luther wrote: *zu nahe.* Literally: "too close to." The English phrases "too close for comfort," or "hitting too close to home" are covered by Luther's phrase. For the translation, see also Götze, *s.v.* nahe.
[37] Literally: "yet." I.e., notwithstanding the statement that they trusted in God.
[38] Luther rejects the interpretation of the Imperial office developed by the Landgrave (see Introduction). He sees in *the emperor* the (major) governmental authority of which St. Paul speaks in Romans 13, and he sees in the territorial sovereigns the (minor) governmental authorities which are derived from the Imperial office. It is an open question how clearly Luther here understood the constitutional basis of the Imperial office and the *de facto* operation of this office in his time.
[39] Luther wrote "Psalm 34" by mistake.
[40] I.e., to bring the troops together for battle.
[41] Literally: "already be in the field [i.e., the field of battle.]."

justifiable[42] disaffection and ill will? In this way would we not finally have made the Emperor really angry at us, and at the same time have given him the best reason to defend himself and to call on the Empire for help?[43] No doubt, writers could then easily be found who would present our case in such a way that the [cause of the] gospel would be injured, insulted, dishonored, and disgraced, while elaborating the Emperor's case in such a way that he would have to [appear] as a sheer angel, and we as sheer devils.

Third, it[44] would be unfair[45] to the opposition and the sovereigns who are in the Empire to attack them and their poor subjects because of the Emperor.[46] For I hear that the Emperor has been petitioned to guarantee peace for the Estates of the Empire. Therefore, if in spite of this the opposition should be attacked, then both God and the world would be greatly angered, and we in all justice would be condemned. They could then in all justice and with excellent arguments present all these matters [as proof of] their innocence, and cover us with disgrace[47] and shame.

It is therefore my opinion that the plan to bring the troops to the battlefield should be dropped, unless many other needs and matters come up.[48] In the meantime one is in an excellent position to sue His Imperial Majesty, in all humility, for peace.

This is my sincere and well-meant opinion, [and] I ask Your Electoral Grace to accept it graciously. Herewith I commend [Your Grace] to God. Amen.

December 24, 1529   Your Electoral Grace's dedicated
MARTIN LUTHER

---

[42] Luther wrote: *billiche*. See note 29.

[43] I.e., the Empire is to help the Emperor maintain peace in the land.

[44] See note 40.

[45] See note 36.

[46] I.e., it would be unfair to wage a preventive war against those sovereigns who had affirmed the resolution of the 1529 Diet of Speyer, and who might function as executors of the Emperor's decision against the Protestants.

[47] Literally: "put us into all [possible] disgrace."

[48] I.e., Luther does not on principle reject the idea of armed resistance to the emperor.

201

To Some Pastors of the City of Lübeck
Wittenberg, January 12,[1] 1530

The Reformation began to infiltrate the Imperial city of Lübeck as early as 1522.[2] By 1525 one of the major preaching positions in Lübeck was occupied by an evangelical preacher. Notwithstanding some setbacks in 1525, the Reformation continued to develop as a people's movement, and by 1528 even one of the preachers of the famous St. Mary's Church was an evangelical. John Walhoff (the preacher at St. Mary's Church) and Andrew Wilms (the preacher at the cathedral) became the spiritual leaders of the movement.[3] The papists did not sit idle, however, and since they dominated the city council the two evangelical preachers were removed from their offices. Yet this action did not stop the evangelical movement. When the city council attempted to levy a new tax, the citizens used this as a club against the council in their struggle for "good" preachers. A spontaneous demonstration, in which the citizens, singing hymns, moved out of the churches and through the streets of the city, forced the authorities to reinstate the dismissed preachers at the end of 1529. In 1530 the church of the Reformation was then officially organized in Lübeck. On May 1 the first evangelical communion was celebrated, and in October John Bugenhagen[4] came to the city to draw up an evangelical church ordinance. The present letter was written by Luther[5] shortly after the two evangelical preachers had returned to Lübeck, and prior to the development which led to the organization of the Reformation in that city. As he had done repeatedly,[6] so now Luther warns the pastors that their primary concern should be sound instruction regarding justifi-

---

[1] On the date, see note 7.
[2] On the Reformation in Lübeck, and for documentation of the following presentation, see W. Jannasch, *Reformationsgeschichte Lübecks vom Petersablass bis zum Augsburger Reichstag, 1515–1530* (Lübeck, 1958).
[3] For some biographical material, see *WA, Br* 13, 120, to *WA, Br* 5, No. 1520.
[4] See *LW* 48, 303, n. 44.
[5] See also note 7.
[6] See e.g., *LW* 48, 400 ff.; Luther's *Invocavit Sermons* of 1522 (*WA* 10III, 1 ff.; *LW* 51, 70 ff.), and his *Against the Heavenly Prophets* of 1525 (*WA* 18, 62 ff.; *LW* 40, 79 ff.).

*cation by faith, rather than liturgical reforms. Once the true faith
has been grasped, Luther says, liturgical reforms will follow natu-
rally, while liturgical reforms without sound doctrinal basis, exciting
though they may be, are of no use at all.*
    Text in Latin: WA, Br 5, 220–221.[7]

To the Ministers of the Word in Lübeck

Christ's grace and peace be with you, [and may you live] in faith
and patience. We have heard[8] good and joyous news concerning
you, excellent Brethren, namely, that through your ministry the
gospel lifts up its head in your town. We rejoice over this, and
thank the Father of mercies;[9] we confidently pray, nevertheless,
that he who has begun his good work[10] among you may continue
to guide [it] with his Spirit, so that the tempter in all his wickedness may not be an obstacle to you. Therefore carry on in awe and
humility, knowing that it is God's Word with which you deal,
which, while it is to be proclaimed to men and devils with utmost
confidence, must also be handled in God's presence[11] with utmost
reverence and awe. Then [God] will give you his blessing, so that
you will bring forth much fruit, and that your fruit will remain,[12]
as is written: "His righteousness endures forever."[13]

Although we believe it unnecessary that you should be admonished by us, we nevertheless both beg and urge you most

---

[7] The WA, Br text is taken from an old manuscript copy which can be found
in a collection of materials entitled: *Ex chirographo Lutheri.* For a description of the collection, see WA, Br 5, No. 1520, Introduction, n. 1. The text is
also extant in another manuscript copy (in addition to the common editions
of Luther's works). In this manuscript copy Bugenhagen (see note 4) is
identified as the writer of this letter, and the date of the letter is given as
March 12, 1530. According to Jannasch, *op. cit.,* pp. 391 f., no decision can be
made regarding the date of this letter. And Hans Volz and Eike Wolgast, the
revisers of WA, Br, suggest (WA, Br 13, 120) that this letter was written
jointly by Luther and Bugenhagen.

[8] How Luther received this news is not clear. He could have had personal
contacts with Lübeck, however, at least since May, 1528, when Andrew
Wilms had visited Wittenberg; see note 3.

[9] II Cor. 1:3.

[10] Phil. 1:6.

[11] Luther wrote: *coram Deo.* On this technical term, which was of fundamental
importance in Luther's theology, see Rupp, *Luther Studies,* pp. 81 ff.

[12] John 15:16.

[13] Ps. 111:3.

earnestly not to deal first with change[s] in the ritual, which [changes] are dangerous, but to deal with them later. You should deal first with the center of our teaching and fix in the people's minds what [they must know] about our justification; that is, that it is an extrinsic righteousness—indeed it is Christ's—given to us through faith which comes by grace to those who are first terrified by the law and who, struck by the consciousness of [their] sins, ardently seek redemption. It does not help to talk to the others[14] of God's grace, for they understand nothing but the external change[s] in the ritual, with which they are titillated for one hour, but as saturated people they soon loathe all sound teachings. Adequate reform of ungodly rites will come of itself, however, as soon as the fundamental[s] of [our] teaching, having been successfully communicated, have taken root in devout hearts. These [devout people] will at once recognize what a great abomination and blasphemy[15] that papistic idol is, namely, the mass and the other abuses of the sacrament, so that it will not be necessary to fish in front of the net,[16] that is, first to tear down [the ritual] before the righteousness of faith is understood. Among the most important things you must constantly impress upon yourselves as well as upon the people, however, are the prayers and litanies, both private and public, for purity and fruitfulness of the Word, for common peace, [good] government, and for all other matters [about which] you can read in the litany.[17]

I pray you to accept graciously these few words of admonition as coming from people who are participating in your gift and ministry.[18] Christ himself, our only preserver, will be with you, and will teach and accomplish through you what will contribute to his honor and the common good. Amen.

Wittenberg, January 12, 1530

---

[14] I.e., those who have not come to terms with justification by faith.

[15] Literally: "sacrilegious blasphemy."

[16] Luther often used the expression: *Fur dem hamen fischen,* i.e., to fish in front of the net (see e.g., p. 279; WA 51, 677, No. 101). This saying can refer to a futile undertaking—looking for something that no longer is there—or it can refer to someone's interference with or spoiling of a legitimate undertaking. Cf. Thiele, *Luthers Sprichwörtersammlung* (see p. 258, n. 32), No. 101.

[17] This is apparently a reference to Luther's *German Litany* and the *Corrected Latin Litany,* which had been published in 1529; WA 30III, 29 ff.; LW 53, 155 ff.

[18] See I Tim. 6:2 (Vulgate; Luther Bible); Rom. 5:15.

202

To Nicholas Hausmann
[Wittenberg, the beginning of February, 1530][1]

Luther reports some news and rumors in this letter and comments briefly on them: the alliance between Strassburg and Zürich, in which Luther sees a sign of the sacramentarians' tendencies toward rebellion; the growing hatred of the upper German and Swiss Reformers for the Wittenbergers and their followers; rumors concerning a "return" of the Turks, and a trip of the Emperor to Spain; the spreading of the gospel in England, France, and Spain; and the downfall of the English lord chancellor, Cardinal Wolsey. Luther concludes his letter by extending greetings from his wife.

On Nicholas Hausmann, see LW 48, 399 f.

Text in Latin: WA, Br 5, 237.

To the man, revered in the Lord, Mr. Nicholas Hausmann, most faithful and sincere bishop[2] of the church in Zwickau, my brother

Grace and peace in the Lord. I have no news which I could write to you, my Nicholas. Perhaps you have more [than I].

The people of Strassburg have defected from the Empire to the Swiss people,[3] and are planning to resist Emperor Charles.[4] I have been a prophet since I always said that the mind[5] of the sacramentarians is full of hidden [leanings toward] insurrection.[6]

---

[1] The extant autograph is undated. For a discussion of various dates assigned to the letter in older editions, and of the arguments favoring the beginning of February, 1530, as the most probable date for this letter, see WA, Br 5, No. 1527, Introduction.

[2] See p. 87, n. 5.

[3] After it had become clear at Marburg and at Smalcald that no alliance of *all* the Protestant Estates of the Empire could be worked out, Strassburg entered into a political and military alliance (*Burgrecht*) with Zürich on January 5, 1530. The purpose of this alliance was mutual protection against any possible attack by any Estate (including the emperor) which might be made for the purpose of enforcing either the Edict of Worms (see LW 48, 210), or the resolution of the 1529 Diet of Speyer (see p. 223). For details, see Fabian, *ESBV* (2nd ed.), p. 91.

[4] See LW 48, 175 f.

[5] Luther used the word *spiritus.*

[6] See p. 231.

[This mind] comes now to the fore and betrays itself. Unless God intervenes they will be another[7] Münzer;[8] but they will be this to their own ruin, so that they, the violators and defilers of the sacrament and the gospel, may receive their punishment. Let the dead bury their dead.[9]

Another rumor has it that the Turk is returning,[10] another that Charles is returning to Spain.[11] Everywhere the ungodly papists are caught in troubles; still they don't repent.[12] England is admitting the gospel while the King[13] looks the other way.[14] The Car-

---

[7] Literally: "Unless God blocks them they will give us a new . . ."

[8] See p. 111, n. 36.

[9] Matt. 8:22; Luke 9:60.

[10] Luther used the word *redire*. On the movements of the Turkish army in 1529, see p. 241, n. 5. To which place the Turks were supposedly returning is not clear. Did the rumor suggest a new Turkish attack against the southeastern border of the Empire, i.e., a return of the Turkish threat for the Empire? Or were the Turks to return to their home base, Constantinople? This latter possibility is suggested by the *WA. Br* editor, who supports his assumption by referring to Luther's letter of February 26, 1530, written to Spalatin, in which Luther tells of receiving the news from Poland that the Turk had returned (*redire*) to Constantinople; *WA, Br* 5, 243.

[11] Emperor Charles was at that time in northern Italy; see Ranke 2[III], 130 ff. Having settled his differences with Pope Clement VII, Charles was crowned emperor in Bologna on February 24, 1530. Thus his Imperial affairs in Italy were settled, at least for the time being, and as well as possible under the circumstances. In order to concentrate on a speedy settlement of the affairs in Germany, the Emperor, on January 21, 1530, called a meeting of the diet to Augsburg: see p. 280. The circumstances surrounding the rumor mentioned by Luther could not be clarified. Ranke (2[III], 135) mentions some plans of Charles to go to Naples, and perhaps the rumor had something to do with these plans. Brandi (1, 236; 2, 204) mentions the urgent requests of Ferdinand (see *LW* 48, 217, n. 17) that Charles come to Germany, and a January 11, 1530, letter of Charles to Ferdinand in which the Emperor attempted to make his brother understand his delay in coming to Germany. The rumor must have been based on some news from the Imperial court. That such a rumor could develop at all at a time when the Emperor's arrival in Germany was expected (see e.g., *C.R.* 2, 15) indicates, perhaps, that there must have been a certain disappointment among the Germans about the fact that the Emperor again delayed coming to Germany, or that Germany had sunk to a minor position because of the broader concerns of Charles.

[12] Literally: "don't return to the heart." See Isa. 46:8, which Luther translates: "gehet in ever Herz." (RSV: "recall it to mind.") Present-day German has the phrase *in sich gehen*.

[13] I.e., Henry VIII. On Luther's relationship to Henry VIII see *ARG* 53 (1962), 60 ff.; E. Doernberg, *Henry VIII and Luther: An Account of Their Personal Relations* (Stanford, 1961); N. Tjernagel, *Henry VIII and the Lutherans: A Study in Anglo-Lutheran Relations from 1521 to 1547* (St. Louis, Mo., 1965), pp. 3 ff.

[14] For reasons of his own, Henry VIII gradually loosened his ties to the

dinal,[15] that demigod of England, even of Europe,[16] has been sentenced to life imprisonment.[17] In France and Spain the Word is also beginning to spring forth.[18]

Since our synod at Marburg[19] the sacramentarians are burning with a worse hatred for us than ever before;[20] apparently they are sorry that we could not be pulled into their abyss, and perhaps

Pope. Among these reasons was certainly the King's disappointment at the procrastination on the part of the Curia regarding his wish to be divorced from Catherine of Aragon. The background of Luther's statement could not be clarified, and perhaps one should not put too much weight on Luther's statement. Nevertheless among Luther's friends the rumor was being circulated that the King himself was arranging for importing some of Luther's writings to England; see WA, Br 5, No. 1527, Introduction. Even though this editor could not substantiate the validity of this rumor, it is interesting to note that Luther knew of the gradual improvement of the cause of the gospel in England, and considered this news important enough to communicate it to Hausmann. On the Reformation in England in the decade from 1520 to 1530, see Tjernagel, op. cit., pp.. 3 ff.; W. A. Clebsch, England's Earliest Protestants (New Haven, 1964).
[15] I.e., Thomas Wolsey. See NCE 14, 989; O.D.C.C., p. 1474.
[16] This is apparently a reference to Wolsey's diplomatic play on the European scene. Wolsey had been lord chancellor since 1515, and since 1518 he had guided English politics toward a rapprochement with France, and thus against the Hapsburg dynasty, a strategy which, together with other factors, led eventually to his downfall. To what degree Luther knew of these diplomatic maneuvers has to remain an open question. Nevertheless since Luther had been periodically engaged in controversy with Henry VIII, and since there were other points of contact between Wittenberg and England, one can be sure that the general situation of the "gospel" in England, and the major political events there, were not totally unknown to Luther.
[17] Apparently this was the news being circulated in Luther's part of the country. On October 17, 1529, Wolsey was dismissed from the office of lord chancellor. He was indicted for offending the statute Praemunire, but was pardoned by Henry. Suspected of intrigues against the King, however, and accused of high treason, Wolsey was brought to the Tower. He died on November 29, 1530.
[18] The background of this statement could not be clarified.
[19] See pp. 234 ff.
[20] The crisis among the Protestants came to a head not in Marburg (as Luther states) but in Smalcald (see p. 250). For at Smalcald the Electoral Saxon delegation presented the upper German city delegates with the ultimatum: accept the Schwabach Articles (see p. 250) or be excluded from an alliance. Since the acceptance of these articles would have meant the abandonment of Zwingli and his theology of the Lord's Supper, and since the delegates were not ready to do this, the negotiations for an alliance finally collapsed there in Smalcald. The city of Ulm then called the upper German cities to a meeting in Biberach, scheduled for December 30; at this meeting the Saxons were blamed for the collapse of the negotiations, and some unkind words were spoken about Luther and his political supporters. On this meeting, see Fabian, ESBV (2nd ed.), pp. 76 ff.; Fabian, ABBP, pp.. 107 ff.

[also for] other [reasons]. Christ, who has begun this work, will also complete it.[21]

Farewell, and pray for me. The empress, my Katie, respectfully greets you. The grace and the gift[22] be with you. Amen.

Yours,

MARTIN LUTHER

203

To Hans Luther
Wittenberg, February 15, 1530

Informed by James, his brother in Mansfeld, of their father's serious illness, Luther wrote the following letter of spiritual counsel. Luther explains why he does not visit his father, and expresses his hope that both his father and mother can come to Wittenberg and stay in the Luther house, apparently for the rest of their days. He even dispatches his nephew (a certain Cyriac Kaufmann, who was then studying at Wittenberg) to Mansfeld to investigate this matter further. Strengthening his father in this time of illness, Luther emphasizes that his father's faith is a sign of God's gracious dealings with him; Luther stresses that God's promises are valid and true, and that in Jesus Christ man has the most faithful helper in the hour of death. Encouraging his father not to become disheartened, Luther admonishes him to hold firmly to God's word of promise. He further points out that death on the one hand means an end to man's pilgrimage through the vale of tears, on the other hand the entrance into the peace of Christ and the certainty of a joyous reunion of all believers.

This letter is among the finest of Luther's writings. It throws a light on the relationship between father and son, a relationship which must have been different than is sometimes suggested.[1] Cop-

---

21 See Phil. 1:6.
22 See Rom. 5:15.
1 See *LW* 48, 330. For a positive evaluation of Erikson's book, cited therein, see F. Meuser and S. Schneider (eds.), *Interpreting Luther's Legacy* (Minneapolis, Minn., 1969), pp. 55 ff.

*ies of the letter were circulated among some of Luther's friends,
and the text is available in several sixteenth century manuscript
copies; the letter can also be found in the earliest collection of
Luther's writings of pastoral counsel.[2] These facts seem to suggest
that even Luther's contemporaries held the letter in high regard.*

On Hans Luther, see LW 48, 329 f.

Text in German: WA, Br 5, 239-241.

To my dear Father, Hans Luther, a citizen at Mansfeld in the valley:[3]
Grace and peace in Christ Jesus, our Lord and Saviour. Amen

Dear Father: James, my brother,[4] has written me that you are
seriously ill.[5] As the weather is now bad, and as there is danger
everywhere, and because of the season, I am worried about you.
For even though God has thus far given to and preserved for you
a strong, tough body, yet your age gives me anxious thoughts at
this time—although regardless of this [worry], none of us is, or
should be, sure of his life at any time. Therefore because of these
circumstances I would have liked to come to you personally, but
my good friends advised me against it, and have talked me out of
it. I myself have to agree, for I did not dare to venture into danger
at the risk of tempting God, since you know how lords and peasants
feel toward me.[6] It would be great joy for me, however, if it were
possible for you and mother[7] to be brought here to us; this my
Katie, too, desires with tears, and we all [join her in this]. I hope

---

[2] For bibliographical details, see WA, Br 5, No. 1529, Introduction, and
Enders, *Briefwechsel* 7, No. 1600.

[3] Mansfeld, just like Eisleben, was located in a valley, and the *Grafschaft*
Mansfeld was divided into three parts, each part belonging to one of the
counts of Mansfeld.

[4] Luther's younger brother, James, was a city councilor in Mansfeld, and
died in 1570. Luther was apparently very close to him. On James Luther see
O. Sartorius, *Die Nachkommenschaft D. Martin Luthers in vier Jahrhunderten*
(Göttingen, 1926), p. A 4; Köstlin-Kawerau 1, 20.

[5] Apparently Luther's father suffered from the English fever. See p. 239, n. 29.

[6] Some manuscript copies offer a text which reads in translation "sovereigns"
instead of "peasants." Other witnesses add a sentence which reads in translation: "I might be able to come to you, but to return home might be
dangerous." See WA, Br 5, 241, nn. b, c. It is not clear whether Luther is
thinking here of some special circumstances, or is talking in general terms
only.

[7] On Luther's mother, see LW 48, 329, n. 1.

we would be able to take care of you in the best way. Therefore I am sending Cyriac[8] to see whether your weakness [will allow you to be moved]. For if according to God's will your illness turns out to be one either to life or to death,[9] it would be a heartfelt joy for me (as would be only right) to be around you in person and to show, with filial faithfulness and service, my gratitude to God and to you, according to the Fourth Commandment.

In the meantime I pray from the bottom of my heart that the Father, who has made you my father and given you to me, will strengthen you according to his immeasurable kindness, and enlighten and preserve you with his Spirit, so that you may perceive with joy and thanksgiving the blessed teaching concerning his son, our Lord Jesus Christ, to which you too have been called and have come out of the former terrible darkness and error.[10] I hope that his grace, which has given you such knowledge[11] and begun his work in you, will preserve and complete [his work] up to the arrival of the future life and the joyous return of our Lord Jesus Christ.[12] Amen. God has also sealed this teaching and faith in you and has confirmed them with marks;[13] that is, because of me, you, together with all of us, have suffered much slander, disgrace, scorn, mockery, contempt, hatred, hostility, and even danger. These are but the true marks with which we have to become identical to our Lord Christ, as St. Paul says,[14] so that we may also become identified with his future glory.

Therefore let your heart now be bold and confident in your illness, for we have there, in the life beyond, a true and faithful helper at God's side, Jesus Christ, who for us has strangled death, together with sin, and now sits [in heaven] for us; together with all the angels he is looking down on us, and awaiting us, so

---

8 I.e., Cyriac Kaufmann, son of Luther's sister, who was married to George Kaufmann, a Mansfeld citizen. This nephew had matriculated at Wittenberg on November 22, 1529. Apparently Cyriac's parents were dead by 1534, and Luther had an active part in guiding Cyriac and his younger brothers and sisters through their years of adolescence. See Sartorius, *op. cit.*, p. A 1.
9 Literally: ". . . God's will it will get you to this or that life . . ."
10 See I Pet. 2:9.
11 I.e., knowledge of redemption.
12 See Phil. 1:6.
13 See Gal. 6:17.
14 See note 13; Rom. 8:17; 6:5.

that when we are to depart, we dare not worry or fear that we might sink or fall to the ground. His power over death and sin is too great for them to harm us. He is so wholeheartedly faithful and righteous[15] that he cannot forsake us, nor would he wish to do so; [he wishes] only that we desire [his help] without doubting his promise, for he has said, promised, and pledged [his help]. He will not and cannot lie to us, nor trick us; there is no doubt about this. "Ask," (he says,) "and it will be given you; seek, and you will find, knock, and it will be opened to you."[16] And elsewhere: "All who call on the name of the Lord shall be saved."[17] The whole Psalter is full of such comforting promises, especially Psalm 91, which is particularly good to be read by all who are sick.

I wished to talk this over with you in writing, because I am anxious about your illness (for we know not the hour),[18] so that I might participate in your faith, temptation,[19] consolation, and gratitude to God for his holy Word, which in these days he has given to us so richly, powerfully, and graciously. Should it be his divine will, however, for you to wait still longer for that better life, [and] to continue to suffer with us in this troubled and sorrowful vale of tears, and to see and hear sadness, or, together with all Christians, to assist [others] in enduring and overcoming [this sadness], then he will also give [you] the grace to accept all this willingly and obediently. This cursed[20] life is nothing but a real vale of tears, in which the longer a man lives, the more sin, wickedness, torment, and sadness he sees and feels. Nor is there respite or cessation of all of this until we are buried;[21] then, of course, [this sadness] has to stop and let us sleep contentedly in Christ's peace, until he comes again to wake us with joy. Amen.

Herewith I commend you to Him who loves you more than you love yourself. He has proved his love by taking your sins upon himself and by paying [for them] with his blood, and he has let

---

[15] Luther wrote *frumb*, i.e., pious, devout. For the meaning which this term had in Luther's time, see Trübner 3, 716.

[16] Matt. 7:7.

[17] Acts 2:21.

[18] Luther wrote *Stündlein*, i.e., the (little, short) hour of death.

[19] Literally: "struggle [or fight]." See also *LW* 48, 28, n. 10.

[20] I.e., cursed through the Fall, but also through God's judgment over sin.

[21] Luther wrote: *bis man uns mit der Schaufel nachschlägt.* Literally: "until one flattens us with the shovel."

you know this through the gospel, and has given it to you freely to believe this by his Spirit.[22] Consequently, he has prepared and sealed everything in the most certain way, so that you are not permitted to worry about or be concerned for anything except keeping your heart strong and reliant on his Word and faith. If you do this then let him care for the rest. He will see to it that everything turns out well.[23] Indeed, he has already accomplished this in the best way, better than we can understand. May he, our dear Lord and Saviour, be with you and at your side, so that (may God grant it to happen either here or there)[24] we may joyfully see each other again. For our faith is certain, and we don't doubt that we shall shortly see each other again in the presence of Christ. For the departure from this life is a smaller thing to God than if I moved from you in Mansfeld to here, or if you moved from me in Wittenberg to Mansfeld. This is certainly true; it is only a matter of an hour's sleep, and all will be different.

I hope that in these matters your pastor and preacher[25] will abundantly demonstrate their faithful service to you, so that you will not need my words. Yet I could not refrain from excusing my physical absence, which (God knows) causes me heartfelt sorrow. My Katie, Hänschen,[26] Lenchen,[27] Aunt Lena,[28] and all my household send you greetings and pray for you faithfully. Greet my dear mother and all my relatives. God's grace and strength be and abide with you forever. Amen.

Your loving son,
MARTIN LUTHER

[Written] at Wittenberg,
February 15, 1530

---

[22] Another possible translation would be: "given grace through his Spirit to believe this."
[23] Ps. 37:5 (Luther Bible).
[24] I.e., either in this life or the life to come, or in Wittenberg or Mansfeld.
[25] It is not clear who is meant here. For possibilities, see WA, Br 5, 241, n. 10.
[26] John Luther; see p. 323, n. 7.
[27] Magdalen Luther; see p. 312, n. 6.
[28] Magdalene von Bora, (an aunt of Luther's wife), a former nun who sometime after 1523 left the nunnery and lived with the Luther household until she died. See WA, Br 5, 241, n. 11; 8, 19.

204

To Elector John
[Wittenberg,] March 6, 1530

At the Smalcald meeting of the Protestants in November, 1529,
the negotiations for a great alliance of all the Estates which had
signed the Protest and Appeal collapsed because of the Eucharis-
tic controversy.[1] On January 6 the "Lutheran" Estates met in
Nürnberg[2] to negotiate whatever common action might be taken
by those Protestants who were willing to subscribe to the Schwa-
bach Articles.[3] The Nürnberg negotiations came to a standstill
when the Franconian theologians[4] and statesmen[5] denied, for
legal and theological reasons, the right of the Estates to take
up arms against the emperor for any reason whatsoever. Thus
the issue was reopened which on the basis of a brief drafted by
Bugenhagen seemed to have been settled at Schleiz, but which,
as the further developments document,[6] was not at all settled.
As a result, on January 27, 1530, Elector John promptly de-
manded a brief on this matter from his Wittenberg theologians.[7]
Luther consulted some of his colleagues and issued his brief
in the following letter.

Critically discussing the reasons given as justification for
armed resistance to the emperor, Luther categorically denies
that, as long as the emperor remains in office and is not removed
from office, there can be any justification of armed resistance to
the emperor. Luther further stringently warns of the bloodshed
and political catastrophe which would be the certain results of

---

[1] See p. 250.
[2] On this Nürnberg meeting, see Schubert, *BRP*, pp. 223 ff.; Fabian, *ESBV* (2nd ed.), pp. 82 ff.; *ABBP*, pp. 118 ff.
[3] See p. 236, n. 14.
[4] Especially Wenceslas Link; see *LW* 48, 169 f.
[5] Especially Lazarus Spengler; see *LW* 48, 184.
[6] See pp. 244, n. 7; 256, n. 17 (Luther's brief for the Nürnberg meeting).
[7] *WA*, Br 5, No. 1522. For Luther's first brief on this issue, see letter No. 200. Not only had the Elector asked the Wittenberg theologians for a brief on this matter, but as early as autumn of 1529, Lazarus Spengler (see p. 245, n. 10) had sent a brief to Melanchthon, requesting an opinion on it. By December 12, 1529, Spengler was eagerly looking forward to a reply; on March 17, 1530, however, he was still waiting. See *WA*, Br 5, 250, and *ibid.*, n. 1.

*any action against the emperor which could be considered as re-
bellion. Luther affirms that, if necessary, one has to endure suffering for one's religious convictions, and emphasizes the necessity of standing up for one's faith by willingly sacrificing one's
life and property should the emperor start any military or police
actions against the Reformers or against the Protestant Estates.
Drawing on Isaiah 30:15 f., Luther lifts the issue of armed resistance out of any political or legal realm and places it into the realm
of faith. He considers the search for justification of armed resistance
to the emperor and for the right to prepare for war against the
emperor as signs of man's gross lack of trust in God's almighty
power.*

*If one compares this brief with Luther's letter to Elector John,
written on December 24, 1529 (letter No. 200), then one has to
ask whether some change in Luther's attitude toward the issues
concerning resistance to the emperor has occurred.[8] In this connection it should be noted that some of the ideas which Luther
here suggests to his sovereign are identical with the advice which
he gave to Elector Frederick as early as March, 1522.[9]*

*Even though this brief was obviously to be treated confiden-
tially,[10] nevertheless firsthand copies did circulate among some of
the more prominent members of the Protestant camp;[11] they in
turn made secondhand copies. Finally and almost inevitably one
of these copies fell into the hands of the "enemies," who published
it at once, in 1531. Cochlaeus,[12] the editor, apparently obtained the
text[13] while attending the 1530 Diet of Augsburg in the entourage*

---

[8] K. Müller, *op. cit.* (see p. 257, n. 25), pp. 22, 85, answers this question
affirmatively; see also Schubert, *BRP*, pp. 25 f.

[9] See note 43.

[10] See e.g., Melanchthon's letter to Camerarius, cited in *WA*, Br 5, 250.

[11] E.g., prior to the middle of March, 1530, Melanchthon sent a copy to
Spengler in Nürnberg, though he intended to show the original to Spengler
on the trip to the Diet of Augsburg. Spengler in turn copied the brief, whether
from Melanchthon's copy or from the original cannot be established. See *WA*,
Br 5, 250; for other copies see *ibid.*, 251 and Enders, *Briefwechsel* 7, 240; see
also *WA*, Br 13, 123, to *WA*, Br 5, No. 1536.

[12] On John Cochlaeus, one of the most famous literary opponents of the
Reformation, see *NCE* 3, 970 f.

[13] Since the Cochlaeus edition (for bibliographical information, see *WA*, Br 5,
256) presents a poor text, and since one may hardly suppose that Cochlaeus
did a poor copying job, one can only assume that his source was already a
poor secondhand copy. See *WA*, Br 5, 251.

of Duke George of Saxony. On the eve of the Smalcaldic War the brief was again published and extensively commented upon, both by the Protestants and by their opponents.[14]

The following translation is based on the text made available by Otto Clemen in the Weimar edition. This text, in turn, is based on an edition of the autograph published in 1802. For verification of this text Clemen used a copy of the autograph made by Veit Dietrich,[15] *most probably in 1530. Clemen also gives the many textual variations which can be found in the Cochlaeus edition.*

On Elector John, see LW 48, 269, n. 8.

Text in German: WA, Br 5, 258–261.

Grace and peace in Christ!

Most Illustrious, Noble Sovereign, Most Gracious Lord! At Your Electoral Grace's request[16] I have questioned my good friends,[17] Dr. Jonas,[18] John Pomer,[19] Master[20] Philip,[21] and discussed [with them] the question of whether one may resist His Imperial Majesty[22] if His Majesty intends to move against someone with force for the sake of the gospel, etc. We have come to the following conclusions: Some might infer,[23] on the basis of the Imperial or secular

---

[14] For details, and for bibliographical information, see WA, Br 5, 252 ff.

[15] See WA, Br 5, 251; 13, 123, to WA, Br 5, No. 1536.

[16] See WA, Br 5, No. 1522.

[17] Literally: "my dear gentlemen and friends."

[18] Justus Jonas; see LW 48, 275, n. 3.

[19] I.e., John Bugenhagen; see LW 48, 303, n. 44.

[20] I.e., Master of Arts.

[21] Philip Melanchthon; see LW 48, 77, n. 3. Melanchthon also forwarded to the Elector a brief in which he presented arguments against armed resistance to the emperor; his arguments were identical to those presented by Luther. See C.R. 2, No. 666; Schubert, BRP, p. 233.

[22] It is somewhat academic to ask whether, throughout this letter, Luther, whenever he mentioned the emperor, or His Imperial Majesty, was thinking of Charles V (see LW 48, 175 f.), or was speaking in general terms only. Since in other circumstances Luther most of the time directed his thoughts to specific incidents, he probably was focusing on Charles V in this letter, too. On the other hand Luther must have been aware that the position set forth in this brief would be important, even if the specific circumstances of the moment and the emperor involved had changed. Consequently Luther might have focused on the Imperial office as such, rather than on the present incumbent.

[23] The following lines are taken over from the Electoral instruction for the brief; see WA, Br 5, 224, lines 29 ff. "Some" may be a reference to Christian

laws,[24] that in such a case one would have the right to resist His Imperial Majesty, especially since His Imperial Majesty has promised and sworn to attack no one with force, but to respect the traditional privileges,[25] etc., as the jurists mean when speaking of *repressalia* and *diffidatio*.[26]

According to Scripture, however, it is in no way proper for anyone who wants to be a Christian to stand up against the authority of his government[27] regardless of whether [that government] acts rightly or wrongly; rather a Christian is to suffer force and injustice, especially from his government. For even if in this case[28] His Imperial Majesty acts unjustly and operates contrary to his duty and oath, this does not nullify the authority of the Imperial government, nor does it nullify [the necessity of] obedience on the part of the Emperor's subjects, as long as the Empire and the electors consider His Majesty to be emperor, and do not remove him from office. Even if an emperor or sovereign acts contrary to all of God's commandments, he still remains emperor and sovereign —and yet he is bound more to God by obligation and oath[29] than to man. If it should be [considered] acceptable to resist His Imperial Majesty when he acts unjustly, then one might as well resist him whenever he acts contrary to God ['s will]. The result of this would be that no governmental authority or obedience would be

---

Beyer, (see p. 349, n. 8), the Electoral Saxon chancellor, who led the Saxon delegation to Nürnberg, and who, on the basis of the Schleiz conference (see note 6), presented the Saxon point of view which affirmed the right of resistance.

[24] See notes 25, 37, 38.

[25] This is a reference to the *Wahlcapitulation* of Charles V of July 3, 1519; see *DRTA.JR* 1, No. 387, Paragraphs 5–6, 21–24. It was Philip of Hesse who in December of 1529 interjected this argument into the discussion in an attempt to convince Margrave George of Brandenburg-Ansbach of the moral and legal right of armed resistance to the emperor; see Schubert, *BRP*, p. 203.

[26] *Repressalia*, i.e., the right of revenge exercised by one state against another which had acted illegally toward the former. *Diffidatio*, i.e., the feudal right of canceling the feudal obligations if one party in the feudal contract did not live up to the contract. See Du Cange, *s.v.* diffidare, diffidatio, repraesaliae; Brinckmeier, *s.v.* diffidare, repraesaliae.

[27] In the text is added: *got gebe*, which means "may God grant [this]." I.e., may God grant that the Christian not stand up against his government; or, may God prevent that the government act wrongly.

[28] I.e., if the Emperor attacked the Protestants; this attack would be unconstitutional because of the *Wahlcapitulation* mentioned in note 25.

[29] I.e., because of the emperor's office, which God has instituted according to Rom. 13:1 f., and to which God has called the emperor.

left in the world, because every subject could use the excuse that his government was acting unjustly [and] against God.

In this matter secular or papal laws do not take into consideration the fact that governmental authority is a divine institution;[30] perhaps this is why [these laws] esteem duty and oaths [to men] so highly that in such a case[31] they seldom support and defend governmental authority. But since[32] the emperor remains emperor, [or] a sovereign remains sovereign, even if he trespasses all of God's commandments, or even if he were a heathen, so he is to be [governmental authority for his subjects][33] even if he does not fulfill his oath and duty, until he has been removed from office, or is no longer emperor.[34] Christ's statement is to stand firm: "Render to Caesar the things that are Caesar's,"[35] and so is I Peter 2 [:17]: "Honor the king." For we ought to be subject in all reverence not only to the kind and just, but also to evil and malicious lords. In summary: sin does not nullify governmental authority nor [the duty] of obeying it, but punishment[36] does nullify them; that is, when the Empire and the electors unanimously remove the emperor from office so that he is no longer emperor. Aside from this, as long as he is unpunished and remains emperor, no one should withdraw obedience from him or oppose him. That would be to start mob action, revolt, and discord.

The legal dictum *Vim vi repellere licet,* "one may fight force with force,"[37] accomplishes nothing here, for it may not be applied

---

[30] It has to remain an open question whether Luther was making a random statement here, or was basing his statement on detailed knowledge.

[31] I.e., in a situation when the emperor has broken his "duty and oath to men."

[32] Clemen (*WA,* Br 5, 261, n. 6) suggests that one should translate "as long as."

[33] For Luther's argument here, see also his 1523 book *Temporal Authority: To What Extent It Should be Obeyed; WA* 11, 245 ff.; *LW* 45, 81 ff.

[34] The necessary consequences of this statement would be that, according to Luther, the emperor holds his office by contract, could be removed from this office, and then could be resisted. It has to be pointed out that Luther does not discuss how this possible removal should be executed. One has to ask how Luther would relate this principle of a possible removal from office to his understanding of governmental authority as being instituted by God.

[35] Matt. 22:21.

[36] I.e., when the unjustly acting emperor is removed from office then he is punished, and this punishment cancels the duty of obedience on the part of the subjects.

[37] *Corpus iuris civilis, Digesta* XLIII: Tit. XVI, Par. 27.

to governmental authority. It is even invalid if applied to [those of] equal [standing], unless self-defense or protection of others, or of subjects, demands [the use of force]. Other legal dictums stand against this [first one]: "No one ought to be judge [of his own case]." And: "He who retaliates is wrong."[38]

The subjects of all the sovereigns are also subjects of the emperor; [they are] even more [the emperor's subjects] than the sovereigns'. It would therefore be wrong for anyone to protect the emperor's subjects against the emperor, their lord, by using force, just as it would not be proper for the mayor of Torgau to protect the citizens [of Torgau], by using force, against the sovereign in Saxony, as long as the same is sovereign in Saxony.[39]

One might argue that the Emperor does not intend to accept the Appeal,[40] or to investigate the matter, or to deal with it in due process. [As a counterargument I propose][41] that His Imperial

---

38 *Corpus iuris civilis, Codex Iustinianus* III: Tit. V. The last quotation is a saying used several times by Luther; WA 18, 304; 32, 331.

39 This argument became of major importance in the debate, since Philip of Hesse and other supporters of the right of armed resistance to the emperor contended that there was equality between the sovereigns and the emperor, and that the territorial subjects were *not* subjects of the emperor. See also p. 254. Consequently the position of the mayor of Torgau and his relationship to the elector of Saxony was radically different from that of the elector of Saxony and his relationship to the emperor. The mayor and citizens of Torgau were subjects of the elector, and if they resisted the Electoral government they would be rebelling. The elector of Saxony and the emperor were equals, the emperor being only first among equals; consequently to resist the emperor could not be considered rebellion on the part of the elector of Saxony. Luther reflected here a more imperial, monarchic understanding of the nature of the Empire, while Philip of Hesse represented a federal understanding of the nature of the Empire. It must be pointed out that Luther does not go into any details of constitutional law, nor does he contrast his position with those consequences which have to be drawn from some of his earlier statements; see note 34. One must ask the questions to what degree Luther was familiar with the constitutional law of the Empire, and to what degree he was able to build a bridge from Romans 13 to the political and legal realities of his time.

40 See p. 245, n. 9.

41 Literally: "due process, for I at once add that His Imperial Majesty did accept." Or: "due process, for I equate [this (i.e., the Emperor's refusal to grant a hearing) with the fact] that his Imperial Majesty did accept." As Clemen (WA, Br 5, 262, n. 13) has suggested, Luther's sentence is incomplete. Luther introduces his own argument with "for." Luther's next phrase (*ich setze gleich*) could mean either that the Emperor's refusal is for him the same as if the Emperor accepted the Appeal, and dealt with it in due process —in either case, the Protestants lose (see the following sentence)—or that

277

Majesty did accept the Appeal and did have the matter properly investigated. What would happen, [I ask,] if we were then nevertheless condemned by an unjust verdict (as certainly would happen)? Then such an excuse[42] would be useless unless one wanted to appeal again and again, and do so forever. For the Emperor certainly knows, and we surely do too, that if the matter receives a due process hearing, we shall surely be condemned, and therefore he deals with us as people who are already condemned.

What then shall one do?

One should do the following: If His Imperial Majesty proceeds against us[43] then no sovereign or lord is to protect us against His Majesty; rather he is to leave territory and people standing open to the Emperor, as belonging to him, and commend the matter to God. No one is to ask his sovereign or lord to do otherwise. But everyone is then to stand for himself and confess his faith by offering his body and life, and not to drag the sovereign into danger or burden him by seeking protection; rather he should let the Emperor deal with his subjects as the Emperor wishes, as long as he is emperor.

If in addition to having land and people open to him, the Emperor wants to go farther and wants to force the sovereigns to attack, imprison, kill, [or] exile their subjects for the sake of the gospel, and the sovereigns believe or know that the Emperor is wrong in this, and is acting contrary to God's will, then this pertains also to the sovereigns' own faith. Then they ought not to obey the Emperor, so that they do not agree and cooperate with him, and make themselves participants of such evil. In such a situation it suffices [for them] to leave the land and people undefended, and the Emperor unobstructed. They ought to say: If the Emperor intends to terrorize our subjects, who are also his own [subjects], then he should do this on his own conscience; we cannot resist him,

---

Luther puts up as counterargument the assumption that the Emperor had accepted the Appeal. But would this do any good?

[42] I.e., the argument that, if attacked for the sake of the gospel, the Protestants may fight the Emperor because he has acted without due process.

[43] As in 1522, Luther envisions that he and his co-workers, wherever they may be found in the Empire, are the real targets of any action taken by the Emperor. For the thoughts presented in this and the following paragraph, see also LW 48, 391 f.

but we also do not wish to help him or agree with him in this matter, for one has to obey God rather than men.[44]

In the meantime, if we conduct ourselves in this way and commend the matter to God, praying in full confidence and daring such danger for his will's sake, then he will be faithful and will not abandon us. He will also find [ways and] means to help us and preserve his Word, as he has done from the beginning of Christendom, especially at the time of Christ and of the apostles. Therefore it seems to me that one would act rashly[45] if one were to oppose governmental authority for the sake of defending the gospel; such action certainly would [document that we have] a false faith which does not trust God that he certainly knows how to protect and help us in many ways without our [own] cleverness and efforts. God preserved King Jehoiachin by even [working] through the [King's] enemy, the Emperor of Babylon,[46] when the King surrendered [to him] at God's Word;[47] [God] also preserved the prophet Jeremiah.[48] For [God's] wisdom and power have neither number nor end,[49] [a fact] which he wants us to learn and experience through such great danger, as he often in the past has let us see and experience. Therefore he says [in] Isaiah 30 [:15 f.]: "If you had remained silent, you would have been helped; through quietness and hope you would have been strong. But you do not want this, and answer: 'We want to escape on horses.' Therefore you shall be fugitives," etc.

Furthermore, this also has to be considered: Even if it were right to resist the Emperor in this way, and if it were done, then we would have to follow through, and chase the Emperor out of the land, and we ourselves would have to become emperor. For the Emperor would fight back, and there would be no end until one party had been fought to the ground; and of course, there is [always] the mob. Even if we had won, then we would have to defeat those who had helped us, for no one would want us for emperor, and in such a wild uproar everyone would want to be

---

[44] Acts 5:29.
[45] Luther uses the same phrase here as on p. 263, n. 16.
[46] See II Kings 25:27.
[47] "Surrendered," i.e., to Nebuchadnezzar; see II Kings 24:12.
[48] See e.g., Jer. 26:24; chapter 38; 39:11 ff.
[49] See Ps. 147:5 (Vulgate).

emperor. What unspeakable slaughter and woe would develop, so that a sovereign should prefer rather to lose three principalities, in fact, he should prefer to be dead three times over, rather than to be the cause of such woe, to assist in it, or to consent to it. For how could any conscience bear this? The devil would like such a development,[50] but may God preserve us from it and graciously help us. Amen.

All this we reply to Your Electoral Grace and humbly submit for Your Electoral Grace's consideration. May Christ our Lord give to Your Electoral Grace strength and wisdom to do what is pleasing to him. Amen.

March 6, 1530   Your Electoral Grace's dedicated
        MARTIN LUTHER

205

To Nicholas Hausmann
Coburg, April 18, 1530

The relationship of the Protestants to the Emperor[1] moved into a new phase[2] when on March 11 the Imperial Summons[3] for a diet, to be convened in the city of Augsburg on April 8, was delivered to the Electoral Saxon residency in Torgau. This Summons, issued by Emperor Charles V in Bologna[4] on January 21, 1530, put three

---

[50] Literally: "games."

[1] I.e., here and throughout this letter, Emperor Charles V; see *LW* 48, 175 f.

[2] See pp. 155 f.; 245, n. 9.

[3] Text: *URA* 1, No. 1; for an excerpt in translation, see Reu[II], No. 15; Kidd, No. 113; Hillerbrand, pp. 401 f.

[4] See p. 265. Charles moved to Italy to restore the Imperial authority there (especially over Florence; see note 31) and was finally crowned emperor on February 24, 1530, in Bologna. See Ranke 2[III], 136. Even though there was to be peace between the Emperor and Pope Clement VII, Charles was no blind papist. He realized the necessity not only of reforms in the church, but also of a religious renaissance of Christendom. A general council of the church was to accomplish this. For Charles's ideas and plans see Brandi 1, 228 ff.; 2, 192 ff., 203 ff. The Diet of Augsburg was to eliminate the one great obstacle to the council, the Protestants. One of the conditions of the Barcelona treaty (see p. 222) was that the Protestants were to be persuaded through negotiations or, if necessary, forced to return to the Roman church. For details, see Walter, RA, 1 ff.

issues on the agenda of the diet: The first was the defense of the Empire against the Turks. The second was the Reformation; this diet was to arrive, on the basis of a "charitable hearing [of] every man's opinion . . . [at] a unity in Christian truth, [and was to] dispose of everything that has not been rightly explained or treated . . . [so] that one single, true religion may be accepted and held by us all, and that we all live in one common church and in unity. . . . " And the third was a number of administrative and judicial matters pertaining to the Empire.[5]

The Electoral Saxon government immediately undertook the necessary steps to prepare for this diet. On March 14 the Elector[6] *instructed his Wittenberg theologians to draft articles concerning the controversies in matters of faith, and concerning ecclesiastical customs and ceremonies, articles which would present the Electoral Saxon "opinion," and which would give a basis for negotiations with other Protestant Estates for the purpose of common action.*[7] *The Wittenberg theologians were further instructed to come to Torgau on March 20 for a strategy session,*[8] *and to do everything necessary in order to be able to accompany the Elector on the trip to the diet. How far the theologians would accompany the Elector*

---

[5] This summons documents a different attitude toward the Protestants on the part of the Emperor than that which he expressed in his treatment of the delegation which was to turn over to him the Protest and Appeal; see p. 245, n. 9. Consequently the Electoral Saxon court expected that the whole Reformation issue would be discussed and perhaps even settled. And yet the Emperor promised very little in this summons, and the hopes of the Protestants that doctrinal matters would be *discussed* certainly were not justified; all the Emperor really promised was that he would *listen* to the opinions of the various parties. His intention had been clear at least since the Barcelona treaty (see note 4), and this intention was to lead the Protestants back into obedience to the Roman church by all means possible, perhaps by some concessions in matters of ecclesiastical practice, or by force if necessary.

[6] I.e., here and throughout this letter, Duke John; see *LW* 48, 269, n. 8.

[7] Eagerly looking forward to the diet, the Elector approached some of the sovereigns who had joined him in signing the Protest and Appeal, and urged them to go to Augsburg if at all possible; URA 1, No. 6. On March 11, or 12, the Elector's councilors prepared a highly detailed plan of action; URA 1, No. 3. Text of the March 14 communication to the Wittenberg theologians: WA, Br 5, No. 1538. For general information, see Gussmann, *QFGAG* 1¹, 87 ff.

[8] See WA, Br 5, 265. This meeting did not take place; consequently on March 21 the Elector for the second time summoned the theologians to Torgau; see WA, Br 5, 269. It is not clear whether this meeting ever took place; it is only known that Melanchthon was in Torgau on March 27, for he wrote a letter from here; see Gussmann, *QFGAG* 1¹, 428, n. 5; *C.R.* 2, 33 f.

would depend upon whether safe-conduct were granted for preachers and theological consultants who were being brought to the diet. The theologians were to accompany the Elector, however, at least as far as Coburg, which at that time was the southernmost residency and castle in the Elector's domain. If the safe-conduct were arranged, then only Luther was to stay at Coburg, or perhaps even at Nürnberg,[9] while the others were to go to Augsburg; if no safe-conduct could be arranged then all were to stay at Coburg in order to be available for consultations.

Some darkness lies over the activities of the Wittenberg theologians in the following weeks.[10] On April 3, however, Luther, Melanchthon,[11] Jonas,[12] and Veit Dietrich[13] left Wittenberg for

---

[9] According to the Elector's March 14 instructions for the Wittenberg theologians (see note 7), Luther was to stay at the Coburg—obviously for security reasons. According to the plan of action drafted by the Electoral councilors (see note 7), Luther and Jonas were to stay at Nürnberg, which was closer to Augsburg than the Coburg. This plan raised the serious question whether the Nürnberg city council would permit Luther, as an excommunicated and banned person, to stay within the city; or to phrase it differently, whether the city council was in a position to guarantee Luther's safety. See further, note 22.

[10] See note 8. One of the questions would be: What happened to the articles which the Elector had requested on March 14? There seems to be agreement that the so-called *Torgau Articles* (*URA* 1, No. 27; Reu II, No. 19) fulfill the Elector's request. The question would be whether they were the work of the Wittenberg theologians, or were solely written by Melanchthon. The material presented in the *Torgau Articles* was later developed by Melanchthon into the second part of the *Augsburg Confession*. For recent literature on the origin of the *Augsburg Confession*, see R. Nürnberger (ed.), *Festschrift für Gerhard Ritter* (Tübingen, 1950), pp. 161 ff.; *ARG* 51 (1960), 158 ff.; 57 (1966), 76 ff.

[11] Philip Melanchthon; see *LW* 48, 77, n. 3.

[12] Justus Jonas; see *LW* 48, 275, n. 3.

[13] Veit Dietrich (1506–1549) of Nürnberg began to study in Wittenberg in 1522, and lived in Luther's home, with a few interruptions, from 1527 to 1534. Having been graduated as Master of Arts in 1529, he accompanied Luther to Marburg and to Coburg. As chief preacher at St. Sebald's Church in Nürnberg, a position to which he was appointed in 1535, Dietrich dedicated all his energy to the development of practical theology, especially catechetics. Among other works he published an altarbook, a summary of all the books of Scripture, a summary of Christian teachings, catechism sermons, and a collection of what today would be called Sunday school materials. More important than this activity, however, was his contribution to our knowledge of Luther. As Luther's trusted friend, sharing with the Reformer the lonely months at the Coburg, he began to note down Table Talks, to collect preliminary and final drafts of letters, as well as copies of letters and briefs, and manuscripts of lectures and sermons. For an excellent biography of Dietrich, see B. Klaus, *Veit Dietrich: Leben und Werk* (Nürnberg, 1958).

Torgau; here they joined the Electoral party for the trip to Coburg, where they arrived safely on April 15.[14] They all stayed in the Elector's residency in the city until April 24, when the Electoral party, with Melanchthon and Jonas, left for Augsburg. On the 24th, about 4:00 A.M.,[15] Luther and Veit Dietrich moved into the Coburg castle.

The following letter is one of those Luther wrote while still living with his friends in the residency. He tells Hausmann what he has done for Martin Sanger, who was to come to Hausmann and report details. Luther also tells of the Emperor's delay in arriving in Germany, and of the fear of many people that the whole diet might be cancelled because of manipulations on the part of the papists. Informing Hausmann of his planned stay at Coburg, Luther includes news about the siege of Florence, and about the possibility of an invasion of the Empire by the Turks. In a postscript Luther mentions that one thousand ducats worth of his books were purchased by the people of Florence at the last Frankfurt book fair.

On Nicholas Hausmann, see LW 48, 399 f.

Text in Latin: WA, Br 5, 277–278.

To the excellent man, Mr. Nicholas Hausmann,
faithful bishop of the church at Zwickau,[16]
my superior in the Lord

Grace and peace in Christ. We have done for Martin Sanger as much as we could, my Hausmann, as he himself will report [to

---

[14] For the itinerary, see Buchwald, *LK*, pp. 70 f.; WA, Br 5, 274, n. 7; see also WA 32, xxviii. On April 8 Emperor Charles wrote from Mantua to Elector John that he expected the Elector to arrive in Augsburg before April was over. Due to pressing business the Emperor had to delay his departure from Italy, but, so he assured the Elector, he had now begun the journey to Augsburg and hoped to arrive there soon. URA 1, No. 45; *St. L.*, 16, 666 f. This letter arrived at Coburg on April 22 (see URA 1, 167; WA, Br 5, 278, n. 2) and was, in turn, responsible for the continuation of the journey by the Electoral party.

[15] This hour was chosen obviously for security reasons, to avoid any public commotion; see WA, Br 5, No. 1552, Introduction. April 23, the date of Luther's move into the Coburg given in Buchwald, *LK*, p. 71, and Schubert, LaK, 116, n. 30, have to be corrected accordingly.

[16] See p. 87, n. 5.

you].[17] In addition, he will tell[18] Cordatus[19] and you that we are still here, and do not know when we shall move on.[20] For yesterday a letter[21] and a messenger arrived [here],[22] informing [us] that the Emperor is still at Mantua and will celebrate Easter there. In addition it is said[23] that the papists are trying extremely hard to stop the diet, since they are afraid that something might be decided against them. Finally it is said that the Pope[24] is angry with the Emperor, since the [latter] intends to interfere with ecclesiasti-

---

[17] The background of this statement could not be clarified. On Martin Sanger, or Sangner, see WA, Br 5, 278, n. 1.

[18] The text of the extant autograph would have to be translated: "In addition, you [i.e., Hausmann] will tell Cordatus and yourself . . ."

[19] Conrad Cordatus (1476?–1546) of Austria had studied theology at Vienna and Ferrara, and came to Ofen in 1510. Because of his evangelical convictions he was removed from office and imprisoned. When he was released from prison he studied at Wittenberg, then returned to Hungary, and was again imprisoned. Later exiled from there, he stayed briefly in Silesia, and then from 1529 to 1531 was a preacher in Zwickau. In 1532 Luther was able to provide a pastorate for him in Niemegk. In 1537 Cordatus became a pastor in Eisleben, and in 1540 superintendent in Stendahl. Cordatus is best known as one of the collectors of Luther's Table Talks (see also note 13), and for his controversy with Melanchthon concerning the doctrine of justification. On Conrad Cordatus, see NDB 3, 356 f. Cordatus was most eager to go to the Diet of Augsburg, but Luther advised against this; see WA, Br 5, 273.

[20] Since it was common knowledge that the Emperor was still in Italy, there was no need to hurry to Augsburg. Finally, on April 22, the Emperor's letter (mentioned in note 14) arrived in Coburg, and this in turn made the Elector continue his journey.

[21] This is a reference to a letter of the Nürnberg city council, dated April 16, in which the following news is reported as coming from some of "our" merchants in Bozen and Augsburg. Text: URA 1, No. 49. "Yesterday" should not be taken literally, since the "messenger" had arrived in Coburg on April 16. See note 22. Either Luther erred regarding the date, or, and this is most probable, he did not hear of the messenger's presence, and of the letter, until April 17, i.e., "yesterday."

[22] I.e., apparently the Nürnberg syndic (see Hilfswörterbuch, s.v. Syndicus) Michael von Kaden (see ADB 14, 782 ff.), who brought the letter and who was to give the answer of the Nürnberg city council to the Elector's inquiry of April 7, namely, whether the city council would permit Luther to stay at Nürnberg during the sessions of the diet (see note 9). Nürnberg absolutely refused to grant this request. See Schubert, LaK, 113 ff.; Schornbaum, Nürnberg, 200. For the Elector's reply to Nürnberg, dated April 18, see URA 1, No. 51.

[23] Apparently the following news came to Luther via von Kaden, who also gave a detailed report on the Emperor's coronation in Bologna (see note 4), which report Luther, in turn, communicated to von Amsdorf; see WA, Br 5, 275.

[24] I.e., here and throughout this letter, Pope Clement VII; see p. 161, n. 12.

cal matters,[25] and to listen to the [various] parties,[26] while the [former] hoped that [the Emperor] would only send his hangman against the heretics and restore the *status quo ante*. For [the papists] want nothing to be changed or to be given up, nor do they want to be judged or examined. [All they want is] that we be simply condemned and destroyed, while they are completely restored.[27] And so they will perish, for in such way one walks toward utter ruin; thus the ungodly have to be blinded since they are to perish. Some even think that the whole diet will be cancelled, and that nothing will come of it.

I am ordered by the Elector to remain at Coburg (once the others[28] have left for the diet)—I don't know for what reason.[29]

---

[25] Luther wrote: *causis ecclesiasticis,* i.e., the technical term in the Canon Law for all matters pertaining to the church, matters which stand under the exclusive jurisdiction of the church.

[26] See the Imperial Summons, quoted in the Introduction.

[27] It is extremely difficult to clarify to what degree Luther's statements are based on solid information. They may have been simply general assumptions. On April 25 the instructions for the papal legate to the diet, Lorenzo Campeggio, were dispatched from Rome, though they had been issued as early as March 16. Text: Gussmann, *QFGAG* 1¹, 249 ff.; see also the special privileges and powers entrusted to Campeggio: *NB* I.Abt.,E.1, No. 1c. This material documents how the Pope wished the Reformation matters to be handled: his plan was to woo the nobility and common people, sharply criticize the laxity of the clergy, and threaten all who would not fall in line—this should bring the sheep that had gone astray back to the flock. (As early as April 28 Clement VII authorized Campeggio to absolve penitent heretics, and to take the necessary steps to eradicate the Protestant heresy by wiping out stubborn heretics; see *NB* I.Abt.,E.1, No. 1e; see also Kidd, No. 112.) According to an April 25 letter of Jacopo Salviati (who was the Pope's secretary and most influential advisor) to Campeggio, the Curia saw in Campeggio's mission a parallel to the efforts to bring the Hussites back to the Roman church; see *NB* I.Abt.,E.1, No. 2. In order to put Luther's statements into the proper perspective, one should also remember the attempt of Aleander, the legate to the Diet of Worms, to obstruct every effort to bring the Luther case before the Emperor during the Diet of Worms; see *LW* 48, 198, n. 3; 193, n. 9. While Luther is perhaps a bit pessimistic in evaluating the situation here, time has shown he was correct in judging the intentions of the papists; the development of the diet—above all the resolution of the diet (see p. 423)—was to confirm his judgment.

[28] I.e., the Electoral party, and Melanchthon, Jonas (see notes 11, 12), and Agricola (see *LW* 48, 220) as the theological consultants and preachers.

[29] Since Luther obviously knew that as a banned person he could not accompany the Elector to Augsburg, the statement here has to be understood as meaning that Luther did not know why he was to stay at the Coburg rather than return to Wittenberg. See also *WA*, Br 13, 125, to *WA*, Br 5, 279, n. 7.

And so all things become uncertain from one day to the next.

Florence has neither been conquered, nor has it been reconciled with the Pope, and the Pope is not sorry about this.[30] For the army inside [the city] always shouted that they too were a part of the Emperor's Empire. And so nothing involving force has been undertaken against the [Florentine army] by the Empire from the outside, but the siege has been lifted and they are free [again].[31] From this you people can see how much good our prayers do, if we are persistent.

It is said that the Turk[32] has promised, or rather threatened, to return to Germany next year with very great forces, even leading against us large numbers of Tartars. But it is written: "The Lord brings the counsel of the nations to naught."[33] Word and prayer will fight against [the Turks].

Pray for me, and farewell in Christ.[34]

Coburg, April 18, 1530   MARTIN LUTHER

The[35] Florentine people have sent a messenger to Frankfurt and ordered him to buy one thousand ducats[36] worth of my books

---

[30] The last portion of this sentence ("and the Pope . . .") has been translated as literally as possible. Apparently Luther wanted to say that the Pope was not sorry over the lack of success on the part of the Imperial army against Florence because of the alleged pro-Imperial tendencies on the part of the Florentine garrison. Obviously such "loyalty" to the Empire was contrary to papal interests.

[31] This news is correct only in part. After the sack of Rome, the republican party of Florence exiled the Medici dynasty and organized a republic. One of the conditions of the Barcelona peace treaty (see note 4) was the restoration of the Medici dynasty in Florence. Pope Clement VII had a definite interest in this since he was a member of the Medici family. On October 24, 1529, the siege of Florence began. Aided by the new fortifications designed by Michelangelo, the city defended itself bravely, but finally had to surrender on August 12, 1530. It is difficult to estimate how tight the siege was (see also note 37), but there is no evidence that the siege was ever lifted during this time. For details, see Ranke, 2[III], 135; Elton, pp. 344 ff.

[32] See p. 265. Nothing could be established about the background of this statement.

[33] Ps. 33:10.

[34] Literally: "and pleasantly farewell in Christ."

[35] This postscript was written on a separate piece of paper which was attached to the autograph. Since the postscript was written on what appears to be the same poor paper as the rest of the letter, there is some jusification for assuming that it is a postscript to this letter.

[36] The ducat was a very valuable gold coin, weighing approximately 3.5 grams; it originated in Venice, and during the later Middle Ages became very

and bring them to Florence;[37] perhaps out of spite for the Pope they will permit [the preaching of] the gospel there. This has been written to us from Frankfurt as certain.

206

To Philip Melanchthon
Coburg,[1] [April 24,][2] 1530

This is the first extant letter which Luther wrote from the Coburg. On April 24, after the morning meal, the Electoral party left the residency in Coburg for the journey to Nürnberg and Augsburg. Prior to their departure Luther, Veit Dietrich,[3] and Cyriac Kaufmann[4] had moved into the Coburg.[5] While waiting for his luggage in the afternoon[6] of the 24th, Luther wrote letters to Melanchthon, Jonas,[7] and then, apparently as an afterthought, also to Spalatin.[8]

popular as currency throughout northern Italy and southern Germany. From 1559 the ducat was the official coin of the Empire.

[37] How Luther received this news about the Frankfurt Easter book fair is unknown. Apparently the siege of Florence could not have been terribly tight if the Florentine people could buy books at Frankfurt and have them shipped back to Italy. Or were the Frankfurt merchants confusing the people of Florence with people from another city? On the book traffic between Frankfurt and Italy, see F. Kapp, *Geschichte des deutschen Buchhandels bis in das 17. Jahrhundert* (Leipzig, 1886), pp. 457 f.

[1] As Luther had done with his letters from the Wartburg, so he did with most of his letters from the Coburg: he gave a fictitious name to the place from which he was writing. The circumstances of the letter make clear, however, where Luther was when he wrote it. The names which he invented for his place of residence sometimes apparently are a sign of humor, sometimes perhaps even a sign of slight sarcasm. It is doubtful that these names should be understood in terms of security, since at least in one case Luther did give the correct name of the place from which he was writing; see WA, Br 5, 341. See however also WA, Br 13, 159, to WA, Br 5, 467, line 12.

[2] For the exact dating of this letter, see WA, Br 5, No. 1552, Introduction, and below, note 38.

[3] See p. 282, n. 13. Dietrich, too, wrote a letter to Melanchthon on April 24; WA, Br 12, 111 f.

[4] See p. 269, n. 8.

[5] On Luther's stay at the Coburg, see Schubert, LaK; W. Schanze, *Luther auf der Veste Coburg* (Coburg, 1927).

[6] See note 38.

[7] WA, Br 5, No. 1553.

[8] Since in his letter to Melanchthon Luther extended greetings to Spalatin, he apparently did not intend to write to him. A short time later he had changed his mind, and also wrote to Spalatin; see letter No. 207.

In the letter to Melanchthon Luther tells his first impressions of the
Coburg, and his working plans. He hopes to work on the Psalter,
on the prophets, and on Aesop's fables. The letter reflects the seri-
ousness of the hour. Luther knows of Melanchthon's worries about
the pending diet; he himself is deeply disturbed about the constant
threat of danger from the Turk. In both circumstances Luther sees
the arrival of the final destruction of the satanic powers, and of
man's complete redemption. Luther assures Melanchthon of his
prayers, and commends him to God's grace.

The autograph of this letter is no longer extant. The text of
the letter is available in several manuscript copies and in the com-
mon editions of Luther's works. These witnesses differ in some
instances, but the variations do not seem to have major bearing on
the meaning of the text.

On Philip Melanchthon, see LW 48, 77, n. 3.

Text in Latin: WA, Br 5, 285–286.

To my dearest brother, Master[9] Philip,
a faithful and skilled servant of Christ

Grace and peace in the Lord Jesus. We have finally arrived at our
Sinai, dearest Philip; but we shall make a Zion out of this Sinai, and
construct here three huts:[10] one for the Psalter,[11] one for the
prophets,[12] and one for Aesop;[13] but this one is only temporal.[14]
This place is certainly extremely pleasant and most suited for

---

[9] I.e., Master of Arts.

[10] This is an allusion to Matt. 17:4.

[11] Apparently Luther planned to work on a commentary on the Psalms.
Beginning on May 4 he started to dictate to Veit Dietrich a commentary on
the (first twenty-five) Psalms. Luther apparently then changed his mind, and
selected individual Psalms, for in July and August he was occupied with work
on Psalm 117. For unknown reasons the Psalm commentary dictated to
Dietrich was never published during Luther's life. Dietrich kept the manuscript, and his heirs finally had it published in 1559. See WA, 31¹, 219 ff.,
258 ff.; LW 14, 3 ff., 40 ff.

[12] This is a reference to the translation of and commentary on individual
prophetic books. By the middle of June Luther had finished Jeremiah, and
then began working on Ezekiel. See WA 30ᴵᴵ, 220 ff.; WA DB 11ᴵᴵ, lv ff.

[13] Luther's translation, with a preface, of some of Aesop's fables (see O.C.D.,
p. 355) was not published until 1557. See WA 50, 432 ff.; WA, Br 13, 125,
to WA, Br 5, 286, n. 4.

[14] I.e., the work on Aesop, a secular work, has only temporal importance in
contrast to the work on the Psalter and the prophets.

studying,[15] except that your absence makes it a sad place.[16] I am beginning to get fired up against the Turk and Muhammad,[17] since I am aware of Satan's fury, which is unbearable and which rages so powerfully[18] against bodies and souls. Therefore I shall pray and weep aloud and will not be silent until I see that my shouting has been heard in heaven. The domestic monsters of our Empire torment you more.[19] But we [together] are the people for whom it has been predestined to see and endure these last two woes,[20] which come down upon us and rage among us with the violence of the last day.[21] But precisely this violence is a witness and prophet of the end [of Satan], and of our redemption.

I am asking Christ to grant you sound sleep, and to liberate your heart from worries, that is, from Satan's flaming darts,[22] and to protect you [against them]. Amen.

I am writing this since I have nothing to do; I have not yet received my trunk with the papers and [other] things, for till now I haven't seen either one of the two officials.[23] Nothing interferes with our solitude, for this whole large house, which stands out from the [rest of the] castle, belongs totally to us, and we have been

---

[15] Literally: "for studies."
[16] Literally: "saddens it [i.e., the place]."
[17] See p. 286. Luther interrupted his work on Jeremiah in order to translate chapters 38 and 39 of Ezekiel (the prophecies concerning Gog and Magog). He added notes and a preface to this translation, and prior to May 12 he sent the manuscript to Wittenberg for printing. See WA 30[II], 220 ff.
[18] Literally: "so haughtily."
[19] This is a reference to Melanchthon's tense anticipation concerning the pending diet and its possible outcome.
[20] See Rev. 9:12. Clemen identifies (WA, Br 5, 286, n. 7) the "two woes" as the Turk and Muhammad. In WA, Br 13, 125, ad loc., the "two woes" are identified as the Turk and the Pope. See also in this vol., p. 217. One may also submit that by the "two woes" Luther meant the external woe, i.e.. the Turk, and the internal, domestic woe, the "monsters of our Empire," i.e., the manipulations of the papists (especially for the pending diet). On the basis of Luther's statements this last suggestion seems to this editor to be the most likely. Luther is deeply disturbed about the gospel's enemy from outside the Empire, the Turk, while Melanchthon is "more" worried about the gospel's enemy inside the Empire; and both Luther and Melanchthon are predestined to experience these two foes, in whose raging Luther sees Satan's fury against bodies and souls. But this final attack of Satan is a sign of "his" doom, and of "our" redemption.
[21] The last portion of this sentence (from "which") is translated quite freely. See also LW 48, 104, n. 7.
[22] Eph. 6:16.
[23] See notes 28, 29.

given the keys to all the rooms.[24] It is said that more than thirty people are working[25] here, among whom are twelve night watchmen and two lookout guards with bugles stationed in different towers.[26] But what is all this?[27] Of course, I have nothing else to write about [now].[28] I do hope the bailiff [or] the tax collector[29] will be here tonight, [and] then we shall perhaps hear some news.

God's grace be with you. Amen.

---

[24] There are two very tall buildings within the Coburg, the so-called *Hohe Haus*, which at that time was the armory, and the *Hohe Kemenate*. According to Schanze, *op. cit.*, p. 20, Luther most probably lived in two of the rooms of the latter building with a view to the north, i.e., the southern slopes of the Thuringian Forest.

[25] Literally: "eat bread."

[26] According to Schanze, *op. cit.*, p. 18, the numbers of the forces stationed in the Coburg do not suggest that the Elector was either especially concerned with Luther's safety (and consequently put more men into the Coburg), or was not sufficiently careful about Luther's safety (by not putting a larger garrison into the castle), since according to contemporary sources (see WA, Br 13, 126, to WA, Br 5, 287, n. 12) the forces in the castle were never much above or below the figures mentioned by Luther.

[27] The meaning of this sentence is unclear. Did Luther want to ask what good these troops would be if an attack were executed against the castle in an attempt to "kidnap" him? This seems to be dubious. Or did Luther mean: What is this "trifle of news" to you, Melanchthon, for you are going to Nürnberg and Augsburg, and will experience all the pomp which is a part of such a journey and of the pending diet? The following sentence seems to suggest this latter interpretation.

[28] Clemen (*WA*, Br 5, 287, n. 13) suggests that in the autograph the following sentence, which can be found only in some witnesses, might have been written on the margin as an afterthought, or as an explanation to the "two officials" mentioned above.

[29] The witnesses which contain this sentence either simply place the two titles next to each other (perhaps because Luther did so in the autograph and assumed that Melanchthon knew of whom he was thinking, or perhaps the "marginal note" was too poorly written so that the "and," or whatever else Luther might have written, could not be read), or omit the two titles completely, thus leaving a lacuna, or give only one title. See Enders, *Briefwechsel* 7, 303, n. t. The *WA*, Br text reads: *cistanista questor. Cistanista*, or *Kastner* in German, has been translated as bailiff. In the case of the *Kastner* of Coburg this term is not quite adequate, since he was not an official of the public administration, as a bailiff is, but of the private administration of the Elector's personal property. In this area he did fulfill the responsibilities which were held by a bailiff. On the various functions of a *Kastner*, see *Hilfswörterbuch, s.v.* Kastner. *Quaestor*, or *Schösser* in German, was the tax collector for the district of Coburg. Paul Bader was *Kastner* in Coburg, and Arnold von Falckenstein was the tax collector. On both officials, see *WA*, Br 13, 125, to *WA*, Br 5, 286, n. 10.

You greet Doctor Caspar[30] for me, and Master[31] Spalatin,[32] for I shall request Jonas[33] to greet Master[34] Agricola,[35] and Aquila.[36] *From the kingdom of the birds,*[37] *at the third hour,*[38] *1530*

MARTIN LUTHER

---

[30] Dr. Caspar Lindemann (who died in 1536) was practicing medicine in Leipzig; he also taught there at the University, and functioned, with some interruptions, as "family doctor" for the Saxon Electors Frederick and John (see *LW* 48, 49 f.; 269, n. 8). In 1532 Lindemann was called to Wittenberg University. Through his mother Luther was related to Dr. Lindemann. For details, see *WA*, Br 5, 287, n. 14; *WA*, Br 13, 126, *ad loc.* Lindemann, like the others mentioned in this paragraph, was a member of the Electoral party which had left for Nürnberg and Augsburg. Some of the witnesses do not contain this paragraph.

[31] See note 9.

[32] George Spalatin; see *LW* 48, 8 f.

[33] See note 7.

[34] See note 9.

[35] John Agricola, see *LW* 48, 220.

[36] I.e., Caspar Aquila (1488–1560), who since 1527 had been a pastor in Saalfeld. Although Aquila was one of the lesser known friends of Luther, the Reformer considered Aquila indispensable for the translation of the Old Testament because of his versatility in Hebrew. During the visitations Aquila was made superintendent of the Saalfeld clergy in 1528. Even though he was a close friend of Agricola, and somewhat supported the latter's position in the Antinomian controversy (see pp. 212 f.), his friendship with Luther and Melanchthon continued. In later years he even became a strong opponent of Agricola, because of Agricola's role in bringing about the Augsburg Interim, and he charged Agricola with abandoning the gospel. For his strong criticism of the Augsburg Interim, Aquila had to go into hiding for awhile, since the Imperial government had put a price on his head. In 1550 he became dean at Smalcald, and in 1552 he returned to Saalfeld, where he died in 1560. On Caspar Aquila, see *NDB* 1, 332 f.

[37] I.e., the Coburg; see note 1. In the following letter to Jonas (*WA*, Br 5, No. 1553) Luther described the noise which the birds made in the early morning hours. See also letter No. 207.

[38] Luther mentioned in his letter to Jonas (see note 37) that from 4.00 A.M., and throughout the whole day, the jackdaws had been making much noise. Consequently the letter to Melanchthon, signed at the third hour, must have been written at approximately 3:00 P.M. In his letters to Melanchthon and Jonas dated April 29 Luther mentioned that he had written letters to them on the first day of their separation; *WA*, Br 5, 297, 298. Since the Electoral party left Coburg on April 24 (see p. 283, n. 15), this date can be established as the date of the letters to Melanchthon, Jonas, and Spalatin. These letters reflect Luther's first impressions after his arrival at the Coburg.

207

To George Spalatin
Coburg, [April 24,]¹ 1530

*Having written to Melanchthon and Jonas in the afternoon of his
first day at the Coburg,² Luther also wrote a letter to Spalatin.
When Luther arrived at the Coburg he apparently was quite impressed with the birds flying around the castle; especially the
jackdaws³ caught his eye. In the letter to Spalatin, Luther interprets
the gathering of the jackdaws outside his window as a picture of
the diet to which his friends are traveling. The letter reveals
Luther's gift of observing and enjoying the seemingly unimportant
things in life, and also his fine sense of humor. But the humor is
only an attempt to chase away his serious concerns for his friends
and the common cause.⁴*

On George Spalatin: LW 48, 8 f.

Text in Latin: WA, Br 5, 290–291.

To the excellent man, Mr. George Spalatin,
a faithful servant of Christ in the gospel, my superior

---

¹ For the date, see p. 291, n. 38.

² See letter No. 206, Introduction.

³ It is not clear whether Luther saw and heard only jackdaws. Luther's statements in the following letter to Spalatin seem to suggest this. But what Luther
has to say about the pleasantness of the sound made by the birds seems to put
this into question, since the crowlike noises made by the jackdaws are anything but pleasant. In his letter to Jonas written just prior to this letter to
Spalatin (see WA, Br 5, No. 1553), Luther mentioned the music made by the
birds as being so powerful that it could outdo the morning storm. Then he
continues by mentioning the *Gekeke* (cackling?) of the jackdaws. WA, Br 5,
289. (This could of course be a play on words referring to his old foe, John
Eck [see LW 48, 80, n. 13] who was also going to Augsburg.) While the
allegory on the diet apparently was closely tied to the jackdaws, this does not
exclude the possibility that Luther also observed other birds, which impressed
him and stimulated his imagination.

⁴ Luther was apparently quite taken by the allegory on the pending diet. In
the letter to Jonas he sets forth some phases of it for the first time; in the
present letter to Spalatin he presents the fully developed picture; and he
repeats it once more in a letter to his friends in Wittenberg (WA, Br 5, No.
1555), if this letter was indeed written by him; see WA, Br 13, 127, to WA,
Br 5, No. 1555. For a similar allegory (this time between a hunted hare and
the persecution of the gospel) see LW 48, 295.

Grace and peace in the Lord. It is not you people alone, my Spalatin, who are traveling to a diet, for we, too, arrived at a diet as soon as we had parted from you, and so we overtook you by far. Therefore our journey to the diet has not been prevented,[5] but only changed.

You people, of course, go to Augsburg, [but] you are uncertain when you will see the beginning [of your diet]; we came here right into the midst of a diet. Here you might see magnanimous kings, dukes, and other noblemen of the kingdom, who seriously care for their belongings and offspring, and who with untiring voice proclaim their decisions and dogmas through the air. Finally, they do not live, or rather they are not locked up, in such holes and caves as you people[6] call—with but little reason—palaces. Rather they live under the open sky, so that the sky itself serves them as paneled ceiling, the green trees as a floor of limitless variety, and the walls [of their palace] are identical with the ends of the earth. They also show contempt for the foolish luxury of gold and silk; rather they all [live] the same way, [have] one color, one [kind of] dress, and one voice, [and all] are dressed in an unbelievable similarity and equality. All are equally black, all have dark blue eyes,[7] all make the same music in unison, yet with a pleasant difference between the voices of the elders and the youngsters. I have not yet seen nor heard their emperor.[8] I see that they openly despise the four-legged cavalry. They have a better [cavalry, one] with wings, through which they can even escape from the wrath of the artillery. As far as I could understand from the interpreter of their resolutions, they have unanimously decided to make war throughout this whole year [first] on the barley, the raw as well as the malted, and then on the summer and winter wheat, and whatever else are the best fruits.

---

[5] I.e., by the fact that Luther could not go as far as Nürnberg; see p. 284, n. 22.

[6] I.e., the people of the court. Luther addresses Spalatin as a member of the Electoral court, even though Spalatin had left the service of the court after the death of Elector Frederick the Wise, and thereafter served the court only on special occasions and for special missions. There is also some sarcasm in Luther's statement here, as in other cases when he speaks of the people at court; see e.g., LW 48, 294 f., 354, 383.

[7] So according to Clemen, WA, Br 5, 292, n. 3. In the letter to his Wittenberg friends (see note 4) Luther calls the eyes grey; WA, Br 5, 294.

[8] I.e., just as you people have not yet seen Emperor Charles; see p. 283, n. 14.

There is danger that they will be victorious in many things, for they are a crafty and cunning race of warriors, marvelously trained in stealing and robbing.

We sit here with great pleasure in [this][9] diet, as idle spectators and listeners.[10] For in addition to the fact that that uniform and beautiful black color wonderfully refreshes us, seeing that these heroes are so magnificently dressed, the unanimity of all their voices, which are saturated with beautiful melodies, also delights us beyond measure. Finally the hope and expectation of their bravery and victories, which we believe they will win over the wheat and barley (and whatever similar things there might be), make these fathers of the fatherland and preservers of the commonwealth extremely agreeable and pleasant to us. [Consequently] if something could be accomplished by wishing it, we would wish that they might be free of that defamatory name *monedula*,[11] or rather from the accusation that they are thievish, and that they might be praised with names worthy of their dignity—that is, that they all together might be called "lancers" or "spearmen"[12] (yet with a passive meaning).[13] Nevertheless if they found a fair interpreter they would derive sufficient glory and praise from [their][14] very name *Mon Edula* if it were taken to mean *man Edel*,[15] or

---

[9] Literally: "their [i.e., the jackdaws'] diet."

[10] See p. 289.

[11] I.e., the Latin term for jackdaw. The defamation lies in the fact that the jackdaw, like the crow, is supposedly a thief. There are a number of German fairy tales and proverbs in which a jackdaw, or a crow, steals something, especially anything made of shiny metal, as, e.g., a ring.

[12] Literally: "armed with a lance or spear."

[13] I.e., be lanced or speared. What Luther meant here becomes clear from his letter to his friends in Wittenberg (see note 4; *WA*, Br 5, 294): "We wish them [i.e., the jackdaws] fortune and success [on their warpath], that they all together may be speared on a fence post. Yet I consider it [i.e., the diet of the jackdaws, or their war against the wheat] to be no different from the sophists and papists with their preaching and writing, whom in this way I am forced to have all in one heap before my eyes, so that I might listen to their dear voices and sermons, and see what a very useful people they [i.e., the papists] are, who devour everything that is on earth. . . ." The meaning of Luther's sentence is, then, that he wishes the papists and their secular hangers-on to be "called" or considered as being "lanced or speared," i.e., as being unable to harm his friends in Augsburg, even more, as being defeated.

[14] Literally: "the."

[15] I.e., a man of noble birth or standing; these two words are written in German.

Edelman[16] if you turn the words around. However at this point begins an affront to your[17] diet, for your *Edelmoni*[18] excel too much through *monedulana* virtue[s].[19] Yet our *Man Edelini*[20] in their diet are better off in one point—they have a less expensive and more tolerable market than your [*Edelmoni*] at Augsburg.[21]

This suffices for a joke, but [it is] a serious and necessary joke which should chase away the thoughts seizing me, if it can repel them [at all]. The rest you will hear from Jonas and Philip.[22]

From the kingdom of the winged jackdaws, the fifth hour,[23] *1530*

Yours,
MARTIN LUTHER

208

To Elector John
[Coburg,] May 15, 1530

The Electoral Saxon delegation arrived in Augsburg on May 2, apparently the first one to do so.[1] *Here it became evident that the Torgau Articles*[2] *(which were to be a defense of the Electoral Saxon position in ecclesiastical matters) would not suffice for the*

---

[16] I.e., the German term for a nobleman; this word is written in German.
[17] See note 6.
[18] I.e., "your" men of noble birth. Luther creates this term by taking the German *Edelman* (see note 16) and supplying a Latin masculine plural ending, carrying through his fanciful association with Latin *monedula*, in order to set the stage for the following *monedulana*.
[19] I.e., the thievish "virtue" of the jackdaw; see note 11.
[20] I.e., a form derived from *man Edel* (see note 15). Again, as with *Edelmoni*, Luther creates this term by taking the German *man Edel* (see note 15) and adding a pseudo-Latin masculine plural ending.
[21] Luther expected that the influx of people would result in a rise in prices in Augsburg, or a scarcity of goods. This indeed did happen, as Jonas reported to Luther on May 4; see WA, Br 5, 301.
[22] See p. 287.
[23] I.e., approximately 5:00 P.M.; for the date, and time of day, see p. 291, n. 38.
[1] See Justus Jonas to Luther: Augsburg, May 4, 1530; WA, Br 5, 301; Hans von Dolzig to Elector John: Innsbruck, May 8, 1530; URA 1, 178.
[2] See p. 282, n. 10.

upcoming business at the diet.[3] Consequently Melanchthon continued to rework this material, changing it radically and incorporating the Schwabach Articles.[4] On May 11 the Apologia, or rather Confession,[5] was sent by a special mounted messenger to Luther at the Coburg, with the request that he study the Confession, correct it where necessary, approve it, and return it by the same messenger.[6]

On May 10 the Elector had received word from his special ambassador[7] at the Imperial court (which was then slowly traveling through Austria)[8] that the Emperor intended to prohibit the indi-

---

[3] Two facts influenced the Electoral Saxon delegation to abandon the *Torgau Articles* as they had been reshaped by Melanchthon (see Reu I, 54 f.; Gussmann, *QFGAG* 1[I], 101 f.): (a) Upon their arrival in Augsburg the Electoral Saxon delegates gained the impression that Emperor Charles V (see *LW* 48, 175 f.) might not be willing to listen to long disputations and arguments. See Philip Melanchthon to Luther: Augsburg, May 11, 1530; *WA*, Br 5, 314; Reu II, No. 25. Consequently a short confession of faith might serve better as a basis for whatever further negotiations might take place. Perhaps such a document might also be more in agreement with the intentions of the *Summons* (see pp. 280 f.). (b) Soon after his arrival in Augsburg, Melanchthon became acquainted with Eck's *404 Articles*. On March 14, 1530, this old enemy of Luther (see *LW* 48, 80, n. 13) had dispatched to the Emperor a beautifully handwritten document containing four hundred and four articles of Protestant teaching which were alleged to be heretical; Eck also offered to debate the Reformers in Augsburg for the purpose of making known to the whole world that the Reformers indeed were heretics. For Eck's *404 Articles*, which were printed in a Latin version in April, and soon thereafter in a German version, see Reu I, 56 ff.; II, Nos. 18, 22; Gussmann, *QFGAG* 2, 99 ff.; *American Society of Church History*. Papers, 2nd Ser., 2 (1910), 19 ff.; *WA*, Br 5, 305 (Melanchthon to Luther: May 4, 1530). Melanchthon and the other members of the Electoral Saxon delegation apparently realized at this point that, if Eck's *404 Articles* were received by the Emperor and became a part of the diet's discussions, then the *Summons* would be invalid, since the Protestants would be considered heretics from the very beginning, and no longer partners in dialogue, as was assumed by the wording of the *Summons*. Consequently it became necessary for the Protestants to give an account of their faith in order to establish the fact that they were Christians. See Walter, RA, 32 ff.; Reu I, 63 ff. As a result of this development, Melanchthon and others started to work on that document which eventually became the *Augsburg Confession*.

[4] See p. 236, n. 14.

[5] Melanchthon in his May 11 letter to Luther (*WA*, Br 5, 314; Reu II, No. 25) called the document *"apologia* or rather *confessio."*

[6] See Elector John to Luther: May 11, 1530; *WA*, Br 5, No. 1564.

[7] Hans von Dolzig to Elector John: Innsbruck, May 8, 1530; *URA* 1, No. 70, esp. pp. 180 f. On the Dolzig mission, through which a rapprochement of the Elector and the Emperor was to be brought about, see Walter, RA, 27; Fabian, *ESBV* (2nd ed.), pp. 84 f.

[8] Emperor Charles arrived in Innsbruck, and thus on German soil, on May 4. Here he was joined by the papal legate, Lorenzo Campeggio, and by many

vidual delegations to the diet from having their own pastors preach in the churches of Augsburg. When forwarding the Confession, Elector John also requested Luther to advise him what to do in this matter.

In the present letter Luther guardedly approves of Melanchthon's work, and suggests to the Elector that he abide by the Emperor's demand in the preaching matter, since in Augsburg, as an Imperial city, the emperor is the lord.

On Elector John, see LW 48, 269, n. 8.

Text in German: WA, Br 5, 319–320.

To the Most Serene, Noble Sovereign and Lord, Sir John, duke in Saxony and elector, landgrave in Thuringia and margrave in Meissen, my Most Gracious Lord

Grace and peace in Christ our Lord! Most Serene, Noble Sovereign, Most Gracious Lord! I have read through[9] Master[10] Philip's[11] *Apologia*,[12] which pleases me very much; I know nothing to improve or change in it, nor would this be appropriate, since I cannot

---

of those sovereigns who were still strongly supporting the papacy. They came to Innsbruck for a "caucus" on how to put the *Summons* of the diet into operation, and how to do it in such way that the unity of Christendom would be restored. Consequently the news coming from Innsbruck to Augsburg was not too promising for the Protestants. For details, see Walter, RA, 13 ff., 19 ff., 27 ff.; URA 1, Nos. 16, 64–70, 72, 79, 80; Gussmann, QFGAG 1¹, 103 f.; Reu I, 78 ff.; II, Nos. 28–30.

[9] Literally: "read over." The word used by Luther suggests that he only skimmed the document.

[10] I.e., Master of Arts.

[11] Philip Melanchthon; see *LW* 48, 77, n. 3. While Melanchthon was indeed the main author of the *Augsburg Confession,* nevertheless there were others who helped him draft this document.

[12] I.e., the first draft of the *Augsburg Confession.* Luther sometimes called this document *apologia,* sometimes *confessio,* sometimes *apologia confessionis.* See *Deutsche Theologie* 3 (1936), 251, n. 9. There is no document extant which has been identified as first draft of the *Augsburg Confession.* On May 22 Melanchthon wrote Luther that "we are daily changing many things in the *Apologia.*" And on June 3 the Nürnberg delegation dispatched a draft of the confession to the city council, and a German translation of this draft is extant; see Reu II, No. 37. It is commonly assumed that there are not too many fundamental differences between the *Apologia* of May 11 and the confession as extant in the German translation of June 3, even though, as is obvious in view of Melanchthon's May 22 statement, the two documents are not identical. See WA, Br 5, 312, n. 1; Reu I, 72 ff.; Gussman, QFGAG 1¹, 442, n. 27.

step so softly and quietly.[13] May Christ, our Lord, help [this *Apologia*] to bear much and great fruit, as we hope and pray. Amen.

On the question [of what to do] if His Imperial Majesty[14] should demand that Your Electoral Grace stop the preaching,[15] it is still my opinion, as it has been before,[16] that the emperor is our lord, and that the city and all belongs to him—just as one should not resist Your Electoral Grace in Torgau, if [Your Grace] should demand or decree to do or not to do something [in that city which belongs to Your Grace].[17] Of course, I would be happy if it were possible for someone in [all] humility, with sound and proper words and ways of arguing, to alter His Imperial Majesty's mind about this demand and plan, so that His Imperial Majesty would not prohibit the preaching without having investigated [the matter], but would have someone listen to the way we preach [prior to deciding]. His Imperial Majestic obviously should not prohibit the preaching of the pure and clear Scripture since, after all, we do

---

[13] Whether there is any slight sarcasm, or criticism, in this evaluation is unimportant. What is important, however, is the fact that Luther approves of Melanchthon's work, even though Luther makes it quite clear that he would have said things differently. Luther acknowledges, however, that Melanchthon has the burden of presenting the gospel in Augsburg, and consequently it would not be appropriate for him, Luther, to interfere. In his writings from Coburg Luther did not "step softly." As Gussmann has pointed out, throughout his life Luther had great admiration for Melanchthon's *Apologia*, but this did not stop him from criticizing the document as a whole; see Gussmann, *QFGAG* 1[I], 442 f. On Luther's evaluation of the *Augsburg Confession*, and of the work of his friends in Augsburg, see esp. *Deutsche Theologie* 3 (1936), 247 ff.

[14] I.e., here and throughout this letter Emperor Charles V; see *LW* 48, 175 f. Augsburg was an Imperial city, and consequently the emperor was lord there, just as Elector John was lord in Torgau. See also p. 277.

[15] See note 7.

[16] In his May 11 letter to Luther, Elector John, while acknowledging a pertinent brief of Luther which had been issued prior to this date, demanded nevertheless that Luther once more deal with this matter. Enders, *Briefwechsel* 7, No. 1613, and Clemen, *WA*, Br 5, No. 1564, Beilage, publish such a brief, which commonly has been ascribed to Luther. Enders dates this brief "End of March, or Beginning of April, 1530." Clemen (*WA*, Br 5, 313) and Rückert (*LB* 264, n. 10) have convincingly challenged Enders' argumentation that the brief mentioned by the Elector on May 11, and by Luther on May 15, is identical with this brief dated "End of March, or Beginning of April, 1530." Now, on May 15, Luther gives the same advice as Melanchthon had given in Augsburg, and of which Melanchthon had informed Luther on May 11; see *WA*, Br 5, 314; Reu II, No. 25.

[17] See also p. 277.

not preach in a seditious and fanatic way.[18] If this accomplishes nothing, then one has to let force prevail over right. We have done what we ought to do, and are excused. This I wanted to reply humbly for Your Electoral Grace's information regarding this question.

May the merciful God be with Your Electoral Grace through his holy, comforting Spirit.[19] Amen.

May 15, 1530   Your Electoral Grace's dedicated

MARTIN LUTHER

209

To Landgrave Philip of Hesse
Coburg, May 20, 1530[1]

Luther assures the Landgrave of his prayers and attempts to confirm the Landgrave in the true faith concerning the Lord's Supper by admonishing him not to be swayed by those who maintain a

---

18 According to Hans von Dolzig's report (see note 7) one of the reasons given by the Emperor for his intention to stop evangelical preaching in Augsburg was the Emperor's fear that this preaching might cause trouble. This was a good cover-up. In reality, however, the Emperor, under the influence of the anti-evangelical forces in Innsbruck, was simply attempting to bring the evangelicals back into line.

19 The mounted messenger immediately returned to Augsburg, carrying with him the *Apologia,* this letter and some books for the Elector (see *WA,* Br 5, 112), a short letter (also of May 15) to be given to Melanchthon personally (*WA,* Br 5, No. 1567), and a short letter (also of May 15) to Agricola (*WA,* Br 5, No. 1569). In the letter to Melanchthon Luther asked that Justus Jonas (see *LW* 48, 275, n. 3), as carefully as possible, be informed of the death of his little son. Luther did not mention the *Apologia* in this letter, and this seems strange. Did Luther omit any mention of the *Apologia* because he thought that Melanchthon would see the letter to the Elector, and thus know his opinion? Or should this silence be understood as a sign of disappointment on Luther's part concerning Melanchthon's too "soft" way of presenting the gospel? The date of the messenger's arrival at Augsburg could not be established. On May 22, however, the Elector acknowledged receipt of Luther's letter (*WA,* Br 12, 112), and Melanchthon reported to Luther how Jonas took the news about his son's death. Melanchthon also mentioned that he wished Luther had evaluated the articles of faith more carefully to make sure that they were correct. See *WA,* Br 5, 336. Obviously Melanchthon was not satisfied with Luther's summary evaluation of the *Apologia.*

1 For the controversial date of this letter, see *WA,* Br 5, 328 f.

symbolic interpretation of the Lord's Supper.[2] *He sees in these attempts the "flaming darts" of the devil (Ephesians 6:16), and he encourages the Landgrave to use the "sword of the Spirit and the armor of God" as defense against them. Then Luther charges that the representatives of the symbolic interpretation of the Lord's Supper lack the necessary sound exegetical basis for their teachings, and that their teachings are new and in opposition to the traditional faith of the church. Luther underscores that the symbolists' teachings are wrong not only about the Lord's Supper, but also about other matters of the Christian faith; he also suggests that their behavior is un-Christian. All who affirm their teachings about the Lord's Supper will automatically be considered their supporters, Luther points out, and consequently they will become participants in all that the symbolists teach and do. Luther briefly mentions the possible consequences to the Landgrave's conscience, should he affirm the symbolists' faith, and urges him to remain steadfast in the true faith.*

On Landgrave Philip of Hesse, see p. 124, n. 18.

Text in German: WA, Br 5, 330–332.

To the Serene Sovereign and Lord, Sir Philip, landgrave in Hesse,
count in Katzenellenbogen, Ziegenhain, Dietz and Nida,
my Gracious Lord

Grace and comfort, peace and joy in Christ our Lord and Savior! Serene, Noble Sovereign, Gracious Lord! Although I hope in cheerful confidence that our dear Lord Christ is living with Your Sovereign Grace in the right, pure faith, and, particularly, is firmly preserving in Your Sovereign Grace's heart the [pure] teachings concerning the sacraments—so that it would actually not be necessary for me to write Your Sovereign Grace about this matter— yet I have heard,[3] and can also well imagine on my own, that our opponents[4] are exceedingly industrious and busy with attempts and efforts to pull Your Sovereign Grace over to their side.[5] And

---

[2] See pp. 94 ff., 223 f., 228 ff., 234 ff., 244, 250.
[3] See WA, Br 5, 329.
[4] I.e., here and throughout this letter, the *Schwärmer*, or sacramentarians, Zwingli, Oecolampadius, and Bucer.
[5] Literally: "to their crowd."

even if their attempts and search for a contact might not be harmful to Your Sovereign Grace, yet I know well what a mighty one and [what a] conjurer the evil spirit is, [who] insinuates [evil] with all kinds of cunning thoughts, and if he cannot win with force or cunning, he finally is able to wear people down with his incessant pushing,[6] and thus to dupe them. Even if all this were not the case —although, of course, there must be something to it—there is still God's commandment which orders us to care and pray for one another, to comfort, warn, admonish, visit, and strengthen one another, and in short to assist one another with aid and counsel, just as we desire it from God and man.

According to the commandment I shall even praise myself with good conscience, to the effect that I am one of the least[7] among the noblemen[8] who from his heart cares and prays for Your Sovereign Grace [and] calls with great fervor to God, the Father of all mercies,[9] graciously to preserve Your Sovereign Grace in the knowledge of God and in the pure Word, especially now in these wicked and dangerous times when you are in the midst of wolves and without doubt [surrounded][10] by evil spirits. In addition, [I pray to God] to protect [Your Grace] from all evil deeds, [and] to send His Spirit to make Your Sovereign Grace an instrument pleasing to Him, through which He might accomplish much great and good gain to the praise and honor of His Word. Indeed, through Your Sovereign Grace much gain and good can be accomplished for many afflicted, deserted, and erring souls. Amen.

In addition to such prayer, I come now with my admonitions and warnings, with all good and humbly conceived intentions. Honestly and from my heart I ask Your Sovereign Grace to put the most charitable construction on my actions, for I owe this [to Your Grace] and I have the best of intentions. And so [I admonish] Your Grace not to be moved by the sweet and fine-sounding words of our opponents, or rather, not to listen to the devil's cunning insinuations and thoughts, which St. Paul in Ephesians 6 [:16]

---

6 This is perhaps an allusion to Luke 18:2 ff.
7 Or: "I am at least one of the noblemen."
8 Literally: "the most noble men." This passage is perhaps an allusion to I Cor. 15:9.
9 II Cor. 1:3.
10 Literally: "is not totally free from."

calls "flaming darts." For against these flaming darts Your Sover
eign Grace has good weapons and armor, that is, the sword of the
Spirit, which is the Word of God.[11]

Further, it is dangerous to accept such new teaching in contrast to lucid and open texts and the clear words of Christ, and
to abandon this old belief (which from the beginning till now has
been maintained in all of Christendom)[12] on the basis of such poor
[Scripture] passages and thoughts as [our opponents] have thus
far brought forth—[material] which certainly is unable to satisfy
any conscience over against the lucid words of Christ. I know for
a fact that [our] opponents themselves cannot silence their consciences with [the poor biblical passages they quote], and I am
convinced that, were the beer in the barrel again, they would now
let it remain there.[13] This was very obvious to me on several occasions at Marburg.[14] But since they have arrived at a negative position, they are unwilling and unable to retreat.[15] Beyond this, Your
Sovereign Grace at that time[16] heard that their two best arguments
were based on the following:[17] Since the sacrament is a sacrament
or sign, it could not be Christ's body itself, as Oecolampadius
argued;[18] and since a body would need some room, Christ's body
could not be present there, as Zwingli argued.[19] These certainly
are absolutely rotten and unsound arguments,[20] and we can hear
them ridiculed even by the papists and sophists. Dear God, how
many Scripture passages did [our opponents] quote in which they
were openly caught as having erred and failed, and now they
have to abandon them! Certainly this demonstrates sufficiently that
there is no solid foundation [for their position], but only their own

---

11 Eph. 6:17.
12 The parentheses have been added by this editor. Obviously in order to press
his point, Luther is generalizing here. He knew very well that this was not
the case.
13 I.e., if the opponents now had a chance to do things over, they would not
present their "poor" teaching, since they see that they are wrong and cannot
prevail against Luther. See also WA 23, 73; LW 37, 19.
14 See pp. 234 ff.
15 For the following, see also WA, Br 5, 340, and WA, Br 13, 136, *ad loc.*
16 This is a reference to the Marburg Colloquy; see note 14.
17 Literally: ". . . heard that their two best pieces stood on it."
18 Literally: "pretended."
19 Literally: "wanted."
20 Or: "foundations."

mere folly. Your Sovereign Grace knows further that [our opponents] did not remain with only this [one] error, but have [also] taught inappropriate things concerning baptism, infant baptism, hereditary sin, the usage of the sacraments, and the external Word; and yet they were so fickle in [these teachings] that (as Your Sovereign Grace knows) at Marburg they conceded all to us, and talked [quite] differently.[21]

All who affirm the faith [of our opponents] have to become participants in this and many other matters.[22] I shall be silent about the unfriendly way in which they deal with us now. [That is,] they receive Karlstadt[23] and believe all the obvious lies which that wretched man dreams up about us—and he must have done a good job at it, since they defend[24] him, God knows for how long.[25]

From the bottom of my heart I would be sorry if Your Sovereign Grace should become a participant in all their unfounded matters, evil folly, and grossly wrong teachings[26] and actions— especially since Your Sovereign Grace already has more than enough to do and to bear, both before God and the people, in fulfillment of Your Grace's own office. Consequently it is not necessary for Your Sovereign Grace to be troubled with this alien and vacillating matter; and in addition to become a great offense for many who would also fall [prey to our opponents' teachings]; and to strengthen and harden the hearts of those who have [already] fallen so that, [even] if the matter [itself] were straightened out,

---

[21] This is perhaps a reference to the *Marburg Articles;* see p. 235, n. 6.

[22] Literally: "Of these and many other [things] must make themselves participants all who care for [or: patronize] their [i.e., the opponents'] faith."

[23] Literally: "They take that Karlstadt to themselves." For Andrew Karlstadt, see *LW* 48, 79, n. 12.

[24] Or: ". . . about us, [and they have to do good to him,] and defend. . . ."

[25] Clemen (*WA,* Br 5, 332, n. 10) explains this passage as follows: Karlstadt had been kindly received by the preachers of Strassburg; see *WA,* Br 5, 246, 298, and *ibid.,* n. 6. Luther could not yet know, however, that according to a decision of the Strassburg city council of May 9, Karlstadt had been requested to leave town, and to go either to Basel or Zürich, i.e., either to the town of Oecolampadius or of Zwingli, where he might be safe. The council gave Karlstadt's quarrel with the electors of Saxony as the reason for this order. Bucer and Capito recommended Karlstadt to Zwingli, and were delighted with the good reception that was given to Karlstadt by Zwingli. See M. Krebs and H. G. Rott (eds.), *Quellen zur Geschichte der Täufer, 7, Elsass: Stadt Strassburg* (Gütersloh, 1959), Nos. 214, 215.

[26] Literally: "talking."

they never could be brought back again. They would remain as an eternal thorn [in the flesh][27] and a sighing in Your Sovereign Grace's conscience, since Your Grace—may God prevent it—would have been the cause of such a fall and hardening of the heart.

O Lord God! It is no joke or jest to teach new [doctrines]; indeed at this point neither illusions, nor folly, nor uncertain [Scripture] passages are to be put in operation; lucid, powerful texts must be available, which thus far [our opponents] have not produced. It is true that I have suffered such great torment and danger for my teachings that I certainly would not want to have done such sour labor in vain, nor [continue] to do it. Therefore I certainly would not resist them because of hatred or arrogance; God, my Lord, knows that I would have accepted their teaching a long time ago, if only they could demonstrate [a sound] foundation [for it]. But [the foundation] on which they stand is something on which I am unable to base my conscience. And so I hope that Christ, our Lord, has accomplished something through me, poor instrument [that I am], so that [our opponents] cannot in any way consider me as someone who has [done] nothing against their actions.

Herewith I shall commend Your Sovereign Grace to our dear Lord God. (I hope) Your Sovereign Grace may see that my intentions are honest and faithful. May God, the Father of all poor wretched souls, grant his peace to all of us, and enlighten us with his truth. To him be praise, honor, and thankfulness in eternity. Amen.

From the wilderness,[28] *May 20, 1530*

Your Sovereign Grace's dedicated
MARTIN LUTHER

---

[27] See Acts 9:5 (Luther Bible).
[28] I.e., the Coburg; see p. 287, n. 1.

210

To Elector John
[Coburg,] May 20, 1530

This is a letter of pastoral counsel[1] for Elector John, who was at that time attending the Diet of Augsburg. In the introduction and in a postscript Luther takes care of some correspondence matters. The body of the letter is dedicated to strengthening in the Elector a feeling of joy and gratitude to God for the many blessings which God has bestowed upon him. Luther points out that whatever the Elector has to endure at the moment he endures exclusively for the sake of the Word of God, and as a result of the Elector's open affirmation of this Word. Luther then focuses on three points in which he sees signs of God's particular blessings on the Elector, and which, in turn, should be reasons for the Elector's comfort, strength, joy, and gratitude. In the first place, the Elector's territory is a place where the gospel is freely at work. This can be seen especially in the preaching and in the religious training of the young people. Consequently Electoral Saxony is a paradise of God, and the Elector is the caretaker of this paradise. This means, secondly, that the Elector, his property and his talents, are engaged in a continuous service to God. And finally, in this service the Elector has the support of the prayers of many people, not only of his own subjects, but even of those people who have to live outside of the paradise, (that is, outside of Electoral Saxony,) but who long to live in it. In contrast to these blessings the troubles created for the Elector by Satan are of no importance.

On Elector John, see LW 48, 269, n. 8.

Text in German: WA, Br 5, 325–327. The following translation, with minor changes, is by Theodore G. Tappert and is used by permission from LCC 18, 140–144.

To the most Serene, Noble Sovereign and Lord, Sir John,
duke in Saxony, elector of the Holy Roman Empire, etc.,
landgrave in Thuringia, and margrave of Meissen,
my Most Gracious Lord

---

[1] From Coburg Luther wrote many letters of pastoral counsel to his friends in Augsburg; only a few examples have been included in the present volume. For others, see *LCC* 18, *passim.*

Grace and peace in Christ, our Lord and Saviour. Amen. Most Serene, Noble Sovereign, Most Gracious Lord: I have for some time delayed answering Your Electoral Grace's first letter from Augsburg,[2] which was so graciously addressed to me, and which contained news and the admonition that I should not let time hang heavily on my hands [here] in this place, etc.[3] Indeed it was not necessary for Your Electoral Grace to be anxious and to think about me so graciously, but it is our duty to remember, be concerned about, and pray for Your Electoral Grace, and this we certainly do, and do faithfully. No, I do not find the days to be long. We live like lords, and these [last] weeks passed so quickly that they seem like no more than three days.[4]

On the other hand, Your Electoral Grace is now, and has to be, in a tiresome situation. May our dear Father in heaven help Your Electoral Grace to remain steadfast and patient [in God's] grace, which he gives us so abundantly. For to begin with, it is certain that Your Electoral Grace must endure all this trouble, expense, danger, and tedium solely for God's sake, inasmuch as none of the raging sovereigns and enemies can find any fault with Your Electoral Grace except on account of the pure, tender, living Word of God; for they know Your Electoral Grace to be a blameless, peaceful, devout, and faithful sovereign. Since this is certain, [the hostility of Your Grace's opponents] may be taken as an important sign of God's love for Your Electoral Grace, [since we see] that he so abundantly grants his holy Word [to Your Grace], and makes [Your Grace] worthy of suffering so much shame and enmity on its account. [All of this] should be a source of comfort. For God's friendship is a bigger comfort than that of the whole world. On the other hand, we see that God does not consider the angry and wrathful sovereigns worthy of knowing and possessing his

---

[2] This is a reference to Elector John's May 11 letter to Luther (see p. 296), in which the Elector informed Luther about the preaching matter (see p. 296, n. 7), and also expressed his hope that Luther would not be bored at the Coburg. Luther apparently did not consider his short May 15 letter, No. 208, a sufficient answer.

[3] Literally: ". . . writing from Augsburg, graciously [addressed] to me, [containing] information of news and the admonition that I, in this place, should not let time get long for me, etc."

[4] Luther had moved into the Coburg on April 24 (see p. 291, n. 38); therefore about three weeks had gone by when he wrote the present letter.

Word. Indeed, they are obliged in their blindness and callousness to revile and persecute it; this senseless raging of theirs is a terrible sign of God's disfavor and wrath toward them. This certainly ought to terrify them in their consciences and cause them to despair; ultimately it will be so.

In addition to this, the merciful God shows himself to be even more gracious by making his Word so powerful and fruitful in Your Electoral Grace's territory. For surely Your Electoral Grace's territory has more excellent pastors and preachers than any other territory in the whole world, and their faithful, pure teaching helps to preserve peace. As a consequence, the young people, both boys and girls, grow up so well instructed in the Catechism and the Scriptures that I am deeply moved when I see that young boys and girls can pray, believe, and speak more of God and Christ than they ever could in the monasteries, foundations, and schools of bygone days, or even of our day.[5]

Truly, Your Electoral Grace's territory is a beautiful paradise for such young people; there is no other place like it in all the world. God has erected this paradise in Your Electoral Grace's [land][6] as a token of his grace and favor for Your Electoral Grace. It is as if he should say: "To you, dear Duke John, I entrust my most precious treasure, my pleasant paradise, and ask you to preside over it as father. I place it under your protection and government, and I give you the honor of being my gardener and caretaker." This is most certainly true, for the Lord God, who has set Your Electoral Grace over this territory to be its father and helper, feeds all [the people] through Your Electoral Grace's office and service, and they all must eat of Your Electoral Grace's bread. This is as if God himself were Your Electoral Grace's daily guest and ward, since his Word, and those children of his who have his Word, are Your Electoral Grace's daily guests and wards.

In contrast to this, one should consider how the fury of other sovereigns harms the valuable youth. They[7] turn God's paradise into sinful, foul-smelling, and ruinous mudholes of[8] the devil; they

---

[5] In his *Sermon on Keeping Children in School*, published in 1530, Luther made similar statements. See *WA* 30[II], 546 f.; *LW* 46, 231 f.
[6] Literally: "bosom." Perhaps this is an allusion to Luke 16:22.
[7] I.e., "other sovereigns."
[8] Literally: "for the devil."

spoil everything, and they have none but devils as their daily guests at table. For in God's sight they do not deserve the honor of giving even a cup of cold water[9] to [God's] Word out of their great wealth.[10] On the contrary, they have nothing better to give to the thirsty Christ on the cross than vinegar, myrrh, and gall.[11] Nevertheless, many devout people, who yearn[12] for Your Electoral Grace's paradise and blessed land,[13] live [in their lands] secretly, and help to pray earnestly for it.

God[14] dwells so richly in Your Electoral Grace's territory as graciously to allow his Word to have free course there; as a result of this Your Electoral Grace's office, property, goods, and all are used in a blessed service and way; actually all this is nothing less than daily alms and offerings presented unceasingly to the honor of God's holy Word. Further, Your Electoral Grace is endowed with a peaceful heart,[15] which is not bloodthirsty and cruel, as the hearts of [Your Grace's] opponents are and must be. Consequently Your Electoral Grace certainly has ample cause to rejoice in God, and to find comfort in these notable marks of his grace. For it is indeed a great and glorious honor that God has chosen, consecrated, and made Your Electoral Grace worthy of using life and possessions, territory and people, and all that Your Electoral Grace owns in this beautiful service of God, so that His divine Word is not only not persecuted, but also cultivated[16] and preserved. It matters not that some among us are lazy,[17] for in spite of this Your Electoral

---

[9] See Matt. 10:42.

[10] I.e., the "other sovereigns" do not deserve the honor of promoting God's Word in their territories, not even in the smallest possible way; on the contrary, they harm the Word of God, just as Christ was harmed on the cross.

[11] Matt. 27:34.

[12] Literally: "longingly yearn."

[13] See also Luther's letter to the Evangelicals in Leipzig, dated October 4, 1532; WA, Br 6, No. 1964; LCC 18, 218 f.

[14] The material in the text which precedes the sentence beginning "For it is indeed . . ." is one long sentence which reads, literally translated: "For since God dwells . . . as graciously to . . . there, so that . . . of God's holy Word, and in addition [repeat: since God] endows Your Electoral Grace . . . are and must be, therefore indeed Your Electoral Grace certainly has ample cause . . . of his grace."

[15] Or: disposition.

[16] Or: nourished.

[17] For the translation, see Trübner 8, 228; WA, Br 13, 134, to WA, Br 5, 329, n. 9.

Grace's service and protection are effective in preserving the Word.

And finally, Your Electoral Grace is now also supported by the earnest and faithful prayers of all Christians, especially [those living] in Your Electoral Grace's territory. We know that our prayers are legitimate,[18] and our cause is just; therefore we are also certain that [our prayers] please [God] and are heard. Indeed, the young people, who lift up their innocent young voices and call from the bottom of their hearts to heaven,[19] faithfully commending Your Electoral Grace as their dear father to the merciful God, will accomplish it.[20] On the other hand, we [also] know that our opponents have an unjust cause, that they are unable to pray, that they employ clever devices [to gain their ends], and that they rely on their own wit and power, as is evident. In short, [they are building] on sand.[21]

May Your Electoral Grace graciously receive this letter from me; God knows that I speak the truth and do not dissemble. I am sorry that Satan is trying to disturb and trouble Your Electoral Grace's heart. I know him very well, and I know how he is used to tossing me around. He is a doleful, sour spirit who cannot bear to see anyone happy or at peace, especially with God. How much less will he be able to endure it that Your Electoral Grace is of good

---

[18] Luther wrote: *dass unser Gebet recht ist,* i.e., that our prayer is right (or: correct, or: just). Tappert's translation, "effectual," does not seem to do justice to the text. This is the case especially if one considers either the context or the parallelism which exists between the sentence beginning "we know," and the sentence beginning "On the other hand." Luther means to say: (a) Our prayers are heard because our cause is just; (b) our prayers are right—i.e., we pray in the right way for something which is just—and consequently our prayers are legitimate prayers. Were "effectual" the appropriate translation, then Luther would say: Our prayers are heard, because our cause is just, and our prayers are effectual, i.e., are heard. This seems to make little sense, especially if one considers the statement concerning the opponents. Luther says that the opponents cannot pray. Obviously this statement does not mean that the opponents are unable to pray. It can only mean that they cannot pray with a good conscience, or legitimately. The reason for this is the evil cause for which the opponents stand; the consequence of this is the knowledge that the opponents' prayers are not heard, and that the opponents have to employ other means to accomplish their goals.
[19] Literally: ". . . [they who] from the bottom of their hearts call and shout to heaven with their innocent little tongues, faithfully commending . . ."
[20] "It" refers either to the fact that "our" prayers are pleasing to God, or it refers generally to the support given to the Elector through the prayers.
[21] See Matt. 7:26.

courage, since he knows very well how much we depend on[22] Your Electoral Grace.[23] And not we alone, but almost the whole world— and, I almost wanted to say, heaven itself, because, in fact, a large part of the Kingdom of Christ is constantly being built up in Your Electoral Grace's territory through [the preaching of] the saving Word. The devil knows this and is angry over it. We are therefore obligated faithfully to support Your Electoral Grace with our prayers, words of comfort, love, and every other possible means at our disposal. For when Your Electoral Grace is happy, we live, but when Your Electoral Grace is sorrowful, we are ill.

Our dear Lord and faithful Saviour, Jesus Christ, whom the Father of all mercies[24] has so abundantly revealed and given to us, grant unto Your Electoral Grace, beyond all my asking, his Holy Spirit, the true and eternal Comforter; may [the Comforter] ever preserve, strengthen, and keep Your Electoral Grace against all the cunning, poisonous, and flaming darts[25] of the sour, grievous, and wicked spirit. Amen, dear God, Amen.

Written on May 20, 1530

Your Sovereign Grace's humbly dedicated

MARTIN LUTHER

Most Gracious Lord: Dr. Apel[26] has requested me to ask Your Electoral Grace, in his behalf, to pardon and to excuse him for

---

[22] Luther wrote: *wie viel an* [Your Electoral Grace's heart] *uns allen gelegen.* On the basis of Trübner 4, 471, another translation would be: "how much we are concerned for Your Electoral Grace's heart. And not we alone [are concerned], but almost . . ."

[23] Literally: "Your Sovereign Grace's heart."

[24] II Cor. 1:3.

[25] Eph. 6:16.

[26] On November 5, 1529, Luther recommended Dr. John Apel to Duke Albrecht of Prussia for the position of chancellor; see WA, Br 5, No. 1490. On Apel, see p. 115, n. 2; WA, Br 3, 292, n. 9; Friedensburg, *GUW*, p. 165 f.; *NDB* 1, 322. When this position was offered to him, Apel accepted it, and left Wittenberg to go to Königsberg. He apparently had a bad conscience (according to Clemen, WA, Br 5, 328, n. 17), since he left the Elector's service rather quickly, and did so only several months after the Elector had appointed him as a member of the Electoral court. Apel sent his resignation to Luther via a messenger, and apparently asked for Luther's help in avoiding the Elector's disfavor. Luther fulfills this request in this postscript. The messenger continued to Augsburg, where he arrived on May 22, obviously bringing this letter for the Elector, a letter of comfort (dated May 19) for Jonas, whose little son had recently died, and a letter for Melanchthon, also dated

taking leave at this time and going to Prussia. He had desired to mention this long ago, but because Your Electoral Grace was always so burdened [with other duties, and since] he himself is a very shy and well-mannered person, he never wanted to impose on Your Electoral Grace. I assume that he himself will write to Your Electoral Grace at greater length. Your Electoral Grace will certainly know how to deal graciously with this matter. Herewith I commend [Your Grace] to God's keeping.

211

To Mrs. Martin Luther
[Coburg,] June 5, 1530

Judging from the following letter we may conclude that it is a great loss for all who are interested in knowing Luther as a person that few of the letters exchanged between Luther and his wife are extant. Letter No. 211 is the first letter still available to us that Luther wrote to his wife from the Coburg. In this hastily written letter Luther confirms receipt of a package from his wife, in which was a picture of their daughter Magdalen. He offers some suggestions for weaning Magdalen, suggestions which he in turn had received from Argula von Grumbach, one of the many visitors he had had recently. Luther also complains about a pair of glasses which he had received, and mentions some correspondence matters. Finally he mentions some news about the diet, which people fear will never actually get started, obviously because of the Emperor's delay and

May 19. See WA, Br 5, 335, and *ibid.*, Nos. 1570 and 1571; see also WA, Br 12, 112. (Clemen, WA, Br 5, 337, nn. 3, 4 has to be corrected accordingly.) Apel's messenger perhaps also carried letter No. 209. According to Melanchthon's May 22 letter to Luther, this messenger of Dr. Apel was to return to Luther with letters; WA, Br 5, 336. The messenger did stop by at the Coburg, but brought no mail, as Luther complained to Melanchthon on June 2 and 5; WA, Br 5, 345, 350; see also in this vol., p. 317. The messenger continued his journey, apparently carrying with him a letter to Apel; see WA, Br 5, 328, n. 16; if he went to Wittenberg (and this is most probable), then he took along letter No. 211, Luther's June 5 letter to his wife.

because of the maneuvers of the papists. He also asks that Bugen-
hagen be shown a certain letter of Wenceslas Link.
Text in German: WA, Br 5, 347–348.

To my dearly beloved[1] Catherine Luther,
mistress of the house[2] at Wittenberg: *Personal*

Grace and peace in Christ! Dear Katie! If I am correct, I have
received all your letters.[3] This is then the fourth letter[4] I am writing
to you since Mr. John has gone from here to you.[5] Together with
the box, I have also [received] the picture of Lenchen.[6] At first
I did not recognize the little strumpet,[7] so dark she appeared to
me to be. I think it would be good if you want [to stop nursing
her],[8] [but] gradually, so that at first you omit one feeding per day,

---

[1] Literally: "heartily beloved."

[2] Literally: "To my heartily beloved housewife [or: mistress of the house],
Catherine Luther at Wittenberg."

[3] None of these letters from Catherine Luther to her husband is extant.

[4] The first three letters are not extant.

[5] The background of this statement could not be clarified.

[6] I.e., Magdalen Luther; see p. 218, n. 4. The German diminutive form
"Lenchen" has been preserved since it conveys a certain attitude of kindness,
affection, and cordial attachment; the literal translation, "little Magdalen," does
not do justice to this meaning. It is impossible to identify the picture mentioned
by Luther. Perhaps a charcoal or ink-drawing, the picture might have been
made on the little girl's first birthday (she was born on May 4, 1529). Lucas
Cranach later painted her when she was apparently a young teenager and
shortly prior to her death in 1542; for a poor copy, see Schwiebert, plate
LIII. This picture can indeed confirm Luther's following statement about the
dark complexion. On June 19, 1530, Luther's companion at the Coburg, Veit
Dietrich (see p. 282, n. 13), wrote to Mrs. Martin Luther: "You did something very good when you sent the picture to Doctor [Luther], for the picture
[helps] him to forget many troubling thoughts. He has attached it to the wall
opposite the table in the . . . chamber where we eat." See WA, Br 5, 379.

[7] Literally: "little whore." One should not be offended by this term, for in his
Against the Heavenly Prophets Luther wrote: "How often does a mother call
her daughter 'little whore' both in wrath and in love?" WA 18, 106; LW 40,
123.

[8] Luther wrote: *wilt absetzen von wehnen. Absetzen* means literally to set, or
put down, to come down from, to depose. The term *wehnen* is unclear, and
apparently was not frequently used by Luther. Modern German uses *ent-
wöhnen* for weaning a child, and the English "wean" is from the same root.
In Middle High German *wenen* means to be, or become, used to something,
or to make something or someone used to something or someone. The meaning
of Luther's statement would be to have a child which was used to feeding on
the mother's breast taken off the breast. Luther's phrase literally translated
would read: "to put down [the child] from being used to [the mother's
breast]." See also Trübner 2, 207.

then two feedings per day, until [the child] clearly[9] stops [nursing by herself]. So George von Grumbach's[10] mother, Lady Argula,[11]

---

[9] Literally: "cleanly."

[10] George von Grumbach, the eldest son of an old Bavarian noble family (see also note 11) was then studying at Wittenberg. On June 19 Luther extended greetings to him; see WA, Br 5, 376.

[11] Argula von Grumbach is one of the few fascinating and truly great women of the Reformation in Germany who is known to us in some detail. Born in 1492 into the old noble family of Ehrenfels-Stauffen, situated near Regensburg, she was raised at the Bavarian ducal court in Munich. As she herself wrote, at age ten she received a German Bible from her father, and later became a dedicated reader of the Bible; and this was before Luther's name was known in Germany. In approximately 1515/16 she married Frederick von Grumbach, a Franconian nobleman who owned some hereditary estates in the area of Würzburg and also at Lenting in Bavaria. He was the Bavarian ducal *Pfleger* (bailiff, or deputy) in Dietfurt, a small town west of Regensburg in the romantic valley of the Altmühl river. Here Argula von Stauffen-Grumbach became a serious student of the gospel, eagerly reading Luther's German writings, which she apparently obtained from Nürnberg. From approximately 1522/23 she corresponded with Luther. Most unfortunately nothing of this correspondence has been preserved. In 1523/24, when Master Arsacius Seehofer, at the University of Ingolstadt—Eck's territory (see LW 48, 80, n. 13) —was forced to recant his evangelical teachings and was then imprisoned, Lady Argula wrote several letters of pamphlet length in his defense, and these letters were at once printed. In these letters, and in the controversies resulting from them, she showed herself to be a fervent and steadfast confessor of the gospel; she combined sound theological insights with wit and great literary ability. Her stand on the gospel resulted in her husband's dismissal from office, and apparently also in great strain for the marriage. (See Luther's fine testimony on Argula von Grumbach in the letter to John Briessman in Königsberg, dated late February 1524; WA, Br 3, 247.) Even though the Grumbachs were able to retain some of their private possessions in Lenting, as well as in Franconia, the family rapidly became impoverished (especially since Frederick von Grumbach apparently abandoned his family in protest against Lady Argula's stand on matters of faith). The burden of holding the family together fell on Lady Argula's shoulders, but she was equal to the task. All the children were well educated, the oldest son George attending the University of Wittenberg, and receiving room and board with the Melanchthon family. Lady Argula was twice widowed, and her later years are under a cloud. Most of her children died while she was still living, the Franconian and Bavarian properties had to be mortgaged, and finally had to be sold in lieu of payments. She spent the rest of her days lonely and poor on an estate at Köffering, near Regensburg, apparently the last estate to remain to her from the once wealthy Stauffen domain. Notwithstanding old age and calamities she was active; a "school" and a "domestic congregation" were organized under her leadership, and she was known for her evangelical convictions throughout Bavaria. In and out of jail (she was apparently at least twice jailed for her confession of faith), she was rescued from more cruel consequences only by the intercessions of some of the Bavarian noble families, as well as by some general political circumstances. She died either in 1554 or in 1568. Lady Argula visited Luther at the Coburg on June 3, 1530; see WA, Br 5, 346, 351. On Argula von Grumbach, see M. Heinsius, *Das unüberwindliche Wort. Frauen der Reformationszeit* (Munich, 1951), pp. 134 ff.; NDB 7, 212.

has advised me; she has been with us here, and had dinner with us. Hans Reinecke from Mansfeld also [has been here],[12] and George Römer.[13] [We are having so much company] that we will have to move to another place; this place is becoming a place for a pilgrimage [for everyone].[14]

Tell Master Christian[15] that in all my life I haven't seen worse glasses than those which arrived with his letter. I couldn't see a thing through them,[16] and so I was unable to write the letter to the father of the Cuntzes.[17] Also, I am not at Coburg,[18] but if I

---

[12] On Hans Reinecke, with whom Luther had attended the school of the Brethren of the Common Life in Magdeburg (see Schwiebert, pp. 117 ff.), see WA, Br 2, 564, n. 3; 8, 281, n. 2.

[13] On George Römer, also of Mansfeld, see WA, Br 3, No. 645, Introduction. The Römers were a respectable Nürnberg family that had emigrated to Mansfeld for business reasons. George Römer did his undergraduate work at the Universities of Leipzig and Wittenberg; while at Wittenberg he became a member of the Luther-Melanchthon circle. By 1525 he had returned to Mansfeld. Reinecke and Römer apparently visited Luther on June 2; see WA, Br 5, 346.

[14] Luther made similar statements in a June 5 letter to Wenceslas Link (LW 48, 169 f.); see WA, Br 5, 350. Even though Luther had a number of visitors at the beginning of June (there were others in addition to those mentioned in the letter above), one may assume that Luther was not serious either in his complaint about the visitors, or in his notion of moving. See also Schubert, LaK, 125.

[15] I.e., master craftsman Christian Düring; see LW 48, 42, n. 8.

[16] According to Clemen (WA, Br 5, 348, n. 14), Luther apparently was referring here to some type of glasses with magnifying lenses. Clemen cites evidence which suggests that Luther had good vision till his last years. Apparently it was not much before July 13, 1545, that Luther stated that "now" he did not see as well as thirty years ago. Schubert suggests (LaK, 128) that the need for some type of reading glasses might have had something to do with Luther's complaint of ringing in his head and ears.

[17] A translation more in keeping with the meaning of Luther's phrase would be: "old man Cuntz." The background of this statement could not be clarified. One possibility of translating and understanding this sentence and the next would be that Luther wants Christian Düring to know that the glasses were no good, and that therefore he had not written the letter to the father of the Cuntzes. Luther would then state that he could not do anything, apparently in a matter pertaining to the father of the Cuntzes, because he was not in Coburg; nevertheless he would be willing to help, if possible. The text can, however, also be translated as: ". . . see a thing through them, and [that] the letter to old man Cuntz didn't get to me." On the basis of the following sentence one may assume, then, that Luther was to transmit a letter, apparently from Düring, to the father of the Cuntzes. Luther could not do this because the letter had not reached him; and further, he could not do it anyway, even if the letter had reached him, because the father of the Cuntzes apparently lived in the city of Coburg while he, Luther, was in the Coburg

can do something further [in this matter], I shall not fail to do it. Nevertheless you, of course, are to [continue to] forward your letters to the bailiff,[19] who will certainly take care to get them to me.

Both at Nürnberg and at Augsburg there is increasing doubt that the diet will get started.[20] The Emperor[21] still procrastinates at Innsbruck;[22] the priests are conniving, and there is foul play.[23] May God grant that the devil cheat them. Amen. Let Mr. Pomer[24] read Dr. Wenceslas' letter.[25] [I am writing] in a hurry [since] the messenger did not want to wait.

---

castle, which was located "high above" the city. Luther nevertheless offers his services. In any case, the person and the circumstances involved are unknown to us.

[18] I.e., in the city.

[19] I.e., Paul Bader; see p. 290, n. 29.

[20] Luther made similar statements in his June 2 or 3 letter to Melanchthon (WA, Br 5, 346), in his June 5 letter to Link (WA, Br 5, 349), and in the letter to Melanchthon, also dated June 5 (see letter No. 212). According to this last letter, Nürnberg was apparently the source of this news. Indeed, the Nürnberg ambassador at the Imperial court, which was then at Innsbruck, had informed the city council of the rumor that the diet might be postponed. The city fathers communicated this information to their delegates at Augsburg, who replied on May 20 in such a way that it is clear that they did not believe this rumor, since in Augsburg there was news to the contrary; C.R. 2, 56. Yet in fact the rumor from Innsbruck was well substantiated. Campeggio, the papal legate, had presented to Emperor Charles a memorandum (dated May 9) in which he strongly suggested postponing the diet. And on May 12 the Papal Legate had informed the Curia of the possibility of having the diet either postponed or moved. See Reu II, 508. NB I.Abt., E.1, p. 30. How did Luther know of this development? One possibility would be that he learned of it through Link, who had traveled from Nürnberg to Coburg, and had visited Luther on May 18; WA, Br 5, 322. The other possibility, and this is the more likely one, is that Luther knew of this news through a no-longer extant letter from Link (see note 25) to which Luther replied on June 5 with WA, Br 5, No. 1583. In this reply Luther wrote that he did not like to hear that the whole diet was now in doubt.

[21] Emperor Charles V; see LW 48, 175 f.

[22] See p. 296, n. 8. It is strange for Luther to have made this statement, for on June 1 Elector John had informed Luther of the rumor that the Emperor had left Innsbruck for Munich; WA, Br 5, 344. It is very doubtful that the messenger, who was to go on to Torgau (see WA, Br 5, No. 1579, Introduction), had not yet delivered this letter at Coburg. See also p. 335, n. 11.

[23] Literally "it deals with herbs." This is perhaps a reference to herbs used in witchcraft.

[24] I.e., John Bugenhagen; see LW 48, 303, n. 44.

[25] For the translation, see WA, Br 13, 137, to WA, Br 5, 348, line 24. Luther's reference is to Link's no-longer extant letter mentioned in note 20. Luther assumed that Bugenhagen would be especially interested in the news concerning the diet.

Greetings, kisses, hugs, and regards²⁶ to all and everyone according to his place.

June 5, in the morning, 1530   MARTIN LUTHER

212

To Philip Melanchthon¹
[Coburg,] June 5, 1530

In the first portion of this letter Luther complains about the lack of letters from his friends in Augsburg, and he communicates several bits of news, or rumors, which he had recently heard: The Emperor has ordered the Augsburg city council to dismiss all specially hired security forces; the Duke of Bavaria is planning an impressive reception for the Emperor; the Emperor is not coming to Augsburg; and the diet is to be canceled. Luther then briefly mentions the possible public reaction to his recently published Exhortation. Finally, in the second part of the letter, Luther mentions his father's death, of which he had just been informed. This is occasion for Luther to reflect on the role his father played in his life. He ponders his father's death, and muses over his own position as one of the oldest living male Luthers. He praises God that his father could have lived to the present, and thus have been enabled to see the light of truth.

On Philip Melanchthon, see LW 48, 77, n. 3.

Text in Latin: WA, Br 5, 350–351.

Grace and peace in Christ

In my last letter, my Philip, I wrote² that we were annoyed because you people had let the messenger³ return to us empty-handed,

---

²⁶ Literally: "and be kind to." This could mean either that on behalf of Luther, Catherine ought to be kind to all, or that Luther is "sending kindness" to all.

¹ The letter is extant in one manuscript copy, and in the common editions of Luther's works. While the address is missing in the manuscript copy, it is clear to whom Luther was writing since the addressee is mentioned in the first sentence.

² See Luther to Melanchthon: June 2, 1530; WA, Br 5, 345.

³ This was Dr. Apel's messenger, who had delivered to Augsburg letter No. 210 and the letters mentioned on p. 310, n. 26. He had returned to the

although there are so many of you, and all are usually eager to write. And now you have also let the second messenger[4] return empty-handed—first the messenger of Apel,[5] and now the carrier of the venison from Coburg.[6] I cannot think enough [about this, asking myself] whether you people are so negligent or [are in some way] indignant; for you must know that we here in the wilderness, as in a dry land, are longing for letters from you people from which we may learn of all your affairs.

Well, we have heard that the Emperor[7] has ordered the Augsburg [city council] to dismiss the hired soldiers, and to remove the chains from the streets.[8] The day before yesterday[9] Argula von

---

Coburg empty-handed; see pp. 334 f. He had arrived at the Coburg prior to June 2, for on that day Luther complained to Melanchthon that Apel's messenger did not bring any letters, and that consequently the friends in Augsburg had broken their promise to send letters with this messenger; WA, Br 5, 345. Since Melanchthon made this promise in his May 22 letter (see WA, Br 5, 336), it is clear that by June 2 Luther had had this May 22 letter at least for several days. See also p. 334, n. 5.

[4] See note 6.

[5] See note 3.

[6] In view of the high prices at Augsburg (see p. 295, n. 21), the Elector brought some of his supplies from Coburg or from other towns in Electoral Saxony. The carrier of these supplies, too, had returned empty-handed from Augsburg. This is the way Rückert, LB, p. 280, n. 18, explains the circumstances. He further suggests that another shipment of venison was at once dispatched from Coburg, and that Luther sent along (among other letters) this June 5 letter to Melanchthon. Rückert's interpretation (which is affirmed in WA, Br 13, 137, to WA, Br 5, 351, nn. 3, 4) is a correction of Clemen's view of the situation. Clemen had identified (WA, Br 5, 351, n. 2) the "second messenger" with the "mounted messenger" of Elector John who brought a letter of the Elector to Luther; see p. 335. One would have to ask whether Luther's statement to the effect that "you have permitted this messenger to return" fits this mounted messenger. Rückert's interpretation, however, does not answer all possible questions either; see p. 336, nn. 14, 20.

[7] Emperor Charles; see LW 48, 175 f.

[8] The Augsburg city council had hired two thousand mercenaries (according to some sources only four hundred), and had made preparations for closing off the streets with chains, obviously to take all necessary precautions for the dignitaries present within the walls. The Emperor, misunderstanding this action, interpreted it as an affront to his rights as lord of the city, and on May 24 complained to the city council through members of the Council of Regency (see LW 48, 70, n. 1). The city council explained its motivations, and the Emperor's representatives were satisfied. Whether or not further pressure was used by the Council of Regency is not known. Shortly before May 28, however, the city council dismissed seven hundred and ninety-five of the hired mercenaries. See BA, p. 52; NB I.Abt.,E.1, p. 31, n. 21a. On June 9 the Frankfurt delegation reported from Augsburg to the city council that the Emperor had hired one thousand mercenaries "whom he wanted here at Augsburg." See BA, p. 394. It is not clear whether these were new soldiers, or

Stauffen[10] was here; she told us about the extraordinary pomp, the theatrical productions, and other new-fashioned honors with which the Duke of Bavaria will receive the Emperor at Munich.[11] And finally, from Nürnberg[12] they begin to convince us that the Emperor will not come to the diet, and further, that the diet will be nullified through the efforts and the conniving of the papists. Should this happen, then it would be a sign of God's implacable wrath against the papists, for [then it is clear] that God does not wish to listen to the prayers which even we have offered in their behalf.

If the opinions on my little book vary,[13] don't be disturbed. My God is a God of fools, and is used to ridiculing the wise;[14] therefore I don't care for them either.

Today Hans Reinecke[15] wrote me[16] that my very dear father,

---

whether the Emperor simply took over those who were hired by the Augsburg city council. One may assume that Luther also heard of this development from Nürnberg through Link's no-longer extant letter; see p. 315, n. 20. On May 26 and 28 the Nürnberg delegation in Augsburg reported this development to the city council. See *C.R.* 2, 66 f., 89 f.; see also Roth, *Augsburgs Reformationsgeschichte* (see p. 146, n. 24), 1, 329 f.

[9] I.e., June 3.

[10] See p. 313, n. 11.

[11] Great preparations were made in Munich, where Emperor Charles V was expected on May 22. He did not reach Munich until June 10. The Nürnberg ambassador at the Imperial court gave a detailed report on the festivities in connection with the Emperor's entry into Munich; *C.R.* 2, 91, n. 3. This report was slightly reworked and published as a one page flier; see *URA* 1, No. 87; *WA, Br* 5, 442 f.

[12] See p. 315, n. 20.

[13] This is a reference to Luther's *Vermahnung an die Geistlichen, versammelt auf dem Reichstag zu Augsburg* (*Exhortation to the Clergy Assembled at the Diet of Augsburg*) (Wittenberg: Hans Lufft, May, 1530), *WA* 30^II, 268 ff.; *LW* 34, 9 ff. This was the first book Luther wrote at the Coburg. On April 29 he reported to Melanchthon that the work on this *Exhortation* was progressing; *WA, Br* 5, 298. On May 12 he wrote to Melanchthon that the manuscript had been finished and shipped to Wittenberg; *WA, Br* 5, 316. Luther received copies of this book on June 2 from a bookdealer who was traveling in a great hurry from Wittenberg to Augsburg to capture the market there before a competitor could do so; *WA, Br* 5, 345. On June 5 Luther presupposed that the books were in the process of being sold in Augsburg. Luther's above remark certainly was not based on any information available to him; Luther wrote in anticipation only. On June 12 and 13 Jonas reported to Luther that five hundred copies of the book had been sold, and that many discerning readers had applauded the book; *WA, Br* 5, 358, 361; see also *WA* 30^II, 237 f.

[14] See I Cor. 1:18 ff.

[15] See p. 314, n. 12.

[16] This letter is not extant. Clemen suggests (*WA, Br* 5, 352, n. 10) that Reinecke, while returning from Coburg to Mansfeld, met the messenger from

Hans Luther[17] the Elder,[18] departed from this life on Exaudi Sunday[19] at one o'clock. This death has certainly thrown me into sadness, thinking not only [of the bonds] of nature, but also of the very kind love [my father had for me]; for through him my Creator has given me all that I am and have. Even though it does comfort me that [Reinecke] writes that [my father], strong in faith in Christ, had gently fallen asleep, yet the pity of heart and the memory of the most loving dealing[s] with him have shaken me in the innermost parts of my being, so that seldom if ever have I despised death as much as I do now. Yet "the righteous man is taken away from calamity, and he enters into peace;"[20] that is, we die many times before we die once for all. I succeed now in the legacy of the name, and I am almost the oldest Luther in my family. Now it is up to me, not only by chance, but also by law, to follow [my father] through death into the kingdom of Christ; may He graciously bestow this on us, for it is for His sake that we are the most miserable among men, and a disgrace for the whole world. Since I am now too sad, I am writing no more; for it is right and God-pleasing for me, as a son, to mourn such a father, from whom the Father of [all] mercies[21] has brought me forth, and through whose sweat [the Creator] has fed and raised me to whatever I am [now]. Indeed I rejoice that he has lived till now so that he could see the light of truth. Praise be to God in all his deeds and councils for ever and ever. Amen.[22]

More at another time. Greet all our friends.

June 5, 1530   MARTIN LUTHER, D.

Mansfeld who was to bring Luther the news of his father's death, and that Reinecke took it upon himself to inform Luther of this event.

[17] On Hans Luther, see *LW* 48, 329 ff.

[18] I.e., in contrast to Luther's uncle, Klein Hans, or Hans Luther the Younger; see also *WA*, Br 5, 350, n. 10.

[19] I.e., May 29, 1530.

[20] Isa. 57:1 f.

[21] II Cor. 1:3.

[22] On June 19 Veit Dietrich wrote to Mrs. Martin Luther: "Within two days [Luther] has gotten over [the death of] his father, although it was very hard for him. Looking at Hans Reinecke's letter, [Luther] says to me: 'So my father is also dead!' Then he hurriedly took his Psalter, went into his room, and wept so greatly that the next day his head [hurt]. Since that time he has not betrayed any further emotion." *WA*, Br 5, 379.

213

To Philip Melanchthon[1]
[Coburg,] June 7, 1530

Luther again complains about the lack of letters from Augsburg, and informs Melanchthon that from now on he too will not write anymore. Luther includes a letter of consolation he had received in connection with his father's death. Finally, Luther communicates the news, received from his wife, that the Elbe river had flooded again even though there had been no heavy rains in the area of Wittenberg.

On Philip Melanchthon, see LW 48, 77, n. 3.

Text in Latin: WA, Br 5, 354.

Grace and peace in Christ

I see that you all have decided to torment us with silence. Consequently, so that we don't pine away unavenged, we announce to you by means of this letter that from now on we shall compete with you in the matter of silence. Should you perhaps despise this, [let me add that] I praise the Wittenbergers who, although they are extremely busy, write three times before you idle people write once.[2]

I have received [a letter of] comfort in regard to the death of my very dear father;[3] if you want to know of it, you may learn about it from this letter[4] of Michael Coelius.[5] I stop my pen here, not to make you [even] more silent by [my] writing.

---

[1] The letter is extant in one manuscript copy, and in the common editions of Luther's works. Although the address is missing in the manuscript copy, and although the text itself does not give any clue as to the addressee, the circumstances mentioned in the letter (complaint about the lack of letters; see pp. 316 f.) suggest that Luther was writing to Augsburg. Further, that Melanchthon or Jonas was the intended recipient of this letter becomes clear from Luther's June 29 letter to Melanchthon; see letter No. 215.

[2] Obviously Luther is being slightly sarcastic here.

[3] See pp. 318 f.

[4] This letter is not extant.

[5] Michael Coelius (1492–1559) had studied at Leipzig, where he was graduated as Master of Arts in 1511. In 1518 he was ordained into the priesthood, and in 1519 he became a priest at Rochlitz. Later he received a pastorate in Bensen (in northern Bohemia), where in 1523 he ran into

Greet all our friends. The grace of God be with you. Amen.
June 7, 1530

My lord Katie writes[6] that the Elbe river has flooded again,[7]
even though not yet a drop of rain has fallen there. Much water
means many monstrosities.

Farewell.

Yours,

MARTIN LUTHER

214

To John Luther
[Coburg, about June 19, 1530][1]

*While Luther was at the Coburg Jerome and Peter Weller,[2] two
brothers, moved in with the Luther family. Jerome Weller took
over the education of Luther's four-year-old son John, and reported*

difficulties because of his evangelical sermons. After he had to flee this
pastorate, Luther recommended Coelius as court chaplain to one of the counts
of Mansfeld in 1525. He remained in the service of the counts of Mansfeld
to the end of his life. Coelius was present at the death of Luther's father, and
at Luther's own death. He also preached one of the funeral sermons for
Luther. Perhaps Coelius' no-longer extant letter was the one brought to Luther
by that messenger whom Reinecke supposedly had intercepted; see p. 318,
n. 16. On Michael Coelius see WA, Br 5, 354, n. 1; WA, Br 13, 138, *ad loc.*
[6] Perhaps in the letter to which Luther replied on June 5; see p. 312.
[7] See also WA 30[I], 329.
[1] For the date of the letter, see note 3.
[2] The Weller family and the Luther family were close friends. Jerome Weller
(1499–1572), even though he was apparently older than most of the students,
studied law and theology at Wittenberg from 1527 to 1535, while also
functioning as tutor in Luther's home. In 1535 Jerome was graduated as
Doctor of Theology from Wittenberg University, and then went as pastor and
teacher to Freiberg in Saxony. Jerome was apparently of a very sensitive, shy,
and modest nature and very easily depressed; his brother Peter was of a
different emotional make-up. Peter started studying theology at Wittenberg as
early as 1525 (see K. Bauer, *Die Wittenberger Universitätstheologie und die
Anfänge der deutschen Reformation* [Tübingen, 1928], p. 108); he was accepted by Duke Albrecht of Prussia (see p. 60) in 1529 as a servant, and
was given a scholarship by the Duke for the purpose of studying law at
Wittenberg. In return, Peter had to obligate himself to remain in the Duke's
service for fifteen years. See WA, Br 3, 419, n. 8; Enders, *Briefwechsel* 8, 8,
n. 1; WA 39[I], 40 f.

in no-longer extant letters to the father about the boy's progress. On June 19 Luther wrote to Jerome Weller, thanking him for two letters.[3] Luther also wrote to his son John. He mentions his pleasure at his son's diligence in studying and praying, and encourages the boy to continue them. Luther further encourages John by promising a present upon his return, and by drawing a verbal picture of a beautiful garden in which children, who studied hard and said their prayers diligently, were permitted to play happily, eat fine fruit, ride horses, play musical instruments, and dance. If John and his friends were good boys, then they would be permitted to enter this garden too, the owner of the garden had promised, and they may even bring Aunt Lena along. Luther closes his letter by commending John to God, and extending greetings to Aunt Lena.

This letter is a very fine example of Luther's ability to be simple and profound at the same time, and in this respect this letter reminds one of Luther's hymn From Heaven above to Earth I Come. While obviously the letter can be sentimentalized, if properly understood it reveals features in Luther's personality which are only too often overlooked. The autograph of the letter is unfortunately no longer extant, but the letter is available in many manuscript copies and printed editions. For his text in WA, Br, Clemen used a manuscript copy which was deposited at Jena; he also gives the variations to be found in a copy deposited in Zwickau. Clemen submits[4] that in the text tradition there is an observable tendency toward intensifying the cordial nature of the letter, and thus perhaps toward sentimentalizing the letter.[5]

On John Luther, see p. 152, n. 7.

Text in German: WA, Br 5, 377–378.

---

[3] WA, Br 5, No. 1593. On the same day Luther also wrote to Peter Weller (WA, Br 5, No. 1594) and to Caspar von Tetleben (WA, Br 5, No. 1592), all in Wittenberg. Since a messenger was available, Luther used the opportunity to communicate with these friends back home. It is also very likely that on this same day he wrote to his wife and to his son, especially since he had heard such good news about the boy from Jerome Weller. The opening sentences in Luther's letter to his son and in the letter to Jerome Weller substantiate June 19 as the approximate date for the present letter.

[4] WA, Br 5, No. 1595, Introduction.

[5] Some of the more striking variants are given below; they appear to substantiate Clemen's argument.

To my beloved[6] son Hänschen[7] Luther at Wittenberg

Grace and peace in Christ! My beloved[8] son: I am pleased[9] to learn that you are doing well in your studies, and that you are praying diligently. Continue to do so, my son, [and] when I return home I shall bring you a nice present from the fair.[10]

I[11] know of a pretty, beautiful, [and] cheerful garden where there are many children wearing little golden coats. [They] pick up fine apples, pears, cherries, [and] yellow and blue plums under the trees; they sing, jump, and are merry.[12] They also have nice ponies[13] with golden reins and silver saddles.[14] I asked the owner of the garden whose children they were. He replied: "These are the children who like to pray, study, and be good." Then I said: "Dear sir, I also have a son, whose name is Hänschen Luther. Might he not also [be permitted] to enter the garden, so that he too could eat such fine apples and pears, and ride on these pretty ponies, and play with these children?" Then the man answered: "If he too[15] likes to pray, study and be good, he too may enter the

---

6 Luther wrote: *hertzlieben*, i.e., literally: "heartily beloved." The Jena manuscript copy originally had a text which would have to be translated as "beloved son." The *hertz* ("from the heart") is written into the free space between the lines. The text of the Zwickau manuscript has to be translated as: "dear son."

7 *Hänschen* is the diminutive of Hans, or John. The German *Hänschen* (or *Hansen*) has been retained in the text of the letter. This form not only suggests little in size, or young in age, but—and this especially—it conveys a certain attitude of kindness, affection, and cordial attachment, a meaning to which the literal translation "little John" cannot do justice.

8 The text of the Jena manuscript copy originally read *hertzliebster*, i.e., most beloved from the heart; this was corrected to read *hertzlieber*, i.e., beloved from the heart.

9 The Zwickau manuscript copy offers a text to be translated as: "very pleased."

10 Literally: ". . . bring along a beautiful [this is missing in the Zwickau manuscript copy] fair for you."

11 For the following lines, see also WA, TR 3, No. 3777.

12 The last part of the sentence (from "sing") is written above the line in the Jena manuscript copy.

13 The text reads: *kleine Pferdlin*, i.e., literally, "little horses," whereby horses also would have to be a diminutive.

14 The Zwickau manuscript copy offers a text to be translated as "little saddles."

15 So on the basis of the Zwickau manuscript copy.

323

garden, and also Lippus[16] and Jost.[17] And when they are all together [there], they will also get whistles, drums, lutes, and all
kinds of other stringed instruments; and they will also dance, and
shoot with little crossbows." And he showed me there a lovely lawn
in the garden, all prepared for dancing, where many gold whistles
and drums and fine silver crossbows were hanging. But it was still
so early [in the morning] that the children had not yet eaten;
therefore I couldn't wait for the dancing. So I said to the man:
"Dear sir, I shall hurry away and write about all this to my dear
son Hänschen so that he will certainly study hard, pray diligently,
and be good in order that he too may get into this garden. But
he has an Aunt Lena,[18] whom he must bring along." "By all
means," said the man, "go and write him accordingly."

Therefore, dear son Hänschen, do study and pray diligently,
and tell Lippus and Jost to study and pray too; then you [boys]
will get into the garden together. Herewith I commend you to the
dear[19] Lord ['s keeping]. Greet Aunt Lena, and give her a kiss for
me.

Your loving[20] father,
MARTIN LUTHER

215

To Philip Melanchthon[1]
[Coburg,] June 29, 1530

*Throughout this long letter Luther comments at length on corre-
spondence matters, reporting especially on those letters from his*

---

[16] I.e., Philip Melanchthon, Jr., who was born on February 21, 1525; see WA,
Br 3, 446, n. 2.
[17] I.e., Justus Jonas, Jr., who was born on December 3, 1525; see WA, Br 3,
630, n. 1.
[18] I.e., Magdalene von Bora; see p. 271, n. 28.
[19] In the Jena manuscript copy the equivalent of "dear" has been written above
the equivalent for "almighty." The Zwickau manuscript copy contains only
the equivalent for "dear."
[20] The Zwickau manuscript copy offers a text to be translated as "most
loving."
[1] The address can be found only in a manuscript copy which is deposited in
the Landesbibliothek in Stuttgart; see WA, Br 13, 147, to WA, Br 5, 405, No.
1609.

*friends in Augsburg which finally had arrived at the Coburg. Luther
had received a copy of the Augsburg Confession (which was presented to the Emperor on June 25), and he comments briefly on
Melanchthon's question as to the points on which concessions
could be made to the papists. At a later point in the letter Luther
again comments on the confession and the events in Augsburg, and
categorically rejects Melanchthon's assertion that he and his co-
workers in Augsburg had followed Luther's authority in this matter.
Luther mentions a letter (once written, but then torn up) to Duke
John Frederick. He also reports in some detail on his general well-
being: in good spirits again, he is now tormented by physical problems. To these business matters Luther adds a long paragraph of
spiritual counsel for Melanchthon, written in some places in an
almost harsh tone. Luther points out that the outcome of the diet
is a matter of faith, and that it cannot be made into a matter which
is perceivable and manageable. People of faith can face Satan and
the whole world. Should Melanchthon lack this faith, as Luther
suggests he indeed does, then Melanchthon at least should draw
strength from the faith of the brethren and of the church at large.
Luther opposes Melanchthon's lack of faith with a brief confession
of his own faith in the form of rhetorical questions. The letter
closes with greetings to all friends, and a short benediction. In a
postscript Luther returns to the question of any concessions to be
made to the papists. Luther explains his comparative silence on
this question by pointing the finger at Melanchthon, who had not
supplied him with sufficient detail for him to be able to deal with
the problem. Almost as if closing the books on the question, Luther
makes a categorical statement: all things can be conceded that are
not contrary to the gospel.*

*The autograph of this letter is not extant; there are many man-
uscript copies available, however, and the letter was printed as
early as 1549 by Matthias Flacius,[2] who used it in his struggle
against the Augsburg Interim. The following translation is based
on the text edited by Clemen in WA, Br. As is often the case,
Clemen does not make clear on which source he based his text, nor
does he give textual variations. Enders, Briefwechsel 8, 41 ff., does*

---

[2] See WA, Br 5, No. 1609, Introduction. On Matthias Flacius, see *O.D.C.C.*,
pp. 507 f.

give a text-critical apparatus which has been consulted for the translation. The German translation presented in St. L. 16, 901 ff., is based on a text which lacks some sentences. In view of the text tradition and the lack of order in the text of the letter itself, one may seriously ask whether the text as it is available is identical with the autograph.

On Philip Melanchthon, see LW 48, 77, n. 3.

Text in Latin: WA, Br 5, 405–407.

To my dearest brother, Philip Melanchthon, at Augsburg[3]

Grace and peace in Christ. I have read your[4] oration,[5] my Philip, with which you people justify yourselves because of your silence. In the meantime,[6] however, I have twice written a letter to you people in which I have sufficiently explained the reason for my silence (at least [I have done so] in the latter letter, the one which the messenger brings who has been sent by our tax collector[7] to the Sovereign).[8] Today your most recent letters have arrived simultaneously, the one delivered by the messenger,[9] and the other[10] by Februarius.[11] In these letters you remind me of your work, dan-

---

[3] See note 1.

[4] "Your," i.e., plural; see note 5.

[5] Luther used *rhetorica*. This is a reference to the attempts by Melanchthon and Jonas to excuse, or explain, the fact that Luther had received no letters from them. According to Luther they had not written to him for three weeks (May 22 to June 12). Luther focused on the following letters: Justus Jonas to Luther, June 12 (WA, Br 5, No. 1587); Philip Melanchthon to Luther, June 13 (*ibid.*, No. 1589, and WA, Br 12, 114 f.). On June 27 Luther mentioned these letters, and promised he would write more about this "*apologia* of your [plural] silence." WA, Br 5, 399. The second group of letters was dated June 25: Philip Melanchthon to Luther (WA, Br 5, No. 1600); Justus Jonas to Luther (*ibid.*, No. 1601).

[6] I.e., while you people in Augsburg were silent; so Rückert, LB, p. 299, n. 2, in contrast to Clemen's highly artificial explanation (WA, Br 5, 407, n. 1).

[7] I.e., Arnold von Falckenstein; see p. 290, n. 29.

[8] I.e., here and throughout the letter, Elector John; see LW 48, 269, n. 8.

[9] Philip Melanchthon to Luther: Augsburg, June 26, 1530; WA, Br 5, No. 1604. Melanchthon sent this messenger at his own expense to the Coburg; see WA, Br 5, 402.

[10] Philip Melanchthon to Luther: Augsburg, June 27, 1530; WA, Br 5, No. 1607.

[11] I.e., Wolf Hornung (Hornung is another name for the month of February; see also p. 348, n. 3) whom Melanchthon mentioned as carrier of the June 27 letter to Luther; see WA, Br 5, 402. Hornung, who had gone to Augsburg to

ger, and tears[12] in such a way that it appears that I, in an unfair way, add insult to injury[13] by my silence, as if I did not know of these things, or sat here among roses[14] and cared nothing [for your troubles]. I wish my cause were such as to permit the flow of tears![15] Indeed, had not your first letters, dealing with the arrival of the Emperor,[16] come here that evening, I too had decided to send a messenger to you the next day at my own expense to find out whether you were alive or dead. Master[17] Veit[18] will testify to this. Still, I believe that all your letters have been delivered to us.[19] For those dealing with the arrival[20] and with the entrance of the Emperor [into Augsburg][21] came finally, though after some delay, and they arrived almost simultaneously.[22] But some devil or

seek redress of some grievance against the Elector of Brandenburg, apparently left Augsburg on June 27 in the morning, and arrived at the Coburg probably in the afternoon of June 29. He must have traveled swiftly, in contrast to Melanchthon's own messenger (see note 9), who was sent on June 26. The "simultaneously" obviously should not be pressed.

12 Both of Melanchthon's letters, especially the one of June 26 (see note 9), are indeed lamentations; so are Jonas' and Melanchthon's June 25 letters to Luther (see note 5).

13 Literally: "add pain upon pain by my silence, [or: sorrow upon sorrow]." See Phil. 2:27.

14 See Seneca *Epistolae morales* 36. 9.

15 Here Luther is obviously needling Melanchthon, who on several occasions mentions his tears and the tears of others in connection with the situation in Augsburg; see WA, Br 5, 387, 396, 403.

16 This is a reference to Melanchthon's and Jonas' letters of June 13 and June 12 (WA, Br 5, Nos. 1589, 1588 [?], 1587), in which Luther was informed of the pending arrival of the Emperor in Augsburg. Luther mentioned below that these letters arrived, after some delay, almost simultaneously with the letters which Jonas and Melanchthon had written on June 18 and 19 (see note 21). See also note 22.

17 I.e., Master of Arts.

18 Veit Dietrich; see p. 282, n. 13.

19 Luther here contradicts Jonas' statement to the effect that letters had been lost, and that this was the reason why Luther had not received the letters which Jonas and Melanchthon had written. Jonas made this statement on June 12 (WA, Br 5, 356), and again on June 25 (WA, Br 5, 389).

20 See note 16.

21 This is a reference to Jonas' June 18 and Melanchthon's June 19 letters (WA, Br 5, Nos. 1590, 1591), in which Luther was informed about the ceremonies connected with the Emperor's entrance into Augsburg.

22 On June 27 Luther reported to Melanchthon that he had "yesterday" sent the letters mentioned in notes 16 and 21 to Wittenberg; WA, Br 5, 400. The date on which these letters arrived at the Coburg cannot be established exactly. On June 19 Luther was still impatiently waiting for any direct news from his friends in Augsburg; see WA, Br 5, 372, 381, 382. On June 25 he had in hand the letters of June 12/13 and 18/19. On that day, under the

Satan may have been at work here; let[23] him do whatever he has to do.

I have received your *Apologia*,[24] and I wonder what it is you want when you ask[25] what and how much is to be conceded to the papists. In connection with the Sovereign it is another question what he may concede, if danger threatens him.[26] For me personally more than enough has been conceded in this *Apologia*. If the papists reject it, then I see nothing that I could still concede, unless I saw their reasoning, or [were given] clearer Scripture passages than I have seen till now. Day and night I am occupied with this matter, considering it, turning it around, debating it, and searching the whole Scripture [because of it]; certainty[27] grows continuously in me about this, our teaching, and I am more and more sure that[28] now (God willing) I shall not permit anything further to be taken away from me, come what may.

---

impression of these letters, Luther wrote to Hausmann and informed him that he had ordered his friends in Wittenberg to send all the news which they received (*sic!*) from him to Hausmann. See WA, Br 5, 385. On June 25 Luther had, then, already written to his friends in Wittenberg, and was envisioning that they would have received the news from the Coburg by the time Hausmann received this letter. Luther's shipment to Wittenberg apparently was delayed until June 26, a fact which he did not anticipate on June 25 when he wrote to Hausmann. It is safe, then, to assume that the letters from Augsburg arrived sometime after the last of Luther's June 19 letters had been written, and prior to June 25.

[23] The following sentence is written in German.

[24] I.e., the *Augsburg Confession*. Text: H. Lietzmann *et. al.* (eds.), *Die Bekenntnisschriften der evangelisch-lutherischen Kirche* (2nd ed.; Göttingen, 1952), pp. 31 ff.; see also H. Bornkamm, *Der authentische lateinische Text der Confessio Augustana* (*Sitzungsberichte der Heidelberger Akademie der Wissenschaften*. Philosophisch-historische Klasse. 1956, II [Heidelberg, 1956]). English text: T. G. Tappert (trans. and ed.), *The Book of Concord. The Confessions of the Evangelical Lutheran Church* (Philadelphia, 1959), pp. 24 ff. On June 26 Melanchthon forwarded to Luther a copy of the *Augsburg Confession*; see WA, Br 5, 397.

[25] On June 26 Melanchthon wrote to Luther: "Now [i.e., after the *Augsburg Confession* had been presented to the Emperor] it seems to me one has to decide, before our opponents may answer, what we are willing to concede to them [in matters of] both kinds, the marriage of priests, private mass. . . . Reply on these matters. . . ." See WA, Br 5, 397. On June 27 Melanchthon repeated this request; see WA, Br 5, 403. Melanchthon's request was the result of the discussions which he conducted with Alfonso Valdes (a member of the Imperial court), and which were intended to lead to peace.

[26] This sentence is missing in some witnesses. For a detailed analysis of this sentence, see *Deutsche Theologie* 3 (1936), 68 ff.

[27] Luther used a Greek word here.

[28] The following part of the sentence is written in German.

I had written to the younger Sovereign[29] as you requested, but I afterwards tore up the letter, since I was afraid to give ideas to this genius, and then to hear excuses which I wouldn't like.[30]

Here I am sufficiently well off, for it seems that that demon, which till now has beaten me with fists,[31] has given up (as if broken by your prayers and those of the brethren), though I suspect that instead of this [demon] another one has followed, which will wear down my body. Yet I would rather tolerate this torturer of the flesh than that executioner of the spirit. And I hope that He who defeated in me the father of [all] lies will also overcome [that] murderer.[32] [The devil] has sworn to kill me,[33] this I certainly know, and he will have no peace until he has devoured me. All right, if he devours me, he shall devour a laxative (God willing) which will make his bowels and anus too tight for him. Do you want to bet? One has to suffer if he wants to possess Christ.[34] It

---

[29] I.e., Duke John Frederick; see *LW* 48, 181 f.

[30] On June 25 Melanchthon wrote to Luther: "The Emperor greets Elector John in a quite friendly way, and I wished our party [literally: ours] would be more courteous [or: obliging] to [the Emperor]. I wish to God that in this matter you would admonish [Duke John Frederick] in a letter . . . no one is more gentle than the Emperor himself." See *WA, Br* 5, 386. Enders (*Briefwechsel* 8, 21, n. 4) suggests that Duke John Frederick opposed Melanchthon's secret negotiations with Valdes (see note 25), and that Luther, so to speak, was to bring the Electoral prince in line. Clemen (*WA, Br* 5, 387, n. 4) rejects this interpretation, and Rückert (*LB*, p. 301) makes no attempt to explain the passage beyond citing the appropriate passage from Melanchthon's June 25 letter. To complicate the situation, Enders, *Briefwechsel* 8, 46, n. 13, connects Luther's statement, above, with Melanchthon's May 4 request that Luther write to Duke John Frederick; see *WA, Br* 5, 305. And finally, the whole sentence is missing in two witnesses, one manuscript copy, and the Flacius edition (see note 2). Does this suggest that the sentence was missing in the autograph? If one does not want to assume this, how is one to understand this passage? It is very dubious that Luther's statement has anything to do with Melanchthon's May 4 request; at least there is no material available which would suggest that there are any connections between Luther's statement and that request. What was Luther to do according to Melanchthon's June 25 request? The circumstances of this request suggest that Luther was (only) to admonish the Electoral prince "to be more polite," or something to this effect, in order not to lose the Emperor's good will. This would leave the question open as to how one should understand the second half of Luther's statement. What kind of excuses did Luther expect? By whom would they be made? And for what?

[31] See II Cor. 12:7 (Luther Bible).

[32] See John 8:44.

[33] Literally: "sworn death to me."

[34] These last three sentences (beginning with "[The devil] has sworn") are written in German.

would be easy indeed for us to triumph if we were willing to deny and calumniate [Christ]. [Yet] it is written:[35] "Through many tribulations," etc.[36] This is no longer just a word; it has become a reality,[37] and we should act accordingly.[38] Yet He is [here] who along with the tribulation brings about the escape[39] for the faithful.

I don't like that you write in your letter[40] that you have followed my authority in this cause.[41] I don't wish to be, or be called, the originator [of] this cause for you people; even though this might be properly interpreted, yet I don't want [to hear] this term ["originator"]. If this is not simultaneously and in the same way your cause, then I don't want it to be called mine and imposed upon you. If it is my cause alone then I will handle it by myself.

I[42] believe that all your letters which you have sent by Dr. Jonas'[43] messenger have been delivered to me. Afterwards none were delivered, except the ones dealing with the Emperor's arrival and his entrance [into Augsburg],[44] and the ones sent thereafter up to this day.[45] Therefore you may also know [now] that I do have the picture of Vienna.[46] Between the messenger of Jonas and the Emperor's entrance [into Augsburg],[47] however, you thoroughly crucified us by your silence.

---

[35] This phrase is written in German.

[36] Acts 14:22.

[37] Literally: "but now has come into the work [i.e., into operation, or working]."

[38] This sentence (beginning with "This is no longer") is written in German.

[39] I Cor. 10:13.

[40] Philip Melanchthon to Luther: Augsburg, June 26, 1530; WA, Br 5, 397. See also Melanchthon's June 27 letter to Luther; WA, Br 5, 403.

[41] "In this cause" is missing in many witnesses.

[42] The following paragraph is missing in some witnesses.

[43] See Philip Melanchthon to Luther: May 22, 1530; WA, Br 5, 335; Justus Jonas to Luther: June 12, 1530; WA Br 5, 355. Only Melanchthon's May 22 letter is extant.

[44] See notes 16, 21.

[45] I.e., Melanchthon's letters, dated June 25, 26, 27; Jonas' two letters dated June 25 (see notes 5, 9, 10); Spalatin's (?) letter (see p. 334, n. 3); and Agricola's letter (see WA, Br 5, No. 1608).

[46] On May 22 (see WA, Br 5, 336) Melanchthon sent to Luther a series of wood cuts by Sebald Beham which were entitled: The Siege of the City of Vienna. For detailed bibliographical information, see WA, Br 5, 338, n. 24. On June 25 Melanchthon inquired from Veit Dietrich whether Luther had received this shipment; see WA, Br 5, 386; WA, Br 13, 136, to WA, Br 5, 338, n. 24, and 142, to WA, Br 5, 386, No. 1600.

[47] I.e., between the letters of May 22 (see note 43), and the June 12/13 letters (see note 16) dealing with the Emperor's entrance into Augsburg.

In my last letter[48] I comforted you with thoughts which I hope do not lead to death but to life. What else can I do? The end and the outcome of this cause torture you because you cannot comprehend them. But if you could comprehend them, then I would not wish to be a partner in this cause, much less its originator. God has placed this cause into a certain paragraph,[49] which you don't have in your rhetoric, nor in your philosophy. This [paragraph] is entitled "Faith"; in this paragraph are contained all the things that[50] cannot be seen and do not appear.[51] Should someone attempt to make these things visible, touchable, and comprehendable, as you do, he will bring back, as the reward of his labor, worries and tears such as those you are bringing back to all of us who are vainly protesting.[52] The Lord has promised that he would live in a cloud,[53] and he has made the darkness his hiding place.[54] If someone wants to, let him try to change it.[55] Had Moses attempted to comprehend the outcome by which he might escape the pharaoh's army, then Israel would perhaps to this day be in Egypt. May the Lord increase faith for you and for all of us. If one has faith what may Satan and the whole world do? But if we don't have this faith, why don't we then console ourselves at least with the faith of others? For by necessity there are others who believe in our stead, unless there is no more a church in the world, and Christ has ceased to be with us prior to the end of the world.[56] For if Christ is not with us, where, I earnestly wish to know, is he then in the whole world? If we are not the church, or a part

---

[48] Luther to Philip Melanchthon: June 27, 1530; WA, Br 5, No. 1605; see also WA, Br 5, 408, n. 23, and WA, Br 13, 147, ad loc.

[49] Luther wrote: in locum quendam communem. This is obviously an allusion to Melanchthon's Loci communes (see LW 48, 232, n. 21). For the translation of locus with "paragraph [of teaching]," or with "category," see LJB 8 (1926), 27 ff.; Q. Breen, Christianity and Humanism, ed. N. P. Ross (Grand Rapids, Mich., 1968), pp. 93 ff.

[50] From here on to the end of the sentence Luther wrote in Greek.

[51] Heb. 11:1, 3. See also Luther's explanation of the first twenty-five Psalms (see p. 288, n. 11), in which on July 1, 1530, he picked up the argument of this June 29 letter; WA 31^I, 347; 345, note to line 26.

[52] I.e., protesting what Melanchthon was doing, or how he was making unnecessary worries for himself.

[53] I Kings 8:12.

[54] Ps. 18:12.

[55] This sentence is written in German.

[56] See Matt. 28:20. Literally: "end of the age."

of the church, where is the church? Are the dukes of Bavaria,[57] Ferdinand,[58] the Pope, the Turk, and those like them, the church? If we don't have God's Word, who are the people who have it? If God is with us, who is against us?[59] We are sinners and are ungrateful, but [God] will not therefore be a liar. And yet in this sacred and divine cause we cannot be sinners, even though in our ways we are evil. But you do not even hear [any of] this, so distressed and weak does Satan make you. May Christ heal you; for this I pray fervently, and without interruption. Amen.[60]

I[61] wish an opportunity would present itself to me to come to you; I am eager to come even without having been asked or invited.[62] These letters to Brenz[63] and Dr. Caspar[64] should have gone with the last letter,[65] but the messenger had [already] left while the letters were being brought down [to the city]. Greet all, for I cannot again write to them all.

God's grace be with you and with all of you. Amen.

June 29, 1530   MARTIN LUTHER

---

[57] The dukes of Bavaria were known for their strong opposition to Luther and his work. On June 19 Melanchthon complained to Luther about the dukes of Bavaria; see WA, Br 5, 371. Further, the dukes were Eck's territorial lords (see p. 296, n. 3). And finally, the dukes were among those German sovereigns who had gone to Innsbruck to meet with the Emperor, prior to the actual beginning of the diet; see Walter, RA, 16.

[58] Ferdinand of Austria, the Emperor's brother; see LW 48, 217, n. 17.

[59] Rom. 8:31.

[60] For a commentary, see *Deutsche Theologie* 3 (1936), 67 ff., 247 ff.

[61] The following sentences, down to "Greet all, for I cannot," are missing in some witnesses.

[62] Luther made a similar statement in his June 27 letter to Melanchthon; see WA, Br 5, 400. On June 25 Jonas had expressed his hope that Luther might be brought to Augsburg under an Imperial safe-conduct; see WA, Br 5, 392. On June 19, however, Luther wrote to Conrad Cordatus that there was little hope that he would be called to Augsburg; WA, Br 5, 381.

[63] John Brenz; see pp. 177 f.

[64] Apparently Dr. Caspar Lindemann; see p. 291, n. 30. Neither the letter to Brenz nor that to Lindemann are extant. See also WA, Br 13, 148, to WA, Br 5, 408, nn. 31, 32. Apparently both letters were still to be given to the messenger who, in great haste, had stopped at the Coburg and picked up Luther's June 27 letters to Melanchthon (WA, Br 5, No. 1605) and to Link (*ibid.*, No. 1606). The messenger went only as far as Nürnberg, and Link was to expedite the Melanchthon letter and the other letters which Luther had received from Wittenberg and had sent along with this messenger.

[65] Luther's June 27 letter to Melanchthon; WA, Br 5, No. 1605.

When[66] I had finished the letter the thought occurred to me that it might perhaps seem to you that I have replied too little to your question as to how much and how far one should make concessions to the opponents.[67] But on the other hand, you have asked in insufficient detail; you have not informed [me] what demands you think will be made of us.[68] As I have always written, I am ready to concede all things [to the opponents] if only the gospel alone is permitted to remain free with us. What is contrary to the gospel,[69] however, I cannot concede. What else should I answer?

216

To George Spalatin
[Coburg,] June 30, 1530

In the first part of this letter, Luther enumerates the messengers who had returned from Augsburg without bringing any letters, and thus substantiates his charge that Spalatin (and his other friends in Augsburg) had ceased writing to him for a long period of time. Then Luther closes the books on this episode which had caused him so much annoyance and worry. In the second part of the letter, which is indirectly addressed to Melanchthon, Luther, referring to Psalm 2:1 ff., points out that the raging of those who oppose the gospel is a sign of their doom, and, says Luther, this in turn should encourage the friends in Augsburg. Luther suggests that Melanchthon views the whole matter in a wrong perspective; even more, Melanchthon's worries are a sign of lack of faith and of man's ambition to be like God. Drawing on Exodus 3:14, Luther emphasizes that the cause of the evangelicals is God's, and God, not Melanchthon, will see the cause through to the end. Luther concludes with a call to repentance, which casts out every ambition to be like God.

On George Spalatin, see LW 48, 8 f.

Text in Latin: WA, Br 5, 414–415.

---

[66] This postscript is missing in many witnesses.
[67] See note 25.
[68] Indeed, in neither letter (see note 25) did Melanchthon give specific information to Luther.
[69] Literally: "What fights [against] the gospel."

To the venerable Mr. George Spalatin, Master [of Arts],[1]
faithful and sincere bishop[2] at Altenburg[3]

Grace and peace in the Lord. "I shall not tolerate" (so you say,[4] my Spalatin,) "being called a man who has ceased writing [letters]." Yet you will endure [this charge] even if you don't like it. For since [the arrival of] Dr. Jonas' messenger—through whom you people promised to write so many letters,[5] both to us and to the people in Wittenberg, [and to send them] via Dr. Apel's messenger, that we expected a forest of letters and were afraid that you would become noisier than our jackdaws[6]—[no letters arrived]. But when this messenger of Apel arrived,[7] he carried only a letter from

---

[1] Literally: "To the venerable man, Mr. Master George Spalatin . . ."

[2] See p. 87, n. 5.

[3] The address, though now missing in the extant autograph, has been supplied on the basis of some manuscript copies. Spalatin himself noted on the autograph that this letter was written by "D. M. L." on June 30, 1530.

[4] Spalatin had apparently done this in a no-longer extant letter which Jonas mentioned in his June 25 letter to Luther; see WA, Br 5, 389. According to the context in which Jonas mentioned this letter, it must have been written on about June 18 or 19. For on June 18 Jonas informed Luther that Spalatin himself was sending to Luther a report on the Emperor's entrance into Augsburg. Jonas corrected here only what he had said earlier in this letter, that in a short time "we" will send this report, a statement which he had already once corrected to read that "we are sending" this report. See WA, Br 5, 367; 369, n. 2. It is therefore safe to assume the following circumstances: While Jonas was writing his June 18 letter to Luther he anticipated sending Spalatin's report "in a short time." Then Jonas was informed that Spalatin was sending the report himself. And on June 25 Jonas informed Luther that he and Spalatin had written a great deal about the entrance of the Emperor into Augsburg; see WA, Br 5, 389. This passage obviously refers to a letter of Spalatin and not to the report mentioned by Jonas on June 18. Perhaps it was a covering letter for that report, for one may hardly assume that Spalatin sent that report without adding a personal greeting. But according to Luther's statement above, this no-longer extant letter must also have contained an attempt on Spalatin's part to refute Luther's charge that Spalatin was not writing any letters. And further, in this no-longer extant letter, according to Luther, Spalatin rejected Luther's description of him as a *Cessator in scribendo* ("a man who has ceased writing [letters]"). Here and at the end of this paragraph Luther used a capital C, although in both instances the small c would have been appropriate. Had Spalatin used this phrase too?

[5] This is a reference to the messenger whom Jonas and Melanchthon had contracted to deliver Melanchthon's May 22 letter to Luther (and a no-longer extant May 22 letter of Jonas; see WA, Br 5, 355, 389). The promise, mentioned by Luther, was made by Melanchthon in his May 22 letter; see WA, Br 5, 335, 336. This "messenger of Dr. Jonas" had arrived at the Coburg at least several days prior to June 2; see note 10.

[6] See pp. 293 ff.

[7] See note 10, and p. 310, n. 26.

Jonas to Wittenberg.[8] When asked, "Aren't you bringing letters?"[9] he answered, "No." "How are the gentlemen doing?" He answered, "Fine." I soon took up this matter with Philip.[10] Thereafter[11] the mounted messenger arrived, who was dispatched to Torgau, and who brought me a letter from the Sovereign[12] directly. When asked, "Aren't you bringing [other] letters?" he answered, "No." "How are the gentlemen doing?" He answered, "Fine." Then I wrote again to Philip,[13] [forwarding the letter] with the carrier of the

---

[8] This letter could not be identified, and apparently is no longer extant. But since the "messenger of Dr. Jonas" (see note 5) was to continue his journey to Wittenberg to deliver Jonas' letter of comfort for his wife on the death of their son (see WA, Br 5, 355; 12, 113, n. 9), it can safely be assumed that Apel's messenger carried a similar (second) letter of comfort for Jonas' wife.
[9] This dialogue is written in German, here and as repeated throughout the paragraph.
[10] According to Clemen (WA, Br 5, 415, n. 6) Luther refers here to his June 2 letter to Melanchthon (WA, Br 5, No. 1580), in which Luther mentioned the fact that his friends in Augsburg had permitted Apel's messenger to return to the Coburg empty-handed. On the basis of Luther's "soon," it is safe to suggest that Apel's messenger had stopped by at the Coburg at least several days prior to June 2, and that the "messenger of Dr. Jonas" (see note 5) had arrived at the Coburg at least a day or two before that date. Consequently Melanchthon's (and Jonas') letter of May 22 could have been in Luther's hands any time after May 26, since it took a messenger not more than approximately four days to travel from Augsburg to Coburg (about two hundred kilometers) if he was not in too great a hurry. If he was in a hurry, the journey could easily be made in two days.
[11] I.e., after June 2. The Elector's letter mentioned by Luther (WA, Br 5, No. 1579) was dated June 1, and was dispatched to the tax collector in Coburg; i.e., this letter was sent with official mail. The date when this mounted messenger arrived at Coburg cannot be established. At any rate, by June 5, when Luther wrote to his wife and to Melanchthon, he had apparently not yet received the Elector's letter. When did he receive it? When did the conversation, on which Luther here reported, take place? The situation becomes even more complicated in view of the fact that the following letter to Melanchthon, of which Luther clearly states that he wrote it *after* he had met the mounted messenger, is commonly identified with the June 5 letter; so in WA, Br 5, 415, n. 8; Rückert, LB, p. 280, n. 18; WA, Br 13, 137, to WA, Br 5, 351, nn. 3, 4; Enders, Briefwechsel 8, 56, n. 5. The easiest way out of the dilemma would be to suggest that on June 30 Luther's memory tricked him, and that the conversation with the mounted messenger took place after the letters of June 5 had been written. Whatever the circumstances may have been, they were not as clear-cut as they appear to be on the basis of the available commentaries. The statement in WA, Br 13, 137, to WA, Br 5, 351, nn. 3, 4, to the effect that on June 30 Luther placed the mounted messenger between Apel's messenger and the venison carrier, who took letter No. 212 along to Augsburg, contributes little, if anything, to a clarification of the text.
[12] I.e., here and throughout this letter, Elector John; see LW 48, 269, n. 8.
[13] If the first letter to Melanchthon was the one of June 2, as is commonly assumed, then this second one was the one of June 5, No. 212; see also note

venison who left from here; he too returned empty-handed. At this point I started to have gloomy thoughts,[14] and assumed that you wanted to hide some bad news from me. [Then] the fourth messenger arrived, Jobst Nymptzen.[15] "Are you bringing letters?" "No." "How are the gentlemen doing?" "Fine." I pass over how often our tax collecter here[16] received letters from his brother, the marshall von Falckenstein,[17] while we in the meantime were thirsty and hungry for more than three weeks, thanks to your silence. If we wanted to find out something we had to learn it from the [marshall's] letters. I ask you if you wouldn't call me a man who had ceased [writing letters], if I had done this to you? I admit that I was angry and full of fear, since I know of Philip's[18] worries and the Sovereign's crosses. Yet I was relieved when I heard that [all of] you were fine;[19] but I couldn't quite believe it. But enough about this; do not even mention it or think of it any more.[20]

That[21] [at Augsburg] kings, sovereigns, and people are raging and howling against the Anointed of the Lord[22] I consider to be a good sign, and much better than if they were flattering. For it

---

11. According to Rückert, *LB*, p. 280, n. 18, letter No. 212 was dispatched to Augsburg by the carrier of the venison, who had returned on or prior to June 5 without bringing letters, and who was immediately to make another trip to Augsburg; Rückert supports his interpretation with Luther's statement made here. When this carrier of venison returned empty-handed for the second time cannot be established.

14 Literally: "sad [things]." Luther's statement concerning the time when he developed these "gloomy thoughts" may not be pressed. He made similar statements in his June 5 letter to Melanchthon (see p. 317), and in his June 2 letter to Melanchthon (*WA*, Br 5, 345); both these letters were written prior to the second time that the venison carrier supposedly returned empty-handed from Augsburg, provided that Rückert's interpretation of the situation is correct.

15 Nothing could be established about this messenger. For Clemen's suggestion (*WA*, Br 5, 415, n. 9) that this messenger might have taken letter No. 213 back to Augsburg, see *WA*, Br 13, 149, to *WA*, Br 5, *ad loc.*

16 I.e., Arnold von Falckenstein; see p. 290, n. 29.

17 I.e., the Electoral Saxon *Hofmarschall* Christopher von Falckenstein; see *WA*, Br 5, 382, n. 3.

18 I.e., here and throughout this letter, Philip Melanchthon; see *LW* 48, 77, n. 3; see also in this vol., pp. 289, 327, 340 f., 370, 395.

19.See p. 327, n. 16.

20 It has to be pointed out that according to the way in which Luther's report here has been interpreted by Rückert, Enders, and in *WA*, Br 13, there is no room in this report for Luther's June 7 letter to Melanchthon (No. 213).

21 For a commentary on and analysis of this second half of the letter, see *Deutsche Theologie* 3 (1936), 249 f.

22 See Ps. 2:1 f.

follows: "He who sits in the heavens laughs at them."[23] Since our Sovereign laughs at them, I do not see why we should shed tears in their[24] presence. For he doesn't laugh on his own behalf, but on our behalf, so that we, too, may laugh more courageously at their ineffectual plans. Only faith is necessary, that the cause of faith be not without faith [on our part]. He, however, who has begun this work,[25] certainly has begun it without our counsel and effort; and until now he has protected and guided his work above and aside from our counsel and effort. He it is who will complete and close it outside and beyond our counsel and effort; concerning this I have not the slightest doubt. I know and I am certain in whom I have believed, for he is powerful [and able] to do beyond whatever we ask and understand,[26] even though Philip thinks and wishes that God should work in the frame of and according to his [Philip's] own counsel, so that he could boast: "It had to come out that way; in such a way I would have done it." No,[27] it should not be: "Thus I, Philip, want it." The "I" is too little. [Rather] it is: "So I [want it], I [who] shall be who I shall be."[28] This is His name: [I shall be] who I shall be. We do not see who He is, but He will be it, and so we shall see it. But enough of this verbosity.

Be strong in the Lord,[29] and on my behalf continuously admonish Philip not to become like God,[30] but to fight that innate ambition to be like God, which was planted in us in paradise by the devil. This [ambition] doesn't do us any good. It drove Adam from paradise, and it alone also drives us away, and drives peace away from us. In summary:[31] we are to be men and not God; it will not be otherwise, or eternal anxiety and affliction will be our reward.

Farewell in Christ.

June 30, 1530   MARTIN LUTHER

---

[23] Ps. 2:4.
[24] I.e., the enemies of the gospel; "Sovereign," i.e., God.
[25] Phil. 1:6.
[26] Eph. 3:20.
[27] Some phrases in the following sentences (down to "But enough") are written in German.
[28] Exod. 3:14 (Luther Bible).
[29] Eph. 6:10.
[30] Gen. 3:5.
[31] Literally: "We are to be men and not God. This is the sum; it will not . . ." This sentence is written in German.

217

To John Agricola
Coburg, June 30, 1530

Luther once more[1] sets forth his opinion on the Emperor's demand that all preaching by the evangelicals in Augsburg be stopped. He sees in this demand an omen for the further development of the diet: At first the Emperor might request that the evangelicals abandon their teachings; should the evangelicals refuse to do this, then a decree would undoubtedly be issued suppressing these teachings. Luther, having the sharp vision of someone who has the necessary distance for seeing things in the proper perspective, realizes that the Emperor, rather than guiding the diet according to the Summons,[2] is himself being guided by the papists, against whose maneuvers only God could help.[3] And so Luther asks Agricola to tell Melanchthon not to ruin himself with worries. While the sacrifice of a contrite and humble spirit is pleasing to God, a destroyed spirit and a ruined soul is not what God wants. To the contrary, Luther suggests that in Melanchthon's worries Satan may be seen at work, just as Satan is at work in the way in which the papists are trying to run the diet. Luther derives comfort from the fact that his friends at Augsburg are not dealing with humans but rather with satanic powers, for in their blindness these powers are attacking God himself and thus will bring their own doom upon themselves. Luther mentions some recent visitors, and concludes his letter with a benediction for his friends in Augsburg, whom he calls Christ's confessors and servants.

The autograph of the letter is no longer extant. The total letter, as well as fragments of it, is extant in many manuscript copies and editions.[4] While the witnesses offer textual variations,[5] none of these

---

[1] See pp. 298 f.

[2] See pp. 280 f.

[3] See also Luther's June 30 letter to Elector John; WA, Br 5, No. 1615; LCC 18, 152.

[4] For information on the witnesses, see WA, Br 5, No. 1613, Introduction; WA, Br 13, 149, *ad loc.*; Enders, *Briefwechsel* 8, No. 1686, Introduction.

[5] Enders, *Briefwechsel* 8, No. 1686, gives some of the more important textual variations.

seems to suggest fundamental differences in the meaning of the text.
On John Agricola, see LW 48, 220.
Text in Latin: WA, Br 5, 416–417.

To the excellent Master[6] John Agricola,[7] a minister of Christ,
[presently] at Augsburg, my brother in the Lord

Grace and peace in Christ. Concerning the letters and the silence,
my Agricola, [I have written] to the others who are with you.[8]

Concerning the Emperor's[9] decree, by which he prohibited all
sermons,[10] I think the following: Our Sovereign[11] has acted correctly in that he, [staying at the moment] in a city which does not
belong to him, has acknowledged the lord [of that city],[12] and has

---

[6] I.e., Master of Arts.

[7] Literally: "To the excellent man, Master John . . ."

[8] See letters No. 215, 216.

[9] I.e., here and throughout this letter, Emperor Charles V; see *LW* 48, 175 f.

[10] See pp. 298 f. By May 15 Luther and Melanchthon agreed that Elector John,
as a guest in the emperor's city and thus a direct subject of the emperor,
should comply with the Emperor's request to abstain from public preaching;
see p. 298, n. 16. While the theologians thus played into the Emperor's hands,
Gregory Brück was of a different opinion; for his (May 10 or 11) brief on
this matter, see *URA* 1, No. 71. For the time being the Elector did not
comply with the Emperor's demand, a fact for which Luther later seemed to
admire the Elector; see *WA*, TR 3, No. 2934a. On June 15 the Emperor
finally arrived in Augsburg. That same evening he summoned to his private
quarters those sovereigns who had signed the Speyer Protest and Appeal, and
personally demanded that the preaching be stopped. The Protestant sovereigns
were shocked. Margrave George of Brandenburg-Ansbach-Kulmbach answered
that he would rather kneel down and have his head cut off than deny God's
Word. Landgrave Philip of Hesse stated that the evangelical preachers
preached nothing evil or new, but preached only God's Word as the fathers
of the early church had done, and that the Emperor could easily convince
himself of this by listening to the evangelical preachers; and further, the
Emperor's conscience was not lord and master over his, the Landgrave's,
conscience. This meeting ended with the postponement of a final answer by the
Protestants. On June 16 the evangelical sovereigns formally protested the
Emperor's demand. After much talk back and forth a compromise was finally
worked out on June 18. According to this solution both evangelicals *and*
papists ceased public preaching, while the Emperor alone was empowered to
appoint ministers for public worship. Luther knew of these developments
from his friends in Augsburg. For documentation, see *WA*, Br 5, 367 (Jonas
to Luther, June 18); 371 (Melanchthon to Luther, June 19); 383 (Osiander
to Luther, June 21); 394 (Elector John to Luther, June 25); *URA* 1, Nos. 93,
94, 96–98, 100; *TP*, pp. 62 ff.; *BA*, pp. 45 ff. For the reconstruction of the
events, see Walter, *RA*, 38 ff.; Reu I, 90 ff.

[11] I.e., here and throughout this letter, Elector John; see *LW* 48, 269, n. 8.

[12] In Augsburg, as an Imperial city, the emperor himself was lord.

not attempted to rule [there],[13] regardless of whatever force seems to be involved in this matter. For one is not permitted to resist evil,[14] and Christ has commanded us to yield when he said: "If they persecute you in one town, flee to another."[15] And also: "Go out from that house."[16] Consequently, I believe that the Sovereign, although as a member [of the diet] he is not permitted physically to leave [Augsburg], by his silence he nevertheless fled, so to speak, into another town and "went out from that house." As Naaman the Syrian did in the temple of Nisroch, so [our Sovereign, too,] can read the Word and worship God at home by himself.[17] Nevertheless [the Emperor's decree] sets an evil example, though it is not an offense.[18] But from this example I suspect the diet might come to an identical end; that is, that first the Emperor will ask the Sovereign to abandon all our teachings, just as he asked [us] at the beginning to refrain from preaching. If, then, after this request [the Sovereign] does not wish to do this, a similar interdict against the teaching will follow. These are my thoughts [on this subject]. Here is where the first real trouble of the diet will show up, and here is where the hand of God is to be expected and implored. For it is absolutely certain that the papists, who have been handed over to the devils, can do nothing else but rage. Abel's blood lies heavily on them, and their abominations harden them, so that they cannot live unless they have drunk blood.

Admonish Philip[19] not to make too big a sacrifice of his contrite spirit[20] so that he does not finally lack the stuff for further

---

[13] Literally: "Our Sovereign, who in a foreign city has acknowledged the lord and has not attempted to rule, has acted correctly, whatever force seems to be in that matter."

[14] Matt. 5:39.

[15] Matt. 10:23.

[16] Matt. 10:14.

[17] Literally: "[Our Sovereign] can, together with Naaman the Syrian in the temple Nisroch and at home by himself, read and honor the Word." Luther, apparently citing from memory, confused II Kings 5:18 with II Kings 19:37; see also WA, Br 5, 609, a September 8, 1530, letter to Jerome Weller, in which Luther also confused these two passages. On June 21 Luther was informed that the evangelicals affirmed the right to have sermons in their quarters; see WA, Br 5, 383.

[18] Literally: "Nevertheless it is a matter of an evil example, though not of an offense."

[19] I.e., here and throughout this letter, Philip Melanchthon; see LW 48, 77, n. 3.

[20] Ps. 51:19. Literally: "to mitigate [or: moderate] the sacrifice of a contrite spirit."

sacrificing. It is, of course, a great comfort to know that one uses up all one's energy for the sake of the best cause, [in fact] for God himself, as long as one cannot doubt that one pleases God [with this], as with a most pleasant odor;[21] but there is a measure to all things.[22] The sacrifice is pleasing, not the ruin, and God does not want souls to be destroyed. [Such destruction of souls] is an addition from Satan. For anything expected from the Emperor's kindness is worth nothing. I think that the papists have urged the Emperor for this reason so that he might examine this case, and, having heard our defense, they might finally decide what they want. In this way they would nevertheless have made the pretense of having listened to us sufficiently, and thus they might so much more easily and plausibly throw the charge of obstinacy at us, as people who have been heard, admonished, and in the end have not obeyed[23] the Emperor. Toward what other end is Satan contriving; for what good are we hoping from him? Or do we not know his thoughts: that through disguise, lies, adroitness, [and] deception he twists everything so that he himself appears glorious, but Christ absolutely dishonored? Certainly you people at Augsburg are not dealing with human beings, but with the very gates of hell,[24] with powers which are not only extremely well taught and exercised but also—and this is comforting—raging in the extreme; blinded by this raging they cannot avoid, in the end, running headlong into God's wisdom,[25] and they cheat themselves by their own cleverness. Amen, Amen.

Caspar Müller[26] has been here with me, with my brother James,[27] and has told me what he had entrusted you to tell me.[28] So, also this evil has to be laid on us, so that everywhere we are tortured by the devil's monstrosities. [More] on this some other time.

---

[21] Phil. 4:18.

[22] See Horace *Satires* i.1, 106.

[23] Literally: "heard [or: listened to]."

[24] Matt. 16:18 (Luther Bible).

[25] From the following "and" to "cleverness," this portion of the sentence has been written in German—apparently in all witnesses.

[26] Caspar Müller was the chancellor of the counts of Mansfeld, who was not continuously present at Augsburg; see *ADB* 22, 648.

[27] James Luther; see p. 268, n. 4. He had visited Luther, apparently in connection with the passing of their father (see pp. 318 f.), as Schubert (LaK, 127) suggests.

[28] The background of this statement, as well as of the following, could not be clarified.

May the Lord Jesus, who has sent you all [to Augsburg] as his confessors and servants, and for whom you offer even your necks, be with you [all]. May he, through his Spirit, grant you the testimony of certainty in the faith[29] to know and not to doubt that you are his confessors. This faith will quicken and comfort you, because you are ambassadors of a great king. These are trustworthy words. Amen.

From the wilderness,[30] *June 30, 1530*

Yours,

MARTIN LUTHER

218

To Philip Melanchthon[1]
Coburg, July 3, 1530

After commending a certain Francis to Melanchthon, Luther evaluates the Augsburg Confession, which he has just reread, and with which he is very pleased. However, citing and paraphrasing Luke 19:14, Psalm 118:22 f., and Mark 15:28, Luther voices certain criticism of Melanchthon and of the confession.

On Philip Melanchthon, see LW 48, 77, n. 3.

Text in Latin: WA, Br 5, 435–436.

To Philip Melanchthon, a servant and confessor of Christ,
my dearest brother[2]

Grace and peace in Christ. I am commending to you, dearest Philip, this man Francis,[3] who has been sent to us from Breslau by Dr.

---

[29] Luther used a Greek word for this phrase.
[30] See p. 287, n. 1.
[1] The letter is extant in many manuscript copies, and in the common editions of Luther's works. Even though the address is missing in all witnesses with the exception of one manuscript copy, it is clear to whom Luther wrote this letter, since the addressee is mentioned at the beginning of the letter, and is corroborated through the circumstances mentioned in the letter. For the textual variations, see Enders, *Briefwechsel* 8, No. 1696, and WA, Br 13, 152, to WA, Br 5, No. 1621.
[2] For the address, see WA, Br 13, 152, to WA, Br 5, No. 1621.
[3] Nothing could be found out about this man.

Hess.[4] [Francis] desires nothing but to see and talk to all of you. He could not be admitted to me.[5]

Yesterday I carefully reread your whole *Apologia*,[6] and I am tremendously pleased with it.[7] You are wrong[8] and commit sin, however, in this one point in that you go[9] against sacred Scripture, where Christ says of himself: "We do not want this one to rule over us,"[10] and you strike out against that "cornerstone, which the

---

[4] John Hess; see *LW* 48, 143, n. 5.

[5] According to Rückert, *LB*, p. 315, n. 17, Elector John (see *LW* 48, 269, n. 8) apparently ordered that the number of visitors to Luther be curtailed. See also p. 314.

[6] I.e., the *Augsburg Confession*. On June 26 Melanchthon had forwarded to Luther a copy of the *Augsburg Confession*, and on June 30 he had asked Veit Dietrich for Luther's opinion of it; see *WA, Br* 5, 397; *ibid.*, No. 1616, Introduction. On June 29 Luther confirmed to Melanchthon the receipt of the confession; see p. 328. In his June 30 letters to Augsburg (see pp. 333 ff., and *WA, Br* 5, Nos. 1610 [?], 1611, 1614, 1615) Luther mentioned the confession only indirectly. Now, on July 3, Luther for the first time mentions the confession to Melanchthon in some detail. Clemen (*WA, Br* 5, 436, nn. 2, 3) suggests that "reread' 'or "read again" has to be understood as a *second* reading of the confession which Luther had read for the first time and in the first form prior to or on May 15; see p. 297. And further, Clemen argues, Luther now read the confession "diligently and totally," because Melanchthon, on May 22, had voiced his unhappiness about Luther's May 15 summary judgment of the confession; see *WA, Br* 5, 336, and *ibid.*, 337, n. 16. Luther now, on July 3, wants to make sure that Melanchthon is aware that this time his, Luther's, judgment is based on a thorough study. Clemen's interpretation is impossible, for Luther does not use two adverbs (diligently, totally) but he uses an adverb and an adjective, which, in turn, have to be connected with *Apologia* and "reread." Clemen's interpretation would also be highly artificial. If we were to accept it, we would have to assume that by July 3 Luther had read the *Augsburg Confession* only once, i.e., in the form in which it was sent to him prior to May 15. This is hardly probable, especially in view of Melanchthon's May 22 statement (*WA, Br* 5, 336) that daily changes were being made in that form of the confession which Luther had seen prior to May 15, of Melanchthon's June 26/27 requests (see p. 328, n. 25) that Luther show where concessions to the papists could be made, and of Luther's tense expectation of news from Augsburg (see p. 336). In contrast to Clemen one may submit that immediately after receiving the confession Luther read it in order to reply to Melanchthon concerning any concessions which could be made to the opponents. His verdict is brief and simple: more than enough has been conceded; nothing further can possibly be conceded. See p. 328. Then Luther "reread" the whole confession diligently, probably several times, perhaps even taking notes, and sharpened his judgment. Finally on July 2 he read it again, and now on July 3 he gives a new verdict.

[7] Literally: "and it [i.e., the *Augsburg Confession*] pleases [me] very much."

[8] Some witnesses offer a text which has to be translated as: "It [the *Augsburg Confession*] errs and sins, however, in this one point in that it goes . . . to rule over us, and it strikes out against . . ." See also Excursus.

[9] Literally: "you make [or: act] against."

[10] Luke 19:14.

builders have rejected."[11] Where there is such great blindness and obstinacy of the demons what would you expect except rejection? For they[12] will not concede to us the title "builders," which they appropriate for themselves, and this is just.[13] We, however, have to be glorified with the title[s] "destroyers," "scatterers," "confusers," so that we might be counted among the evil-doers, since even the stone itself has been rejected, counted among the robbers, and condemned [as one of them].[14] Therefore we have no other hope for salvation than in the Lord alone;[15] he has to do the wondrous deeds, and he will not desert this stone, for it follows: "This [stone] has been made the cornerstone. This has been done by the Lord, however, not by us; therefore it is marvelous before our eyes."[16] But more on this at another place.[17]

May Christ strengthen you and us,[18] comfort [you] with his Spirit, and deal with us according to all his wondrous deeds. Amen.

Give my respectful greetings to all our friends.[19]

From the wilderness,[20] *July 3, 1530*   Yours,

MARTIN LUTHER

---

[11] Ps. 118:22.

[12] I.e., the papists.

[13] I.e., because the papists are the builders of Ps. 118:22 who have rejected Christ, the cornerstone.

[14] Mark 15:28. Literally: ". . . rejected [and] with the robbers condemned and counted [as one of them]."

[15] While this is a statement of Luther's faith, it is also directed against Melanchthon's hopeful efforts to work out, by concessions, a peaceful solution of the whole Reformation issue.

[16] Ps. 118:22 f.

[17] It is not clear to what Luther is referring here. He could have been thinking of a future letter, or some book(s) on which he was working, or, and this seems to be most probable, of his *Das schöne Confitemini, an der zal der 118 Psalm* (*The Beautiful Confitemini, The 118th of the Psalms*) (Wittenberg, Hans Lufft, August, 1530), WA 31[1], 65 ff., esp. 171 ff.; LW 14, 43 ff., esp. 96 ff. On June 30 Luther wrote of this booklet to John Brenz, saying that he had been verbose in writing it, and that it was now being printed at Wittenberg. See WA, Br 5, 418 f.; see also WA, Br 5, 401.

[18] Literally: "you, with us, and comfort."

[19] Literally: "Greet respectfully all our [friends]."

[20] See p. 287, n. 1.

Excursus

On July 8 Melanchthon answered letter No. 218 (WA, Br 5, No. 1629). It has to be pointed out that Melanchthon in no way mentioned Luther's criticism. Did Melanchthon properly understand Luther's criticism, but simply bypass it because he saw that, in view of his own hopes to accomplish religious peace through negotiations (see p. 328; WA, Br 5, 475), any discussions between himself and Luther would be futile? Or did Melanchthon misunderstand Luther's criticism, and see in it "only" the growling of the "old man" who was still in a bad mood because of the long period of silence (see pp. 326 ff.; WA, Br 5, No. 1616, Introduction)? More important than these questions, however, is the nature of Luther's criticism itself, especially since it stands in sharp contrast to Luther's repeatedly voiced enthusiastic approval of the *Augsburg Confession* (see e.g., pp. 297, 354, 368). While it is not the task of this Excursus to unravel this knot, the text of the letter requires some commentary on Luther's criticism voiced above, pp. 343 f.

There is a parallel between Luther's opinion concerning the final form of the *Augsburg Confession* and that which he voiced on May 15 about the first draft of the final form of the confession (see pp. 297 f.). In both cases Luther approves of and is pleased with the confession, in both cases he is critical. On May 15 he is critical when he states that he could not have "stepped so softly and quietly"; one may submit that Luther meant to say that he certainly would not or could not have presented the issues in the way in which Melanchthon did. Now, on July 3, Luther is more specific in his criticism: something is wrong and contrary to Scripture. But what is wrong?

Von Schubert (LaK, 151 f.) sees here a criticism of the *Augsburg Confession* itself. Developing this argument, one may submit that Luther apparently misses a clear rejection of the false doctrine of the papists about Christ's fundamental position in the process of salvation and the life of the church. For according to von Schubert, in a July 21 letter to Jonas, Luther clarifies his criticism of July 3. In this letter to Jonas Luther points out that the confession "steps softly" (WA, Br 5, 496) by not openly dealing with purgatory, with the veneration of the saints, and especially with the pope as Antichrist. The citation of Luke 19:14 and Psalm 118:22 f. on July 3 would then have to be understood in the light of this July 21 statement. Luther criticizes the confession for not dealing with a "theology of the papacy"; he sees here a fundamental weakness and a dimming of the *solus Christus,* the sovereign rule of Christ (Luke 19:14), and this for the sake of "stepping softly." Purgatory and the veneration of the saints, while important, would have to be considered as adjuncts to this.

Clemen seems to affirm von Schubert's interpretation (see WA,

Br 5, 436 n. 4). Both von Schubert and Clemen could have strengthened their argumentation by referring to the textual variations cited above in note 8. At this point it would have been necessary for them to investigate the text tradition of this letter in order to answer the question whether the witnesses according to which Luther's criticism was directed against the confession itself do not make available a text of which it can reliably be shown that it was copied from the autograph, or from a source closer to the autograph than the source(s) used by the other witnesses, according to which the criticism was directed against Melanchthon personally.

Von Schubert's interpretation has not remained unchallenged. Rückert argues (*Deutsche Theologie* 3 [1936], 72 ff.) that Luther's criticism does not refer to the confession itself, but to Melanchthon's overall behavior, that is, to his worries, hopes, and actions. According to Rückert, Luther meant to say that Melanchthon should not complain that the disciples of Christ are exposed to the same fate as the master.

It is irrelevant whether Luther directs his criticism (exclusively) toward the confession itself, or (exclusively) toward Melanchthon's behavior, because Luther did not in the past, nor does he now, separate Melanchthon and the confession. For Luther the confession is Melanchthon's work (see pp. 298, n. 13; 330), and it is written in a Melanchthonian and not a Lutheran way. The object of criticism is Melanchthon, the man, the theologian, the author of the confession, and consequently the product of this man's pen, that is, the confession itself.

Suffice it to say that Luther's statement was puzzling to those who read it. Since it is unlikely that the textual variations cited above in note 8, are copy errors, one can submit that the copyist, perhaps being puzzled by Luther's statements and perhaps even having an insight into Luther's attitude toward Melanchthon and the confession, altered their source(s) somewhat in an attempt to clarify the text and to free Melanchthon from Luther's criticism. This assumption presupposes, of course, that Luther indeed wrote in such a way that the criticism was directed against Melanchthon personally. On the other hand, if this assumption is wrong, and if Luther had written in such a way that the criticism was directed against the confession rather than against Melanchthon personally then those copyists who furnish the text according to which Melanchthon was the target of Luther's criticism would have tampered with their sources(s) in an attempt to free the confession from Luther's criticism. Only a careful analysis of the text tradition can—perhaps—answer this question.

As Vogelsang has convincingly demonstrated (*Deutsche Theologie* 3 [1936], 247 ff.) the "Melanchthon—confession" alternative does not do justice to Luther's criticism. A look at the text confirms this argument. Luther wrote (see p. 343; "and I am tremendously pleased. . . ."):

et placet vehementer [subject: *tua apologia*]. *Sed erras et peccas in uno.* . . . The adversative conjunction *sed* denotes the opposition to *placet vehementer* for which *tua apologia* is the subject. Consequently the opposition is connected with the *placet* regarding the *Apologia,* and not with anything that is mentioned in the following sentence. One has to add, then, after *sed* something like *in tua Apologia,* or *in scribendo tuae Apologiae,* so that the sentence would have to be paraphrased: "Your *Apologia* pleases me tremendously. But notwithstanding this, my honest approval of your work, I have to tell you that in writing the *Apologia* [understood in the broadest sense possible, that is, a context provided in the following sentences] you err and sin. . . ." The *man and his work* are the target of Luther's criticism, not only here in this letter but also in Luther's general reactions to the events in Augsburg.

On the one hand, having received the confession, Luther voiced his wholehearted approval and simply stated that "we" have made enough concessions, that nothing further was to be conceded, and that not a hair's breadth was to be abandoned (see pp. 328, 333; WA 30^{II}, 390; Schubert, LaK, 152). As early as July 15, 1530, Luther admonished Jonas, Spalatin, Melanchthon, and Agricola not to speculate that unity in doctrinal matters might be accomplished, but to return home (see letter No. 224). Luther was then quite taken aback when he found out that his friends remained in Augsburg, and that the negotiations were to be continued (see p. 382). While Luther expected nothing from these negotiations conducted at Augsburg (see especially p. 413), he did hope that peaceful coexistence of evangelicals and papists could be accomplished (see p. 369).

On the other hand, Luther apparently decided to make up for Melanchthon's "softness." As von Schubert has pointed out (LaK, 152), Luther was working on a booklet on purgatory (WA 30^{II}, 360 ff.) at least as early as June 30 (see also WA 31^{I}, 339). Luther was thus dealing with one of the topics which he said on July 21 was not sufficiently dealt with in the confession. Luther intended to begin a "new struggle" against the papacy (see WA, Br 5, 419 [to John Brenz, June 30, 1530]; WA 30^{II}, 367 f.). He started out by dealing with purgatory, which had been controversial since the days of the indulgence controversy. Apparently he was thinking of then treating the mass and other *historien,* among them apparently the papacy as Antichrist. (See WA 30^{II}, 390, 471, n. 2). Whatever Luther's literary plans at this point were, his literary productivity of 1530 certainly compensated for Melanchthon's "softly stepping;" one of the reasons for Luther's comparatively general statements, both in his July 3 letter to Melanchthon, and in his July 21 letter to Jonas, might have been the fact that Luther did not consider it necessary to go into details, in view of the booklets which he was about to write or to publish.

To Nicholas Hausmann
Coburg, July 6, 1530

*Taking advantage of an available messenger, Luther reports some
of the news he has received concerning the Diet of Augsburg: The
Augsburg Confession, to which seven sovereigns and two city councils have subscribed, has been read in the Emperor's presence; now
a reply to the confession is being written; many bishops wish
peace; at least one bishop supposedly considered the confession a
document of truth, and the Duke of Brunswick affirmed the truth
of "certain articles"; the friends in Augsburg are being treated well,
and all are full of praise for the Emperor's kind attitude toward the
evangelicals. Luther ends the letter with a brief reference to a correspondence matter, a blessing, and greetings to the friends.*
On Nicholas Hausmann, see LW 48, 399 f.
Text in Latin: WA, Br 5, 440.

To the venerable Mr. Nicholas Hausmann,[1]
a faithful and most sincere bishop of the church[2] at Zwickau

Grace and peace in Christ. Better than I can write it, this our
February, or Hornung,[3] will tell you, excellent Sir, all the things
which happened both at Augsburg and here at my place. After
Hornung's arrival here,[4] however, Dr. Jonas wrote[5] to me that our
confession[6] (which our Philip[7] prepared) has been publicly read

---

[1] Literally: "To the venerable man, Mr. Nicholas . . ."
[2] See pp. 87, n. 5; 61, n. 9.
[3] I.e., Wolf Hornung; see p. 326, n. 11. He had brought to the Coburg
Melanchthon's June 27 letters to Luther and Dietrich (WA, Br 5, No. 1607).
Hornung, a different name for February, is one of the names from Charle-
magne's calendar which is still occasionally used in present-day German.
[4] He arrived at the Coburg on June 29; see p. 326. Clemen suggests (WA,
Br 5, 441, n. 1) that Hornung apparently stayed with Luther at the Coburg
till July 6. See also WA, Br 5, 403, n. 2.
[5] Justus Jonas (see LW 48, 275, n. 3) to Luther: Augsburg, June 30, 1530
(?); WA, Br 5, No. 1618. This letter is extant only as a fragment. Not all the
news reported by Luther to Hausmann can be found in this fragment. "D.
Jonas" has been added on the margin of the autograph.
[6] I.e., the *Augsburg Confession.*
[7] I.e., here and throughout this letter Philip Melanchthon; see LW 48, 77,

348

by Dr. Christian,[8] our Sovereign's[9] chancellor, right in the palace of the Emperor,[10] [and] in the presence of the Emperor and of the sovereigns and bishops of the whole Empire; only the crowd of the common people were excluded. To the confession have subscribed:[11] first, the Sovereign [and] Elector of Saxony, then Margrave George of Brandenburg, John Frederick, the Electoral prince,

---

n. 3. Luther considered the *Augsburg Confession* to be Melanchthon's work, even though he was aware of the facts that in drafting the confession Melanchthon was assisted by others, and that Melanchthon worked in behalf of "all of us" (see the two references to "our confession" and "our Philip").
[8] I.e., Dr. jur. Christian Beyer, the chancellor of the Electoral Saxon government. Beyer had been chancellor since approximately February 1, 1529. At that date Gregory Brück (see pp. 51 f.) "retired" from the office of chancellor and became "Alt-Kanzler," i.e., senior chancellor, or chancellor emeritus. Notwithstanding this retirement Brück remained very active in the political affairs of Electoral Saxony. Freed from the administrative duties of the chancellery, which were taken over by Beyer, Brück functioned as "consultant" to the Elector, and concentrated on shaping policy. See Fabian, *ESBV* (2nd ed.), pp. 344 f. On Christian Beyer, see *NDB* 2, 204.
[9] I.e., here and throughout this letter, Elector John; see *LW* 48, 269, n. 8.
[10] I.e., here and throughout this letter, Emperor Charles V; see *LW*, 48, 175 f. See also Elector John to Luther: Augsburg, June 25, 1530, in the morning; *WA*, Br 5, 395; Reu II, 309. The Elector reported in this letter that in spite of many efforts, the public reading (i.e., the reading in a plenary session of the diet) of the German version of the confession could not be accomplished because Ferdinand of Austria (see *LW* 48, 217, n. 17, and in this vol., p. 223) and the papists were successful in fighting against this public presentation of the confession. Consequently the confession would be read in the Emperor's chambers (located in the palace of the bishop of Augsburg) during a private audience, where not many people could be present. The confession was read on Saturday, June 25, between 3:00 or 4:00 P.M. and 6:00 P.M., in the Emperor's private chapel, in the presence of approximately two hundred sovereigns and officials. See Justus Jonas to Luther: Augsburg June 25, 1530; *WA*, Br 5, 392; Reu II, 308. See also the fragment of the Jonas letter mentioned in note 5 (*WA*, Br 5, 427), and *WA*, Br 5, 393, n. 7. For further details concerning the reading of the confession, see Reu I, 110 ff.; II, 310 ff.; Walter, RA, 52 f. For a view of the events set forth by the opponents of the evangelicals, see *TP*, pp. 76 ff.; *NB* I.Abt.,E.1, No. 18 (Campeggio's report to Rome, dated June 26).
[11] On the subscribers to the *Augsburg Confession*, and the negotiations that preceded their signing, see *Die Bekenntnis-Schriften, op. cit.* (see p. 328, n. 24), pp. xvi ff., 136 f.; Gussmann, *QFGAG* 1¹, *passim;* Walter, RA, 48 ff.; Reu I, 95 ff. The list of subscribers given by Luther cannot be found in Jonas' letter mentioned in note 5. As early as June 25 Jonas had given Luther a list of the names of those who had signed the confession, in which list the name of Duke Francis of Brunswick-Lüneburg was missing, however; see *WA*, Br 5, 392; Reu II, 308. Perhaps in the no-longer extant part of Jonas' letter, mentioned in note 5, Jonas had given another, complete list; or perhaps Luther knew of the fact that Duke Francis had signed the confession from Spalatin or Agricola; see *WA*, Br 5, Nos. 1608, 1617; see also Enders, *Briefwechsel* 8, 82, n. 3.

and the Landgrave of Hesse, Ernest and Francis, the dukes of Lüneburg, the Sovereign Wolfgang of Anhalt, the city of Nürnberg, and the city of Reutlingen. Now the Emperor's party[12] is deliberating on an answer [to the confession].[13] Many bishops[14] are inclined to peace and despise the sophists Faber and Eck.[15] It is said that one bishop stated in a private conversation: "This is the pure truth, we cannot deny it."[16] The [Archbishop of] Mainz is said to be very concerned for peace.[17] So is the Duke of Brunswick,[18] who in a friendly gesture invited Philip to dinner [and] testified[19] that

---

[12] Literally: "the Imperials."

[13] Luther knew this from two of Melanchthon's letters; one was dated June 26 (WA, Br 5, 397), the other was dated June 30 (WA, Br 5, 423). In the fragment of the Jonas letter mentioned in note 5 this information does not appear. Even though the opponents of the evangelicals, especially the theologians, refused at the beginning of the diet to abide by the Summons (see pp. 280 f.), and to submit an "opinion," they were forced to do so by the Emperor after the Augsburg Confession had been presented. On June 27 the opposition issued a memorandum, and the papal legate, Campeggio, also drafted a memorandum; this material was presented to the Emperor, who forwarded it to the pro-papal Estates of the diet on July 5. On July 7 these Estates issued an opinion to the effect that a general council of the church should deal with the Augsburg Confession, that in the meantime the common grievances against the Roman See should be settled, and that the Emperor should seek peace and unity with the evangelicals, a task for which the pro-papal Estates offered their help. Apparently as early as June 27 these Estates had suggested that the theologians prepare a refutation of the confession, and on July 5 Campeggio reported to Rome that the work on the refutation had begun. See Reu I, 115 ff.; II, No. 41; Walter, RA, 58 ff.; TP, pp. 79 ff.; NB I.Abt.,E.1, No. 19.

[14] For an example see note 16.

[15] I.e., John Faber (see p. 41, n. 35) and John Eck (see LW 48, 80, n. 13, and in this vol., p. 296, n. 3). This news cannot be found in the fragment of the Jonas letter mentioned in note 5, even though Luther could read there of Faber's and Eck's agitations against the evangelicals; see WA, Br 5, 427. See also Philip Melanchthon to Luther: Augsburg, June 30; WA, Br 5, 423.

[16] According to the fragment of the Jonas letter mentioned in note 5, this was Christopher Stadion, the bishop of Augsburg; WA, Br 5, 427. See also Philip Melanchthon to Luther: Augsburg, June 30; WA, Br 5, 423. On Stadion, who was a strong supporter of the Erasmian reform program, see H. P. Schmauch, Christoph von Stadion (1478–1543), Bischof von Augsburg, (1517–1543) und seine Stellung zur Reformation (Munich: Phil. Diss., 1956).

[17] On Cardinal Albrecht von Brandenburg, archbishop of Mainz, see LW 48, 44 f.; see also note 19.

[18] On Duke Henry of Brunswick, see also p. 82, n. 4.

[19] Luther's sources for the news concerning the Archbishop of Mainz and the Duke of Brunswick were the following letters: Justus Jonas to Luther: Augsburg, June 13, 1530; WA, Br 5, 362 (the meeting between Melanchthon and the Duke); Philip Melanchthon to Luther: Augsburg, June 13, 1530; WA, Br 5, 365 (the meeting between Melanchthon and the Duke, which took

he certainly could not deny the articles dealing with "both kinds," the marriage of priests, and the [religiously] indifferent quality of [all] food.[20] There is no one in this whole diet whom our friends praise more highly for his placidness than the Emperor himself.[21]

---

place on June 13); Justus Jonas to Luther: Augsburg, June 18, 1530; WA, Br 5, 369 (the Archbishop and the Duke are behaving decently); Philip Melanchthon to Luther: Augsburg, June 19, 1530; WA, Br 5, 371 (the Archbishop and the Duke have sympathy for "our" situation); Philip Melanchthon to Luther: Augsburg, June 30, 1530; WA, Br 5, 423. In the fragment of the Jonas letter mentioned in note 5 the news concerning the Archbishop and the Duke is missing. To strengthen the Archbishop's sympathy for the cause of the evangelicals, Luther addressed him on July 6, 1530, in an open letter. Luther urged the Archbishop to become a German Gamaliel (Acts 5:34 ff.), and to take the initiative in promoting a drive for peaceful coexistence within the Empire between evangelicals and papists, and thus to avoid the spectacle of civil war, which would give the highest pleasure to the Pope and the Italians. Luther added a brief exposition of Psalm 2 to impress on his addressee the utter futility of struggling against the sovereignty of Christ and the gospel. Text: WA 30^{II}, 397 ff.; Reu II, 319 ff.

[20] See *Augsburg Confession*, Arts. XXII, XXIII, XXVI; for "both kinds," see LW 48, 143. In his June 13 letter to Luther, Jonas wrote: "Among other things, this Duke [Henry] of Brunswick has discussed with Philip [Melanchthon] certain excellent ideas concerning the common [public] cause. For he said that for sometime now . . . he has been reading in the New Testament and has gained much fruit from this reading. He realizes that the freedom of "both kinds," etc., the marriage of priests, the freedom concerning monastic [vows], etc., the abolition of bought masses, etc., [and] freedom in [matters of] food are articles of such nature as could not in justice be condemned, and that in these matters, with God's help, ways to unity could be found." WA, Br 5, 362. According to this report, the Duke had an "evangelical" attitude also concerning the mass, a fact which Luther did not communicate to Hausmann. It would be another question whether Melanchthon had correctly interpreted the Duke's position to Jonas, or whether Melanchthon did not see more in the Duke's position than was actually there. In the letter fragment mentioned in note 5 Jonas reported to Luther (WA, Br 5, 427 f.) that the Archbishop of Salzburg supposedly had said the following in private: "I would wish that "both kinds," and matrimony were [a matter of choice]; I [also] would wish that the mass be reformed, [and] that there be freedom in matters of food [i.e., the fasting regulations] and other traditions [i.e., ecclesiastical customs], and that so [good] order would prevail. But that one corner [in the Empire, i.e., Wittenberg and Luther] should reform us all, this is disturbing the peace; this cannot be tolerated." This is an interesting statement, since in other letters from Augsburg Luther's friends describe the archbishop of Salzburg, Matthew Lang (see LW 48, 99, n. 14), as an enemy of their cause; see WA, Br 5, 387, 389 f.; see also, *ibid.*, 412. On the other hand it is very probable that Lang made such a statement, because he was a supporter of the Erasmian reform program, and the statement attributed to him was typical of that program.

[21] The sources for this information are the letters from Augsburg written by Luther's friends after the Emperor had arrived in Augsburg on June 15. See WA, Br 5, 371, 386, 427 (the fragment mentioned in note 5), 435.

This is the way things are now at the beginning [of the diet]. The Emperor treats our Sovereign not only with kindness, but almost respectfully; so writes Philip.[22] It is astonishing how all are filled with affection and applause for the Emperor. Perhaps, by God's will, as the first emperor was a very bad one,[23] so this last [emperor] will be a very good one.[24] Let us only pray, for the power of prayer is certainly felt.

Since all this [news is] true, you may communicate it to Cordatus[25] and all the brethren. I believe that you have in the meantime received my letter to you,[26] and [the one to] your brother.[27]

The Lord be with you. Amen. Greet all our [friends].

From the wilderness,[28] *July 6, 1530*   Yours,

MARTIN LUTHER

---

[22] See Philip Melanchthon to Luther: Augsburg, June 25, 1530; *WA*, Br 5, 386. The Emperor had good reasons for attempting to gain Elector John's good will (especially after the rather sharp confrontation concerning the matter of preaching; see p. 339, n. 10) and his cooperation, especially for the matter of defending the Empire against the Turks. Tetleben recorded on June 22 a conference of sovereigns in which it was decided that the matter of faith was to be settled first, before any other business would be enacted; *TP*, p. 71. See also *WA*, Br 5, 428, n. 1.

[23] This is perhaps a reference to the Diet of Worms (the *first*, and until the Diet of Augsburg the only diet over which Emperor Charles personally presided) and the Edict of Worms (see *LW* 48, 210). See also note 24.

[24] In the letter fragment mentioned in note 5 Jonas wrote to Luther that he, Jonas, had this time studied the Emperor's face more carefully than ten years ago at Worms, and it seemed that all things pointed toward the fact that the Emperor had a gracious royal heart and a certain *humanitas*; see *WA*, Br 5, 427. Perhaps this reference to Worms prompted Luther's statement above. "First emperor" would have to be understood as a reference to Charles V's first diet (i.e., the Diet of Worms), while "last [emperor]" would have to be understood as a reference to the latest diet at which the Emperor was present, i.e., the Diet of Augsburg.

[25] Conrad Cordatus; see p. 284, n. 19. See also letter No. 220.

[26] Luther to Nicholas Hausmann: Coburg, June 25, 1530; *WA*, Br 5, No. 1599; Luther enclosed with this letter a no-longer extant letter of comfort for Hausmann's brother.

[27] I.e., Valentin Hausmann, with whom Luther repeatedly exchanged letters, none of which seems to be extant. For some information on Valentin Hausmann, who in 1560 became the city judge in Freiberg/Saxony, see *WA*, Br 3, 304, n. 1; 13, 66, *ad loc.*

[28] See p. 287, n. 1.

220

To Conrad Cordatus[1]
Coburg, July 6, 1530

*Announcing Wolfgang Hornung as the carrier of a letter to Haus-
mann and as source for news concerning the Diet of Augsburg,
Luther informs Cordatus that the Augsburg Confession has been
read in the Emperor's presence, notwithstanding great efforts on
the part of the papists to prevent this. Meditating on the public
presentation of the confession, Luther expresses his joy over the
fact that he could have lived to this day and have experienced this
moment; for him Psalm 119:46 is fulfilled, and this is for him a
pledge that Matthew 10:32 will be fulfilled. In the last paragraph
Luther mentions a book which describes the pomp surrounding the
Emperor's entrance into Augsburg. He encourages Cordatus to
pray, especially for the Emperor, for Elector John, and for Philip
Melanchthon. In closing, Luther assures Cordatus that he will call
him to come to Augsburg if he, Luther, is summoned there, and
adds a brief benediction.*

On Conrad Cordatus, see p. 284, n. 19.

Text in Latin: WA, Br 5, 441–442.

Grace and peace in Christ

Here you have, dearest Cordatus, one living and one not living
letter; that is, February[2] in person, and my letter to your bishop,[3]
from which you will be able to find out all that I now know about
this diet. Therefore I have nothing further to write to you.

Jonas writes[4] that he was in the audience when, for two whole
hours,[5] the confession[6] of our [friends] was read by Dr. Christian,[7]

---

[1] The autograph of this letter is no longer extant. While in all witnesses the
address is missing, it is clear to whom Luther was writing, since the name of
the addressee is mentioned in the first sentence.
[2] I.e., Wolfgang Hornung; see p. 326, n. 11.
[3] See letter No. 219.
[4] Justus Jonas; see LW 48, 275, n. 3, and in this vol., p. 348, n. 5.
[5] See p. 349, n. 10.
[6] I.e., the *Augsburg Confession.*
[7] I.e., Christian Beyer; see p. 349, n. 8.

and that he had studied[8] the facial expressions of all [present],[9] about which he promises to give me a personal report.[10] I have a copy of the confession here,[11] but I am under orders to retain it.[12] The opponents[13] certainly finagled and struggled[14] to keep the Emperor[15] from permitting [the confession to be read], or from listening to it. And so, the confession could not be read publicly in a plenary session of the diet;[16] this [our opponents] accomplished. Finally, by the Emperor's order the confession was presented[17] and read before the [whole diet],[18] that is, [only] before the sovereigns and estates of the Empire.

I am tremendously pleased to have lived to this moment when Christ, by his staunch confessors, has publicly been proclaimed in such a great assembly by means of this really most beautiful confession.[19] And [so the word] is fulfilled: "I spoke of your testimonies in the presence of kings." What follows will [also] be fulfilled: "And I was not put to shame."[20] For "whoever will confess

---

[8] Literally: "seen."

[9] In the extant fragment of the Jonas letter mentioned on p. 348, n. 5, Jonas said only that he had "contemplated" the Emperor's facial expression; the whole context in which this statement can be found in the fragment suggests that this contemplation took place during the reading of the *Augsburg Confession*.

[10] In the fragment of the Jonas letter mentioned on p. 348, n. 5, this promise does not appear.

[11] See p. 328.

[12] See Melanchthon's letters to Veit Dietrich and to Luther, dated June 26 and 27, 1530; *WA*, Br 5, Nos. 1604, 1607. According to these letters the Emperor had ordered that the confession not be published; according to Melanchthon, Elector John had promised the Emperor to make great efforts to keep the confession from being spread among the public. In forwarding a copy of the confession to the Coburg, Melanchthon therefore admonished his friends not to release it to anyone else. Immediately after the reading of the confession, the Emperor informed the subscribers and others present not to publish the confession without his special permission; see *URA* 2, No. 108. See also *WA*, Br 13, 145, to *WA*, Br 5, 396, n. 1.

[13] I.e., the papal party in Augsburg.

[14] Literally: "It has certainly been provided for and extraordinarily worked for by the opponents that the Emperor neither admit nor listen to [the confession]. . . ."

[15] I.e., here and throughout this letter, Emperor Charles V; see *LW* 48, 175 f.

[16] Literally: "before the common Empire." For the diet, see *LW* 48, 70, n. 1.

[17] Literally: "turned over [i.e., to the diet]."

[18] Literally: ". . . be read in the presence of the whole Empire . . ."

[19] See perhaps I Tim. 6:12.

[20] Ps. 119:46. See also Luther's letter to Cardinal Albrecht, archbishop of Mainz (see p. 350, n. 19); *WA* 30[II], 398; Reu II, 320. This verse became the motto of the *editio princeps* of the Latin text of the *Augsburg Confession*.

me" (so he who does not lie states) "before men, him I also shall confess before my Father who is in heaven."[21]

Concerning other matters, (I believe) you will have found out all the news from others.[22] Now[23] [a booklet has been published] describing the pomp of the Emperor's entrance into Augsburg.[24] I have to see and feel with my hands that in truth God is called [in] Psalm 62[25] "listener to prayers"; it is right and deserved that God be praised throughout the whole world with this title. Therefore do continue to pray and to kindle all [you meet] to prayer, especially for the Emperor,[26] that excellent young man who is worthy of God's and man's love; and then [also] for our Sovereign,[27] who is not less good, [yet] carries a heavier cross, and for Philip,[28] who miserably tortures himself with worries.[29]

---

[21] Matt. 10:32.

[22] Persons or letters? While it is not certain of which specific source of information Luther was thinking, it is most probable that he was referring here either to any one of the following letters and circumstances, or to all of them together: June 19, 1530, to Cordatus (WA, Br 5, No. 1596; the next sentence above [see note 24] suggests strongly that Luther was especially thinking of this June 19 letter); perhaps a no-longer extant letter to Valentin Hausmann (see p. 352, n. 27), of which Luther announced on June 19 to Cordatus that he hoped to write it "one of these days" (WA, Br 5, 381); on June 25 Luther informed Hausmann that this letter had been written (WA, Br 5, 385); June 25, 1530, to Hausmann (WA, Br 5, No. 1599); the direct forwarding of letters and news to Hausmann from Wittenberg, of which Luther said on June 25 to Hausmann that he, Luther, had ordered the friends in Wittenberg to do this (WA, Br 5, 385); July 6, 1530, to Hausmann (letter No. 219); and the messengers for some of these letters.

[23] Literally: "Indeed."

[24] In his June 19 letter Luther informed Cordatus of the Emperor's entrance into Augsburg; WA, Br 5, 381. As if to continue this letter, Luther informs Cordatus on July 6 that "now indeed" this entrance has been described in a booklet. For bibliographical information on the pamphlets which describe this event, see WA, Br 5, 442 f.; for texts, see URA 1, No. 92. It is dubious whether one may connect this passage with Spalatin's report (mentioned on p. 334, n. 4), as do Rückert, LB, p. 319, n. 15, and WA, Br 13, 154, to WA, Br 5, 442, n. 7.

[25] Some witnesses read: Ps. 82. It cannot be established of which passage Luther was thinking. Enders, Briefwechsel 8, 84, n. 9, suggests Ps. 61:5; St. L. 16, 915, suggests Ps. 65:3; Rückert, LB, p. 319, n. 17, suggests Ps. 62, even though Rückert argues that the key phrase "listener to prayers" cannot be found in this Psalm; yet according to Rückert the whole mood of the Psalm would fit Luther's thought.

[26] See also p. 352.

[27] Elector John of Saxony; see LW 48, 269, n. 8.

[28] Philip Melanchthon; see LW 48, 77, n. 3; see also, in this vol., 336, n. 18.

[29] On June 19, 1530, Luther asked Gabriel Zwilling (see LW 48, 39, n. 3) and his congregation to pray for the Elector and the whole diet; WA, Br 5, 382.

Should I be summoned [to Augsburg], I shall call you too; don't doubt it.[30]

The Lord be with you. Amen.

From the wilderness,[31] *July 6, 1530*   Yours,

MARTIN LUTHER

221

To Lazarus Spengler[1]
Coburg, July 8, 1530

In reply to a question from Spengler as to whether the seal had turned out to be correct, Luther gives a detailed interpretation of his seal, the Luther rose, in which he sees a "compendium" of his theology.

On June 25, 1530, Jonas informed Luther[2] that the Electoral prince, Duke John Frederick,[3] had ordered that Luther's rose be executed in a "beautiful stone," and mounted in gold, and that the Duke had the intention of presenting this Petschaft (seal) to Luther in person. An entry in the Electoral Saxon financial records, noting for August 22, 1530, expenses for a signet ring, could most probably be applied to this information.[4] On September 15, 1530, Luther in-

---

[30] See p. 284, n. 19.

[31] See p. 287, n. 1.

[1] To the many printed witnesses listed in *WA,* Br 5, No. 1628, Introduction, (see also Enders, *Briefwechsel* 8, No. 1701), has to be added a manuscript copy which seems to have its origin with Spengler's descendants, and which in contrast to most of the other witnesses dates from the 16th century. Consequently chances are excellent that the text of this manuscript copy (which hereafter is referred to as Spengler manuscript copy) is more closely related to the no-longer extant autograph than the text of any other extant witness. The readings of the Spengler manuscript copy which differ from the *textus receptus* are printed in *WA,* Br 13, 155, to *WA,* Br 5, 444, No. 1628. The address and the signature are missing in the *textus receptus.* In the Spengler manuscript copy there follows after the date: *Martinus Luther suo Spenglero,* i.e., "Martin Luther to his [friend] Spengler."

[2] *WA,* Br 5, 393.

[3] *LW* 48, 181 f. He was also in Augsburg.

[4] See *ARG* 25 (1928), 50, 85 f.; H. Volz (*WA,* DB 11[II], 377, n. 11; *WA,* Br 13, 154, to *WA,* Br 5, 444, No. 1628; 13, 144, to *WA,* Br 5, 394, n. 17) suggests that this entry is to be connected with this ring, and he is more positive in suggesting this than Clemen in *WA,* Br 5, 394, n. 17. There is no material available, however, which is compelling enough to assume that this suggestion is more than a probability.

formed Melanchthon that the Duke (who had left Augsburg before the other members of the Electoral Saxon party, and who had visited Luther) had presented him with a golden ring.[5] It cannot be said with certainty[6] that this ring was a signet ring, and that this gift was the seal which Jonas mentioned on June 25; it is probable that the ring of which Luther wrote on September 15 and the seal of which Jonas wrote on June 25 were identical. However, Jonas wrote of a Petschaft (seal)[7] in which the rose would be cut in a (precious ?) stone, which was to be mounted in gold. Luther, on the other hand, wrote of a golden anulus, which means first of all a finger ring; it can also mean a signet ring, though for this term signatorius would usually be added, or even used as a synonym. And further, it has to remain an open question whether the ring, which Luther mentioned on September 15, has to be seen in connection with this present letter to Spengler. Had Luther ordered a seal[8] in Nürnberg? Or did Luther's friends in Nürnberg want to make a present to Luther? Only the fact that Spengler sent a drawing of the Luther rose to the Coburg is certain. It is generally assumed[9] that Duke John Frederick had a signet ring made in Nürnberg, and that Spengler sent a drawing of it to the Coburg.[10]

---

[5] WA, Br 5, 623. Another of Luther's rings was his "doctor ring" which shows in a heartlike shield the symbol of the Trinity, the three interwoven rings; for a picture, see P. Schreckenbach et al. (eds.), Martin Luther. Ein Bild seines Lebens und Wirkens (Leipzig, 1921), p. 57.

[6] As, e.g., Rückert (LB, p. 389, n. 27) and Clemen (WA, Br 5, 623, n. 12) did.

[7] Petschaft (see Trübner 5, s.v. Petschaft), originating in the language of the Bohemian chancellery, is the equivalent of the Latin sigillum which, if used in connection with diplomatics, means seal (see Trübner 6, s.v. Siegel). Already in medieval sphragistics sigillum could mean a seal as this term is understood at present, and not a signet ring. One may not simply equate Petschaft with signet ring, even though a ring functioned very often as a Petschaft.

[8] Luther used several seals. O. Thulin (A Life of Luther Told in Pictures and Narrative by the Reformer and His Contemporaries [Philadelphia, 1966], p. 35) reproduces three forms of the rose and two antique cameos (one representing a yoke of horses, and one an antique goddess). Unfortunately Thulin does not say, nor do the pictures give any definite clues, whether these seals were seals as this term is understood at present (i.e., Petschaft), or whether they were signet rings; from the pictures they appear to be seals.

[9] WA, Br 5, No. 1628, Introduction; Rückert, LB, p. 320, n. 2; WA, Br 13, 154, to WA, Br 5, 444, No. 1628.

[10] Before the readings of the Spengler manuscript copy had been printed in WA, Br 13, the fact that Spengler had sent a drawing of the seal to Luther was only assumed. See note 16. Whether this drawing had anything to do with the Duke's gift for Luther cannot be documented.

Luther created his own coat of arms by taking one symbol from his family's coat of arms. The Luther family coat of arms, supposedly granted to the family in 1413, shows a half of a crossbow standing to the right of two white roses which are placed one above the other.[11] The shield, which leans slightly to the left, is open to the left, and is crowned by a helmet which, in turn, is decorated with two horns. It is not known when Luther created his own coat of arms.[12] Some of the theological thoughts expressed in the present letter to Spengler can be found as early as 1516.[13] By 1519/20 the single rose was known to be Luther's emblem.[14]

On Lazarus Spengler, see LW 48, 184.

Text in German: WA, Br 5, 445.

Grace and peace in Christ!

Honorable, kind, dear Sir and Friend! Since you ask whether my seal[15] has come out correctly,[16] I shall answer most amiably and tell you of those thoughts which [now] come to my mind about my seal as a symbol of my theology.

There is first to be a cross, black [and placed] in a heart, which should be of its natural color, so that I myself would be reminded that faith in the Crucified saves us. For if one believes from the heart he will be justified.[17] Even though it is a black cross, [which] mortifies and [which] also should hurt us, yet it leaves the heart in its [natural] color [and] does not ruin nature; that is, [the

---

[11] For a picture, see Thulin, *op. cit.*, Illustration No. 1.

[12] Without any documentation, Thulin, *op. cit.*, p. 26, states that Luther did this in 1516.

[13] See e.g., Luther's April 8, 1516, letter to George Spenlein; *LW* 48, No. 4.

[14] Wolfgang Stöckel in Leipzig published one of Luther's sermons in 1520. The title page shows a woodcut of Luther (one of the oldest extant portraits of the Reformer) with the rose emblem. Since the woodcut is not too clear, one cannot determine whether the rose was already shown in the form now commonly known. For a picture, see Schreckenbach, *op. cit.*, p. 84.

[15] Luther wrote: *Petschaft.* This suggests a connection with the *Petschaft* mentioned by Jonas on June 25 (see note 2), and not with the *anulus* mentioned by Luther on September 15 (see note 5).

[16] The translation is based on the *textus receptus.* The text of the Spengler manuscript copy reads in translation: ". . . whether my coat of arms or seal (*Petschaft*) in the picture, which you have sent to me, has come out correctly . . ."

[17] Rom. 10:10.

cross] does not kill but keeps [man] alive. For the just man lives by faith,[18] but by faith in the Crucified One. Such a heart is to be in the midst of a white rose, to symbolize that faith gives joy, comfort, and peace; in a word it places the believer into a white joyful rose; for [this faith] does not give peace and joy[19] as the world gives and, therefore, the rose is to be white and not red, for white is the color of the spirits and of all the angels.[20] Such a rose is to be in a sky-blue field, [symbolizing] that such joy in the Spirit and in faith is a beginning of the future heavenly joy; it is already a part [of faith], and is grasped through hope, even though not yet manifest. And around[21] this field is a golden ring, [symbolizing] that in heaven such blessedness lasts forever and has no end, and in addition is precious beyond all joy and goods, just as gold is the most valuable[22] and precious metal.[23]

May Christ, our dear Lord, be with your spirit until the life to come.[24] Amen.

From the wilderness[25] *Grubok,*[26] *July 8, 1530*

222

To Elector John
[Coburg,] July 9, 1530

On July 3, in the evening, the Emperor consulted with those Imperial Estates who had remained faithful to the papal church, and set forth a program of action concerning the Augsburg Confession

---

[18] Rom. 1:17. This quotation and the continuation of the sentence (to "Crucified One") are written in Latin.

[19] John 14:27.

[20] See WA, Br 13, xxxii, to WA, Br 5, 445, n. 5.

[21] The translation is based on the Spengler manuscript copy.

[22] Literally: "the highest."

[23] In the Spengler manuscript copy a sentence is added which reads in literal translation: "I wished to have told you of this, my compendium of theology, in good friendship, and you will [accept it] in good part."

[24] Literally: ". . . your spirit until into that life [i.e., the life in the eschatological fulfillment just described]."

[25] These two words are written in Latin. See p. 287, n. 1.

[26] I.e., "Koburg" spelled backwards.

and its subscribers.[1] *News about this meeting reached Elector John of Saxony, who on July 4 requested Luther's opinion on the situation.*[2] *On July 5 the Elector's letter was dispatched to the tax collector in Coburg, Arnold von Falckenstein, with the request that Luther's answer be sent to Augsburg immediately.*[3] *Having received the Elector's letter on July 9, Luther replied that same day, and on July 15 Elector John acknowledged the receipt of letter No. 222.*[4]

On July 5 the Emperor, through some of his officials, presented to the pro-papal Estates a memorandum in which the program of action which had been discussed on July 3 was exactly formulated.[5] *On July 6 these Estates replied to the Emperor and, having suggested some modifications, endorsed this program.*[6] *Then, on July*

---

[1] See Elector John to Luther: Augsburg, July 4, 1530; WA, Br 5, 437. Besides the consecration of a bishop, Tetleben records for July 3 only a private meeting between the Emperor and the evangelical sovereigns (Elector of Saxony, Landgrave of Hesse, Margrave of Brandenburg-Ansbach); he gives no detailed information about this meeting, but he mentions his fears that nothing good came out of it. See TP, p. 81. On the events of July 3, see also BA, p. 100. On July 3 the Nürnberg delegation reported to the city council that the Elector of Saxony and the Landgrave of Hesse had met several times with the Emperor, who had attempted to influence them to abandon the confession; see C.R. 2, 161. On July 5 the Frankfurt delegates reported home about the business at Augsburg, the conferences between the Emperor and individual sovereigns, and the general secrecy concerning what was going on behind closed doors. While they admitted that they had little concrete to report, they also hinted that they knew something which they could not entrust to a letter. See BA, pp. 407 f. The July 3 meeting between the pro-papal Estates and the Emperor, mentioned by the Elector to Luther, indeed must have been a secret one.

[2] See Elector John to Luther: Augsburg, July 4, 1530; WA, Br 5, No. 1622.

[3] *Ibid.*, Introduction.

[4] Elector John to Luther: Augsburg, July 15, 1530; WA, Br 5, No. 1650.

[5] According to the report of the Frankfurt delegation, the Emperor and his brother Ferdinand, together with "the ladies," went hunting by 10 A.M. on July 5; see BA, p. 408. The meeting at which the memorandum was presented was an official session of the diet at city hall, from which the evangelicals were excluded; when very important questions were discussed, then even those members of the diet who were considered not absolutely "safe" were excluded from the deliberations. See BA, p. 101. For the meeting, the business transacted, and the memorandum, see ZKG 12 (1891), 120 ff.; TP, pp. 81 f.; Walter, RA, 55 ff.

[6] For the full text of the Estates' answer, see ZKG 12 (1891) 130 ff.; for a report on the July 6 meeting and an abstract of the Estates' answer, see TP, pp. 82 ff. (In Walter, RA, 58, July 7, given as date of the Estates' answer, has to be corrected to July 6.) For the Emperor's reply to the Estates' answer, see URA 2, No. 110. According to Elector John's July 4 letter to Luther, in their July 3 meeting the pro-papal Estates were not unanimous in their reaction to the program presented by the Emperor; see WA, Br 5, 438.

9, *the Imperial policy toward the confessors shifted into action.*
On that day the confessors were officially asked whether they would
wish to submit additional articles.[7] *Thus began the official negotia-*
tions between the Emperor and those who had signed the Augs-
burg Confession.
  On Elector John, see LW 48, 269, n. 8.
  Text in German: WA, Br 12, 117–119.[8]

To the Most Serene, Noble Sovereign and Lord, Sir John,
  duke in Saxony and elector, landgrave in Thuringia
  and margrave in Meissen, my Most Gracious Lord

Grace and peace in Christ. Most Serene, Noble Sovereign, Most
Gracious Lord. Today, on July 9, I have received your Electoral
Grace's letter, written on July 4,[9] and I have read[10] with joy that
Your Electoral Grace's general disposition has improved.[11] For
God knows that I write such letters[12] to Your Electoral Grace for
no reason other than that I worry that Satan (who is a master of
evil thoughts) might afflict Your Electoral Grace. Beyond this, I
certainly know and believe that our Lord Jesus Christ himself
comforts Your Electoral Grace's heart better than I or anyone else
would be able [to do]. This is established before our eyes by
facts.[13] For the opponents[14] think they have definitely won a vic-

---

[7] See URA 2, No. 113; WA, Br 5, No. 1637, Introduction.
[8] This text is based on the autograph, while the text in WA, Br 5, 453–455
is based on a manuscript copy.
[9] See note 2.
[10] Literally: "heard."
[11] Literally: "Grace's thoughts have been softened."
[12] To justify the plural Luther must have been thinking of at least two letters.
Certainly one of the letters has to be Luther's "letter of comfort," written on
June 30, for which Elector John thanked Luther on July 4; WA, Br 5, 437.
According to Rückert, LB, p. 314, n. 17, and WA, Br 13, 151, to WA, Br 5,
421, No. 1615, this "letter of comfort" is no longer extant; Clemen's arguments
concerning Luther's June 30 letter (WA, Br 5, No. 1615) are not convincing.
(According to the text tradition, this June 30 letter was addressed to the
Electoral prince, Duke John Frederick; Clemen argues, however, that this letter
was addressed to the Elector himself.) The other letter could not be identified. Was Luther perhaps thinking of his May 20 letter to Elector John
(No. 210)?
[13] Luther wrote: *Das werck gibts auch und zeuget fur augen.*
[14] I.e., here and throughout this letter, the papal party and its ecclesiastical
and political representatives and supporters at the diet.

tory,[15] in that, through His Imperial Majesty's[16] decree, they have prohibited the preaching.[17] On the other side, however, these miserable people do not see that by the presentation of the written confession[18] more has been preached than might have otherwise been done by perhaps ten preachers. Is it not deep wisdom and high irony that Master Eisleben[19] and others have to be silent, while[20] instead the Elector of Saxony, together with other sovereigns and lords, arrives on the scene[21] with the written confession,[22] and preach[es] unhindered before [His] Imperial Majesty[23] and the whole Empire, right under our opponents' noses, so that they have to listen to it and are unable to say anything against it? I am of the opinion that by this fact the prohibition of the preaching is well revenged. Our opponents do not wish to permit their servants to listen to [our] preachers, but they themselves have to listen to something even worse (as they call it) from such great lords, and have to be mute. Christ certainly is not silent at this diet, and even if [the opponents] rave, they will have to hear more from the confession than they would have heard in a whole year through the preachers. This is how it goes, as St. Paul says: God's Word will yet be unfettered.[24] If [the Word] is prohibited from being preached in the pulpits, then one must hear it in the palaces. If poor preachers are not to speak the Word, then great sovereigns and lords will speak it. In summary: if all is silent, then the stones will shout [the Word], says Christ himself.[25]

[About the matter][26] concerning which Your Electoral Grace

---

15 Literally: "have hit it very well." The phrase "to hit a bull's eye" comes closest to what Luther said.

16 I.e., here and throughout this letter, Charles V; see LW 48, 175 f.

17 See p. 339, n. 10. Perhaps one may assume that in the no-longer extant "letter of comfort" (see note 12) Luther had already dealt with this matter, and that he now places it in a different light, i.e., the situation created by the presentation of the Augsburg Confession.

18 I.e., here and throughout this letter, the Augsburg Confession.

19 John Agricola; see LW 48, 220, and in this vol., pp. 339 ff.

20 Literally: "yet."

21 Luther wrote: tritt auff. Auftreten is used, e.g., to designate the entrance of an actor to the scene.

22 See note 18.

23 See p. 349, n. 10.

24 II Tim. 2:9.

25 Luke 19:40.

26 In his July 4 letter (see notes 1, 2) the Elector informed Luther confidentially that he had heard from a trusted person the following: (1) The

requests [an answer] from me, I shall humbly give my opinion:

First, should his Imperial Majesty demand that His Imperial Majesty be allowed to be the judge in this matter,[27] because His Imperial Majesty does not intend [to permit] much debate in this matter, then I think that Your Electoral Grace could reply to this that His Imperial Majesty's *Summons*[28] implies that the matter will be graciously investigated. If this should not take place, then this *Summons* would not have been necessary, and His Imperial Majesty could very well have done such judging in Spain, and ought not to have summoned Your Electoral Grace to come at great trouble and expense to Augsburg; likewise he could have spared other Imperial Estates [this expense]. For if there were no more to be accomplished or expected [than such a verdict], His Imperial Majesty could certainly have delivered such an answer by a messenger.[29] It would cause His Imperial Majesty and the whole Empire great disgrace, however, and perhaps great offense and trouble, if His Imperial Majesty, without having investigated the matter simply wished to interfere in it, be its judge, and give absolutely no other answer.[30] (Of course such clever counsel originates with no one else than Your Electoral Grace's good friend,

---

Emperor does not intend to have the matter (i.e., the *Augsburg Confession* and the whole Reformation movement) debated. (2) The Emperor would attempt to get "us" (i.e., the signers of the confession,) to accept him as judge, who would simply pass a verdict on the matter. (3) Should "we" refuse to accept him as judge, then he would issue a mandate according to which the ecclesiastical *status quo ante* would have to be restored. (4) Then the Emperor would proclaim a council. (5) Should "we" refuse to abide by the mandate, then the Emperor would actively see to it that the mandate would be obeyed. The Elector requested that Luther give his opinion on these points, even though the Elector mentioned that he was well aware that his information might not be correct; that he had indeed received correct information can be seen from the June 5 memorandum mentioned in note 5.

[27] "Matter" designates here, and throughout the remaining portions of the letter, the faith confessed in the *Augsburg Confession*, as well as the ecclesiastical practices which had developed during the decade from 1520 to 1530 in the evangelical portions of the Empire.

[28] See pp. 280 f.

[29] The suggestion has been made (see *WA, Br* 5, 455, n. 6) that this statement, as well as the reference to the possibility of judging the matter in Spain, has to be seen against the background of the mandate issued on July 15, 1524, in Burgos/Spain. In this mandate Emperor Charles prohibited an assembly of the German Estates, which was to settle the Reformation issue. See *St. L.* 15, 2268 ff.

[30] I.e., other than the one he could have sent from Spain by a messenger.

N.N.)[31] Certainly it is not the Emperor [who is behind this], as everyone will and must say.[32]

Second, should His Imperial Majesty (that is, [rather,] N.N.)[33] indeed wish to insist that His Imperial Majesty simply be admitted as the judge in this matter, then Your Electoral Grace may state in all frankness: Yes, His Imperial Majesty is to be the judge in this matter, and Your Electoral Grace is willing to accept and endure everything to the extent and provided that His Imperial Majesty does not pass a verdict [which is] contrary to Scripture, or God's Word.[34] For Your Electoral Grace is unable to put the emperor above God,[35] or to accept the emperor's verdict if it is in opposition to God's Word. By saying this, sufficient respect for His Imperial Majesty has certainly been shown, since nothing but God alone (who is, ought to be, and must be above all) will be placed above[36] His Imperial Majesty.

Third, should [the opponents] argue that with this [reply] we intend to dishonor His Imperial Majesty [by making the Emperor] look like a person inclined to act against God, and that we should believe that His Imperial Majesty as a Christian sovereign would make no decision or judgment contrary to the divine Word ([for] they also answered me thus at Worms,[37] just as they now answer Your Electoral Grace), to this argument Your Electoral Grace certainly will know [how] to reply, namely, that God has strictly prohibited trust in sovereigns and men; as Psalm 118[38] and Psalm 142[39] say: "Do not put your trust in sovereigns."[40] Indeed also God's first commandment in which [God] says: "You shall

---

[31] This is apparently a reference to Duke George of Saxony, Luther's bitter foe; see *LW* 48, 110; n. 20.

[32] For the opinions about Emperor Charles set forth by Luther and his friends in Augsburg, see, e.g., pp. 329, n. 30; 351 f.; 355.

[33] See note 31.

[34] For a commentary, see *Deutsche Theologie* 3 (1936), 92 ff., 251 ff., 254 ff.

[35] Acts 5:29.

[36] Literally: "will be preferred to."

[37] For the background of this statement (which is explained neither in Enders, *Briefwechsel*, nor in *WA*, Br, and Rückert, *LB*), see Fife, pp. 683 ff. See also *LW* 48, 205; *Deutsche Theologie* 3 (1936), 92, n. 15.

[38] V. 8 f.

[39] Luther apparently was thinking of Ps. 146:3.

[40] This quotation is written in Latin.

have no other gods, etc.,"[41] does not permit this [trust]. Further, if the word of their own mouths is honest, and [if] they are Christian sovereigns, then they cannot prove this more convincingly than to judge with and according to Christ's word and say: "Thus says Christ, etc." But if they judge without Scripture, or demand that one accept their verdict without Scripture, then their own words[42] convict them [of lying, since] they want to be Christian sovereigns, [yet] without and contrary to Christ. This is worse than being a lord without a territory, the Empire without money, being trained without being artistic. But we read:[43] "Their folly is made plain."[44]

But may Your Electoral Grace be of good cheer. Christ is present, and he will also confess Your Electoral Grace before his Father, just as Your Electoral Grace now confesses [Christ] before this wicked generation.[45] As [Christ] says: "Whoever honors me, him I shall also honor."[46] That same Lord who has begun [his work] will also complete it.[47] Amen.

I am praying studiously and ardently in behalf of Your Electoral Grace. If I could do more, it would be incumbent upon me to do it. May God's grace be with [Your Grace], as it has been until now, and be multiplied in Your Electoral Grace. Amen.

Saturday, July 9, 1530   Your Electoral Grace's dedicated
MARTIN LUTHER

---

[41] Exod. 20:3.
[42] Literally: "their own mouths' word."
[43] II Tim. 3:9. The following quotation is written in Latin.
[44] It has to be pointed out that Luther deals only with points (1) and (2) of the five points mentioned by the Elector on July 4; see note 26. Perhaps point (3) can also be considered as having been touched upon by Luther. For Luther's opinion in connection with points (4) and (5), see e.g., pp. 220, 435.
[45] Matt. 10:32; 12:45.
[46] Mark 8:38; see also note 45, and I Sam. 2:30.
[47] Phil. 1:6.

223

To Justus Jonas
Coburg, July 9, 1530

Having expressed his appreciation for some recent letters, Luther sets forth some of his thoughts on the Diet of Augsburg and its possible outcome. Interwoven with these thoughts is a challenge to his friends in Augsburg to remain steadfast, and this challenge is supported with a brief exegesis of Psalm 110:1. Luther expects that the diet will rapidly reach its climax and crisis. Since he is convinced that opposing statements of faith cannot be reconciled, he hopes that the diet, notwithstanding dissension in matters of faith, will work out political peace in the Empire. If this could be accomplished, then, Luther affirms, the diet would have been a full success, and this for three reasons: Through the Augsburg Confession Christ has been publicly, and within sight of his enemies, confessed; "we" have been established as men of peace, that is, as God's children, while the opponents have been established as men of war and bloodshed; and Christ's sovereignty, and the defeat of his enemies, prophesied in Psalm 110:1, have been truly manifest. Do "we" dare to make a liar out of the psalmist? Therefore in concluding Luther boldly challenges Jonas to believe that Christ is indeed King of kings; if Christ loses this title at Augsburg, then he has also lost it in heaven and on earth.

The autograph of the letter is no longer extant; in view of the difficult text passage in connection with the exegesis of Psalm 110:1,[1] this loss is especially unfortunate. The letter is available in several manuscript copies, in some special editions, and in the common editions of Luther's works.[2]

On Justus Jonas, see LW 48, 275, n. 3.

Text in Latin: WA, Br 5, 458–459.

To Dr. Justus Jonas, a servant of Christ, and [my] brother[3]

---

[1] See note 32.

[2] For the witnesses, see Enders, *Briefwechsel* 8, No. 1706; WA, Br 5, No. 1635, Introduction, and WA, Br 13, 158, *ad loc.*

[3] For the address, which is missing in most witnesses, see WA, Br 13, 158, to WA, Br 5, 458.

Grace and peace in Christ. In these days we have received many letters from you,[4] excellent Jonas, and since those days of silence[5] I in turn have written four, even five times;[6] and now I am writing for the sixth time. Your letters were extremely welcome to me. Indeed I see that now after the synopsis[7] the first act[8] of the diet is being recited; the uproar,[9] and the highlight or crisis[10] will follow.[11] While we shall await a happy end, [the opponents][12] will [get] a tragic end. Not of course that unity on statements of faith[13] will ever be brought about (for who would hope to have Belial reconciled with Christ?),[14] except that perhaps the marriage [of priests] and "both kinds" will be conceded[15] (but even in this connection the adverb "perhaps" has to stand, and even a very strong

---

[4] I.e., you people at Augsburg. The letters mentioned by Luther were dated June 30, and were written by Melanchthon (WA, Br 5, No. 1616), Spalatin (ibid., No. 1617), Jonas (ibid., No. 1618), and Osiander (ibid., No. 1619). Perhaps Luther was also thinking of the July 4 letter of Elector John (see p. 360).

[5] See pp. 324 ff.

[6] Luther counted here according to his letters to Melanchthon. Luther to Philip Melanchthon: (1) June 27 (WA, Br 5, No. 1605); (2) June 29 (ibid., No. 1609); (3) June 30 (ibid., No. 1611); (4) July 3 (ibid., No. 1621); (5) July 5 (ibid., No. 1623); (6) July 9 (ibid., No. 1634). On June 29 Luther apparently also wrote to Jonas (WA, Br 5, No. 1610), and on June 30 he also wrote to some of his other friends in Augsburg (WA, Br 5, Nos. 1612, 1613, 1614), and to the Electoral prince, Duke John Frederick (see p. 361, n. 12).

[7] Luther wrote argumentum.

[8] Luther wrote prologum.

[9] Luther wrote turba.

[10] Luther wrote: epitasis vel paroxysmus.

[11] According to Rückert (LB, p. 325, n. 4) and Clemen (WA, Br 5, 459, n. 3), Luther here applies the divisions of the Greek comedy to the phases of the diet. According to Aelius Donatus (a grammarian of the 4th cent. A.D.) in his De comoedia Graeca, VII, a comedy has four parts: prologus—Luther calls it argumentum—i.e., the synopsis or table of contents; protasis—Luther calls it prologus—i.e., the first act in which only a part of the prologus (i.e., Luther's argumentum) is unfolded; epitasis—Luther calls it turba—i.e., the act in which the story is further unfolded and becomes more complicated; katastrophe—Luther calls it epitasis vel paroxysmus—i.e., the act in which the story is finally completely unfolded and brought to an end. For the Donatus passage, see Poetarum Graecorum fragmenta 6[I], ed. Kaibel (1899), 69. In his June 25 letter (see WA, Br 5, 386) Melanchthon had written of the prooimia of the diet, i.e., the prologue of the diet. Luther took up this term, and spoke several times about the diet in terms of a drama or comedy; see e.g., p. 362, and Luther's July 13 letters to Jonas and Spalatin (WA, Br 5, 471, 472), and his July 27 letter to Jonas (WA, Br 5, 500).

[12] See p. 361, n. 14.

[13] Literally: "on dogmas."

[14] See II Cor. 6:15.

[15] On "both kinds," see LW 48, 143, and in this vol., p. 377, n. 29.

"perhaps"),[16] but that I wish and almost hope that the dissension in matters of statements of faith[17] may be set aside and a political unity be brought about. If with Christ's blessings this could be done, then more than enough would have been accomplished[18] at this diet.

For, first of all, and this is most important, Christ has been proclaimed through this public, glorious confession,[19] and has been affirmed in bright daylight and in the very presence[20] of these, [his opponents,] so that they may not boast that we have run away, have been afraid, or have hidden our faith. I only envy you this opportunity, for I could not be present at this [time when] the beautiful confession [was presented].[21] And so that same misfortune happened to me which happened a year ago at Vienna to those supreme commanders of the war, so that no credit or victory could be granted to them for the resistance and defense of the city against the Turks.[22] Yet I am pleased and comforted[23] that

---

[16] Rückert, *LB*, p. 325, n. 8, suggests that Luther here is making reference to the events in Augsburg. In the fragment of the letter of June 30 (see p. 348, n. 5), Jonas informed Luther of consultations among the signers of the *Augsburg Confession* concerning a brief summary of those teachings in which one might be able to make concessions to the papists, and that this summary was to be turned over to the Emperor. For these consultations Melanchthon had drawn up articles which soon would be forwarded to Luther for his judgment; *WA*, Br 5, 428. As early as June 29 the Nürnberg delegation reported to the city council that Melanchthon had drawn up a brief summary of the *Augsburg Confession* which was to be presented privately to the Emperor; *C.R.* 2, 153 f. These "summary articles" are no longer extant. According to a letter of Veit Dietrich, Luther did indeed at the beginning of July receive some articles by a special messenger, who immediately took them back to Augsburg; see Enders, *Briefwechsel* 8, 70, n. 17; *WA*, Br 5, 429, n. 10. Whether these were the articles mentioned by Jonas, as Enders (*loc. cit.*) suggests, or some other material, cannot be substantiated. And further, Clemen (*WA*, Br 5, 429, n. 10; 426) contradicts himself when on the one hand he suggests June 30 as the date for this Jonas fragment, while on the other hand he suggests that perhaps as early as June 27 the articles were sent to Luther. Apparently Luther's brief, which is published in *WA*, Br 5, 430 ff., is to be connected with the event mentioned by Jonas. See also Walter, *RA*, 67 ff.; Schubert, *LaK*, 153.

[17] Literally: "in dogmatic dissension."

[18] Literally: "been done and enacted."

[19] I.e., the *Augsburg Confession*.

[20] Literally: ". . . affirmed into the light and into the face of . . ."

[21] Literally: ". . . be present in this beautiful confession."

[22] See p. 242, n. 10. The supreme commander of the Imperial army which was to aid in Vienna's defense against the Turks arrived at Vienna too late, i.e., after the siege of the city had been lifted. Even if he had arrived earlier, he could not have accomplished much since the "army" under his command was not yet at battle strength. So he had to stay at Linz during the crucial

in the meantime this, my Vienna,[24] has been defended by others.

Secondly, it is certain that we always have sought peace, and, as the Psalm says,[25] have pursued it, offered it, [and] prayed for it, while our opponents indeed have sought nothing other than war, bloodshed, and disaster. This is a definite sign that we are God's Children, because we are men of peace.[26]

If we obtain the third point, [that is,] that we part from one another in political peace, then we have clearly defeated Satan for this year. This is not a prediction on my part, but is [a reflection of] my thinking about the diet.[27] For how should I hope that our opponents would do anything good? What should I expect from the Emperor,[28] however excellent he may be,[29] since [his way] is blocked [on all sides]?[30] Christ[31] lives and sits, not at the right hand of the emperor (for then we would have perished a long time ago), but at the right [hand] of God. If this is true then it is a big lie.[32] Nevertheless I am delighted in this lie, and I am definitely ready[33] to die on the basis of it.[34] Why should I then not

---

first days of October. When the Imperial army was finally ready to move, the Turks had already lifted the siege. See Ranke 2[III], 123 f., 127 f.; F. B. von Bucholtz, *Geschichte der Regierung Ferdinands I.*, 3 (Vienna, 1832), 294.
23 Literally: "It pleases [me] and I am comforted [by the fact] that . . ."
24 I.e., Luther's teaching concerning the gospel.
25 Ps. 34:14.
26 See Matt. 5:9.
27 Luther wrote: *Haec mea est non praedestinatio, sed cogitatio de istis comitiis.*
28 I.e., here and throughout this letter, Emperor Charles V; see *LW* 48, 175 f.
29 See p. 364, n. 32.
30 Or: ". . . since he is possessed [perhaps one has to add: by the papists, or: by evil spirits]."
31 Luther begins here a brief exegesis of Ps. 110:1: "The Lord says to my lord: Sit at my right hand, till I make your enemies your footstool." Luther works with the Vulgate text: *"Dixit Dominus Domino meo: Sede a dextris meis, donec ponam inimicos tuos scabellum pedum tuorum."* He keeps the Hebrew text in mind, however, and derives his main observation from it; see Excursus.
32 This sentence is written in German. In some witnesses, this sentence and the first half of the next sentence, up to "lie," are replaced by a Latin text which reads in translation: "This [i.e., Christ's sitting at the God's right hand] is something unbelievably great. Yet I am delighted in this unbelievable fact. . . ." As Clemen (*WA*, Br 5, 429, n. 11) has pointed out, this text is apparently an attempt to circumvent the difficulty of the sentence above, which obviously puzzled the copyist. One may, then, safely assume that the sentence as translated above was indeed a part of the autograph. See also Excursus.
33 Luther uses a Greek word here.
34 Literally: "die in it."

also live on the basis of it?[35] If God would only grant that Philip[36] believed this, at least with my faith, if he doesn't have some other[37] faith. "At the right hand" may be unimportant,[38] but "[at] *my* [right hand]"—devil! Where does this have an end?[39] The[40] pronoun[41] is the important factor,[42] for the noun *adonai*[43] which follows the "He said" will certainly preserve the precious "Sit[44] [at my right hand]" until the "footstool" also comes [about]. Do you want to bet that David will lie?[45] [No, he doesn't lie,] unless this month Augsburg has begun to be the master [of things] all by itself, or to evade God's right hand, so that one would have to believe that Christ has been dethroned there by the sacramentarians,[46] and David[47] has been corrected by the papists. If this has happened, then we here at Gruboc[48] don't know it. Therefore, my Jonas, write this to us, and then I shall search for another Christ and think of another David, who does not fool me in this way and ridicule me with empty words.

But blasphemous joking aside, for [we are] not blasphemous but in earnest. Farewell to you in Christ, and believe with us, as you do, that Christ is the King of kings and Lord of lords.[49] If he loses this title now at Augsburg then he has also lost it in heaven and on earth. Amen.[50]

    Gruboc,[51] *July 9, 1530*   Yours,

                                                MARTIN LUTHER

---

[35] Literally: "live in it?"
[36] Philip Melanchthon; see *LW* 48, 77, n. 3.
[37] I.e., his, Melanchthon's, own faith.
[38] Literally: "be a small thing."
[39] Except for the quotations, this sentence is written in German; "my" is italicized by this editor.
[40] Except for the quotations and the words listed in notes 41, 43, and 44, this sentence is written in German.
[41] This word is written in Latin.
[42] Literally: "will accomplish it."
[43] These two words are written in Latin. See Excursus.
[44] This word is written in Hebrew.
[45] This sentence is written in German.
[46] I.e., Zwingli and the upper German Reformers; see pp. 94 f. Clemen suggests (*WA, Br* 5, 460, n. 15) that in the fragment mentioned in note 16 Jonas perhaps wrote something about the activities of the sacramentarians in Augsburg.
[47] I.e., David as author of Ps. 110.
[48] See p. 359, n. 26.
[49] I Tim. 6:15; Rev. 19:16.
[50] This sentence is written in German.
[51] See note 48.

The understanding of Luther's exegesis of Psalm 110:1 is made difficult by the sentence: "If this is true, then it is a big lie." Clemen rejects the available variant as an attempt to make the understanding of this sentence easier (see p. 369, n. 32). He suggests that Luther perhaps wanted to say the following: If Psalm 110:1 really means that Christ sits at the "right hand of God," then this statement is "a great lie," for Christ's sovereignty is neither manifestly revealed in this world, nor confessed by all people; while for the believer Christ's sovereignty is indeed real, for the unbeliever the statement concerning this sovereignty is a lie.

On the basis of the following sentences, "Nevertheless I am delighted . . ." and "Why should I then not . . ." one may go one step further and suggest that for Luther the Christian lives and dies in this "lie;" that is, the Christian lives by something which is a lie for the man without faith. Even to the believer Psalm 110:1 appears to be a lie, namely in the hour of spiritual struggle (Anfechtung). It is for this struggle that Luther wants to strengthen his friends at Augsburg through prayer, intercession, and an example of courageous daring faith which takes God at his word. Luther's statement concerning the "big lie" has to be seen in the eschatological frame which is basic for his theology. In the eschaton it will be established before the eyes of all people that the "lie" (in which Luther can now delight, in which he can die, and for which he is ready to live) is not a lie, but is truth. Why? Because God himself stands behind the lie.

It may seem strange but it is God who does the lying. Here is one of the central themes of Luther's theology, a theme which Luther had learned from the Apostle Paul (see I Corinthians 1:18 ff.), and which he developed in great detail in his *First Lectures on the Psalms* (see *LW* 48, 18, n. 3), and then again in the material prepared for the Heidelberg Disputation (see *LW* 48, 60; 31, 39 ff.). For Luther, God hides himself in death in order to reveal truth. God makes this statement, "Sit at my right hand," by which for the unbeliever really nothing happens, at least so the unbeliever thinks. Consequently for Luther the important word in Psalm 110:1 is *"my,"* and the important factor is that it is *God* who speaks in this Psalm. Nothing can escape the right hand of God, not even the devil. But who is this God? He is *my* Lord and God, whose word is true, and who will finally put all of Christ's enemies down and make them the footstool of the King of kings and Lord of lords. Is there anyone here who wants to doubt, then, that Christ indeed is lord? Any bets that David's words in Psalm 110:1 will turn out to be lies? To have any doubts about Christ's lordship is to have doubts concerning God, who is *my* God, that is, the God and father of each believer. And Augsburg will be the great test for this, our faith. If God is God, then the statements of Psalm 110:1 are true, notwithstanding what happens at Augsburg, that is, how timid Melanchthon might act, or how much the opponents rage, Christ is king at Augsburg, unless he is not Christ, that is, not the one to whom Psalm 110:1 is spoken. If this is the case, then forget about Christ. Here is the point from which the sentence, "[No, he doesn't lie,] unless this month Augsburg has begun . . . ," has to be understood. Luther challenges his reader with the question: "Will David in Psalm 110:1 turn out to be a liar?" If God is God, then David will not be a liar, you can literally bet your life on it. But David will be a liar if Christ has been dethroned in Augsburg by a victory of the sacramentarians, or if you people at Augsburg don't take God and his Word seriously anymore; then David and Psalm 110:1, that is, God himself, indeed will turn out to be liars.

Luther arrives at this understanding of the Psalm verse by interpreting the Vulgate text in the light of the Hebrew text. The Hebrew text reads in translation: "Jahweh [God] says to my *adonai* [lord] . . ." Luther simply exchanges the consonants of Jahweh for those of *adonai*, (thus dissolving the *Quere perpetuum*), and places the tone of *adonai* on the "i," thus making it into the personal pronoun suffix "i." Consequently "the pronoun is the important factor" for Luther so that he paraphrases: "Said *my* lord [God] to my lord [Christ] . . ." (The text of the Luther Bible reads: *Der Herr sprach zu meinem Herrn.* . . .) Through this linguistic operation "God" of Psalm 110:1 becomes "*my* lord [God]," and this "my (lord) God," in turn, is for Luther the important factor, that is, the assurance that the sovereignty of Christ will come about and that Christ will triumph at the diet.

224

To Justus Jonas, George Spalatin, Philip Melanchthon, John Agricola[1]
Coburg, July 15, 1530

Luther confirms the receipt of letters from Augsburg. He anticipates that the signers of the Augsburg Confession have received a reply

---

[1] The autograph of this letter is no longer extant. The address is found only in the editions of the letter, but is missing in the manuscript copies. A Luther autograph of a July 15 letter to Spalatin is extant, however, in which Luther writes: "I am awaiting you people here, my Spalatin, as happy returners, that is, as people condemned by the Emperor's edict, which orders the restitution [of all things]." See WA, Br 5, 481. The plural "you people" suggests that in this letter to Spalatin Luther was hoping that all the friends in Augsburg would return. In the opening sentence of the present letter Luther does not name the addressee by name, and this is contrary to the way in which

from their opponents, and sketches the probable answer and what might follow next. He conjectures that the answer will not be based on biblical material, and will be followed by a mandate and by threats. Since Luther is convinced that further discussions would be utterly pointless, he urges his friends to seek a gracious dismissal from the Emperor and to return home, since they have done all they could. By going to Augsburg the evangelicals have given to Caesar what is Caesar's, and by confessing Christ they have given to God what is God's. The most important accomplishment of the diet will have been the presentation of the confession, and nothing further could be accomplished in matters of faith. Should their opponents intend to use military force against the evangelicals, then God will show what to do about it. Elector John's councilors should stay at Augsburg to deal with the remaining issues. In closing Luther again exhorts his friends to return home, and adds a brief benediction.

For the addressees, see note 1.

Text in Latin: WA, Br 5, 479–480.

To Justus Jonas, George Spalatin, Philip Melanchthon, and
John Agricola Eisleben,
my colleagues at Augsburg

Grace and peace in the Lord. Yesterday we received the letters brought both by Arnold and the messenger from Coburg.[2] I believe

Luther usually begins his letters. Further, throughout the letter Luther uses the plural when speaking to the addressee. This seems to suggest that the present letter was indeed jointly addressed to the friends in Augsburg, though it must be added that the foundation in the text tradition for the individual addressees is weak. On Justus Jonas, see *LW* 48, 275, n. 3; on George Spalatin, see *ibid.*, 8 f.; on Philip Melanchthon, see *ibid.*, 77, n. 3; on John Agricola, see *ibid.*, 220.

[2] On July 14 Luther received July 10 letters from Melanchthon and Spalatin; WA, Br 5, Nos. 1636, 1637. Apparently he also received July 10 (?) letters (extant only in fragmentary manuscript copies) from Jonas and Agricola; WA, Br 5, Nos. 1638, 1639. This material was delivered by a certain Arnold Burenius (see *ADB* 3, 586 ff.), who returned from Augsburg; see WA, Br 5, 461, n. 3. On July 14 Luther also received Melanchthon's letter of July 8, together with the letters from Jonas and Brenz which were also dated July 8; WA, Br 5, Nos. 1629, 1630, 1631. These letters were delivered by an unknown messenger from Coburg, who had not yet left Augsburg on July 9; see WA, Br 5, 461. Perhaps this messenger was the one used (regularly?) by the Electoral Saxon government for its dispatches between Augsburg and Torgau, with Coburg functioning as relay station.

that by now you have that answer of the opponents, which, as you write, you were expecting;[3] that is, you will have to hear "fathers,

---

[3] In their letters from Augsburg (see note 2) the friends had informed Luther that they were expecting the answer of the opponents to be released in the near future. What is meant by "answer" is unclear. On July 8 the "answer" was, according to Melanchthon, *one* of three plans of action which the opponents were discussing at that time. (On July 8 Melanchthon informed Luther of the following: After the presentation of the confession three plans were developed in the diet's College of Sovereigns [see *LW* 48, 70, n. 1]. The harshest plan was that the Emperor should insist that the Edict of Worms [see *LW* 48, 210] be strictly enforced. The second plan was somewhat gentler; according to this plan the confession was to be evaluated by honest, learned, and non-partisan scholars, and on the basis of their evaluation the Emperor would then pass a verdict. The third plan, the one which probably would be accepted, was that a refutation of "our" confession would be read to "us," and that then the Emperor would pass judgment on the differences between "our" confession and its refutation. Should "we" be unwilling to accept this, then the Emperor would order the *status quo ante* to be restored until a council should meet. "I don't expect anything better." See *WA*, Br 5, 446; see also the fragment of Jonas' July 8 letter to Luther, *WA*, Br 5, 449. That the friends in Augsburg informed Luther correctly can be seen from *NB* I.Abt.,E.1, No. 22.) According to Brenz, the "answer" was a "confession" on the part of the opponents; see *WA*, Br 5, 451 (July 8). On July 10 Melanchthon simply informed Luther that the opponents had not yet answered; *WA*, Br 5, 461. Jonas informed Luther that the *Augsburg Confession* had been sent to Rome, and that an answer was expected daily. In a narrower sense the "answer" (envisioned by Luther) would, then, be a reply to the *Augsburg Confession* (as it was eventually given in the *Confutation*). In a wider sense, the "answer" would be the opponents' planned procedure against the signers of the *Augsburg Confession*. Therefore neither Luther's friends in Augsburg, in their expectations, nor Luther, in his assumption, were correct, since the *Confutation* was not promulgated until August 3; see *TP*, pp. 98 ff. Yet both Luther and his friends *were* correct in that they realized that the opponents would make some moves which would show their intentions. This the opponents indeed had done by the time this present letter reached Augsburg. On July 9 the evangelicals were asked whether they intended to submit any articles other than those presented in the *Augsburg Confession* (see p. 361, n. 7). On July 10 the evangelicals replied negatively to this question; see *URA* 2, No. 113. On July 16 Elector John was informed by the Emperor that he would not grant the Elector the solemn investiture as long as the Elector supported the Lutheran teachings. See *URA* 2, No. 121. On July 10 the Emperor announced to the pro-papal Estates (see *URA* 2, No. 110) that he would not function as an arbiter between papists and evangelicals, but that he would act as supreme protector of the church and of the Christian faith. I.e., the Emperor intended simply to show the evangelicals (on the basis of the still-to-be-written *Confutation*) that they were wrong, and to demand their return to the *status quo ante*. This return was to be brought about both through gentleness and threats (see, e.g., the matter of investiture). The Emperor envisioned a general council of the church to deal with the whole Reformation issue, and to bring about concessions to the evangelicals and redress those grievances which the public had against the church. On July 12 the Emperor received the first draft of the *Confutation,* and on July 14 the Emperor himself wrote to the Pope requesting a general council. See Walter, RA, 62 ff.

fathers, fathers, church, church, church, usage, custom." Moreover
you will hear nothing taken from Scripture. Based on these arbiters
and witnesses, the Emperor[4] will pronounce a verdict against you.
Then will follow threats and boastings till kingdom come.[5] But the
Lord will give you voices and wisdom.[6]

Since you write: "In a short time we shall report in person on
other matters"—do so now![7] More has happened [at this diet] than
could have been expected. For instance, you have given to Caesar
the things that are Caesar's, and to God the things that are God's:[8]
perfect obedience to Caesar by appearing [at the diet] at such great
expense, hardship, and trouble; and to God the precious sacrifice
of the confession,[9] which will force its way through all the courts of
kings and sovereigns, will rule in the midst of [God's] foes,[10] and
by his voice will go out into all the earth,[11] so that those who do not
believe are without excuse;[12] and [all] this, in turn, will be the fruit
of the silence commanded at the beginning of the diet.[13] If now this
reward be added,[14] that, according to the testimony of the opponents, not one article of faith has been violated, then we will have
accomplished much more than I have hoped, that is, we will have
been liberated from the disgrace of the name "heretics."[15] May

---

4 I.e., here and throughout this letter, Emperor Charles V; see *LW* 48, 175 f.
5 Literally: "boastings to heaven and hell."
6 Luke 21:15.
7 This is an almost verbatim quotation from Melanchthon's July 8 letter; *WA*,
Br 5, 446, and Luther uses this quotation to admonish his friend to do as he
had promised.
8 Matt. 22:21.
9 I.e., here and throughout this letter, the *Augsburg Confession*.
10 Ps. 110:2.
11 See Ps. 19:5.
12 Rom. 1:20.
13 This is a reference to the Emperor's prohibition of preaching on the part
of the evangelical preachers; see p. 339, n. 9.
14 See also p. 369.
15 The background of this statement is not clear. Was Luther thinking here,
e.g., of a remark by one of the papists as quoted on p. 350? This is suggested
by Rückert, *LB*, p. 332, n. 14. Enders, *Briefwechsel* 8, 114, n. 7, cites a statement made by Spalatin on July 2 (see *WA*, Br 5, 481, n. 9), according to
which the opponents stated that the confessors had not erred in the articles of
faith. But how did Luther know about this statement? Was Luther perhaps
being sarcastic here? (He certainly did not expect that the opponents would
declare the faith confessed in the *Augsburg Confession* to be orthodox.) If
the opponents declared the confession to be heretical, then "we" would be
freed from the disgrace of the name "heretic," because "we" would be condemned by those who in reality are heretics.

Christ himself confess you as you confessed him,[16] and honor them that have honored him.[17] Amen. Therefore in the name of the Lord I free you from this diet. Home, and again, home![18]

Do not hope for unity or concession[s]. For this I have never pleaded at God ['s throne], since I know that it is an impossibility. [I have prayed] only that they, while themselves remaining in their godlessness, may permit you to teach, and may concede peace, and if they wish to help us, to do it in whatever way they can. If the Emperor intends to issue an edict, let him do it;[19] he also issued one at Worms.[20] We shall listen to the Emperor as emperor, nothing more, nothing beyond [this]. Why are we concerned with that masked emperor, that boor?[21] He who opened the Emperor's and kings' door to our confession will counsel us, and He will again counsel us if, contrary to my hopes, the Emperor drives against us with military force.[22] We shall, of course, yield to the [true] emperor; it will be something else, however, if the masked emperor[23] should attempt anything.[24] Therefore obtain[25] from the

---

[16] Matt. 10:32.

[17] See I Sam. 2:30.

[18] This sentence is written in German.

[19] See note 3 (Melanchthon's July 8 letter to Luther).

[20] See *LW* 48, 210. Luther does not anticipate that a new edict would be more effective in stopping the Reformation movement than was the Edict of Worms.

[21] This apparently is a reference to Duke George of Saxony (see *LW* 48, 110, n. 20; *WA*, Br 5, 481, n. 11), who is seen, on the basis of his agitations against the confessors (see e.g., pp. 363 f.; *WA*, Br 5, 446, 461), as someone who plays the emperor's role without actually being the emperor.

[22] Literally: "with force and arms."

[23] See note 21.

[24] Luther expresses here his readiness to yield to the Emperor's army if attacked for the sake of the gospel, but not to yield to the army of Duke George. Though it has not been commented upon in great detail, this particular passage is important for Luther's understanding of the equality of the Imperial sovereigns, and of the emperor's overlordship. The passage throws light also on Luther's understanding of the problems concerning war within the Empire for the sake of defending the evangelical teachings.

[25] Luther used the plural, and addressed it to his friends, i.e., the "theological consultants" of Elector John. Yet it seems that Luther was also suggesting that the Elector himself return from Augsburg, and this for the following reason: The theologians stood under the Elector's jurisdiction; consequently the Emperor could neither grant nor refuse them a dismissal. Only the Elector himself had to receive permission to leave the diet prior to its closing. And further, the second part of the sentence (". . . and let the sovereign's councilors . . .") seems to suggest that the main contingent of the Electoral Saxon

Emperor permission [to leave], and let the Sovereign's councilors[26] remain there to work on the rest of the issues.[27] Our case has been made, and beyond this you will not accomplish anything better or more advantageous. To Campeggio's[28] boast that he has the power to grant dispensations,[29] I reply with Amsdorf's[30] words: "I don't give a hoot for the legate and his lord's[31] dispensations;[32] we shall find sufficient dispensations [elsewhere]."[33] Since the lord[34] gives the orders, pay no attention to the servant's[35] dispensation—if such a robber and invader of the Empire may be called a servant.

Home, home![36] May the Lord Jesus preserve and comfort you, who for his name's sake have worked hard, and have been sufficiently afflicted. Amen.

Gruboc,[37] *July 15, 1530*   MARTIN LUTHER, D.

---

delegation was to return home, and only a small delegation of councilors was to remain at Augsburg to work on the rest of the issues. See note 27.

[26] Elector John of Saxony; see *LW* 48, 269, n. 8. While it cannot be said with certainty, it may be assumed that by "councilors" Luther was first of all thinking of the chancellor, Christian Beyer (see p. 349, n. 8). For a list of the other councilors who were to accompany the Elector to Augsburg, see *URA* 1, 13.

[27] See the issues mentioned in the *Summons* (pp. 280 f.); see also p. 352, n. 22.

[28] I.e., the papal legate; see p. 126, n. 6.

[29] Melanchthon, who on July 8 was received by the Papal Legate in a private audience, reported on that day to Luther's companion, Veit Dietrich (see p. 282, n. 13), that the Legate had the power to make concessions on the marriage of priests and "both kinds." *WA, Br* 5, 447; see also *ibid.*, 449.

[30] Nicholas von Amsdorf; see *LW* 48, 218.

[31] I.e., the pope.

[32] Literally: "I defecate on the legate's and his lord's dispensation." "Defecate" is a rather polite word for the term used by Luther! It cannot be established under what circumstances von Amsdorf supposedly made this statement. Perhaps, as Rückert, *LB*, p. 333, n. 8, suggests, one has to assume that Luther wanted to say: "I reply with that coarseness [or: bluntness] which is typical of Amsdorf. . . ."

[33] The quotation is written in German.

[34] I.e., the pope.

[35] I.e., Campeggio.

[36] This exhortation is written in German.

[37] See p. 359, n. 26.

225

To Philip Melanchthon[1]
Coburg, July 21, 1530

On July 14, 1530, Melanchthon wrote[2] to Luther: "Concerning us and our case, nothing has been decided till now. New deliberations take place daily. May Christ grant that [these deliberations] lead to peace. Eck[3] . . . has presented to the Emperor[4] a confutation[5] of our confession.[6] Even though this confutation has not yet been made public,[7] yet I hear from friends that it is a long document and full of insolence. . . . I am forwarding to you an inquiry concerning [ecclesiastical statutes],[8] and I wish you to reply in detail on this matter.[9] For in all our discussions[10] no topic troubles me more

---

[1] The autograph of this letter is no longer extant. The letter is available in several manuscript copies, in some special editions, and in the common editions of Luther's works. For the witnesses, see Enders, *Briefwechsel* 8, No. 1724; WA, Br 5, 492; WA, Br 13, 164, to WA, Br 5, 492, Fundorte. The variants offered by the witnesses do not make substantial contributions to the content, or the understanding of the text. Even though the address is missing in all witnesses, it is clear to whom Luther was writing, since the addressee is mentioned in the opening sentence of the letter.

[2] WA, Br 5, 475 f.

[3] John Eck; see p. 296, n. 3.

[4] Emperor Charles V; see LW 48, 175 f.

[5] This is a reference to the first draft of the *Confutation*, which had been presented by the papal theologians to the Emperor on July 12; see p. 374, n. 3.

[6] I.e., the *Augsburg Confession*.

[7] The draft of the *Confutation* was forwarded by the Emperor to a meeting of the pro-papal Estates of the Empire, who began discussing it on July 14; see TP, p. 87.

[8] Melanchthon wrote: *de traditionibus*, i.e., traditions. What Melanchthon meant here was expressed in German writings of that time with the term *Menschensatzung*, i.e., statutes made by man. These were those statutes of the Canon Law by which the life of the individual Christian and the existence of the church at large were regulated, and which did not originate in specific divine commandments. These statutes dealt, e.g., with fasting; with the rights, privileges, and duties of the clergy; and with details in the liturgy.

[9] This request was underscored in Melanchthon's July 14 letter to Luther's companion at the Coburg, Veit Dietrich (see WA, Br 5, No. 1646, Introduction); and on July 20 Melanchthon urged Luther to deal with these questions (see WA, Br 5, 490).

[10] Literally: "debates." Neither Enders, *Briefwechsel* 8, 107, nor Clemen, WA, Br 5, 476, comments on this passage. When and between whom did these discussions take place? What was their purpose? Rückert, LB, p. 337, n. 17, identifies "discussions" with Melanchthon's private negotiations with the papal legate, Cardinal Campeggio (see p. 377, n. 29), which took place on

than this one, which appears to be the least important topic.[11]
Certainly it is a matter of small significance. [The statutes] are only
ropes [with which to hang] consciences . . . regardless of whether
they are observed or abolished."

Melanchthon then briefly mentioned justification by faith and
the freedom of a Christian as foundations of the Christian life, and
continued: "This I call freedom, as Paul observed the law when he
was among the Jews. I have set forth several reasons for setting up
statutes, so that you may more easily see at which point I am
especially perplexed. For instance, if statutes are made without
ungodly intention, then it seems [to me] that they have to be
observed by necessity because of the ius potestatis,[12] *and not*

---

several occasions during the first ten days of July; see Walter, RA, 67 ff. Too
little about these negotiations is known to make any definite statements. For
details see ZKG 9 (1888), 68 ff. On July 7 Melanchthon wrote a letter to
Campeggio personally, and perhaps also to the Legate's secretary, and the
letter seems to throw some light on the passage above. In this letter
Melanchthon abandoned his former demand that the marriage of priests and
"both kinds" be publicly granted to the evangelicals, and only asked that both
matters be tolerated until a general council of the church had finally decided
the issues. He further stated that the problem of the mass could be settled
without difficulties. And finally, he promised that ecclesiastical jurisdiction
would be restored in the territories of the evangelicals. C.R. 2, 172 f.; for a
July 6 letter to the Legate, see C.R. 2, 169 ff.; see also Reu I, 127 f. Since
the ecclesiastical jurisdiction hung together closely with the "statutes," one is
justified in assuming that the discussions mentioned above by Melanchthon
have to be seen against the background of Melanchthon's negotiations with
Campeggio. On the other hand Melanchthon could also have had in mind
discussions which had taken place between himself and his colleagues. We
know, for example, from a letter by Jonas (of which only a fragment is extant),
and which is generally given the date of June 30, 1530 (see WA, Br 5, 428),
that prior to the discussions between Melanchthon and Campeggio, Melanchthon disagreed quite strongly with Jonas on the validity of the ecclesiastical
jurisdiction.

11 Or: ". . . appears to be the easiest [topic] of all [the topics]."

12 St. L. 16, 1011, translates this term with "Recht der Obrigkeit," i.e., law
of the governmental authority. This translation would have to be seen against
the background of Rom. 13:1, where the Vulgate used potestas for the Greek
exousia, and the RSV used "governing authority," or simply "authority,"
while Luther used Obrigkeit. With this translation of potestas in mind one
would have to paraphrase Melanchthon's statement as follows: If the bishops
make statutes for the life of the faithful, and do this with the right intention
(i..e., not contrary to the teaching concerning justification; see the following
paragraph of the text), then these statutes necessarily have to be obeyed, not
because this obedience is a matter of faith and worship of God, but because
the law of the government is involved, for we see that the bishops rule *iure
humano*, i.e., by man-made law (in contrast to divine law). Another possibility
of interpreting *ius potestatis* would be to see in this phrase the technical term

because of the worship [of God] itself. For we see that the bishops indeed rule by man-made law. [In treating the teaching] concerning the mass, and in the first catalogue of the articles of faith, it seems to me that I have been sufficiently careful; concerning the matter of the statutes, I am not yet satisfied with [my work] in this [piece of] writing.[13] *I suspect that the opponents will also make much noise about the ecclesiastical orders."*

In the attached material[14] Melanchthon gave five reasons for the existence of ecclesiastical statutes: *(1) They deal with works by which man can be reconciled with God; (2) they are a necessary part of the worship of God; (3) they are a means of ensuring good order; (4) they help to develop bodily discipline; (5) they deal with means of demonstrating publicly the fact that faith is active in love and gratitude.* Although Melanchthon rejected the first two reasons, he wrote[15] concerning the last three reasons: *"There is no doubt that in these last three cases statutes justly can be made. Since this is so, our opponents can argue [the following]: Such statutes are permitted and commanded a potestate;*[16] *therefore they are necessarily to be observed, just as the Jews were forced by necessity to observe the [festival of] consecration [of the altar], instituted by the Maccabeans,*[17] *and the Ninivites were forced by necessity to observe the fasting decreed by the king,*[18] *and the Jews [were*

---

for the *potestas iurisdictionis* of the church, which according to the Canon Law is exercised by the bishop, and which Melancthon, contrary to the Canon Law, affirms as being *iure humano*. Melanchthon would then mean the following: The ecclesiastical statutes (if they do not contradict the teachings of the faith) are by necessity to be obeyed because they were made by the bishops who *iure humano* hold the *potestas iurisdictionis* in the church, and this obedience is not a matter of *faith* and *worship*, but a matter of *obedience* (see in the text, the last paragraph of Melanchthon's letter) to the law of ecclesiastical jurisdiction. For the translation of *potestas* as "jurisdiction," see Lewis and Short, *s.v.* Potestas, I: B, 3; E. A. Gooder, *Latin for Local History* (London, 1961), p. 131; Du Cange, *s.v.* Potestas, Rector (1).

[13] Melanchthon wrote: *In loco de Missa et in primo catalogo articulorum fidei videor mihi satis cautus fuisse; in traditionum materia nondum* (according to one witness: *nunquam;* see Ender's, *Briefwechsel* 8, 108, line 36, n. r) *mihi satisfeci in hoc scripto.* See Excursus.

[14] *WA*, Br 5, 476 f.

[15] *WA*, Br 5, 477.

[16] I.e., by the *potestas jurisdictionis* of the church; see note 12.

[17] I Macc. 4:59.

[18] Jonah 3:7.

forced to observe the fasting] decreed by Jehoshaphat.[19] *For we are forced to confess that the bishops are potestates*[20] *by man-made law. The statutes are therefore obligatory, not because they themselves are [a part of] the worship [of God], but because they deal with works which are permitted,*[21] *and because they are commanded by a potestas.*[22] *Not the nature of the work itself, but the ius potestatis*[23] *interjects the element of necessity."*

"*Here you will say that there [are] reason[s] why statutes may be abolished, not only because they are contrary to the doctrine of justification, but also because the freedom given [us] through the gospel cannot be taken away from us, just as Paul freely observed the law among the Jews only so that he would not offend anyone.*[24] *But this [argument] does not seem to suffice, or else it certainly is offensive to average people. If obedience is required, then there is no freedom, for freedom and obedience contradict one another. This knot has to be untied; for that freedom seems totally to dissolve obedience, [and this] should not be."*

"*I am arguing as follows: The Jews would have sinned by violating Jehoshaphat's fasting edict. . . . Therefore we also sin*[25] *if we violate the ordered fasting in the permissible cases. It was a different thing that Ahab*[26] *established when he instituted a cult. He instituted this cult for appeasing God, which is contrary to the teachings of faith. Had he instituted something which was not contrary to faith, but in agreement with faith, as Jehoshaphat did, then one certainly would not have been permitted to violate [this statute]. So one may also argue concerning the statutes of our [opponents]. For I now consider that the bishops may rule on the basis of man-made law."*

---

[19] II Chron. 20:3. The center of Melanchthon's argument would be the fact that in all cases (the bishops' statutes, the law to observe the festival of consecration of the altar, and the fasting law of the king of Ninivites and of Jehoshaphat) a *potestas,* a jurisdiction, was involved, which in turn has to be obeyed, according to Rom. 13:1 ff.

[20] I.e., men empowered with jurisdiction; see note 12.

[21] I.e., the nature of the works does not conflict with the teachings concerning justification by faith.

[22] I.e., are commanded by those who have the *potestas;* see note 12.

[23] See note 12.

[24] See Acts 16:3; 21:26; I Cor. 9:20.

[25] Because "we" would go contrary to the *potestas,* which according to Rom. 13:1 is from God.

[26] This is perhaps a reference to I Kings 21:9.

"[Please] answer whether the statutes, if made according to the three [specifications mentioned above],[27] *are necessarily to be observed because of the authority and command of the potestas, and if such statutes are binding on the conscience."*

These inquiries about the value of man-made statutes for the existence of the church were prompted by Melanchthon's search for a solution to the problem of the validity of the Canon Law in the church of the gospel. Luther replied promptly on July 21. While he does deal with Melanchthon's concern, Luther actually pushes beyond this concern to deal with the larger question of the nature of the Canon Law. Luther illustrates his arguments with a detailed discussion of episcopal authority. Thus he develops principles for an evangelical ecclesiastical law, while at the same time critically evaluating the Canon Law.

On Philip Melanchthon, see LW 48, 77, n. 3.

Text in Latin: WA, Br 5, 492–495.

Grace and peace in Christ

Through your previous letters,[28] my Philip, you made me hopeful that you would have received the answer of the opponents as early as Monday a week ago,[29] and that soon [thereafter] you would be dismissed through a subsequently issued edict. Almost with certainty I therefore expected that you would return that same week. Now this letter[30] shows [another picture]. But concerning this and other matters at some other time.

[Now] to the discussion of the statutes.[31] You treat correctly the five reasons for ceremonies. Where the difficulty lies, however, and here you do have [problems], is indeed in the fact that the person or the effective cause for statutes is debatable. The problem of the final cause[32] is an easy question. On this whole problem I think the following:

---

[27] See points (3), (4), and (5) above in the second paragraph of the text of Melanchthon's letter.

[28] This is a reference to the July 8 letters mentioned on p. 373, n. 2.

[29] I.e., July 11. Melanchthon mentioned this date in his July 8 letter; see WA, Br 5, 446.

[30] I.e., Melanchthon's July 14 letter; see Introduction.

[31] See Introduction.

[32] Luther uses here the Scholastic technical terms *causa efficiens,* and *causa finalis.* Applied to the problem under discussion, this means that Luther sees

First, it is certain that these two governments[33] are separate and different, that is, the ecclesiastical one and the secular[34] one; Satan, through the papacy, has fundamentally confused and mixed them. We have to be sharply alert here, neither to have them brought together so that the two governments may again be mixed, nor to give an inch to any one or consent that he may mix [them]. For this would mean to make common cause with thieves and robbers, because in this connection we have the divine Word,[35] which says, "But not so with you."[36] It is the authority, and it commands that the two governments be preserved separate and unmixed.

Second, from this it follows that the same person cannot be a bishop and a sovereign, nor simultaneously a pastor and a housefather.[37] You understand sufficiently well what I want to say here. I want to keep the persons separate, just as the governments, even though the same man can represent both persons, and the one Pomer[38] can be a parish pastor and a householder. For I do not wish to disquiet the bishops, since there are good ones among them. So the same man, Conrad von Thüngen,[39] is duke of Franconia and

---

the crux of the problem not in the final outcome (i.e., the situation created by the statutes, their purpose, and what to do with them) on which Melanchthon had focused in the five points mentioned in the July 14 letter (cited in the Introduction), but rather in the circumstances which make it possible for the statutes to develop at all; and these circumstances are secured by the Canon Law, which in turn is administered by the bishops.

33 Literally: "administrations."

34 Literally: " political."

35 Literally: "authority."

36 Luke 22:26.

37 Obviously Luther does not want to say that a pastor may not be married. Luther's statement here has to be seen against the background of his argumentation in section five.

38 I.e., John Bugenhagen; see LW 48, 303, n. 44.

39 Conrad von Thüngen, a member of an old noble family of Franconia, was bishop of Würzburg from 1519 to 1540; see ADB 16, 632 ff. At the beginning of the eleventh century the bishop of Würzburg began to absorb royal rights in eastern Franconia, i.e., the area east of the upper Rhine valley. By 1120 the bishop functioned as viceroy in the area which today is known as Franconia, and in 1168 Emperor Frederick Barbarossa bestowed the title "Duke in Franconia" on the bishop of Würzburg. In contrast to the situation in Bavaria, or Saxony, where ducal power rapidly developed into a centralized office, in Franconia the ducal title was merely of ceremonial importance. Luther apparently chose this example not because of the actual coexistence of secular and ecclesiastical power in the man Conrad von Thüngen—for in Luther's time the political or legal power (or the "secular jurisdiction") of the

bishop of Würzburg, even though the duke of Franconia cannot be bishop of Würzburg. I have been so verbose on this matter to you because you knew that I have in great detail dealt[40] with these effective causes of statutes, and not only with the final causes[41] which you have listed.[42]

Third, as bishop, a bishop has no authority[43] to impose on his congregations[44] any statute or ceremony, except with the expressed or silent agreement of the church.[45] For the church is free and is the lord of all, and the bishops ought not to dominate the faith of

---

bishop of Würzburg was rapidly declining, if not non-existant. Luther apparently chose this example because, on paper at least, the "duke of Franconia" held the lordship over a highly complex group of people where one lordship crossed with another, and where even the duke's lordship (i.e., the lordship of the bishop of Würzburg) was everywhere challenged or eliminated by other lordships. See also in the text of the letter, in section five.

[40] Literally: ". . . knew that our most powerful word has also dealt with . . ."

[41] See note 32.

[42] Luther sees in the mixing of secular and ecclesiastical governments the *causa efficiens* (see note 32) of the statutes issued by the bishops. In this argument Luther is not so much concerned with the coexistence of bishop and sovereign in one man, but rather with the mixing of the principles by which both governments operate, or should operate. Secular governments operate with rights, laws, and force, and consequently of necessity obedience on the part of the citizens is involved. Ecclesiastical government is to operate through love, equality, and freedom of all believers, and not by force. Consequently bishops have *no right, or power* (*potestas*), to *impose* statutes on the faithful, and these statutes are not *necessarily* to be obeyed. In the sentence above, Luther also corrects Melanchthon, who in his July 14 letter had suggested that until now Luther has dealt primarily with the *causa finalis* character of the statutes, i.e., with the argument of the papists to the effect that statutes are to be considered parts of worship; see *WA, Br* 5, 476. While Luther confirms that he has dealt with this matter (see e.g., his *Address to the German Nobility* and his *On the Babylonian Captivity of the Church*), he affirms that he has also dealt with the question of the *causa efficiens* of the statutes, i.e., with the reason why these statutes were made at all. He sees this reason in the mixing of the principles by which the two administrations ought to operate. According to Luther this mixing creates a tyranny in the church, which, in turn, is manifested in the exercise of the ecclesiastical jurisdiction. In making the affirmation that he has also dealt with the *causa efficiens* of statutes Luther could have been thinking again of his *Address*, but also of his 1523 booklet concerning the authority of a Christian congregation and its right to judge all doctrine and to call and dismiss pastors and teachers (*WA* 11, 401 ff.; *PE* 4, 75 ff.). For details, see *LJB* 31 (1964), 29 ff.; *SMRH* 5 (1968), 152 ff.

[43] Luther used *potestas*; see notes 12, 42.

[44] Luther used *ecclesia*; see also p. 61, n. 9.

[45] For more details on this principle, see the references cited in note 42.

the congregations,[46] nor burden or oppress the congregations against their will. The bishops are, after all, only servants and stewards,[47] and not the lords of the church. If the congregations, as one body, have agreed with the bishop, however, then the bishop may impose upon the faithful whatever the bishop wishes, as long as [the principles of] faith[48] remain unviolated, and he can also abolish [such rules] according to [his] judgment. But the bishops are not looking for this [type of] jurisdiction;[49] they only want to dominate, and to keep all matters under their sole power. This we may not concede, nor may we have any part in this iniquity and affront to, or oppression of, the church and truth.

Fourth, as sovereign, a bishop[50] may impose even less on the church, since this would mean fundamentally to mix these two jurisdictions.[51] [Should he do it anyway] then he would really be a pseudo-bishop,[52] and we, were we to give in to this, would likewise be guilty of this sacrilege. Against this godlessness and iniquity one must [fight and] die rather [than give in]. [Of course,] I speak of the church as a church which already has been separated from the political commonwealth.[53]

Fifth, as sovereign, a bishop may impose upon his subjects, as subjects, whatever seems appropriate to him, as long as it is godly and permissible;[54] the subjects are required to obey, since [under these circumstances] they obey not as members of the church, but as citizens. For the church is a twofold person in one and the same man. [For instance,] by prescribing, as duke of Franconia, a fast or something else permissible to his Franconian people, Conrad von Thüngen[55] forces to obedience those who acknowledge him as duke, but not those who acknowledge him [only] as bishop, as do [the

---

[46] See II Cor. 1:24; I Pet. 5:3.
[47] I Cor. 4:1.
[48] Literally: "godliness."
[49] Luther used *potestas;* see notes 12, 42.
[50] Luther here grants the possibility that a bishop might also be a sovereign of the Empire.
[51] See note 49.
[52] See I Pet. 4:15 (Greek text, Luther Bible).
[53] Luther speaks here of the church of the gospel, for which the mixing of the principles of secular and ecclesiastical administrations has been abolished.
[54] I.e., is not in conflict with God's Word and the principles of faith; see Acts 5:29.
[55] See note 39.

people] who are under the authority of other sovereigns, even though they belong to the diocese of Würzburg.[56] It is the same as if Pomer[57] forces his servant to abide by his house rule, but does not force his Wittenberg parish [to abide by this house rule].

Concerning your argument about the king of Nineveh,[58] you can see that this is a purely secular law,[59] regardless of whether a Christian[60] or pagan people is under [the king's authority]. It is the same as if the emperor universally ordered all people to fast; then the members of the church would obey him too, since according to the flesh the church is under the emperor, but the church does not obey as church. It is the same situation concerning King Jehoshaphat. Concerning the Maccabeans, however, it is clear that they did not institute their [festival of] consecration [of the altar] by themselves, but with the unanimous agreement of all the people. This agreement could again have abolished [this consecration festival]. I grant that in this matter much of secular law was involved, even more, almost all of it was a secular matter, since of course the Maccabeans were ruling; and yet nothing was instituted without the agreement of the people.[61]

We are unable, therefore, either on the basis of the ecclesiastical[62] or the secular[63] law, to grant to the bishops the power[64] to

---

[56] And consequently acknowledge Conrad von Thüngen only as bishop. They would not have to obey the order given by Conrad von Thüngen as bishop of Würzburg.

[57] See note 38.

[58] See Introduction.

[59] Consequently this law is not of the quality that an ecclesiastical statute should be. Of all the examples cited by Melanchthon (see Introduction), Luther accepts only the law of the Maccabeans concerning the annual commemoration of the festival of the consecration of the altar (I Macc. 4:59) as being equal to an ecclesiastical statute.

[60] Literally: "a church [or: congregation]."

[61] And this is for Luther the only way in which ecclesiastical statutes are to be enacted; see the references cited in note 42. If this is the case with "almost secular" legislation, how much more should it be the case with statutes for the church.

[62] I.e., according to those principles which *should* govern an evangelical ecclesiastical law and which Luther had detailed above, in sections three and four.

[63] Rückert, *LB*, p. 340, n. 18, sees in this whole sentence a contradiction to Melanchthon's repeated statement that the bishops rule *iure humano*; see Introduction. I.e., Rückert understands Melanchthon's *iure humano* as synonym for the *profano iure* used here by Luther. This seems to be impossible. Melanchthon's *iure humano* is related to the *potestas* which the bishops

impose[65] anything on the church, even if it is permissible and godly, since one ought not to do evil so that good may result.[66] Should [the bishops] wish to enforce and exact [this jurisdiction] by force, then we ought not to obey or consent to it, but rather we ought to die for the purpose of maintaining the differentiation of these two governments, that is, for God's will and law, against godlessness and sacrilege.

Moreover, should [the bishops] say (which, of course they will not do) that they are ready to burden us, and even to be considered by us as tyrants, at their own responsibility, and thus demand that we not resist this evil,[67] etc., then we must resist anyhow and must not obey with a single deed;[68] we must do the opposite [of what they demand of us]. Because in this case[69] not only would an evil be endured, but iniquity would be strengthened and godliness denied through the very work and endurance. Should they, however, compel us to fast by actual force, for instance by taking away food or by jailing us, then the evil is endured [without harm to one's conscience], since neither by word nor deed has agreement been given to it.

In this connection thoughts come to my mind, however, that

---

exercise and which qualifies those statutes of the Canon Law which are man-made in contrast to God-given; Melanchthon's *iure humano* belongs therefore in the realm of ecclesiastical law. Luther's *profano iure*, however, is to be the opposite of the ecclesiastical law. Luther wants to say here that neither according to an evangelical ecclesiastical law (for which he had outlined some principles in [3] and [4]) nor according to the secular law of the state may one grant to bishops that *potestas* or jurisdiction which the bishops were claiming. It could not be established whether, when Luther used the term "secular law," he was thinking of any specific paragraph or was making a rather general statement. See also WA 30[II], 420 ff.

[64] See note 43.

[65] This is the key to Luther's criticism of Melanchthon and of the Canon Law. For Luther ecclesiastical law had nothing to do with legislation or with force; see also the references given in note 42. Consequently Luther rejects the *potestas jurisdictionis* (which according to Canon Law is exercised by the bishops), and also rejects the necessary obedience which was advocated by Melanchthon on condition that the ecclesiastical statutes do not jeopardize the teachings of the faith.

[66] Rom. 3:8. The "good result" would be the *obedience* to the *potestas* (see Rom. 13:1 ff.).

[67] Matt. 5:39.

[68] Literally: ". . . and not obey with any work but to do the contrary . . ."

[69] I.e., if one accepted the argumentation of the opponents, and did as they demand.

we might come into danger through the deceits and tricks [of the bishops], if they pretend that the emperor as emperor, and they as sovereigns, wish to legislate such things, or wish to have such laws retained by the church, not as by the church itself but as by subjects. Under this pretense they could revive and strengthen that whole tyranny of the mixture [of the two governments]; in this way they would nevertheless have the whole church oppressed and subject to the episcopal jurisdiction.[70] Here my opinion is that we are by divine authority forbidden to believe them.[71] For Christ forbids considering the godless and the sinner as a just man, unless he has publicly repented. Matthew 18[:17]: "If he does not listen to the congregation, let him be to you as a gentile and a tax collector." Since the bishops are openly guilty of this mixture [of the two governments], of this tyranny and oppression of the church, we cannot believe them[72] unless they have first, through public repentance, rescinded and condemned the former laws and all the things they did on the basis of this mixture and tyranny.[73] Should they refuse to do this, then it is clear that they wish to rejoice in impenitence and freedom from punishment, and to restore all their abominations by guile and fraud, and wish to lie about the fact that they order these things as sovereigns, or the emperor as emperor. We should therefore be alert and deal carefully[74] with those who are full of every deceit and villainy[75] of their god Satan, so that they do not catch some of us, and afterwards leave behind pain which cannot be healed[76] because the church has been ruined and the abomination has been rebuilt.[77] [Their] deceit (if it is entirely thrust [on us] with full force) could also be seen if the

---

[70] See note 49.

[71] According to Rückert, *LB*, p. 341, to line 1, one would have to translate: "forbidden to yield to them."

[72] According to Rückert, *LB*, p. 341, to line 6, one would have to translate: "yield to them."

[73] Literally: "mixed tyranny."

[74] See Eph. 5:15.

[75] Acts 13:10.

[76] Literally: "pain and unhealable crying."

[77] In the fragment of the June 30 letter (see note 10), Jonas, reporting confidentially to Luther that he, Jonas, and Melanchthon disagreed in matters of the ecclesiastical jurisdiction, wrote: "But in this matter you should counsel us, so that the matter may not be harmful for future generations and afterwards sear our conscience[s]." *WA*, Br 5, 428.

bishop of Würzburg[78] enjoined [laws] not only upon those for whom he is duke, but simultaneously also upon those for whom he is [only] bishop. [This would be the same] as if the pope enjoined [laws on all], not only upon the subjects of his temporal dominion.[79] And likewise in other cases.

Only to this extent[80] may you safely concede to the bishops the authority [to enjoin] statutes. If then by some pretense the church were oppressed, then [at least] this would be without our consent or guilt. I wish that [the opponents] would insist and demand that they and their statutes be obeyed as law of the sovereigns, but not as law of the bishops. But Satan will not do this, since he knows in advance that in the long run this noose will strangle him. But it would be good for Duke George,[81] who in this way would become bishop of Meissen, Merseburg, and Prague, because obviously he could order, in his name, that the bishops be obeyed as if [their orders] were his orders. It would be much better for the Landgrave of Hesse,[82] who would concede nothing to [the Archbishop of] Mainz,[83] except Amöneburg[84] and Fritzlar, and in Thuringia nothing would be left to [the Archbishop of] Mainz except the episcopal court at Erfurt.[85]

---

[78] See note 39.

[79] I.e., the citizens of the Papal States.

[80] I.e., that a bishop as a *secular sovereign* enjoins *statutes of a secular nature* upon the citizens subject to his *secular authority.*

[81] Duke George of Saxony; see *LW* 48, 110, n. 20. Parts of the dioceses of Merseburg and Prague stood at that time under the political lordship of the Albertine branch of the ruling Saxon family, of which Duke George was a member, while parts of the territory of the diocese of Meissen stood under the joint lordship of the Albertine and Ernestine branches. See "Die wettinischen Länder 1485–1554," a map prepared by K. Blaschke, in H. Eberhardt *et. al.* (eds.), *Die Reformation in Dokumenten* (Weimar, 1967), Appendix.

[82] Philip of Hesse; see p. 124, n. 18.

[83] Cardinal Albrecht; see *LW* 48, 44 f.

[84] Luther wrote *Amelburgum.* "Luther (or perhaps only the copyist) confuses at this point Amöneburg, near Marburg, which belonged to Mainz, with Hammelburg in Franconia, which belonged to the abbey of Fulda." Enders, *Briefwechsel* 8, 132, n. 12. In Hesse only Amöneburg and Fritzlar stood under the secular jurisdiction of Mainz, while in terms of ecclesiastical administration all of Hesse was a part of the diocese of Mainz. See Rückert, *LB,* p. 341, n. 28.

[85] As far as secular jurisdiction was concerned, the Landgraviate Thuringia was a part of Electoral Saxony; but as far as ecclesiastical jurisdiction was concerned, Thuringia was a part of the diocese of Mainz. The city of Erfurt and its surrounding territory at one time were totally (i.e., ecclesiastically and secularly) subject to the archbishop of Mainz. Over the centuries, however, Erfurt had gained a certain independence by carefully playing off the arch-

But you despise [these thoughts] as rude and boorish. Nevertheless they are valuable as answers to your prying and pointless questions, since you can see that these people do not wish, or are unable to wish, anything other than to rule the church according to secular law, or to be considered only as secular sovereigns.[86] [And yet] they want to be bishops, and if they do not want to be that, what would they be? What would they continue to be? Therefore I wish you would be of a little more peaceful mind. Also, you are wearing me out with your vain worries, so that I am almost tired of writing to you, since I see that I accomplish nothing with my words. "I am unskilled in words, but not in knowledge."[87]

The Lord Christ be with you. Amen.

From the wilderness,[88] *July 21, 1530*   Yours,

MARTIN LUTHER

---

bishop of Mainz against the elector of Saxony. By the time Luther was writing, the archbishop held total jurisdiction (i.e., ecclesiastical as well as secular jurisdiction) only in the area of the "episcopal court," i.e., the collegiate cathedral chapter. In these last sentences Luther seems to say the following: I wish that the opponents would insist that the evangelicals accept the necessity of ecclesiastical statutes being obeyed as law of the sovereigns. If this were accepted, it would have some positive results for the Duke of Saxony, the Landgrave of Hesse, and the Elector of Saxony (the lord of Thuringia). Duke George could then exercise control over parts of the dioceses of Merseburg, Meissen, and Prague, because episcopal statutes would be proclaimed as ducal statutes, so that Duke George would in reality be bishop, and the statutes of the local bishops would be subject to ducal approval. The Landgrave of Hesse would be even better off, for he could simply eliminate the jurisdiction of the archbishop of Mainz (under whose ecclesiastical jurisdiction Hesse stood), except in the cases of Amöneburg and Fritzlar (towns in which the archbishop of Mainz was both secular and ecclesiastical lord). In Thuringia the archbishop could function as secular and ecclesiastical lord only in the area of the Erfurt collegiate cathedral chapter. Everywhere else the Elector of Saxony would take over.

[86] I.e., endowed with (secular) power to rule the church with force.
[87] See II Cor. 11:6.
[88] See p. 287, n. 1.

In his July 14 letter Melanchthon mentioned a "first catalogue of the articles of faith." What was this? This question becomes complicated by the context, in which Melanchthon mentioned that it seems to him that he had been sufficiently careful when he dealt with the mass, and that he had also been sufficiently careful in this first catalogue. But "careful" with what? This Melanchthon did not say. Then Melanchthon continued that in the matter of the statutes he was not yet satisfied (or according to one witness, he never was satisfied) with the work he did "in this [piece of] writing." This raises the second question: "What was "this piece of writing?"

Neither Enders (*Briefwechsel* 8, 108), nor Clemen (*WA*, Br 5, 476), nor Rückert (*LB*, p. 337, n. 17) establishes the identity of either the "first catalogue," or "this [piece of] writing." In *WA*, Br 13, 162, to *WA*, Br 5, 476, lines 27 f., the "first catalogue" is identified with the first part of the *Augsburg Confession* which is entitled: "Articuli Fidei Praecipui," that is, "Chief Articles of Faith." Melanchthon supposedly was thinking of Article XV, in which "Church Usages," or "Ecclesiastical Rites" were discussed; the reference to the mass supposedly is to Article XXIV. According to this commentary one would have to paraphrase Melanchthon's statement as follows: It seems to me that in Article XXIV of the *Augsburg Confession,* and in the first part of the confession, I have been sufficiently careful. But why did Melanchthon use this extremely clumsy way of presenting his ideas? Further why did he single out the mass, while thus far he had never spoken of the mass, but only of ecclesiastical statutes in general? Why would he in one case refer to a specific dogmatic *locus* and the pertinent article in the *Augsburg Confession,* but in the other case refer to a whole part of the confession, (that is, to twenty-one articles,) and leave it up to Luther to pick the pertinent article? This question, of course, presupposes that Melanchthon was indeed thinking of Article XV of the *Augsburg Confession,* an assumption for which *WA*, Br 13, *loc. cit.,* does not give any foundation. And finally, what is "this [piece of] writing" in the second half of the sentence? Does it refer to the "first catalogue"? That is, according to *WA*, Br 13, *loc. cit.,* does it refer to the *Augsburg Confession?* If so, what is the meaning of this statement?

In order to find a way out of this dilemma one has to begin with "this [piece of] writing." It is extremely dubious that this phrase refers to the "inquiry concerning ecclesiastical statutes" of which Melanchthon said that he was forwarding it to Luther (see p. 378). Why would Melanchthon refer to this "attached material" which he had mentioned a long time ago, that is, at the beginning of this paragraph? And further, why would Melanchthon do this in the same breath in which he mentioned the "first catalogue?" The only natural reference for "this [piece of] writing" is the "first catalogue" which Melanchthon had mentioned.

In order to establish the identity of "first catalogue," what Melanchthon does say, and does not say, has to be pointed out. He says that he thinks that in treating the mass he was sufficiently careful; he does not say where or when he treated the mass in such a way that he feels justified to make this assertion. Then he says that he thinks he was sufficiently careful (not only) in treating the mass, (but) also in the "first catalogue"; he does not say what points in the first catalogue he treated in such way that he feels justified to make this assertion. In one case Melanchthon speaks of a specific instance, in the other case he speaks in general terms of a whole document, and in both cases he is sure that he has acted with sufficient care. Then Melanchthon goes on to say that he is still dissatisfied with the way in which he treated the matter of the statutes in this document. If one adopts the interpretation of *WA, Br* 13, *loc. cit.*, that "first catalogue" is identical with the first part of the *Augsburg Confession,* then one would make Melanchthon contradict himself, for he dealt with the statutes in Article XV, that is, an article of the first part, of which Melanchthon had just said that he thought he was sufficiently careful, that is, of which he had just approved. If one wishes to nullify this argument by pointing to the fact that Melanchthon dealt with statutes also in Article XXVIII, then one would have to prove that for Melanchthon "this [piece of] writing," in which his dealing with statutes dissatisfied him, referred *only* to the *second part* of the confession (Arts. XXII–XXVIII) or *only* to *Art. XXVIII* of the confession. This will be extremely difficult, for a careful analysis of Melanchthon's thoughts on the nature of ecclesiastical law could substantiate the fact that Melanchthon had no reason for being dissatisfied with the position on ecclesiastical law which he had developed in *Augsburg Confession,* Arts. XV and XXVIII—unless he had any wish suddenly to modify this position for the purpose of meeting the demands of the opponents. And this was apparently the case in the discussions with the papal legate, Campeggio, and in those with Jonas (see above, note 10). The "first catalogue of the articles of faith" seems to be, then, that document which, on June 30(?), Jonas called *summa doctrinae in quo cedere possint, in quo non,* or the *articuli* which Melanchthon drafted for the negotiations between the evangelicals and the papists, and which were sent to Luther for his judgment (see *WA, Br* 5, 428). Unfortunately these *articuli* are no longer extant. If, however, the document published by Clemen as appendix to *WA, Br* 5, No. 1618, is indeed Luther's judgment on these *articuli,* and there is no reason to question this assertion, then one may make some observations concerning these no-longer extant *articuli,* which, in turn, substantiate the assumption that the "first catalogue" mentioned by Melanchthon on July 14 was identical with these no-longer extant *articuli* mentioned by Jonas on June 30.

In his judgment, Luther dealt at great length with matters concerning the Lord's Supper, while his treatment of matters which can be related to ecclesiastical law is comparatively brief. Whenever Luther did deal with matters pertaining to the statutes, he dealt with details but not with principles. In no way were the problems touched which on July 14 Melanchthon outlined in his "inquiry concerning ecclesiastical statutes." This fact does suggest that in the document which Luther evaluated these matters were also treated rather briefly. And this observation suggests that Melanchthon's thinking regarding these matters had progressed in the period from June 30 (that is, the approximate date of the *articuli*; see WA, Br 5, No. 1618) to July 14, and would justify Melanchthon's July 14 statement to the effect that he was dissatisfied with the way in which he had handled this matter in the *articuli*. Further, in Melanchthon's July 14 statement concerning the mass (a statement which is quite abruptly interjected into the general statements concerning the nature of ecclesiastical statutes) has to be seen a reflection of Melanchthon's July 7 letter (see note 10) to Campeggio (in which Melanchthon, quite optimistically, assumed that the problems pertaining to the mass could easily be straightened out), and a reflection of the fact that apparently in the *articuli* Melanchthon had dealt at length, and to his satisfaction, with the mass. This assumption is substantiated if one considers Luther's judgment on the *articuli*. And finally, after Melanchthon had voiced his dissatisfaction with his treatment of ecclesiastical statutes in his *articuli*, he mentioned (see the text of the letter) his anticipation that the opponents might also make much noise about the ecclesiastical orders. Melanchthon would not have made this statement unless he had realized that his own position on this matter was not sufficiently enough developed, and unless he expected Luther to deal with this issue. Judging by Luther's reaction to the *articuli*, one has to say that the paragraphs of the *articuli* which dealt with ecclesiastical orders apparently were rather brief, so that Melanchthon indeed could have felt poorly prepared for the negotiations with the papists.

In view of this material one would have to paraphrase Melanchthon's July 14 statement: It seems to me that I have been sufficiently careful, in particular in treating the mass, in general in all that I wrote in that first list of articles which we used as basis of our discussions with the opponents, and which you, Luther, have seen and evaluated. But I am dissatisfied with the way in which I had treated in that list matters concerning ecclesiastical statutes. I also suspect that I will have a difficult time regarding ecclesiastical orders, if and when the opponents raise this issue, as they certainly will. Hence my request that you, Luther, deal with the attached inquiry concerning ecclesiastical statutes.

226

To Gregory Brück[1]
Coburg, August 5, 1530

The following letter is one of the fine expressions of Luther's faith, and was written to the Electoral Saxon chancellor emeritus[2] (who was in Augsburg) at a time when Luther was waiting for definite news regarding the Confutation. In this letter Luther deals with two themes. The one theme which runs throughout the letter could be phrased as an exhortation: Trust in God, who will work out the dangerous situation which has developed even though there is no tangible reason for such trust aside from God's word of promise. Luther illustrates this theme with two observations of nature: the vault of the heavens does not collapse even though it does not rest on pillars which can be touched; a thin rainbow holds up heavy rainclouds, and assures mankind that the world will not be destroyed by a flood. The second theme, set as counterpoint to the first, could be phrased as a question: What will happen if the hopes of the evangelicals for a political peace do not materialize? Answering this question, Luther develops three thoughts: (1) The present dangerous situation serves only to test the extent of "our" trust in the mercy and love of God, who, in his time and with his methods, will bring about peace. (2) Consequently "we" can only pray and hope that the Emperor will enact nothing which would be contrary to God's law and to the Imperial law. (3) Should the Emperor, however, do this, then it is "our" task to differentiate between those actions undertaken by the Emperor himself, and

---

[1] The autograph of this letter is no longer extant. The letter is available in many manuscript copies, in some special editions, and in the common editions of Luther's works. Little is known about the external circumstances of the letter. On June 27, 1530, Melanchthon mentioned to Luther that Brück was depressed; WA, Br 5, 403. It is very doubtful, however, that this present letter has to be seen against the background of this Melanchthon statement. Once the letter had arrived at Augsburg it became generally known among the evangelicals; see WA, TR 2, Nos. 1324, 2426. On September 2 John Brenz (see pp. 177 f) apparently sent a copy of this letter (seemingly together with a copy of letter No. 210, or of Luther's no-longer extant June 30 letter to the Elector [see p. 361, n. 12] to the mayor of Schwäbisch Hall; see WA, Br 5, No. 1675, Introduction.

[2] See p. 349, n. 8.

those undertaken by tyrants usurping the Emperor's authority;
thus we would maintain the Emperor's honor and the validity of
the Imperial law. In the concluding paragraphs Luther points out
that the opponents of the evangelicals are a long way from reaching
their goals, and that only after all is finished can one develop a
proper perspective on the events. He closes with greetings to his
friends in Augsburg, and a short benediction.

On Gregory Brück, see pp. 51 f.

Text in German: WA, Br 5, 530–532. For the following trans-
lation, Theodore G. Tappert's translation (LCC 18, 155 ff.) has
been consulted.

To the honorable and learned Sir Gregory Brück,
doctor of law, Electoral Saxon chancellor and councilor,
my gracious lord and dear friend[3]

Grace and peace in Christ! Honorable, learned, dear Sir and Friend:
I have now written several times to my Most Gracious Lord[4] and
to our friends, so that I almost think I may have overdone it—
especially with my Most Gracious Lord—and may have created
the impression of doubting that His Electoral Grace has more en-
couragement and help from God than I have. But I wrote at the
urging of our friends,[5] some of whom[6] are so discouraged and
worried that they act as if God has forgotten us—although he cannot forget us without having first forgotten himself, unless it should
be that our cause is not his cause, and our word not his. But if
we are sure and do not doubt that it is his cause and word, then
our prayer has certainly already been heard, and help for us
already has been decided upon and prepared; this cannot be
wrong. For [the Lord] says: "Can a woman forget her child, that
she should not have compassion on the fruit of her womb? Even

---

[3] Luther wrote *Gevatter*; see *LW* 48, 201, n. 2.

[4] I.e., here and throughout this letter, Elector John of Saxony; see *LW* 48,
269, n. 8; the letters mentioned are Nos. 210, 222, and the no-longer extant
letter of June 30 (see note 1).

[5] How literally this passage should be taken is not clear.

[6] This is obviously a reference to Melanchthon (see p. 336), and perhaps also
to Jonas (although Jonas is not known for a lack of courage while at Augsburg; see however p. 388, n. 77), and perhaps to Brenz (see p. 327,
n. 15).

if she should forget it, yet I will not forget you; behold, I have graven you on my own hand."[7]

I have recently seen two miracles. The first [was this]: Looking out of the window, [I saw] the stars in the sky and the whole beautiful vault of heaven,[8] but I saw nowhere any pillars on which the master had rested this vault; yet the sky did not collapse, and this vault still stands fast. But there are some people who look for such pillars, and would very much like to clutch and feel them. Yet since they are unable to do this, they are alarmed and tremble[9] for fear [that] the sky will definitely fall down—for no other reason than that they can neither see nor clutch[10] the pillars. If they could touch [the pillars], then the sky would stand fast, even for them.

The second [miracle was this]: I also saw great, thick clouds hovering over us, so heavy that they could be compared with the waves of an ocean. Yet I saw no ground on which the clouds rested, or stood, nor any tubs in which their water could be caught.[11] Nevertheless the clouds did not fall on us but merely greeted us with a sour face, and drifted on. When the clouds had passed by, both the floor and our roof[12] which had held them up—[namely,] the rainbow—were shining through. Yet the floor and roof were so weak, thin, and little that they were lost in the clouds, and looked more like a ray [of light], which sometimes shines through a stained-glass window, than a strong floor; and so it was as difficult to believe that [a floor] was there, as to believe that the weight of the clouds was suspended there. Nevertheless it actually happened that this (seemingly) frail ray [of light] held up the weight of water and protected us. Yet there are some people who would rather look at, pay attention to, and be afraid of the water, and

---

[7] Isa. 49:15 f.

[8] Literally: "vault of God."

[9] Luther wrote: *zappeln und zittern sie,* i.e., they struggle (with hands and feet, like a fly caught in a spider web, or behave like a struggling eel) and tremble for fear.

[10] Literally: "neither clutch nor see."

[11] Literally: ". . . nor [did I see any] tubs in which they [i.e., the clouds] would be framed [or: set]."

[12] The clouds were resting on a floor, so that they did not fall down on "us"; "we" were protected from the clouds by a roof. Both "floor" and "roof" were symbolized by the rainbow.

the thickness, and the heavy weight of the clouds, than consider this thin, narrow, and fragile ray [of light]. They would very much like to feel the strength of this ray; since they cannot do this they fear that the clouds will bring on an eternal deluge.[13]

I am having some fun as I write this to Your Honor, and yet I am serious, for I found special pleasure in learning that Your Honor, above all others, has been of good courage and stout heart in this trial of ours.[14] I had certainly hoped that peace at least in a political sense[15] could be accomplished, but God's thoughts are far above our thoughts.[16] This is as it should be, for God (says St. Paul)[17] hears and does far more than we think or ask,[18] because we do not know how we should pray; Romans 8 [:26]. If God should grant our prayer that the Emperor[19] give us peace, then one might perhaps say [that God does] less[20] rather than[21] more than we think, and the Emperor would certainly get the glory instead of God. God himself, however, desires to give us peace, so that the glory might be his alone, as is fitting. Not that we should therefore think the less of His Imperial Majesty; but we ask and desire that His Imperial Majesty undertake nothing against God and the Imperial law.[22] Should [His Majesty] do this, however,

---

[13] Luther wrote *Sündflut*, i.e., the technical term for the flood of Genesis, chaps. 7 and 8.

[14] Even though the source for this statement could not be established, Luther is correct here. In the August 5 negotiations between Emperor Charles and the signers of the *Augsburg Confession* Brück delivered the decisive speech for the evangelicals, a speech which a contemporary said went through the heart of each Christian; see *WA, Br* 5, No. 1675, Introduction. On August 25 Melanchthon praised Brück's strength to Luther (see *WA, Br* 5, 562), while the Nürnberg delegates reported home that the Elector of Saxony had no one more capable for "these matters" than Brück (see *Realencyklopädie für protestantische Theologie und Kirche* 3 [3rd ed. Leipzig, 1897], 442).

[15] Luther wrote: *pax politica*. See also p. 369.

[16] See Isa. 55:8 f.

[17] Eph. 3:20.

[18] From "far more . . ." the sentence is written in Latin.

[19] "Emperor" or "His Imperial Majesty" refers throughout this letter to Charles V; see *LW* 48, 175 f.

[20] This word is written in Latin.

[21] From here to "think," the sentence is written in Latin.

[22] It is not clear exactly what Luther meant by "Imperial law." In contrast to the law of the church, the Canon Law, which at Luther's time was exactly defined and documented in the collections making up the *Corpus iuris canonici*, the law of the Empire was a highly complex and ambiguous collection of statutes maintained by custom or by decision. In his July 3, 1519, election contract with the electors, Charles V simply promised to maintain the

(may God forbid it,) then we as faithful subjects will nevertheless not believe that it is His Imperial Majesty who acts, but assume that other tyrants do it using the name of His Imperial Majesty. Thus we will distinguish between the name of His Imperial Majesty and the acts of the tyrants, even as we distinguish between God's name used by heretics and liars, and honor God's name but pay no heed to lies. Under no circumstances ought we or are we able to approve or accept the designs of the tyrants which they enact under the cloak of His Imperial Majesty's name,[23] but we are bound to defend His Imperial Majesty's name, and help to maintain [His Majesty's] honor; we are neither to permit nor approve any abuses against God and the Imperial law, in order that we may not become participants [in guilt] and heap on our consciences such sins, abuses, and dishonor of His Imperial Majesty's name [as are committed by others]. For sovereigns are to be honored,[24] and we may not permit them to be dishonored.

By his Spirit God will bless and further this work which he has graciously given us to do; he certainly will find the ways, time, and place to help us, [and] he will neither forget nor forsake [us]. Those men of blood[25] have not yet brought to an end what they are now beginning, nor have they all achieved security, or whatever it is that they desire.[26] Our rainbow is frail; their clouds are mighty; but in the end it will be clear which type of music is being played.[27]

May Your Honor make allowance in my behalf for my idle

Golden Bull, the laws concerning public peace, and "the other ordinances and laws" of the Empire; see *DRTA.* JR 1, 866. But then a long list of detailed promises was added, which in turn the electors considered as binding on the Emperor, i.e., as Imperial law. It is very doubtful that in mentioning the Imperial law Luther was thinking of any particular legal paragraph; most probably he used the term in the way that the term "law and order" is used today.

[23] See also p. 376.
[24] See Rom. 13:7.
[25] See Ps. 55:23; 139:19; see also *WA,* Br 13, 170, to *WA,* Br 5, 532, line 75.
[26] A literal translation of the last part of this sentence following "nor have they . . ." would be: ". . . also they all are not yet home again [in the sense of returning safely home, or bringing one's ship home safely] nor [have they come] to the place [where] they would like to be."
[27] From "in the end . . ." the sentence is written in Latin. Literally: ". . . clear whose tunes [are being played]."

talk. [Please] comfort Master[28] Philip[29] and all the others. May Christ in my stead comfort and preserve also our Most Gracious Lord. To [Christ] be praise and thanks forever. Amen. To his grace I also faithfully commend Your Honor.

From the wilderness,[30] *August 5, 1530*

MARTIN LUTHER, D.

227

To Mrs. Martin Luther[1]
[Coburg,] August 14, 1530

Luther takes advantage of a hurriedly passing messenger to send this brief note to his wife, and he promises to write more soon. He mentions the rumor that in Augsburg the Confutation has been made public, but that no copy has been made available to the evangelicals. He reports that since August 10 he has been completely healthy again, and that consequently he is now eager to write—whether he means letters or other writings is not clear. He closes with a brief benediction and an exhortation to pray confidently.

Text in German: WA, Br 5, 544–545.

Grace and peace in Christ!

My dear Katie: This messenger passed hurriedly by, so that I couldn't write anything further; yet I didn't want to let him go without a personal note. You can tell Mr. John Pomer[2] and all [the others] that I shall soon write more. We have not yet received anything from Augsburg, but are waiting all hours [of the day]

---

28 I.e., Master of Arts.

29 Philip Melanchthon; see *LW* 48, 77, n. 3. Title and name are written in Latin.

30 See p. 287, n. 1.

1 The autograph of this letter is no longer extant, and the text is available only in printed form. Even though none of the witnesses gives an address, the text itself makes clear to whom Luther was writing .

2 John Bugenhagen; see *LW* 48, 303, n. 44.

for a message or letter.[3] Rumor has it[4] that the answer of our opponents supposedly has been publicly read, but that they did not wish to give a copy to our friends so that they could answer it.[5] I don't know whether this is true. Since [our opponents] shy away from the light in such a way, our friends will not remain for long [at Augsburg]. Since St. Lawrence day[6] I have been completely healthy and did not feel any throbbing in my head. This has made me really eager to write, for until then the throbbing tortured me too much.[7]

Greetings to all.[8] [I shall write] more some other time. God be with you all. Amen. Pray confidently, for all is under control,[9] and God will help [us].

Written on August 14, 1530   Martin Luther

228

To Mrs. Martin Luther
Coburg, August 15, 1530

After letter No. 227 had been sealed, Luther received several letters from Augsburg. He now forwards these to Wittenberg along with a second short personal note to his wife. Promising to write more soon, Luther asks his wife to extend greetings to all, and to take care that a student, a certain John Polner, should behave obediently. He also tells of eating ripe grapes, even though it has been

---

[3] Literally: "writing."
[4] The source of this rumor could not be traced in Luther's correspondence, even though as early as July 30, 1530, Melanchthon had informed Luther of the rumor that "today" the *Confutation* was to be made public, but that this was a false rumor; see WA, Br 5, 515.
[5] See p. 401, n. 5.
[6] I.e., August 10.
[7] Since the end of July Luther had complained to his friends in Augsburg of severe headaches, which forced him to rest a great deal; see WA, Br 5, 516 f., 520, 522, 524. While traveling to and from Augsburg, Peter Weller (see p. 321, n. 2) had visited Luther at the Coburg at that time. Luther assumed that Peter Weller, having returned to Wittenberg, had informed Catherine Luther of the headaches.
[8] Literally: "Greet all [people] and all [things]."
[9] Luther wrote: *denn es ist wohl angelegt,* i.e., for it is well organized, or planned.

a wet summer. In a postscript Luther complains about the tardiness of Nickel Schirlenz, one of his printers in Wittenberg, and repeats his instruction to transfer the job of printing the manuscript of his Sermon on Keeping Children in School from Schirlenz to George Rhau; he also asks his wife to see to it that the sermon is printed at the earliest possible time.

Text in German: WA, Br 5, 545–546.

To my dear lord, Mrs. Catherine Luther at Wittenberg:
Personal

Grace and peace in Christ! My dear Katie! After I had sealed the letter,[1] these letters from Augsburg[2] came to me. At this point I held the messenger back,[3] so that he would take them along.[4] From these letters you will certainly be able to see how things are going for us at Augsburg—very much as I wrote in the other letter.[5] Have Peter Weller[6] read the letters to you, or Mr. John Pomer.[7]

---

[1] I.e., letter No. 227.

[2] These were letters dated August 6, written by Jonas, Melanchthon, and perhaps also Spalatin and Camerarius, and letters dated August 8, written by Melanchthon and Agricola. See WA, Br 5, Nos. 1676–1681.

[3] See p. 399. This messenger obviously had not come from Augsburg, and had not delivered the letters mentioned in note 2; he had begun his trip to Wittenberg, or perhaps Torgau, from somewhere else. Why he was in such a great hurry in the beginning, yet could then be delayed for a whole day, could not be ascertained.

[4] While it could not be established which of the letters mentioned in note 2 the messenger took along to Wittenberg, on the basis of the following statements it is certain that Luther at least forwarded the August 6 letters of Jonas and Melanchthon; WA, Br 5, Nos. 1676, 1677.

[5] On August 6 Melanchthon and Jonas reported to Luther that the final draft of the *Confutation* had been turned over to the Emperor on July 30, and was read in a plenary session of the diet on August 3; that the evangelicals had asked for a copy of the *Confutation,* and that sometime later the Emperor expressed his willingness to give them a copy, provided that it would not be published or copied, a condition unacceptable to the evangelicals; and that by August 6 the evangelicals had not yet seen the *Confutation.* See WA, Br 5, 533, 537. The friends in Augsburg reported the events as Luther, on August 14, had guessed them to be on the basis of a rumor; see letter No. 227. On the events surrounding the presentation of the *Confutation,* see Walter, RA, 71 ff.; Reu I, 119 ff.; TP, pp. 97 ff.; NB I.Abt.,E.1, Nos. 25, 26, 27; URA 2, No. 137; BA, pp. 167 ff., 190 ff. 415 ff. Text of the *Confutation*: J. Ficker, *Die Konfutation des Augsburgischen Bekenntnisses* (Leipzig, 1891); for an English translation see Reu II, Nos. 45, 48.

[6] See p. 321, n. 2.

[7] John Bugenhagen; see LW 48, 303, n. 44. Both Rückert, *LB,* p. 361, n. 22, and Clemen, WA, Br 5, 546, n. 2, suggest that Catherine Luther, though she

May God continue to help, as he has graciously begun to do. Amen. I cannot write any more now for the messenger is sitting here ready to leave, and hardly [is willing] to wait any longer.

Greet our dear *sack*.[8] I have read your letter to the wife of the bailiff,[9] and she thanks you very much. I have recommended John Polner[10] to Peter Weller;[11] take care that he behaves obediently. Greet Hansen Luther[12] and his teacher,[13] to whom I shall also write soon.[14] Greet Aunt Lehne,[15] together with all the others. Here we are eating bunches of ripe grapes, even though outside it has been very wet this month.

God be with you all. Amen.

From the wilderness,[16] August 15, 1530

MARTIN LUTHER

---

knew some Latin (see e.g., *WA*, TR 5, No. 5567, and in this vol., p. 237), was to have help either from Weller or from Bugenhagen in translating the letters. Since little is known of Catherine Luther's ability to handle Latin, we must be careful in suggesting that she was in need of help. Luther could very well have meant that she might have difficulty in reading the handwriting in the letters, or in understanding the details of their content.

[8] Literally: "bag [or: sack]." What Luther means here is unclear. Enders, *Briefwechsel* 8, 187, n. 2, suggests (on the basis of some older commentary) that Luther was thinking here of a certain Nickel Sack von Geilsdorf; on him see *WA*, Br 3, 251, n. 2; 7, 9 f. Rückert, *LB* p. 362, n. 3, and Clemen, *WA*, Br 5, 546, n. 3, take over this suggestion, though with some doubt; Rückert asks whether at that time there were such close relationships between the Luther family and this Nickel Sack as to warrant such greetings from Luther. Could *sack* also designate the sack-like pillow or bag in which a baby sleeps, or could be carried around? Luther would then perhaps be thinking here of his little daughter Magdalen, who was approximately fifteen months old, having been born on May 4, 1529.

[9] This is a reference to a no-longer extant letter to Barbara Bader, nee Hiltner, the wife of the Electoral Saxon bailiff for Coburg; see *WA*, Br 5, 546, n. 4.

[10] John Polner, or Pelver, was one of Luther's relatives; he was the son of Klaus Polner, who had married one of Luther's sisters. Apparently John Polner was to stay with the Luther family while he was at Wittenberg University. Clemen has collected (*WA*, Br 5, 546, n. 5) some data from the *Table Talks*, according to which both Klaus Polner and his son seem to have been heavy drinkers; hence Luther's remark. John Polner matriculated at Wittenberg on November 22, 1530, and studied theology. In later years he was one of Luther's assistants (*famulus*; see *LW* 48, 164, n. 4). After some teaching on the pre-university level, he finally was ordained and took over a pastorate. See also *WA*, Br 13, 172, to *WA*, Br 5, 546, n. 5.

[11] See note 6.

[12] John Luther; see p. 152, n. 7.

[13] I.e., Jerome Weller; see p. 321, n. 2.

[14] Still on August 15 Luther wrote to Jerome Weller; see *WA*, Br 5, No. 1684.

[15] I.e., Magdalene von Bora; see p. 271, n. 28.

[16] See p. 287, n. 1.

How disgusted I am that our printers delay so miserably the work on the manuscript! I sent this manuscript [to the publishing house] so that it should soon be finished [being printed], and [instead the printers] store it away for the winter.[17] If I had wanted to store it in this way, I certainly would have known how to keep it here with me. I have written to you[18] to take the sermon[19] away from Schirlenz (if he has not begun [to work on it]), and to give it to George Rhau. Yet I can well imagine that Schirlenz may hardly have the money to spend for the necessary paper to print this long manuscript. If this has not yet happened, then see that it is done soon, and that the sermon is completed as quickly as possible.

229

To Elector John[1]
[Coburg,] August 26, 1530

The Confutation was intended to demonstrate that the Augsburg Confession was a document of heretical faith, and to try to entice the evangelicals to come to terms with the papal church. This intention becomes especially clear from the concluding paragraph of the Confutation, in which it is written: "His Holy Imperial Majesty[2] is fully convinced, and hopes that the result will be that

---

[17] Literally: ". . . they [i.e., the printers] make for me out of it [i.e., the manuscript] fruit which is stored [i.e., obviously for the winter]." Freely paraphrased, Luther meant to say: while I intend that the printers immediately go to work on the manuscript which I sent, the printers in turn play a dirty trick on me by shelving the manuscript.

[18] Like so many other letters exchanged between Luther and his wife, this one too is no longer extant.

[19] *Eine Predigt, dass man Kinder zur Schulen halten solle* (A Sermon on Keeping Children in School) (Wittenberg: Nickel Schirlenz, 1530), WA 30[II], 517 ff.; LW 46, 213 ff.

[1] The extant autograph does not give an address because the address was written on an envelope-like wrapper, and this wrapper has obviously been lost. The content of the letter, however, makes sufficiently clear to whom Luther was writing.

[2] I.e., here and throughout this letter, Emperor Charles V (see LW 48, 175 f.), in whose name the *Confutation* was made public. Thus the *Confutation* had the quality of a proclamation by the Emperor, and amounted to an Imperial verdict against the *Augsburg Confession*.

when the Elector, princes, and cities [i.e., the signers of the Augsburg Confession] have heard . . . this Reply [i.e., the Confutation] they will agree with united minds in regard to those matters also in which they perhaps have not yet agreed hitherto with the Roman Catholic Church, and that in all other things above mentioned they will obediently conform to the Catholic and Roman Church and the Christian faith and religion. . . . For (which may God forbid) if this admonition, so Christian and indulgent, be unheeded, the Elector, princes, and cities can judge that a necessary cause is afforded His Imperial Majesty that, as becometh a Roman Emperor and Christian Caesar and a defender and advocate of the Catholic and Christian Church, he must care for such matters as the nature of the charge committed to him and his integrity of conscience require."[3]

This intention immediately lost its momentum when the signers of the Augsburg Confession demanded the right to study the Confutation prior to giving any answer to the Emperor's demand.[4] *On August 5 the Emperor's plan was completely nullified when the evangelicals would not abandon their demand to study the Confutation, and the Emperor refused to hand the Confutation over to the confessors without attaching conditions, which in turn the confessors rejected.*[5] *At this point one way*[6] *out of the dilemma would have been the use of force, as was envisioned in the closing paragraph of the Confutation. Apparently neither the Emperor nor the pro-papal Estates of the Empire were willing to take this step.*[7] *After some negotiations, the evangelicals finally suggested on Au-*

[3] Reu II, 382 f. The last sentence was obviously a threat against the signers of the *Augsburg Confession,* who were thus faced with the alternatives: either accept the *Confutation,* or face the wrath of the Emperor who would use (military) force to restore the *status quo ante.* See also *NB* I.Abt.,E.1, No. 27.
[4] See *TP,* p. 99.
[5] See *TP,* pp. 100 f.; *URA* 2, No. 137 (the Emperor's August 5 answer to the confessors); *BA,* p. 190.
[6] Other ways out of the dilemma would have been to recognize the *Augsburg Confession* as a valid expression of Christian faith (an action impossible for the Emperor to take because of his own personal religious convictions), or to promote the idea of a council and work for an armistice which should last until the council had decided all issues. Since the pope's cooperation would be needed for the calling of a council, this possibility would not have been an easy one to bring about. On the idea of having a council resolve the Reformation issues (as this idea developed during the first half of August), see Walter, RA, 74 ff.; *NB* I.Abt.,E.1., No. 27.
[7] See Walter, RA, 73 ff.; see however also *NB* I.Abt.,E.1, No. 27.

gust 13 the forming of a committee of seven representatives from each party which should work out a compromise between the Augsburg Confession and the Confutation. This committee was created on August 14, and began its work on August 16.[8] Due mostly to Eck's flexibility and Melanchthon's willingness to make concessions, this committee made good progress, and reached tentative agreement on 15 articles of the first part of the Augsburg Confession. However when the committee worked on the second part of the confession (the articles dealing with the "corrected abuses") difficulties arose, which in turn had a negative effect upon the work already accomplished.[9] The evangelicals were unable to accept the proposals made by the papists on August 19,[10] and the papists were unable to accept the proposal made by the evangelicals on August 20.[11] Consequently the work of the Committee of Fourteen collapsed on August 21, and on August 22 the diet was informed of this collapse.[12]

On that same August 22 Elector John dispatched a special messenger to Arnold von Falckenstein (the tax collector at Coburg) with copies of the August 19 and 20 proposals, and a letter to Luther requesting Luther's opinion on these proposals by return mail.[13] Letter No. 229 of August 26 is Luther's reply to the Elector. As could be expected, Luther rejected the proposals made by the papists. In letters written on the same day to Spalatin,[14] Melanchthon, and Jonas, Luther reiterated this rejection, using a mixture of slight sarcasm, serious exhortation, precise analysis of the situation, and strengthening comfort.[15] Von Walter has called these

---

[8] See TP, pp. 116 ff.; BA, pp. 208 ff.; URA 2, Nos. 142, 143.

[9] Spalatin was secretary of the Committee of Fourteen; see URA 2, 220. He kept a record which he edited after September, 1532. For this record see URA 2, Nos. 144, 145. For another record, see BA, pp. 211 ff., 214 ff.

[10] Text: URA 2, No. 152; TP, pp. 126 f.

[11] Text: URA 2, No. 153; TP, pp. 128 ff.

[12] For the events, see TP, pp. 130 f.; URA 2, Nos. 154, 157, 158; BA, pp. 229 ff.

[13] Text of the Elector's letter: WA, Br 12, 124 ff.; of the covering letter to Arnold von Falckenstein, ibid., 126, n. 20. The package apparently also contained Melanchthon's August 22 letter to Luther; WA, Br 5, No. 1691. In this letter Melanchthon gave a brief sketch of the negotiations of the Committee of Fourteen.

[14] See letter No. 230.

[15] See WA, Br 5, Nos. 1698–1700; for excerpts in English, see Reu II, 386 ff.

letters *"ein kräftiges Donnerwetter,"* that is, powerful thunderclaps which exploded over the evangelical politicians and theologians who were so eagerly seeking a compromise, and which gave them the proper perspective on the events.[16]

The package of letters arrived at Augsburg on August 29 or 30.[17] There the situation had, in the meantime, developed from the August 22 deadlock to a new crisis. On August 22 the pro-papal Estates had suggested the creation of a committee of three representatives from each party which was to take up the negotiations, and was to concentrate on those articles on which the Committee of Fourteen had reached no agreement. This Committee of Six began its work on August 23. By August 31 the Committee of Six was also deadlocked, and informed the diet accordingly.[18] Now it was again up to the Emperor to act. The situation became most serious when on August 31 Elector John requested from the Emperor permission to leave the diet.[19] The lines had been clearly drawn, and it had been established that the discrepancies between confessors and papists were too fundamental, and thus too important, for anyone to have any hope of finding a compromise.[20]

On Elector John, see LW 48, 269, n. 8.

Text in German: WA, Br 5, 572–574. For the following translation that by Schmauck-Benze in Reu II, 383 ff. has been consulted.

Grace and Peace in Christ!

Most Illustrious, Noble Sovereign, Most Gracious Lord! I have received Your Electoral Grace's letter,[21] together with the copies

---

[16] Walter, RA, 81.

[17] On August 29 Melanchthon was still awaiting Luther's "opinion"; see WA, Br 5, 597.

[18] TP, pp. 131, 132 ff., 137 f.; URA 2, Nos. 162–166, 168–169; BA, pp. 242 ff.; NB I.Abt.,E.1, No. 32.

[19] TP, p. 130, already mentions for August 22 that the confessors were determined to leave Augsburg. For the Emperor's negative answer of August 31 to Elector John, see URA 2, No. 170.

[20] It has to remain open whether and to what degree Luther and his August 26 letters, and a brief issued shortly thereafter, decisively influenced the negotiations of the Committee of Six, or only confirmed and strengthened the evangelicals. The latter is suggested by the fact that for the negotiations of the Committee of Six the signers of the Augsburg Confession instructed Melanchthon not to make further concessions; see BA, p. 242.

[21] See note 13.

[of the proposals prepared by] the two parties of the committee.[22] Since Your Electoral Grace requests my opinion on this material, I shall herewith humbly present it.

First of all, the condition or means [of compromise] proposed by the other party[23] is by no means to be accepted,[24] (as our party[25] has [already] recognized),[26] and I am quite surprised that such a proposal could have been made.

On the articles of our party, [the following] is my approving opinion: That the opponents demand that we teach that "one kind" of the sacrament[27] is also correct, and that to use "both kinds"[28] should not be a matter of commandment but of indifference and free choice, etc.,[29] Your Electoral Grace certainly knows that one of our principal tenets is that nothing is to be taught or done unless it is firmly based on God's Word,[30] so that we do not (as Paul says)[31] run aimlessly or shadow box.[32] For it is still enough of an effort for us to remain steadfast when acting according to a sure word [of Scripture]. It is, of course, certain that "one kind" of the sacrament is a purely human invention, and is in no way confirmed by God's Word; the contrary, however, that is "both kinds," is confirmed by a lucid and clear Word of God. Therefore

---

22 See notes 10, 11.

23 "Other party" or "our opponents" refers throughout this letter to the pro-papal delegation on the Committee of Fourteen in particular, or to the opponents of the evangelicals in general. For a list of the members of the pro-papal delegation on the Committee of Fourteen, see TP, p. 117; URA 2, 219.

24 Or: "tolerated," or "endured."

25 "Our party" or "our friends" refers throughout this letter to the signers of the Augsburg Confession and their supporters in general, or to the evangelical delegates on the Committee of Fourteen in particular. For a list of the members of the evangelical delegation on the Committee of Fourteen, see TP, p. 118; URA 2, 219, 220.

26 I.e., "our party" in Augsburg has rejected the August 19 proposal of the pro-papal delegation on the Committee of Fourteen, just as Luther is doing now.

27 I.e., that in the Lord's Supper only bread is to be given to the communing laymen.

28 See LW 48, 143 f.

29 For the appropriate passage in the August 19 proposal of the pro-papal delegation on the Committee of Fourteen, see URA 2, 251 f. See also Melanchthon's August 22 letter to Luther; WA, Br 5, 555.

30 Literally: "wrapped in God's Word."

31 I Cor. 9:26.

32 Literally: "run uncertainly and strike vain blows."

we are able neither to approve nor to teach that "one kind" is correct. For there stands Christ, [saying in] Matthew 15[:9]: "In vain do they serve me with man-made teachings," etc. In addition they intend to treat Christ's word, "Do this in remembrance of me," etc.,[33] as a matter of indifference—[that word] which he so sincerely and honestly commanded[34] [us to observe].

But they themselves do not believe that ["one kind"] is a matter of indifference, because on account of it they have burnt, exiled, and persecuted many people, and condemned them because of this "great heresy."[35] Therefore we must not allow this matter to be considered indifferent, not only for the sake of God and ourselves, but also for their own sakes. For in consenting, we also would have to denounce them as murderers and scoundrels who have condemned and persecuted as heresy something that is [supposedly] a matter of indifference. Since they themselves do not believe that ["one kind"] is a matter of indifference, we really are in no position to teach that it is, unless they would recant and could bring back to life all those whom they have persecuted on account of it.

It is a wonderful assertion when [our opponents] complain that they cannot control[36] the people if we do not teach that they, too, are correct.[37] Such profound reasoning I hear gladly. It is just as if God should have his Word taught for the purpose of allowing [the papists] to control their people and remain tyrants.

Concerning private masses[38] the same answer is to be given,

---

[33] I Cor. 11:24 f.

[34] Literally: "commanded cordially [or: "from the heart"], seriously."

[35] Luther was obviously thinking here of the fate of John Huss (see LW 48, 143 f.) and that of the Hussites.

[36] Luther wrote *halten,* i.e., hold something, hold together, hold on to something.

[37] As Enders, *Briefwechsel* 8, 216, n. 5, has pointed out, this argument can be found neither in the August 19 nor the August 20 proposals. In his August 22 letter (see note 13) Melanchthon also does not mention this argument. In the August 22 letter of the Elector to Luther this argument does appear, however; see WA, Br 12, 125. And on August 29, i.e., while the Committee of Six was still working, Melanchthon informed Luther that Eck was insisting that the evangelicals accept the validity of "one kind," since the common man could not be kept obedient if "we" do not free consciences in this matter, and teach that it is perfectly correct to celebrate the Lord's Supper by giving and receiving only the bread; see WA, Br 5, 598.

[38] In the August 19 proposal the pro-papal delegates insisted that the evangelicals accept the celebration of general and private masses and maintain

for they, too, are a human invention, [and] apart from other abuses in them, have arisen without any foundation in God's Word. That [our opponents] state,[39] however, that they would not compel us to establish [private masses], but desire only that we do not prevent them, [we counter]: "We do not prevent them from doing anything; but that we should approve of [private masses], this we are unable to do. For were one to permit the practice of only one human work, one would have to permit all the others also. Consequently, [our opponents' argument] would be the shortest way [for the opponents to accomplish all they wish]. If we permit the practice of private masses, then we might as well abandon the whole gospel and adopt purely human works, for there is no reason why only one and not all human works should be adopted. But He who has forbidden and condemned them all has also forbidden and condemned this one.

That [our opponents] state[40] that a sovereign's competency does not include preventing [the celebration of private masses, we counter:] We certainly know that the office of a sovereign and the office of preaching are not one and the same, and that it is not a sovereign's responsibility [to prevent the celebration of private masses]. But the present question is whether a sovereign as a Christian wishes to consent in this matter; the question is not whether he is acting here as a sovereign. There is a difference between whether a sovereign is to preach, or whether he wishes to consent to the preaching. Not the sovereign, but Scripture is to oppose the private mass. Whether a sovereign wishes to agree with Scripture or not is up to him, and no one on earth forces him to do it.

Concerning the Canon [of the mass], if it is to be tolerated, provided that it is properly interpreted,[41] [I answer]: Blah! If in

---

the Canon of the mass; see *URA* 2, 252. For the private mass see *LW* 48, 281, n. 26. For the text of the Canon, see B. Thompson (ed.), *Liturgies of the Western Church* (New York, 1961), pp. 72 ff. For a historical and theological commentary, see J. Jungmann, *The Mass of the Roman Rite: Its Origins and Development* 2 (New York, 1955), 101 ff.

39 This argument does not appear in the August 19 proposal (see note 10), but it does appear in the Elector's August 22 letter; see *WA*, Br 12, 125.

40 See note 39.

41 See the August 19 proposal of the pro-papal delegation (*URA* 2, 252 f.), and the enclosure in Melanchthon's August 25 letter to Luther (*WA*, Br 5, 564).

this matter things depended on a good exegete, I would long since have interpreted the belief of the Turks properly and would have turned all unbelief into Christian faith. Everyone knows very well how [our opponents] have sold the mass as a sacrifice[42] and [good] work.[43] Now they wish to interpret it away. But, in summary, this, too, is a human invention, which one may not tolerate in God's matters; and in addition, it is dangerous and offensive. Since they are abandoning the matter itself,[44] and agree with us that the mass is not a sacrifice,[45] why is it then necessary for them to retain the offensive word, since [the word][46] is, after all, unnecessary, and dangerous besides? One should not run into danger unnecessarily, for this is prohibited, and would mean tempting God. St. Augustine says:[47] "He has the meaning [but] he should improve the word." He is speaking [here] of the word "fate,"[48] and says: he who understands "fate"[49] as "will of God"[50] understands it correctly; yet [Augustine] does not wish to accept the word ["fate"] and [therefore argues]: "he should improve the word."[51] Do we want to use[52] dark and ambiguous words when we have a hard time staying with lucid and clear words?

Further, nothing is accomplished by leaving the word "sacrifice"[53] in the Canon, for even without this word the Canon clearly interprets the mass as a true sacrifice, so that no one is able to understand or interpret it otherwise than that the mass is a sacri-

---

[42] Luther uses a Latin word here.
[43] See note 42.
[44] I.e., the affirmation that in the mass the body and blood of Christ are sacrificed in an unbloody, sacramental way, as, e.g., Thomas Aquinas (*Summa theologica* III, qu. 79 a. 7; a. 1 ad 3; qu. 81 a. 4) taught and the Council of Trent (Sess. XXII, cap. 2) dogmatized. Did Luther at this point understand the proposal correctly? Or was he being slightly sarcastic? For John Eck's interpretation of the Lord's Supper (he was the leading papal theologian in the Committee of Fourteen), see E. Iserloh, *Die Eucharistie in der Darstellung des Johannes Eck* (Münster, 1950).
[45] See note 42.
[46] I.e., the word "sacrifice."
[47] *The City of God*, 5:1. The quotation is written in Latin.
[48] See note 42.
[49] See note 42.
[50] Luther uses a Latin phrase here.
[51] This portion of the quotation is written in Latin.
[52] Literally: "Do we want first to erect dark and uncertain words."
[53] See note 42.

fice. For among other things[54] it is written in the Canon that God, through the hands of his angel, should let this sacrifice of the sacrament be brought up before his divine altar.[55] This, of course, cannot be interpreted to mean a memorial of Christ's sufferings, because [such a memorial] is to be accomplished through the sermon. In short, the Canon beseeches God[56] to accept such a sacrifice, even though [this sacrifice] is the body and blood of his dear son. [And so we act] as if a man had to intercede with God in behalf of Christ. This is blasphemous and abominable, and [consequently] the Canon is not to be tolerated.

Finally, we are ready to accept and yield everything that is in our power. But we beg [our opponents] not to demand of us those things that are not in our power. What belongs to God's Word is, of course, not within our power. And what has been instituted as a service of God,[57] yet is without [basis in] God's Word, is also not in our power to accept. Therefore we are no longer able to accept fastings and festivals,[58] by which one is edified,[59] unless they are ordained by the secular government as a secular ordinance. All that which is adorned with ceremonies such as vestments, ritual, fasting, [and] feasting, is secular, since God has subjected such matters to reason and has ordered that [reason] may deal freely with them; Genesis 2.[60] For it is worldly matter and earthly existence which are subjected to reason through the word: "Have dominion over the earth."[61] Since secular government is reason's highest product, [the government] is able to be creative and give orders in these matters.

---

[54] Literally: "words."
[55] This is a reference to Rubric 27: *Supplices te rogamus*, i.e., "Humbly we ask it of thee." *Liturgies, op. cit.* (see note 38), p. 76.
[56] This is a reference to Rubric 19: *Te igitur*, i.e., "And so, . . . we humbly pray . . . thee. . . ." *Liturgies, op. cit.* (see note 38), p. 72. See also WA, TR 3, No. 3556; Bainton, pp. 40 ff.
[57] Or: "for the worship of God."
[58] See the August 19 proposal (*URA* 2, 250), where in Section One the *potestas iurisdictionis* (see p. 379, n. 12) of the bishops is maintained; against this Luther now flatly states that these "secular matters" are to be handled by the secular government.
[59] Or: "by which one builds oneself up." I.e., fastings and festivals are used to build up one's religious value.
[60] Was Luther thinking of Gen. 2:8, 15?
[61] Gen. 1:28. This quotation is written in Latin.

This is what I wish now to answer[62] humbly and hurriedly to Your Electoral Grace regarding the questions [sent to me]. Herewith I commend [Your Grace] to God's grace. Amen.

August 26, 1530   Your Electoral Grace's dedicated
MARTIN LUTHER

230

To George Spalatin[1]
Coburg, August 26, 1530

Luther returns to Spalatin a letter from Elector John and asks that the Electoral seal, which had been forgotten, be added to the letter, which is then to be returned to the Coburg. In the second paragraph Luther, with some slight sarcasm, discusses the negotiations that had recently taken place in Augsburg. He is amazed by the strange attempts to bring about unity between himself and the pope; of course the friends in Augsburg are not eager to agree to these compromise negotiations, but were only tricked by some ghosts into this business. Should the parties in Augsburg succeed, even though they are unwilling workers, then he will attempt to reconcile Christ and Belial. Luther cuts through the fog of false hopes for unity with incisive logic: the pope does not want unity, and Luther sees no possibility of it. In closing Luther affirms that Christ is the wisdom of the friends in Augsburg, and will guide them so that the conniving of the papists will be fruitless. He adds greetings and a blessing.

On George Spalatin, see LW 48, 8 f.
Text in Latin: WA, Br 5, 575–576.

To my dearest brother in the Lord, Master[2] George Spalatin,
a disciple of Christ

Grace and peace in the Lord. I have something, my Spalatin, for which I need your service and conscientiousness, namely, that you

---

[62] Literally: "now to have answered humbly."
[1] For this letter, which is extant as autograph, see also letter No. 229, Introduction.
[2] I.e., Master of Arts.

see to it that this letter from our Sovereign[3] to me is carefully notarized[4] with the seal of the Sovereign and returned to me. For even though it was sufficient for me that the letter had been personally signed by the excellent Sovereign, yet it delights me to charge the Chancellor[5] with sloppiness since he has dispatched the Sovereign's letter unsealed. I well remember writing to the Sovereign one time and not signing [the letter], and being reprimanded for being so negligent.[6] Now I have my perfect revenge with this unsealed letter—oh sweet revenge! Knowing your conscientiousness, I am confident that this matter will be taken care of.[7]

I hear[8] that you people, like it or not,[9] have begun a strange project, that is, to bring about unity between the pope and Luther. But the pope will not want it, and Luther sees no possibility of it. Watch out that you don't use all this effort for absolutely nothing. If you people can accomplish [this unity], even though it is contrary to the will of both parties, then I shall soon follow the example you set, and reconcile Christ and Belial.[10] Of course I know that you were not pushed into this pointless work by your own will, but by chance—or rather by the masked ghosts of Speyer.[11]

---

[3] I.e., here and throughout this letter, Elector John of Saxony; see LW 48, 269, n. 8. For the Elector's letter, see p. 405, n. 13.

[4] Apparently the Elector's letter was dispatched in a great hurry, so that the chancellery had forgotten to seal the letter. This was not a great mistake, since the letter was part of a package dispatched to Coburg for forwarding to Luther; see p. 405, n. 13.

[5] Enders, Briefwechsel 8, 218, n. 2, suggests that Luther was thinking of Chancellor Brück, and this is possible. In view of the material presented on p. 349, n. 8, however, it is more likely that Luther was thinking of Christian Beyer.

[6] The background of this statement could not be clarified.

[7] It is possible that in this paragraph Luther was "mocking" Spalatin's pedantry (so according to Clemen, WA, Br 5, 576, n. 5), or was joking about some personal matter between Luther and Spalatin (so according to Rückert, LB, p. 375, n. 18.).

[8] See letter No. 229, Introduction.

[9] It seems to be extremely awkward, and perhaps grammatically impossible, to assume (as Clemen, WA, Br 5, 576, n. 6, does) that "like it or not" could belong either to "I hear," or to "you people have begun."

[10] See II Cor. 6:15. As early as July 9 Luther had used this passage in connection with the negotiations in Augsburg; see p. 367. See also WA, Br 5, 470 (July 13); see also Deutsche Theologie 3 (1936), 78 ff., 248 ff.

[11] On August 8 Agricola mentioned to Luther the contents of a pamphlet (see WA, Br 5, 542, n. 10, 543; BA, pp. 194 ff.) which was circulating in Augsburg. This was the story: During July of 1530, two fishermen were working on the Rhine, near Speyer, when, one night, a monk came and asked one of them to ferry him across the Rhine. When the fisherman came to his boat

Christ, who thus far has been your strength, will now also be your wisdom,[12] so that those Italian intrigues[13] may accomplish nothing against you. For "the evil counsel will turn out to be worst for him who gives it."[14]

Greet Master[15] Eisleben,[16] Dr. Brenz,[17] Schnepf,[18] and all our [friends]. God's grace be with you. Amen.

From the wilderness,[19] *August 26, 1530*

Yours,

MARTIN LUTHER

---

there were many monks to be transported to the other side. When he had transported a boatload across the river, the fisherman saw many more monks on the other shore, and was ordered to ferry them across, too. The fisherman became terrified and apparently fell to the ground and became lame. The next night the fisherman's companion had the same experience. But when the first boatload of monks had almost reached the opposite shore, this fisherman demanded his reward. At this the one monk, apparently the spokesman, replied by hitting the fisherman in the ribs with a white staff, saying angrily that no one was any longer willing to give anything free to monks. The fisherman was forced (apparently by means of a divine spell) to continue with his services until all the monks had been ferried across. Both fishermen affirmed their stories when questioned by the city council of Speyer. The first fisherman recuperated, but the face of the second fisherman was terribly scratched, and he eventually died. Both fisherman affirmed overhearing that the monks had come from Cologne and were on their way to the diet in Augsburg. Once the monks had been ferried across the Rhine, they disappeared, and there were many who believed that they had been evil spirits. Referring to Agricola's letter, Melanchthon wrote to Luther on August 8: "The ghost of the monks at Speyer . . . definitely signifies a terrible tumult." WA, Br 5, 542. It was this ghost (signifying a terrible tumult), Luther now argues, who pushed the friends into losing all perspective, and into negotiating for unity in doctrinal matters.

12 See I Cor. 1:30.

13 I.e., the intrigues of the Italian clergy, or, more specifically, of the papal legate, Campeggio. Throughout the second half of the fifteenth and the first half of the sixteenth centuries there were heard throughout Germany loud protests against the manipulations, especially the financial ones, of the papacy and the Italians, i.e., the Curia; see also LW 48, 82. These protests were summarized in the *Gravamina* (i.e., grievances) of the German nation against the Roman See. Luther here characterizes the negotiations at Augsburg as an intrigue on the part of the (Italian) papacy for the purpose of subverting the church of the gospel (in Germany).

14 Luther here cites a saying often documented in classical literature, and recorded and analyzed by Erasmus of Rotterdam in his *Adagia*; Clericus 2, 73 f. See also WA, Br 11, 328, to WA, Br 5, 576, n. 10.

15 I.e., Master of Arts.

16 I.e., John Agricola; see LW 48, 220.

17 John Brenz; see pp. 177 f.

18 Erhard Schnepf (1495–1558), one of the Reformers of Württemberg, was born in Heilbronn and studied theology at Erfurt and Heidelberg, where it is

231

To Mrs. Martin Luther
Coburg, September 8, 1530

Taking advantage of a messenger who is hurriedly passing through, Luther writes this quick note. He voices his hope of coming home soon since the negotiations at Augsburg on "our case" are at an end. Now it is only necessary to wait for the Emperor's final statements. Luther says some expect that this final verdict will defer all matters until a general council of the church can be convened, while others hope that this verdict may provide an excuse for making war against the evangelicals. Luther gives instructions to his wife about publication arrangements for some of his manuscripts,

---

possible he became acquainted with Luther during the Heidelberg Disputation (see *LW* 48, 60 ff.). After he held several pastorates in southwest Germany, he was (from 1527 to 1534) one of the theological professors at the newly founded University of Marburg, and also functioned as preacher in Marburg. As theological consultant to Landgrave Philip of Hesse, Schnepf attended the 1529 Diet of Speyer and the 1530 Diet of Augsburg. In 1534 Duke Ulrich of Württemberg called Schnepf to Stuttgart as preacher, and entrusted him with the organization of the evangelical church in a part of the Duchy of Württemberg. Together with John Brenz, Schnepf prepared the *Württemberg Church Ordinance* of 1536, and other legal, liturgical, and catechetical materials. In 1544 Schnepf went as a theological professor and pastor to Tübingen, where he also became principal of the world-famous *Stift*. In the aftermath of the Smalcaldic War, Schnepf had to leave Tübingen. In 1549 he found refuge at the University of Jena, which was just then in the process of being established, and soon he took over ecclesiastical responsibilities in the newly formed Duchy of Saxony. The last decade of his life was overshadowed by the doctrinal controversies (which became increasingly bitter) between the Wittenberg followers of Melanchthon and the theological faculty at Jena. Schnepf, like Brenz, represented that type of Lutheranism which flourished in the southwestern parts of Germany, thoroughly Lutheran, strong in faith and piety, and always trying to avoid controversy and maintain peace in the church. He signed the *Syngramma Suevicum* and strongly opposed Zwinglianism. In Augsburg he was one of the few theologians who in the negotiations of August and September 1530 did not lose their heads either to false hopes or to lack of confidence; he made such a fine impression that, on September 13, e.g., one of the Nürnberg delegates wrote home: "Schnepf [i.e., the snipe, or woodcock] is the only one who still has a beak to sing [as a steadfast Christian]." *C.R.* 3, 364. On the other hand, in 1534 (i.e., two years prior to the *Wittenberg Concord*) Schnepf signed an agreement with Ambrosius Blaurer, the Reformer of Constance, who was known for his inclination to Zwinglianism, and who became, on the basis of the agreement, Schnepf's co-worker in the Reformation of Württemberg.
[19] See p. 287, n. 1.

and also announces that he has a big piece of sugar candy for their son John. Puzzled by the fact that someone had told his wife that he was ill, Luther points to his literary productivity as proof of his good health. Luther closes the letter with general greetings, a brief blessing, and an exhortation to prayer. As an afterthought he suggests that his wife deal with John Polner according to Bugenhagen's and Weller's advice.

Text in German: WA, Br 5, 608–609.

To my dearly beloved[1] mistress of the house,
Catherine Luther, at Wittenberg: *Personal*

Grace and peace in Christ. My dear Katie: This messenger hurriedly passed by, so that I was[2] unable to write much. However, I hope that I myself shall soon come, for this messenger brings us letters from Augsburg[3] [to the effect] that the negotiation[s] on our case have come to an end, and that they are now awaiting the Emperor's[4] decision and verdict. [The general opinion is] that everything will be postponed until a future council, for the [Arch]-bishop of Mainz and [the Bishop of] Augsburg are still standing firm, and the Count Palatine [and the Archbishops of] Trier and Cologne are also not willing to consent to strife and war. The others eagerly wish to rage, and expect the Emperor definitely to command this. May God's will be done. If only there will [finally] be an end to the diet![5] We have done and offered enough; the

---

[1] See p. 312, n. 1.
[2] Luther wrote from the point of view of the letter's recipient, for whom the act of writing had been past.
[3] The background of this statement is unclear.
[4] Emperor Charles V; see *LW* 48, 175 f.
[5] On August 29 the negotiations of the Committee of Six (see p. 406) had collapsed because of the unwillingness of the evangelicals to accept the conditions stipulated by the opposition in connection with "both kinds," private mass, the Canon of the mass, celibacy, and ecclesiastical jurisdiction; see *TP*, pp. 132 ff.; *BA*, p. 247; *C.R.* 2, No. 869. On August 31 the Estates referred the matter back to the Emperor; he now had the difficult task of either making a decision himself, or getting the negotiations off dead center. The Imperial and papal policy machine was at once shifted into high gear (see *TP*, p. 137 f.; *NB* I.Abt.,E.1, No. 32; *BA*, p. 248; Walter, *RA*, 82 f.), while the evangelicals sat back and waited, with Elector John repeatedly asking to be excused from the diet (see *URA* 2, No. 170; *C.R.* 2, 339), thus making it clear that he saw no possibility for further fruitful negotiations. In

papists do not want to give a hair's breadth. Thus someone will come who will teach them to give in and yield [the field].

I wonder why Hans Weiss[6] did not accept the Psalm.[7] I would not have expected that he would be so choosy,[8] since it is

---

these first days of September, when the diet's final phase had begun, four groups with four possible solutions to the Reformation issues were clearly discernable. There were the evangelicals, by now convinced of the fruitlessness of further negotiations in ecclesiastical matters, who pushed for a "benevolent" resolution of the diet (see LW 48, 70, n. 1) with an unconditional guarantee of peace until such time as a general council of the church could be convened to deal with all the ecclesiastical issues raised by the Reformation; see TP, p. 137; URA 2, 309. The evangelicals were opposed by the die-hard papists, led by the papal legate, Cardinal Campeggio, who did all in his power to stifle the council plan and to convince the Emperor that he should pursue a hardline policy which eventually would result in war against the stubborn heretics; see Walter, RA, 83. Between these two extremes stood the Emperor, and a group of moderate papists, especially some bishops. Though the Emperor was fundamentally opposed to granting anything significant to the evangelicals, he was in no military or political position to pursue a hardline policy against them; see Walter, RA, 83. And the group of moderates simply wanted peace on the basis of coexistence.

In the August 31 meeting, in which the collapse of the negotiations of the committee was announced to the Emperor, the Archbishops of Mainz, Cologne, and Trier, and the Count Palatine declared their basic inclination to peace, and their unwillingness to advise making war, or to assist in waging war against the evangelicals; see BA, p. 248. Apparently Aurifaber's "History of the Diet of Augsburg" (reproduced in BA) and Luther's statement above are the only precise witnesses of this incident. Even though the friendly attitude toward the evangelicals on the part of at least two of these bishops was generally known, so that the incident is probable, one has to be careful and not stretch Aurifaber's and Luther's statement. On September 7 the Emperor was ready to make his next move. On the condition that the evangelicals restore the ecclesiastical *status quo ante,* and thus block the further development and spread of the Reformation, the Emperor was ready to offer them an armistice until a general council could be convened; see TP, pp. 140 f.; URA 2, No. 179. In a plenary meeting of the diet on September 9, the evangelicals rejected this proposal publicly. They also rejected any further negotiations, insisted on a final pronouncement by the Emperor, and expressed their hope that this pronouncement would unconditionally guarantee them peace until a general council of the church would deal with the Reformation issues. See TP, pp. 142 f.; URA 2, Nos. 179, 180, 184. Now it was again up to the Emperor to act.

6 Hans Weiss was one of Luther's printers in Wittenberg.

7 This is a reference to Luther's Der 117. Psalm ausgelegt (*Explanation of Psalm 117*) (Coburg: Hans Beern, August, 1530), WA 31¹, 223 ff.; LW 14, 4 ff. Hans Weiss was to publish a second edition, which differed from the first only in a letter of dedication.

8 Hans Weiss's attitude becomes understandable if one remembers that what he was to publish was really only a reprint, and he was to do this only a very short time after the first edition had appeared on the market.

an important manuscript. I am herewith sending the rest of it,[9] and I am glad that George Rhau[10] is getting [the business]. If Mr. John Pomer[11] and Cruciger[12] approve of the manuscript concerning the keys,[13] then go ahead and have it printed. There is no reason for taking a vacation just to please the devil.[14]

I am really amazed that someone has told you I am ill,[15] [since] you [can] see with your own eyes the books I am writing. For I have finished the prophets, except for Ezekiel;[16] I am working on [Ezekiel] now, and [also] on a sermon on the sacrament,[17] not to speak of the writing of letters and whatever more there is to be done.[18]

I could not[19] write any more now because of the hurry. Greet

---

[9] On August 27 Luther dated the letter of dedication; see *WA* 30[I], 223 ff.; *LW* 14, 4 ff. He sent this letter, together with a first installment of the manuscript, to Wittenberg at a date which could not be established. It is probable that Luther sent the manuscript to the printer via his wife (as Clemen *WA, Br* 5, 609, n. 4 states), though this cannot be verified. If Luther did send this first installment to his wife, then he probably added a no-longer extant covering letter to which, by September 8, his wife had replied (in an also no-longer extant letter), informing him of Weiss's refusal to accept the manuscript.

[10] George Rhau was another of Luther's publishers in Wittenberg. He did publish the *Explanation of Psalm 117,* and the work came off the press in the first half of October; see *WA* 30[I], 219.

[11] I.e., John Bugenhagen; see *LW* 48, 303, n. 44.

[12] Caspar Cruciger; see p. 104, n. 12.

[13] This is a reference to Luther's *Von den Schlüsseln* (*On the Keys*) (Wittenberg: Hans Lufft, October, 1530), *WA* 30[II], 435 ff.; *LW* 40, 325 ff.

[14] Rückert, *LB* p. 384, n. 7, suggests that this statement has to be seen against the background of Elector John's strong suggestion (made in a July 21 letter to Luther) that Luther should not publish anything at this point that might aggravate the situation, provided that Luther could reconcile this with his conscience; see *WA, Br* 5, 497 f.

[15] Apparently in the no-longer extant letter mentioned in note 9 Luther's wife voiced concern for her husband's health.

[16] At this point Luther had finished the translation of all the prophets (see p. 288) except for the book of Ezekiel. On August 15 Luther had announced to Melanchthon that he hoped to finish the work on the minor prophets within a week, that only the work on Malachi and Haggai was left, and that then the work on Ezekiel (which he had interrupted because of linguistic [?] trouble and illness) would be taken up again. See *WA, Br* 5, 548. On Luther's work in translating the prophets, see *WA, DB* 11[II], lvii ff.

[17] This is a reference to Luther's *Vermahnung zum Sakrament des Leibes und Blutes unsers Herrn* (*Admonition Concerning the Sacrament of the Body and Blood of Our Lord*) (Wittenberg: Joseph Klug, November, 1530), *WA* 30[II], 595 ff.; *LW* 38, 97 ff.

[18] Or: "there is to be written."

[19] See note 2.

everyone and all! I have for Hansen Luther[20] a big fine piece of sugar [candy][21] which Cyriac[22] has brought from Nürnberg from the pretty garden.[23] With this be commended to God, and [all of you] pray! Deal with Polner[24] according to Pomer's [25] and Weller's[26] advice.

From the wilderness,[27] September 8, 1530

MARTIN LUTHER

232

To Nicholas Hausmann
Coburg, September 23, 1530

Answering Hausmann's request for news about the diet, Luther briefly reports on the developments that had taken place in Augsburg during the last part of August. He tells of the collapse of the negotiations between the committees, since the conditions of the papists and their concessions were unacceptable to the evangelicals, and the concessions made by evangelicals were unacceptable to the papists. So the matter was referred back to the Emperor for a final decision. Luther gives a summary evaluation of the conduct of the papists, and concludes that their conduct is a sure sign of satanic arrogance. While writing this letter Luther receives a letter from Elector John in Augsburg, informing him that the Emperor has given a gracious dismissal to the Elector. Luther is now expecting the return of his friends. In closing Luther gives a brief evalu-

---

[20] John Luther; see p. 152, n. 7.

[21] Literally: "book of sugar." Luther makes a pun here. He had just listed his literary productions. Continuing, he says that he also has a "book" for his son, but it is a book made of sugar.

[22] On August 3 Luther sent his nephew, Cyriac Kaufmann, who was staying with him at the Coburg, to Augsburg, so that the young man might experience the pomp and excitement of a diet. On his return trip to the Coburg Cyriac must have bought the gift mentioned by Luther.

[23] This is obviously a reference to letter No. 214.

[24] See p. 402, n. 10.

[25] See note 11.

[26] Peter Weller; see p. 321, n. 2.

[27] On this phrase, written in Latin, see p. 287, n. 1.

*ation of Emperor Charles, whom he considers to be a man of good
will, yet a man who is harassed by demonic monsters.*
On Nicholas Hausmann, see LW 48, 399 f.
Text in Latin: WA, Br 5, 631–632.

To Mr. Nicholas Hausmann, venerable in the Lord,[1]
bishop of the church at Zwickau,[2] my revered elder

Grace and peace in the Lord. Even though I think, excellent
Nicholas, that, since the younger Sovereign[3] has returned home
and no doubt has brought with him in abundance all [that is
newsworthy], all events at Augsburg are known at your place, yet
I shall briefly write as much as I know,[4] since you ask this of me.[5]

I believe you have heard that arbiters—among whom was
Philip[6]—had been charged with deliberating on unity in teaching
and on peace.[7] Since they could not agree, the matter has been
again referred back to the Emperor,[8] whose verdict is expected,[9]
although in the last letter [our friends in Augsburg] wrote that in
the meantime they had once more deliberated on conditions for
peace. However, they did not communicate what the conditions
were.[10] In the prior negotiations for unity the opponents[11] de-

---

[1] Literally: "To the man, venerable in the Lord, Nicholas Hausmann."
[2] See pp. 87, n. 5; 61, n. 9.
[3] I.e., the Electoral prince, Duke John Frederick; see LW 48, 181 f. He had
left Augsburg on September 12 (see TP, p. 148) and arrived at the Coburg
on September 14 (see WA, Br 5, No. 1719, Introduction; URA 2, No. 196).
Apparently he continued his trip on the fifteenth, for on that day Luther wrote
to Melanchthon that Duke John Frederick *had* given him a golden ring and that
he *had* wanted to take him, Luther, along to Wittenberg; see WA, Br 5, 623.
This suggests that the Electoral prince and his party had left the Coburg by
the time Luther was writing to Melanchthon.
[4] Literally: "briefly communicate as much as I have."
[5] Nothing could be established about the background of this statement.
[6] Melanchthon (see LW 48, 77, n. 3) had been a member of the Committee
of Fourteen and of the Committee of Six; see pp. 404 ff.
[7] For the following sentences see pp. 403 ff.
[8] I.e., here and throughout this letter and the Excursus, Emperor Charles V;
see LW 48, 175 f.
[9] See also Excursus.
[10] The background of this statement is not clear because the letter mentioned
by Luther cannot be identified with certainty. On September 4 Melanchthon
informed Luther that the matter had been referred back to the Emperor but
that "we [i.e., the evangelicals] were deliberating today certain peace conditions, which, should the opponents insist on them, [Elector John] would

manded that we allow private masses; also, that we preserve both Canons with a proper interpretation, that is, that the term "sacrifice" be understood as a representative memorial sacrifice; also, that we should teach that it is a matter of choice to take one or both elements [in the celebration of the Lord's Supper]; also, that we should leave it up to the married monks, nuns, and priests whether to abandon their spouses, return to the monasteries, and not be considered as married people. If we were willing to accept these conditions, then [the opponents] would be willing to permit us [to give] both elements [in the celebration of the Lord's Supper], and, for the sake of the children who had been born, to tolerate, just as brothels are tolerated, those [of the clergy, monks, and nuns] who had married—[but only] until a council.

You see, my Nicholas, Satan's absolutely secure arrogance, who, like a tyrant with his captives, dares to suggest such foul, filthy, dishonorable conditions. Our friends have conceded nothing of these points. They have offered,[12] however, to restore the ecclesiastical jurisdiction on condition that the bishops take care that the gospel be taught, and all corruption be eliminated; and also

---

forward to you before allowing anything to be decided." WA, Br 5, 604. Was Luther thinking of this letter and these deliberations, of which nothing else seems to be known? The similarity of the phrases used by Melanchthon on September 4 and by Luther on September 23 makes highly probable that on September 23 Luther was indeed thinking of these deliberations mentioned by Meianchthon on September 4. But as suggested by Clemen (WA, Br 5, 632, n. 3), there is also another possibility for interpreting this passage. On September 10 Melanchthon sent a letter to Nürnberg in which he included a no-longer extant letter for Luther which was to be forwarded to the Coburg; see C.R. 2, 358. In a September 10 letter to Luther's companion, Veit Dietrich, Melanchthon mentioned that either peace could be brought about under certain conditions, or the *status quo ante* would be restored by Imperial edict; WA, Br 5, No. 1720, Introduction. What Melanchthon wrote in the no-longer extant September 10 letter to Luther is unknown; and so it cannot be established how much Luther knew of the events in Augsburg, especially of the September 10 negotiations (see Excursus). Apparently Luther knew something of the September 10 negotiations, since in the next sentence he refers to the *"prior* negotiations," which is obviously a reference to the work done by the committees in August. At any rate, as he himself states to Hausmann, Luther had not received exact information, i.e., the text of those conditions which, it was hoped, would form a basis for a peaceful solution to the religious controversy.

11 This is a reference to the work of the Committee of Fourteen and of the Committee of Six (see note 6).

12 In the Committee of Fourteen; URA 2, No. 153; see also above, p. 405, n. 11, and WA, Br 5, 556, 564.

[to restore] certain feast days, etc. But nothing has been accomplished [by this]. The opponents simply want to perish; an inescapable fate pushes them.

While I am writing this line, a letter of our Sovereign[13] from Augsburg arrives[14] in which the excellent Sovereign informs me that he has been permitted by the Emperor to depart from Augsburg today, Friday.[15] Therefore we are now expecting our returners.[16] Emperor Charles is an excellent man; he hopes to restore unity and peace. I don't know whether he will be able to do this, besieged as he is by so many demonic monsters.

Farewell in the Lord, dearest friend.

From Coburg, September 23, 1530   Yours,

MARTIN LUTHER

---

[13] I.e., here and throughout this letter and the Excursus, Elector John; see *LW* 48, 269, n. 8.

[14] Literally: "interrupts me [or: obstructs me]." The letter is no longer extant. Extant, however, is a September 19 letter of Elector John to his son, Duke John Frederick (see note 3), in which the Elector tells of the constant delays regarding the granting of permission for him to leave the diet. According to this letter, Elector John was finally granted permission to leave Augsburg on Friday, September 23. *URA* 2, No. 198.

[15] The Elector left Augsburg, with his advisors, on September 23 in the (late?) afternoon (*BA*, p. 321; *TP*, p. 165), after he had empowered a legation to represent him in the final negotiations of the diet; *URA* 2, Nos. 197, 217.

[16] The Electoral party relaxed somewhat on its return trip. On September 27 the Elector arrived at Nürnberg (*BA*, p. 321). On October 1, in the late afternoon, the Electoral party arrived at the Coburg. On October 4 in the morning the Electoral party, with Luther, began the return trip to Torgau, where they arrived on October 11. See *WA*, Br 5, 644, n. 2; *ibid.*, No. 1732, Introduction; *BA*, p. 321. Luther arrived at Wittenberg on October 13; see *WA* 32, xvii f., lxx.

Excursus

At the time that Luther was writing to Hausmann, the final phase of the diet had reached its climax. In the evening of September 22 Charles V proposed a diet resolution which dealt exclusively with the religious issue, however, and completely bypassed the other issues for which the diet had been convened.

Much frustration and many negotiations preceded the Emperor's proposal. After the negotiations were again deadlocked on September 8 and 10 (see p. 416, n. 5), the Emperor tried once more on September 9 and 10 through intermediaries to get the situation off dead center. From September 10 to 14 these efforts were kept alive, even though only half-heartedly. (See Walter, RA, 84 f.; URA, 2, Nos. 185, 186, 188–192; BA, pp. 293 ff.; TP, pp. 146 ff.) On September 14, however, the papal legate, Cardinal Campeggio, nullified all plans in this connection. He was at the end of his patience (see Walter, RA, 85), and so were the evangelicals. Duke John Frederick's departure from Augsburg on September 12, without a final audience with the Emperor, the increasing criticism of Melanchthon voiced by some of the evangelicals (especially by the Nürnberg delegation), and the Elector's repeated attempts to receive a gracious dismissal—all serve to identify the situation.

On September 22 in the late afternoon the Estates were summoned to the Emperor's quarters for a plenary meeting, and were presented with the resolution. (For the events of September 22, see TP, pp. 152 ff.; BA, p. 309; URA 2, No. 205.) This resolution (text: URA 2, No. 206; BA, 310 ff.; English translation: Reu II, No. 51) provided for a general armistice till April 15, 1531; at that date the evangelical Estates were to inform the Emperor of their decision whether they would return to the faith of the Roman church. Further, the Emperor promised to exert all possible efforts with the Curia for a council which was to bring about a Christian reformation. The *Augsburg Confession* was considered to have been refuted by the *Confutation,* and further publications on the part of the evangelicals were prohibited. Inhabitants of evangelical territories who wanted to maintain the faith and practices of the Roman church were to be granted the privilege of doing so, while subjects of pro-papal sovereigns were not to be enticed into becoming evangelical or into moving into evangelical territories. And finally, the evangelicals were to assist the Emperor in political or military undertakings against the Zwinglians and Anabaptists. After a brief consultation Gregory Brück rejected this resolution on behalf of the evangelicals. (See TP, pp. 157 f.; URA 2, Nos. 207, 208; BA, pp. 313 ff.) In order to demonstrate that the *Augsburg Confession* was not refuted, Brück wanted to hand over to the Emperor the first draft of the *Apologia* by Melanchton. Even though the Emperor was already reaching for it, he pulled his hand back—apparently after his brother, Ferdinand of Austria, had whispered something into his ear. (See *BA*, p. 314; *URA* 2, 481; *TP*, p. 158.) To accept the *Apologia* at this moment would obviously have meant an admission that the *Augsburg Confession* was not necessarily refuted, and that the *Confutation* need not have been the final word on the issue.

On the morning of September 23 the pro-papal Estates met in the Emperor's quarters and accepted the resolution, with some minor changes. (For the events of September 23, see *BA*, pp. 315 ff.; *TP*, pp. 159 ff.; *URA* 2, Nos. 211–216.) Though not unanimously (see Water, *RA*, 87), they also founded an alliance to defend the Empire and the faith of the Roman church to the extent of their properties and lives, an alliance in which the Emperor joined immediately. Then the evangelicals were summoned and officially informed of this alliance, and were again requested to accept the resolution. The evangelicals, in turn, offered once more to defend their theological position. But the Emperor insisted on the acceptance of the resolution. Elector John affirmed that his confession was based on God's Word, so that all the gates of hell could accomplish nothing against it. (It is not clear whether this incident occurred at the end of the meeting, or sometime during the meeting. Aurifaber still adds that prior to their departure the Emperor and the evangelicals shook hands; see *BA*, p. 320.) The evangelicals commended their cause to God and left. A short while later Elector John departed from Augsburg. (See *TP*, pp. 164 f.; see also above, notes 14–16.)

233

To Mrs. Martin Luther
[Coburg,] September 24, 1530

Referring to a letter written "yesterday" and to a letter by Elector John, Luther announces to his wife that he hopes to be home again in two weeks, if it is God's will. He anticipates that his cause will be condemned in one way or the other, and informs his wife (a former nun) that his opponents insist on preserving monastic life and on forcing back into it those monks and nuns who had abandoned monastic life. Luther also tells of news according to which some people hope that the diet will bring about peace; he considers this peace a sign of God's great grace, especially in view of the Turkish menace. He closes with a brief benediction.

Text in German: WA, Br 5, 633–634.

To Doctor Luther's Mrs. Catherine,[1] at Wittenberg: *Personal*

Grace and peace in Christ! My dear Katie! Yesterday I wrote to you[2] and sent along a letter of my Most Gracious Lord,[3] from which you can learn that our friends at Augsburg are intending to set out. According to this [letter] I hope to be with all of you at home in fourteen days,[4] (if God gives [his] grace).[5] Even though I think that our cause will not remain absolutely free from condemnation, yet this matters little. [The opponents][6] definitely intend to have the monks and nuns back in the monasteries.[7] Yet Rietesel[8] has written to us[9] that he hopes that [our party][10] will depart from Augsburg with peace [reigning] in all streets. May God grant this. It would be a [sign of] great grace, [and] we all certainly are in need of it, since the Turk is such a menace.[11]

No doubt you will hear more from Hornung.[12] With this may you all be commended to God. Amen.

September 24, 1530   MARTIN LUTHER

---

[1] Luther wrote: *frawen Katherin Doctor Lutherin.*

[2] This letter is no longer extant.

[3] I.e., Elector John; see *LW* 48, 269, n. 8. This is obviously a reference to the letter which Luther had received on September 23; see p. 422.

[4] See p. 422, n. 16.

[5] Literally: "According to this [letter] I hope (if God gives [his] grace) we shall be in fourteen days with you [plural] at home."

[6] See p. 407, n. 23.

[7] See p. 421.

[8] John Rietesel was Elector John's chamberlain and confidant.

[9] Literally: "to here," i.e., Coburg. The no-longer extant letter of Rietesel was apparently directed to one of the Electoral Saxon officials at Coburg.

[10] See p. 407, n. 25.

[11] See p. 265.

[12] Wolf Hornung; see p. 326, n. 11. Apparently he was the letter carrier.

234

To Louis Senfl[1]
Coburg, October 4, 1530[2]

Throughout his life the Psalter was one of the sources of Luther's rich devotional life. During his stay at the Coburg, Psalm 118:17 was for Luther a special comfort.[3] Since Luther was very fond of music, it is not surprising that he used the Psalter, sung according to the liturgical regulations and in the musical settings of the church, for prayer and meditation. While at the Coburg Luther apparently did much thinking about the nature of music and its relationship to church and theology; this resulted in a sketch entitled "On Music" which is extant only as a copy by Veit Dietrich.[4] Luther also contacted Louis Senfl, one of the leading composers and conductors of his time.

In this letter Luther briefly sets forth his ideas on the spiritual value of music. For Luther music and theology are of equal importance, since both chase away the devil and disperse the spiritual anxieties created by the devil. Music and theology have the same function, that is, they proclaim truth, and this is the reason, Luther says, why the old Testament prophets did not use any of the liberal arts except music. In a second paragraph Luther asks Senfl for an arrangement of the antiphon taken from Psalm 4:8. This antiphon, Luther assures Senfl, has been dear to him since the days of his youth, and now, when he feels the end of his life approaching, it means even more to him. He encloses the plainsong version of this antiphon in case Senfl does not have it, and closes the letter with a brief benediction, and with greetings to Senfl's choir.

---

[1] According to the textual variations reproduced in Enders, *Briefwechsel* 8, 278, the address is missing in all witnesses. The circumstances of the letter (see *WA, Br* 5, No. 1727, Introduction) corroborate the tradition which has designated Senfl as the addressee of this letter.

[2] On the date, which is controversial, see *WA, Br* 5, No. 1727, Introduction, and Rückert, *LB*, p. 403, n. 31.

[3] See also *WA*, 31[I], 146 ff.; *WA, TR* 5, No. 5247. Well-established tradition reports that while at the Coburg Luther wrote Ps. 118: 17 ("I shall not die, but I shall live and recount the deeds of the Lord") on the wall of his living quarters, with the notes for the plainsong; see *WA, Br* 5, 638, n. 4; *WA* 48, 283 f.; Schanze, *op. cit.* (see p. 287, n. 5), pp. 20 f.

[4] See *WA* 30[II], 695 f.

Louis Senfl (ca. 1486–1543), apparently from Zürich or Basel, joined the court choir of Emperor Maximilian in 1496. He soon advanced to the position of official composer and conductor. Soon after the death of Maximilian, Senfl joined the court of Duke William of Bavaria in Munich, where in 1523 he became chief conductor and court composer, positions he held to the end of his life. Senfl is considered one of the German masters of the sixteenth century polyphonic hymn and song; he is also famous for his compositions of motets and masses. Even though Senfl did not join the Reformation, he maintained friendly connections with some of the evangelicals. On Louis Senfl see Die Musik in Geschichte und Gegenwart 12 (Kassel, 1965), 498 ff.; Grove's Dictionary of Music and Musicians 7 (5th ed.; New York, 1955), 698 f.

Text in Latin: WA, Br 5, 639.[5]

Grace and Peace in Christ

Even though my name is detested, so much that I am forced to fear that this letter I am sending may not be safely received and read by you, excellent Louis, yet the love for music, with which I see you adorned and gifted by God, has conquered this fear. This love also has given me hope that my letter will not bring danger to you.[6] For who, even among the Turks, would censure him who loves art and praises the artist? Because they encourage and honor music so much, I, at least, nevertheless very much praise and respect above all others your dukes of Bavaria, much as they are unfavorably inclined toward me.[7]

There is no doubt that there are many seeds of good qualities in the minds of those who are moved by music. Those, however, who are not moved [by music] I believe are definitely like stumps

---

[5] The letter is extant in many manuscript copies, in some special editions, and in the common editions of Luther's works. The many witnesses demonstrate the popularity of this letter and its far-flung distribution.

[6] See note 7.

[7] The Bavarian dukes were among the leading opponents of Luther, and were most active in combating the Lutheran teachings; see, e.g., p. 332, n. 57. For the cultivation of music in Munich, see O. Ursprung, *Münchens musikalische Vergangenheit* (Munich, 1927), pp. 33 ff.; WA 30[II], 696; *Die Musik in Geschichte und Gegenwart* 9 (Kassel, 1961), 879 ff.

[of wood] and blocks of stone. For we know that music, too,[8] is odious and unbearable to the demons. Indeed I plainly judge, and do not hesitate to affirm, that except for theology there is no art that could be put on the same level with music, since except for theology [music] alone produces what otherwise only theology can do, namely, a calm and joyful disposition. Manifest proof [of this is the fact] that the devil, the creator of saddening cares and disquieting worries, takes flight at the sound of music almost as he takes flight at the word of theology. This is the reason why the prophets did not make use of any art except music; when setting forth their theology they did it not as geometry, not as arithmetic, not as astronomy, but as music, so that they held theology and music most tightly connected, and proclaimed truth through Psalms and songs.[9] But why do I now praise music and attempt to portray, or rather smear, such an important subject on such a little piece of paper? Yet my love for music, which often has quickened me and liberated me from great vexations, is abundant and overflowing.

Returning to you, I ask if you would have copied and sent to me, if you have it, a copy of that song: "In peace [I will both lie down and sleep]."[10] For this tenor melody[11] has delighted me from youth on, and does so even more now that I understand the words. I have never seen this antiphon arranged for more voices. I do not wish, however, to impose on you the work of arranging; rather I assume that you have available an arrangement from some other source.[12] Indeed, I hope that the end of my life is at hand; the world hates me and cannot bear me, and I, in turn, loathe and detest the world; therefore may the best and [most] faithful shepherd[13] take my soul to him.[14] And so I have already started to sing this antiphon and am eager to hear it arranged. In case you should

---

[8] I.e., in addition to sound theology.
[9] See e.g., Isa. 5:1; I Sam. 10:5; see also WA 30[II], 696.
[10] Ps. 4:8.
[11] I.e., the *cantus firmus* of the plainsong which Luther wanted to have arranged for more voices; see also *LJB* 15 (1933), 80 f.
[12] I.e., some other source than Senfl's immediate work.
[13] See John 10:11 f.; I Pet. 2:25.
[14] I Kings 19:4.

not have or know it, I am enclosing it here with the notes;[15] if you wish you can arrange it—perhaps after my death.

The Lord Jesus be with you forever and ever. Amen. Forgive my temerity and verbosity. Extend respectful greetings to your whole choir on my behalf.[16]

From Coburg, October 4, 1530   MARTIN LUTHER

235

To the Electoral Saxon Government[1] [Torgau, about October 27, 1530][2]

The diet resolution, presented to the evangelicals on September 22, and the alliance founded by some of the pro-papal Estates[3] brought the evangelicals into a most dangerous situation. While returning from Augsburg, Gregory Brück[4] wrote on October 3 to Landgrave Philip of Hesse[5] about plans of action during the period of the armistice.[6] While this letter did not contain any concrete suggestions for dealing with the military threat possibly involved in the alliance of the pro-papal Estates, it nevertheless established grounds for further common action. Meanwhile, however, on October 2

---

[15] I.e., the notes for the tenor voice of the plainsong.

[16] For this whole letter, see also WA, 35, 535 ff; LW 53, 332 ff.

[1] The address and signature are missing since Luther did not send this document, but personally gave it to the Electoral Saxon councilors while he was in Torgau.

[2] The circumstances surrounding this note and its contents help establish the place from which it was written and its approximate date. That Luther was in Torgau from approximately October 26 to 28 can be seen from his October 26 letter to Nicholas Hausmann (WA, Br 5, No. 1739), and his October 28 letter to Landgrave Philip of Hesse (see letter No. 236), for in this letter Luther referred to his opinion, given to the Elector, on the issue of resistance. And finally, on October 27 Brück wrote and dispatched to other evangelical Estates letters which clearly reflect the new situation created by Luther's note; see Fabian, ESBV (2nd ed.), p. 125, n. 632. While it is possible that Luther wrote the letter on October 26, it is very dubious that such an important document was issued so early in the conference, i.e., at its beginning. See also p. 435, n. 17.

[3] See pp. 423 f.

[4] See pp. 51 f.

[5] See p. 124, n. 18.

[6] Text: Fabian, ESBV (1st ed.), pp. 140 f.

the Landgrave himself had written to Elector John,[7] to the Electoral prince, Duke John Frederick,[8] and to Brück, suggesting an immediate conference to prepare a joint defense against any possible attack.[9] The Landgrave envisioned an alliance of all the Protestants, as he had done in Speyer in the spring of 1529.[10] To accomplish this, the Eucharistic controversy had to be settled, along with other problems;[11] therefore the Landgrave apparently also wrote to Luther on October 2 or 3, although no such letter is extant.[12] The reaction of the Electoral Saxon Court to this move on the part of the Landgrave was evasive. The Elector and his councilors had to be on guard against the Landgrave's hotheadedness and political ambitions.[13] And further, they had to contend with a fundamental problem, namely, the matter of the legal and theological-moral right of taking up arms against the emperor,[14] should he attack. In the negotiations of 1529/30 the Electoral Saxon court first affirmed and then denied that such a right existed.[15] Luther's negative position on the right of armed resistance to the emperor was known.[16] The situation in Augsburg, however, made Luther aware of new legal dimensions of this issue, as may be seen from his August 5 letter to Brück.[17] Under the impact of the development in Augsburg, especially the emergence of the political and military alliance of pro-papal sovereigns, the attitude on the part of the leading political

---

[7] See *LW* 48, 269, n. 8.

[8] See *LW* 48, 181 f.

[9] Text of the letters: Fabian, *ESBV* (1st ed.), pp. 137 ff.

[10] See pp. 223 f.

[11] This was especially emphasized in the letter to Elector John; see Fabian, *ESBV* (1st ed.), p. 137.

[12] See Fabian, *ESBV* (2nd ed.), pp. 106 f. Luther apparently answered this letter on October 15, 1530; *WA, Br* 5, No. 1735.

[13] Text of the Elector's answer: Fabian, *ESBV* (1st ed.), pp. 141 f.

[14] While obviously here and throughout this letter "emperor" can refer to Charles V (see *LW* 48, 175 f.), the problem is of fundamental importance regardless of the incumbent of the Imperial office, or the particular circumstances involved.

[15] See pp. 244, n. 7; 246.

[16] See p. 255, n. 10.

[17] See letter No. 226. The problem raised by this letter could be formulated as follows: What does the Imperial law say about the emperor, his relationship to the elector of Saxony, and the elector's right to resist the emperor with arms if and when the emperor acts as a tyrant who nullifies the Imperial law? The brief prepared by Brück for the Torgau conference (see note 21) takes exactly this problem as its point of departure.

and military men at the Electoral Saxon court became increasingly determined. As early as September 30 Hans von Dolzig[18] submitted to Duke John Frederick a preliminary defense and mobilization plan for Electoral Saxony.[19] Gregory Brück incorporated this material into a substantial brief, in which he set forth plans for political and military action to defend the territory in case of an attack, even by the emperor; he submitted this brief to Duke John Frederick on October 23.[20] With the aid of the legal councilors at the Electoral court Brück drafted another brief[21] in which, on the basis of principles of judicial procedure, a legal basis for armed opposition to the emperor was established. In order to gain moral support for this position, a conference was held in Torgau from approximately October 25 to 28 between the Wittenberg theologians, led by Luther, and the Electoral Saxon councilors, led by Brück.[22] During this conference the theologians were presented with an abstract of the last of the briefs just mentioned,[23] and on the basis of it the theologians endorsed the right of armed resistance to the emperor. In the name of his colleagues Luther wrote the following lines,[24] extant in his own handwriting, in which the armed opposition to the emperor was approved, provided that the circumstances were as the legal experts had analyzed them.

Text in German: WA, Br 5, 662.

A piece of paper[25] has been presented to us[26] from which we see what the Doctors of Law[27] are concluding regarding the question:

---

[18] See p. 69, n. 7.

[19] See Fabian, *ESBV* (1st ed.), p. 48 f.; *op. cit.* (2nd ed.), pp. 114 f.

[20] Fabian, *ESBV* (2nd ed.), pp. 114 f., 342 f.

[21] For Brück's authorship, see Fabian, *ESBV* (2nd ed.), pp. 117 f.; for the text, see *ARG* 13 (1916), 231 ff.; Müller, *op. cit.* (see p. 257, n. 25.), pp. 89 ff.; *St. L.* 10, 558 ff.; *Widerstandsrecht*, pp. 63 ff.

[22] On this conference, see Fabian, *ESBV* (2nd ed.), pp. 118 ff.; Müller, *op. cit.*, pp. 33 ff.

[23] See note 25.

[24] The protocol of the conference contains, of course, more than this short note of Luther; for the text, see *WA*, Br 5, 662 f.

[25] It is doubtful whether the whole brief (see note 21) was presented to Luther, for he would hardly have called it a *zetel*, i.e., a piece of paper. See also note 31.

[26] I.e., Luther himself, and Melanchthon, Jonas, and perhaps also Spalatin; see Fabian, *ESBV* (2nd ed.), p. 121, n. 616.

[27] I.e., Brück (see note 21) and his staff.

In what situations may one resist the governing authority? If, then, [this issue] has been settled by these Doctors of Law or experts in this way,[28] and [since] we certainly are in those situations in which (as [the legal experts] demonstrate) one may resist the governing authority, and [since] we have always taught that as long as[29] the gospel does not go contrary to secular law one is to let secular law be effective, valid, and competent [in those matters which it is able to handle],[30] we therefore are unable to oppose [anyone with arguments taken from] Scripture, if in this instance it is necessary to fight back, even if the emperor himself [attacks us], or whoever else may do so in his name.

Further, now everywhere there is the danger that any day other incidents might occur, as a result of which one has to defend oneself immediately, not only because of the secular law, but also because of the duty and distress of conscience. Therefore it is also fitting to arm oneself, and to be ready to meet a force which might suddenly arise, as could easily occur judging by the present pattern and course of events.

That until now we have taught absolutely not to resist the governing authority was due to the fact that we did not know that the governing authority's law itself[31] grants [the right of

---

[28] The main arguments of the brief were as follows: (a) The emperor is not competent in matters of faith; he can only execute a decision of a council, and for such a decision the evangelicals have asked in their Protest and Appeal of 1529, but have not yet received it. (b) Even if the emperor were competent in matters of faith, his jurisdiction would have been nullified by the appeal of the evangelicals to a higher authority, i.e., the council. (c) Should the emperor, or his followers, try to enforce the resolution of the Diet of Augsburg in any way, then their actions would be unjust, because they would be acting contrary to principles of court procedure. (d) Then the emperor would no longer be acting as just judge, but as tyrant; even more, he would be acting as a private person, and contrary to the Word of God. (e) Therefore armed resistance to the emperor is permitted.

[29] Or: "because the gospel." Luther wrote weil. The presented translation is more strongly supported by Luther's usage of weil than the alternative. See also Trübner 8, 89 f.

[30] Literally: ". . . effective, valid, and maintain [or: "keep"] what they [i.e., the secular laws] are able to do."

[31] I.e., as this law was interpreted by Brück and his staff. The legal validity of the legal experts' arguments and of Luther's reaction is a matter by itself. Luther apparently was presented only with an abstract of the brief (see note 25), which contained, perhaps in the form of theses, only the conclusions and not the arguments or the documentations. This documentation was almost completely drawn from Canon Law and not from secular law. Müller, op. cit.,

armed resistance]; we have, of course, always[32] diligently taught that [this law] must be obeyed.

236

To Landgrave Philip of Hesse
Torgau, October 28, 1530

While at Torgau,[1] Luther received an October 21 letter of Landgrave Philip of Hesse.[2] In this letter the Landgrave exhorted Luther to publish a book which would deal with the Diet of Augsburg.[3] Then the Landgrave discussed the problem of armed resistance to the emperor.[4] In an attempt to convince Luther that the evangelical Estates did have the right of armed resistance even against the emperor, the Landgrave gave a list of five major arguments which were taken from constitutional law,[5] rather than from the law of

---

p. 49, n. 2, points out that only two references were taken from Roman Law, all the rest from Canon Law. Were one to assume that Luther saw the whole brief, then Müller's observation would raise serious questions. Did Luther simply accept the Canon Law as valid because of certain reasons (e.g., in order to cooperate with the court)? Did Luther base his reaction only on the few passages from Roman Law? How could Luther then say that secular law grants the right of resistance? If Luther saw only an abstract, then one has to ask why? Was he to be tricked? And was he therefore a victim, as Müller (*op. cit.*, pp. 52 f.) suggests? This may hardly be affirmed, because in Luther's own mind new dimensions of the resistance problem had appeared, at least since the August 5 letter to Brück (see note 17). And further, Luther puts the responsibility on the legal experts when he begins his opinion on the matter by stating *"if"* the situation is as the legal experts describe it, *then* armed resistance to the emperor cannot be rejected on biblical grounds.

32 Or: "everywhere."

1 See letter No. 235, Introduction.

2 *WA*, Br 5, No. 1737. On October 20 the Landgrave had written to Elector John (see note 14), requesting that in view of the dangerous development at the diet (see note 10) the Elector immediately call a conference of the evangelicals for the purpose of discussing a military alliance, and further requesting that he take the necessary first steps of mobilization. See Fabian, *ESBV* (2nd ed.), p. 119.

3 In case Luther should not have sufficient material for such a booklet, the Landgrave offered to send any material necessary; see *WA*, Br 5, 653.

4 The Landgrave took as his point of departure Luther's brief for Chancellor Brück, issued on March 28, 1528 (*WA*, Br 4, 421 ff.), in connection with the Pack affair (see pp. 189 ff.).

5 See *WA*, Br 5, 653 ff.

court procedure, as were the reasons of the Electoral Saxon legal experts.[6] In the present letter, his rather short reply to Landgrave Philip, Luther points out that he is ready to publish a booklet on the diet resolution, in which he would exhort people not to obey the resolution so that they would not thereby become involved in devilish plots. On the resistance issue, Luther simply refers to his opinion given to Elector John, which, he is sure, will soon become known to the Landgrave. In closing, Luther asks for the Landgrave's understanding regarding "our" willingness to make concessions to the papists on certain matters. Since these concessions would not be accepted anyway, they would serve as good propaganda for the evangelicals.

On Landgrave Philip, see p. 124, n. 18.

Text in German: WA, Br 5, 660–661.

To the Illustrious, Noble Sovereign and Lord, Sir Philip, landgrave in Hesse, count in Katzenellenbogen, Ziegenhain, Dietz, and Nida, my Gracious Lord

Grace and peace in Christ! Most Illustrious, Noble Sovereign, Gracious Lord! I have received Your Sovereign Grace's letter,[7] and some information concerning matters presently under discussion.[8]

First, regarding Your Sovereign Grace's request to publish a booklet in order to comfort the weak, I do not wish to conceal from Your Sovereign Grace that [even] without this request I was planning to publish a booklet[9] shortly in which I intend to deal

---

[6] See p. 432, n. 28.

[7] See note 2.

[8] This is obviously a reference to the resistance issue. What Luther meant by "some information" is unclear. Enders, *Briefwechsel* 8, 296, n. 1, suggests that "information" was identical with a brief on the resistance matter issued by the Hessian theologians, and forwarded by the Landgrave to Luther. This is possible, though it seems more probable that Luther was thinking of the detailed information concerning the resistance matter which had been given to him by the Landgrave himself in the October 21 letter. See note 5.

[9] This is a reference to Luther's *Warnung an seine lieben Deutschen* (*Warning to His Dear German People*), WA 30[III], 276 ff.; LW 47, 11 ff. Luther was working on this booklet as early as October 1; see WA 30[III], 254. According to Luther's statement above, he was now approaching the end of his work. It was published by Hans Lufft, and came off the press sometime during the first ten days of April, 1531.

with the resolution[10] and with the evil plans of the sovereigns. I shall admonish everyone's conscience that no subject is bound to offer obedience, should His Imperial Majesty[11] insist on [obedience to the resolution]; I shall rather (as much as my pen is able) discourage [people] from [offering] such obedience, so that no one gets involved in such blasphemous, murderous, and devilish plots. God grant that I create much fruit with this [booklet]. Amen. Yet it will have to be written carefully[12] so that it cannot be condemned as seditious.

Second, I am hoping that God will hit on a way that no bloodshed might occur because of this matter.[13] Therefore (in case it should ever—God forbid—come to this) I have also presented to my Most Gracious Lord, the Elector,[14] my opinion about what may be done in the matter of resistance;[15] no doubt [this opinion] will not remain unknown to Your Sovereign Grace, because I clearly see and recognize that there will be a general deliberation on this [issue].[16] For many reasons it is dangerous for me, as an ecclesiastical person, to present such [an opinion] in writing; [therefore I have given it personally to the Elector].[17]

---

[10] For the resolution (see LW 48, 70, n. 1) of the Diet of Augsburg, see pp. 423 ff. After most of the evangelicals had departed from Augsburg, the pro-papal Estates dominated the business activities of the diet (see NB I.Abt.,E.1, Nos. 34, 36, 37, 39), and drafted a second resolution (URA 2, No. 249), which was presented to a rump diet on October 13 (see TP, pp. 193 ff.; BA pp. 322 ff.). This resolution (of which Elector John was informed by the chief of his Augsburg legation, Count Albrecht of Mansfeld, who came personally to Torgau on approximately October 22; see Fabian, ESBV [1st ed.], pp. 47 f.) suggested an even tougher course of action against the evangelicals. It is not clear, but it is also unimportant, whether Luther was thinking of the September 22 version of the resolution, or of the October 13 version.

[11] Emperor Charles V; see LW 48, 175 f.

[12] Luther wrote verwaret; this term is used in connection with the safekeeping of a prisoner, of a town, of precious jewels, or of any other important objects. Luther meant to say that the booklet had to be written in such a way that no one could successfully attack it and charge that it was seditious.

[13] I.e., the gospel as it had been confessed in the Augsburg Confession.

[14] Elector John; see LW 48, 269, n. 8.

[15] Literally: ". . . opinion as to what one may do with the resistance."

[16] Or: ". . . general deliberation on the basis of [this opinion]." The sentence is quite awkwardly structured. More freely translated the sentence would read: ". . . recognize that one intends to make a general brief out of my opinion."

[17] As Clemen has suggested (WA, Br 5, 661, n. 5), in contrast to Enders (Briefwechsel 8, 296, n. 3), Luther apparently is not referring here to the written statement issued during the Torgau conference (letter No. 235), but

I ask Your Sovereign Grace not to be shocked that we have once more offered concessions in some matters, as for instance, fasting,[18] feast days, [differentiations in matters of certain] foods,

---

to a conversation with the Elector, a conversation of which nothing further could be established other than that it took place sometime prior to this October 28 letter to the Landgrave. If this is the case, and there is no reason to deny this possibility, then one must ask why Luther wrote letter No. 235 at all, and whether letter No. 235 was perhaps written *after* this letter to the Landgrave had been written. The matter becomes even more complicated if one considers Luther's statements that his opinion would become known to the Landgrave, and would become the basis for general deliberations, and that he did not write down his opinion in order to avoid endangering himself. How could even Luther's orally expressed opinion be safe, i.e., not become public, or endanger him? While in Torgau, Luther certainly became acquainted with the alliance negotiations of the evangelicals, which were planned for Nürnberg on November 13; see *WA, Br* 5, 663; Fabian, *ESBV* (2nd ed.), pp. 126 f. So he also must have known of the correspondence between the Electoral court and the evangelicals, especially with the Landgrave and the city council of Nürnberg. (In fact, Luther's letter was probably sent to the Landgrave together with the October 28 letter of the Elector to the Landgrave; see Fabian, *ESBV* [2nd ed.], p. 125, n. 632.) While in this correspondence letter No. 235 is not directly mentioned, the readiness of the Electoral Saxon court to affirm the right of resistance to the emperor on the basis of a "new brief" on this matter (see Fabian, *ESBV* [2nd ed.], p. 127) was so shocking to the Nürnberg city council that it canceled the planned conference (see Fabian, *ESBV* [2nd ed.], pp. 134 ff.), obviously to gain time for studying the new position of the Electoral Saxon court; this meant, however, that eventually the city council would demand to study the brief on which this new position was based. It is then not clear why Luther on the one hand expected that either his written statement (letter No. 235), or his orally expressed opinion, given to the Elector and developed by the Elector's councilors into a brief, would not become generally known, yet on the other hand said that he recognized very well that there would be a general deliberation on the resistance matter, and that in this way his opinion would become known to the Landgrave. Did Luther expect that only his orally-transmitted opinion would become known to the evangelicals, and that they would be satisfied with hearsay? It seems that Luther was not thinking of letter No. 235 when in his October 28 letter to the Landgrave he mentioned his "opinion" on the resistance matter as being given to the Elector. For letter No. 235 was not directed to Elector John, but was directed to Brück and his staff as a part of the conference transactions. What could Luther have told the Elector personally (if a personal meeting did indeed take place) that he did not wish to become public? Why did he hope or think that it would not become public, and thus endanger him? How could Luther hope not to be put on the spot in this matter? This question is especially important because Luther himself states that his opinion would become public! Luther's statements raise questions which have been bypassed in all available editions of this letter. The "opinion" mentioned by Luther here, and the circumstances under which it was given, cannot be identified, though certainly Luther's statements have to be seen in connection with the Torgau conference.

18 Literally: "to accept the fasting."

and hymns,[19] for we know, of course, that [the opponents] cannot accept [these concessions] in this way. Our purpose in doing this is to increase our respectability all the more, so that I can emphasize their infamy all the more powerfully in my booklet.[20] Even if all [these concessions] should be accepted this would not be dangerous for us.

With this I commend [Your Grace] to God. Amen.

Torgau, October 28, 1530   Your Sovereign Grace's
                                     willing [servant],
                                     MARTIN LUTHER

---

[19] This is a reference to the willingness of the evangelicals to make concessions (see p. 421), a willingness which had been strongly criticized by the Landgrave in the past; see e.g., WA, Br 5, 619, 651.

[20] See note 9.

INDEXES

INDEX OF NAMES AND SUBJECTS

[References to biographical sketches are in boldface type.]

INDEX TO SCRIPTURE PASSAGES